Frommer's®

LONDON
FROM $75 A DAY

Here's what the critics say about Frommer's:

"Amazingly easy to use. Very portable, very complete."
—Booklist

♦

"The only mainstream guide to list specific prices. The Walter Cronkite of guidebooks—with all that implies."
—Travel & Leisure

♦

"Complete, concise, and filled with useful information."
—New York Daily News

♦

"Hotel information is close to encyclopedic."
—Des Moines Sunday Register

Frommer's® 99

LONDON
FROM $75 A DAY

The Ultimate Guide to
Comfortable Low-Cost Travel

by Marilyn Wood

MACMILLAN • USA

ABOUT THE AUTHOR

Marilyn Wood came to the United States from England to study journalism at Columbia University. The former editorial director of Prentice Hall Travel, she has also worked as a reporter, ranch hand, press officer, and book reviewer. In addition, Marilyn is the author of *Wonderful Weekends from New York City, Wonderful Weekends from Boston,* and *Frommer's Toronto,* and she is the co-author of *Frommer's Canada.*

MACMILLAN TRAVEL

A Simon & Schuster Macmillan Company
1633 Broadway
New York, NY 10019

Find us online at **www.frommers.com**

ISBN 0-02-862641-9
ISSN 1055-5331

Editor: Kelly Regan
Production Editor: Suzanne Snyder
Design by Michele Laseau
Digital Cartography by Gail Accardi and Ortelius Design
Page Creation by Carrie Allen, Jena Brandt, Laura Goetz, and Sean Monkhouse

Photo Editor: Richard Fox

SPECIAL SALES

Bulk purchases (10+ copies) of Frommer's and selected Macmillan travel guides are available to corporations, organizations, mail-order catalogs, institutions, and charities at special discounts, and can be customized to suit individual needs. For more information write to Special Sales, Macmillan General Reference, 1633 Broadway, New York, NY 10019.

Manufactured in the United States of America

Contents

7 Strolling Around London 239

8 Shopping 252

9 London After Dark 269

10 Easy Excursions from London 290

Index 316

List of Maps

AN INVITATION TO THE READER

In researching this book, we discovered many wonderful places—hotels, restaurants, shops, and more. We're sure you'll find others. Please tell us about them, so we can share the information with your fellow travelers in upcoming editions. If you were disappointed with a recommendation, we'd love to know that, too. Please write to:

Frommer's London from $75 a Day
Macmillan Travel
1633 Broadway
New York, NY 10019

AN ADDITIONAL NOTE

Please be advised that travel information is subject to change at any time—and this is especially true of prices. We therefore suggest that you write or call ahead for confirmation when making your travel plans. The authors, editors, and publisher cannot be held responsible for the experiences of readers while traveling. Your safety is important to us, however, so we encourage you to stay alert and be aware of your surroundings. Keep a close eye on cameras, purses, and wallets, all favorite targets of thieves and pickpockets.

WHAT THE SYMBOLS MEAN

✪ Frommer's Favorites

Our favorite places and experiences—outstanding for quality, value, or both.

The following abbreviations are used for credit cards:

AE	American Express	EURO	EuroCard
CB	Carte Blanche	JCB	Japan Credit Bank
DC	Diners Club	MC	MasterCard
DISC	Discover	V	Visa

FIND FROMMER'S ONLINE

Arthur Frommer's Budget Travel Online (www.frommers.com) offers more than 6,000 pages of up-to-the-minute travel information—including the latest bargains and candid, personal articles updated daily by Arthur Frommer himself. No other Web site offers such comprehensive and timely coverage of the world of travel.

The London Experience

London—and indeed all of Britain—is in the midst of a sea change. After 18 years of Tory rule, Prime Minister Tony Blair and his New Labour party have proclaimed the dawn of a "Cool Britannia." And who can blame him? London is humming with electricity, a buzz sparked by cultural revolutions both grand and small. Alexander McQueen and Stella McCartney lead a wave of maverick fashion designers, their impact felt from the most exclusive haute couture houses right down to the funky stalls of Kensington Market. Britpop's invasion, led by the likes of Oasis and Blur, may be on the wane, but the music biz is riding high, buoyed by the success of groups like the Spice Girls (minus one, still strong) and the Verve. Perhaps most surprising, British chefs have gotten with the program; English cuisine is no longer considered an oxymoron. Aged, dismal pubs have morphed into trendy-hip eateries, thanks to minimalist, blond-wood makeovers and unapologetically innovative menus. One thing's for certain—this is *not* your father's pub grub. Even the economy—once the butt of French and German jokes—is booming, attracting (gasp!) a large community of French businesspeople who prefer (another gasp!) doing business in Britain.

The media has trumpeted this renaissance, dubbing everything "new" to such an extent that some wags have taken to calling the game "new tennis" whenever Tony takes to the courts. On the other hand, London has yet to forsake the timeless traditions and institutions that have shaped the city throughout its two thousand–year history. The Tower, Big Ben, Buckingham Palace, and Westminster Abbey still preside solemnly over London's heart. The weather's still schizophrenic, cabs look the same (although many now sport Day-Glo colors and advertisements), and the narrow streets still wind past grand houses and vivid gardens. It's the streetscape that has changed. Pinstriped entrepreneurs hustle down the street, glued to their cell phones; hipsters sip decaf lattes at sidewalk java joints; and daredevil skateboarders defy the traffic along Oxford Street.

Through it all, the character of London's people remains much the same—pragmatic, stoic, proud, disputatious, bawdy, and ironic. The vaunted "stiff upper lip" wilted noticeably with the outpouring of grief that followed the 1997 death of Diana, the "people's Princess." The media continues to debate whether such emotional displays signify the replacement of a reasonable, responsible society with one mired in navel-gazing self-indulgence.

Central London

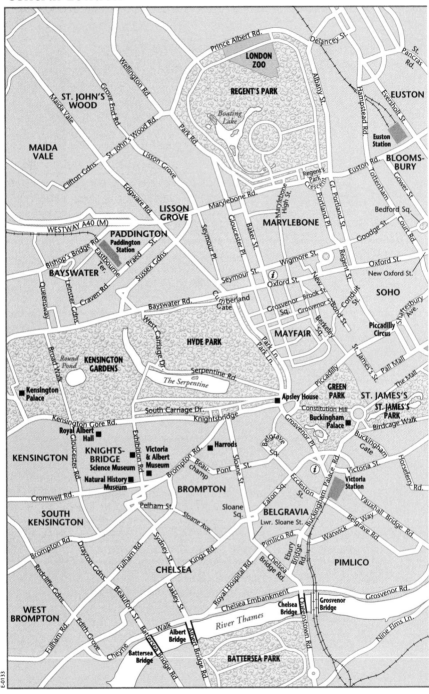

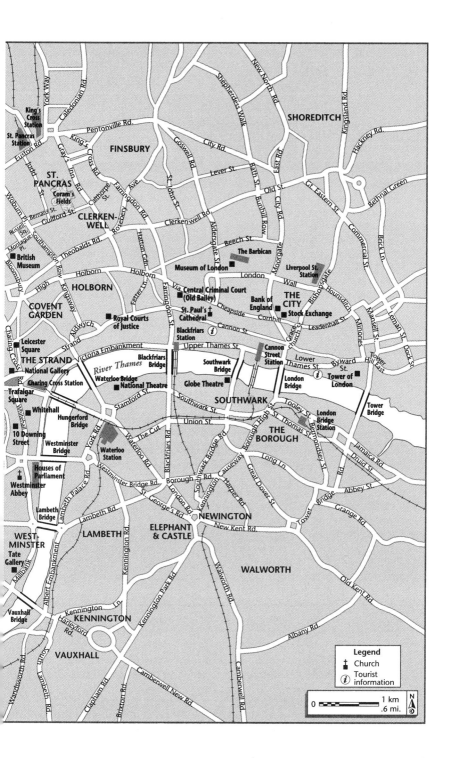

But in pubs around town, the topic of conversation is likely to be football—say, the standing of London's Arsenal against Manchester United, or whether David Beckham's game has been adversely affected by his impending marriage to Posh Spice. Whatever the outcome of these swirling arguments, London remains a marvelous amalgam of techno and pomp. You're sure to be enchanted by the many juxtapositions contained within this sprawling 600-square-mile city. Welcome to the dynamic, creative, modern London, a brilliant fusion of past and present.

1 Frommer's Favorite Affordable London Experiences

- **Visit the East End:** Home to London's famous Cockneys and gateway for most of the city's immigrants, the East End is best visited on a Sunday, when a lively outdoor market takes over Petticoat Lane.
- **Observe a Parliamentary Debate:** You wouldn't expect lawmakers to make catcalls and boo, but that's exactly what they do in the House of Commons. Debates here can be exciting, not sleep-inducing as they are Stateside.
- **Browse Harrods,** touching down particularly in the exquisitely decorated and lavishly tiled and stocked food halls, the kids' department, and the hunting and shooting plus sports department.
- **Attend Evensong at One of London's Classic Churches:** Evensong is quintessentially English. The service lacks any sermon or serious preaching, and there's no Eucharist, so it's not too taxing for the average visitor. Instead, it's a glorious musical celebration that takes place in the beautiful surroundings of a (perhaps) Wren-designed church. Go to St. Martin-in-the-Fields, for example, and hear the Magnificat sung. You're sure to feel better afterwards.
- **Sit in at the Courts of the Old Bailey:** Watch the bewigged judges and barristers argue a criminal case or similarly peruked barristers do the same for civil cases at the Royal Courts of Justice.
- **Ride atop the Number 188 Bus from Euston to Greenwich:** With the whole of London practically at your feet, this is the best—and cheapest—tour in town.
- **While away an Afternoon in Hyde Park or St. James's Park:** Meander along the Serpentine, stopping to admire Epstein's statue of Pan; admire the numerous waterfowl and other birds in St. James's Park, and check out the view of Buckingham Palace from the bridge across the lake.
- **Catch a Promenade Concert at the Royal Albert Hall:** It's only £3 to stand, which is the place to be at this emotionally charged summer series of concerts given under the great dome of the Royal Albert Hall.
- **Spend a Day in Greenwich:** Take the river launch down to what arguably is one of the great architectural complexes in London, if not in Britain.
- **Get Up Early Saturday Morning For the Portobello Market:** Browse through the stalls and the many stores tucked down passageways and in nooks and crannies. Also check out the many antique stores along Westbourne Grove—still a treasure trove of beautifully crafted, if expensive, antiques.
- **Enjoy A Pint in One of the City's Historic or Riverside Pubs:** Try the Dove at Hammersmith, the George Inn near Waterloo, or the Spaniards on the edge of Hampstead Heath.
- **Attend a Performance at the Royal Court Theatre:** Go on a Monday night when it's only £5 to see what will assuredly prove a cutting-edge, possibly even disturbing piece of theater.
- **Meander through the British Museum or the National Gallery of Art:** Both are free; can you believe it in this most sophisticated of cities?

- **Experience one of London's great events:** Some of my favorites are the Oxford and Cambridge Boat Race (in April), the Notting Hill Carnival (in August), and the Lord Mayor's Procession (in November); see the Calendar of Events in chapter 2 for a complete listing.
- **Devote an Afternoon to Oxo Tower Wharf,** and check out the bars and shops that include a branch of Harvey Nichols. From here, you'll enjoy great views of the Thames.

2 The City Today

In Europe, London is the place to be. It's chic and dynamic, and crackles with life and creativity. The Brits have emerged from the fuddy-duddy doldrums and have rediscovered art, style, fashion, design, music, food, and modernism. And London has become, once again, the center of it all. It's almost hard to believe that British fashion designers are wooed and feted in Paris—Alexander McQueen at Givenchy, Stella McCartney at Chloe, and John Galliano at Dior. Fashion is hot at home too, with such names as Jasper Conran, Ally Capellino, Amanda Wakeley, Pearce Fonda, Antonio Berardi, David Emanuel, Ben de Lisi, and Ghost. The Britpack artists, painters, and musicians create waves of excitement and controversy. Damien Hirst (of the formaldehyde sheep fame) has taken to putting his installations in such restaurants as Quo Vadis and is also opening a restaurant of his own. Liam and Noel Gallagher continue to create waves wherever they go and the Spice Girls, despite the departure of Ginger, keep pumping out that girl power around the world. Even Nelson Mandela recently admitted that it was a thrill to meet them. Bold building schemes, mega restaurants, new politics, and lots of money are making London the place for movers and shakers of all sorts.

Still, it's also the place for tradition and history. It can't help itself in this regard. Walk down any London street, and you will encounter homes of famous writers, artists, or scientists; views that you might recognize from paintings by Canaletto, Turner, Monet, Pissarro, and Whistler; squares haunted by the spectres of riot and mayhem; and streets that have witnessed the footsteps of great personalities and the rituals of grand pageants.

Most first-time visitors arrive in London with preconceived notions—about bowler-hatted businessmen clutching their black umbrellas as they briskly walk down the street; about politicians cheering, shouting, and insulting each other in the Commons; about scandals, royal and otherwise (Remember Profumo, Christine Keeler, and more recently, Sir Anthony Blunt?); about afternoon tea, bangers and mash, and lager and lime; about football, rugby, cricket, and tennis; about the Beatles, punk, Britpop, and Sir Michael Tippett; about palaces, pageantry, and peers. Before we leave home, our heads are already filled with a seemingly endless panoply of images, characters, sounds, and stories that have been passed along to us from literature, film, music, the media, photography, and more. The real-world examples of these preconceptions speak more to the past than to the future.

And the future is what consumes London right now; grand preparations are under way for the millennium celebration at Greenwich and throughout the city and nation. It seems everything is being rearranged, expanded, and refurbished for the big event, including practically all of the great museums and galleries. And the makeover is not just structural; the very definition of Englishness is also being redefined. It's pretty clear that while London still conveys stability, confidence, solidity, masculinity, and love of tradition, there are radical societal shifts taking place, as everyone jostles to join the mainstream and define their particular kind of Englishness, from the black and Asian communities in Brixton and Tower Hamlets

Impressions

An American in London . . . cannot but be impressed and charmed by the city.
The monumentality of Washington, the thriving business of New York, the antique
intimacy of Boston, plus a certain spacious and open feeling reminiscent of Denver
and San Francisco—all these he finds combined for his pleasure.
  —John Updike, "London Life," in *Picked Up Pieces* (1976)

homosexuals and girl power adherents. Necessarily, some noses are out of joint, and conflicting signs of unrest are surfacing.

In many ways, they are indications of how this once-powerful city that ruled an empire and claimed half the world has embraced that social and technological change. London is more technically advanced, fast-paced, and internationally minded than it ever was.

Newer, more intense conflicts, though, are coming to the fore. Communities of new Londoners, especially women, people of color, and gays, are contributing to the changes and the creation of Britain's new self image and refreshing energized outlook. These groups are all working to break down the old bastions of prejudice.

Added to the mix are many of the problems that afflict any big multicultural city—homelessness, poverty, drugs, and violence. You will find homeless people on the streets and in the Tube stations; crime is more common than it was; and if you visit the outer boroughs, especially the East End, you'll stumble on unrepaired sidewalks and see graffiti-splattered walls. You won't be able to go inside an attractive, historic church because the doors will be bolted against you on account of vandalism.

In the heart of London, though, everything is more sanguine. The city still crackles and pulsates. People hang out in wine bars, cafes, and pubs at lunch and after work. Somehow, Londoners seem to be even more in love with technology than their American counterparts; the number of cellular phones that one encounters on the streets is astonishing. Shopping has become a major pastime, and home decorating and dining out are natural extensions of this thriving consumer society. London has become a serious food town, and now can boast chefs who have earned three stars from Michelin—among them Marco Pierre White and Nico Ladenis. Ethnic food is more commonplace, with cuisines from Afghan to Sudanese popping up everywhere, joined also by the advent of cyber cafes, where you can reserve a computer terminal and sign on to the Internet. And due to the real estate boom, historic residences are being widely renovated and loft living has come to some parts of town, notably Docklands, Clerkenwell Bow, and Battersea.

Although Covent Garden, Soho, and Camden are still the major hangouts, other areas have been vigorously gentrified or rescued from decay; Islington, Clerkenwell, and even Hackney, have all been touted as up-and-coming neighborhoods. Other formerly stodgy residential areas like Marylebone are being reenergized by commercial retail development and the arrival of such merchandisers as Sir Terence Conran. London is even gearing up for a mayoral election that will give it the first democratically elected mayor in its history. Such candidates as Jeremy Archer and Glenda Jackson will ensure an interesting campaign. Between the promise of a new mayor and the restoration of the Greater London Council which Maggie Thatcher simply abolished in 1986 (because it was a Labour thorn in her flesh), London pride is sure to return with a vengeance.

The election of Tony Blair has already provided a shot in the arm to this sense of pride. His popularity outstrips that of any PM to date. So far he has scored some

One Nation, One Currency . . . Sort of: Britain's Euro Reluctance

The only club it seems that the British aren't too sure about joining wholeheartedly is the Common Market. It's easy to forget that London is the capital of an island nation. Britain is separated from the rest of Europe by the English Channel, a swath of water that historically (at least until the Blitz) served to protect the British people from foreign invasion, but also acted as a barrier to closer communication with the nations on the Continent. Such isolation led to the development of a separate culture, significantly different from those on the Continent in various aspects—food, fashion, and social and political customs. Eel pies and bowler hats are as distinctly English as are the Church of England and the House of Commons. Since Britain joined the EEC in 1973, much of this insularity has faded, and Britain increasingly looks and feels more European with its outdoor cafes and brighter colors and fashions.

But the assimilation hasn't been a smooth one. Battles raged against the EEC during the tenure of Prime Minister John Major, from the demonstrations against shipping cattle to Europe because they were not dealt with compassionately aboard the boats, to the uproar over Spanish fishermen accused of invading English fishing grounds. Under Tony Blair, skepticism has persisted with Britain's reluctance to leap in and join in the first wave of adopting the Euro standard, a single EEC-wide currency that's slated to take effect in 2002.

Old rivalries resurface over seemingly trivial issues—say, chocolate. Recently the Europeans, led by the Belgians, Swiss, and French, demanded that British chocolate should not be labeled as such, because it did not contain the requisite ingredients. Likewise, wrangling continues about British beef and the dangers of mad cow disease. Such ill will reared its head again in the summer of 1998 during the World Cup soccer matches in France, when advance ticket sales for the matches were restricted largely to French residents. In response, the British government spent millions of pounds on a campaign to warn British soccer fans not to go to France unless they had tickets. Then the French, a month or so before the game, invited fans to come even if they didn't have tickets just to see Paris and France. The whole brouhaha culminated with a British tabloid trumpeting the headline "Frogs need a good kicking."

In short, the Brits haven't quite made up their minds about Europe—a fact which continues to make the European Community a sometimes uneasy alliance.

enormous successes with his commitment to peace in Northern Ireland. He's young compared to other European leaders, his wife is a QC, and he represents the new, youthful Britain, a political image that he has taken great pains to cultivate by hobnobbing with the luvvies or celebrities of the art, fashion, theater, literary, and music worlds—Damien Hirst, Alexander McQueen, Alan McGee, Lord and Lady Rogers, the Gallagher brothers, and Fay Weldon—and persuading them to support him and his New Labour. Blair has launched a campaign to change the image of Britain from a "backward-looking country with bad weather, poor food, and arrogant, unfriendly people," according to Demos, a Labour think tank.

Besides the campaign to change the country's image, serious constitutional changes are also afoot. There's serious talk about abolishing (or certainly reforming) the House of Lords. Scotland already has been granted a parliament of its own. And most notably, there is continuing talk about abolishing the monarchy. In the '90s, the House of Windsor has become the subject of unusually intense tabloid coverage. The divorce of Princess Ann and Mark Phillips and the scandal surrounding the divorce of Prince Andrew and Sarah Ferguson were nothing compared to the furor that erupted over the separation, and eventual divorce, of Prince Charles and Princess Diana. As details of the breakup were revealed, the royal family's dirty linen came tumbling out of the closet, and both Diana and Charles appeared on television to tell their stories. In the face of all this bad news and bad publicity, the queen, upon the advice of her ministers, finally agreed to start paying taxes on her income and also opened Buckingham Palace to the public to help pay for the repairs needed at Windsor Castle.

It was after the divorce (and the stripping of her royal title) that Diana truly came into her own. Many people, especially women, had identified with the princess's problems, appreciated her maternal, compassionate, and more intuitive approach to family life, and admired her vigorous charity work on behalf of AIDS victims, the sick and disabled, and the abolition of landmines.

When Diana was killed in a car crash with her companion, Dodi al-Fayed, in 1997, the nation was inconsolable, and the royal family came under intense fire for their initially cool reaction. Vacationing at Balmoral at the time, the Queen announced that she would not return to London until the Saturday morning of the funeral. Meanwhile, Kensington Palace was mobbed with mourners from all walks of life and from all segments of society—blacks, Asians, gays, old and young, male and female, upper, middle, and working class. Flowers, candles, and notes carpeted the sidewalk outside the palace gates.

The Windsors were completely shocked by the outpouring of grief. Finally, under pressure from Charles and Tony Blair, the queen returned to London to address the nation the evening before the funeral and in that address she offered a personal tribute to the Princess. This gesture was followed by several others intended to placate her subjects, including a walkabout in front of Kensington Palace during which Princes William and Harry were mobbed like rock stars. At the funeral the Queen made a point of bowing to the cortege as it passed in front of Buckingham Palace, and the Duke of Edinburgh chose to walk behind the gun carriage carrying the coffin to Westminster Abbey. It was a belated effort from the royal family to regain the respect and love of their people and to reburnish the tarnished image of the monarchy.

And other institutions besides the monarchy are also in retreat. With fewer people attending services, many churches have closed and congregations have been combined. However, while the Church of England and the Roman Catholic Church are in decline, there are signs of life among other faiths; the impressive Hindu temple in Neasden is testament to that. And more and more Londoners are turning to New Age philosophies and pop psychology à la the late Princess Diana.

Impressions

London is the epitome of our times, and the Rome of today.
—Ralph Waldo Emerson

We would rather see London laid in ruins and ashes than that it should be tamely and abjectly enslaved.
—Prime Minister Winston Churchill, in defiance of German war attacks, 1940

The city has a network of spiritualist churches at which mediums appear regularly, and aromatherapy shops seem to be on every street corner.

Other institutions which haven't already been dismantled by Maggie Thatcher are also fast disappearing—the dole, for one. Already the honeymoon between Tony Blair and the luvvies has dissolved over such issues as reduced benefits for single mothers, welfare-to-work plans, and the end of free university education. The committee formed to "modernize" Britain and recast its image has come under fire largely because it is composed of singularly stodgy people who couldn't recognize half of the celebrities in today's news, and wouldn't know cool if it came up and bit them them on the nose.

Still, despite all this, change is in the air. Tony Blair continues to lead Britain on a program of constitutional reform without parallel in this century, though critics charge that Blair will one day preside over a "disunited" Britain, with Scotland breaking away and Northern Ireland forming a self-government. And while the abolition of the monarchy may not be imminent, it is no longer a wild idea of the Left. People are seriously questioning the wisdom of supporting a royal family in imperial style. At the very least, perhaps a more modest, Europeanlike monarchy would do. At the very least it's good for the tourist trade, on which Britain is increasingly dependent, and what would the tabloids do without the royal family to pin headlines on?

3 A Look at the Past

London is full of history—yet many visitors, faced with the traffic-clogged streets and the many ugly, modern buildings, wonder where exactly history can be found, and if it only exists in the blue plaques attached to so many buildings in celebration of some remarkable personage or event. But it is there, in living color, in the pageantry of the monarchy, in the pubs, in the gentlemen's clubs, in the Houses of Parliament, in the Inns of Court, and in the people's very bones, it seems. Although London has always been a commercial city and the mercantile spirit has always placed commerce and development ahead of urban planning (which has meant that much of the past was destroyed), still a great heritage remains. History is to be found everywhere, tucked away secretly down tiny alleyways or more openly at St. Paul's or Westminster. Here in London you will see history at work in the institutions that play major roles in the daily life of the city.

The City of London proper is contained in one square mile, which today is the financial district. The story of London is how that one square mile grew to be what it is today, a 600-mile conurbation in which 6.4 million people live. Early in its history, villages grew up outside the original walled city with names like Kensington, Clerkenwell, Knightsbridge, Hampstead, Highgate, and many

Dateline

- **A.D.43** Londinium settled by Roman invaders.
- **50** London Bridge built across the Thames.
- **61** Boudicca sacks London.
- **190–220** City walls built.
- **350** Saxons invade.
- **410** Romans retreat.
- **457** Londoners take refuge behind city walls.
- **604** First St. Paul's built. Mellitus appointed Bishop of London.
- **886** Alfred the Great takes London from the Danes.
- **1066** William of Normandy (the Conqueror) crowned king.
- **1078** Construction of White Tower begun.
- **1097** William Rufus builds Westminster Hall.
- **1123** St. Bartholomew's Hospital founded.
- **1176–1209** London Bridge built of stone.

continues

- **1192** Henry FitzAilwin elected first mayor of London.
- **1214** King John grants city a charter.
- **1215** Magna Carta signed.
- **1348–49** Black Death sweeps London.
- **1381** Peasants' Revolt.
- **1397** Richard Whittington, a wealthy merchant, elected lord mayor.
- **1401** Water piped in from Tyburn.
- **1455** Wars of the Roses begin.
- **1461** Edward of York crowned king.
- **1483** Richard, Duke of Gloucester, imprisons (and possibly murders) crown prince Edward V and his brother; crowns himself Richard III.
- **1485** Henry Tudor defeats Richard at Bosworth. Henry VII launches Tudor dynasty.
- **1509** Henry VIII succeeds to the throne. Marries first of six wives.
- **1513** Henry VIII builds navy and opens dockyards at Deptford and Woolwich.
- **1536–40** Dissolution of the monasteries. Church of England established, with king at head.
- **1553** Mary Tudor made queen. Lady Jane Grey, the "Nine Days' Queen," is executed.
- **1558** Elizabeth I (1558–1603) succeeds throne.
- **1588** Spanish armada defeated.
- **1599** Globe Theatre built.
- **1600** London expands to areas south of the Thames.
- **1605** Guy Fawkes and his Gun-powder Plot to blow up King James I and Parliament are foiled.
- **1631** Inigo Jones builds Covent Garden.

continues

others. Today, of course, those villages have all been incorporated into London and yet each area does still have a distinct history and flavor of its own, making it worthwhile to explore in depth particular London neighborhoods that interest you. The section that follows tells the story of how the fabric of contemporary London was woven over the last 2,000 years.

EARLY ROMAN, SAXON & DARK AGE LONDON By any measure, London is a very old city. Archaeological excavations have proved that there were early settlements here as far back as 2500 B.C. Although most scholars debate the origin of London's name, most people think it's derived from the Celtic words *Llyn Din*, meaning "lakeside fortress."

Origins notwithstanding, most historians agree that the British Isles began to fall under Roman control in A.D. 43. Julius Caesar visited twice and camped on the very ground where Heathrow stands today. The Romans built a bridge across the Thames to their Kentish Highway, which ran from Canterbury via London to Chester. Some of these original Roman routes are still in use today— Oxford Street, Bayswater Road, and Edgeware Road, for example. It's believed that the London stone set into the wall at 111 Cannon Street was the milestone used to fix all distances in Roman Britain. First a military base, London was transformed by the Romans into an important trading center. They constructed buildings with tiled roofs, mosaic floors, and public baths. If you want to see what it looked like then, visit the Museum of London, which has a very effective model of Roman London. To protect the city against the "barbarians," the Romans built a wall around it (between A.D. 190 and 220), fragments of which can also be seen in the Museum of London. When the empire started to crumble around A.D. 410, the Romans withdrew, leaving Londoners and the Britons to resist the Anglo-Saxon invasions.

Confusion followed the Romans' departure. From the 7th to the early 9th centuries, the tribal kingdoms of Kent, Mercia, Northumbria, and the West Saxons fought each other for control of Britain. Meanwhile the Vikings began their invasions initially along the coasts. From 871 to 872 they occupied the Saxon city that had grown up around Charing Cross outside the original Roman walls. The Saxon king Alfred the Great fought back and, in 886, was able to make peace with the

Danes. The Londoners abandoned their Saxon settlement and returned to the area within the old Roman walls. The population of the city at this time was about 12,000, and the town was large enough to be divided into 20 wards, each with aldermen who in turn reported to the town reeve. Few traces of this early period remain.

In the late 10th century, the Vikings began raiding again. London resisted, but finally accepted first Sweni in 1013, and later his son Canute. After Canute's death, Edward, the son of Ethelred the Unready, became king and it is he who is largely responsible for the creation of Westminster. He built a palace on the site of today's Westminster Hall, transferred his court here, and spent a tenth of his income rebuilding the abbey of St. Peter at Westminster. He was known as Edward the Confessor because of his piety. When his beloved wife, Eleanor of Castile, died in Nottinghamshire in 1290, her funeral cortege traveled to London, and at every overnight stop Edward had a cross erected. Only one stands in London today and it is, of course, Charing Cross, the last stop on the funeral route.

Today you can visit his tomb in Westminster Abbey. Edward, whose mother was Norman, died on January 6, 1066, and after his death a battle for the throne raged between Saxon and Norman. The merchants and barons in the city supported the Saxon king, Harold, primarily because they had extracted a guarantee of rights and privileges from him, but Harold was defeated at the Battle of Hastings and William the Conqueror marched on London, burned Southwark, and forced the city to surrender.

MEDIEVAL LONDON   William had himself crowned in Westminster. He was smart enough to understand the power vested in the city, and he maintained the rights that had been previously granted to the city by Harold, including the right to elect its own leaders, as it had done for centuries. That right is still intact today and every year the Lord Mayor of the City is elected and makes a grand procession from the city to the law courts in the Strand for investiture. Such was the strength of the city barons that even the monarch had to ask permission to enter the city; that is still true to this day. Under William, favored Norman barons were granted tracts of land on which they built huge, fortified stone houses, known as *burhs*. None of these mansions survive, but street names such as

- **1637** Hyde Park opened to public.
- **1642–58** Oliver Cromwell leads Parliamentary forces during Civil War and later Protectorate.
- **1649** King Charles I beheaded before the Banqueting House in Whitehall.
- **1660** Monarchy restored under Charles II.
- **1665** Great Plague strikes 110,000 Londoners.
- **1666** Great Fire destroys 80% of the medieval city.
- **1675–1710** Wren rebuilds 51 churches, including St. Paul's.
- **1688** Bloodless Revolution: James II banished; William and Mary invited to throne.
- **1694** Bank of England established.
- **1725** Mayfair developed.
- **1739–53** Mansion House built.
- **1759** British Museum founded.
- **1780** In Gordon Riots, mobs protest against Papists.
- **1801** First census. Population: 959,000.
- **1802** West Indian Dock opens.
- **1826** University College established.
- **1829** Metro Police established.
- **1832** First Reform Bill enfranchises some property owners.
- **1837** Victoria, 18, succeeds her uncle, William IV.
- **1840s** Influx of Irish immigrants, who come to flee famine and political repression.
- **1847** British Museum opens.
- **1851** Hyde Park hosts the Great Exhibition, which finances development of South Kensington.
- **1858** The Great Stink. Royal Opera House opens.

continues

- **1863** The first Underground connects Paddington to the City.
- **1877** First Wimbledon Tennis Championship.
- **1882** Law Courts built in the Strand.
- **1888** London County Council established.
- **1889** Great Dock Strike.
- **1894** Tower Bridge opens.
- **1901** Queen Victoria dies. Edward VII ascends throne.
- **1907** Central Criminal Court (the Old Bailey) constructed.
- **1910** King Edward VII dies and is succeeded by George V.
- **1914–18** World War I. London bombed from planes and airships.
- **1922** BBC begins broadcasting.
- **1936** King George V dies. Prince of Wales succeeds throne as Edward VIII, but abdicates to marry Wallis Simpson.
- **1937** Edward's younger brother crowned King George VI.
- **1939–45** World War II. Air raids and rocket attacks destroy much of the city: 30,000 killed, 50,000 injured.
- **1947–48** New Commonwealth influx.
- **1948** London hosts Summer Olympics.
- **1951** Royal Festival Hall opens.
- **1952** King George VI dies.
- **1953** Queen Elizabeth II crowned in first nationally televised coronation ceremony.
- **1955** Heathrow Airport opens.
- **1956** Clean Air Act.
- **1960s** Swinging London— Mary Quant, the Beatles, et al. The controversial Centre

continues

Bucklersbury and Lothbury tell us where they once stood.

During the 11th century, the old Saxon London of wood and thatch was converted into Norman stone. William began the massive, impregnable White Tower (of the Tower of London) in 1078, not only as a fortification against invaders, but also to intimidate his new London subjects.

The 12th, 13th, and 14th centuries were dominated by overseas wars—the Crusades, the Hundred Years' War with France—and at home by the Wars of the Roses—the struggle between the House of Lancaster and the House of York for the English throne. Despite all this strife, London continued to grow and thrive largely through trade even though there was only one bridge—London Bridge—across the Thames. The original bridge was built of wood and replaced many times, but in 1176 a stone bridge was begun. It took 33 years to complete and cost 200 lives. It was 940 feet long with 20 arches and had upon it a chapel dedicated to Thomas à Becket. Timbered houses lined the cobbled roadway that was only 12 feet wide and the only way southeast out of the city. Across this bridge the medieval kings of England set out to Crécy, Potliers, and Agincourt. At the southern end of the bridge, heads of traitors were impaled on the turrets of the gate (one foreign visitor in the 16th century noted 30 heads on display).

The River Thames was the city's main highway, and you could travel from London to Westminster in 1372 for only two pence. It was lined with wharves, each assigned a particular type of cargo— hay, fish, and wool—the commodities that made London rich. Road travel was difficult. Some roads were wide enough for 16 knights to ride abreast (these were dubbed royal roads), but most were narrow, made of dirt, and poorly maintained. In the late 14th century, it took 4½ days to ride from London to York, traveling about 44 miles a day. Wagons took even longer.

The wealth of the city was built on trade—on wool in particular. Indeed, sheep outnumbered people 300 to 1. But only a handful of merchants controlled this trade, which by the 1480s was exporting via London a million yards of cloth to Europe. Other trades flourished, too. In 1422, the clerk of the Brewers Company recorded 111 trades being carried on in the city—drapers, soapmakers, cord wainers, goldsmiths, haberdashers, vintners, and many more. Guilds set standards, trademarks, and prices, and they arranged pensions for their members. As the guilds grew prosperous, they built impressive halls, many of which survive today like Drapers' Hall, Fishmongers' Hall, and Goldsmiths' Hall. Today you can still see the banners of the principal companies flying in Guildhall; many of their halls have survived, like the Drapers', Fishmongers', and Goldsmiths' Halls (usually their 19th-century versions, not the originals).

Daily life was hard for most. Londoners lived in constant fear of plague and fire. In 1348–49, the Great Plague carried off 30% to 40% of the population. At the height of the epidemic, 200 dead were buried each day in one London cemetery. Drink was the common relief from the hardships and terrors of daily life. In 1309, the city had 1,334 taverns, each brewing its own individual ale. Religion also provided solace. In 1371, London had 106 churches and numerous monasteries. Holy Days, royal celebrations, and fairs, like the famous St. Bartholomew fair, provided relief. For example, on the occasion of the visit of Henry VI in 1432, young women representing Mercy, Grace, and Pity dispensed the wine of joy and pleasure at the Great Conduit water pump in Cheapside; at every coronation the conduits flowed with wine, and celebrations lasted for days.

The Court had its own pleasures. Jousting tournaments were held in Smithfield and Cheapside. The king went hunting for deer, boar, and hare in what are now our favorite London parks. Among the wealthy classes, chess was so popular that *The Rules of Chess* was the second book Caxton chose to print.

Westminster, linked to London by Whitehall and the Strand (but primarily via the Thames), was the center for the court and the government. From the early 14th century on, the king summoned his nobles to council at Westminster. The treasury and the courts were in Westminster Hall; here, too, the exchequer functioned, using tally sticks to keep the accounts. The sum of money owed was marked in notches along the stick, which was then split in half, one half being retained by the exchequer and the other by the debtor. It was the later burning of these old sticks in 1854 that destroyed the original buildings at Westminster.

Point Tower and Barbican Centre constructed.
- **1965** Churchill (b. 1874) dies. Greater London Council formed.
- **1973** Britain joins European Community.
- **1974** Covent Garden Market moves out to Nine Elms.
- **1976** Royal National Theatre opens.
- **1979** Margaret Thatcher becomes Britain's first female prime minister, heading a Conservative government.
- **1981** Charles, prince of Wales, marries Lady Diana Spencer in St. Paul's Cathedral. Docklands Development Corporation established.
- **1982** The Thames Flood Barrier is completed downstream at Woolwich. Barbican Arts Centre opens.
- **1988** Museum of the Moving Image opens.
- **1989** Design Museum opens.
- **1990** Thatcher steps down as prime minister. Conservative John Major replaces her.
- **1992** Royal family rocked by scandals. Queen agrees to pay income tax.
- **1993** IRA bomb explodes in London.
- **1994** Channel Tunnel officially opens.
- **1997** Tony Blair wins election for New Labour. Princess Diana killed in Paris car crash; nation mourns with huge outpouring of grief.
- **1998** Londoners approve a measure that would allow for a democratically elected mayor.

By the early 14th century the population had reached 50,000. City living conditions were awful: Pigs and poultry roamed the streets along with packhorses and dogs; the streets were open sewers; there was no clean water supply since water was drawn directly from the Thames at the Great Conduit in Cheapside; and fires were frequent. In the Plantagenet era there's a record of one street being piled so high with garbage that passage was impossible. Many individuals scraped by as rakers and gong farmers (that is, by digging through the garbage and excrement).

TUDOR AND ELIZABETHAN LONDON The modern history of London begins with the Tudors, who ascended the throne at the end of the 15th century. The first Tudor, Henry VII, laid the solid administrative foundations on which the later Tudors built a great nation under a strong monarchy.

Between 1500 and 1600, the population of London rose from 50,000 to 200,000. The wealth of the city grew, much of it acquired by the English Company of Merchant Adventurers, who traded in Antwerp. These merchants traded wool to the Dutch and shipped back to England in the mid–16th century such items as tennis balls, licorice, Bruges silks, warming pans, thimbles, and dye for cloth. The richest men in England were the 800 or so wholesale traders who carried on this trade, and it was they who founded, in 1571, the first financial institution in the city, the Royal Exchange, which functioned until 1939.

Under the Tudors, England grew in economic and political power. Henry VII's son, Henry VIII, was a powerful Renaissance prince who competed with archrival Francis I of France and also dared to challenge the pope when he was refused a divorce. He also laid down the foundations of both the British Army and Navy when he incorporated the Fraternity of Artillery in 1537, established dockyards at Deptford and Woolwich, and commissioned ships like the *Great Harry*.

Patronage of the arts and architecture was an important way to display power, and Henry invited great painters like Holbein to his court, built Nonsuch Palace (long gone), and embellished Whitehall and St. James. He also enclosed Hyde Park, St. James's Park, and Green Park for his own hunting and other pleasures.

He is, of course, best known for separating the English church from Rome and for dissolving the monasteries and confiscating church wealth and lands, including Wolsey's Whitehall Palace (he'd already taken over Hampton Court, Wolsey's country place, in 1529). Frustrated in his desire for a male heir, he married six times, executing two of his wives. Anne Boleyn passed through Traitor's Gate at the Tower in 1536 on the way to her execution, performed by a headsman from Calais, who used a sword instead of an ax. It is said that the severance was so swift that her lips were still moving in prayer when her head was on the ground. Catherine Howard was also beheaded, but she tested the block first and died proclaiming her love for Culpepper, who had already been executed for his dalliance with her.

Henry VIII's appetite was prodigious and his reputation for extravagance well earned. His kitchen, which you can see at Hampton Court Palace, was 100 feet long and 38 feet wide, and had ceilings 40 feet high. Every year £300,000 was spent on food and £50,000 on drink. At each of the two main meals of the day the Great Master of the Household was allotted 10 gallons (80 pints) of ale and 6 quarts (12 pints) of wine; the Lord Chamberlain, however, was only entitled to 4 gallons of ale and a quart and a half of wine at each meal, while a female member of the court was allowed 3 gallons of ale and a pitcher of wine every day, in addition to what she could drink at the table. Little wonder that people died of apoplexy brought on by overeating (as did Queen Anne much later).

Although Henry VIII confiscated the Church's wealth and property, the greatest physical destruction of the wealth of London's parish churches occurred under his son Edward VI (1547–53), a fanatic Protestant who presided over the stripping of church sculptures and other decorative elements. For example, at Grayfriars Church 100 tombs and monuments were ripped out. In 1549 the cloister of St. Paul's was demolished and the Lord Protector Somerset used the materials to build Somerset

House in the Strand. The bishopric of Westminster was dissolved by Edward VI in 1550 and the church returned to the Dean, but at the same time part of its revenues were transferred to St. Paul's; this is the origin of a common English saying, "robbing Peter to pay Paul." In 1553 Mary reestablished Catholicism and many public executions were carried out at Smithfield.

In 1558, Elizabeth ascended the throne, ushering in a period marked by colonial expansion, economic growth, and the flowering of the arts. A popular queen and a master politician, she secured the country 30 years of peace as she advanced England's interests against those of Catholic France and Spain; in 1588 her navy defeated a large Spanish armada that had set out to attack England. For this victory, Elizabeth gave thanks in St. Paul's.

During the Elizabethan period, literature and the arts flourished. Edmund Spenser published his epic poem, *The Faerie Queene*, dedicating it to Elizabeth, while the statesman and philosopher Francis Bacon; the soldier, explorer, and poet Sir Walter Raleigh; and others of equal versatility wrote books on history, science, and philosophy. At the same time, the English theater came into its own. In 1576, the first playhouse, called "The Theatre," was built by James Burbage in Shoreditch, followed by the Rose on Bankside in 1587, the Swan in 1595, and the Hope in 1614. Play-going became central to London life, with as many as 40 plays a year being presented at the Rose, including works by Christopher Marlowe, John Webster, Ben Jonson, Thomas Middleton, and of course, William Shakespeare, who had joined Burbage's company in 1599. Today Bankside is experiencing a similar cultural revival.

STUART LONDON   Political instability followed the death of Elizabeth, as an increasingly assertive, and largely Puritan, Parliament sought to promote its prerogatives and limit those of the monarch. The initial struggle between king and Parliament was played out in London. During James I's reign the conflict simmered, but under Charles I, the conflict exploded. The king was forced to dissolve several parliaments. In response, Parliament brought the king's ministers to trial, including Thomas Wentworth, Earl of Strafford, who was charged with 28 crimes and defended himself for 18 days in Westminster Hall. Charles fled to York and raised his standard at Nottingham in 1642. London prepared for a Royalist attack. Trained bands were called out, armed boats patrolled the Thames, and 100,000 men were pressed into digging 18 miles of trenches linking 24 bastions. The attack never came. Instead, the battle between Royalist and Parliamentary troops was fought around the country—at Edgehill, Oxford, Marston Moor, Naseby, and Preston. The king was defeated and, in 1649, stood trial in Westminster Hall, where he was condemned to death. On January 30, 1649, Charles I took his last walk through St. James's Park, flanked by guards and a troop of halberdiers in front and behind, with colors flying and drums pounding. The procession crossed a gallery at what is now Horse Guards Parade and entered the Banqueting House of Whitehall Palace. Four hours later, Charles I stepped via a window onto the wooden scaffold. After saying his prayers, he pulled off his doublet, lay down his head, and was dispatched with an ax. Legend has it that his last words were: "To your power I must submit, but your authority I deny." Today, an equestrian statue stands at the head of Whitehall looking down to the spot where he died; at the other end of Whitehall outside Westminster Hall stands a statue of Oliver Cromwell, the Puritan general who, as Lord Protector, ruled England from 1649 to 1658 following Charles's execution.

Charles I had been a great patron of the arts and invited Rubens and Van Dyck to his court. In 1621, Rubens painted the ceilings of the Banqueting House in Whitehall for £3,000 and a gold chain. Under Cromwell the arts died. Theaters were closed and the city fell under a pall until Cromwell's funeral in 1658, described by the diarist John Evelyn as the "joyfullest funeral that ever I saw." The heads of Cromwell and his generals Ireton and Bradshaw were impaled and placed above the roof of Westminster Hall. It's said that his head remained there for 25 years until it was blown down and stolen by a sentry.

The Restoration of the Merry Monarch, Charles II, restored the city to life. The theaters reopened. The king kept a lavish court at Whitehall Palace. Political and social climbers flocked there to curry favor either directly with the king or with one of his many mistresses. Courtiers came to chat with Charles while his wig was being combed and his cravat tied. One courtier might be awarded a frigate, another a company or a favorable judgment.

All the merrymaking was interrupted by two major catastrophes—the Great Plague (1665) and the Great Fire (1666). The first victim of the plague died on April 12, 1665; by December of that year, 110,000 had died. The king and his court left for Hampton Court, and other members of the upper class dismissed their servants and fled. In the city, the unemployed roamed the city looting and pillaging. Day and night, grave diggers dug mass graves but were unable to keep up with the corpses that piled up in mounds. The stench of death was horrid. When a person was diagnosed with the plague, everyone in that household was locked up for 40 days, which only increased the number of sick. Eventually, the plague ran its course, and in February 1666 the king deemed it safe enough to return to London. We all probably know the nursery rhyme "ring a ring o' roses," which refers to the first sign of the disease—a rash.

The king had hardly been in the city a few months when the Great Fire broke out in the early morning of September 2, 1666, at the bakery of Robert Farriner in Pudding Lane (a monument marks the spot today). Fanned by strong easterly winds, it quickly spread throughout the city. Samuel Pepys described flames leaping 300 feet into the air, warehouses blazing, and people jamming the river and roads in vain attempts to flee. The lord mayor, Sir Thomas Bludworth, had been awakened with the news but returned to bed with a dismissive, "a woman might piss it out." By mid-morning when the fire had consumed 300 houses, Pepys described the mayor running hither and thither wailing, "Lord, what can I do? I am spent. People will not obey me. I have been pulling down houses but the fire overtakes us faster than we can do it." The Duke of York (later James II) was put in charge of fire fighting, and the king himself also helped. The fire burned for four days, ranging over 400 acres within the city walls and 60 more acres outside, totally destroying 87 churches, 44 livery halls, and 13,000 half-timbered houses. Ten thousand were left homeless. The fire wiped out medieval London. From then on, it was decreed that all buildings be constructed of stone and brick.

Although the king saw an opportunity to create an elegantly planned city and invited architects—Sir Christopher Wren among them—to submit plans, London needed immediate rebuilding. The medieval plan was retained, and to this day London's streets follow the same routes they did in the Middle Ages—which doesn't help the flow of traffic at all. Streets were widened, though, and pavements were laid for the first time.

Six commissioners were appointed to rebuild the city. Wren was one of them. He rebuilt 51 churches (23 survive today along with the towers of six) and designed the 202-foot-high monument commemorating the fire. His greatest achievement was the rebuilding of St. Paul's.

In 1688, England experienced the "Bloodless Revolution" when James II, who had tried to reintroduce Catholicism, was driven from the throne. The Dutch

Dr. Johnson—The Man Who Invented the English Language

A most extraordinary Londoner and a wonderful character, Samuel Johnson captured the life of 18th-century London in his writings. Born in Lichfield, Johnson (1709–84) was the son of a bookseller. He went to Oxford but was forced to leave as he couldn't pay the tuition. In 1737, he arrived in London and began a journalism career, writing essays and articles for *The Rambler*. In 1755, after nine years of labor in his Gough Street quarters, he produced his famous *Dictionary of the English Language*, which set down the spellings and meanings of English words for the very first time. In that respect, Johnson could be said to have created the English language in a standard form. Before this time, there was no comprehensive source an English speaker could turn to for the accepted spellings and meanings of words. The dictionary is still considered an important authority on the language today.

Johnson met the Scottish diarist James Boswell in 1763, and it's Boswell who documented the lexicographer's habits and attitudes in the *Journal of the Tour to the Hebrides* (1785) and *The Life of Samuel Johnson* (1791). Intensely human, generous, and compassionate, Johnson was a cat lover and would buy oysters for his cat Hodge himself, just so that his servants did not "take against the poor creature," if he ordered them to do so.

Unfashionable, he usually wore a drab brown suit. (Unlike most of his contemporaries, Johnson possessed "no relish for clean linen.") Still, he once shocked the audience at a performance of his *Mahomet and Irene* by appearing in his box at Drury Lane in a brilliant scarlet waistcoat embroidered with gold lace.

A gregarious man, Johnson frequented many taverns and coffeehouses. He had a regular seat at the Turk's Head in Gerrard Street, where he formed the Literary Club with Joshua Reynolds. Regular members were David Garrick, Oliver Goldsmith, Edmund Burke, and Boswell. Among his companions, he indulged his passion for conversation and aphorism. Many of the latter are still fresh and hard to improve upon like his definition of *angling*—a stick and a string with a worm on one end and a fool on the other.

prince William and his wife, James's sister Mary, were invited to take the throne.

From 1660 to 1690, London underwent a property boom, especially in Piccadilly, the Strand, and Soho. In 1656, Covent Garden Market opened as a temporary market in the garden of the Earl (later the Duke) of Bedford. In fleeing from the Great Fire and the Great Plague, many of the gentry had discovered the advantages of living outside London in the villages north and west of the city, such as Bloomsbury, Kensington, Hackney, Islington, and Hampstead. During this period, London began to take on the appearance that it has today as the aristocracy developed their estates. They built houses for rent and laid out squares like Bloomsbury (1666) and St. James (1665)— the first of many squares developed in the late 17th and early 18th centuries.

18TH-CENTURY LONDON   During the 18th century the city of London experienced explosive growth, the population jumping from 490,000 in 1700 to 950,000 in 1800. In the process the city was transformed. Mayfair and the West End were developed. Squares were laid out as the focal points of private and

Mayhem & Riot

London has had a long tradition of riots. One of the early uprisings, the Peasants' Revolt (1381) was brought on by the introduction of the poll tax—a fact Margaret Thatcher would have done well to recall! Wat Tyler and John Ball led a peasant army to London, assembling at Black Heath and Mile End beyond Aldgate, to demand an end to serfdom and feudalism. Such was the commotion that young King Richard II, who had decided to meet with the rebels, was unable to land his barge at Greenwich. Frustrated, Tyler and his men went to Southwark, where they freed the prisoners of Marshalsea. Then they burned the Chancery at Lambeth Palace and marched down Fleet Street, sacking Savoy Palace, the home of the corrupt and hated politician John of Gaunt. They tossed Gaunt's furnishings, jewelry, and silver into the Thames. Whomever they disliked and who happened to cross their path—especially lawyers—they killed. The rebels took the Tower of London and beheaded both Sudbury, the Archbishop of Canterbury, and Hales, the royal treasurer.

Again, the king tried to appease the mob and met with them at Smithfield, but Tyler arrogantly increased his demands. The lord mayor, William Walworth, who had accompanied the king, stabbed and killed Tyler. Richard made concessions to the mob and eventually they dispersed, but once they did, the king's promises were revoked.

In 1517, the Evil May Day riots occurred when a preacher at St. Paul's Cross stirred up a crowd against foreigners. Troops were called out to control the disturbance. Guns were fired from the tower, and 400 were taken as prisoners. The ringleaders were hanged, then drawn and quartered, and finally gibbetted.

In the 17th century, mobs were an ever-present chorus on the political stage. Foreign visitors were surprised to observe how passionate and voluble the normally taciturn, complacent Englishman became on political issues. Religious conflicts were often at the heart of many of the ugly riots that broke out, like the torchlit pope-burning processions of 1673 to 1680. To stop disturbances, the Riot Act was passed in 1715, but not to much avail. In 1736, the Irish living in London were targeted. In 1743, the Gin Act provoked riots. Nearly every election was a cause for riot.

Even ministers of Parliament have incited riots. In 1778, a mob led by Lord George Gordon, MP, marched to Westminster agitating against the repeal of anti-Catholic laws in the Catholic Relief Act. More than 50,000 Gordon rioters ran amok, pillaging and burning the homes and private chapels of Roman Catholics. Storming Newgate, they freed prisoners. Breaking into Langan's distillery in Holborn, they consumed and burned 120,000 gallons of gin. In Bloomsbury, they burned down the home of Lord Chief Justice Mansfield. Moving on to the city, they attacked the Bank of England, where they were met with a volley of gunfire. Three hundred people were killed, 450 jailed, 160 tried, and 25 hung. MP Gordon was acquitted on treason charges.

In the 1880s, the early trade unionists rallied in Trafalgar Square and then went on a binge terrorizing the West End. London's tradition of rioting has continued in the 20th century, with the latest probably being the 1990 demonstrations in Trafalgar Square to protest and overturn Thatcher's poll tax.

corporate estates. Each was associated with a particular oligarchy—Hanover Square with the Whig aristocracy and the Earl of Scarborough; Cavendish with the Tories under the Earl of Oxford; and Lincoln's Inn, New Square, and Bedford Square with lawyers. If you walk down Bedford Row, to this day you will find shingles marking the chambers of many a lawyer-peer. Wealth flowed back from overseas colonies in America and also from colonies established by the East India Company, the Royal Africa Company, and the Hudson's Bay Company—all of which had been formed in the 17th century. The Port of London flourished. Between 1720 and 1780 port trade tripled. Eighteen hundred vessels were jammed into the Upper Pool of the Thames in a space for 500, while larger ships lay downriver at Woolwich, offloading their cargoes onto 3,500 lighters, or barges. Because of the congestion, it sometimes took three or four weeks to unload one vessel. The River Thames was the city's supreme highway and the source of its great wealth. As the century progressed, the role of the Thames was systematically reduced as other forms of transportation—from the stage and hackney coach to the sedan chair—were developed and new bridges were added to the one and only London bridge, like the one at Westminster in 1749. Other social developments also helped change the face of the city. Increased wealth and an incipient concern for the poor led to the establishment of major public institutions like the Foundling Hospital (1742), Chelsea Hospital (1692), and Greenwich Hospital (1705); the British Museum (1755); and the Royal Academy of Arts (1768), all of which survive to this day. A rudimentary fire department was begun. Charity schools, including august institutions that still operate today—such as St. Paul's, Westminster, and Christ's Hospital—already accommodated 3,000 pupils by 1710.

In the 18th century the major social institution, other than the church, was the coffeehouse, where literary and powerful men gathered to exchange views and gossip about politics and society. Addison, Steele, and Swift all frequented Burtons in Russell Street; Samuel Johnson could be found in the Turks Head at no. 142 the Strand; East India Company merchants frequented the Jerusalem Coffeehouse in Cornhill; and indeed, the first stock exchange was informally started at Jonathan's Coffeehouse in 1722. London's first newspaper, the *Daily Courant*, was launched in 1702 and was reaching 800 readers by 1704. Later in the century the *Guardian*, *Spectator*, and *Rambler* were all being published regularly, and for a fee Grub Street hacks would produce anonymously any kind of libel or satire—a tradition that continues to this day in the tabloids.

The politics of the age, which can best be summed up in one word, corruption, were captured by Hogarth most acidly in his series entitled *The Election*. Votes were bought and sold. Politicians stole from the public purse. Walpole, for example, was reckoned to have remodeled his house from proceeds he gained while he was prime minister. It was ever so and today the Lord Chancellor is taken to task for spending millions on the restoration of his chambers. Riots were common; during the worst, the Gordon Riots in 1780, several prisons were burned and the Bank of England and Downing Street were attacked.

In the 18th century, social life was gruesome for many. In Spitalfields, the center of silk-weaving, masters hired out looms, employing female and child labor. Workhouses and prison workshops were common too. To see the seamier side of London life, just look closely at Hogarth's *Gin Lane* or *The Rake's Progress*.

Those who could afford it took their leisure at Vauxhall Gardens (1660) or at Ranelagh Pleasure Gardens (1742). Horse racing, archery, cricket, bowling, and skittles, along with less salubrious pastimes like bullbaiting and prizefighting, were favored pursuits. Freak shows were also popular and could be found at Don Saltero's Coffee House in Chelsea. Mrs. Salmon's waxworks in Fleet was another popular venue.

Theater continued to thrive under actor-managers like David Garrick and Richard Brinsley Sheridan, both at Drury Lane. Musicians and composers were welcomed at the courts of the Hanoverian kings (George I, II, and III). Johann Christian Bach, Franz Joseph Haydn, and Mozart were all invited to perform at the court. The composer most identified with the London of this period is, of course, Handel, and it was during the reign of George III that the annual performance of that composer's *Messiah* was inaugurated. Outside of the court and the church, the city's musical traditions were launched by one Thomas Britton, who from 1678 to 1714 arranged weekly concerts in a loft above his Clerkenwell coal house.

Under the Georges, a great many artists and literary figures rose to prominence, among them, the painters Sir Joshua Reynolds (who became head of the Royal Academy of Arts, founded by George III in 1768), Thomas Gainsborough, William Turner, and William Hogarth; the great lexicographer and wit Samuel Johnson; his biographer, James Boswell; the poet Alexander Pope; the novelists Samuel Richardson and Henry Fielding; and the historian Edward Gibbon. Gibbon's multivolume *History of the Decline and Fall of the Roman Empire*, one of the great achievements of English literature, caused George III to remark, "Always scribble, scribble, scribble. Eh, Mr. Gibbon?"

19TH-CENTURY LONDON   In the 19th century, London became the wonder of the world—a wonder that was based on imperial wealth and power. In 1811, at the age of 58, the Prince of Wales, son of George III, was made regent for his father, who had become totally insane. He set up an alternate court at Carlton House and also at his extravagant palace in Brighton. At both, he lavishly and openly entertained his mistresses, including the famous Mrs. Fitzherbert (whom he had married illegally), but treated his wife Caroline abominably, to the point of banning her from his coronation, which took place in 1820 at an extraordinary cost of £238,238. In the light of today's royal scandals one might say, as the French do, *Le plus ça change le plus c'est la même chose.* Largely condemned by the populace for his extravagance and dissolute behavior, George IV did, however, contribute to the city's architectural growth and harmony, working with architect John Nash to bring some urban planning to the city. Together they laid out Regents Street, a grand highway leading from Carlton House to Piccadilly.

Plump as a partridge, Victoria ascended the throne in 1837. As the century progressed, London was further transformed into a modern industrial society, the center of an empire that ruled half the world. Victorian London was shaped by the growing power of the bourgeoisie and the queen's moral stance. The racy London of the preceding three centuries seemed to disappear, but in actuality it just went underground.

Extremes of wealth and poverty marked life in Victorian London. Thirty percent of the population lived below the poverty level. Children worked long hours in factories and sweatshops or as chimney sweeps and shoeblacks. Immigrants—Irish and European—poured into the overcrowded and foul slums. People lived in appalling conditions graphically depicted in many of Charles Dickens' novels. Gin consumption was prodigiously high in the 1820s. In an effort to reduce this, a tax on beer was abolished, and many beer houses opened as a result, which perhaps accounts for the multitude of pubs that still exist today. The River Thames was the city's main sewer and the source of its drinking water. In 1858, the Great Stink caused by the hot summer drew sensational attention to this fact.

As the century progressed, both political and social reforms were slowly applied. In 1832, the First Reform bill was passed. Social reformers worked to improve living conditions. Lord Shaftesbury strove for improvements in labor and education, Elizabeth Fry in prisons, and Florence Nightingale in hospitals. In 1870 the Education Act made elementary education compulsory.

Transportation was revolutionized. In 1829 Shillibeer's horse-drawn omnibus had been launched. In 1863 the first underground railway ran from Paddington to Farringdon, carrying 12,000 passengers in its first year. In 1890, the first electric tube ran on the Northern Line. Railway networks spread out across the country, and all entered central London at impressive gateways—Victoria, Charing Cross, St. Pancras, and Euston stations—which still stand today.

In 1851, the iron-and-glass Crystal Palace was built in Hyde Park to house the Great Exhibition, which showcased the industrial and technological wonders of the age. More than six million people flocked to see the display. With the encouragement of Prince Albert, science and technology advanced. Beginning in 1880, electric lighting illuminated London interiors.

The middle class enjoyed theater, music halls, dining out, and sports. By 1850, London had more than 50 theaters, which produced everything from popular blood-and-thunder melodramas to pageants at Christmas and Easter. Toward the end of the century, the works of Oscar Wilde, Arthur Wing Pinero, James Barrie, and George Bernard Shaw improved the repertory. Actor-manager Henry Irving and actress Ellen Terry made the Lyceum in the Strand the most exciting theater anywhere in the world. The music hall was even more popular than the theater. By 1870, the city had more than 400 music halls, compared with 57 theaters. People flocked to the Hackney Empire and the London Coliseum to hear Marie Lloyd, Dan Leno, and other stars belt out Cockney tunes and ribald folk songs. Eating out was also becoming an upper-middle-class pastime. It had been an exclusively male domain but was slowly opened to women too. At Simpsons, which opened in 1848, women had been allowed to dine in a separate room, but at the new hotel restaurants that opened—The Savoy in 1889, the Ritz in 1906, and the Cafe Royal in 1870—ladies could dine with impunity. The last became a fashionable and famous mecca for artists and writers from the 1890s to the 1920s—Augustus John, Aubrey Beardsley, Oscar Wilde, Max Beerbohm, and James McNeill Whistler. Both Edward VIII and George VI also dined here, and later patrons included Sir Compton McKenzie, T. S. Eliot, and J. B. Priestley. Eating out became a popular phenomenon with the opening of the first Joe Lyons in 1894, famous for its corner houses which provided anything from a snack to a five-course meal in a pleasant atmosphere. By 1910 there were 98 corner houses in the London area and dining out had come to the masses. Spectator sports were also popular—football, rugby, and cricket in particular. Tennis became so when the All England Croquet Club, desperate to revive its sinking fortunes, added tennis to its rostrum in 1874. So successful was the ploy that the first Wimbledon Championship was held in 1877. The manufacture of the safety bicycle in 1885 launched a biking craze that started women on the way to liberation. The "New Woman" of the 1890s took to the road on a bike without a chaperone. Shopping, too, was becoming a pastime, and already department stores were opening to satisfy the need—Whiteleys (1863, now converted into one of London's best shopping malls), Harrods (the 1860s), Liberty (1875), and Selfridge (1909)—all famous names that have survived to this day.

Here in this energetic capital, Victoria celebrated her golden jubilee before ushering in the 20th century.

THE EARLY 20TH CENTURY   The opening years of the century during the reign of Edward VII (1901–10) were filled with confidence. Britain was at the height of its power and Londoners looked forward to a radiant future. Some historians, though, have pinpointed the economic decline of Britain as early as the turn of this century, arguing that the country was already losing markets and trade to the United States.

At home, social revolution marched on. The trade union movement gained recruits. Women campaigned vigorously for the vote, chaining themselves to railings and protesting at the Houses of Parliament. In November 1911, 223 women were arrested when, angered by the government's failure to introduce a suffrage bill, they went on a window-smashing spree. Between 1905 and 1914, 1,000 suffragettes were imprisoned at Holloway. Ultimately, World War I and the social changes it wrought would help women gain the franchise.

Rivalry between Britain and Germany had been building for many years, and war broke out in 1914. British men marched off expecting the victory to be sure and fast. Instead, the war bogged down in the trenches, and terrible slaughter was committed. Back home, 900 bombs were dropped on London, killing 670 people and injuring almost 2,000. The Great War shattered the liberal middle class's illusion that peace, prosperity, and social progress would continue indefinitely in a strong and beneficent British Empire.

The peace imposed on the Germans at Versailles led inexorably to economic dislocation and ultimately to the Crash of 1929 and the Great Depression that followed in the 1930s. The country's stability was further threatened by a grave constitutional crisis in 1936, when the new and immensely popular king, Edward VIII, abdicated after refusing to renounce his love for Wallis Simpson, an American divorcée. His brother succeeded him as George VI.

Meanwhile, fascism was rising in Germany and threatening the peace with its expansionist ambitions. British and French attempts at appeasement failed and, in 1939, World War II began when Hitler marched into Poland. In 1940–41 and again in 1944–45 London lived through the Blitz. More than 20,000 people were killed and vast areas of the city were destroyed. Even the House of Commons, that redoubtable symbol of British democracy, was hit. But the spirit of the Londoners proved indomitable. They dug trenches in public parks to resist an invasion, and night after night, as waves of German planes approached, they ran for their shelters. One hundred and fifty thousand slept in the Underground, others stayed home, and still others continued partying defiantly.

The indomitable spirit of those war years (1940–45)—personified by Prime Minister Winston Churchill and by the royal family itself, which chose to remain in London despite the dangers—still evokes proud memories among Londoners. But for many, these memories are bittersweet: Britain had won the war but lost the peace. Unlike Germany and Japan, which received help under the Marshall Plan and infusions of American capital, Britain was impoverished, her industrial plant antiquated and obsolete. Dissolution of the empire followed swiftly and the nation's morale plummeted.

POSTWAR AND CONTEMPORARY LONDON   Postwar London was a glum place. Rationing continued until 1953. Only the coronation of Queen Elizabeth II in June 1953, watched by 20 million on their TV screens, seemed to lift London's spirits. Heathrow was formally opened in 1955, and in that same year Mary Quant opened her boutique on the King's Road. The coffee bar, the comprehensive school, rock and roll, and antinuclear protests all arrived in the 1950s, setting the stage for the Swinging London of the 1960s. Wowing young people around the world were the Beatles, the Kinks, the Rolling Stones, The Who, Eric Clapton's Yardbirds, and the Animals. Sixties London was suddenly the fashion and arts capital of the world.

The pace dropped in the 1970s when the Beatles disbanded, but the trendy movement continued with the establishment of Terence Conran's Habitat chain,

The Blitz

Hitler launched his blitz of London on September 7, 1940. Bombs fell on the Woolwich Arsenal, the Victoria and Albert Museum, and the East India and Commercial Docks. In the second week of the assault, more than 1,400 incendiary canisters were dropped on the Docklands. The philosopher Bertrand Russell predicted that pandemonium would sweep the city. The government prepared for the worst, anticipating as many as 18,750 casualties if bombing was continued for a week. Three lines of defense were prepared to be manned by the army and the Home Guard. A last stand was even planned in Whitehall, where machine guns were mounted on key buildings.

The government issued 2.25 million Anderson shelters, intended to be buried in the backyard—the only trouble was that most Londoners didn't have backyards. Children were evacuated to the country.

Abandoning plans to invade England, Hitler continued to bomb London. More than 3,000 incendiary bombs were dropped on December 8, 1940. Twenty-one days later, the heart of London was destroyed, but St. Paul's stood out surrounded by flames—a symbol of London's endurance.

In May 1941, the city experienced its worst bombing, when 1,436 people were killed. The House of Commons, Westminster Abbey, and the Tower of London were all hit. Thousands were left homeless, and local authorities struggled in vain to rehouse them. From September 1940 to May 1941, 20,000 tons of bombs rained down on London—20,000 died and 25,000 were injured. Hitler's attempt to demoralize the nation failed. Spirits remained high and, although people complained about the ineptitude of the authorities, daily life continued. Londoners were told to "dig for victory." Dig they did, planting their allotments. Londoners kept chickens and rabbits, and the swimming pool at the Ladies Carlton Club in Pall Mall was used as a pigsty.

The attack was renewed in 1944, but this time with "doodle bugs," or missiles. These were devastating, more destructive than anything launched before. On November 25, 1944, a crowded Woolworths at New Cross was hit and 160 people were killed.

In total, the blitz destroyed or damaged 3.5 million homes, close to half of London's housing. It wiped out whole communities like Stepney and Bermondsey. However, it couldn't conquer the spirit of the Londoners.

Anita Roddicks's Body Shop, and Saatchi and Saatchi, the world's largest advertising empire. In 1976, the city finally got its Royal National Theatre, first conceived of in 1848. The Barbican Arts Centre opened in 1982 and the Museum of the Moving Image in 1988.

Other less heart-warming developments also occurred during the postwar years. When the United States closed its doors to immigration from the West Indies in 1952, the annual number of West Indians heading for Britain rose from 1,000 to 20,000. They settled in particular areas—the Jamaicans in Brixton and Stockwell, Trinidadians and Barbadians in Notting Hill. The presence of these new immigrants brought calls to slow immigration from such right-wing politicians as Conservative Enoch Powell. In summer 1958, London experienced its first race riots in Notting Hill. Parliament responded by limiting immigration but prohibiting discrimination in housing and employment. More race riots followed in 1981 and 1985, and the race issue continues to fester as second- and third-

What'd Ya Say?

For many Americans it's a shock to discover that the British in fact speak British English, not American English; as George Bernard Shaw succinctly put it, America and England are two nations separated by a common language. Believe it or not, there are enough differences to cause, if not total communications breakdowns, then some embarrassing or amusing exchanges. For although the English use words and phrases you think you understand, they often have denotations quite different from their U.S. equivalents.

When the British call someone "mean," they mean stingy. And "homely," meaning ugly or plain in America, becomes cozy and comfortable in England. "Calling" denotes a personal visit, not a phone call; however a person-to-person phone call is "a personal call." To queue up means to form a line, which the British do at the drop of a hat. And whereas a "subway" is an underground pedestrian passage, the actual subway system is called "the Underground" or "the Tube." The term theatre refers only to the live stage; movie theaters are "cinemas" and the films themselves are "the pictures" or "the flicks." And a "bomb," which suggests a disaster in America, means a success in England.

In a grocery store, canned goods become "tins," potato chips "crisps," rutabagas "swedes," eggplants "aubergines," green squash "courgettes," while endive is "chicory" (and, conversely, chicory is "endive"). Both cookies and crackers become "biscuits," which can be either "dry" or "sweet," except for graham crackers, which are "digestives."

The going gets rougher when you're dealing with motor vehicles. When talking about the actual vehicle, very little means the same, except for the word "car," unless you mean a truck which is called a "lorry" or a station wagon which is called a "shooting brake." In any case, gas is "petrol," the hood is the "bonnet," the windshield is the "windscreen," and bumpers are "fenders." The trunk is the "boot" and what you do on the horn is "hoot," while what you do when you turn is "indicate."

Luckily, most of us know that an English apartment is a "flat" and that an elevator is a "lift," and that you don't rent a room or an apartment, you "let" it. And in any building the first floor is the ground floor, the second floor is the first floor. Once you set up housekeeping, you don't vacuum, you "hoover."

Going clothes shopping? Then you should know that undershirts are called "vests" and undershorts are "pants" to the English, while long pants are called

generation black youths find themselves treated as second-class citizens in what they regard as home. Immigrants also arrived from India and Pakistan in the 1950s and 1960s; the Punjabi Sikhs gathered in Southall and the Bengali Muslims around Brick Lane in Tower Hamlets. Their communities have also been under attack; at first they turned the other cheek, but today the Asians, who have become extremely successful entrepreneurs and businesspeople, are fighting back and demanding justice. In contrast to other European countries, though, the experience of the violence of the '80s does seem to have shocked the British into reality and to have helped mold a much more honest cross-cultural society than most, despite what the tabloid references to "frogs" and "krauts" might suggest to the contrary.

Economically, the postwar years were hard. The economic decline of the country, though, was initially masked by the nation's continued reliance on preferential "trousers," their cuffs are called "turnups" and suspenders are "braces." Panties are "knickers" and panty hose are "tights." Pullovers can be called "jumpers," little girls' uniforms called "pinafore dresses." If you want diapers, ask for "nappies."

The education system offers such varied types of school and terminology that to explain them all to the visitor would be too confusing. Briefly, however, the large English public schools such as Eton and Harrow are similar to American large private prep schools such as Andover. But the English also have other private or "independent" schools on all levels. And all of the above charge tuition. In addition, there are "state schools," which Americans would call public schools. These include "primary schools" and "secondary comprehensive schools," "secondary moderns," and "grammar schools" that are all roughly equivalent to American junior and senior high schools.

In school and elsewhere, the letter Z is pronounced "zed" and zero is "nought." And if you want to buy an after-school treat, a Popsicle is called an "iced lolly" while a box of snacks is referred to as "tuck."

Please note that none of the above terms are slang. If you really want a challenge you can always try and learn the Cockney rhyming slang. The cockneys are the indigenous Londoners, although strictly speaking they need to be born within the sound of St. Mary le Bow in Cheapside to warrant using the name.

The derivation of the word "cockney," which became synonymous with "Londoner" in the 17th century, is believed to be the Middle English "coke-ney," meaning cock's egg, a misshapen egg laid sometimes by young hens. In reference to human beings it suggested a simpleton or an effeminate townsman in contrast to a sturdy countryman. In other words, an "odd fellow." And the oddest feature about this fellow is undoubtedly the rhyming slang he has concocted over the centuries based on the rhyme—or the rhyme of the rhyme—that goes with a particular word or phrase. So take my advice and don't try to delve further, unless you happen to be Professor Higgins—pardon me, 'iggins.

Other slang can get you in trouble too. In England "pissed" isn't angry, it's drunk; "stuffed" isn't full, it's pregnant; and a rubber refers to an eraser, not what you think it refers to; while "fag," refers to a cigarette. "Fanny" in English is definitely not what you think it means—but we can't tell you what it means—we'll leave that up to you. Fanny Hill might give you a clue.

Commonwealth trade. In 1950 most Commonwealth exports flowed through London, making the port one of the busiest in the world. But in the 1960s many Commonwealth countries gained their independence and began to create their own industries and to diversify their markets. Germany, Japan, and the United States were competing, too, and London was hit hard. The death blow came for the Dockyards when they fought against containerism. The East India dock closed in 1967, followed by St. Katharine's in 1968, and the Royals in 1981. Only Tilbury, which had containerized, survived. At the same time, manufacturing jobs were lost as major companies like Thorne-EMI and Hoover relocated to other areas. Unemployment in the poorer boroughs of London like Tower Hamlets and Southwark rose from 10,000 in the 1960s to 80,000 in the 1980s.

Promising to revitalize the economy, Margaret Thatcher and the Conservatives came to power in 1979, intent on reversing what observers saw as Britain's decline.

Impressions

London, that great cesspool into which all the loungers of the Empire are irresistibly drained.

—Sir Arthur Conan Doyle, *A Study In Scarlet*

Thatcher's reforms included the privatization of major industries—from insurance companies to British Airways and British Rail—which had been nationalized by the Labour government after World War II. She reduced the power of the trade unions, traditional supporters of the Labour Party, and dismantled parts of the welfare state. At the height of her power in the early 1980s, she stood her ground defending the Falkland Islanders against the invading Argentinians. For a brief moment, gunship diplomacy returned, resuscitating English pride. Later, fiercely protective of British sovereignty, Thatcher refused to agree to a German-backed monetary union within the European Community and opposed other moves toward the creation of a federal entity. In doing so, however, she angered many backbenchers in her own party. In 1990, after the longest tenure of any modern British prime minister, Thatcher was forced out of office and replaced by her chancellor of the exchequer, John Major. Major's tired government staggered along under the weight of sexual and financial scandal and internal party strife over Britain's role in the European Union. After 18 years of Tory rule, the British people were ready for a change. In 1997 Tony Blair, who had succeeded in moving the Labour Party to the center, triumphed in the election. (For more on this, see "The City Today," above.)

4 The Architectural Landscape

Little remains, at least aboveground, of Roman or Saxon London, although at the Museum of London visitors can view substantial Roman archaeological finds unearthed during building developments. The story of London's buildings really begins with the Normans and with the finest extant example of Norman military architecture, the **White Tower** at the Tower of London. It has massive walls that are 20 feet wide at their base, while the four stories rise to a height of 90 feet. Inside, the chapel of St. John is a classic early Romanesque design complete with a line of cubiform capitals supporting the nave.

The Gothic style that followed was practiced in England from 1170 to 1560, longer than in Continental Europe, largely because the break with Rome effectively cut off England from the full influence of the Renaissance. There are three periods of English Gothic—Early, Decorated, and Perpendicular, the last reigning from 1375. The greatest masterpiece of Perpendicular design in London is the Henry VII chapel at **Westminster Abbey,** with its ornate fan vaulting. Other examples of Perpendicular Gothic are St. George's Chapel in Windsor and King's College in Cambridge. Other great Tudor Gothic buildings include **Westminster Hall** (1395) with its incredible hammer-beam roof, and the great hall at **Hampton Court Palace** (1535). To get a good sense of what Tudor London looked like, visit **Staple Inn**, a wonderful gabled-timber building in Holborn. It was Inigo Jones (1573–1652) who brought the Renaissance style to England. Jones had traveled to France and Italy and directly experienced those countries' Renaissance buildings. Appointed surveyor to the royal family, he designed the **Queen's House at Greenwich** and the **Banqueting Hall** (1619–22) in Whitehall, which both display pure Roman classicism. For the most part, though, English architects did not excel at classicism.

Christopher Wren (1632–1723) dominated the second half of the 17th century. A founding member of the Royal Society, Wren was initially interested in science and astronomy; he was 30 years old before he began his architectural career. After the Great Fire of London in 1666, Wren presented an urban plan for a new London. Rejecting his plan—the costs were deemed too high—London lost the opportunity to rebuild on a grand open scale. The city was rebuilt according to its original medieval plan of narrow streets lined with tall buildings, which contributes mightily to the problems of congestion today. Still, Wren did build 53 churches in addition to **St. Paul's.** The most outstanding examples of his work are St. Bride's (1680–1701); St. Mary Le Bow (1671–80); St. Stephen Walbrook (1675–87); St. Lawrence Jewry (1670–86); Christ Church, Newgate Street (1704); and St. Magnus Martyr, London Bridge (1670–1705).

Among Wren's team of artisans were wood-carver Grinling Gibbons, ironworker Jean Tijou, and painter Sir James Thornhill. Wren also expanded Hampton Court Palace, and he designed **Kensington Palace** and the **Royal Hospital** at Greenwich. The early 18th century ushered in a more traditional baroque form of architecture, practiced by a famous trio, John Vanbrugh, Nicholas Hawksmoor, and Thomas Archer. Vanbrugh is best known for Castle Howard in Yorkshire and Blenheim Palace in Oxfordshire. Famous for his bold steeples, Hawksmoor built **St. Mary Woolnoth** in London. Archer is responsible for **St. John, Smith Square.**

In the 1720s, baroque faded and was replaced with Palladianism, a classical style based on the works of Andrea Palladio, which was very popular from 1720 to 1760. Its major practitioners were Colen Campbell and William Kent, both of whom concentrated on country houses. These estates were usually landscaped by England's famous Capability Brown.

One architect who favored neither baroque nor Palladianism was James Gibbs (1682–1754), who designed **St. Martin-in-the-Fields** (1722) and **St. Mary-le-Strand** (1714–17), two churches that were copied throughout New England and the colonies.

During the second half of the 18th century, a revival in classicism occurred. Sir William Chambers (1723–96), the surveyor-general, created the Thames-side **Somerset House** in grand Palladian style. Today it houses the Courtauld Galleries. For his designs of domestic homes, the more innovative Robert Adam (1728–92) drew his inspiration from Greek temples and Roman villas. Adam's decorative team embellished them with stucco, metalwork, and murals. His work, albeit substantially modified by a later neo-classicist, can be seen at Apsley House.

The most familiar architectural "look" recognized by visitors to London—the symmetrically designed terrace set around a garden square—was also developed in the 18th century. It had first been used in Bath by John Wood and his son. In London a series of squares was laid out: Grosvenor, Hanover, Berkeley, Cavendish, Bedford, and Portman. Sadly, one of the greatest examples of the style—the Adelphi, a riverfront terrace designed by Robert Adam—was destroyed in 1937. John Nash (1752–1835) was another exponent of the style and some of his work survived. He designed Regent's Park and the terraces around it, along with **Regent Street**, which he laid out for the Prince Regent.

One of Britain's most individual architects was Sir John Soane (1753–1837), and anyone who is interested in architecture ought to visit his home in Lincoln's Inn Fields. Among his more famous works besides the house are **Dulwich Picture Gallery** and the **Bank of England.**

After 1840, England was swept by a Gothic Revival and, later, a series of revivals of Renaissance and baroque. The best example of the Gothic Revival in London is the **Palace of Westminster**, designed by Sir Charles Barry (1795–1860) and decorated in a marvelous manner by Pugin (1855–85). Other exponents of the style were Edmund Street (1824–81), who designed the **Law Courts in the Strand**; Alfred Waterhouse (1830–1905), who built the richly decorated Romanesque **Natural History Museum;** and Sir George Gilbert Scott (1811–78), who designed the impressive **St. Pancras Station** and Midland Hotel, as well as the **Albert Memorial.** The Albert Memorial can now be seen in all its glory thanks to a major refurbishment. Other late Victorian architects include Thomas Collcutt, whose work can be seen in the **Palace Theatre** (1890) on Cambridge Circus, the **Savoy Hotel** (1889–91), and the **Wigmore Hall** (1890). Another amazing building of this period is the Byzantine **Westminster Cathedral** (1895–1903), designed by J. F. Bentley.

In the last two decades of the 19th century, architects abandoned the ornate heaviness of Gothic Victorian and returned to greater simplicity. The Queen Anne style that evolved was most used by Norman Shaw; his work can be seen at **New Scotland Yard**, which incorporates some baroque elements. Shaw also designed a great number of brilliant London houses.

Throughout the 19th century, as science and manufacturing progressed, architects experimented with new building materials like glass and iron. At the **Palm House** at Kew, visitors can see one of the early experiments with glass, but the most dramatic example of this experimentation was the Crystal Palace built for the Great Exhibition of 1851. It was 1,851 feet long and 450 feet wide and contained 900,000 feet of glass that was supported on 3,300 iron columns with 2,224 girders. Sadly, this magnificent example of engineering was destroyed in 1936.

The 20th century opened with a return to traditionalism and a revival of baroque, considered an appropriate style for such a great imperial capital. The buildings that most exemplify this are: the **Old Bailey**, the War Office in Whitehall, and both **Victoria** and **Waterloo Stations**.

A revival of French Renaissance followed. Designed by Arthur J. Davis, the **Ritz Hotel** (1903–06) is a true Beaux Arts building, with mansard roof and a rhythmical sequence of spaces, ending with the restaurant that overlooks Green Park. Between the wars Sir Edward Lutyens dominated the architectural scene. Beginning as an Arts and Crafts sympathizer, he later advocated free-style classicism. Among his London buildings are **Britannic House** (1920–26), the **Reuter's Building** in Fleet Street, and the **Cenotaph** in Whitehall.

The only pioneering work was done at the turn of the century by William Morris and Philip Webb, who founded the Arts and Crafts movement as an alternative to historicism. They argued that buildings should relate to their sites and that local materials and elements of style should be employed (something that Frank Lloyd Wright was to do in the United States). Morris and Webb rejected mass production and called for a revival of individual craftsmanship in the decorative arts. They were largely ignored, and as a consequence, English architecture stagnated, dominated by neoclassical and other historical forms that expressed the grandiosity of empire. In fact, there was no real modern architecture in London until after 1945. The only major Arts and Crafts buildings of note were created by C. F. A. Voysey and Harrison Townsend—most of their work is out in the suburbs, but Townsend's **Horniman Museum** is on London Road, Forest Hill in South London.

The **Royal Festival Hall** designed by R. H. Matthew and J. L. Martin for the Festival of Britain in 1951 went a long way to converting the public to acceptance of modern architecture and has stood up well. It consists of a series of flowing interior spaces and was the first building in London to apply acoustical science. The **Royal National Theatre** (1967–77) by Denys Lasdun is another well-designed and highly functional building that blends in well with its riverside location. In contrast, the **Barbican** (begun in 1955) looks brutish and ugly and is impossible to navigate unless you're carrying a map of the complex, and even then it's notoriously difficult. Designed by Chamberlin, Powell, and Bon, the Barbican incorporates an arts center, a school, and housing for 6,000.

Two of the more famous modern British architects are Sir Basil Spence (1907–76) and Sir Hugh Casson (b. 1910), both of whom were influenced by the International School. Most of the former's major buildings are outside London, but the brutish approach can be seen at his **Knightsbridge Barracks** (1967–69) in Kensington. Sir Hugh Casson designed the Elephant House at the zoo. Architects Philip Powell (b. 1921) and John Hidalgo Moya (b. 1920) built the **Museum of London.** Other influential architects include Peter and Alison Smithson, who designed the **Economist Buildings** in St. James's Street; James Stirling, responsible for the Tate Gallery Extension; and Sir Norman Foster, who designed the Channel 4 buildings and has won the commission for a £100 million extension at the British Museum.

Perhaps the most infamous building in London, designed by R. Seifert in the 1960s, is the **Centre Point** (1962–66) office block, which looms over Tottenham Court Road. For many years it stood vacant and was the focus of a protest by the homeless. Today it has become a landmark of sorts, but it stands, as do most of Seifert's skyscrapers, including his **National Westminster Tower** (1981), as an example of what Pevsner has called the ruination of the London skyline. Other monstrosities on the skyline have been contributed by non-British architects, like the **Canary Wharf Tower** designed by Cesar Pelli in 1988.

Architectural innovations have always generated controversy, with the Prince of Wales throwing in his comments for good measure. Under the Tories, free development was encouraged, and as a consequence, ugly concrete blocks were thrown up around St. Paul's and strung along Marylebone Road. Developers also built tower blocks to house the poor which have turned into eyesores and fail dismally to create community. The terraces and houses that the poor were moved from have now been gentrified from Hammersmith to Hackney and south of the river in Greenwich, Camberwell, and Battersea. The yuppies who gentrified these areas brought their cars into the city and today the traffic problems are serious and getting worse every day with no sign of relief given the Britishers' stubborn attachment to their wheels. In 1981 the London Docklands Development Corporation was established to redevelop the abandoned Docks. Sadly, even though the Olympia and York's Canary Wharf are fine examples of modern urban design, much of the rest of the infrastructure is still being created.

Today, the battles continue. The latest laughing stock after the new **British Library,** which critics berated until they actually got to go inside, is the **Millennium Dome** which is being designed by Sir Richard Rogers. Dear to the heart of one of the more despised friends of Tony Blair, Peter Mandelson, the Minister without Portfolio, it has become the butt of jokes and severely criticized as wasteful. While we will have to wait until 2000 to actually see the outcome, there will be plenty of entertaining satirical commentary between now and then.

5 Pies, Puddings & Pints: The Lowdown on British Cuisine

Gone is the sodden cabbage and the gray meat that used to lay on every English dinner plate. In its place, London can finally boast of thrilling food from all over the world. And furthermore, challenged by the ethnic cuisines of their immigrant population, the English have responded by improving and reinterpreting their own food to create "Modern British," as they call it. Suffice it to say that the late humorist George Mikes' comment that "the Continentals have good food; the English have good table manners" is no longer deserved. Even Michelin agrees, having awarded some of its coveted stars to several English restaurants.

MEALTIMES & DINING CUSTOMS   Mealtimes in England are much the same as in the United States. England is still famous for its huge breakfast—bacon, eggs, grilled tomato, and fried bread, preferably fried in the bacon fat. Toast will be served cold in toast racks—another strange British habit that persists at finer dining establishments. Other traditional breakfast dishes are kippers or smoked herring. The finest kippers come from the Isle of Man, Whitby, and Loch Fyne in Scotland. The herrings are split open, placed over oak chips and smoked slowly to produce a nice pale-brown smoked fish which is delicious.

Lunch, usually eaten between noon and 2pm, is often taken at the pub—or else consists of a sandwich on the run. Pub fare used to consist of old stalwarts like bangers and mash, pasties, Scotch eggs, curry or lasagna, but the new or renovated pubs are offering much better and fresher fare. The food has been given a new look and a new treatment in such pubs as the Chapel off the Edgware Road, The Engineer in Primrose Hill, or the Eagle in Clerkenwell. Here you will find menus that change daily and dishes that are innovative and flavorsome. Of course, standard pub fare still exists and may include cornish pasties (a pastry envelope filled with seasoned chopped potatoes, carrots, and onions, which was traditionally taken down the mines or to the fisheries by Cornishmen), Scotch eggs (a hard-boiled egg surrounded by breaded sausage meat, or a Ploughman's (a plate of cheese, bread and pickles). Other light meal oddities include a dark, foul-smelling paste called Marmite which is spread on bread by some Brits, who swear by its health-giving properties. Watercress and anchovy paste is another combination often celebrated at the tea table.

Afternoon tea, still enjoyed by many, may be limited to a simple cup of tea accompanied by biscuits or cakes, or it can be a much more formal affair starting with delicate tiny crustless cucumber or watercress sandwiches, followed by scones or crumpets with jam and possibly cream, and finishing with a selection of cakes and pastries—all accompanied by a properly brewed pot of tea. Don't refer to it as high tea. High tea is a working man's meal taken at the end of the day around 6 or 7pm consisting of such atrocities as spaghetti on toast and similar hot snacks. Dinner, usually enjoyed around 8pm, may consist of traditional English dishes or any number of ethnic cuisines that are currently found in London, the hands-down favorite still being Indian. If there is one ethnic cuisine to taste in London, then it should be Indian, for London has the best in the world. Go to Cafe Spice Namaste, Chutney Mary's, or Veeraswamy.

Supper is traditionally a late-night meal, usually eaten after the theater.

SOME TRADITIONAL FAVORITES

You don't have to travel around England to experience regional English dishes—you can find them all over London. On any pub menu you're likely to encounter such dishes as shepherd's pie, a deep dish of chopped cooked beef mixed with onions and seasoning, covered with a layer of mashed potatoes, and served hot. You might also find Lancashire hot pot, a stew of mutton, potatoes, onions, and carrots, the English equivalent of a *pot au feu*.

Among appetizers the most typical are potted shrimp (small buttered shrimp preserved in a jar), prawn cocktail, and smoked salmon served with lemon and brown bread. You might also be served pâté or fish pie, which is a very light fish pâté. If you're an oyster lover, try some of the famous Colchester variety. Most menus will also feature a variety of soups, including cock-a-leekie (chicken soup flavored with leeks, actually Scottish in provenance), a game soup (such as turtle flavored with sherry), or any number of others.

The most traditional main course is roast beef and Yorkshire pudding—the pudding made with a flour base and cooked under the joint to absorb the fat flavor from the meat. The beef might be a large rolled sirloin which, so the story goes, was named by James I (not Henry VIII as some claim) when he was a guest at Houghton Tower, Lancashire. "Arise Sir Loin," he cried as he knighted the joint with his dagger. Another dish that makes similar use of a flour-based batter is toad-in-the-hole, in which sausages are cooked. Game is also a staple on English tables, especially pheasant and grouse.

On any menu you'll find fresh seafood too—cod, haddock, herring, plaice, or Dover sole, the aristocrat of flat fish, delicious served on the bone. Skate is another flat fish rarely found on American menus. It has a wonderful flavor and moist, fleshy texture. Look for it in black butter—that is, with capers and butter. Cod and haddock are the most popular for use in the traditional fish and chips (chips, of course are fried potatoes, or thick French fries) which the true Briton covers with salt and vinegar.

The East End of London has quite a few interesting old dishes, among them tripe and onions. East Enders can still be seen on Sunday at the jellied eel stall by Petticoat Lane devouring their share of eel or cockles, mussels, whelks, and winkles, all small shellfish/snails eaten with a touch of vinegar. Eel-pie and mash shops can still be found in London purveying what is really a minced beef pie topped with flaky pastry and served with mashed potatoes and a portion of jellied eel.

The British call desserts "sweets," with trifle topping the list. It consists of sponge cake soaked in sherry or brandy, coated with fruit or jam, and topped with a cream custard. A "fool" such as gooseberry fool is a light cream dessert whipped up from seasonal fruits. Fruit crumbles are made with a variety of fruits—apple, rhubarb and blackcurrant—topped with a "crumble" which contains all the ingredients of normal pastry but has not been rolled into a pastry sheet. Other old favorites are bread and butter pudding, and, of course, the traditional British plum pudding served at Christmas, which is suet, dried fruit, and other ingredients steamed together and enriched with brandy or similar. Variations of this include a richly sweet treacle pud, and then, of course, there's spotted dick, everyone's nightmare.

Cheese is traditionally served after dessert as a savory. There are many regional cheeses, the best known being Cheddar. Although the country doesn't produce as many cheeses as France, there are still many regional cheeses, and a trip to Neal's Yard Dairy in Neal's Yard or to the food counters at Harvey Nichols' Fifth Floor Cafe, Harrods, or Fortnum & Masons will introduce you to some you've probably never heard of. Among the more common are County cheeses that include Cheshire, Leicester, Double Gloucester, and many more. Caerphilly, a mild, crumbly cheese, comes from Wales; while Stilton, the king of British cheeses, a blue-veined cheese often enriched with port, comes from Leicestershire, Derbyshire, and Nottinghamshire.

TEA & THEN SOME: DRINKS GALORE

The quintessential British drink is, of course, tea, which is used by the British to assuage any and all problems or stressful situations. Tea in Britain does not consist of a tea bag in a tea cup; it is served in a pot which is properly warmed and in which the tea is brewed. All kinds of tea are available. Afternoon tea is still one of the great British rituals. Other oddly British soul-quenchers include something called Bovril and Horlicks.

Beer is an Englishman's solace. But there are beers and then there are beers. The primary distinction is made between lager and bitter. Lager is a German-style beer that Americans are used to, light, slightly carbonated, and served cold; but most British prefer bitter, which is higher in alcohol, more flavorful, less carbonated, and usually served at room temperature. In recent decades the English have consolidated a Campaign for Real Ale to protest the centralization and standardization of beers by the large breweries. Many pubs now offer these "real" ales, distinguishable at the bar by hand-pumps that must be "pulled" by the barkeep as opposed to taps that are just flipped on. Real ales are natural "live" beers, allowed to ferment in the cask. They are in many ways the equivalent of American microbrews. Cocktails are not drunk quite in the same way as they are in America, although that has changed in cool Britannia too. Simple drinks like whisky and soda and gin and tonic in summer are still common, but bars are increasingly offering an array of martinis and tropically inspired drinks, including margaritas, daiquiris, and punches. In summer, a great thirst-quencher, although it sounds awful, is the shandy, which is half lager and half lemonade or ginger beer; the lager and lime is 90% lager and 10% or less Rose's lime juice. Other unique British combinations are the Black Velvet—Irish in this case—which consists of Guinness and champagne; or a rum and black, which is dark rum with blackcurrant juice added. A drink associated with special summer occasions is a Pimms cup, which consists of Pimms mixed with lemon or other ingredients. Cider is also served and there is something called "scrumpy," produced in the West Country, which is extraordinarily powerful stuff.

The English have also long had a reputation for being great wine connoisseurs, primarily because they controlled the Bordeaux wine region for so many centuries. Claret has been their wine of choice for centuries, but today wines from all over the world can be found on wine lists and in wine stores. In fact, the Brits are very savvy about wine. Because taxes and other factors make wine expensive, the Brits have been the first to seek out good-tasting, reasonably priced wines from Chile, Uruguay, South Africa, New Zealand, and other new wine-growing regions. Madeira and port are also favorites and the port is still passed around at traditional dinners. The English do make their own wines but they are the fruit variety made from such ingredients as elderberry. Soft drinks, of course, are also available. If you order water in a restaurant, you'll be asked if you want still or carbonated. Both are bottled and carry a price tag. If you want plain free tap water you'll need to ask specifically for it.

6 Are You Clubbable?

Perhaps it has to do with the weather, but whatever the reason, a lot of English life seems to take place behind closed doors in clubs. From membership-only bars and nightclubs to more organized affairs (including the House of Commons, if the comments of the new female MPs are to be believed), the English love the notion of clubs and they're adept at forming them. Whatever the activity, there's a club for it—political, social, professional, or sporting. It seems gentlemen like to have a place to escape from their wives—particularly in London, where a number of gentlemen's clubs still steadfastly refuse to allow women. The women-at-clubs issue has become a hot controversy, with some members resigning to protest what they consider benighted policies.

Impressions

Would I were in an alehouse in London!
I would give all my fame for a pot of ale, and safety.

—Shakespeare, *Henry V*

Unless you're invited by a member, you'll not be allowed to enter the hallowed portals of most clubs. To give you an edge if you find yourself engaged in conversation with a high-born English gent, I'll name a few.

Boodle's is the quintessential St. James club to which country gentlemen repair when they visit London. Founded in 1762 by Edward Boodle, it has counted among its members the historian Edward Gibbon, the Duke of Wellington, slave abolitionist William Wilberforce, and both the elder and younger Pitts of English politics.

The **Carlton Club,** also in St. James, is the Conservative club par excellence founded in 1832 by the Tories after they had taken a severe beating in the election. Club rules require that members share the views and principles of the Conservative party. Among its early members were Disraeli and, oddly enough, Gladstone—until 1860, when he resigned after being insulted for his more liberal views. Important decisions made here include the election of Bonar Law as leader and the withdrawal from Lloyd George's coalition in 1922.

The **Reform Club** in Pall Mall is the counterpart for radicals. It was founded in 1836. Fans of the movie *Around the World in 80 Days* might remember that Phineas Fogg accepted the bet in this club's smoking room. Today, the Reform is more social than political. It's been open to women since 1981.

On Garrick Street, the **Garrick** is a club for actors, painters, and writers. Thackeray, Dickens, and Irving were all members. Today, its membership is drawn primarily from publishing, TV, and film. It's been a hotbed of controversy for its stern refusal to admit women.

The **Travellers** was indeed started for travelers by Lord Castlereagh in 1819. Particularly for diplomats, this was a place to share stories and findings. Today, this social club is not restricted to "travelers."

The most aristocratic of them all is **White's** in St. James. Its membership rolls have included several kings—George IV, William IV, and Edward VII. Admirals and prime ministers have all gathered here, too. Originally White's Chocolate House, it was founded in 1693. The essayist Richard Steele, the poet and satirist Alexander Pope, and poet and dramatist John Gay all frequented it. Pope wrote in his *Dunciad* (1728) that this was "a place to teach oaths to youngsters and to nobles wit." Jonathan Swift thought ill of White's and is reckoned to have shook his fist at the building every time he passed by. Members dined here or went on drinking binges or gambled all night. Bets were placed on anything—births, marriages, and deaths. Lord Arlington placed a bet on which of two raindrops would reach the bottom of a window first. White's has remained largely a social club, except for a spree of partisan politics in the 1790s when supporters of William Pitt the younger gathered here.

A list of all of London's clubs would get very long—especially if one includes the many livery companies (professional societies), which maintain grand halls and traditions that are centuries old. Clubs are part of the English landscape, and pubs in their own way operate as such. Then, there are the sports clubs—soccer, cricket, and rugby— which also excite the great passions of Londoners.

7 Famous Londoners

Martin Amis (b. 1949)   Son of Kingsley Amis, he has bitterly satirized English society in such novels as *The Rachel Papers, Dead Babies, Money, London Fields* and *Times Arrow.* A few years ago his demand for a £500,000 advance for his latest novel and his leaving of his longtime agent caused a major literary storm.

Francis Bacon (1909–92)   Born in Dublin, he came to London at age 14 and taught himself to paint. This Expressionist painter first caused a furor with his *Three Studies for Figures at the Base of a Crucifixion* displayed at the Tate in 1944. His work—such as his famous series of carcasses—explores grotesque and satirical themes.

Aubrey Vincent Beardsley (1872–98)   The most famous Victorian illustrator and a master of art nouveau. He illustrated editions of both Alexander Pope's *Rape of the Lock* and Oscar Wilde's *Salome.* He died at age 26 of tuberculosis.

Annie Besant (1847–1933)   An atheist and Fabian in her youth, she discovered theosophy in 1889 and became a disciple of the spiritualist Helena Blavatsky. She went to India and established the Indian Home Rule League and later introduced her protégé Krishnamurti to the West.

William Blake (1757–1827)   This Romantic poet is known for visionary, symbolic poems such as his *Songs of Innocence* (1789) and *Songs of Experience* (1794). He also received critical acclaim for his illustrations of *The Book of Job*, Dante's *Divine Comedy*, and Milton's *Paradise Lost.*

William Booth (1829–1912)   Minister and social worker, he founded the Salvation Army in 1878.

James Boswell (1740–95)   He wrote the classic English biography *The Life of Samuel Johnson* (1791), and his *London Journal* established him as a colorful portrayer of 18th-century London.

Thomas Carlyle (1795–1881)   A Scottish historian, he moved to London in 1834 to gain access to reference works for his manuscript on the French Revolution, which took him more than three years to write. He developed a great friendship with Emerson and became an influential social critic.

Thomas Chippendale (1718–79)   The most famous furniture designer in English history, he set up a workshop in St. Martin's Lane.

Sir Noel Coward (1899–1973)   This wit and gossip wrote and produced plays, such as *Private Lives*, that still delight audiences. He also wrote the screenplay for *Brief Encounters*, several novels, and many songs, including "Mad Dogs and Englishmen," which he performed himself.

Charles Dickens (1812–70)   This master of English literature portrayed the social ills of Victorian London, from his first book *Sketches by Boz* to his last, *The Mystery of Edwin Drood.* While residing at 48 Doughty Street in WC1 for only two years (1837–1839), he produced *Pickwick Papers, Nicholas Nickleby*, and *Oliver Twist.*

Sir Arthur Conan Doyle (1859–1930)   Creator of Sherlock Holmes, fiction's most famous sleuth, Conan Doyle resided at 12 Tennison Rd. in SE 25. Besides his popular mysteries, he wrote serious historical novels. A professed spiritualist, he was knighted in 1902.

Margaret Drabble (b. 1939)   In her early novels, such as *The Millstone* and *The Middle Ground*, Drabble explored the conflict between tradition and modernity. Her later works have focused largely on the role of women in English society.

Henry Fielding (1707–54)   His early career as a writer of comedy, farce, and burlesque ended when the Licensing Act was passed in 1737—the law partly inspired by his own attacks on Walpole. Fielding then turned to the novel and helped make it the most popular form of literature in England. He produced the classics *Joseph Andrews* (1742) and *Tom Jones* (1749). He also served as a magistrate in London and established an early type of police force.

Elizabeth Fry (1780–1845)   This Quaker philanthropist worked to improve the conditions of women at Newgate prison. Fry also set up soup kitchens.

David Garrick (1717–79)   A great Shakespearean actor, theatrical producer, and playwright. He is buried in Poets' Corner in Westminster Abbey.

William Hogarth (1697–1764)   A painter and engraver, Hogarth revived the medieval art form of morality pictures. His *Harlot's Progress*, *The Rake's Progress*, and *Marriage à la Mode* are a series of satirical engravings.

Jack the Ripper (???)   Although his identity has never been confirmed, there has been much speculation that he might have been a member of the royal family. He murdered six prostitutes, all found in the East End in 1888.

Glenda Jackson (b. 1936)   She first won acclaim in the 1960s for her stage performances with the Royal Shakespeare Company. Then she garnered two Academy Awards for her roles in *Women in Love* and *A Touch of Class*. In 1992, she gave up acting to take her seat in Parliament as Labour MP for Hampstead. She is also running for mayor of London.

Elton John (b. 1947) Born Reginald Dwight in Pinner North London, he took the name Elton John in the late '60s. He conquered the U.S. and Britain with such early albums as *Elton John, Honky Chateau,* and *Goodbye Yellow Brick Road*. A great showman and a major glitter rock star, he suffered severe emotional and drug problems but recovered. A friend of Princess Diana's, he performed a touching eulogy at her funeral, a version of "Candle in the Wind" that he had rewritten for the occasion and that went on to break music records as the best-selling single of all time.

Samuel Johnson (1709–84)   Most famous for his *Dictionary of the English Language* and his complete edition of Shakespeare, Johnson left Oxford without a degree. He came to London at age 28. While residing at 17 Gough Square, he frequented London's coffeehouses and founded what is still the most famous London eating club. Original members of the "Club" included playwright Oliver Goldsmith, political philosopher Edmund Burke, and painter Joshua Reynolds. Johnson was a master of aphorism, as evidenced by his definition of fishing: "A stick and string with a worm on one end and a fool on the other."

John Keats (1795–1821)   Born in London, Keats gave up a career in surgery to become a poet. When *Endymion* was published in 1818, he was called "a Cockney poet." Shelley argued that these vicious attacks caused the breakdown of his health. He contracted tuberculosis, sailed for Italy in 1820, and died in Rome in 1821.

Lillie Langtry (1852–1929)   The greatest English beauty of her era, she achieved fame as the publicly acknowledged mistress of the Prince of Wales, the son of

Queen Victoria (later Edward VII). She became a stage actress and reigned as an arbiter of taste from her town house near Cadogan Square.

Karl Marx (1818–83)   After being expelled from Paris, Marx moved to London in 1849. Extremely poor, he lived with his family in two small rooms at 28 Dean St. in Soho, often subsisting on potatoes and bread. His studies in the British Museum Reading Room were his primary occupation, and it was here that he wrote his most famous work, *Das Kapital*. In September 1864, he took part in the first meeting of the International Working Men's Association, held at St. Martin's Hall in London. He is buried in Highgate Cemetery.

George Orwell (1903–50)   Born in India as Eric Arthur Blair, he attended Eton and moved to Burma before returning to live penuriously in Europe—an experience he described in *Down and Out in Paris and London* (1933). He is most famous for *Animal Farm* (1946) and *1984* (1949).

Samuel Pepys (1633–1703)   In his celebrated *Diaries* (1660–69), Pepys meticulously and vividly recorded the events of his day. He founded the civil administration of the Royal Navy, converting it from an occasional service to a permanent and efficient military force. He resided at what is now 12–14 Buckingham St.

Alexander Pope (1688–1744)   Born in London to Catholic parents, he contracted Pott's disease early in life. This caused a curvature of the spine and stopped him from growing taller than 4 feet 6 inches. Barred from education because of his religion, he taught himself. His poem "The Rape of the Lock" (1714) mocked the fashionable society of the day. His translations of the *Iliad* and the *Odyssey* brought him great wealth. In *The Dunciad* (1728), he scolded literary hacks and other enemies; his *Essay on Man* (1734) was his most ambitious work.

Henry Purcell (1659–95)   The major figure of English baroque music, Purcell was an organist at Westminster Abbey. Composer of the opera *Dido and Aeneas*, he also wrote many odes, the most famous of which is *Sound the Trumpets*, composed for James II's birthday.

George Bernard Shaw (1856–1950)   Born in Ireland, Shaw came to London in 1876 and worked as a journalist and music critic. He revolutionized the theater with his issue-oriented plays that satirized the institutions and philosophies of the period. *Pygmalion*, which mocked the class system, has become his most famous play. *Saint Joan* and *Heartbreak House* are two other major works that still find an audience.

Sir Arthur Seymour Sullivan (1842–1900)   This composer was the musical half of the enormously popular duo Gilbert and Sullivan—famous for such operettas as *The Mikado*, *The Yeoman of the Guard*, and *H.M.S Pinafore*. Sullivan also composed one of the most famous Anglican hymns, "Onward Christian Soldiers."

William Makepeace Thackeray (1811–63)   Born in Calcutta, India, he studied at Cambridge and at the Middle Temple (law). His novels appeared in serial form in magazines. *Vanity Fair* (1848) is a brilliant satire of early 19th-century upper-middle-class life; it was followed by *Pendennis*, *Henry Esmond*, and *The Newcomes*.

Joseph Mallord William Turner (1775–1851)   Son of a London barber, J. M. W. Turner became Britain's greatest landscape painter. At 14, he entered the Royal Academy and went on to paint landscapes in watercolors and seascapes in the Dutch tradition. His interest in the violent moods of nature has been attributed to the effect his mother's madness had on him. He lived at 23 Queen Anne St.

Evelyn Arthur St. John Waugh (1903–66)   This London-born author satirized the madcap frivolity of the English aristocracy in such works as *Vile Bodies*, *The Loved One*, and, most famous of all, *Brideshead Revisited.*

Oscar Wilde (1854–1900)   Born in Dublin, he is most famous for his witty, sophisticated plays *The Importance of Being Ernest*, *Lady Windermere's Fan*, and *An Ideal Husband.* He also wrote two collections of fairy tales and a novel, *The Picture of Dorian Gray.* In 1891, the Marquess of Queensberry accused him of having homosexual relations with the Marquess's son, Lord Alfred Douglas. In response, Wilde brought a libel action against him. In turn, Wilde was charged with homosexual offenses and served two years in jail, where he wrote his most famous poem, *The Ballad of Reading Gaol.* Released in 1897, he went to live in Paris and died in poverty.

Virginia Woolf (1882–1941)   In her writing, such as the essay *Street Haunting* or the novel *Mrs. Dalloway*, Woolf's excitement about her city appears in almost every line. From about 1906, Woolf was identified with a brilliant circle of writers and artists who called themselves the Bloomsbury Group. She lived at 29 Fitzroy Sq.

Sir Christopher Wren (1632–1723)   Mathematician and astronomer, Wren became a celebrated architect responsible for rebuilding much of London after the Great Fire of 1666. He designed 51 churches, including St. Paul's Cathedral, St. Bride's in Fleet Street, and St. Mary Le Bow in The City. He was also responsible for the Royal Hospital in Chelsea and the Royal Naval College in Greenwich. Knighted for his service, Wren is buried in St. Paul's Cathedral.

8 Recommended Books & Films

BOOKS

GENERAL HISTORY   For a very personal portrait of London, John Russell's *London* is filled with entertaining anecdotes and fascinating observations; it's enhanced by large color photographs and illustrations. For a drier but nevertheless interesting discussion of all of the social institutions of England, Anthony Sampson's *Anatomy of Britain* and his later *Changing Anatomy of Britain* can't be beaten. If you're a lover of fascinating minutiae, then you'll love *The London Encyclopedia* (Macmillan, 1983), edited by Ben Weinreb and Christopher Hibbert. Hibbert's *London: The Biography of a City* (Penguin, 1969) is also another treasure from this great and very accessible historian. *London: A Social History* (Hamish Hamilton, 1994) by Roy Porter brings the history of this great city to life. For children, *The Wonderful Story of London* (Odhams, 1956) will capture the imagination; it may only be available in secondhand bookstores. Other favorites of mine include novelist and literary critic V. S. Pritchett's *London Perceived* (Hogarth, 1986) and Virginia Woolf's *London Scene: Five Essays* (Random House, 1986), which depicts the city in the 1930s and is a literary gem.

For 17th-century history, nothing compares to Pepys and Evelyn. For the flavor of the 18th century, read Daniel Defoe's *Tour Through London About the Year 1725.* For insight into 19th-century England from an outsider's point of view, pick up Taine's fascinating *Journey Through England.* A magnificent, not-to-be missed work of modern history is E. P. Thompson's *The Making of the English Working Class.* For a turn-of-the-century portrait of London's East End, see Jack London's portrait. For a modern insightful interpretation of recent events, particularly Thatcherism, read novelist Julian Barnes' *Letters from London.*

So poetry, which is in Oxford made
An art, in London only is a trade.

—John Dryden

Other great historical works worth reading are *London Life in the Eighteenth Century* by M. Dorothy George, an enlightened and readable study of life in the Georgian period; *The Making of Modern London*, by Gavin Weightman and Steve Humphries, on the Victorian development of London; and *The Long Weekend*, by Robert Graves and Alan Hodge, a fascinating and straightforward account of Britain between the wars. Specialty books include *Americans in London* (William Morrow, 1986) by Brian N. Morton, a street-by-street guide to the clubs, homes, and favorite pubs of more than 250 famous Americans. Many literary guides are available, too. *The Writer's Britain*, by Margaret Drabble, is an illustrated favorite, although not strictly about London.

ARCHITECTURE   For an easy and succinct overview, read the sections on England in Doreen Yarwood's excellent *The Architecture of Europe* (Batsford, 1974). For exclusive coverage of England, there's *A History of English Architecture* (Penguin, 1979) by Peter Kidson, Peter Murray, and Paul Thompson. Among the many books on London, the giant of them all is Pevsner's *London* (Penguin, 1957) a two-volume survey. This labor of love recently has been revised (1993) by Bridget Cherry; it's only available in England. The *Architects of London* (Architectural Press, 1979) by Alistair Service brings those master builders to life. Nairn's *London* (Penguin, 1988) is another very personal book about London, its history, and buildings. Donald Olsen's *The City as a Work of Art: London, Paris and Vienna* (Yale University Press, 1986) is a well-illustrated text tracing the development of these great cities. The poet John Betjeman has always concerned himself with the preservation of England's history and heritage, especially its buildings; his *Victorian and Edwardian London* (Batsford, 1969) expresses his love for that era in particular.

FICTION   It's hard to know where to begin, because of all the arts, England is probably richest in literature. Chronologically, start with Chaucer, who delivers a wonderful portrait of medieval London in his *Canterbury Tales*. Follow with Shakespeare and Ben Jonson. Then the essayists Addison and Steele, whose *De Coverley Papers* portray 17th-century society and its concerns in graphic detail. Pepys and Evelyn, of course, are wonderful friends with which to explore the London of this period. For the 18th century, Fielding is a great companion, as are Swift and Defoe. Boswell's *London Journal* and his other books also make wonderful reading. Anything by Dickens or Thackeray will provide insight into Victorian London. The period from the turn of the century to the 1920s and 1930s is best captured in the works of Virginia Woolf, Henry Green, Evelyn Waugh, P. G. Wodehouse, and Elizabeth Bowen. Contemporary authors who provide insight into London society are Muriel Spark, Iris Murdoch, Angus Wilson, V. S. Naipaul, Margaret Drabble, Martin Amis, Angela Carter, Ian McEwan, Jeanette Winterson, Graham Swift, Anita Brookner, Kazuo Ishiguro, Hanif Kureishi, Allan Hollinghurst, Nick Hornby, and a legion of others.

BIOGRAPHY   As for biographies, again there are so many to choose from. Among the great ones are Jackson Bate's portrait of Samuel Johnson, and the many royal portraits that have been written by Antonia Fraser, as well as her book on Oliver Cromwell. Other marvelous political biographies include Blake's *Disraeli*.

For a portrait of Disraeli's opponent Gladstone, see those written by Richard Shannon or H. C. Matthews. When it comes to Winston Churchill, you can read his autobiography written in brilliant English, or turn to Martin Gilbert's *Churchill: A Life* (St. Martin's, 1991). Richard Ellman's life of *Oscar Wilde* (Knopf, 1988) captures turn-of-the-century society. As for the royals who have been so much in the tabloids, two books dredge up all the lurid details—Anthony Holden's *The Tarnished Crown* (Random House, 1993) and A. N. Wilson's *The Rise and Fall of the House of Windsor* (W. W. Norton & Company, 1993). For Diana's perspective on the whole family and her role in it, read *Diana Her True Story* (Simon & Schuster) by Andrew Morton.

FILMS

Britain has a venerable independent film industry that has risen and fallen since the 1930s, when the Korda brothers rescued it from its first trough. Today it is supported by the government and by such institutions as the British Film Academy, (which awards a female version of Oscar known as the Stella) and the British Film Institute.

Here are some suggestions for movie favorites to put you into a British/London mood. If you haven't already seen it, start with the 1997 hit *The Full Monty*. More insight into the changes in British and London life can be gleaned from such fairly recent films as *Secrets and Lies, Naked, Trainspotting, Four Weddings and a Funeral, The Crying Game, Mona Lisa, My Beautiful Laundrette, Educating Rita,* and *A Clockwork Orange.*

Period dramas have always been a British strong suit and they still are. Recent worthies include the many film interpetations of Jane Austen's novels, *Pride and Prejudice, Persuasion,* and *Sense and Sensibility,* and such older grand historic spectacles as *Becket, A Man for All Seasons,* and *The Lion in Winter.* Transplanting dramas from one era to another is another favorite British ploy, whether on the musical or film stage. See Richard Loncraine's 1996 film *Richard III,* for example.

To relive the last time London was as swinging as it is now, watch a variety of takes on the '60s: *This Sporting Life* (1963), *The Pumpkin Eater* (1964), *Darling* (1965), *Georgy Girl* (1966), *Alfie* (1966), *The Knack, The Jokers, Blow-Up* (1966), *Up the Junction* (1967), *If* (1968), *Kes* (1969), *To Sir with Love,* and *Sunday Bloody Sunday.*

The Brits are also well known for turning out better-than-most mysteries and crime and spy thrillers. After all, Alfred Hitchcock did get his start here and film makers have had plenty of writers to draw from, whether it be Graham Greene, John Le Carre, Agatha Christie, or P. D. James. Among the classics are the *Lodger* (1926), *Dr. Jekyll and Mr. Hyde* (1931), *The Man Who Knew too Much* (1934), *The Thirty-Nine Steps* (1935), *The Adventures of Sherlock Holmes* (1939), *The Ipcress File* (1965), *Frenzy* (1972), and *The Long Good Friday* (1979).

And then there are my favorite Golden Oldies that may have something or nothing to do with London: *Brief Encounter* (1946), *The Ladykillers* (1955), *Passport to Pimlico* (1948), and *The Bridge on the River Kwai* (1957).

2 Planning an Affordable Trip to London

London is expensive, more expensive than any American city (even New York). But this doesn't mean that you can't enjoy a marvelous, affordable vacation here; that's the raison d'être for this guidebook. Your trip will be much more enjoyable—and certainly a lot smoother—if you plan it properly. This chapter is designed to help you do so, step-by-step.

1 The $75-a-Day Premise

Our premise is that two people traveling together can have a fine vacation for $75 a day per person. That $75 is meant to cover the price of a double room and two meals a day. (The budget takes into account that you'll most likely be served a full breakfast at your hotel.) This budget will provide you with adequate accommodations (sometimes even with an in-room bath), a decent lunch at a pub or cafe, and a fine repast at an ethnic restaurant in the evening. Sticking to this budget, you won't feel at all deprived. If you want to, you can do it for less. Naturally, you can also do it for more. I've included some recommendations for taking either the higher or lower route in this book, too.

Having an affordable vacation doesn't mean that you'll have to stay in dingy accommodations, eat fast food, and generally have a less-than-fun vacation. Twenty years ago, you might have had to do just that, but today you don't. Because London has changed radically.

There are still bed-and-breakfasts that provide comfy lounges; crisp, clean rooms; and full, hearty breakfasts. True, they're harder to find, because so many B&Bs and small hotels have upgraded to add ensuite bathrooms (and subsequently increased their prices), but such gems do exist, and this book will help you find them. I have scoured the neighborhoods of London to find the very best. In Bloomsbury, for example, you'll find typically English hotels for modest travelers. And if you don't mind staying farther out, in the beautiful neighborhood of Hampstead, you can enjoy a great value there, at La Gaffe (see review in chapter 4). If you're on a very strict budget, consider staying at a youth hostel or at any one of several fine university accommodations like the London School of Economics Holborn Residence—they're all options that are included here too.

The biggest revolution for frugal travelers, though, has occurred in the food industry. The British have discovered food in a big way; every day it seems a hot new restaurant opens to a popular buzz. World cuisine has come into its own— French, Indian, Chinese, Italian, Greek, and many other ethnic groups are bringing good-quality budget food to Londoners long starved for such. The Brits themselves have been prodded into reexamining their own cuisine, and the results can be seen in the many new restaurants heralding what's been called "modern British" cooking. Even pubs now offer much better fare, and many have been redesigned to bring in the sunlight, instead of hiding behind smoked-glass windows and dark exteriors. You'll also notice these watering holes have become much more family-friendly. The selections contained in this book will guide you to the best low- and moderate-cost options available, as well as the favorite, good-value places frequented by locals. I've also thrown in some splurge choices and will suggest affordable ways to sample the fare prepared by the many celebrity chefs who have contributed to the current frenzied dining scene.

As for sightseeing, well, you can't get around the fact that some of the stock-in-trade sights are overpriced (like Buckingham Palace and the Tower of London). But you could still enjoy a splendid, eye-opening vacation even if you visited only the many free attractions of the city: such major museums as the British Museum, the National Gallery, the Tate, and the Wallace Collection; the half dozen or so lovely parks; the hundreds of churches (many of which offer free concerts); the many street and antiques markets; the time-honored pageants conducted at the Old Bailey, the Houses of Parliament, Buckingham Palace and Whitehall; and of course, the city streets themselves, lined with buildings that resonate with literary and historical associations.

2 Fifty-Five Money-Saving Tips

PRETRIP PLANNING AND TRANSPORTATION SAVINGS

1. Information pays; forewarned is forearmed. These adages apply to travel today— so read as much as you can about London before you go, talk to people who have been there recently, and get as much free information from the **British Tourist Authority** as you possibly can. Visit their offices in New York or Chicago (see "Visitor Information & Entry Requirements," below, for addresses and phone numbers) and pick up a wealth of information. The office will send you a package containing information about London's White Card, a three- or seven-day saver pass to major museums and galleries (see tip no. 28, below), and the London for Less discount card and guidebook (see tip no. 9, below). You'll also be able to get maps and such helpful booklets as *Britain for Cyclists, Britain for Walkers,* and more.

2. Travel off-season. London is great in the winter. Cultural life is at full throttle. Rooms are easier to find and are cheaper. Dining and sightseeing are less frenetic. You don't have to go in darkest February—in April or October you'll still reap the financial benefits.

3. Reserve and pay in advance, especially if you plan to rent a car. If you book with an agency like **Europe by Car,** One Rockefeller Plaza, New York, NY 10020 (☎ **212/581-3040**), or 9000 Sunset Blvd., Los Angeles, CA 90069 (☎ **213/272-0424**), you can secure a subcompact car with manual shift for as little as $135 per week, including tax, insurance, and unlimited mileage. If you wait to book with a local British company, you'd pay at least $270 per week.

4. Shop around for your airfare. This will no doubt be the most expensive part of your trip, so it pays to do some legwork. Great bargains can be had by searching the Internet (for specifics see the box "Cyber Deals for Net Surfers," below). Alternatively, scour your newspaper for such consolidators as **TFI Tours International** (34 W. 32nd St., 12th floor, New York, NY 10001; ☎ 212/736-1140), which sells airline seats at a substantial—as much as 60%—discount. Certainly consult with your travel agent, who often can be privy to special deals and package rates. Air carriers are motivated to fill every seat on each flight, so they adjust pricing frequently. Also investigate charter flights on scheduled airlines offered by such reliable operators as the **Council on International Educational Exchange** (205 E. 42nd St., New York, NY 10017; ☎ 212/822-2600).

5. Fly during the week. It's about $25 cheaper than flying on a Friday, Saturday, or Sunday.

6. If you have plenty of time and schedules are not of any great consequence, then consider going as a **courier.** Such companies as Now Voyager (74 Varick St., Suite 307, New York, NY 10013; ☎212/431-1616) or Halbart Express (147–05 176th St., Jamaica, NY 11434; ☎ 718/656-8189) might be able to send you to London for as little as $350 in high season. The catch is that you must agree to forfeit your baggage allowance (one carry-on allowed only) so the company can use it to transport their shipment to the country you're flying to. Also, courier companies generally seek solo passengers, so if you're traveling with a companion, it might be difficult to coordinate your flights.

7. Consider taking a **package tour.** Often you can secure a week or more in London for one low price that includes airfare, transfers, accommodations, and some sightseeing discounts. You needn't join the group activities—just enjoy the price tag, which would be a lot higher if you assembled the trip yourself. For example, in 1998 **Globus** offered 8 days and 7 nights in London for as little as $439 (traveling in January) to $649 (from May to September). The price includes round-trip airfare, hotel with continental breakfast, guided half-day tour, theater seats for a show selected from a list provided, two-day Travelcard, and Globus travel bag. Those prices can't be beat—except perhaps by Cosmos, which offers the same package for $348 and $523 respectively. This actually represents little more than you'd pay for just airfare, and a discounted airfare at that. Contact your travel agent for Globus-Cosmos and for other tour operators such as Trafalgar Tours (☎ 212/689-8977) or Frames Rickard (☎ 800/992-7700). Most major airlines also do packages. For example, in 1998 British Airways (☎ 800/247-9297) was offering six-night packages, including airfare, for $809; American Airlines Vacations (☎ 800/832-8383) also was offering six nights including round-trip air for $889; and Virgin Vacations (☎ 800/364-6466) was offering three nights for $629.

8. Pack light. You won't need a porter and you're less likely to succumb to the desire for a taxi. *Note:* Luggage carts are free in London's airports.

9. Purchase a **London for Less Card and guidebook** for $19.95. This grants you discounts to many different facilities—attractions, theater and concert tickets, restaurants, shops, tours, car rental, hotels, fees at foreign currency exchanges, and telephone calls. Of course, you may not use a lot of the coupons, and you may not find yourself wanting to dine or shop at the particular selections in the book. But with discounts on tickets to the Royal Shakespeare Company, Royal Opera, Royal Ballet, and Royal Philharmonic, *plus* savings on admissions or tours at Buckingham Palace, the Tower of London, Westminster Abbey, Hampton Court Palace, Kensington Palace, and Kew Gardens, you're sure to save the $19.95 you paid for the book, and then some. Any additional hotel, shopping,

and dining discounts will only be a bonus. You can purchase the card and book at any tourist info center in London; in the states, call ☎ **888/GO-FOR-LESS,** or contact the BritRail Travel Office, 551 Fifth Ave., 7th floor, New York, NY (☎ **212/490-6688**), next to the BTA office.

10. Before you leave, you should also purchase a 3-, 4- or 7-day **London Transport Visitor Travelcard,** which offers virtually unlimited travel on London-area transport plus discount vouchers for attractions and restaurants. This card cannot be bought in the United Kingdom and can be obtained through your travel agent or from BritRail Travel International. If you buy it here rather than in London, there are definite advantages: you don't have to provide a passport photo; the day card allows you to travel at any time (in London it's only after 9:30am); and the weekly card allows travel in all zones, not just one or two.

11. Before you leave home, check out calling card options. There are usually surcharges for using cards abroad but they are still often the best bet for calling home from abroad. If you carry an American Express Card, investigate the charges using the "Connections" plan. Check out AT&T, MCI, and Sprint, and see what current international calling programs they have, and whether it's worth switching your residential service to one of them. Currently, the cheapest option appears to be **Voicenet** (☎ **800/864-2363**), which charges under $3 for a 10-minute call from London.

ONCE YOU ARRIVE

12. Take public transportation from the airport and from the airport to the city. The Piccadilly Line of the Underground runs directly from Heathrow to downtown and costs only £3.30 ($5.30) instead of the £40 or more ($64) that a taxi would cost. It's a savings of $59—close to a whole day's budget.

13. Once in the city, purchase one of the many calling cards available that offer discounted rates on international calls to various countries. For example, First USA charges only 10¢ per minute for calls to the U.S. These cards can be purchased at newsagents; there's also a booth on the street at Piccadilly. The London Tourist Board information center in the forecourt at Victoria Station also sells a discount card.

14. Don't use traveler's checks or money changers like American Express, or other bureaux de change. Instead, withdraw money from your bank account at home (if you can) using an overseas ATM. Exchange rates at ATMs are far more advantageous, because banks use a special wholesale rate—but check with your bank before leaving to make sure you won't be charged a fee for overseas withdrawals. Above all, don't draw cash from your credit card; you'll pay exorbitant interest rates for that privilege.

ACCOMMODATIONS

15. When you're seeking out potential hotels, look in a university area, such as Bloomsbury. Other London neighborhoods worth investigating for the supply of budget hotels are Earl's Court, Victoria, and Paddington/Bayswater.

16. Think about what you really want in a hotel room. If a private bathroom is not crucial to you, you can save anywhere from £5 to £10 ($8–$16) per night.

17. Negotiate the price. Ask the management if they'll give you a discount if you stay three nights or more; suggest trade-offs—a lower price for a smaller room or a room minus TV and so on. If you're a student or senior, ask for special discounts. If you're on a hotel-lined street like Sussex Gardens in Bayswater, or Ebury Street near Victoria, keep checking out rooms until you find one you like for your price.

18. Depending on your particular peccadilloes, consider staying at a youth hostel or at any one of several university accommodations. One of the finest examples of the latter is **High Holborn Residences,** which charges only $64 to $80 for a double, and provides all these extra facilities: two TV lounges, a bar with two pool tables, table tennis, 24-hour Laundromat, computer, and access at special discounted rates to a nearby gym with indoor/outdoor pools and squash courts.

19. Don't call home from a hotel phone unless you know that you can access USA Direct or a similar company; and even then, check to see if there's a charge for the connection to USA Direct. Similarly, don't call from a pay phone, which is often connected to carriers charging super high prices.

DINING

20. Stay at a hotel that provides a full breakfast, not a continental one. More and more hotels are offering only continental breakfast. We have noted which hotels still serve a traditional English breakfast of cereals, breads, fruit, bacon, eggs, sausage, mushrooms, and tomatoes, which would be worth at least £5 ($8) per person outside the hotel.

21. Bring a knife, fork, plate, and corkscrew so that you can enjoy the wares from the city's splendid food halls at Harrods, Fortnum & Mason, Selfridges, or from more humble establishments like Tesco Metro and Marks & Spencer.

22. If picnicking in a park or eating in your hotel room is not your style, then opt for one of the many low-cost and moderately priced restaurants which have multiplied in the last few years. Pubs also have reinvented themselves and many now offer good fare at lunch, as do wine bars. Sandwich and light-fare cafes and other eat-on-the-run shops abound. At dinner, the options range from some of the best Indian in the world to Chinese, Malaysian, Greek, Italian, Middle Eastern, and Japanese. There is also a whole range of new and old tried-and-true chains—from the newer Cafe Sofra and Cafe Rouge to the venerable Stockpot, which has been keeping Londoners happy for years. They offer excellent value.

23. At many a London restaurant, you'll find the English equivalent of the French prix fixe: the table d'hôte or the two-course or three-course set menu. Depending on the neighborhood, you can find a two-course meal for as little as £5.95 ($9.50) and as much as £12.50 ($20). These set meals offer excellent value at lunch and dinner, and at the more fashionable restaurants a luncheon prix fixe can provide an affordable way to try the cuisine of some of London's most celebrated chefs. For example, Alastair Little in Soho offers a luncheon for only £23 ($36.80), one of the city's greatest food values. Note, though, that most of these menus offer very limited choices—that's why they are the price they are.

24. Restaurants also offer pre-theater menus or what might be called early bird menus in the United States; these are also great dining buys.

25. At most restaurants, service is included—don't make the mistake of tipping twice.

TRANSPORTATION AROUND TOWN

26. Walk—it's the best way to explore a city and meet its citizens. Though the city is large, with a little advance planning, your localized battle plan can focus your sightseeing, shopping, and meals in a few adjacent neighborhoods, which will allow you to explore on foot and save on Tube costs. Use public transportation, too. Take advantage of whatever discounts are available, like the one-day or one-week TravelCard which allows you to ride the buses and Underground throughout the two zones of Central London for £3.50 ($5.60) and £16.60

($26.55) respectively. Just knowing you can hop a bus or a train at any time will inculcate a much more spontaneous approach to sightseeing.

27. For London's cheapest tour, ride the no. 188 bus from Euston to Greenwich, or any of the other routes, for that matter. If you have a bus pass, you can go wherever you please within the zones for which your pass applies.

SIGHTSEEING & ENTERTAINMENT

28. Purchase a **London White Card.** Cards cost £16 ($25.60) for three days, £26 ($41.60) for seven days, and £32 ($51.20) and £50 ($80) respectively for family cards. The card is good at 16 institutions: Apsley House, Barbican Art Gallery, Courtauld Institute, Design Museum, Hayward Gallery, Imperial War Museum, London Transport Museum, Museum of London, Museum of the Moving Image, National Maritime Museum, Old Royal Observatory & Queen's House, Natural History Museum, Royal Academy of Art, Science Museum, Theatre Museum, and the Victoria & Albert Museum. If you visited all the museums you would have to shell out £76.95 ($123.10). Thus the savings are a huge £50.95 ($81.52) on a seven-day card. Of course you may not be able to visit all the museums in the allotted time, but even if you visited only six or seven you will have gotten more than your money's worth. The White Card can be bought before you go at the BritRail Travel Shop across from the BTA office at 551 Fifth Ave., 7th floor, New York, NY (☎ **212/490-6688**), or in London from the participating museums and at the London Tourist Information Centres.

29. Make creative sightseeing choices. Some of the best things in life are free. In London, a walk down any street will likely turn up a number of buildings that are marked with blue plaques, indicating that someone famous lived there or some historic event took place there.

30. Students can present their student ID to obtain discounted admissions, wherever granted. Men and women age 60 and older can receive senior citizen discounts at some attractions.

31. Most churches are free to the public. Take time to contemplate the brilliant interiors of Wren's churches or the many memorials that every church seems to have.

32. London has loads of world-class free attractions and museums—the main galleries of the British Museum and the National Gallery, and the permanent collection of the Tate Museum, to name only three.

33. Enjoy the free entertainment that's invariably given at Covent Garden—be it a jazz trio or a couple of young music students delivering Mozart arias with much more than amateur aplomb.

34. Tour the historic monuments and attend the pageantry events—the daily Changing of the Guard at Whitehall, or any of the other colorful free pageants that take to the streets, like the Lord Mayor's Show or the Notting Hill Carnival (see "Calendar of Events" for details).

35. Enjoy the architecture of London. The nave of Westminster Abbey is still free (though you must pay a hefty price to see the crypts of famous people and the Poets' Corner), as are the many buildings that line the streets of London, from the Tudor Staple Inn to the modern Lloyd's building. Don't overlook the squares and terraces in every neighborhood from Trafalgar to Bloomsbury.

36. Explore the parks. Don't sit on a deck chair though—there's a charge. Opt for the classic park bench.

37. Visit the Old Bailey and the Royal Courts of Justice in the Strand and, of course, the Houses of Parliament. They're all free and will provide an introduction to the institutions and social issues of contemporary London.

Cyber Deals for Net Surfers

It's possible to get some great deals on airfare, hotels, and car rentals via the Internet. So go grab your mouse and start surfing before you take off—you could save a bundle on your trip. The Web sites highlighted below are worth checking out, especially since all services are free.

Microsoft Expedia (www.expedia.com)   The best part of this multi-purpose travel site is the "Fare Tracker": You fill out a form on the screen indicating that you're interested in cheap flights from your hometown, and, once a week, Expedia will e-mail you the best airfare deals. The site's "Travel Agent" will steer you to bargains on hotels and car rentals, and you can book everything, including flights, right on-line. This site is even useful once you're booked: Before you go, log on to Expedia for oodles of up-to-date travel information, including weather reports and foreign exchange rates.

Preview Travel (www.reservations.com and www.vacations.com)   Another useful travel site, "Reservations.com" has a "Best Fare Finder," which will search the Apollo computer reservations system (a huge database used by travel agents worldwide) for the three lowest fares for any route on any days of the year. Say you want to go from Chicago to Orlando and back between December 6th and 13th: Just fill out the form on the screen with times, dates, and destinations, and within minutes, Preview will show you the best deals. If you find an airfare you like, you can book your ticket right on-line—you can even reserve hotels and car rentals on this site. If you're in the pre-planning stage, head to Preview's "Vacations.com" site, where you can check out the latest package deals around the world by clicking on "Hot Deals."

Travelocity (www.travelocity.com)   This is one of the best travel sites out there. In addition to its "Personal Fare Watcher," which notifies you via e-mail of the lowest airfares for up to five different destinations, Travelocity will track the three lowest fares for any routes on any dates in minutes. You can book a flight right then and there, and if you need a rental car or hotel, Travelocity will find you the best deal via the SABRE computer reservations system (another huge travel agent database). Click on "Last Minute Deals" for the latest travel bargains, including a link to "H.O.T. Coupons" (**www.hotcoupons.com**), where you can print out electronic coupons for travel in the U.S. and Canada.

38. Visit the cemeteries. Not just Highgate—there are several that contain the remains of many other worthies who chose London as their home. Check out Brompton Cemetery on Old Brompton Road, the Dog's Cemetery in Kensington Gardens, and Hampstead Cemetery on Fortune Green Road.

NIGHTLIFE

39. Go to venues early or very late and you'll receive a discount. For example, at the Limelight it's free before 11pm on Monday and Thursday and half-price before 10:30 and 10pm on Friday and Saturday, respectively.
40. Go to the kiosk in Leicester Square for half-price theater tickets, which range from £12 to £20 ($19.20–$32).
41. Attend matinees instead of evening performances. A top-price matinee will cost at least £5 ($8) less than a top-price evening ticket.

Trip.Com (www.thetrip.com)   This site is really geared toward the business traveler, but vacationers-to-be can also use Trip.Com's valuable fare-finding engine, which will e-mail you every week with the best city-to-city airfare deals on your selected route or routes.

Discount Tickets (www.discount-tickets.com)   Operated by the ETN (European Travel Network), this site offers discounts on airfares, accommodations, car rentals, and tours.

E-Savers Programs   Several major airlines, most all of which service London, offer a free e-mail service known as **E-Savers,** via which they'll send you their best bargain airfares on a weekly basis. Here's how it works: Once a week (usually Wednesday), subscribers receive a list of discounted flights to and from various destinations, both international and domestic. Here's the catch: These fares are available only if you leave the very next Saturday (or sometimes Friday night) and return on the following Monday or Tuesday. It's really a service for the spontaneously inclined and travelers looking for a quick getaway. But the fares are cheap, so it's worth taking a look. If you have a preference for certain airlines (in other words, the ones you fly most frequently), sign up with them first.

Here's a list of airlines and their Web sites, where you can not only get on the e-mailing lists but also book flights directly:

- **American Airlines:** www.americanair.com
- **British Airways:** www.britishairways.com
- **Continental Airlines:** www.flycontinental.com
- **Delta Airlines:** www.delta-air.com
- **Northwest Airlines:** www.nwa.com
- **TWA:** www.twa.com
- **US Airways:** www.usairways.com
- **Virgin Airways:** www.virgin.com

One final caveat: You'll get frequent-flier miles if you purchase one of these fares, but you can't use miles to buy the ticket.

—Jeanette Foster

42. On Monday nights when all tickets are only £5 ($8), go to the Royal Court Theatre, which offers some of the city's most exhilarating and controversial contemporary drama.

43. Attend performances at London's alternative theaters like the Almeida, which has produced some of the most acclaimed cutting-edge contemporary drama. Tickets range from only £6.50 to £19.50 ($10.40–$31.20) in contrast to the £8 to £35 ($12.80–$56) price tag for a West End production.

44. Seek out performances at the many drama and music schools in London. For example, students of Trinity College give free concerts in Hinde Street Church on most Thursday lunchtimes during term. Call for information on student concerts and productions at the following places: The Central School of Speech and Drama, 64 Eton Ave., NW3 (☎ 0171/722-8183); the Guildhall School of Music and Drama, the Barbican, EC 1 (☎ 0171/628-2571); the Royal Academy

of Dramatic Art, 62–64 Gower St., WC1 (☎ 0171/436-1458); Royal Academy of Music, Marylebone Rd., NW1 (☎ 0171/873-7373); or Trinity College of Music, 11–13 Mandeville Place, W1 (☎ 0171/487-9647). Who knows, you may spy the next Emma Thompson, Helena Bonham-Carter, or Kate Winslett.

45. Attend free lunchtime concerts in the churches or at the Royal Festival Hall. For listings see *Time Out.*

46. At many a jazz or other music club, sitting at the bar instead of at a table can save you anywhere from £6 to £12 ($9.60–$19.20) cover charge.

47. London has developed a happy hour culture. Most bars offer discounted drinks anywhere from 3 to 7pm, slashing prices anywhere from 30% to a full 100%, or two-for-one.

SHOPPING

48. If you're interested in antiques, window-shop along New Bond Street, Westbourne Grove around Portobello, and Camden Passage in Islington. Check out Fulham Road if you want to see how the fashionable set are furnishing their homes.

49. Hang out at the outdoor markets. There's a variety to choose from—Camden Town on the weekends for a youth-oriented avant-garde experience akin to Canal Street in New York City; Bermondsey and Portobello for antiques; and Billingsgate and New Covent Garden for produce.

50. Come to London to shop in January during the sales, when bargains on quality merchandise can be found at all of the major stores.

51. Window-shop along some of the city's most famous retail streets—New and Old Bond Streets, Jermyn Street, and Savile Row, or in such new trendy areas as Notting Hill.

52. Just for fun, drop into one or more of the auction houses to preview the objects—Sotheby's, Phillip's, or Christie's.

53. For antique browsing, go to one of the great centers like Westbourne Grove around Portobello, Camden Passage, or the Bermondsey market.

54. Charity shops are great places to look for bargains on all kinds of items, from furniture and household gear to clothes and accessories. The best stuff will be found at the stores that are in the wealthy neighborhoods—Chelsea, Knightsbridge, and so on, although the others are worth checking out too.

55. Get your VAT refund—a whopping 17.5%. Fill out the appropriate forms in the shop; get the form and your receipt stamped at customs; and mail them back to the retailer.

3 Visitor Information & Entry Requirements

VISITOR INFORMATION

Information about travel in London and elsewhere in Great Britain can be obtained from the **British Tourist Authority (BTA).** The BTA has two offices in the United States. The main office is at 551 Fifth Ave., 7th Floor, at 45th St., New York, NY 10176-0799 (☎ 800/462-2748 or 212/986-2200; phone lines are open Mon–Fri 9am–6pm). The visitor office is open Monday to Friday from 9am to 6pm. A second office is located at 625 N. Michigan Ave., Suite 1510, Chicago, IL 60611 (**no phone**). Office hours are weekdays only 9am to 5pm. The BTA also has a Web site at www.visitbritain.com.

You can also purchase a **London for Less™** card at the Britrail store adjacent to the Manhattan BTA office, or order by credit card from ☎ **888/GO-FOR-LESS.**

This card gives you discounts on some major attractions, restaurants, hotels, tours, concerts, and theater performances—it also allows you to make commission-free currency exchanges at Travelex branches. The card costs $19.95 and can save you considerably more. The card is valid for either a 4- or 8-day period, and comes with a nice fold-out map and guidebook. You can also purchase it at Tourist Information Centres in London.

The BTA also maintains offices in **Australia,** at 210 Clarence St., Sydney, NSW 2000 (☎ 02/267-4555); in **Canada,** at 111 Avenue Rd., Suite 450, Toronto, ON M5R 3J8 (☎ 416/925-6326); in Ireland, at 18/19 College Green, Dublin 2 (☎ 01/670-8000); and in **New Zealand,** at Suite 305/3rd Floor, Dilworth Building, Cnr. Customs and Queens Sts., Auckland 1 (☎ 9/377-6965).

In London, visit the main British Tourist Authority office in the British Travel Centre, 4–12 Lower Regent St., London SW1 (**no phone**). In addition to information on all of Britain, this center has a British Rail ticket office, a travel agency, a theater ticket agency, a hotel-booking service, a bookstore, and a souvenir shop. Hours are 9am to 6:30pm Monday through Friday and 10am to 4pm Saturday and Sunday. Weekend hours are extended from June through September.

ENTRY REQUIREMENTS
DOCUMENTS
Citizens of the United States, Canada, Australia, and New Zealand need only a valid passport to enter Great Britain.

CUSTOMS
Overseas visitors are allowed to import duty-free 200 cigarettes, 100 cigarillos, 50 cigars, or 250 grams of tobacco; 2 liters of table wine plus 1 liter of alcoholic drinks over 22% volume, or 2 liters of alcoholic drinks over 22%; 2 fluid ounces of perfume and 9 fluid ounces of eau de cologne. Most other items can be imported free of tax, provided they are for your personal use. Live animals, plants, and produce are forbidden. When returning to the United States, citizens are allowed to bring back $400 worth of merchandise duty-free. After that amount, you will be charged a flat 10% tax on the next $1,000 worth of goods. If you do shop in London, make sure you retain your receipts to show Customs officials.

4 Money

CURRENCY
POUNDS & PENCE   The English **pound (£),** a small, thick, round coin, is divided into 100 **pence.** Pence (abbreviated "p") come in 1p, 2p, 5p, 10p, and 50p coins. Notes are issued in £5, £10, £20, and £50 denominations.

At press time, it costs $1.60 to buy one English pound ($1.60 =£1). To make budgeting easier, prices quoted in this book are accompanied by their equivalents in U.S. dollars. Exchange rates are volatile, so remember that these conversions are to be used as a guide only.

CREDIT CARDS/ATMS
All major credit cards—American Express, Diners Club, MasterCard, and Visa— are widely accepted. In England, MasterCard is called Access and Visa is known as Barclaycard. Using plastic can be economical as well as convenient. Credit cards eliminate commissions for currency exchange and allow for later billing. Later billing can work out to your advantage or disadvantage, depending on whether the dollar goes up or down with time.

The British Pound & the U.S. Dollar

At this writing, $1 = approximately 62p (or $1.60 = £1), and this was the exchange rate used to calculate the dollar values in this book (rounded to the nearest nickel).

£	U.S.$	£	U.S.$
.05	.08	6.00	9.60
.10	.16	7.00	11.20
.25	.40	8.00	12.80
.50	.80	9.00	14.40
.75	1.20	10.00	16.00
1.00	1.60	15.00	24.00
2.00	3.20	20.00	32.00
3.00	4.80	25.00	40.00
4.00	6.40	30.00	48.00
5.00	8.00	35.00	56.00

Similarly, today you'll save money if you secure currency from an ATM rather than change it at the old-fashioned traditional currency exchange offices. The fees are generally lower and also the rate of exchange used is the "wholesale" rate, which is better. Obviously you'll pay out less in fees if you minimize the number of transactions. Instead of taking out a small amount on several occasions, take out a larger amount on fewer occasions. Check with your bank before you leave regarding the fees charged and anything else you may need to know. For the name of banks overseas that belong to the **CIRRUS** network, call ☎ **800/424-7787.** For **Plus** locations, call ☎ **800/843-7587,** or access the VISA/PLUS International ATM Locator Guide via the Internet at **www.visa.com.**

TRAVELER'S CHECKS

Although traveler's checks in foreign currencies are still easily exchanged in London, ATMs offer an easier and cheaper way to secure cash. Still, some more cautious and safety-conscious travelers may prefer to purchase traveler's checks. Banks and companies like American Express and Thomas Cook offer the best rates. *Beware:* Chequepoint and other private currency-exchange businesses which stay open late charge high commissions.

Traveler's checks issued in British pounds are accepted at most shops, restaurants, hotels, theaters, and attractions. For the foreign traveler, however, there are two drawbacks to carrying them. First, you'll have to exchange your money into pounds at home, a transaction that usually proves more costly than in London. Second, you'll have to re-exchange your unused pounds after your trip, thus incurring a second transaction fee.

5 When to Go

Spring and fall are the best seasons to go to avoid the crowds that descend on the major sights in summer. In winter, the weather in London can be very dreary, but the cultural calendar is rich and the attractions are less crowded.

What Things Cost in London	U.S. $
Taxi from Heathrow Airport to London	64.00
Underground from Heathrow Airport to central London	6.10
Local telephone call	.16
Double room at Tophams Ebury Court (splurge)	155.00
Double room at Oakley Hotel (budget)	65.10
Lunch for one, Bahn Thai (moderate)	12.40–26.35
Lunch for one at most pubs (budget)	7.00–9.00
Dinner for one, without wine, at English House (splurge)	32.15
Dinner for one, without wine, at Chester (moderate)	30.00
Dinner for one, without wine, at Khan's (budget)	6.20–10.85
Pint of beer	3.20
Coca-Cola in a restaurant	1.60
Cup of coffee	1.60
Roll of ASA 100 film, 24 exposures	7.70
Admission to the British Museum	Free
Movie ticket	14.40
Cheapest West End theater ticket	8.00

THE CLIMATE

London's infamous thick fog was never fog at all. It was smog from coal-burning residential chimneys and power plants. Today, rigidly enforced air pollution controls make it an offense to use a fireplace for its intended purpose, so "fog" is no longer in the forecast. However, rain, drizzle, and showers are. A typical weather forecast any time of year predicts "scattered clouds with sunny periods and showers, possibly heavy at times." Temperatures are temperate and rarely go below freezing in winter or above 70° Fahrenheit in summer—although recently there have been some major heat waves. El Niño and other natural phenomena have caused unusual weather patterns, including spring in February, for example, and snow and hail in April.

London's Average Daytime Temperature (°F) & Rainfall (inches)

	Jan	Feb	Mar	Apr	May	June	July	Aug	Sept	Oct	Nov	Dec
Temp.	40	40	44	49	55	61	64	64	59	52	46	42
Rainfall	2.1	1.6	1.5	1.5	1.8	1.8	2.2	2.3	1.9	2.2	2.5	1.9

HOLIDAYS

Most businesses are closed for Christmas on December 25 and for Boxing Day the day after; on New Year's Day, January 1; on Good Friday as well as Easter Monday; and on May 1, which is generally regarded as Labor Day in Europe. In addition, many stores close on bank holidays, which are scattered throughout the year. There's no uniform policy for museums, restaurants, and attractions with regard to closing for holidays.

LONDON CALENDAR OF EVENTS

January
- **Charles I Commemoration.** Banqueting House, Whitehall. Hundreds of men march through central London dressed as cavaliers to mark the anniversary of the 1649 execution of King Charles I. Last Sunday in January.

February
- **Chinese New Year Parade.** Chinatown, at Gerrard and Lisle Streets. Festive crowds line the decorated streets of Soho to watch the famous Lion Dancers. Late January or early February (based on the lunar calendar).

March
- **The Easter Parade.** Battersea Park. London's largest parade features brightly colored floats and marching bands, kicking off a full day of activities. Easter morning.

April
- **The Oxford vs. Cambridge Boat Race.** The dark blues and light blues compete over a Thames course from Putney to Mortlake. The race has been held since 1829, and crowds line the towpaths along the banks of the river and fill the riverside pubs to cheer the teams on. First Saturday in April.

May
✪ **Chelsea Flower Show.** This international spectacular features the best of British gardening, with displays of plants and flowers for all seasons. The location, on the beautiful grounds of the Chelsea Royal Hospital, helps make this exposition a world-class affair.
   Where: Chelsea Royal Hospital, Chelsea. **When:** Late May. **How:** For ticket information, write Shows Department, Royal Horticultural Society, Vincent Square, London SW1P 2PE. ☎ **0171/630-7422;** fax 0171/630-6060, or call (for tickets only) 0171/344-4343.

June
- **The Derby.** The highlight of the flat racing season at Epsom Racecourse in Surrey. The Coronation Cup and Oak Stakes are run at the same meet. Usually the first weekend in June.
- **Royal Ascot.** A 4-day midweek event held at Ascot Racecourse in Berkshire. The glamorous event of the racing season, as renowned for its fashion extravaganzas as for its high racing standards. The royal family attends. Remember the scene in *My Fair Lady*? Usually the third week of June.
✪ **Trooping the Colour.** The official birthday of the queen. Seated in a carriage (no longer on horseback), the royal monarch inspects her regiments and receives their salute as they parade their colors before her. A quintessential British event religiously watched by the populace on TV. The pageantry and pomp are exquisite. Depending on the weather, the young men under the bearskins have been known to faint from the heat.
   Where: Horse Guards Parade, Whitehall. **When:** A day designated in June (not the queen's actual birthday). **How:** Tickets are free and are allocated by ballot. Apply in writing between January and the end of February, enclosing an International Reply Coupon to: The Ticket Office, HQ Household Division, Chelsea Barracks, London SW1H 8RF. Canadians should apply to Royal Events Secretary, Canada House, Trafalgar Square, London SW1Y 5BJ.
✪ **Wimbledon Lawn Tennis Championships.** Ever since the players in flannels and bonnets took to the grass courts at Wimbledon in 1877, this tournament has

drawn a socially prominent crowd. Although the courts are now crowded with all kinds of tennis fans, there's still an excited hush and certain thrill at Centre Court. Savor the strawberries and cream that are part of the experience.

Where: Wimbledon, SW London. **When:** Late June/early July. **How:** Advance booking required for Centre and Number One Courts. Write in October for an application form for inclusion in ticket ballot for following year. The ballot closes at the end of December. A few tickets for the center and number 1 courts are available (except during the last four days of the tournament) along with tickets for the outside courts daily at the gates—be prepared for a line. For more information call ☎ **0181/946-2244.** Fax 0181/947-8752. For a complete list of ticket prices, write to the All England Club, 98 Church Rd., Wimbledon, London, SW19 5AE.

- **Henley Royal Regatta.** A major social event at which international crew teams compete. Held at Henley-on-Thames, Oxfordshire, it's rowed on an upstream course, against the current, from Temple Island to Henley Bridge—more than a mile. Tickets are obtainable from the Secretary ☎ **01491/572153.** Fax 01491/575509. Late June or early July.

July

- **Royal Tournament,** Earl's Court Exhibition Centre in SW5. The British military puts on dazzling displays of athletic and military skills. A mixture of pomp, showbiz, and outright jingoism in aid of service charities. For information write to the Royal Tournament Box Office, Earl's Court Exhibition Centre, Warwick Road, London SW5 9TA. ☎ **0171/373-8141.**
- **Henry Wood Promenade Concerts.** Royal Albert Hall, SW 7. A summer musical event that's been running since 1895. The concerts, from jazz to the classics, are given from late July to mid-September and are famous for their Last Nights. The audience stands in the rotunda of the hall and the orchestra ends with a rousing interpretation of Elgar's "Pomp and Circumstance." Tickets go on sale in May. From late July to mid-September.
- **Doggett's Coat & Badge Race.** Instituted in 1715 by Thomas Doggett, comedian and manager of Drury Lane Theatre, to celebrate the accession of King George. The race is rowed in single sculls from London Bridge to Cadogan Bridge, Chelsea, a more than 4½-mile course. The winner is awarded a scarlet uniform and silver badge. Mid- to late July.

August

✪ **The Notting Hill Carnival,** Ladbroke Grove. One of the largest annual street festivals in Europe, this African-Caribbean fair attracts more than half a million people to its two-day celebration. Live reggae, steel bands, and soul music combine with great Caribbean food, camaraderie, and a charged atmosphere. Free.

Where: Notting Hill, London. **When:** Late August. **How:** Just show up.

September

- **Horse of the Year Show,** Wembley Arena, Wembley. A six-day indoor event that attracts the world's top showjumpers. Usually the last week in September.

November

- **State Opening of Parliament,** Whitehall and Parliament Square. Although the ceremony itself is not open to the public, crowds pack the parade route to see the royal procession. Late October or early November.

✪ **Fireworks Night.** Commemorates the anniversary of the "Gun-powder Plot," a Roman Catholic conspiracy to blow up King James I and his parliament. Huge organized bonfires are lit throughout the city. Guy Fawkes, the plot's most famous conspirator, is burned in effigy. Free.

Where: Hyde Park, Battersea Park, and other public areas in London. **When:** November 5. **How:** Follow the crowds and the smoke.

- **London to Brighton Veteran Car Run.** More than 300 veteran car owners from all over the world compete in this 57-mile run from London's Hyde Park to Brighton. Usually the first Sunday in November; starts at 7am.
- **The Lord Mayor's Procession and Show,** The City. An elaborate parade celebrating the inauguration of the new lord mayor, who travels in a magnificent gilded coach from Guildhall to the Royal Courts of Justice. Usually second Saturday in November.

December

- **Caroling under the Norwegian Christmas Tree.** There's caroling most evenings beneath the tree in Trafalgar Square. Early December.
- **Harrods' After-Christmas Sale,** Knightsbridge. Call ☎ **0171/730-1234** for exact dates and hours. Late December.
- **Watch Night,** St. Paul's Cathedral, where a rather lovely New Year's Eve service takes place on December 31 at 11:30pm; call ☎ **0171/248-2705** for information.

6 Health, Insurance & Other Concerns

MEDICAL REQUIREMENTS

Unless you are arriving from an area known to be suffering from an epidemic, no inoculations or vaccinations are required to enter Britain. If you are currently on medication, carry a doctor's prescription along with any controlled substances you possess.

HEALTH INSURANCE

Citizens of Australia and New Zealand are entitled to free medical treatment and subsidized dental care while in Britain. Americans and other nationals will usually have to pay up-front for services rendered. Doctors and hospitals can be expensive, so although it is not required of travelers, health insurance is highly recommended. Most American travelers are covered by their hometown policies in the event of an accident or sudden illness while away on vacation. Also, some credit card companies offer free, automatic travel-accident insurance, up to $100,000, when you purchase travel tickets on their cards. Before you purchase additional protection, check to see if you are already covered in foreign countries by your health maintenance organization (HMO) or insurance carrier.

OTHER TRAVEL-RELATED INSURANCE

You can also protect your travel investment by insuring against lost or damaged baggage, and trip cancellation or interruption costs. These coverages are often combined into a single comprehensive plan and sold through travel agents and credit card companies. Contact the following companies for more information: **Access America,** 6600 W. Broad St., Richmond, VA 23230 (☎ **800/284-8300**); **Travelex,** P.O. Box 9408, Garden City, NY 11530-9408 (☎ **800/228-9792**); **Travel Guard International,** 1145 Clark St., Stevens Point, WI 54481 (☎ **800/826-1300**); and **Wallach & Co.,** 107 W. Federal St., P.O. Box 480, Middleburg, VA 20117 (☎ **800/237-6615**).

7 Tips for Travelers with Special Needs

FOR TRAVELERS WITH DISABILITIES

Most of London's major museums and tourist attractions are now fitted with wheel-chair ramps to accommodate physically challenged visitors. It's common in London for theaters, nightclubs, and attractions to offer discounts, called "concessions," to people with disabilities. Ask for these before paying full price.

For information on traveling in Britain, call **Holiday Care Services,** 2nd floor, Imperial Buildings, Victoria Road, Horley, RH6 7PZ (☎ **1293/774535,** fax 1294/784647), during regular office hours. If you know where you intend to travel, you can request a couple of their regional information sheets which cover four or five counties. If you want more than two they charge 50p per sheet. They also publish a book that lists Accessible Accommodations in the United Kingdom and Ireland. It costs £7.50 ($12) plus £6.75 ($10.80) for shipping.

Artsline (☎ **0171/388-2227**) offers free information on accessibility to the-aters, galleries, and events around the city. The phone line is open Monday to Friday from 9:30am to 5:30pm.

FOR GAY & LESBIAN TRAVELERS

The Pink Paper is nationally distributed and is free. It's available at gay bars, book-stores, and cafes. The glossy monthly magazine *Gay Times* is available at news-stands and is the general news magazine for the gay community. For London listings, gossip, and scenes look for the free *Boyz* at gay clubs, bars, and cafes. It always features a nude pin-up. **Thud** and **QX (Queer Extra),** which also post London listings, are also available at gay businesses. *Time Out* also provides excel-lent coverage. **The Lesbian and Gay Switchboard** (☎ **0171/837-7324**) offers information, advice, and counseling, as well as a free accommodations agency. The line is open 24 hours and is almost always busy. **The Lesbian Line** (☎ **0171/251-6911**) offers similar services to women only. Officially it's open weekdays between 7 and 10pm but hours are somewhat erratic and often you will reach a machine telling you which days the office will be open.

FOR SENIORS

In Britain, "senior citizen" usually means a woman at least 60 years old and a man at least 65. Seniors often receive the same discounts as students. Some discounts are restricted to British citizens only.

London's youth hostels welcome older guests. These are some of the cheapest accommodations in the city, and are listed under "Super-Cheap Sleeps" in chapter 4, "Accommodations You Can Afford."

Members of AARP have access to a purchase privilege discount program on hotels, car rentals, tours, and other travel facilities. For information write or contact the **American Association of Retired Persons (AARP),** 601 E St. NW, Wash-ington, D.C. 20049 (☎ **800/424-3410**).

FOR STUDENTS

Time Out: London Student Guide is published at the beginning of each school year; it's available from most large newsagents and costs £2.50 ($4). The **University of London Student Union (ULU),** Malet Street, WC1 (☎ **0171/580-9551,** fax 0171/436-4604, E-mail: general@ULU.ucl.ac.uk), caters to more than 70,000 stu-dents and may be the largest of its kind in the world. In addition to a gym and fit-ness center with squash and badminton courts, the Malet Street building houses several shops, two restaurants, a bank, a ticket-booking agency, and an STA travel office. Concerts and dances are also regularly scheduled here. Stop by or phone for information on university activities. The student union building is open Monday to Friday from 8:30am to 11pm, Saturday 9am to 11pm; Sunday 9am to 10:30pm. Take the tube to Goodge Street.

The **International Student Identity Card (ISIC)** is the most readily accepted proof of student status. In the United States, it's available from Council Travel Offices nationwide, as well as from the **Council on International Educational Exchange,** 205 E. 42nd St., New York, NY 10017 (☎ 212/822-2600). The card entitles its holders to an array of travel benefits, including reduced student airfares (offered through Council Travel), discounts on public transportation, telephone calls (via AT&T), international shipping (using FedEx), museum and cultural event admissions, and other tourist services. When purchased in the United States, the card comes with emergency medical and accident insurance coverage. To be eligible for the ISIC, you must be enrolled in a high school or college degree program. Your application must include proof of student status; such proof may be provided by an official letter from the school registrar or high school principal stating that you are enrolled for the following academic year. Enclose the letter with a $20 registration fee and a single passport-size photo. The Council's Go 25 and ITIC cards provide similar benefits respectively for those 25 and under and teachers. The fee is the same.

The council has a London office at 28A Poland St., London W1 V3DB (☎ 0171/437-7767).

London's youth hostels are not only some of the cheapest places to stay, they are also great spots to meet other student travelers. You have to be a member of **Hostelling International (International Youth Hostel Federation)** to lodge at official youth hostels but joining is easy as membership cards are issued at every hostel in London. To apply for membership in the United States, contact Hostelling International, P.O. Box 37613, Washington, D.C. 20013-7613 (☎ 202/783-6161). Membership costs $25 a year for people 18 to 54; those 17 and younger pay just $10 and those 55 and older pay $15.

FOR WOMEN

Silver Moon Women's Bookshop, 64–68 Charing Cross Rd., WC2 (☎ 0171/836-7906), is Soho's only dedicated feminist bookseller featuring a huge selection of fiction and nonfiction titles by and for women. Europe's largest women's bookshop, it is open Monday through Saturday from 10am to 6:30pm (until 8pm on Thursday), Sunday noon to 6pm. Tube: Leicester Sq.

Women-only dance events occur a couple of nights a week in London at clubs all around the city. These clubs are designed for lesbians and straight women who are not looking to attract the attention of men. Check the listings in the gay mags or *Time Out* for details.

The **London Rape Crisis Centre** (☎ 0171/837-1600) offers immediate help, advice, and counseling to victims.

8 Organized Tours & Packages

Tours and packages are offered by tour operators, airlines, hotels, and transportation companies. A tour usually includes transportation, sightseeing, meals, and accommodations; the entire group travels together and all share the same pre-planned activities. A package, on the other hand, may include any or all of the above components, but travelers are usually unescorted and make their own itinerary.

Even if you are an independent traveler, don't shy away from a package; it can be a very good value because packagers buy in bulk and share the discount with the consumer. Check the ads in the travel section of your newspaper. Most of the airlines listed in "Getting There," below, offer both escorted tours and on-your-own packages. Other top London tour operators include **Globus Gateway Cosmos** (☎ 800/556-5454), Trafalgar Tours (☎ **800/854-0103**), and Trophy Tours, the agent for Frames-Rickards (☎ **800/527-2473**).

9 Finding an Affordable Place to Stay

When you select a hotel, one obvious rule is to look in those areas where you're most likely to find affordable hotels, like Bloomsbury, which is the heart of London's student community. Don't call or head for Mayfair or Belgravia. "Accommodations You Can Afford," in chapter 4, will guide you to the best budget hotels, hostels, and B&Bs. You may, however, want to consider some alternatives to the standard budget hotel or B&B.

HOMESTAYS   Homestays can provide a much deeper insight into the host culture than staying at a typical hotel. The following organizations make this experience possible. **Servas** (from the Esperanto word meaning "to serve") seeks to promote friendship and goodwill through homestays of at least two nights. Contact the **U.S. Servas Committee,** 11 John St., Suite 407, New York, NY 10038 (☎ **212/267-0252**). Yearly membership is $65 plus $25 for the host list.

Several London-based homestay agencies can also set you up with a local family. Prices range from £16.50 to £35 ($26.40–$56) per person per night for a double room, most of which are located away from the city's tourist center. The higher prices apply to rooms in central London. The agency charges anywhere from £15 to £50 ($24–$80) per couple depending on the number of nights booked. Contact **Host and Guest Service,** Harwood House, 27 Effie Rd., London SW6 1EN (☎ **0171/731-5340**); and **London Homestead Services,** 3 Coombe Wood Rd., Kingston-upon-Thames, Surrey KT2 7JY (☎ **0181/949-4455;** fax 0181/549-5492), which lists more than 200 rooms and requires a minimum of three nights.

HOME EXCHANGES   HomeLink, P.O. Box 650, Key West, FL 33041 (☎ **800/638-3841;** fax 305/294-1448; E-mail: 72520.1414@compuserve.com), can help you set up a home swap—your house or apartment for a residence in London, in England, or in any other country. Listings are concentrated in Europe and North America. The $88 cost of a membership entitles you to a listing sans photograph and receipt of a directory. If you want to post a photograph of your home, it will cost an additional $18 to $22.

EDUCATIONAL TRAVEL   The **American Institute for Foreign Study,** 102 Greenwich Ave., Greenwich, CT 06830 (☎ **800/727-2437** or 203/863-6087), offers 3- to 12-week study/travel programs starting at about $3,199, including round-trip airfare from New York, all meals, and housing. Add-ons from other U.S. cities are available.

The **Institute for International Education,** 809 United Nations Plaza, New York, NY 10017 (☎ **212/883-8200**), also administers students' applications for study-abroad programs in England and other European countries. Write or call ☎ 800/445-0443 for their free booklet, "Basic Facts on Study Abroad."

The **Council on International Educational Exchange,** 205 E. 42nd St., New York, NY 10017 (☎ **212/661-1414**—ask for the Information and Student Services Department), publishes a free magazine entitled *Student Travels.* The council also runs a "Work in Britain" program for U.S. college and university students.

Those 60 and older, along with their spouses of any age (or a "significant other" 50 or older), can take advantage of an educational program sponsored by **Elderhostel,** 75 Federal St., Boston, MA 02110 (☎ **617/426-7788**). This organization sends almost 16,000 people to school abroad every year. Courses last two to four weeks. Fees start at $2,050 for a two-week course and include airfare, meals, lodging, daily classroom instruction, and admission fees.

It's also possible to enroll yourself in summer courses at **Cambridge** or **Oxford University.** For info contact Dr. Joann Painter, 714 Sassafras St., Erie, PA 16501 (☎ **814/456-0757**).

10 Getting There

BY PLANE

Close to 90 scheduled airlines serve London, including almost every major American and international carrier.

THE MAJOR AIRLINES

The major American carriers offering regularly scheduled London flights include: **American Airlines** (☎ 800/433-7300), **Continental** (☎ 800/231-0856), **Delta Airlines** (☎ 800/241-4141), **Northwest Airlines** (☎ 800/447-4747), **TWA** (☎ 800/892-4141), and **United Airlines** (☎ 800/538-2929). **British Airways** (☎ 800/247-9297), the largest British airline, offers a good standard of service from about a dozen cities. **Virgin Atlantic Airways** (☎ 800/862-8621) flies from New York and Newark, New Jersey, as well as from Boston, Washington, D.C., Los Angeles, San Francisco, Orlando, and Miami.

FINDING THE BEST AIRFARE

London's popularity and the number of airlines flying there mean that the airlines compete heavily for customers. Always check local and national newspapers for special promotions and always shop around to secure the least expensive fare.

The lowest-priced standard economy-class fare usually carries some restrictions like advance-purchase, minimum stay, or a Saturday stopover, as well as penalties for altering dates and itineraries. Note too, that weekday flights are slightly cheaper than weekend flights.

You can also purchase tickets from consolidators who buy blocks of seats from airlines and sell them at a discount. The tickets are restrictive, valid only for a particular date or flight, nontransferable, and nonrefundable except directly from the consolidator. In addition, they may not always earn frequent flier miles. These tickets are rarely restricted by advance-purchase requirements; if space is available, you can buy your ticket just days before departure. Always pay with a credit card, though, to protect yourself in case the consolidator goes bankrupt.

The lowest-priced bucket shops are usually local operations with low profiles and overheads. Look for their tiny ads consisting of a list of cities and prices in the travel or classified section of your local newspaper.

Nationally advertised consolidators are usually not as competitive as the smaller, back-room operations, but they often have toll-free telephone numbers and may be more reliable. In early 1998 you could secure a round-trip to London for as little $290. Here are some of the most reliable consolidators operating:

Make the Airline Pricing System Work for You

Ever since the airlines introduced Sabre, increasingly sophisticated computer software has enabled the airlines to practice what's called yield management. This enables the airlines to adjust the pricing of each individual seat on a particular flight according to the demand at any given moment. Thus, fares can change from one hour to the next depending on relative demand for a particular flight. Whatever price you pay for your ticket, you can bet that the person sitting next to you paid either a higher or lower price for what is in effect the same piece of merchandise. It's virtually impossible to state accurate prices for airfares because so many variables come into play. Still, you can play this game to your advantage by making use of the latest computer technology, either via the Internet, a reliable travel agent, or one of the companies that specialize in searching out low airfares.

Among the latter are: **A Better Airfare** (☎ 800/238-8371, www.better1. com); **AAAAbsolute Savings** (☎ 800/359-4537); **Airline Bargain Finder & Ticket Sales** (☎ 800/727-1147); **800 Travel System Inc.** (☎ 800/569-2473); **Fare Busters International** (☎ 800/618-0571); **Global Discount Travel Services** (☎ 800/497-6678); and **1-800 Fly Cheap** (☎ 800/359-2432).

If you want to secure the best possible deal available at the time you make your booking, then shop the discount specialists listed above. If you have access to the Internet, in addition to the sites listed in "Cyber Deals for Net Surfers," above, visit these addresses. **Priceline** (www.priceline.com) allows travelers to post the fares they're willing to pay and see if the airlines are willing to fly them at that price. **Travelbids** (www.travelbids.com) operates in a similar fashion; customers post their itineraries and agents bid on them, with the lowest bid winning the fare (there's a $5 registration charge plus a $5 charge for each listing). **Intellitrip** (www.intellitrip.com) scans for the cheapest fares to your destination.

Arrow Travel, 280 Madison Ave., New York, NY 10016, ☎ 212/889-2550; **Cheap Tickets Inc.,** 115 E. 57th St. at Park, New York, NY 10022, ☎ 212/570-1179 or 800/377-1000; **TFI Tours International,** 34 W. 32nd St., 12th floor, New York, NY 10001, ☎ 212/736-1140 in New York State, or 800/745-8000 elsewhere in the United States; **Travel Land International Inc.,** 19 W. 34th St., no. 603, New York, NY 10001, ☎ 212/268-6464; **UniTravel,** 1177 N. Warson Rd., St. Louis, MO 63132, ☎ 800/325-2222; and **Up & Away Travel,** 347 Fifth Ave., Suite 202, New York, NY 10016, ☎ 212/889-2345.

Charters   Another cheap way to cross the Atlantic is on a charter flight. Most charter operators advertise and sell their seats through travel agents, making them your best source of information for available flights. Two well-known operators that sell tickets directly to passengers include **Travac,** 989 Sixth Ave., New York, NY 10018 (☎ **800/872-8800** or 212/563-3303, or 888/872-8327 for current fare quotes); and **Council Travel Charters,** 205 E. 42nd St., New York, NY 10017 (☎ 800/226-8624, www.counciltravel.com).

Going as a Courier   Companies transporting time-sensitive materials, such as film, blood, or documents for banks and insurance firms, regularly hire air couriers. Flying as a courier can mean that you fly to London in high season for as little as $350 round-trip and in low season for $250 round-trip. To take advantage of this opportunity, you should call the courier service at least a month in advance of your

---

Onward! Flying to & from the Continent & Around Britain

If you want to fly to Europe, the cheapest options will be offered on such no-frills airlines as Debonair, Easyjet, Ryanair, Virgin Express, and British Airways GO. Look for their ads in local newspapers and also on Underground trains.

The first three fly from Luton, the last two from Stansted Airport. A fare war sees lower prices being posted practically every day. For example, you can currently fly to Rome for as little as £100 ($160) round-trip on GO or for £119 ($190.40) round-trip on Debonair. Keep an eye out for ads offering ever lower fares in newspapers and in the Underground.

---

planned trip. The downside of this savings is that you will have to give up your checked-baggage allowance to the courier company and make do with a carry-on. It also means flying alone, although you may be able to coordinate with a friend or partner by making arrangements to leave as couriers on two consecutive days. The courier company will handle the check-in and pickup of packages at each airport.

Two popular courier services are **Now Voyager, Inc.,** 74 Varick St., Suite 307, New York, NY 10013 (☎ **212/431-1616,** 11:30am–6pm); and **Halbart Express,** 147–05 176th St., Jamaica, NY 11434 (☎ **718/656-8189,** 9am–3pm). Note that Now Voyager also operates noncourier discount flights. In summer 1998 you could fly as a courier to London for $399 round-trip but the length of stay was restricted to seven days; the company also offered round-trip flights aboard Air India for $625, a good price for high-season transatlantic travel.

Most flights depart from New York, so you may have to tack on the additional cost to get to the gateway city. Prices change all the time, from low to very low. If a company needs emergency courier service and you can fly immediately, you could travel for next to nothing—say, $50 round-trip.

LONDON'S AIRPORTS

London is served by two major airports: Heathrow and Gatwick. Both have good public transport links to central London.

The cheapest route from **Heathrow Airport** to London is by Underground ("the tube"). The 15-mile journey takes approximately 45 minutes and costs £3.80 ($6.10) to any downtown station. Service is convenient, as the Underground platforms are directly below the airport's four terminals. Most transatlantic flights arrive (and depart) from Terminals 1 and 2. Terminal 3 is home to most intra-European flights, while Terminal 4 is the long-haul hub for British Airways exclusively. Heathrow is big, so even those with light luggage would be well advised to use one of the free baggage carts for the long walk to the Underground. Trains depart every 4 to 10 minutes from 6am to midnight.

There is also a **FastTrain** (☎ **0845/600-1515**), which began service in 1998. It takes only 15 minutes and operates every 15 minutes from Heathrow nonstop to Paddington. Tickets are £10 ($16) one way and £20 ($32) round-trip.

The **Airbus Express** (☎ **0181/400-6655**), which takes between 1 and 1½ hours, costs £10 ($16) round-trip, £6 one way; it travels from all terminals to Baker Street, Euston, Victoria, King's Cross, and 19 other central London stops and hotels. It operates about every 30 minutes from 5am to 10pm. A cab will cost about £40 ($64).

There are two ways of making the 25-mile trek from **Gatwick Airport** to the city center. The first, and more popular, is the **Gatwick Express** train (☎ **0990/**

30-15-30), which takes 30 to 45 minutes to reach Victoria Station. Unfortunately, it costs a hefty £9.50 ($15.20) each way. The station is just below the airport, and trains depart every 15 minutes from 6am to 10pm (hourly, on the hour, at other times). You can also take the **Flightline** bus (☎ **0181/668-7261** or 0990/747-777). The 70-minute journey costs £7.50 ($12) one-way, or £11 ($17.60) round-trip. Buses destined for Victoria Coach Station depart from Gatwick's North Terminal hourly, at different times throughout the day.

If you are flying to London on a no-frills flight, you may land at Stansted Airport. Flightline operates buses from Stansted to central London for £8 ($12.80) single and £12 ($19.20) return, and from Stansted to Victoria for £9 ($14.40) single and £13 ($20.80) return. The journey will take about 1¼ hours. For information call ☎ **0990/747-777.**

BY TRAIN

Each of London's train stations is connected to London's vast bus and Underground network, and each has phones, restaurants, pubs, luggage-storage areas, and London Regional Transport Information Centres.

If you're **arriving from France,** the fastest way to get to London is by taking the HoverSpeed connection between Calais and Dover (see "By Ferry & Hovercraft," below), where you can pick up a BritRail train into the city. If you prefer the ease of one-stop travel, you can take the Chunnel train directly from Paris.

Via the Chunnel from the Continent   Queen Elizabeth and President François Mitterrand officially opened the Channel Tunnel in 1994, and the **Eurostar Express** began twice-daily passenger service between London and both Paris and Brussels. The $15-billion tunnel, one of the great engineering feats of all time, is the first link between Britain and the Continent since the Ice Age.

Rail Europe (☎ **800/94-CHUNNEL** for information) sells tickets on the *Eurostar* direct train service between Paris and Brussels and London. A round-trip first-class fare between Paris and London, for example, costs $398 ($278 in second class); but you can cut costs to $182 with a second-class, 14-day advance purchase (nonrefundable) round-trip fare, and I've seen special published fares as low as $160 round-trip. In London, make reservations for *Eurostar* at ☎ **0345/300003;** in Paris, at ☎ **01-44-51-06-02;** and in the United States, at ☎ **800/EUROSTAR.** *Eurostar* trains arrive and depart from London's Waterloo Station, Paris's Gare du Nord, and Brussel's Central Station. On the French side the train rips along at 186 miles an hour; on the British side it slows down to 100 miles an hour, at least until the track is upgraded.

If you are traveling to London from elsewhere in the United Kingdom, consider buying a **BritRail Classic Pass,** which allows unlimited rail travel during a set time period (8 days, 15 days, or 1 month). (Eurailpasses aren't accepted in Britain, although they are in Ireland.) For 8 days, a pass costs $375 in first class, $259 in standard class; for 15 days, it's $575 and $395, respectively; for 22 days, it's $740 and $510; and for 1 month, it's $860 and $590. If a child age 5 to 15 is traveling with a full-fare adult, the fare is half the adult fare. Children under 5 travel free if not occupying a seat. Senior citizens (60 and over) qualify for discounts, but only on first-class travel: It's $319 for an 8-day pass, $489 for a 15-day pass, $630 for a 22-day pass, and $730 for a 1-month pass. Travelers between 16 and 25 can purchase a BritRail Classic Youth Pass, which allows unlimited second-class travel: $205 for 8 days, $318 for 15 days, $410 for 22 days, or $475 for 1 month.

You must purchase your BritRail pass before you leave home. Americans can secure BritRail passes at **BritRail Travel International,** 500 Mamaroneck Ave.,

Suite 314, Harrison, NY 10528 (☎ **800/677-8585** in the U.S., 800/555-2748 in Canada), or you can get booking information on the Internet at www.raileurope.com.

Travelers who arrive from France via ferry or hovercraft (see "By Ferry & Hovercraft," below) and pick up a British Rail train at Dover arrive at **Victoria Station,** in the center of London. Those journeying south by rail from Edinburgh arrive at **King's Cross Station.**

BY BUS

Whether you're coming from the Continent or from another part of England, London-bound buses almost always go to (and leave from) **Victoria Coach Station,** Buckingham Palace Road, located one block from Victoria Railway Station.

If you're traveling to London from elsewhere in the United Kingdom, consider purchasing a **Britexpress Card,** which entitles you to a 30% discount on National Express (England and Wales) and Caledonian Express (Scotland) buses. Contact a travel agent for details.

Bus connections to Britain from the Continent are generally not very comfortable, although some lines are more convenient than others. One line with a relatively good reputation is **Euroways Eurolines, Ltd.,** 52 Grosvenor Gardens, London SW1W OAU (☎ **0171/730-8235**). Euroways books passage on buses traveling three times a day between London and Paris (9 hours); two times a day from Amsterdam (12 hours); four times a week from Munich (24 hours); and three times a week from Stockholm (44 hours). On the longer routes, which employ two alternating drivers, the bus proceeds almost without interruption, taking occasional breaks for meals.

BY FERRY & HOVERCRAFT

For centuries, sailing ships and ferryboats have traversed the English Channel bearing supplies, merchandise, and passengers. Today, the major carriers are P&O Channel Lines, Hoverspeed, and Sealink. Note that here, too, discounts are offered for early booking usually before the end of March. The shortest and closest routes from London are Dover to Calais, and Folkestone to Boulogne and Calais. On the Dover–Calais route expect to pay anywhere from £102 ($163.20) to £198 ($316.80) (depending on the season) round-trip for car and driver, and £24 ($38.40) for passenger round-trip.

Once you arrive in Dover, you can pick up a BritRail train to London (see "By Train," above).

Car & Passenger Ferries   **P&O Channel Lines** (☎ **0990/980980**) operates car and passenger ferries between Portsmouth and Cherbourg, France (three departures a day; 4¼ hours each way, 7 hours at night); between Portsmouth and Le Havre, France (three a day; 5½ hours each way, 7 hours at night); and between Dover and Calais, France (25 a day; 75 minutes each way).

P&O's major competitor is **Stena Sealink** (☎ **01233/615455**), which carries both passengers and vehicles. This company is represented in North America by **Rail Europe** (☎ **800/677-8585** or 212/575-2667). Stena Sealink operates conventional ferryboat service between Cherbourg and Southampton (one or two trips a day taking 6 to 8 hours) and between Dieppe and Newhaven (four departures a day taking 4 hours each way). Very popular are Sealink's conventional car ferries between Calais and Dover, which depart 20 times a day in either direction and take 90 minutes for the crossing. Typical one-way fares between France and England are £25 ($40) for adults, £22 ($35.20) for senior citizens, and £12 ($19.20) for children.

Hovercraft & Seacats   Traveling by Hovercraft or SeaCat cuts your journey time from the Continent to Britain. **HoverSpeed** operates at least 12 daily 35-minute Hovercraft crossings, as well as slightly longer crossings via SeaCat (a catamaran propelled by jet engines; these go four times daily and take about 55 minutes), between Boulogne and Folkestone. A Hovercraft trip is definitely a fun adventure, as the vessel is technically "flying" over the water. SeaCats also travel from the mainland of Britain to the Isle of Wight, Belfast, and the Isle of Man. For reservations and information, call **HoverSpeed** at (☎ **01304/240241**). Typical one-way fares are £25 ($40) per person.

BY CAR

If you plan to take a rented car across or under the Channel, check carefully with the rental company about license and insurance requirements before you leave.

Ferries from the Continent   There are many "drive-on, drive-off" car-ferry services across the Channel. The most popular ports in France for Channel crossings are Boulogne and Calais, where you can board Stena **Sealink ferries** taking you to the English ports of Dover and Folkestone. For details, see "By Ferry & Hovercraft," above.

Le Shuttle   You can take Le Shuttle (☎ **0990/353535** or 01304/288617) under the English Channel. The tunnel not only accommodates trains but passenger cars, charter buses, taxis, and motorcycles, all taken under the English Channel from Calais, France, to Folkestone, England, or vice versa. It operates 24 hours a day, 365 days a year, running every 15 minutes during peak travel times and at least once an hour at night. With Le Shuttle, gone are weather-related delays, seasickness, and a need for reservations. Motorists drive onto a half-mile-long train and travel though an underground tunnel built beneath the seabed through a layer of impermeable chalk marl and sealed with a reinforced-concrete lining.

Before boarding Le Shuttle, you'll stop at a toll booth to pay, then pass through Immigration for both countries at one time. During the ride, you'll stay in bright, air-conditioned carriages, remaining inside your car or stepping outside to stretch your legs. When the trip is completed, you'll simply drive off toward London. The total travel time between the French and English highway system is about 1 hour.

The cost of moving a car on Le Shuttle varies, according to the season and the day of the week, between £80 and £265 ($128 and $424) each way. Discounts are granted to passengers who return to France with their cars within 5 days of their departure; otherwise, the round-trip fare is twice the price of the one-way fare.

Stores selling duty-free goods, restaurants, and service stations are available to travelers on both sides of the Channel. A bilingual staff is on hand to assist travelers at both the British and French terminals.

Hertz offers **Le Swap,** a service for passengers taking Le Shuttle. At Calais, you can switch cars for either a left-hand- or right-hand-drive vehicle, depending upon which country you're heading for.

Once you've arrived from the Continent, you can quickly connect with a motorway into London. London is encircled by two inner roads, the A406 and the A205, and the M25 farther out. The M25 connects with the M1 to Birmingham, the M40 to Oxford, the M4 to Bristol, the M3 to Southampton, the M20 to Dover, and the M11 to Cambridge. Once in the city, I would suggest you dispense with the car, because parking is difficult and expensive and the city is a maze of one-way streets.

3 Getting to Know London

London is a huge city that spreads out over 600-plus square miles. It sounds intimidating, but it really isn't, given the city's efficient Underground and bus system. London grew up around The City—the financial center equivalent to Wall Street—which occupies one square mile near the Tower of London and Tower Bridge. From here, the city grew west when the monarch's palace was built at Westminster. Around The City and Westminster, a series of villages sprang up—Bloomsbury, Hackney, Holborn, Highgate, and Hampstead, for instance. Over the centuries, these villages were absorbed into the city proper. Today, it's easy to get around from one area to another via public transport.

This chapter will help you get your bearings. It provides a brief orientation and a preview of the city's most important neighborhoods. It answers questions about getting around London by public transportation and also contains a Fast Facts section covering everything from bookstores to shoe repairs.

1 Orientation

VISITOR INFORMATION

The **London Tourist Board (LTB)** operates several information offices. On arrival, stop into the office at the Underground Station Concourse (Terminals 1, 2, 3) at Heathrow (☎ **0839/123456**), open daily 8am to 6pm; or the office in the arrivals concourse in Terminal 3 (☎ **0181/759-9113**), open from 6am to 11pm. Those arriving via Gatwick can visit the office in Victoria Station's forecourt. The Victoria office (☎ **0839/123456;** fax 0171/931-7768) is open daily from 8am to 7pm from Easter to October; the rest of the year, it's open Monday through Saturday from 9am to 6pm, and on Sunday from 9am to 5pm. Other LTB Information Centres are located at Liverpool Street Station (☎ **0839/123456;** open Mon–Fri 8am–6pm, Sat–Sun 8:45am–5:30pm); and at Waterloo Station (☎ **0171/620-1550;** fax 0171/928-6221; open daily 8:30am–10:30pm).

The **British Travel Centre,** 12 Lower Regent St., SW1 (**no phone**), near Piccadilly Circus, provides information on all of Britain. It's open from 9am to 6:30pm Monday through Friday and 10am to 4pm Saturday and Sunday. Weekend hours may be extended slightly in summer. Additional travel centers are located at Canary Wharf, Greenwich, Southwark, and Islington.

London Street Names

Unlike most American cities where numbers hold sway, the street names of London tell its story from Roman and Norman times. Bucklersbury and Lothbury were named after *burhs,* the stone mansions of Norman barons. Ludgate, Aldgate, Cripplegate, refer to the original gates of the city. The Barbican is so called because it stands on the site of a watchtower. In the Middle Ages, *cheaps* were markets: hence modern street names like Eastcheap and Cheapside. As the city grew and more crafts were practiced, artisans and merchants gathered in particular streets and so today you still have Milk Street, Bread Street, and Friday Street (where fish was sold). Clink Street was the site of a prison, hence the expression "in the clink." Cock Lane, in the 14th century, was the only street licensed for prostitution.

For information about travel by bus, tube, or British Rail, visit a **London Transport Information Centre** in any of the major train stations; or call the **London Regional Transport Travel Information Service** (☎ **0171/222-1234**), open 24 hours daily.

CITY LAYOUT
MAIN DISTRICTS, ARTERIES & STREETS

Most visitors won't need to explore the vast area that is Greater London. Instead, they'll concentrate on an area stretching from the Thames Embankment north to Camden Town and Islington, west to Kensington, and East to Tower Bridge. Within this area are located all of the major tourist sights and facilities. The logical—although not geographical—center of this area is **Trafalgar Square.** On the north side of the square is the National Gallery, England's most important repository of fine art, and beyond lies cinema-laden **Leicester Square,** restaurant-packed **Soho,** and London's **theater district.** The city's literary and intellectual center, **Bloomsbury,** is farther north still. This district is anchored by the massive British Museum and dotted with a good number of moderately priced hotels.

The Strand branches east from Trafalgar Square, and connects the **West End** with **The City.** A stroll down this street will reveal an eclectic mix of hotels, restaurants, shops, and office buildings. **Covent Garden Market,** a landmark for tourists and shoppers alike, is located just a few blocks north of the Strand.

South of Trafalgar Square is **Whitehall,** the address of many of Great Britain's most important government buildings. No. 10 Downing Street, the official residence of the prime minister, is just off Whitehall; and Big Ben, Westminster Abbey, and Parliament Square are all located at the bottom of the street along the riverbank. Farther west along the riverbank stands the Tate Gallery.

The Mall is a long road that runs west from Trafalgar Square along the edge of St. James's Park to Buckingham Palace. **Knightsbridge, Kensington,** and **Hyde Park** lie farther west still.

FINDING AN ADDRESS

No doubt about it—you *will* get lost in London. To the chagrin of tourists and postal workers alike, the city's tangle of streets follows no discernible pattern whatsoever. Furthermore, there seems to be little logic to street naming or house numbering. Be warned that Park Walk is not necessarily near Park Crescent, to say nothing of a similarly named street, road, mews, and close. Sometimes odd-

Impressions

It is my belief, Watson . . . that the lowest and vilest alleys of London do not present a more dreadful record of sin than does the smiling and beautiful countryside.
—Sir Arthur Conan Doyle, *The Adventures of Sherlock Holmes*

numbered houses are on one side of a street, while even-numbered homes are on the other. Other times, numbers will run straight up one side of a street, then down the other so that, for example, no. 1 and no. 300 will be opposite one another.

STREET MAPS

A London street map is essential, even if you are staying on the beaten track. If you need a more detailed map than the one bound into the back of this guide, you'll find that bookstores, food markets, souvenir shops, and most sidewalk newsagents sell local maps. Expect to pay £2 to £5.95 ($3.20–$9.50). The London Tourist Board Book and Gift Shop in the Victoria Station information center stocks many maps and guidebooks too.

If you're planning to stay a while in London, you're advised to purchase an **A to Z London Guide,** available at newsstands and bookstores.

NEIGHBORHOODS IN BRIEF

The City (EC1, EC2)   One square mile, The City is the original walled city, still ruled by the lord mayor. It stretches from Temple and Holborn Bars (gates) on the west to Aldgate and Tower Hill on the east and from the Thames to Smithfield and Moorfields in the north. Today, The City is London's financial center, bustling during the day but deserted at night. Here you'll find Guildhall, the Old Bailey, the Bank of England, the Stock Exchange, Lloyd's, St. Paul's, the Barbican, the Museum of London, and at its eastern riverside perimeter, the Tower of London.

The Strand (WC2)   In early London, this thoroughfare connected The City to Westminster and was lined with the palaces of bishops and aristocrats. Today, along this broad street, you'll find the Royal Courts of Justice, King's College, Somerset House (the Courtauld Institute), the Savoy Hotel, and the Inner Temple, as well as shops, hotels, theaters, and restaurants. From Trafalgar Square, it runs east into Fleet Street.

Holborn/Clerkenwell (WC2, EC1)   North of the Strand, this area has long been associated with the legal profession. Both Gray and Lincoln's Inn are located here. Clerkenwell, an old small manufacturing area, is one of the centers of London's new loft living and is becoming a fashionable new neighborhood.

Islington (N1)   Once a dowdy neighborhood, it has now become home to successful young couples and their families. Islington's considered the bastion of New Labour, one of Tony Blair's favorite stomping grounds. It's worth coming to visit the Camden Passage Market, which is open Saturday.

Westminster/Whitehall (SW1)   The heart of governmental London. Home of the Houses of Parliament, Westminster Abbey, 10 Downing Street, Scotland Yard, and government ministries and offices.

Covent Garden (WC2)   Ever since the market moved out in 1974, this has become a tourist mecca for shopping, dining, and entertainment. Site of the Royal Opera House and also of the Actors' Church, St. Paul's.

Bloomsbury (WC1)   A genteel neighborhood anchored by the British Museum and Library and the University of London. You'll find streets and squares lined with terraced houses, antiquarian bookstores, and plenty of academic life. Also home to the Percival David Foundation of Chinese Art.

Piccadilly Circus, Leicester and **Trafalgar Squares (W1, WC2)**   The heart of London's theater district is filled with fast-food restaurants and other services.

Soho (W1)   Between Piccadilly and Oxford Circuses and Cambridge and St. Giles Circuses, this fascinating neighborhood of narrow crooked streets was originally London's foreign quarter. Today, it contains some of the city's finest restaurants, both budget and luxury. Chinatown is just across Shaftesbury Avenue, along Gerrard and Lisle Streets. The sex trade is also part of the Soho scene, but it's been substantially cleaned up in recent years.

St. James (SW1)   The Court of St. James says it all. The Mall leads from Buckingham Palace right along the southeastern boundary of St. James. Home to St. James's Palace, Christie's auctioneers, and such streets as Jermyn, which is lined with stores selling bespoke items for gentlemen.

Mayfair (W1)   Bounded by Piccadilly, Hyde Park, and Oxford and Regent Streets, this area is considered London's most elegant. It's home to the American Embassy, Savile Row, and the Royal Academy. New Bond Street is lined with galleries and auction houses and other top-quality stores.

Marylebone (W1, NW1)   This quiet residential area which incorporates the famous Harley Street is suddenly being rediscovered by such retailers as Conran, who is opening another one of his flagship stores in the High Street. Signs are the neighborhood is on the verge of becoming trendy.

Regent's Park (NW1)   The focal point of this residential area, marked by many John Nash terraces, is the 487-acre park, which also shelters the London Zoo.

Paddington/Bayswater (W2, W9, W10)   This north London residential area has experienced its ups and downs. In the 1950s, it became identified with poor housing and poverty, but today it's enjoying a revival. Bayswater occupies the southern boundaries of Paddington. It's a residential area with a shopping area stretching along Westbourne Grove. Here, you'll find a number of budget hotels and budget restaurants along Sussex Gardens.

Notting Hill (W11)   Adjacent to Bayswater and Kensington, to the west of Kensington Palace and Gardens, this area is associated with a Caribbean community and its famous Caribbean carnival, held on August Bank Holiday. The Portobello Market is also here. The neighborhood has started to become very trendy; fashionable restaurants and stores have been opening here.

Hampstead (NW3)   Originally a village to which Londoners retreated for the waters, Hampstead retains a villagelike ambience. Home to the wealthy and the famous, it encompasses the glorious 800-acre heath. Several homes of famous writers and artists are open to the public.

Camden Town (NW1)   An area of small manufacturers in the late 19th and early 20th centuries, it was home to Greek and Irish communities. In more recent times it has been home to Britpop. Today it's undergoing gentrification. On weekends, its streets are jammed with people visiting the stalls of the youth-oriented Camden Market. The canal adds charm to the area.

Highgate (N6, N19)   Another west London village that retains a separate identity. Home to the famous and also to Highgate Cemetery.

London's Neighborhoods

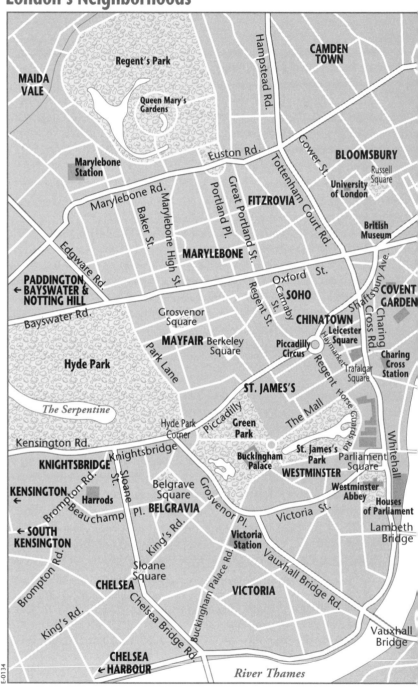

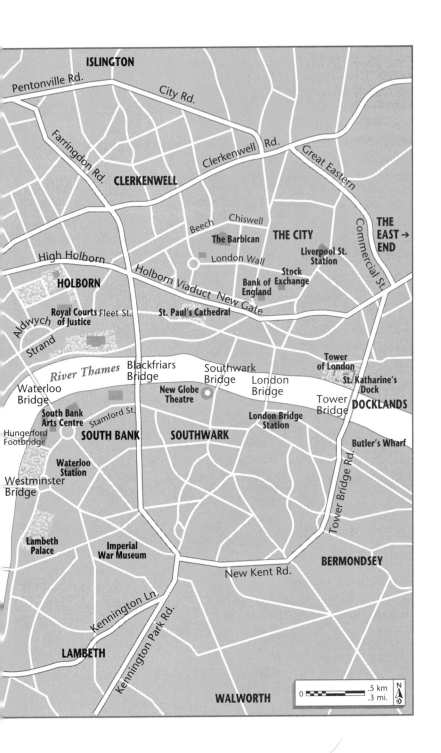

Belgravia (SW1)   Southeast of Knightsbridge, this aristocratic residential quarter rivals Mayfair in prestige and money. It backs onto Buckingham Palace Gardens.

Knightsbridge (SW1)   A premier residential and shopping area, just south of Hyde Park. It's famous for Harrods.

Kensington/South Kensington (W8, W10, W11, W14, SW5, SW7 SW10)   Both lie south of Kensington Gardens. South Kensington is known for being the home of the Victoria and Albert, the Science, and the Natural History Museums.

Chelsea (SW3, SW10)   A stylish district stretching along the Thames, southwest of Belgravia. Many artists and writers have lived in the stately terraced homes that line its quiet streets and mews: Thomas Carlyle, for one. Its major artery is the King's Road, which was the premier fashion street in the '60s days of Swinging London.

Earl's Court (SW5)   This residential area, clustered around the station and exhibition building of the same name, is referred to as both Kangaroo Valley (because of its Australian community) and Bedsit Jungle (because of its largely transient population). Today it is slowly being gentrified as well.

South Bank/Southwark (SE1)   The National Theatre, Royal Festival Hall, Queen Elizabeth Hall, and the Hayward Gallery can all be found here, just across Waterloo Bridge. To the east of the entertainment complex you'll find the Globe Theatre in the heart of Southwark. Here in Bankside the new extension of the Tate is being built. Waterloo station is the departure point for Eurostar trains to Paris and Brussels.

The East End (E1, E2, E3)   One of London's poorest areas and the home of the true Cockney. Most of the immigrants that came to England—the Jews and Huguenots, for example—settled here. In earlier centuries, this area was undesirable, as the prevailing winds and the west-to-east flow of the River Thames carried stench and pestilence from the city to the East End.

Docklands   This modern development was built on and around the London docks which closed in the late '70s. The landmark building is Cesar Pelli's Canary Wharf Tower. Although it went through a brief economic trough in the '80s, the '90s have revived its fortunes again.

2 Getting Around
BY PUBLIC TRANSPORTATION

Getting around London is easy, thanks to the extensive Underground and bus networks. The system is organized by zone. Most visitors need only concern themselves with zone 1, or Central London. This zone extends from the Tower in the east and Notting Hill on the west, from Waterloo in the south to Baker Street, Euston, and King's Cross on the north. A one-way fare within this area is £1.30 ($2.10); a round-trip fare is £2.60 ($4.20). The fare for buses within zone 1 is the same. If you intend to use public transportation several times in a day, then it's cheaper to buy one of the many passes that are available for use on the Underground, buses, and the Docklands Light Railway. Carnets, which are books of 10 tickets, are available for travel on the Underground in zone 1 only. A carnet costs £10 ($16) adult and £5 ($8) children ages 5 to 15 and will save about £3 ($4.80) on the cost of buying single tickets. A one-day travelcard for zones 1 and 2 costs £3.50 ($5.60) adult, £1.80 ($2.90) children ages 5 to 15. It allows you to travel as often as you like in those zones after 9:30am Monday to Friday and all day Saturday, Sunday, and holidays. If you want to travel for a day before 9:30am, the LT card is available for zones 1 and 2 for £4.50 ($7.20) adult, £2.20 ($3.50) children 5 to 15. A weekly travelcard which can be used any time for zone 1 will cost £13 ($20.80) adult, £5.20 ($8.30) child; £16.60 ($26.55) and £5.80 ($9.30) respectively for zones 1 and 2. Monthly and annual cards are also available at Underground stations, Travel Information Centres, and certain tobacconists and newsagents who display a pass agent sign. To secure a weekly pass you'll need a passport-size photograph, which can be obtained at one of the machines located in most stations.

Bus passes valid for travel only on London Transport buses are available for all zones for one day at £2.70 ($4.35) adult, £1.40 ($2.25) children 5 to 15, and for one week for £12 ($19.20) and £5.20 ($8.30) children 5 to 15.

London Regional Transport Travel Information Centres are located in most of the major Underground stations, including Heathrow Central, King's Cross, Oxford Circus, Piccadilly Circus, and Victoria. Off-hour times vary, but all provide service weekdays from 9am to 5pm. LRT also maintains a 24-hour telephone information service (☎ 0171/222-1234).

THE UNDERGROUND

Except for Christmas Day when the tube is closed, subway trains run every few minutes beginning at about 5:30am Monday through Saturday and 7am or so on Sunday. Closing times vary with each station, but the last trains always leave between 11:30pm and 1am. Last train times are posted at the entrance of each station. Tickets can be purchased at the station ticket window or from an adjacent coin-operated machine. An alphabetized fare chart is posted next to most ticket machines. Hold onto your ticket throughout your ride; you'll need it to exit. Pick up a handy tube map, distributed free at station ticket windows. Pick out your destination and note the color of the line that stops there (Bakerloo is brown, Central is red, and so on). Then follow the line back to where you are, noting where you'll have to change to reach your destination. *Note:* The Docklands Light Railway operates from The City to the Docklands area. It only runs Monday to Saturday.

LONDON BUSES

The private bus network is as extensive as the subway. Red buses operate within London; the green buses travel outside the London area. The red double-deckers were going to be phased out gradually, but tourists protested so vehemently that they have been saved on some routes. Note that there are two kinds of bus stops—the compulsory stop (which has a white background) and the request stop (red background). At the first, the bus will stop without being hailed, but at the second you'll need to put your arm out to signal the bus to stop. On a double-decker, the

Tube Tip—Buy That Travelcard Before Leaving Home

If you plan to use public transit extensively, then you should purchase a **Visitor Travelcard** which allows unlimited travel throughout the bus and Underground system, including the link to Heathrow Airport. The pass must be purchased overseas and is available for three, four, or seven days and includes some tourist discount vouchers. In contrast to the travelcards that you can purchase in London, this pass, only available overseas, carries certain benefits. It allows you to travel at any time in all zones and does not require a passport picture. Contact the nearest BTA or Britrail office (see "Visitor Information & Entry Requirements," in chapter 2 for addresses and phone numbers).

conductor will come to your seat to take your fare. On the buses that have no conductors, you pay as you enter. Fares range from 60p (98¢) to £2 ($3.20). Weekly passes are available. You can secure a bus map from any London Transport Information Centre and from many Underground stations, although they are in short supply. For schedule and fare information, call ☎ **0171/222-1234.**

Regular bus service stops after midnight. Night buses have different routes and different numbers than their daytime counterparts. Night service is not as frequent; most routes are serviced only once per hour. Unlike weekly and monthly travelcards, one-day passes are not valid on night buses. The central London night-bus terminus is Trafalgar Square.

BY CAR

Rentals   It's a nuisance to keep a car in London, but for excursions, a rental car can come in handy. Making a reservation in the United States is, of course, cheaper. **Avis** (☎ 800/331-1084) will guarantee a dollar rate at the time of payment, which must be two weeks in advance of the rental. In summer 1998, Avis was offering an economy car for $189 per week, exclusive of a 17½% VAT and CDW (which is about $15 a day), or $399 including tax and CDW. The lowest summer rate at **Hertz** (☎ 800/654-3001), guaranteed in U.S. dollars, was $158 plus CDW and £12 surcharge or $353 all-inclusive plus a £12 surcharge. The best rates can be found at **Europe by Car,** One Rockefeller Plaza, New York, NY 10020 (☎ **212/ 581-3040**); or 9000 Sunset Blvd., Los Angeles, CA 90069 (☎ 213/272-0324), which was charging $135 per week all-inclusive in 1998 for a Ford Fiesta manual shift. Relatively low rates are also offered at **AutoEurope,** P.O. Box 7006, Portland, ME 04112 (☎ **207/828-2525**), which was offering an economy car with stick shift for only $173.90 per week plus CDW and $286.95 all-inclusive.

Gasoline   One of the few city gas stations open 24 hours, **Dorset House Service Station,** 170 Marylebone Rd. (☎ 0171/486-6389), accepts all major credit cards.

Parking   Parking is difficult. Most parking meters are enforced from 6am to 6:30pm. Blue signs point the way to **National Car Parks (NCP),** which are located throughout the city. To find the closest, call NCP (☎ 0171/499-7050). Fines for illegal parking can be stiff. Even worse are the wheel clamps that immobilize violators until the ticket is paid. If you find your car clamped, take the ticket and attached penalty notice to the nearest car pound (the address is on the ticket) to pay your fine.

Special Driving Rules   In Britain, wearing a seat belt is the law. You may not turn right on a red light, and automobiles must stop whenever a pedestrian steps into a crosswalk. Many crosswalks are located in the middle of the block, not at the corner. They're usually marked by white stripes on the pavement (zebra striping) and flashing orange lights on either sidewalk.

BY TAXI

For three or four people traveling a short distance, cabs can make economic sense. A taxi is available when the yellow sign on its roof is illuminated. Hail a cab by raising your arm. The driver will lower the window when he pulls to the curb, so you can state your destination before climbing in. You can also order a cab (☎ 0171/253-5000 or 071/286-0286), but the rates will be higher.

The meter begins at £1.40 ($2.25) for the first 505 yards, and then it's 20p for each additional 293 yards or 51 seconds. An extra person is 40p (64¢) and luggage 10p (16¢) per bag. On evenings, weekends, and holidays, there's a 40p to 60p

(65¢–95¢) surcharge. Since meter rates keep changing, you might want the number of the public carriage office: ☎ **0171/230-1623.**

Minicabs are meterless cars driven by any entrepreneur with a license. Technically, these taxis are not allowed to cruise for fares, but must operate from sidewalk offices—many of which are centered around Leicester Square. Minicabs are handy after the tube shuts down for the night and when black cabs are unavailable. They are available 24 hours, are cheaper than black cabs, and can be ordered in advance (☎ **0171/602-1234**). Always negotiate the fare with the office beforehand. If you're approached by a driver (away from the sidewalk offices), hard bargaining is in order.

If you need a taxi from your hotel early in the morning, it is advisable to make a reservation the night before. Try **Computer-cab** (☎ **0171/286-0286**) or Radio Taxicabs (☎ **0171/272-0272**). These outfits do charge a small booking fee.

BY BICYCLE

Bike lanes are unheard of and cars are unyielding—still, some people do ride. For a rental, try **On Your Bike,** 52–54 Tooley St., SE1 (☎ **0171/378-6669**). A 10-speed goes for £15 ($24) per day and £60 ($96) per week, plus a £200 ($320) deposit. The shop is open Monday through Friday from 9am to 6pm, Saturday from 9:30am to 5:30pm, and Sunday 11am to 4pm. More centrally located is **Bikepark,** 14 Stukeley St., Covent Garden, WC2 (☎ **0171/430-0083**). This place rents a variety of bikes charging £10 ($16) for the first day, £5 ($8) for the next day, and £3 ($4.80) for each day thereafter; they require a £200 ($320) deposit. Open daily in summer; Monday to Saturday in winter.

Serious cyclists should check out the **London Cycling Campaign,** Tress House, 3 Stamford St., SE1 9NT (☎ **0171/928-7220**), for information and advice on biking in the city. Pick up their booklet "On Your Bike," which shows bike paths and quiet streets for cyclists and costs £5.70 ($9.10).

FAST FACTS: London

Airport   See "Getting There" in chapter 2.

American Express   American Express has almost a dozen city offices, including 6 Haymarket, SW1 (☎ **0171/930-4411**). Most are open Monday to Friday 9am to 5:30pm, Saturday 9am to noon (some open all day Saturday and Sunday too, but for currency exchange only). To report lost or stolen cards, call **0127/369-6933,** 24 hours.

Bookstores   Dillons the Bookstore, 82 Gower St., WC1 (☎ **0171/636-1577**), is one of the biggest and best chain bookshops in town. It's open Monday to Friday 9am to 5pm, Saturday 9:30am to 6pm, and Sunday noon to 6pm. See chapter 8, "Shopping A to Z," for more bookstore information.

Business Hours   Most banks are open Monday to Friday 9:30am to 3:30pm. Some are also open Saturday 9:30am to noon. Offices are generally open Monday to Friday from 8:30 or 9am until 5 or 5:30pm. By law, pubs can open Monday to Saturday 11am to 11pm, and Sunday noon to 10:30pm. Note, however, that some pubs in quieter areas may close in the afternoon from 3 to 5:30pm. There is currently talk of bringing Britain in line with Europe and extending the pub hours until early morning; this may well have happened by the time you arrive. Restaurants usually open for lunch at 11am, and stay open until 11pm or midnight. A very few stay open later (see chapter 5, "Great Deals on Dining"). Stores are usually open Monday to Saturday 10am to 6pm, but most stay open at least one extra hour one night during the week. The major stores now also stay open Sunday. Some shops around touristy Covent Garden stay open until 7 or 8pm nightly.

Cameras   See "Photographic Needs," below.

Climate   See "When to Go," in chapter 2.

Currency   See "Money" in chapter 2.

Currency Exchange   As a rule, you will get a better rate for traveler's checks than you will for cash. Banks generally offer the best exchange rates, but American Express and Thomas Cook are competitive and do not charge a commission for cashing traveler's checks, no matter what the brand. Also, don't hesitate to use your credit cards at ATMs. Although you gamble on the rates not swinging too much, the charge for the service—for now, at least—is minimal. **American Express** maintains several offices throughout the city (see above). A conveniently located **Thomas Cook** office is at 1 Woburn Place, Russell Square WC1 (☎ **0171/837-5275**); open Monday to Friday 8am to 5pm, Saturday 9am to noon. The office at King's Cross and the one in front of the British Museum on Great Russell Street (☎ **0171/636-1903**) stay open from 8am to 7pm on Saturday. Beware of **Chequepoint** and other high-commission bureaux de change.

Customs   See "Customs" in chapter 2.

Doctors and Dentists   If you need a physician or dentist and your condition is not life-threatening, call the operator (☎ **100**) and ask for the local police. They will put you in touch with a specialist. You can also visit **Medical Express**, 117A Harley St., Chapel Place, W1 (☎ **0171/499-1991**). This private walk-in clinic is open Monday to Friday 9am to 6pm, Saturday 9:30am to 2:30pm. Consultations begin at £70 ($112). Citizens of Australia and New Zealand are entitled to free medical treatment and subsidized dental care while in Britain.

Driving Rules   See "Getting Around," earlier in this chapter.

Drugstores   **Bliss Chemist,** 5 Marble Arch, W1 (☎ **0171/723-6116**), is open daily 9am to midnight year-round. Call the operator (☎ **100**) and ask for the opening hours and addresses of other late-night "chemists."

Electricity   English appliances operate on 220 volts, and plug into three-pronged outlets that differ from those in America and on the Continent. Hair dryers, irons, shavers, and other American appliances require an adapter and transformer. Do not attempt to plug an American appliance into a European electrical outlet without a transformer; you will ruin your appliance and possibly start a fire.

Embassies/Consulates   The **U.S. Embassy,** 24 Grosvenor Sq., W1 (☎ **0171/499-9000**), does not accept visitors—all inquiries must be made by mail or phone. The **Canadian High Commission,** Macdonald House, 1 Grosvenor Sq., W1 (☎ **0171/258-6600**), is open Monday to Friday 8am to 11am. The **Australian High Commission** is in Australia House on the Strand, WC2 (☎ **0171/379-4334**), and is open Monday to Friday 9am to 1pm. The **New Zealand High Commission** is in New Zealand House, Haymarket, SW1 (☎ **0171/930-8422**), open Monday to Friday 10am to 4pm.

Emergencies   Dial **999** for police, fire, and ambulance from any phone. No money is required.

Eyeglasses   Several spectacle shops line Oxford Street, King's Road, and other major shopping streets. The department stores Harrods and Selfridges (see chapter 8, "Shopping") also have opticians on duty and a good selection of frames. The Contact Lens Centre, 32 Camden High St., NW1 (☎ **0171/ 383-3838**), is one of the cheapest shops for contacts as well as glasses. Depending on your prescription and whether or not the lenses are in stock, you can secure replacement lenses in one hour. It's open Monday to Friday 9:30am to 6:30pm, Saturday 9am to 5pm, and Sunday 11am to 4pm.

Hairdressers and Barbers   The **Hair Beauty,** 5th floor, Harrods department store, Knightsbridge, SW1 (☎ **0171/584-8881**), is a specialty department within the store's hair and beauty salon. Cuts cost £50 to £65 ($80 to $104) and up. Open Monday, Tuesday, and Saturday 10am to 6pm; Wednesday to Friday 10am to 7pm.

Holidays   See "When to Go," in Chapter 2.

Hospitals   In an emergency, dial **999** from any phone; no money is needed. **University College Hospital,** Grafton Way, WC1 (☎ **0171/387-9300**), is one of the most centrally located. A dozen other city hospitals also offer 24-hour walk-in emergency care. Dial **100** and ask the operator to connect you with the police. They'll tell you which hospital is closest.

Hot Lines   The **Restaurant Switchboard** (☎ **0181/888-8080**) makes restaurant recommendations and reservations free of charge. It's open Monday to Friday 9am to 7pm. At **Capital Radio Helpline** (☎ **0171/484-4000**), a live human being will answer any legitimate question about London, the universe, or anything. The helpline is open Monday to Friday 10am to 10pm, Saturday 8am to 8pm, and Sunday 10am to 4pm.

Information   See "Visitor Information," earlier in this chapter.

Laundry/Dry Cleaning   Most laundries open every day. Near Russell Square, try **Red and White Laundries,** 78 Marchmont St.(☎ **0171/387-3667**), open daily 6:30am to 8:30pm; a wash costs £1.20 to £3 ($1.90–$4.80), and dryers and soap are £1 ($1.60). Bring plenty of 20p pieces.

Dry cleaning is expensive in London. Expect to pay about £2.39 ($3.85) for laundering a shirt, £4.49 ($7.20) for dry cleaning a pair of pants, and £6.49 ($10.40) for dry cleaning a silk shirt. With more than 40 branches, **Sketchley,** 49 Maddox St., W1 (☎ **0171/629-1292**), is one of the city's largest cleaning chains. Check the telephone directory for other locations.

Libraries   The British Library, Great Russell Street, WC1 (☎ **0171/ 636-1544**), is one of the largest in the world, holding at least one copy of every book published in Britain. The library is not open to the casual reader, so you'll need a special pass to gain entry, obtainable if you're a bona fide scholar or author. Use the city's many smaller and more accessible local or specialized libraries.

Liquor Laws   Under British law, no one under 18 years of age may legally purchase or consume alcohol. Beer and wine are sold by supermarkets, liquor stores (called "off licenses" or "bottle shops"), and food shops advertising "off-license" sales. Some supermarkets also sell stronger spirits, at excellent prices. Admission-charging nightclubs are allowed to serve alcohol to patrons until 3am or so. By law, hotel bars may serve drinks after 11pm to registered guests only. See "Business Hours," above, for pub hours.

Lost Property   If you lose something on the bus or tube, wait three working days before contacting London Regional Transport, 200 Baker St., NW1 (☎ 0171/486-2496), open Monday to Friday 9:30am to 2pm. The **Taxi Lost Property Office,** 15 Penton St., N1 (☎ 0171/833-0996), is open Monday to Friday 9am to 4pm. Lost-property offices are also located in all the major British Rail stations and at the Victoria Coach Station.

   To report a loss or theft, call the operator (☎ 100) and ask for the police.

Luggage Storage/Lockers   The **Gatwick Airport Left Luggage Office** (☎ 0129/353-5353) never closes, and charges £3 ($4.80) per item for 24 hours, £21 ($33.60) per week. The **Heathrow Airport Left Luggage Offices** (☎ 0181/759-4321), at Terminals 1, 3, and 4, are open daily from about 6am to 10:30pm. They charge £3 ($4.80) per item for 24 hours. Luggage lockers are also available at Waterloo and Victoria (☎ 0171/928-5151), **King's Cross** (☎ 0171/922-9081), and other major British Rail stations. Lockers cost £3 to £7 ($4.80–$11.20) per day, depending on size.

Mail   Post offices are normally open Monday to Friday 9am to 5:30pm, Saturday 9am to 1pm. The **Main Post Office,** St. Martin's Place, Trafalgar Square, WC2 (☎ 0171/930-9580), is open Monday to Saturday 8am to 8pm. Mailboxes, which are usually round red pillars, are well distributed throughout the city. Airmail letters weighing up to 10 grams cost 43p (70¢), and postcards require a 37p (59¢) stamp to all destinations outside Europe. If you ask for special-issue stamps, you'll probably get something pretty. Budget travelers can get more post for the pound by purchasing aerograms for 36p (58¢) each. The deal is even sweeter at £1.99 ($3.20) per half dozen. For information you can also call ☎ 0171/250-2888.

   You can receive mail in London, marked "Poste Restante" and addressed to you, care of the London Trafalgar Square Post Office, 24 William IV St., London WC2N 4DL (☎ 0171/930-0438). It's open Monday to Saturday 8am to 8pm. You will need to show identification to collect your mail. If you have an American Express card or are carrying traveler's checks issued by that company, you can receive mail care of American Express, 6 Haymarket, London SW1, England.

Maps   See "City Layout," earlier in this chapter.

Money   See "Money" in chapter 2.

Newspapers/Magazines   The extraordinarily large number of local newspapers in London is generally divided into two categories—broadsheets and tabloids. In general, tabloids like the *Sun* and the *Daily Mirror* sensationalize news more than the larger-format papers. The *Daily Mail* is a middle-of-the-road paper. The *Times* is the granddaddy of London's opinionated papers, and features a particularly hefty Sunday edition. It's conservative in tone and philosophy, owned as it is by Rupert Murdoch. The *Guardian* is the city's largest left-of-center paper, with in-depth investigative stories and good reporting. The other liberal-leaning paper is *The Independent,* which always seems to be teetering on the brink of closure. The *Daily Telegraph,* known in some circles as the "Torygraph," leans right politically, and is particularly strong in foreign coverage.

   The weekly listings magazine *Time Out* is indispensable for comprehensive coverage of what's happening in the city. The *Evening Standard* also publishes an excellent supplement every Thursday on what's happening.

Photographic Needs   Photo processing in London is more expensive than similar services Stateside. For example, at Dixons you'll pay £4.99 ($8) for processing a roll of color negative film containing 36 exposures. However, **Dixons,**

88 Oxford St., W1 (☎ **0171/636-8511**), with more than 80 branches in London, is the best source for most photographic needs.

Police   Dial **999** in an emergency from any phone; no money is needed. At other times, dial the operator (☎ **100**) and ask to be connected with the police.

Radio   Deregulation has improved London radio, and more and more stations have appeared on the radio dial, but variety is still limited. The dozen or so sanctioned stations—heavy on current pop music, talk, and news—are supplemented by a handful of adventurous "pirate" broadcasters. The legal FM stations include: BBC1 (98.8), featuring a Top 40 format; BBC2 (89.1), a middle-of-the-road music station; BBC3 (91.3), Britain's best classical; BBC4 (93.5), news, talk, humor, and call-in shows; BBC Greater London Radio (94.9), album-oriented rock and talk; Capital FM (95.8), American-format pop rock; Heart (106.2), oldies and easy listening; Kiss (100) dance sounds; Classic (100.9), classical; Jazz FM (102.2), blues, R&B, big band, and the like; Melody (105.8), middle-of-the-road/easy listening; News Direct (97.3), 24-hour news; Virgin (105.8), album-oriented rock.

Religious Services   It sometimes seems that churches in London are almost as ubiquitous as pubs. Protestant houses of worship are on almost every street in the city, and you are welcome to attend Sunday services in any one of them. The London Tourist Board can provide you with a complete list. For a special treat, think about spending Sunday morning in St. Paul's Cathedral (☎ **0171/ 236-4128**) or Westminster Abbey (☎ **0171/222-5152**). Services are held at the abbey at 8am, 10am, 11:15am, 3pm, and 6:30pm. Times vary at St. Paul's; call for information.

Westminster Cathedral, Ashley Place, SW1 (☎ **0171/798-9055**), is England's Roman Catholic headquarters, and a worthy sight. Services are held Sunday at 7am, 8am, 9am, 10:30am, noon, 5:30pm, and 7pm.

The **Liberal Jewish Synagogue,** 28 St. John's Wood Rd., NW8 (☎ **0171/ 286-5181**), holds services Friday at 6:45pm and Saturday at 11am.

The **Buddhist Society,** 58 Eccleston Sq., SW1 (☎ **0171/834-5858**), holds regular lectures and meditations. Call Monday to Friday 2 to 6pm, Saturday 2 to 5pm for information.

Rest Rooms   Even if you don't drink, you'll find London's many pubs handy for their facilities. The most lavish rest rooms, however, are found in the lobbies of the major hotels. Automatic toilets—which are automatically sterilized from top to bottom after each use—are also available in most areas throughout the city. They are well lit, have piped-in music, and cost just 20p (32¢).

Safety   Take particular caution when exploring the East End and Brixton. Avoid the parks after dark.

Shoe Repair   Most of the major tube stations have "heel bars" that can make quick repairs. More extensive work can be performed in any of the major department stores (see Chapter 8, "Shopping") or at **Jeeves Snob Shop,** 10 Pont St., SW1 (☎ **0171/235-1101**); it's open Monday to Friday 8:30am to 6:30pm, Saturday 8:30am to 5pm.

Taxes   A 17.5% Value-Added Tax (VAT) is usually already figured into the price of most items. For example, hotels and restaurants usually include the VAT in their quoted prices. Occasionally they don't, so note the policy, which is usually on the menu/tariff. Tax has been included in all hotel rates quoted in this book. Foreign tourists can reclaim the VAT for major purchases that are being taken out of the UK. You need to fill out the form from the store sales clerk and show it and the goods at the VAT desk at the airport; you'll receive the refund on the spot or by mail. Note that VAT refunds cannot be processed after you arrive home.

Taxis   See "By Taxi," above in this chapter.

Telephone and Fax   The area code is 0171 in central London, 0181 in outer London. (Area codes are necessary when dialing from outside the code.) To dial London from the United States, dial 011, then 44 (the country code), then drop the first 0 and dial either 171 or 181, then the phone number.

London has two kinds of pay phones. One accepts coins and the other uses a phonecard, available from newsagents and green BT phonecard machines in £2, £5, £10, and £20 denominations. The minimum cost of a local call is 10p (16¢) for the first two minutes (during peak hours). You can deposit up to four coins at a time, but telephones don't make change, so unless you are calling long distance, use 10p coins exclusively. Phonecard telephones automatically deduct the price of your call from the card. Cards are especially handy for making long-distance and international calls. Some large hotels and tourist areas have credit-card telephones that accept major credit cards. Lift the handle and follow the instructions on the screen.

To reach the **local operator,** dial **100.** The **international operator** is **155. London and UK phone information** (called "directory inquiries") can be reached by dialing **192** and is free of charge; for international information, dial 153.

The best way to save money on international phone calls is to purchase one of the discount cards available at many variety stores and newsagents. Among the cheapest are the First America and First Europe cards, which charge extremely low rates in comparison to AT&T or British Telecom.

If you need to communicate by fax and your hotel is not equipped, contact **Chesham Executive Centre,** 150 Regent St., W1 (☎ **0171/439-6288**). They charge £4.25 ($6.80) per page plus VAT to fax the United States; the center is open Monday to Friday 9am to 6pm.

Television   London has only six local TV stations: four BBC channels and one independent commercial channel. Many hotels now offer cable/satellite stations including Bravo, UK Gold, and Granada Plus, showing films and classic British TV; Eurosport, a sports channel; Sky News, a 24-hour news channel; and MTV, a clone of the American version.

Time Zone   London's clocks are set on Greenwich Mean Time, five hours ahead of U.S. Eastern Standard Time. Daylight saving time is used in England, though the semiannual changeover occurs on a slightly different schedule from the U.S. To find out the exact time by phone, dial **Timeline** (☎ **123**).

Tipping   Most **restaurants** automatically add a service charge. The restaurant's policy will be written on the menu. When a service charge is not included, a 10% to 15% tip is customary. **Taxi drivers** expect 10% to 15% of the fare. Note that tipping is rare in both pubs and theaters.

Transit Info   The **London Regional Transport (LRT) Travel Information Service** (☎ **0171/222-1234**) offers schedule and fare information for bus, Underground, and British Rail service within Greater London. Open 24 hours.

Water   London's water is safe to drink. Mineral waters, both carbonated and still, are popular at restaurants and will be offered to you for a price; specify tap water, which is free, if that's what you want.

Accommodations You Can Afford

London's hotel scene is changing as profoundly as the city itself. More and more small hotels and bed-and-breakfasts are installing "en suite facilities," which has reduced the number of accommodations that have less expensive rooms without bathrooms. Similarly, whereas at one time every B&B served a large breakfast of bacon and eggs and such, these days more places are switching to the less extensive continental breakfast. Still, plenty of traditional B&Bs have spruced up their facilities, and you'll find the very best of them listed here in this chapter.

Sadly, there is no way of getting around the hard truth that many of London's budget hotels are often poorly maintained and do not offer as much value for money as you might expect. Rooms are often, but not always, small and worn and the furnishings are frequently old-fashioned and utilitarian. The price goes up if you want "decor" of any sort. All these facts were underlined when Britain's own *Sunday Times* reported extensively on the Britain's Good Hotel Guide's condemnation of the rock-bottom standards in London's budget hotels.

RESERVING IN ADVANCE: ROOM BOOKING SERVICES

The demand for budget hotels is so great that most of these hotels, which are often small, have high occupancy rates. In summer, you're well advised to book several months in advance. During the off-season, if you want the top-of-the-line budget places, you still need to book well in advance. Except where noted, the hotels listed in this chapter accept advance reservations. Rooms are typically held with a nonrefundable deposit (preferably in pounds) equaling the cost of one night's stay. When sending a deposit, ask for a confirmation. You may also wish to follow up your reservation request with a telephone call to the hotel. *And if you call from the United States, remember to drop the initial zero from the London area code: dial 171 or 181, not 0171 or 0181.*

If you arrive in London without a reservation, call for room availability before setting out to individual hotels. Most hotels will hold a room for you for an hour or so.

If you're having difficulty securing a room, you can always call the London Tourist Board's telephone accommodation service at ☎ **0171/932-2020.** It operates Monday to Friday from 9:30am to

Strategies for Saving on Your Hotel Room

In London, it'll take some effort to save on your hotel room while securing the best possible value. Here are some tips to keep in mind:

- First, it is worth **trying to bargain for a lower rate** than the one quoted. Remember that a room unsold represents loss of income to any hotelier. You might not have much luck in summer, when most hotels are perpetually booked, but in winter (when prices may fall as much as 30% from summer highs) it may secure you an additional discount.

- Always **ask for long-term discounts** on stays of five nights or longer. Other discounts may apply—student, senior, and veteran, for example.

- You're more likely to secure a decent value if you **look in a neighborhood where there are a lot of budget hotels competing with each other.** So head to Bloomsbury, and Earl's Court in particular, and then Paddington/Bayswater and, as a last resort, Victoria.

- Think about **what you really want in a hotel room.** If a private bathroom is not crucial to you, you can save anywhere from £5 to £10 ($8–$16) per night. Stay at a hotel that provides a full breakfast, not a continental one. More and more hotels are only offering continental breakfast. We have noted which hotels still serve a traditional English breakfast of cereals, breads, and fruit, plus bacon, eggs, sausage, mushrooms, and tomatoes, which would be worth at least £5 ($8) per person outside the hotel.

- Seriously **consider alternatives to small hotels.** Small bed-and-breakfasts are a great option and offer the bonuses of staying in a Londoner's or suburban home and really getting to know the culture. See below for organizations that can arrange such an accommodation for you. Some youth hostels are perfectly acceptable, have double rooms, and offer additional facilities like kitchens, which can help you save even more money. If you come during the Easter or summer school breaks, there are some great university residences to stay at. One of the finest is **High Holborn Residences,** which charges only $64 to $80 double and provides all these extra facilities: two TV lounges, a bar containing two pool tables, table tennis, 24-hour Laundromat, computer, and access at special discounted rates to a nearby gym with indoor/outdoor pools and squash courts. See below for details.

5:30pm; or you can go to one of their information centers, which offer room booking service for a small booking fee of £5 ($8), along with a deposit that is applied to the price of the room.

London Tourist Board centers are located at **Victoria Station Forecourt,** SW1, open Easter to October daily 8am to 7pm (shorter hours in winter); **Heathrow Terminals 1,2,3, Underground Station Concourse,** open daily 8am to 6pm; **Heathrow Terminal 3 Arrivals,** open daily 6am to 11pm; **Liverpool Street Underground Station,** EC2, open Monday to Friday 8am to 6pm and Saturday to Sunday 8:45am to 5:30pm; and the **Waterloo International Arrivals Hall,** Waterloo International Terminal, SE1, open daily 8:30am to 8:30pm. The **British Travel Centre,** 12 Regent St., Piccadilly Service, SW1, also operates a booking service.

Thomas Cook also operates a hotel booking service at **Victoria Station** (☎ 0171/828-4646). The company works with budget-priced properties, but their best rates are for London's fancier rooms. By negotiating for blocks of rooms at some of the city's best hotels, this service can offer special reduced-price rooms. Unfortunately, in season, few if any rooms are available, but you may luck out in the off-season by saving up to 50%. There is a £5 ($8) booking fee. There's another office at **King's Cross Rail Station** (☎ **0171/837-5682**), next to the Pullman Lounge, at the head of platform 8; and also at the Euston, Charing Cross, and Earl's Court Underground stations.

BED & BREAKFAST ORGANIZATIONS

Uptown Reservations, 50 Christchurch St., Chelsea, London, SW3 4AR (☎ **0171/351-3445,** fax 0171/351-9383), operates a B&B reservation service. All of the rooms are in private homes and have bath or shower. Many are in elegant residences in such areas as Knightsbridge, Chelsea, and Kensington. The prices range from £63 ($100.80) single and £83 ($132.80) double with private bathroom and continental breakfast.

London Homestead Services, Coombe Wood Road, Kingston upon Thames Surrey, KT2 7JY (☎ **0181/949-4455,** fax 0181/549-5492), offers the opportunity to stay in a London home for anywhere from £16 to £35 ($27.20–$56) per person. The rooms are all within 20 minutes of Piccadilly on the Underground. Higher priced rooms are in central London and have private bathrooms.

HOSTELS, Ys, AND UNIVERSITY ACCOMMODATIONS

The International Youth Hostel Federation (IYHF) has four establishments in central London, all of which are very crowded during the summer. These are clean but sterile in atmosphere. Breakfast is an additional fee. You can save around £2 by bringing and using your own sheets. MasterCard and Visa are accepted at all London hostels.

You must obtain a membership card to stay at one of IYHF's hostels. Cards are available for £9.30 ($14.40) at the **YHA Shop,** 14 Southampton St., WC2 (☎ **0171/836-8541**). Open hours are Monday to Wednesday 10am to 6pm; Thursday to Friday 10am to 7pm.

In addition to youth hostels, some hotels offer dormitory accommodations (often called "multishares") where visitors share a room with other travelers. If you are traveling with a backpack and arrive at one of London's major railroad stations, you may be handed advertisements for these "unofficial" hostels. These are usually legitimate, but investigate the location before you commit. In addition to Hotel

A Note for Travelers with Disabilities

Depending on the extent of the disability, disabled travelers will find it difficult to locate a budget hotel that caters adequately to them. Most London budget hotels are located in old buildings which have steps at their entrances. Room and bathroom doorways are usually too narrow to accommodate wheelchairs, and the bathrooms that are equipped with support wall bars are often too tiny to accommodate wheelchairs. Few budget hotels have elevators, or the elevators are rarely large enough to accommodate a wheelchair. However, there are some sources that disabled travelers can turn to for help—notably **Holiday Care Services,** which will offer advice. Holiday Care Services also publishes a book about travel in Britain for the disabled. See "Tips for Travelers with Special Needs" in chapter 2 for more information.

Boka in Earl's Court, the Oakley Hotel in Chelsea, and the Repton House Hotel in Bloomsbury, the following hotels offer multishare accommodations and private rooms.

Several YMCA and YWCA hotels offer reliable accommodations at great prices, and most include dinner daily. Because they offer low weekly rates, most Ys are filled with longtimers throughout the year. More than a dozen Ys are found in London, but they're not all well located. In a pinch, phone the **National Council of YMCAs** (☎ 0181/520-5599) for a list of Ys in London.

From early July to late September (and sometimes during Christmas and Easter), dozens of centrally located dormitories open their doors to visitors. Almost always, bedrooms are spartan. Some residence halls only offer singles, and these are relatively inexpensive. Try to reserve months in advance as the dorms soon fill up. Even if you don't have reservations, though, it can't hurt to call and see if they have a cancellation or a "no-show."

1 Best Bets on a Budget

- **Best Overall Value:** The **Thanet,** 8 Bedford Place (☎ 0171/323-6676), in the heart of Bloomsbury, has to be one of the city's very best values. The rooms are spacious and well maintained, and have completely modern facilities and pleasant decor.
- **Best Place to Stay on a Shoestring:** You can't beat the location of the **Holland House Youth Hostel,** Holland Walk (☎ 0171/937-0748), an old mansion right in the center of Holland Park. The accommodations are dorm style but the added bonuses are low-cost cafeteria, Laundromat, and more.
- **Best Bloomsbury B & B:** Right around the corner from the British Museum, the **Morgan,** 24 Bloomsbury St. (☎ 0171/636-3735), is located in a typical terrace house and offers nicely furnished rooms and friendly attentive management.
- **Best for the Theater Buff: Fielding,** 4 Broad Court, Bow St. (☎ 0171/836-8305), is a great base for opera lovers since it's right around the corner from the Royal Opera House, tucked away in a quiet alley. The exterior has great charm with its diamond-pane windows. Inside, rooms are small but furnished with some idiosyncrasy at least.
- **Best Hampstead Hideaway:** A little remote, **La Gaffe,** 107–11 Heath St. (☎ 0171/435-4941), is a characterful establishment in this most appealing of London's villages.
- **Best for Long-Term Stays:** At **Aston's Studios,** 39 Rosemary Gardens (☎ 0171/370-0737), £43 ($68) secures a room with a compact but complete kitchenette, fully equipped with refrigerator, sink, electric stove, and cooking utensils.
- **Best Bathless Choices:** Both the **Vicarage Private Hotel,** 10 Vicarage Gardens (☎ 0171/229-4030), and the Abbey House, 11 Vicarage Gate (☎ 0171/727-2594), have real Victorian style and offer large, spacious rooms with soaring ceilings, in a quiet location on a small garden cul-de-sac.
- **Best University Residence:** The supermodern **High Holborn Residence,** 178 High Holborn (☎ 0171/397-5589), is in a great location near Covent Garden. Apartments housing four or five persons in single rooms have a kitchen, dining room, and bathroom. Other conveniences include a launderette, TV lounge, and bar.
- **Best Budget B & B with meals on hand: Hotel La Place,** 17 Nottingham Place (☎ 0171/486-2323), benefits from having a mother/son professional hotel

management team. The decor is stylish, and the small bar is a pleasant haven; but what makes this B&B unusual is that tasty pizzas, salads, and sandwiches are available 24 hours a day. (Hotel La Place serves dinner in addition to breakfast.)

- **Best for Families:** The **James Cartref House,** 129 Ebury St. (☎ **0171/730-6176**), has three attractive rooms for families. Two each have a double and a single bed, and the other can accommodate five people with one double, one single, and two bunk-style beds. Prices for these range from £85 to £107 ($136–$171.20). In addition, they offer private bathrooms (showers), color TVs, and tea/coffeemaking facilities.
- **Most Friendly B & B: Norfolk Court,** 16–20 Norfolk Sq. (☎ **0171/723-4963**), is owned and operated by George Neokleous, who will welcome you warmly and also swears to cook whatever you want for breakfast.
- **Best Gay-Friendly B & B:** It's a toss-up between the **Philbeach,** 30 Philbeach Gardens (☎ **0171/373-1244**), and the **New York,** 32 Philbeach Gardens (☎ **0171/244-6884**). But we give the edge to the latter, just because of the hot tub and the beautiful garden with fountain. Both have restaurants and friendly management.
- **Best Splurge:** The **Rushmore,** 11 Trebovir Rd. (☎ **0171/370-3839**), just because the rooms are beautifully decorated, each with individual style using fine fabrics, trompe l'oeil, and other painting styles. The tasteful ambience extends also to the serene Tuscan-inspired breakfast room.

2 Victoria

The main—if not the only—reason for staying in this area is the proximity to Victoria Station, and to toney Belgravia to the northwest and the more accessible Pimlico to the southeast. As with most areas adjacent to major stations, hundreds of hotels proliferate, but many are not up to snuff.

The first street to try in this neighborhood is Ebury, and if you can't secure a room there, Warwick Way is another hotel-lined street.

FOR A FEW POUNDS MORE

Collin House. 104 Ebury St., London, SW1W 9QD. ☎/Fax **0171/730-8031.** 13 units (8 with bathroom/shower). £45 ($72) single with bathroom (shower); £60 ($96) double without bathroom, £70 ($112) double with bathroom (shower). All rates include English breakfast. No credit cards. Tube: Victoria.

This hotel is located in a mid-Victorian townhouse in the heart of Belgravia, a lovely upscale residential district. The rooms vary in size, but all are bright and clean with firm comfortable beds and decent lighting, including reading lights. The wall-papered rooms are furnished adequately, and most have wall-to-wall carpeting. Among the furnishings there will be a desk of some kind and often a couple of chairs. Bathrooms are tiled.

Elizabeth House. 118 Warwick Way, London, SW1V ISD. ☎ **0171/630-0741.** Fax 0171/630-0740. 30 units (9 with bathroom). £30 ($48) single without bathroom, £40 ($64) single with bathroom; £50 ($80) twin without bathroom, £60 ($96) twin with bathroom; £20 ($32) per person in multishare room. All rates include continental breakfast. MC, V. Tube: Victoria.

This is a friendly, if very basic, bed-and-breakfast. The rooms are clean but spartanly furnished, with built-in closets and a chest of drawers. Guests can use the television lounges. Laundry facilities are available.

James Cartref House. 129 Ebury St., London, SW1W 9DU. ☎ **0171/730-6176.** Fax 0171/730-7338. E-Mail: James Cartref@Compuserve.com. 11 units (8 with bathroom/shower). TV. £50 ($80) single without bathroom; £65 ($104) double without bathroom, £75 ($120) double with bathroom (shower); £82 ($131.20) triple without bathroom, £92 ($147.20) triple with bathroom (shower). All rates include English breakfast. AE, MC, V. Tube: Victoria.

Derek and Sharon James offer warm hospitality to their guests. All rooms are pleasantly decorated and have sinks and teamakers. No more than three rooms share separate toilet and showers located in the hallways. The proprietors also offer similar accommodations and rates at the **James House** at 108 Ebury St., London SW1W 9QD (☎ **0171/730-7338**).

Leicester Hotel. 18/24 Belgrave Rd., London, SW1V 1QF. ☎ **0171/233-6636.** Fax 0171/932-0538. 57 units (42 with bathroom [shower], 2 with shower only). TV TEL. £30 ($48) single without bathroom, £35 ($56) single with bathroom (shower); £40 ($64) double without bathroom, £45 ($72) double with bathroom (shower). All rates include English breakfast. MC, V. Tube: Victoria.

An excellent value. Decently kept and furnished, nearly all the rooms have bathrooms—tiny, it's true—but with showers. Coffeemakers and hair dryers are found in all rooms with showers.

Luna Simone Hotel. 47–49 Belgrave Rd., London, SW1V 2BB. ☎ **0171/834-5897.** Fax 0171/828-2474. 35 units (30 with bathroom/shower). TV TEL. £40–£45 ($64–$72) single with bathroom (shower); £46–£55 ($73.60–$88) basic double, £55–£65 ($88–$104) double with bathroom (shower). All rates include English breakfast. MC, V. Tube: Victoria.

This family-run hotel is recognizable by the bright orange lettering on the columns out front. The rooms are adequate; most have desks, beds have built-in units behind them, and some attempt at coordinating the overall decor has been made. A hearty breakfast is served in twin dining rooms, separated into smoking and nonsmoking sections.

Oxford House Hotel. 92–94 Cambridge St., London, SW1V 4QG. ☎ **0171/834-6467.** Fax 0171/834-0225. 17 units (none with bathroom). £34–£36 ($54.40–$57.60) single; £44–£46 ($70.40–$73.60) double; £57–£59 ($91.20–$94.40) triple; £76–£78 ($121.60–$124.80) quad. The higher prices are for if you stay only one night. All rates include English breakfast. MC, V. Add 5% if you pay by credit card. Tube: Victoria.

Oxford House is owned by interior designer Yanus Kader, his wife, Terri, and their two sons. It's a warm and friendly accommodation. The pretty, comfortable rooms are decorated in chintz. The beautiful dining area, with its open kitchen, may remind travelers of home. There's also an appealing TV lounge upstairs. In the backyard, guests can visit the hotel's friendly rabbit and two cats. South of Belgrave Road near Gloucester Street.

MODERATELY PRICED CHOICES

Comfort Inn, Westminster. 82–86 Belgrave Rd., London, SW1V 2BJ. ☎ **0800/44-44-44** in the U.K. or 0171/828-8661. Fax 0171/821-0525. 60 units (all with private bathroom). TV TEL. £79 ($126.40) single; £99 ($158.40) double; £119 ($190.40) triple. AE, MC, V. Tube: Victoria.

If you're looking for a typical modern room that happens to be in a Victorian building with classic portico, then this will fit your bill. The rooms feature good beds with floral spreads and bland modern desk-dressers. Extras include room service, fax and photocopying, newspaper delivery, and Internet facilities. Facilities include a bar and restaurant overlooking the courtyard garden.

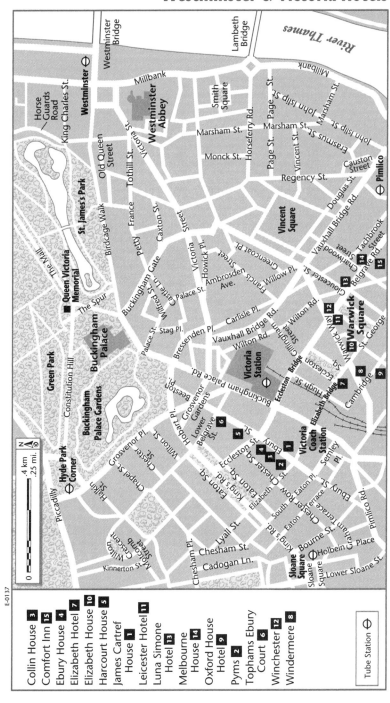

River Thames

Lambeth Bridge

Westminster Bridge

Millbank

⊖ Westminster

Horse Guards Road

King Charles St.

Westminster Abbey

Smith Square

Marsham St.

Page St.

John Islip St.

Marsham St.

Erasmus St.

John Islip St.

⊖ Pimlico

Old Queen Street

Tothill St.

Victoria St.

Monck St.

Horseferry Rd.

Page St.

Vincent St.

Marsham St.

Causton Street

St. James's Park

The Mall

Birdcage Walk

France

Caxton St.

Petty

Buckingham Gate

Street

Victoria

Howick Pl.

Street

Greencoat Pl.

Regency St.

Vincent Square

Douglas St.

Vauxhall Bridge Rd.

Charlwood Street

Tachbrook Street

Belgrave Rd.

14

13

15

Queen Victoria Memorial

The Spur

Castle Lane

Palace St.

Ambrosden Ave.

Francis St.

Willow Pl.

Gloucester St.

Wilton Rd.

Warwick Way

12

11

Warwick Square

St. George

Green Park

Constitution Hill

Buckingham Palace

Buckingham Palace Gardens

Palace St.

Stag Pl.

Bressenden Pl.

Carlisle Pl.

Vauxhall Bridge Rd.

Wilton Rd.

Gillingham Street

Wilton St.

Eccleston Sq.

10

St. George

8

9

Victoria Station

Eccleston Bridge

Hugh St.

Elizabeth Bridge

Cambridge

7

Hyde Park Corner ⊖

Piccadilly

Halkin St.

Chapel St.

Grosvenor Pl.

Chester St.

Wilton St.

Hobart Pl.

Beeston Pl.

Grosvenor Gardens

Lower Belgrave St.

6

5

Buckingham Palace Rd.

Eccleston St.

Chester Sq.

Ebury St.

4

3

2

1

Victoria Coach Station

Semley Pl.

Eaton Sq.

King's Rd.

Eaton Pl.

Elizabeth St.

Chester Row

Chester St.

South Eaton Pl.

Ebury St.

Graham Terrace

Bourne St.

Pimlico Rd.

Pimlico Place

Lyall St.

Chesham Pl.

Chesham St.

Cadogan Ln.

Kinnerton St.

Motcomb Street

Wilton Crescent

Sloane Square ⊖

Holbein Pl.

Sloane Square

Lower Sloane St.

N

.4 km
.25 mi.

0

E-0137

Ebury House. 102 Ebury St., London, SW1W 9QD. ☎ **0171/730-1350.** Fax 0171/259-0400. 12 units (5 with bathroom/shower). TV. £45 ($72) basic single; £60 ($96) basic double; £85 ($136) basic family rooms with a double and bunk beds; £75 ($125) double with bathroom (shower); £90 ($144) triple with bathroom (shower). MC, V. Tube: Victoria.

A pleasant bed-and-breakfast operated by Peter Evans, who offers clean, decent rooms at reasonable prices. Hair dryers are available in all rooms.

Harcourt House. 50 Ebury St., London, SW1W 0LU. ☎ **0171/730-2722.** Fax 0171/730-3998. 10 units (all with bathroom/shower). TV. £60 ($96) single; £70 ($112) double; £85 ($136) triple. All rates include English breakfast. MC, V. Tube: Victoria.

Although the rooms have a somewhat drab decor, Harcourt House is a good value. The rooms contain brass beds and feature hair dryers, too. A full breakfast is served in a cozy dining room at tables with floral tablecloths.

✪ **Melbourne House.** 79 Belgrave Rd., London, SW1V 2BG. ☎ **0171/828-3516.** Fax 0171/828-7120. 15 units (13 with bathroom/shower). TV TEL. £25–£30 ($40–$48) single without bathroom, £40–£45 ($64–$72) single with bathroom (shower); £60–£70 ($96–$112) double with bathroom (shower); £75–£95 ($120–$152) triple with bathroom (shower). All rates include English breakfast. No credit cards. Tube: Pimlico/Victoria.

Melbourne House is far and away the best B&B on Belgrave Road and the only one to earn a listing here. The management is extremely helpful and friendly and wins warm appreciation from guests. Rooms are spacious and clean. The decor lacks coordination and is old fashioned, but each room has the convenience of a desk plus hair dryer, and tea/coffeemaking facilities.

Pyms. 118 Ebury St., London, SW1W 9QQ. ☎ **0171/730-4986.** Fax 0171/730-2357. 12 units (2 with bathroom/shower). TV. £45–£50 ($72–$80) single without bathroom, £75 ($120) single with bathroom (shower); £70–£75 ($112–$120) double without bathroom, £85 ($136) double with bathroom (shower). All rates include English breakfast. AE, MC, V. Tube: Victoria.

This hotel, in a terraced Victorian, has sparkling clean rooms that are maintained by friendly Ms. Ikuko Sakai, who will provide you with a free breakfast if you arrive during breakfast hours. The rooms are furnished with crisp white painted pieces. TVs are small. Good quality showers feature glass doors. All rooms have fridge, hair dryer, and tea/coffeemaking facilities. Breakfast is served in a bright-white dining room with bentwood chairs. There's also an apartment with sitting area and kitchen available for stays of five days or longer. A Japanese breakfast (miso soup, rice, and fish) is offered on request.

Winchester Hotel. 17 Belgrave Rd., London, SW1 1RB. ☎ 0171/828-2972. Fax 0171/828-5191. 18 units (all with bathroom/shower). TV. £68 ($108.80) single, £90 ($144) double; £100 ($160) multi-bed units. Rates include full English breakfast. No credit cards. Tube: Victoria.

The rooms at this terraced Victorian hotel are clean and modestly decorated in '50s Scandinavian style. Moldings add a touch of character to the rooms, along with porcelain lamps. The bathrooms are tiled, with glass-door showers. There's an attractive dining room furnished with polished wood tables and Windsor chairs.

✪ **Windermere.** 142–44 Warwick Way, at the corner of Alderney St., London, SW1V 4JE. ☎ **0171/834-5163.** Fax 0171/630-8831. www.windermere-hotel.co.uk. E-mail: 100773. 1171@compuserve.com. 23 units (20 with bathroom). TV TEL. £59 ($94.40) single without bathroom, £70–£77 ($112–$123.20) single with bathroom; £69 ($110.40) double without bathroom, £85–£99 ($136–$158.40) double with bathroom; £99 triple with bathroom ($158.40). All rates include English breakfast. AE, MC, V. Tube: Victoria.

An attractive, small hotel with clean and pretty rooms, decked out in pinks and grays and white-painted furniture. Beds have padded headboards and you'll usually find at least two sitting chairs. Bathrooms are tiled and also feature hair dryers. The higher-priced, superior rooms are large and accommodate king-size beds. There's a cozy lounge with leatherette furnishings for guests. In the spacious dining room, Windsor-style chairs are set at tables covered with rose-colored cloths. Here break-fast, snacks, and modestly priced evening meals are served (main courses from £7 to £9/$11.20 to $14.40). Room service and laundry/valet also offered.

WORTH THE SPLURGE

✪ Elizabeth Hotel. 37 Eccleston Sq., London, SW1V 1PB. ☎ **0171/828-6812.** 38 units (33 with tub or shower only). TV. £40 ($64) single without bathroom, £60 ($96) single with bathroom; £65 ($104) double without bathroom, £70–£80 ($112–$128) double with bath-room; £100 ($160) triple with bathroom. All rates include English breakfast. Quads, quints, and apartments also available. No credit cards. Tube: Victoria.

On a beautiful and historic square arranged around lovely gardens, the Elizabeth is immaculately kept. The well-decorated rooms have pine desks, candlewick-covered beds, and handsome drapes on the floor-to-ceiling windows. The bathrooms are tiled. A few rooms have balconies. A comfortable lounge has a TV for guests to use. An elevator is an added convenience. All throughout, engravings and prints por-traying such historic figures as Elizabeth I and Sir Francis Drake impart a distinctly English atmosphere. Winston Churchill lived in a house a few doors down from 1909 to 1913. Guests may also use the gardens and tennis court at the center of the square.

Tophams Ebury Court. 28 Ebury St., London, SW1W 0LU. ☎ **0171/730-8147.** Fax 0171/823-5966. E-Mail: Tophams-Belgravia@Compuserve.com. 36 units (all with bathroom). TV TEL. £110 ($176) single with bathroom; £120–£130 ($192–$208) double with bathroom; £160 ($256) triple with bathroom. All rates include English breakfast. AE, DC, MC, V. Tube: Victoria.

A quintessential English hotel that's very traditional in tone. All the rooms are indi-vidually decorated with fine fabrics and comfortable furnishings. Some have four-poster canopy beds. Room 9 is very private; it's tucked away in the back and has pretty pink walls and a dramatic fabric treatment above the bed. All rooms have cof-feemakers and hair dryers. The lounges are extremely comfortable and are furnished with chintz and English antiques. Guests are given honorary membership in Tophams Club, where they can enjoy drinks in the bar. The casual bar-brasserie spe-cializes in modern English food. The hotel also offers laundry/valet, baby-sitting, and a 24-hour porter.

3 Bloomsbury/Fitzrovia

Bloomsbury's proximity to the West End (and to Soho in particular) has long made it a desirable area for tourists. The University of London and the British Museum are also located here. Although a steady demand for rooms keeps prices elevated, some great bargains are still to be found, but you'll need to book well in advance in season.

The two premier hotel streets in the neighborhood are Bedford Place and Cartwright Gardens. Gower Street also has many popular budget hotels.

SUPER-CHEAP SLEEPS

Carr Saunders Hall. 18–24 Fitzroy St., London, W1P 5AE. ☎ **0171/323-9712.** Fax 0171/580-4718. 157 units (3 with bathroom; 78 self-contained apts). £21–£25 ($33.60–$40)

West End Hotels

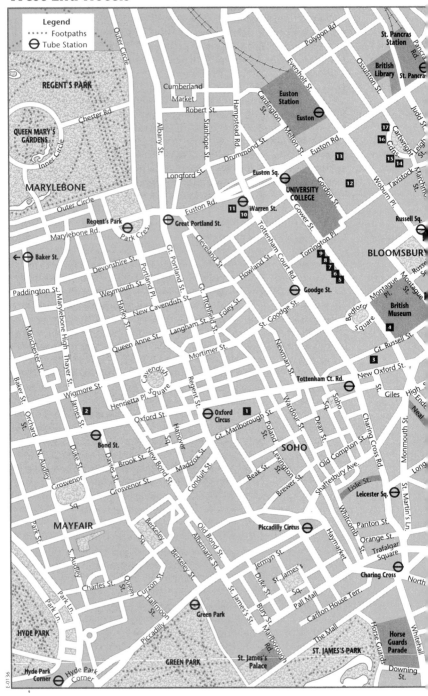

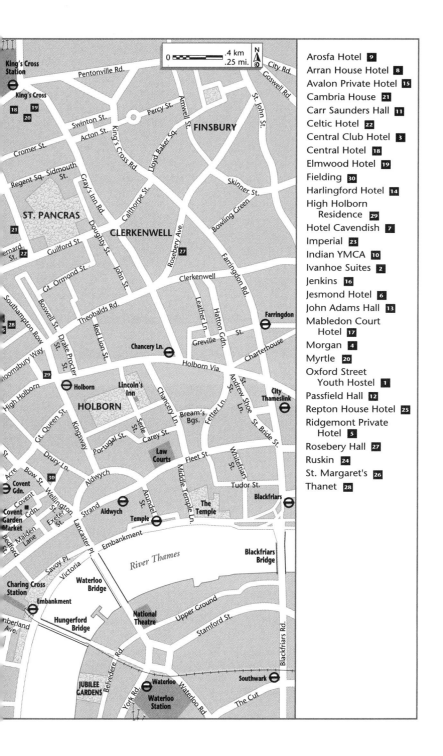

Arosfa Hotel **9**
Arran House Hotel **8**
Avalon Private Hotel **15**
Cambria House **21**
Carr Saunders Hall **11**
Celtic Hotel **22**
Central Club Hotel **3**
Central Hotel **18**
Elmwood Hotel **19**
Fielding **30**
Harlingford Hotel **14**
High Holborn Residence **29**
Hotel Cavendish **7**
Imperial **23**
Indian YMCA **10**
Ivanhoe Suites **2**
Jenkins **16**
Jesmond Hotel **6**
John Adams Hall **13**
Mabledon Court Hotel **17**
Morgan **4**
Myrtle **20**
Oxford Street Youth Hostel **1**
Passfield Hall **12**
Repton House Hotel **25**
Ridgemont Private Hotel **5**
Rosebery Hall **27**
Ruskin **24**
St. Margaret's **26**
Thanet **28**

single; £39–£44 ($62.40–$70.40) twin; £43 ($68.80) twin with bathroom. All rates include English breakfast. MC, V. Open early July–late Sept and also at Easter for 4 or 5 weeks. Tube: Warren St./Goodge St.

The best thing about this London School of Economics residence hall is its location, near inexpensive restaurants and the West End. The rooms, mainly singles, are all small and basic. On the plus side, there's a bar, TV lounge, communal kitchen, and laundry facilities.

Indian YMCA. 41 Fitzroy Sq., London, W1P 6AQ. ☎ **0171/387-0411.** Fax 0171/383-7651. 100 units (4 with bathroom). £33 ($52.80) single without bathroom; £42 ($67.20) double without bathroom, £48 ($76.80) double with bathroom. An additional membership fee of £1 and a reservation fee of 50p will also be charged. All rates include continental breakfast and Indian dinner. No credit cards. Tube: Warren St.

As its name implies, this hotel caters to Indian citizens. It also prefers long-term stays. Nevertheless, it does maintain a few beds for visitors of other nationalities and shorter stays. There's a TV lounge, reading room, and laundry.

John Adams Hall. 15–23 Endsleigh St., London, WC1H 0DP. ☎ **0171/387-4086.** Fax 0171/383-0164. E-Mail: jah@ioe.ac.uk. 146 units (2 with bathroom). July–Sept 3, £23.10 ($36.95) single; £39.90 ($63.84) twin, £44 ($70.40) twin with bathroom. Mid-Mar–Apr, £22 ($35.20) single; £38 ($60.80) twin, £40 ($64) twin with bathroom. All rates include English breakfast. MC, V. Open early July–late Sept, and Easter holiday. Tube: Euston Sq./Euston/Russell Sq.

Housed in a Georgian building, the rooms in this residence are plain and simple, but appear spacious because of their high ceilings and large windows. Facilities include kitchenettes equipped with microwaves and a lounge with satellite TV.

Passfield Hall. 1–7 Endsleigh Place, London, WC1H 0PW. ☎ **0171/387-3584.** Fax 0171/387-0419. 195 units. Easter, £19.50 ($31.20) single; £36 (57.60) twin. Summer, £21–£25 ($33.60–$40) single; £40–£44 ($64–$70.40) twin. All rates include English breakfast. MC, V. Open early July–late Sept and also 4 or 5 weeks at Easter. Tube: Euston Sq./Euston.

A London School of Economics residence, this hall is somewhat cheaper and much more basic than the nearby John Adams Hall. Passfield occupies 10 late-Georgian buildings. Most of the rooms are singles, although there are a few twins and a handful of triples. The rooms have washbasins and central heating. Bed linens and towels are provided. Additional facilities include two TV lounges, launderette, game room, and free tea and coffee.

FOR A FEW POUNDS MORE

Arosfa Hotel. 83 Gower St., at Torrington Place, London, WC1E 6HJ. ☎ **0171/636-2115.** 15 units (2 with bathroom). TV. £31 ($49.60) basic single; £44 ($70.40) basic double; £58 ($92.80) double with bathroom; £59 ($94.40) basic triple. All rates include breakfast. No credit cards. Tube: Goodge St.

This 1950s-style hotel is the least expensive on the block; the rooms are clean and neat, and every one is nonsmoking. This was once the home of John Everett Millais, painter and founder of the Pre-Raphaelite Brotherhood. Although the rooms lack amenities, guests have use of a TV lounge with a tea/coffeemaker. Prices here include a breakfast of eggs, toast, and coffee or tea. In all, a good value.

Arran House Hotel. 77 Gower St., London, WC1E 6HJ. ☎ **0171/636-2186.** Fax 0171/436-5328. www.proteusweb.com/arran. E-Mail: arran@dircon.co.uk. 28 units (9 with bathroom/shower, 4 with shower only). TEL. £35 ($56) basic single, £46 ($73.60) single with bathroom (shower); £47 ($75.20) basic double, £65 ($104) double with bathroom (shower).

Triples, quads, and quints available. All rates include English breakfast. MC, V. Tube: Goodge St.

Arran House stands out on the block because of its exceptionally kind resident proprietor, Maj. John Richards. He has ensured that even guests in the front rooms get a quiet night's sleep by soundproofing all the windows, a modification that I can assure you really works! The rooms are decently furnished and also feature tea/coffeemaking facilities. Other features that make this an appealing choice are the rose garden, the comfortable lounge with cable and satellite TV, and a guest laundry.

Avalon Private Hotel. 46–47 Cartwright Gardens (at Burton Place), London, WC1H 9EL. ☎ 0171/387-2366. Fax 0171/387-5810. 25 units (4 with bathroom/shower). TV TEL. £39 ($62.40) basic single, £55 ($88) single with bathroom (shower); £55 ($88) basic double, £69.65 ($110.40) double with bathroom (shower). English breakfast. AE, MC, V. Tube: Russell Sq., Euston, or King's Cross.

Rooms have okay 1950s-style furnishings and pink satin coverlets on the beds. In addition to the standard amenities, they feature tea/coffeemaking facilities and convenient safes. Breakfast is served in an attractive basement dining room, and there's also a small sitting room. The best thing about this accommodation is its location. It has an attractive outlook across the gardens at the center of the crescent and guests can play tennis on the courts located there.

Cambria House. 37 Hunter St., London, WC1N 1BJ. ☎ 0171/837-1654. 37 units (3 with bathroom). £29 ($46.40) single without bathroom; £45 ($72) double/twin without bathroom, £56 ($89.60) double with bathroom (shower). Weekly discounts available, e.g., £299 ($478.40) for a double without bathroom. All rates include English breakfast. MC, V. Tube: Russell Sq.

Located at the corner of Tavistock Place, south of Cartwright Gardens, Cambria House is a Salvation Army establishment in a large, redbrick building. Simple rooms with wash basins and tea/coffeemaking facilities are located on three floors. Two bathrooms are located on each floor. Light snacks are available all day, and photocopying and fax services are available at reception. Guest facilities include dining room and TV lounge. No alcohol or smoking are allowed here, and the doors are locked at 11pm; to get around this, obtain a late-night key for a £5 ($8) refundable deposit and visit the pub around the corner.

Celtic Hotel. 61–63 Guilford St., London, WC1N 1DD. ☎ 0171/837-6737. 40 units (none with bathroom). £36.50 ($58.40) single; £48.50 ($77.60) double; £68 ($108.80) triple; £78 ($124.80) quad. Rates include full English breakfast. No credit cards. Tube: Russell Sq.

This clean and well-maintained hotel is run by Mr. and Mrs. Gerra, a warm and very hospitable couple, who make sure that everything operates smoothly. The plain rooms are on the small side and contain sinks only. There's a large lounge with TV for guests' use and also a small sitting room. The breakfast is cooked to order and served in an attractive ground-floor room.

Central Club Hotel. 16–22 Great Russell St., London, WC1B 3LR. ☎ 0171/636-7512. Fax 0171/636-5278. 105 units (none with bathroom). £33.75 ($54) single; £61.25 ($98) double; £21.50 ($34.40) per person in multi-bed unit. Weekly discounts are substantial. MC, V. Tube: Tottenham Court Rd.

The big old building dates to 1932 and was designed by Sir Edwin Lutyens. The corridors are wide. Rooms are basic but more spacious than most, and most feature a washbasin, TV, and telephone (for incoming calls only). Hall bathrooms are located on every floor. Additional facilities include coffee shop, bar lounge, Laundromat, gym, and nondenominational chapel.

Central Hotel. 16–18 Argyle St., London, WC1H8 HEQ. ☎ **0171/837-9008** or 0171/278-8682. 31 units (none with bathroom). TV. £26 ($41.60) single; £38 ($60.80) double; £48 ($76.80) triple. All rates include English breakfast. MC, V. Tube: King's Cross.

One of the four Caruana brothers, the hotel's proprietors, will happily show you to a simple, reasonably sized room. If the Central is full, the staff will show you to the Fairway, their other hotel across the street. That one's not quite as nice, so if you can, be choosy.

Elmwood Hotel. 19 Argyle Sq., London, WC1H 8AS. ☎ **0171/837-9361.** 11 units (none with bathroom). TV. £23 ($36.80) single; £32 ($51.20) double. All rates include English breakfast. No credit cards. Tube: King's Cross.

This nice B&B has been owned by the same resident proprietors for more than 15 years. It's of a higher standard than most in the area. An orange-and-yellow sign out front announces it.

Hotel Cavendish. 75 Gower St., London, WC1E 6HJ. ☎ **0171/636-9079.** Fax 0171/580-3609. 20 units (none with bathroom). £28–£32 ($44.80–$51.20) single; £38–£48 ($60.80–$76.80) twin. Triples and quads available. All rates include English breakfast. AE, MC, V. Tube: Goodge St. or Russell Sq.

This is a nicely furnished, clean, and cozy place run by the Edwards family. Breakfast is served in a pleasant dining room. Guests also have use of a TV lounge and, best of all, the garden in the summer. Rooms have electric kettles for tea-making.

Jesmond Hotel. 63 Gower St., London, WC1 6HJ. ☎ **0171/636-3199.** Fax 0171/323-4373. 16 units (3 with bathroom/shower). TV. £31 ($49.60) basic single; £41 ($65.60) single with bathroom (shower); £45 ($72) basic double/twin; £55 ($88) double with bathroom (shower). MC, V. All rates include English breakfast. Tube: Goodge St.

The hotel's proprietors, Mr. and Mrs. Beynon, have been to the United States many times and are acutely aware of American habits and desires. All rooms have hair dryers and tea/coffeemaking facilities.

Myrtle Hotel. 20 Argyle Sq., King's Cross, London, WC1. ☎ **0171/837-5759.** 14 units (none with bathroom). TV. £27 ($43.20) single; £33 ($52.80) double. All rates include English breakfast. No credit cards. Tube: King's Cross.

Accommodations are spartan but clean, and feature washbasins. With regard to comfort, services, and price, the Myrtle is typical of the area.

Ridgemont Private Hotel. 65–67 Gower St., London, WC1E 6HJ. ☎ **0171/636-1141.** Fax 0171/636-2558. 34 units (8 with bathroom). TV. £31 ($49.60) single without bathroom, £40 ($64) single with bathroom; £44 ($70.40) double without bathroom, £55 ($88) double with bathroom; £57 ($91.20) triple without bathroom, £72 ($115.20) triple with bathroom. All rates include English breakfast. No credit cards. Tube: Goodge St.

Its friendly atmosphere and warmhearted Welsh proprietors, Royden and Gwen Rees, make the Ridgemont another good choice along Gower Street. Complimentary coffee and tea are available in the lounge. Other conveniences include laundry facilities. An additional bonus is access to the garden in summer.

MODERATELY PRICED CHOICES

Imperial. Russell Sq., London, WC1B 5BB. ☎ **0171/278-7871.** Fax 0171/837-4653. 448 units (all with bathroom). TV TEL. £70 ($112) single; £90 ($144) double. MC, V. Tube: Russell Sq.

This full-facility hotel is used by lots of group tours. The rooms here are sparkling clean and feature all the modern amenities—plus a kettle for tea-making, pants press, and hair dryer. Occasionally you might find a piece of slashed or torn furniture—not surprising, given the traffic at this hotel. The Atrium Lounge serves afternoon tea and snacks; the Grill is open till 2am.

Jenkins. 45 Cartwright Gardens, London, WC1H 9EH. ☎ **0171/387-2067.** Fax 0171/ 383-3139. E-Mail: Reservation@Jenkinshotel.demon.co.uk. 15 units (7 with bathroom/ shower). MINIBAR TV TEL. £45 ($72) single without bathroom, £59 ($94.40) single with bathroom (shower); £59 ($94.40) double without bathroom, £69 ($110.40) double with bathroom (shower); £80 ($128) triple with bathroom (shower). MC, V. Tube: Euston or King's Cross.

The rooms at this gracious white Georgian hotel are fairly spacious by London standards and contain comfortable furnishings. Although attractive brass bedside lamps and handsome antique reproductions grace rooms, there's the occasional scratched-up piece, too. Overall this hotel offers superb value; the furnishings, at least in style, are superior to those at most other budget places. Fridges, tea/coffeemakers, and hair dryers are standard in all rooms. An additional draw for many guests are the tennis courts, which are open to guests in the gardens opposite. The Jenkins has served as a hotel since the 1920s and has been featured in the PBS Mystery series *Poirot.*

Mabledon Court Hotel. 10–11 Mabledon Place, London, WC1H 9BA. ☎ **0171/ 388-3866.** Fax 0171/387-5686. 32 units (all with bathroom). TV TEL. £60 ($96) single; £70 ($112) double. All rates include English breakfast. MC, V. Tube: Euston or St. Pancras.

A good value. Rooms are modern and bright and show some attempt at color coordination between carpeting and drapes. Guests have use of a comfortable lounge. Breakfast is served in a pretty dining room featuring tables with pink tablecloths. Hair dryers and tea/coffeemakers are found in all the rooms. There's an elevator, too.

Repton House Hotel. 31 Bedford Place, London, WC1B 5JH2. ☎ **0171/436-4922.** Fax 0171/636-7045. 31 units (all with bathroom). £49 ($78.40) single; £69 ($110.40) double; £16.50 ($26.40) per person in a multi-bed unit. All rates include continental breakfast. MC, V. Tube: Russell Sq.

Clean rather than fancy—that's the owner's philosophy—the Repton's basically furnished rooms are spotless. Guests have use of a TV lounge, which also contains a drink vending machine. From the Russell Square Tube stop, turn left, and walk to the square's south side.

Ruskin. 23–24 Montague St., Russell Sq., London, WC1B 5BH. ☎ **0171/636-7388.** Fax 0171/323-1662. 33 units (6 with bathroom/shower). TV TEL. £42 ($67.20) single without bathroom; £60 ($96) double without bathroom, £75 ($120) double with bathroom (shower). All rates include English breakfast. AE, DC, MC, V. Tube: Russell Sq. or Tottenham Court Rd.

Right across from the British Museum, this hotel has modern accommodations and is exceptionally clean. Sink areas are tiled. Tea kettles and hair dryers are added amenities in all rooms. The window boxes out front add a welcome touch.

۞ St. Margaret's. 26 Bedford Place, London, WC1B 5JL. ☎ **0171/636-4277.** Fax 0171/ 323-3066. 65 units (10 with bathroom/shower). TV TEL. £44.50 ($71.20) single without bathroom; £56.50 ($90.40) double without bathroom, £66 ($105.60) double with shower only, £70 ($112) double with bathroom (shower). All rates include English breakfast. No credit cards. Tube: Russell Sq. or Holborn.

The rooms are clean and pleasant at this fine characterful hotel and include such extra amenities as hair dryers. Several comfortable lounges are open to guests. In the attractive breakfast room, the tables are set with fine linens and a bountiful breakfast is served.

✪ **Thanet.** 8 Bedford Place, Russell Sq., London, WC1B 5JA. ☎ **0171/636-2869.** Fax 0171/323-6676. www.freepages.co.uk/thanet_hotel/. 14 units (12 with bathroom). TV TEL. £46 ($73.60) single without bathroom, £57 ($91.20) single with bathroom; £75 ($120) double with bathroom; £89 ($142.40) triple with bathroom. All rates include English breakfast. AE, MC, V. Tube: Russell Sq.

Ideally situated close to the British Museum, between Russell and Bloomsbury Squares, this is a lovely small hotel in a terraced row of Georgians. The spacious rooms are immaculately kept. The high ceilings give an additional sense of space, and the tall windows open. Bathrooms are tiled. Floral fabrics and wall-to-wall carpeting create a comfortable English atmosphere. Tea/coffeemakers and hair dryers are standard room features. Breakfast is served in a pretty, dusty-rose room; tables are set with rose-colored cloths and have bud vases of fresh flowers.

WORTH THE SPLURGE

Harlingford Hotel. 61–63 Cartwright Gardens, London, WC1H 9EL. ☎ **0171/387-1551.** Fax 071/387-4616. 44 units (all with bathroom). TV TEL. £65 ($104) single; £80 ($128) double; £90 ($144) triple; £100 ($160) quad. All rates include English breakfast. AE, DC, MC, V. Tube: Russell Sq. Three blocks north of the Russell Square Underground.

The Harlingford is the nicest hotel on this Georgian crescent in Bloomsbury, a convenient location. A hearty breakfast is served in a particularly pleasing, bright dining room on the ground floor. The cozy and well-furnished communal lounge will entice you away from the TV in your room. Tea/coffeemakers are standard and hair dryers are available on request. Guests also have access to an ice dispenser.

✪ **Morgan.** 24 Bloomsbury St., London, WC1B 3QJ. ☎ **0171/636-3735.** 15 units (all with bathroom). TV TEL. £50–£60 ($80–$96) single; £75 ($120) double; £110 ($176) triple. All rates include English breakfast. No credit cards. Tube: Goodge St./Tottenham Court Rd.

Located in an elegant 18th-century terrace around the corner from the British Museum, this hotel offers excellent value. The beds are covered with pretty floral spreads; the walls are edged with decorative borders. Bathrooms feature glass-doored showers and hair dryers. Breakfast is served at comfortable wooden booths in an appealing oak-paneled dining room.

4 Chelsea, Kensington & S. Kensington

Chelsea stretches along the Thames on its southern border. It's a wealthy residential district with an artsy flavor even though most of the artists and writers that gave it its raffish reputation have long gone—Thomas Carlyle, George Eliot, Oscar Wilde, Henry James, and James McNeill Whistler. It's a lovely neighborhood in which to stay, composed of tree-fringed streets lined with elegant pastel-colored homes.

If you choose to stay in South Kensington, you'll be close to more than half a dozen top museums and the smart boutiques of Beauchamp Place and Knightsbridge.

SUPER-CHEAP SLEEPS

Imperial College. Vacation Accommodation Office, Watts Way, Prince's Gardens, London, SW7 1LU. ☎ **0171/594-9507** and 9511. Fax 0171/594-9504/5. E-Mail: vacation. accommodation@ic.ac.uk. 724 units (none with bathroom). £28 ($44.80) single; £45 ($72) twin. All rates include English breakfast. MC, V. Open late June to late Sept and 4 or 5 weeks at Easter. Tube: South Kensington.

This South Kensington dormitory offers luxurious accommodations close to Hyde Park and Royal Albert Hall. Most are study bedrooms containing wash basin, desk, chair, and wardrobe, and most share shower and bathroom facilities with three other rooms. Kitchenettes are shared with seven other rooms. Rooms with private bathrooms are planned for 1999. The dorm offers some great extras too—indoor pool, squash courts, fitness center, and two tennis courts, plus a pizzeria. Laundromat, hair salon, bureau de change/bank and safe deposit are available too.

FOR A FEW POUNDS MORE

More House. 53 Cromwell Rd., London, SW7 2EH. ☎ **0171/584-2040.** Fax 0171/ 581-5748. 55 units (none with bathroom). £25 ($40) single; £40 ($64) double; £46 ($73.60) triple. 10% discount for stays of one week or more. All rates include English breakfast. No credit cards. Open July–Aug only. Tube: South Kensington/Gloucester Rd.

This Catholic-run dormitory with an institutional feel is home to foreign students during the school year, but singles and twins are rented to visitors of all faiths from July to August. Well located, the house is across from the Science Museum, and it offers several amenities. There is a refrigerator on every floor, microwave ovens for guests' use, and laundry facilities. Turn right from Gloucester Road Underground and walk five short blocks along Cromwell Road.

MODERATELY PRICED CHOICES

✪ Abbey House. 11 Vicarage Gate, London, W8 4AG. ☎ **0171/727-2594.** 16 units (none with bathroom) TV. £40 ($64) single; £65 ($104) double. Triples and quads available. All rates include English breakfast. No credit cards. Tube: High St. Kensington.

Abbey House occupies a lovely, white 1860 Victorian on a quiet garden square. The entryway makes an impression with its black-and-white flooring, potted ferns, and statuary at the top of the staircase landing. The neat and clean rooms are spacious and individually decorated. They feature good-quality, well-lit beds; hair dryers are available on request. The hallway bathrooms are modern and have recently been refurbished and redecorated in Laura Ashley. The staff is extremely helpful and tea and coffee are available round-the-clock.

✪ Aston's Budget Studios and Aston's Designer Studios and Suites. 39 Rosary Gardens, London, SW7 4NQ. ☎ **0171/370-0737.** Fax 0171/835-1419. 60 units (38 with bathroom). A/C TV TEL. Budget studios £43 ($68.80) single with shared bathroom (shower), £52 ($83.20) single with bathroom (shower); £65 ($104) double with shared bathroom (shower), £76 ($121.60) double with shower/wc; designer studios £110–£120 ($176–$192) single or double. AE, MC, V. Tube: Gloucester Rd.

This establishment offers an assortment of studios and suites, which are rented for stays longer than one night. Each unit has a compact but complete kitchenette, concealed behind doors. It's fully equipped with refrigerator, sink, electric stove, and cooking utensils. Some of the budget studio units share bathrooms. The more lavish designer studios and suites boast rich fabrics, marble bathrooms, and lots of electronic equipment, including a telephone answering machine. Laundry and secretarial services available.

Atlas Apollo Hotel. 18–30 Lexham Gardens, Kensington, London, W8 5JE. ☎ **0171/ 835-1155.** Fax 0171/370-4853. 99 units (93 with bathroom/shower). £30 ($48) single without bathroom; £70 ($112) single with bathroom; £85 ($136) double; £96 ($153.60) triple. Rates include continental breakfast. AE, DC, MC, V. Tube: Gloucester Rd.

By combining several buildings into one hotel, the management has created a typical modern hotel, almost Holiday Inn–style in its approach. The rooms all have new modern furniture and carpeting and such standard furnishings as desks and luggage stands.

Hotels from Knightsbridge to Earl's Court

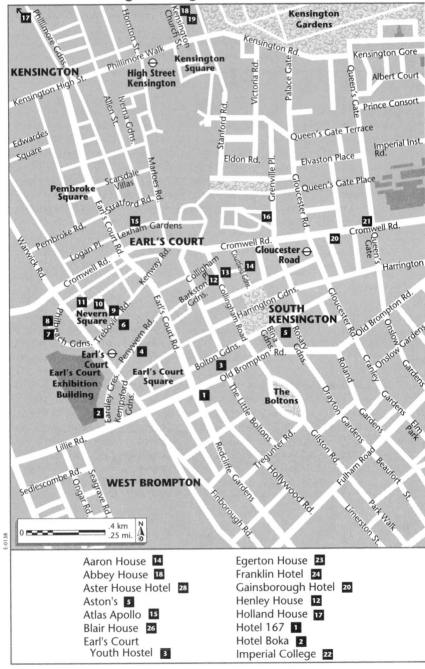

Aaron House **14**
Abbey House **18**
Aster House Hotel **28**
Aston's **5**
Atlas Apollo **15**
Blair House **26**
Earl's Court
  Youth Hostel **3**

Egerton House **23**
Franklin Hotel **24**
Gainsborough Hotel **20**
Henley House **12**
Holland House **17**
Hotel 167 **1**
Hotel Boka **2**
Imperial College **22**

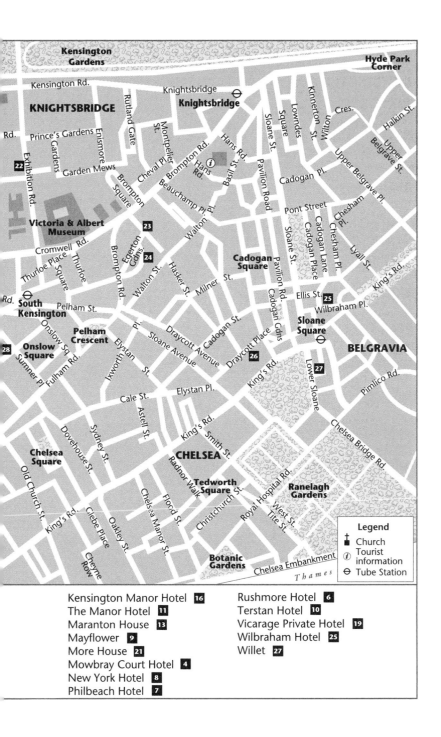

Kensington Gardens

Hyde Park Corner

Kensington Rd.

Knightsbridge

KNIGHTSBRIDGE

Knightsbridge

Prince's Gardens

Rutland Gate

Kinnerton St.

Lowndes Square

Sloane St.

Wilton St.

Cres.

Halkin St.

Rd.

Ennismore Gardens

Montpelier St.

Cheval Pl.

Brompton Rd.

Hans Rd.

Upper Belgrave St.

22

Exhibition Rd.

Garden Mews

Brompton Square

Beauchamp Pl.

Hans Rd.

Basil St.

Pavilion Road

Cadogan Pl.

Upper Belgrave Pl.

Chesham Pl.

Victoria & Albert Museum

Cromwell Rd.

23

Egerton Gdns.

Walton Rd.

Pont Street

Cadogan Lane

Cadogan Place

Lyall St.

Thurloe Place

Thurloe Square

Brompton Rd.

24

Walton St.

Hasker St.

Milner St.

Cadogan Square

Sloane St.

Pavilion Rd.

Cadogan Gdns.

King's Rd.

Rd.

South Kensington

Pelham St.

Sloane Avenue

Cadogan St.

Draycott Ave.

Draycott Place

Ellis St.

25

Wilbraham Pl.

28

Onslow Square

Pelham Crescent

Onslow Sq.

Fulham Rd.

Elystan St.

Ixworth Pl.

Draycott Avenue

Sloane Square

BELGRAVIA

Sumner Pl.

Cale St.

Astell St.

Elystan Pl.

King's Rd.

26

Lower Sloane

27

Pimlico Rd.

Dovehouse St.

Sydney St.

King's Rd.

Smith St.

Chelsea Bridge Rd.

Chelsea Square

Radnor Walk

CHELSEA

Flord St.

Tedworth Square

Christchurch St.

Royal Hospital Rd.

West St.

Ranelagh Gardens

Old Church St.

King's Rd.

Glebe Place

Oakley St.

Chelsea Manor St.

Tite St.

Cheyne Row

Botanic Gardens

Chelsea Embankment

T h a m e s

Legend

✝ Church
ⓘ Tourist information
⊖ Tube Station

Kensington Manor Hotel **16**
The Manor Hotel **11**
Maranton House **13**
Mayflower **9**
More House **21**
Mowbray Court Hotel **4**
New York Hotel **8**
Philbeach Hotel **7**

Rushmore Hotel **6**
Terstan Hotel **10**
Vicarage Private Hotel **19**
Wilbraham Hotel **25**
Willet **27**

Hotel 167. 167 Old Brompton Rd., London, SW5 0AN. ☎ **0171/373-0672.** Fax 0171/ 373-3360. 19 units (all with private bathroom). TV TEL. £66 ($105.60) single; £82–£90 ($131.20–$144) double; extra person £15 ($24). Rates include continental breakfast. AE, DC, MC, V. Tube: Gloucester Rd./South Kensington.

Located in a Victorian terraced residence on the corner of Old Brompton Road and Cresswell Gardens, this hotel offers attractive rooms that retain much of the original architectural character of the building. Each has been individually decorated in a modest way with assorted beds and such decorative accents as country wreaths, lithographs, and plants. A continental breakfast is served.

✪ **Vicarage Private Hotel.** 10 Vicarage Gate, London, W8 4AG. ☎ **0171/229-4030.** Fax 0171/792-5989. E-Mail: reception@londonvicaragehotel.com. 18 units (none with bathroom). £42 ($67.20) single; £66 ($105.60) double; £85 ($136) triple; £92 ($147.20) family room. All rates include English breakfast. No credit cards. Tube: High St. Kensington.

On a quiet residential garden square just off Kensington Church Street, this Victorian house retains many of its original features. A gracious staircase leads to the individually decorated rooms. With typical English floral wallpapers and fabrics, they're a mixture of modern and older pieces and represent some of the best value accommodations in London. Guests can use the comfortable lounge with a TV. Some rooms have TVs, too, and there are plans afoot to add some private bathrooms. Hair dryers and ironing facilities are available on request.

WORTH THE SPLURGE

Aster House Hotel. 3 Sumner Place, London, SW7 3EE. ☎ **0171/581-5888.** Fax 0171/ 584-4925. E Mail: Asterhouse@BTinternet.com. 12 units (all with bathroom). TV TEL. £60–£80 ($96–$128) single; £110–£145 ($176–$232) double. All rates include buffet continental breakfast. MC, V. Tube: South Kensington.

Of a number of small B&Bs on this quiet South Kensington street, Aster House is the most beautiful. The pride with which manager Simon Tan runs this hotel is evident the moment you step into the plushly marbled interior. All rooms have private bathroom and feature amenities usually found in more expensive hotels—fridge, mini-safe, and ceiling fans. Take special note of the award-winning garden in the rear; it's where the fresh flowers found in each room come from. The enormous breakfast buffet includes eggs as well as fresh fruits, cold meats, cheeses, yogurt, muesli, and other cereals. The morning repast is served in L'Orangerie, the beautiful glass-covered pièce de résistance of this special hotel. It also serves as a delightful lounge during the day.

From the South Kensington Station, walk one block down Old Brompton Road to Sumner Place on your left.

Blair House. 34 Draycott Place, London, SW3 2SA. ☎ **0171/581-2323.** Fax 0171/ 823-7752. 17 units (all with bathroom/shower). TV TEL. £87.50 ($140) single; £110–£117.50 ($176–$188) double (the higher price is for a larger room located at the back of the hotel); extra bed £18 ($28.80). All rates include continental breakfast; English breakfast £6 ($9.60). AE, DC, MC, V. Tube: Sloane Sq.

Although the rooms are pleasant enough here, the prices reflect the Chelsea location; you can secure better values in Bloomsbury. Still, the rooms feature high ceilings and elegant moldings. They're furnished in a modern style with floral fabrics that are coordinated for bed and curtains, and, occasionally, antique reproductions. Additional room amenities include a coffeemaker, hair dryer, and pants press. Breakfast is served in the basement dining room or delivered to your room for an additional charge.

The Egerton House Hotel. Egerton Terrace, Knightsbridge, SW3 2BX. ☎ **0171/ 589-2412.** Fax 0171/584-6540 or 800/473-9492. 30 units, all with private bathroom. A/C TV TEL. £130 ($208) single; £170–£210 ($272–$336) double. AE, DC, MC, V. Tube: Knightsbridge/South Kensington.

A small, personal, traditional hotel which offers beautifully appointed and furnished rooms. Each has been individually decorated, some with fully dressed fourposters, others with tented treatments above the beds. Fine linens and fabrics are found throughout. Oil paintings, porcelain lamps, and flowers add charm to the rooms. Each room has a marble bathroom plus a private bar. The drawing roomstudy has been graciously furnished with comfortable antiques, and guests can enjoy afternoon tea or drinks here. Services include concierge and laundry/valet. Breakfast can be served in your room or in the light airy dining room. The hotel is only two minutes' walk from Harrods and Brompton Road and Sloane Street.

The Franklin Hotel. 28 Egerton Gardens, London, SW3 2DB. ☎ **0171/584-5533.** Fax 0171/584-5449 or 800/473-9487. 40 units (all with bathroom). A/C MINIBAR TV TEL. £140 ($224) single, £165–£210 ($264–$336) double. Tube: South Kensington.

This elegant Knightsbridge hotel exhibits good taste and comfort throughout. Public areas are furnished with antiques, oil paintings, and other objets d'art. Fine fabrics are used throughout. The sitting room is exceptionally comfortable and opens onto a garden. Afternoon tea, drinks, and light snacks are served in both. There's also a small bar. The rooms are very beautifully decorated. Some have fourposters that are dressed in fine chintz fabrics. Room features include marble bathroom, fax facilities. 24-hour-room service, laundry/valet, and secretarial service are available.

Gainsborough Hotel. 7–11 Queensberry Place, London, SW7 2DL. ☎ **0171/957-0000.** Fax 0171/957-0001. www.eeh.co.uk. E-Mail: Gainsborough@eeh.co.uk. 49 units (all with bathroom). TV TEL. £76 ($121.60) single; £135 ($216) double; from £200 ($320) junior suite. All rates include buffet English breakfast. AE, MC, V. Tube: South Kensington.

The small elegant hotel occupies a gleaming white mid-Georgian English town house featuring classic portico and balustrades. Each room here has been individually decorated in a very English style with rich floral fabrics and handsome reproduction furniture. Each has been harmoniously color coordinated. Several rooms have fully draped canopy beds; others have coronet treatments above the beds. Nice extra touches include fresh flowers in the rooms, a well-lit desk, and porcelain or similarly elegant lamps among the decor. Standard features include VCR, hair dryer and tea/coffeemaking facilities. 24-hour room service, laundry/valet, baby-sitting, and secretarial services are available. There's also a restaurant, wine bar, and club on the premises for the convenience of guests.

Kensington Manor Hotel. 8 Emperor's Gate, London, SW7 4HH. ☎ **0171/370-7516.** Fax 0171/373-3163. 14 units, 1 suite (all with bathroom). TV TEL. £55–£65 ($88–$104) single; £82 ($131.20) double. All rates include English breakfast. AE, DC, MC, V. Tube: Gloucester Rd.

Located in a cul-de-sac, the Kensington Manor offers good value for money. The rooms are individually decorated and named after counties of England. Some of them even have elegant four-posters. Additional amenities include hair dryer and tea/coffeemaker plus a refrigerator in some rooms. The full English breakfast is served buffet-style and consists of a spread of breads, cereals, fruits, cheese, bacon, eggs, tomato, and more.

Wilbraham Hotel. 1–5 Wilbraham Place, off Sloane St., London, SW1 9AE. ☎ **0171/ 730-8296.** Fax 0171/730-6815. 51 units (all with bathroom). TV TEL. £68–£75 ($108.80–

$120) single; £85–£90 ($136–$144) double; £105–£113 ($168–$180.80) triple. No credit cards. Tube: Sloane Sq.

This is a very British hotel situated appropriately in Belgravia a short walk from Knightsbridge and Victoria. The rooms are traditionally decorated in attractive, color-coordinated decor and have such additional amenities as hair dryers. Additional services include 24-hour room service, laundry/dry cleaning, and newspaper delivery. Baby-sitting can be arranged and families are welcome. There's a comfortable TV lounge plus a bar and buttery serving customary British dishes like Dover sole and lamb cutlets, with main courses priced from £7 to £15 ($11.20–$24). It's open for lunch and dinner, except Sunday. A continental breakfast is £4 ($6.40), a full breakfast £6 ($8.40).

Willett. 32 Sloane Gardens, Sloane Sq., London, SW1 8DJ. ☎ **0171/824-8415.** Fax 0171/730-4830. www.eeh.co.uk. E-Mail: willett@eeh.co.uk. 19 units (all with bathroom). TV TEL. £76 ($121.60) single; £105–£135 ($168–$216) double. All rates include English breakfast. AE, DC, MC, V. Tube: Sloane Sq.

A mansard roof and bay windows give character to this well-restored Victorian London town house hotel, complete with its own garden. It's in a superb location only a short walk from the King's Road and Harrods. Rooms have been recently renovated; some are lavishly decorated with tented fabric treatments above the beds. Others contain beds with fabric-padded headboards and color-coordinated spreads and curtains. Room service, laundry/valet, and complimentary newspapers are provided. Standard room amenities include coffeemaker, hair dryer, and safe. Some of the larger doubles have refrigerators.

5 Earl's Court

Although located just west of exclusive South Kensington, Earl's Court has never achieved the social status of its neighbor. Today, despite distinct signs of gentrification, this is still a great area to hit for budget-oriented hotels.

SUPER-CHEAP SLEEPS

Earl's Court Youth Hostel. 38 Bolton Gardens, London, SW5 0AQ. ☎ **0171/373-7083.** Fax 0171/835-2034. 154 units. £18.70 ($29.90) per person per night for travelers over 18 years, sheets and breakfast included; £16.45 ($26.30) otherwise. Add £1.70 ($2.70) membership fee. MC, V. Tube: Earl's Court.

These basic dormitory accommodations are located near Holland House, in a historic Victorian residence. Bathrooms are shared, but additional facilities include a kitchen and a cafeteria that serves packed lunches and decent low-cost, three-course evening meals. There's also a Laundromat, photocopier/fax, pay phone, luggage storage, tour desk, game room, and lounge with cable TV. Another plus is the small courtyard garden, where barbecues are held in summer. Breakfast (continental or English) is included in the rate. The area around the hostel is lively, and local stores stay open late.

Exit Earl's Court Underground and turn right. Bolton Gardens is the fifth road on your left.

FOR A FEW POUNDS MORE

Aaron House. 17 Courtfield Gardens, London, SW5 0PD. ☎ **0171/370-3991.** Fax 0171/373-2303. 23 units (15 with bathroom). TV. £35–£38 ($56–$60.80) single without bathroom, £45–£49 ($72–$78.40) single with bathroom (shower); £49–£52 ($78.40–$83.20) double without bathroom, £59–£63 ($94.40–$100.80) double with bathroom (shower); £69–£72

($110.40–$115.20) triple with bathroom (shower). All rates include continental breakfast. MC, V. Tube: Earl's Court.

Announced only by a small, gold sign to the left of the hotel's front door, Aaron House is perhaps the nicest budget hotel in Earl's Court. Beveled glass and beautiful moldings and cornices add a touch of style to this understated B&B. The front rooms, all with bathrooms, are particularly large and overlook a peaceful Victorian square. All rooms come with tea/coffeemaking facilities and hair dryers. Furnishings, in general, are pleasant, and small, comfy touches are sprinkled throughout the hotel—a carved mantel here, a gilded mirror there, perhaps even hardwood floors.

The hotel is about three blocks east of Earl's Court Underground, on the west side of Courtfield Gardens.

Henley House. 30 Barkston Gardens, London, SW5 0EN. ☎ **0171/370-4111.** Fax 0171/ 370-0026. E-Mail: henleyhse@aol.com. 20 units (all with private bathroom). TV TEL. £69 ($110.40) single; £89 ($142.40) double. Rates include continental breakfast. Tube: Earl's Court.

Flower-filled terra-cotta window boxes welcome you to this Victorian-style hotel. The appealing lobby has mahogany paneling and fully stocked bookcases. Rooms have been decorated with flair. You'll find built-in beds (sometimes with attractive fabric treatments overhead) and chintz comforters color-coordinated with curtains, all accented with dried flower arrangements and attractive prints. Cushions add a little extra luxury to the beds, and desks and wicker chairs are often in evidence. Tea/coffeemaking facilities and hair dryers are standard amenities. Bathrooms are tiled. The elevator is a distinct plus, too.

Hotel Boka. 33–35 Eardley Crescent, London, SW5 9JT. ☎ **0171/370-1388.** Fax 0171/ 912-0515. 52 rms (10 with bathroom/shower). £28 ($44.80) single without bathroom, £35 ($56) single with bathroom (shower); £38 ($60.80) double without bathroom, £46 ($73.60) double with bathroom (shower); £14 ($22.40) per person in multi-bed room. All rates include English breakfast. AE, MC, V. Tube: Earl's Court.

Boka's bright, blue-tiled columns stand out in the middle of a pretty Victorian crescent. Inside, you'll find rooms with unusually high ceilings, furnished with an eclectic mix of old pieces. The staff is friendly, and guests have the convenience of kitchen facilities and a TV lounge. The mostly student clientele means it can get pretty loud in here.

From Earl's Court Underground, take the Warwick Road exit, cross the street, and turn left to Eardley Crescent.

The Manor Hotel. 23 Nevern Place, London, SW5 9NR. ☎ **0171/370-6018.** Fax 0171/ 244-6610. 27 units (11 with bathroom). TV. £30 ($48) single without bathroom, £45 ($72) single with bathroom (shower); £50 ($80) double without bathroom, £60 ($96) double with bathroom (shower); £60 ($96) triple without bathroom, £75 ($120) triple with bathroom (shower only). Discount for stays of 1 week or more. All rates include continental breakfast. MC, V. Tube: Earl's Court.

Happily devoid of the dark, Dickensian feeling that plagues most of the area's hotels, the Manor is light and airy. In the rooms, the carpeting coordinates with the wallpaper and hair dryers are among the amenities. If you want a tea/coffeemaker there's a small additional charge. The hotel is located two blocks north of the Underground station, at the corner of Templeton Place.

Maranton House Hotel. 14 Barkston Gardens, London SW5 0EN. ☎ **0171/373-5782.** Fax 0171/244-9543. 15 units (all with private bathroom). TV. £60 ($96) single; £70 ($112) double; £90 ($144) triple. MC, V. Tube: Earl's Court.

This hotel, on a quiet garden square, has to be one of London's best values. The owner is extremely friendly and the property is well maintained—even down to the colorful window boxes. It boasts smart, modern rooms with built-in bed units; bedspreads and drapes are color-coordinated. The bathrooms are tiled in elegant black. Some rooms have small balconies. Hair dryer and tea/coffeemaking facilities are standard. Coffee and tea are provided in the morning. Breakfast is not included but it's available at a restaurant just down the road for about £3 ($4.80).

Mayflower Hotel. 26–28 Trebovir Rd., London, SW5 9NJ. ☎ **0171/370-0991.** Fax 0171/370-0994. 48 units (46 with bathroom). TV TEL. £53–£59 ($84.80–94.40) single; £79–£85 ($126.40–$136) double. Rates include continental breakfast.

An attractive exterior with bright yellow awnings and flower-filled baskets draw attention to this hotel. The rooms are light and airy, and thankfully, some attempt has been made to coordinate the décor (i.e., matching bedspreads and curtains in such soothing colors as pale yellows and blues). Furniture is mostly white painted, and beds have padded headboards. Most likely the room will also contain a glass top desk. Some rooms have extra-large tiled bathrooms; all have tea/coffeemaking facilities. An elevator is on the premises.

Mowbray Court Hotel. 28–32 Penywern Rd., Earl's Court, London, SW5 9SU. ☎ **0171/373-8285.** Fax 0171/370-5693. 82 units (70 with bathroom). TV TEL. £43 ($68.80) single without bathroom, £48 ($76.80) single with bathroom; £53 ($84.80) double without bathroom, £60 ($96) double with bathroom (shower); £72 ($115.20) triple with bathroom. All rates include continental breakfast. AE, DC, MC, V. Tube: Earl's Court.

Hotel managers Tony and Peter make this extra-friendly establishment a particularly good choice for this area. Located a few minutes' walk from Earl's Court Station on a reasonably quiet side street, the hotel offers comfortable rooms featuring hair dryers, safes, and even a pants press. The rooms vary in size, but each is brightly decorated and furnished with built-in armoires, desk, and at least one chair. The hotel also has a bar and a TV lounge for guests. Same-day laundry/dry cleaning is available for an additional charge.

New York Hotel. 32 Philbeach Gardens, London SW5 9EB. ☎ **0171/244-6884.** Fax 0171/370-4961. 14 units. £50–£60 ($80–$96) single; £80–£90 ($128–$144) double.

The most appealing feature of this hotel is its grassy garden, which features a fountain, hot tub, and, in season, some glorious wisteria. The elegant dining/breakfast room decorated with potted palms overlooks the garden. Rooms here are clean and simply furnished. Bathrooms are tiled and feature showers with glass doors. There's a TV lounge for guests, as well.

Philbeach Hotel. 30 Philbeach Gardens, London, SW5. ☎ **0171/373-1244.** Fax 0171/244-0149. 40 units (15 with bathroom/shower). TV TEL. £45 ($72) single without bathroom, £50 ($80) single with bathroom; £55 ($88) double without bathroom, £70 ($112) double with bathroom. All rates include continental breakfast. AE, DC, MC, V. Tube: Earl's Court.

Europe's largest and most gay-friendly hotel is located in the heart of Earl's Court. Well run and well located, it's the most recommendable budget accommodation of its kind. Window boxes and plant-filled urns draw the eye to the positively gleaming brass steps at the entrance to this clean, cordial establishment. It offers basic rooms, 24-hour reception, and an international clientele. The TV in the guest lounge offers a Europe-based cable movie channel. A small, conservatory-style restaurant, Wilde About Oscar, overlooks the rear English garden. It serves up good French fare for dinner (duck in a cherry sauce, chicken Provençale) priced from £9 to £13 ($14.40 to $20.80).

MODERATELY PRICED CHOICES

Terstan Hotel. 30 Nevern Sq., London, SW5 9PE. ☎ **0171/835-1900.** Fax 0171/373-9268. 48 units (36 with bathroom). TV TEL. £38 ($60.80) single without bathroom, £52 ($83.20) single with bathroom; £68 ($108.80) double with bathroom; £78 ($124.80) triple with bathroom. All rates include English breakfast. AE, DC, MC, V. Tube: Earl's Court.

The Terstan Hotel is located on a pleasant square in a modernized Victorian terrace house. The half-paneled rooms here are far from stylish, but they're worth considering. They have desks and coffeemaking facilities. Bathrooms are tiled. A lounge, a licensed bar, and a game room are also on the premises. Nonsmokers beware: The rooms I saw definitely had a smoky odor.

WORTH A SPLURGE

Rushmore Hotel. 11 Trebovir Rd., London, SW5 9LS. ☎ **0171/370-3839.** Fax 0171/370-0274. 22 units (all with bathroom). TV TEL. £70 ($112) single; £80 ($128) double; £90 ($144) triple. All rates include continental breakfast. MC, V. Tube: Earl's Court.

This gracious hotel occupies an Italianate-style residence built in 1876. Each of the rooms has been individually decorated in grand style using dramatic colors and a variety of painting techniques, including faux marbling and trompe l'oeil. Fine fringed and tasseled fabrics and furnishings have been used throughout. One room might feature a fully-draped canopy bed; another a bed with coronet or some other fabric treatment. On the top floor are particularly nice, large, skylit family rooms. Marble and brass are used in all the bathrooms, and all rooms contain hair dryers as well as tea/coffeemaking facilities. The conservatory breakfast room is equally delightful and unusual. Tuscan-style wrought iron chairs and glass tables fill a room featuring French limestone and granite slabs, along with floor lighting and large urns filled with saguaro cactus. The Rushmore also offers laundry/valet service.

6 Paddington, Bayswater & Notting Hill

From Paddington Station, Bayswater extends southwest to the northern boundary of Hyde Park. It's a mixed neighborhood, home to Indian, Pakistani, and Arab communities as well as numerous budget hotels. The area's proximity to the park and to good inexpensive restaurants (especially along Queensway and Westbourne Grove), plus direct transportation from Paddington to Heathrow and to the West End via the Central & District line, make Bayswater a desirable location for budget travelers. Among the streets to canvas in this neighborhood is Sussex Gardens, which starts at the traffic circle south of Paddington Station and runs straight up to Edgware Road. Along both sides of Sussex Gardens, you'll see one hotel after another. Accommodations are uniformly nondescript, but rates are good. The fierce competition in the off-season means everything's negotiable.

Just a short walk south of Paddington Station, Norfolk Square's another good hunting ground. Again, few individual hotels among the legions of them stand out.

SUPER-CHEAP SLEEPS

Dean Court Hotel. 57 Inverness Terrace, London, W2. ☎ **0171/229-2961.** 16 units (17 multishare beds; 4 with bathroom). £42–£45 ($67.20–$72) double/twin; £60 ($96) triple; £17 ($27.20) per person per night, £75 ($120) per week in multishare. If you stay 6 nights in a double/twin you receive the seventh night free. All rates include a full English breakfast. AE, MC, V. Tube: Bayswater or Queensway.

This hotel overlooks a quiet Bayswater street, just 50 yards from bustling Queensway. Recently renovated rooms, a large breakfast, and capable management are all hallmarks of this top budget hotel. There are rarely, if ever, more than four

Marylebone, Paddington, Bayswater & Notting Hill Gate Hotels

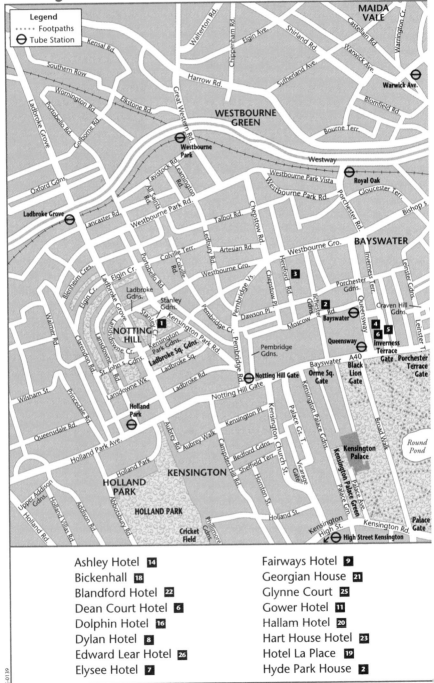

Ashley Hotel **14**
Bickenhall **18**
Blandford Hotel **22**
Dean Court Hotel **6**
Dolphin Hotel **16**
Dylan Hotel **8**
Edward Lear Hotel **26**
Elysee Hotel **7**

Fairways Hotel **9**
Georgian House **21**
Glynne Court **25**
Gower Hotel **11**
Hallam Hotel **20**
Hart House Hotel **23**
Hotel La Place **19**
Hyde Park House **2**

E-0139

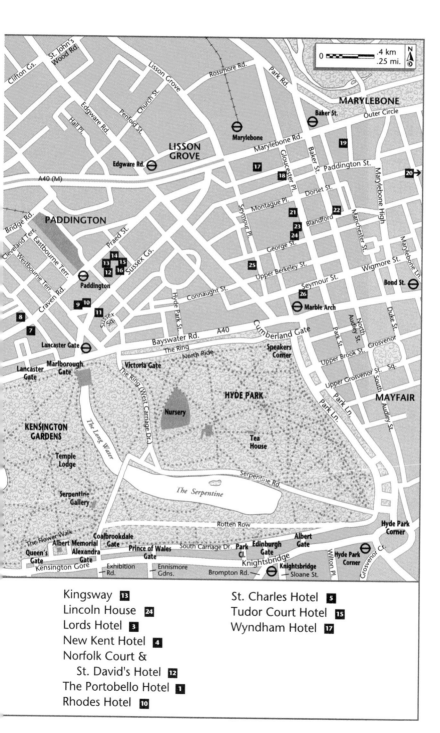

Kingsway **13**
Lincoln House **24**
Lords Hotel **3**
New Kent Hotel **4**
Norfolk Court &
 St. David's Hotel **12**
The Portobello Hotel **1**
Rhodes Hotel **10**

St. Charles Hotel **5**
Tudor Court Hotel **15**
Wyndham Hotel **17**

people staying in a multishare; if you require more privacy, ask for one of the well-furnished twins. Guests also enjoy a lounge equipped with TV, VCR, books, games, and access to a kitchen. A fax, public telephone, and ironing facilities are also available. Free tea and coffee are supplied all day.

✪ **Holland House Youth Hostel.** Holland Walk, Holland Park, London, W8 7QU. ☎ **0171/937-0748.** 200 units. £18.70 ($29.90) per person per night for travelers over 21. All rates include English breakfast. MC, V. Tube: Holland Park.

You can't beat the setting of this hostel, right in the center of Kensington's Holland Park. Half of the hostel is located in a 400-year-old mansion; the other half is in a vintage 1950s building. Accommodations are in dorms housing a maximum number of 12 people. Additional amenities include kitchen, TV room, quiet room, and laundry facilities, plus a cafeteria that is open from 5 to 8pm for inexpensive meals.

New Kent Hotel. 55 Inverness Terrace, London, W2. ☎ **0171/229-2913.** Fax 0171/727-1190. 16 units (19 multishare beds; none with bathroom). £42–£45 ($67.20–$72) double/twin; £60 ($96) triple; £17 ($27.20) per person per night, £75 ($120) per week in multishare. If you stay 6 nights in a double/twin you receive the seventh night free. All rates include English breakfast. MC, V. Tube: Bayswater or Queensway.

Under the same ownership as the adjacent Dean Court (see above), this hotel is just as clean and friendly. It has been recently repainted and refreshed.

From Bayswater Underground, cross Queensway onto Inverness Place. Inverness Terrace is just one block away.

FOR A FEW POUNDS MORE

Dolphin Hotel. 34 Norfolk Sq., London, W2 1RP. ☎ **0171/402-4943.** Fax 0171/723-8184. www.dolphinhotel.co.uk. E-Mail: info@dolphinhotel.co.uk. 32 units (12 with bathroom). TV TEL. £38 ($60.80) single without bathroom, £48 ($76.80) single with bathroom (shower); £48 ($76.80) double without bathroom, £60 ($96) double with bathroom (shower); £63 ($100.80) triple without bathroom, £72 ($115.20) triple with bathroom (shower). All rates include full buffet breakfast. AE, DC, MC, V. Tube: Paddington.

Refrigerators and coffeemakers help the Dolphin stand out from its neighboring hotels. The newly wallpapered and recarpeted rooms (about half of the 32) are a good bet. In general, rooms vary in size from very small to modest, with built-in furniture and tiled bathrooms. Guests have access to a lounge equipped with a TV and a soft-drink vending machine.

Dylan Hotel. 14 Devonshire Terrace, London, W2 3DW. ☎ **0171/723-3280.** Fax 0171/402-2443. 18 units (11 with bathroom). TV TEL. £32–£45 ($51.20–$72) single without bathroom; £50–£52 ($80–$83.20) double without bathroom, £54–£56 ($86.40–$89.60) double with bathroom (shower), £62–£65 ($99.20–$104) double with bathroom (shower/tub). All rates include English breakfast. AE, DC, MC, V. Tube: Paddington.

The proprietors want travelers to think of the Dylan as a "home away from home," and you probably will. Mr. and Mrs. Felfeli live here themselves, and their little touches give budget-oriented guests the comforts of home. Floral drapes and lace curtains hang at the windows in the rooms. Standard amenities include tea/coffeemaking facilities. In the breakfast room, tables are covered with cloths and a cup-and-saucer collection is displayed. Soft drinks are available in the guest lounge from a vending machine.

From Paddington Station, follow Craven Road six blocks; Devonshire Terrace is on your right.

Elysee Hotel. 25–26 Craven Terrace, London W2 3EL. ☎ **0171/402-7633.** Fax 0171/402-4193. 42 units (all with bathroom/shower). TV TEL. £4 ($64) single; £45 ($72) double. MC, V. Tube: Lancaster Gate.

The Elysee Hotel is a good value right on the edge of Hyde Park. It's located in a building with an elevator. Rooms are adequately furnished with typical modern furnishings. All have tea/coffeemaking facilities.

Gower Hotel. 129 Sussex Gardens, London, W2 2RX. ☎ **0171/262-2262.** 21 units (19 with bathroom). TV TEL. £34 ($54.40) basic single, £40 ($64) single with bathroom; £42 ($67.20) basic double, £58 ($92.80) double with bathroom. All rates include English breakfast. MC, V. Tube: Paddington.

The Gower has only two rooms without a bathroom—both are on the top floor. Although the sloping ceilings make these two small, they're good, clean, and worth the climb. Other rooms have the amenities above plus tea/coffeemakers. The management is extremely friendly and supplies such niceties as reasonably priced cold drinks in the lobby and a satellite channel on the TV in your room.

Hyde Park House. 48 St. Petersburgh Place, London, W2 4LD. ☎ **0171/229-1687.** 15 units (one with bathroom). TV. £28 ($44.80) single without bathroom; £42 ($67.20) twin without bathroom; £55 ($88) double with bathroom. All rates include continental breakfast. No credit cards. Tube: Bayswater.

This family-run B&B offers good, clean, quiet accommodations. In the middle of a block of row houses, it's announced by a small awning. There's a quilt on every bed and a hair dryer and tea/coffeemaking facilities in every room. Prices include free use of the kitchen, and you'll receive unlimited attention from the family's friendly small dogs.

From Bayswater Underground, turn left onto Moscow Road and left again at the church.

Lords Hotel. 20–22 Leinster Sq., London, W2 4PR. ☎ **0171/229-8877.** Fax 0171/229-8377. 68 units (62 with bathroom/shower). A/C TV TEL. £30 ($48) single without bathroom, £40 ($64) single with bathroom (shower); £44 ($70.40) double without bathroom, £60 ($96) double with bathroom (shower); £55 ($88) triple without bathroom, £72 ($115.20) triple with bathroom (shower). All rates include continental breakfast. AE, DC, MC, V. Tube: Bayswater or Queensway.

Lords is a well-run budget establishment, offering basic rooms that are both clean and neat. A few rooms have balconies overlooking the gardens at the center of the square, at no extra charge. The view is nice, but the traffic noise will be louder than if you chose a rear room.

From the Bayswater Underground, turn left onto Moscow Road, then right at the Russian Orthodox Church (Ilchester Gardens); Lords is two blocks up on your left.

☯ Norfolk Court & St. David's Hotel. 16–20 Norfolk Sq., London, W2 1RS. ☎ **0171/723-4963.** Fax 0171/402-9061. 69 units (20 with bathroom/shower). TV TEL. £35 ($56) single without bathroom, £45 ($72) single with bathroom (shower); £50–£60 ($80–$96) double with bathroom (shower). AE, MC, V. Tube: Paddington.

This hotel on a quiet square is operated by one of the friendliest owners in town, George Neokleous, who has lived in London for more than 25 years. He takes great pride in his hospitality, and the building is well cared for—as evidenced by the pretty flower boxes and plants on the entrance steps. The historic building retains such original features as moldings and mantels—there's even a room with a domed ceiling. The rooms are modestly outfitted, with tiled bathrooms and beds with tufted padded headboards. At breakfast, George will cook whatever you want. The standard breakfast, though, is one of the best in town—fruit juice and a choice of cereals followed by eggs, bacon, sausage, mushrooms, tomatoes, and baked beans! It's served in a large, attractive dining room that can accommodate 60 or more, so guests rarely have to wait for a table.

St. Charles Hotel. 66 Queensborough Terrace, London, W2 3SH. ☎ **0171/221-0022.** 17 units (all with shower; 8 with bathroom/shower). £32 ($51.20) single with shower only; £45 ($72) double with shower only, £49 ($78.40) double with bathroom (shower). All rates include English breakfast. MC, V. Tube: Queensway.

Mr. and Mrs. Wildridge are the St. Charles's caring proprietors, and the interior of this 1840 heritage home is beautifully kept. They have retained and restored many of the original architectural features, including the oak paneling and fireplace in the comfortable guest lounge. A staircase with an ornate wrought-iron banister leads to the rooms, which are comfortably furnished and also retain such homey features as fireplaces and handsome molded alcoves. Some rooms have balconies. Note there is no elevator access to the four floors. The hotel is situated a few minutes from Hyde Park and Kensington Gardens. The Airbus stop at Queensway is only two blocks from the hotel.

Tudor Court Hotel. 10–12 Norfolk Sq., London, W2 1RS. ☎ **0171/723-6553.** Fax 0171/723-0727. 36 units (10 with bathroom/shower, 3 with shower only). TV. £30 ($48) single without bathroom, £52 ($83.20) single with bathroom (shower); £46 ($73.60) double without bathroom, £69 ($110.40) double with bathroom (shower). All rates include English breakfast. AE, DC, MC, V. Tube: Paddington.

This B&B is owned and managed by outgoing Dave Gupta. The single rooms tend to be on the small side, but doubles are fair-sized. All rooms are neat and clean and several have recently been upgraded with new French-style modular units in the bathrooms. Public phones are available on each floor.

MODERATELY PRICED CHOICES

Ashley Hotel, Tregaron and Oasis Hotels. 15–17 Norfolk Sq., Hyde Park, London, W2 1RU. ☎ **0171/723-9966,** 3375 or 5442. Fax 0171/723-0173. 51 units (39 with bathroom/shower). TV. £33.50 ($53.60) single w/shared bathroom, £44 ($70.40) single with bathroom (shower); £57 ($91.20) double w/shared bathroom, £68 ($108.80) double with bathroom (shower). Triples and family room available. All rates include full breakfast. MC, V. Tube: Paddington.

This hotel occupies three buildings on an attractive quiet garden square. Rooms are decorated with armchairs, white painted furniture, floral coverlets on the beds, and, on occasion, matching curtains at the windows. All rooms have tea-making facilities. Most of the bathrooms are tiny, with minuscule sinks. Downstairs at the self service Butler's Tea Shop, guests can secure hot and cold drinks at any time and enjoy the comforts of a lounge. A good breakfast is served at individual tables in a large breakfast room.

Fairways Hotel. 186 Sussex Gardens, London, W2 1TU. ☎ **0171/723-4871.** Fax 0171/723-4871. www.freepages.co.uk/fairways_hotel/. 17 units (12 with bathroom). TV. £42 ($67.20) single without bathroom; £60 ($96) double without bathroom, £66 ($105.60) double with bathroom. All rates include English breakfast. MC, V. Tube: Paddington.

Fairways occupies a John Nash–style Georgian. The rooms are decorated in English florals, and have a certain flair. Furnishings include a couple of comfortable armchairs for relaxing and tea/coffeemaking facilities. Limited guest parking available.

The Kingsway. 27 Norfolk Sq., London, W2 1RX. ☎ **0171/723-5569.** Fax 0171/723-7317. E-mail: kingsway.hotel@btinternet.com. 35 units (33 with bathroom/shower). TV TEL. £38 basic single ($60.80), £54–£58 ($86.40–$92.80) single with bathroom (shower); £52 ($83.20) basic double, £74–£78 ($118.40–$124.80) double with bathroom (shower). Triples and four-bedded rooms available. AE, DC, MC, V. Tube: Paddington.

This hotel occupies an elegant building dating from the 1850s on a quiet garden square. The rooms, though decorated in a modern style with matching drapes and bedspreads, have high ceilings and some original accents that add a certain charm and character to the place. Extras include pants press, iron/ironing board, tea/coffeemaking facilities, and hair dryer. Bathrooms vary in size but are nicely tiled. There's an attractive lounge for guests. The elevator is an added convenience.

Rhodes Hotel. 195 Sussex Gardens, London, W2 2RJ. ☎ **0171/262-0537.** Fax 0171/723-4054. 18 units (16 with bathroom). TV TEL. £35–£40 ($56–$64) single without bathroom, £47–£50 ($75.20–$80) double without bathroom; £50–£60 ($80–$96) single with bathroom, £65–£80 ($104–$128) double with bathroom. Special rates for families of up to 5 people. All rates include continental breakfast. MC, V. Tube: Paddington.

Most of the rooms here are equipped with private bathrooms, but a few basic singles and doubles are within our budget. Nice additional in-room amenities include fridge, tea/coffeemaking facilities, and hair dryer. Some even have small balconies. The continental breakfast is more substantial than most, featuring ham and cheese as well as breads. If Rhodes Hotel is full, owner Chris Crias will direct you to **Argos House,** his other hotel around the corner. This one has 18 rooms, all with private bathrooms and pleasantly decorated in light colors. You'll pay £10 ($16) less if you stay here, merely because you'll have to walk over to the Rhodes for breakfast.

WORTH THE SPLURGE

The Portobello Hotel. 22 Stanley Gardens, London, W11 2NG. ☎ **0171/727-2777.** Fax 0171/792-9641. 22 units (all with bathroom). TV TEL. £110 ($176) single; from £150 ($240) double. AE, DC, MC, V. All rates include continental breakfast. Tube: Notting Hill Gate.

An extraordinarily elegant Victorian, conveniently located near the Portobello Market. The rooms vary from compact cabins to luxurious suites with ornately carved four-posters and antiques. Many of the rooms feature beds luxuriously swathed in fine fabrics, while the bathrooms contain hand-painted sinks and old-fashioned clawfoot tubs with shower. Adding to the beauty and atmosphere is a garden out back. Guests have access to a nearby health club with a pool and Nautilus equipment. Amenities include laundry/valet, 24-hour restaurant, and bar.

7 Marylebone/Baker Street

FOR A FEW POUNDS MORE

Wyndham Hotel. 30 Wyndham St., London, W1H 1DD. ☎ **0171/723-7204.** Fax 0171/723-7204. 11 units (all with bathroom/shower). TV. £34 ($54.40) single; £44 ($70.40) twin; £54 ($86.40) triple. All rates include continental breakfast. No credit cards. Tube: Baker St.

Tucked away on a quiet Marylebone street, this hotel stands apart from others for its value and appearance. Additional amenities include tea/coffeemakers, and fridges are available on request.

From the Baker Street Underground, cross Marylebone Road and turn right. Wyndham Street is the fifth on your left.

MODERATELY PRICED CHOICES

Bickenhall Hotel. 119 Gloucester Place, London, W1H 3PJ. ☎ **0171/935-3401.** Fax 0171/224-0614. 18 units (14 with bathroom/shower). £55–£60 single with bathroom (shower or tub); £75–£80 double with bathroom (shower); £90 triple or quad with bathroom. Rates include full English breakfast. Tube: Baker St.

This Georgian townhouse has a certain elegance; among its bonuses are a pleasant shaded courtyard garden in the rear that's furnished with wrought-iron chairs and tables. Rooms are extraordinarily spacious with high ceilings. Some possess such decorative features as fireplaces with large mirrors above the mantels. Expect to see such furnishings as antique reproduction desks and chests, or perhaps tufted Victorian chairs. Drapes, bedspreads, and carpeting are color-coordinated. The bathrooms are nicely tiled and feature modern showers and fitments. Additional features include pants presses, tea/coffeemaking facilities, plus hair dryers. You might come across some peeling wallpaper or scuffed paint, but rooms are large by London standards and represent very good value.

Edward Lear Hotel. 28–30 Seymour St., London, W1H 5WD. ☎ **0171/402-5401.** Fax 0171/706-3766. 31 units (12 with bathroom), 4 suites. TV TEL. £40.50 ($64.80) single without bathroom, £80.50 ($128.80) single with bathroom; £60 ($96) double without bathroom, £89.50 ($142.40) double with bathroom; £79.50 ($126.40) triple without bathroom, £105 ($168) triple with bathroom. All rates include English breakfast. MC, V. Tube: Marble Arch.

A block from Marble Arch, this establishment occupies a pair of brick Georgian houses. In the one on the left once lived Edward Lear, famous for his limericks and illustrations. Rooms are small but comfortable and well kept. They have tea/coffeemaking facilities and hair dryers. The public areas are decorated with floral arrangements.

Georgian House Hotel. 87 Gloucester Place, London, W1H 3PG. ☎ **0171/935-2211.** Fax 0171/486-7535. 20 units (all with private bathroom). TV TEL. £70 ($112) single; £85 ($136) double; £95 ($152) triple. Rates include buffet continental breakfast. AE, MC, V. Tube: Baker St.

Rooms in this elevator building are decorated in a bland Scandinavian modern with desk, sitting chairs, and reading lights above the bed. All have tea/coffeemaking facilities. Hair dryers are available on request. At the Georgian House, breakfast is more bountiful than most, featuring eggs, cheese, and ham as well as cereals and juice. It's taken at tables attractively covered with pink tablecloths.

Glynne Court Hotel. 41 Great Cumberland Place, London, W1H 7LG. ☎ **0171/262-4344.** Fax 0171/724-2071. 15 units (all with bathroom). TV TEL. £60 ($96) single; £70 double ($112); £90 ($144) triple. All rates include continental breakfast. MC, V. Tube: Marble Arch.

I find the Glynne Court very appealing. The high-ceilinged rooms are fresh and comfortable, with attractive moldings, sizeable armoires, and color-coordinated fabrics. Leaded windows add a touch of character. Some rooms even have small balconies. Bathrooms are small, but well equipped. Among the standard amenities are tea/coffeemaking facilities and hair dryers. A continental breakfast is served in your room.

Lincoln House. 33 Gloucester Place, London, W1H 3PD. ☎ **0171/486-7630.** Fax 0171/486-0166. www.lincoln-house-hotel.co.uk. E-mail: reservations@lincoln-house-hotel.co.uk. 22 units (19 with bathroom/shower). TV TEL. £49–£59 ($78.40–$94.40) single without bathroom, £72–£80 ($115.20–$128) single with bathroom; £65–£75 ($104–$120) double without bathroom, £90–£105 ($144–$168) double with bathroom; £110–£120 ($176–$192) triple with bathroom. Rates are slightly less from Jan to June. Rates include full English breakfast. MC, V. **Tube:** Marble Arch.

The Lincoln House is another Georgian charmer. It's well-maintained and the care shows—from the polished brass plaque and clean fanlight at the entrance to the finely polished wood paneling in the hallway. The rooms feature ceiling moldings and are furnished with slightly bland built-in desks and dressers and bed headboards. Additional in-room features include pants presses and hair dryers; some rooms even have a fridge. If you prefer a continental breakfast, it will be delivered to your room. The full breakfast is served in an attractive dining room furnished with wheelback Windsor chairs set at tables covered with green checked tablecloths.

WORTH A SPLURGE

Blandford Hotel. 80 Chiltern St., London, W1M 1PS. ☎ **0171/486-3103.** Fax 0171/487-2786. 33 units (all with bathroom). TV TEL. £65 ($104) single; £85 ($136) double; £97 ($152) triple. All rates include English breakfast. AE, MC, V. **Tube:** Baker St.

Located only a minute or two from the tube, this hotel offers excellent value. The rooms have recently been refurbished and feature modern decor—beds with padded headboards, desk, and built-in closets. Five rooms rented as triples are suitable for families. Coffeemakers and hair dryers are standard amenities, and the TV carries Spectravision movie channels. A full breakfast is served in an attractively decorated dining room furnished with elegant chairs and polished wood tables.

Hart House Hotel. 51 Gloucester Place, Portman Sq., London, W1H 3PE. ☎ **0171/935-2288.** Fax 0171/935-8516. 16 units (11 with bathroom). TV TEL. £55 ($74.40) single without bathroom, £67 ($96.10) single with bathroom; £78 ($111.60) double without bathroom, £97 ($133.30) double with bathroom. Triples and quads available. All rates include English breakfast. AE, MC, V. **Tube:** Marble Arch or Baker St.

Owned and operated by the Bowden family, this hotel is in a historic Georgian row house just a short walk from Oxford Street and the British Museum. Many original architectural elements have been retained, including Palladian-style windows in some rooms. Rooms are clean, modern, and comfortable. They are equipped with hair dryers and tea/coffeemakers; among the furnishings you'll usually find two armchairs for relaxing. Some rooms have small balconies. Breakfast is served in an attractive room furnished with polished wood tables and Windsor chairs and lit by a diamond-pane window.

✪ **Hotel La Place.** 17 Nottingham Place, London, W1M 3FF. ☎ **0171/486-2323.** Fax 0171/486-4335. 24 units, 4 suites (all with bathroom). MINIBAR TV TEL. From £79 ($126.40) single; from £95 ($152) double; from £125 ($200) family suite. All rates include English breakfast. AE, DC, MC, V. **Parking** £8.50 ($13.60). **Tube:** Baker St.

This traditional English hotel is a good choice—it's in a quiet neighborhood within walking distance of Oxford Street. A traditional redbrick Victorian, the Hotel La Place offers clean and traditionally furnished rooms featuring such elegant touches as swag draperies and other fine fabrics on the chairs and beds. Standard room features include fridges, computer hook-ups, hair dryers, tea/coffeemaking facilities, and pants presses. Suites have an additional TV, plus phone and fax. The proprietors provide such extra amenities as free coffee/refreshments in the lobby. There's an elegant wine bar on the premises that's open 24 hours, and a restaurant. Not surprisingly, this is a popular choice, so book well in advance. Room service and laundry/valet service are available. The elevator and air-conditioning in the public areas are also welcome features.

8 Barbican/City

SUPER-CHEAP SLEEPS

Barbican YMCA. 2 Fann St., London, EC2Y 8BR. ☎ **0171/628-0697.** Fax 0171/638-2420. E-mail: admin@barbican.ymca.org.uk. 196 units (none with bathroom). £23 ($36.80) single, £40 ($64) twin for bed and breakfast. Weekly rates including bed, breakfast, and evening meal are £140 ($224) per week single and £122 ($170.80) per person in a twin. DC, MC, V. Tube: Barbican.

This well-located hotel can accommodate almost 250 people. Most of the space, though, is occupied by long-term residents, so you'll need to book as far in advance as possible. Accommodations are basic and bathrooms are shared. Phones are available on several floors. Linens are changed weekly. Facilities include a cafeteria/dining room, TV lounge, and fitness center (to which residents are given free membership). The center offers a variety of classes, plus tanning beds, massage, sauna, and sundeck.

City of London Youth Hostel. 36 Carter Lane, London, EC4. ☎ **0171/236-4965.** Fax 0171/236-7681. 199 units. £19 ($30.40) per person in a dormitory with 10–15 beds; £21.30 ($34.10) per person in a dorm with 5 to 8 beds; £22.50 ($36) per person for a 3- to 4-bed unit; £24.50 ($39.20) twin, £25 ($40) single. MC, V. Tube: St. Paul's.

This hostel is situated smack-dab in the heart of the City of London, on a small back street near St. Paul's Cathedral. (In fact, it was formerly the school for the cathedral's choir boys.) Accommodations are in dormitories of various sizes, with some singles and twins available. Additional facilities include laundry room, cafeteria, TV lounge, baggage storage room, rooftop terrace where barbecues are held in summer, and office that sells bus tickets and other travel-related items.

From St. Paul's Underground, turn right and make your way toward the front steps of the cathedral; follow Dean's Court, a small street, to the corner of Carter Lane.

London City YMCA. 8 Errol St., London, EC1Y 8SE. ☎ **0171/628-8832.** Fax 0171/628-4080. 110 units (4 twins with shower). TV. £27 ($43.20) per person per night, £182 ($291.20) per week. All rates include English breakfast. MC, V. Tube: Barbican or Moorgate.

Located near the Barbican Y, this hotel offers a similar standard of accommodation. All the rooms are singles and are arranged in such a way that two adjoining rooms share a bathroom. The facility is generally fully occupied with students during the school term, but you may secure a room during the summer. The on-premises cafeteria is open for breakfast, lunch, and dinner. Additional facilities include laundry room and TV lounge.

9 Oxford Circus

SUPER-CHEAP SLEEPS

Oxford Street Youth Hostel. 14–18 Noel St., London, W1. ☎ **0171/734-1618.** 75 units. £18.70 ($29.90) per person per night in a 3- or 4-bedded room; £20.30 ($32.50) in a 2-bedded room. MC, V. Tube: Oxford Circus.

London's newest "official" hostel is also the smallest and most centrally located. Not surprisingly, it costs more than the others, but if you can get a reservation, it's well worth it. The accommodations are comfortable and are furnished and decorated in a fresh, modern style.

WORTH THE SPLURGE

Hallam Hotel. 12 Hallam St., Portland Place, London, W1N 5LJ. ☎ **0171/580-1166.**
Fax 0171/323-4537. 25 units (all with bathroom). MINIBAR TV TEL. £81.50 ($130.40) single;
£97.50 ($156) double. AE, DC, MC, V. Tube: Oxford Circus.

In a stone-and-brick Victorian, this comfortable and nicely maintained hotel is
run by the Baker family. The rooms vary in size and shape from super small,
with just enough space for a bed, to large twins. The modern furnishings have
been color-coordinated so that drapes and bedspreads actually match. You can
expect each room to contain a desk, at least one sitting chair, and reading
lights above the bed. Tea/coffeemakers and hair dryers are standard room amenities.
The breakfast room overlooks a pleasant patio. Guests have use of a comfortable sitting room. The hotel is also one of the few small hotels that has a nonsmoking
policy.

Ivanhoe Suite Hotel. 1 St. Christophers Place, Barrett Street Piazza, London, W1M 5HB.
☎ **0171/935-1047.** Fax 0171/224-0563. 7 suites. TV TEL. £58–£64 ($92.80–$102.40)
single; £68–£76 ($108.80–$121.60) double. Rates include continental breakfast. Tube:
Bond St.

This hotel is ideally situated just south of Oxford Street and has the added attraction of offering small suites that have sitting areas and private bathrooms. Each
room also has a fridge/bar, tea/coffeemaking facilities, and VCR. The decor is
modern and simple.

10 Covent Garden/Holborn

SUPER-CHEAP SLEEPS

High Holborn Residence. 178 High Holborn, London, WC1. ☎ **0171/379-5589.** Fax
0171/379-5640. 496 units (24 with bathroom/shower). TEL. £25–£30 ($40–$48) single; £40–
£50 ($64–$80) twin; £48–£60 ($76.80–$96) twin with bathroom (shower). Open late June to
late Sept. The higher prices apply from early July to early Aug. Rates include continental buffet
breakfast, except in June. Tube: Holborn/Tottenham Court Rd.

This tall, super-modern residence occupies a great location right across from the
Shaftesbury theatre close to Covent Garden. The accommodations are in apartments housing four or five persons in single rooms. Each bedroom has a washbasin;
the apartment has a kitchen, dining room, and bathroom which are shared by the
occupants. Additional facilities include two TV lounges, a bar which is open nightly
and contains two pool tables plus table tennis, 24-hour Laundromat, and computer
room so guests can obtain their e-mail. Guests also have access at special discounted
rates to a nearby gym with indoor/outdoor pools and squash courts. The continental buffet breakfast is served in the lounge.

WORTH THE SPLURGE

✪ **Fielding.** 4 Broad Court, Bow St., London, WC2B 5QZ. ☎ **0171/836-8305.** Fax 0171/
497-0064. 24 units (all with bathroom). TV TEL. £68 ($108.80) single; £88 ($140.80) double.
Breakfast not included. AE, DC, MC, V. Tube: Covent Garden.

This small hotel is very centrally located—and ideally so for opera lovers as it's right
around the corner from the Royal Opera House. It's tucked away on a pedestrian
lane between Bow Street and Long Acre. The vine-covered trellis at the entryway
and the mullioned windows give it a country air. Inside, rooms are small but clean,
pleasantly outfitted in English florals. The licensed bar, presided over by Smokey,

an African Grey parrot, is open to residents only. Full English breakfast costs £4 ($6.40); continental is £2.50 ($4).

11 Islington

SUPER-CHEAP SLEEPS

✪ **Rosebery Hall.** 90 Rosebery Ave., London, EC1R 4TY. ☎ **0171/278-3251.** Fax 0171/278-2068. 383 units (17 with bathroom). Easter £20–£24 ($32–$38.40) single; £32–£38 ($51.20–$60.80) twin; £50 ($80) twin with bathroom; £51 ($81.60) triple. Summer £20–£30 ($32) single; £32–£46 ($51.20–$73.60) twin; £50–£56 ($80–$89.60) twin with bathroom; £49–£60 ($78.40–$96) triple. All rates include English breakfast. No credit cards. Open early July to late Sept and for 5 weeks around Easter. Tube: Angel.

Of the lot of university accommodations, this may be the fanciest. Owned by the London School of Economics, the hall has well-furnished modern single rooms, a nice breakfast room, and a bar. Evening meals—three courses for £6 ($9.60)—are served daily between 6 and 7pm. Facilities include Laundromat and TV lounge. It's well located near the Camden Passage antiques market.

12 Hampstead & Highgate

SUPER-CHEAP SLEEPS

Hampstead Heath Youth Hostel. 4 Wellgarth Rd., London, NW11 7HR. ☎ **0181/458-9054.** Fax 0181/209-0546. 200 units. Bed only £15.60 ($24.95) adults, £13.35 ($21.35) under 18; bed and breakfast £18.55 ($29.70) and £16.30 ($26.10) respectively. Tube: Golders Green.

This youth hostel is located in a quiet residential area. It was formerly a college and offers a variety of room configurations—twins, triples, and quads plus dorm rooms with anywhere from 5 to 10 beds. All rooms have a washbasin and reading lights above the bed. Bathrooms are located on each floor. Additional facilities include a TV lounge, cafeteria, laundry, kitchen, and, best of all, large garden in which barbecues are held throughout the summer.

WORTH THE SPLURGE

✪ **La Gaffe.** 107–111 Heath St., Hampstead, London, NW3 6SS. ☎ **0171/435-4941.** Fax 0171/794-7592. E-mail: La Gaffe@msn.com. 18 units (all with bathroom). TV TEL. £60 ($96) single; £85 ($136) double. All rates include continental breakfast. AE, MC, V. Tube: Hampstead.

Dating from 1734, this comfortable, informal inn was once a shepherd's cottage. Rooms are small, but they are attractively decorated with coordinated furnishings. All are nonsmoking, a rarity among small, budget-oriented London hotels. Each also has a hair dryer and tea/coffeemaking facilities. The higher-end rooms have four-poster beds, and one even has a Jacuzzi, but these fall out of our price range at £115 ($184). The continental breakfast is fairly hearty, featuring cereals, yogurt, fruit, breads/pastries, cheese, and ham. A full breakfast is an additional £3.95 ($6.30). On the ground floor, there's an Italian restaurant and wine bar. In all, a good value, and only minutes from the Hampstead tube station.

13 Camping

In the unlikely event you're arriving in an RV, the London Tourist Board can supply you with a free brochure listing the many RV sites in and around London that offer full hookup facilities.

Tent City. Old Oak Common Lane, London, W3 7DP. ☎ **0181/743-5708.** Fax 0181/
749-9074. www.btinternet.com/-tentcity/. Email: tentcity@btinternet.com. 270 beds, 130
sites. £6 ($9.60) per person in beds located in men's, women's, and mixed field tents, or in
your own tent. No credit cards. Open June to early Sept. Tube: East Acton. It's a 10-minute
walk from East Acton Underground on the Central Line.

A party atmosphere prevails when hundreds of visitors camp here in the summer.
The main building has showers and toilets, plus cooking facilities and a cafeteria
that provides low-cost evening meals. Additional facilities include laundry, free baggage storage, and shop/snack bar.

Tent City—Hackney. Millfields Rd., London, E5 0AR. ☎ **0181/985-7656.** Fax 0181/
749-9074. www.btinternet.com/-tentcity/. E-mail: tentcity@btinternet.com. 200 sites. £5 ($8)
per person. No credit cards. Open June 1 to late Aug. From Victoria Station take bus no. 38
to Clapton Pond, then walk down Millfields Rd. to Mandeville St. and over the bridge to the
site.

Four miles from central London in an East End park, this large, traditional site is
set beside a canal. You can either bring your own tent, or sleep under one of their
large marquees. The campground offers toilets, showers, cooking facilities, laundry,
baggage storage, and a shop. Canalside pubs are nearby, and there are other recre-
ational opportunities nearby—swimming and fishing, for example.

14 Long-Term Stays

When staying for a month or more, it's economical to rent an apartment (called a
"flat") or a bed-sitting room ("bed-sit"). The latter is usually a room in a house, with
cooking facilities provided. Landlords usually require a security deposit equal to one
month's rent. It's returned when you vacate the place (in good condition, of course).
The magazines the **London Weekly Advertiser** and **Daltons Weekly** contain good
listings; these two publications hit the newsstands on Thursdays. The free, alternative papers *Boyz* and *Thud* also have listings.

Another good place to look for apartments and flat shares is on bulletin boards
posted around London. The largest and most famous of these is at 214 Earl's Court
Rd., next to the Earl's Court Underground.

Finally, there are a number of accommodation agencies that will do the footwork
for you. One is the **Jenny Jones Agency,** 40 S. Molton St., London, W1 (☎ **0171/
493-4801**), which specializes in low-cost rentals of six months or more, and charges
no fees to renters. The office is open Monday through Friday from 9:30am to
5:15pm (closing for lunch from 1:30 to 2:30pm). Contact the London Tourist
Board for a list of all of London's rental agencies.

5 Great Deals on Dining

The story goes that an anonymous 18th-century visitor to London dismissed English cuisine, noting wryly that there were 40 religions in England but only one sauce. If that visitor were to return today, he'd no doubt celebrate the combination of chic surroundings, bold ingredients, robust flavors, and ethnically diverse culinary styles that now make dining out in London an exciting and memorable experience. Exciting modern British food is now being served (at all price levels) throughout the city. Cafes, pubs, and restaurants alike—the rebirth is thrilling. Several restaurants now can boast several Michelin stars, while celebrity chefs and restaurateurs—Terence Conran, Marco Pierre White, Nico Ladenis, Gordon Ramsay, Jean Christophe Novelli, Eric Crouillere-Chavot, Philip Neal, Ruth Rogers, Rose Gray, and Alastair Little, to name just a handful of the leading lights—continue to open new and exciting rooms.

Most of these grand dining rooms are beyond our budget, but there are still a number of ways to secure marvelous meals at modest prices, and to sample the artistry of some of the most talked-about chefs on the current scene.

A few hints to maximize your dining dollar: **Select the prix fixe, or set menu,** usually offered at lunch and often pre- and post-theater. To take advantage of them, plan to take your main meal at lunch or to eat dinner early or late. Many of the ultra-expensive spots offer only a prix fixe lunch, and although it's still expensive, it's a more affordable way to sample some of that exciting cuisine.

The other watchwords? **Think ethnic.** Ethnic restaurants offer some of the greatest bargains and truly terrific food. London in particular has the best Indian cuisine in the world (well, perhaps outside of India), but there are plenty of other routes to go—African, Chinese, Eastern European, Filipino, Greek, Japanese, Malaysian, Spanish, Thai, Turkish, and Vietnamese.

Think also fish and chips, pizza, pasta, and noodles. Many of these specialty restaurants offer reasonably priced and good tasting meals. Similarly, at cafes you can also secure fresh sandwiches and other light meals at a decent price.

Think pub grub. Pubs are quintessentially English and some of them offer great food. Even the traditional fare is satisfying and very affordable. (See "Where to Get That Good, Old-Fashioned Pub Grub," below.)

On a clement day **assemble a picnic** at anywhere from Tesco Metro to more upscale Harvey Nichols and head into one of the squares, like Grosvenor or Golden Square in Soho, or into one of the parks. Don't overlook the chains either. Some of them offer the best affordable meals in the city. (See "The Chains & Java Joints," below, for recommendations.)

1 Best Bets on a Budget

- **Best for the View:** Dine on the terrace overlooking the Thames and Tower Bridge at the **Pont De La Tour,** Butler's Wharf, 36D Shad Thames, SE1 (☎ **0171/403-8403** or 403-9403)—Tony Blair's choice of icon for Bill and Hillary on one of their visits.
- **Best Break on Three-Star Cuisine:** At **Aubergine,** 11 Park Walk, SW10 (☎ **0171/352-3449**), the three-course £25 ($40) menu offers you the chance to sample the cuisine of one of the the city's most celebrated chefs for a fraction of the dinner price. And you can select from two different menus.
- **Best Indian: Cafe Spice Namaste,** 16 Prescot St., E1 (☎ **0171/488-9242**), for the subtle and careful blending of spices, the quality ingredients, and the scrumptious breads and pickles—all served in an Alhambra ambience.
- **Best Pub: The French House,** 49 Dean St., W1 (☎ **0171/437-2477**), because of its traditions and associations with the bohemian life of Soho. The food's good too. For New Wave pub food, I vote for **The Chapel,** just off Edgware Road.
- **Best Pacific Rim: Vong,** Berkeley Hotel, Wilton Place, SW1 (☎ **0171/235-1010**), for its superb marriage of flavors. Even though it's expensive, go at lunch and take advantage of the set menu.
- **Best Thai:** Tiny storefront **Chiang Mai,** 48 Frith St., W1 (☎ **0171/437-7444**), has some of the best Thai going. I love the wonderful combination of chili and tamarind in the *pla lat prik.*
- **Best Pastries & Desserts:** At **Maison Bertaux,** 28 Greek St., W1 (☎ **0171/437-6007**), the pastries and cakes are sublime, even if the service can be erratic.
- **Best Offbeat Dining: Cafe in the Crypt,** Crypt of St. Martin in the Fields, Duncannon St., WC2 (☎ **0171/839-4342**), is my favorite. The salads are super-fresh, and the location can't be beat. St. Martin in the Fields is just *so* London; you can stop and browse the stores afterward, or perhaps do a brass rubbing. Plus, you're doing something for charity when you eat here.
- **Best Burgers/Shakes:** If you must, then the best slabs o' beef (and that's not saying much) can be found at **Ed's Easy Diner,** 12 Moor St., W1 (☎ **0171/439-1955**), along with a classic turquoise-chrome diner look and real milk shakes.
- **Best Traditional British: Rules,** 35 Maiden Lane, WC2 (☎ **0171/836-5314**), still does it right after 200 years. You can't beat the comfort of this room and the impeccable quality of the service, style, and cuisine. And if you go early you can select from the whole menu at a discount.
- **Best for Kids:** If the food is secondary—and it usually is—then the kids will always vote for the **Rainforest Cafe,** 20 Shaftesbury Ave., W1 (☎ **0171/434-3111**), which has a jungle stage set complete with live parrots and frequent downpours. Kids get a free coloring book, too.
- **Best for Carnivores:** Those Argentinian steaks at **Gaucho Grill,** 19 Swallow St., W1 (☎ **0171/734-4040**), are worth the jump in cholesterol.

A Note on Tipping & Reservations

Many restaurants automatically add a 12.5% to 15% service charge to the bill, so look for this and avoid double tipping. Tax is always included in the prices.

At London's finer restaurants, reservations are accepted; these are essential on weekends and recommended throughout the week at fashionable spots.

- **Best Fish & Chips:** In now toney Islington, **Upper Street Fish,** 324 Upper St., N1 (☎ 0171/359-1401), gives you your money's worth. It's fresh and cooked in good clean oil, and the chips are great.
- **Best Budget for Romance:** For a touch of Left Bank Parisian romance, **Andrew Edmunds,** 46 Lexington St., W1 (☎ 0171/437-5708), is a low-lit, intimate spot complete with dripping candles in wine bottles.
- **Best Pizza:** Even though it's a chain, I vote for **Pizza Express,** 30 Coptic St., WC1 (☎ 0171/636-3232), because it's reliable, the pizzas are great, and there are scores of them around the city. As a bonus, you can enjoy them in an attractive ambience. Oh yes, and catch some good jazz too.
- **Best Seafood:** The fish at **Livebait,** 21 Wellington St., WC2 (☎ 0171/836-7161), is certainly bait for any seafood lover. The method of preparation always enhances the fresh fish cooked here.
- **Best Moderately Priced Set Menu: Vasco & Piero's Pavilion,** 15 Poland St., W1 (☎ 0171/437-8774), in Soho, offers more choices than usual on its set menus. Furthermore, the food is terrific and you may just catch a celebrity here.
- **Best *Really* Affordable Set Menu:** Islington's **Le Mercury,** 140A Upper St., N1 (☎ 0171/354-4088), has to have one of London's absolutely best values, offering a set lunch menu which allows you to select from the whole à la carte menu for a mere £5.95 ($9.50).
- **Best Modern Noodle Parlor:** People are proud to wear T-shirts from **Wagamama,** 4 Streatham St., WC1 (☎ 0171/323-9223), because it's one of the most fun dining places in London while being health conscious and serving some great good noodle dishes.
- **Best for Breakfast:** One of the divine croissants or pastries at **Patisserie Valerie,** 44 Old Compton St. (☎ 0171/437-3466), will give you a speedy start to the day; or choose something more substantial from the menu.
- **Best (and Only) Outdoor Barbecue in London: The Market Place,** at Chelsea Farmer's Market, 125 Sydney St., SW3 (☎ 0171/352-5600), is the only place where you can sit out in summer and enjoy a perfect barbecue.
- **Best Wine Bar:** I favor the **Ebury,** 139 Ebury St., SW1 (☎0171/730-5447), because the food is consistently good. And unlike many London wine bars, it's not in a subterranean, claustrophobic cellar. Great wine selections, too.

2 Restaurants by Cuisine

AFRICAN/CARIBBEAN
Cottons Rhum Shop (Camden)

AFRICAN/SUDANESE
Mandola (Notting Hill)

AFTERNOON TEA
Brown's Hotel (Mayfair)
Cafe Valerie (Covent Garden)
Fortnum & Mason (Piccadilly)
Maison Bertaux (Soho)

Patisseries Valerie (Chain)
Ritz Hotel (Mayfair)

AMERICAS/AMERICAN

Big Easy (Chelsea)
Blues Bistro and Bar (Soho)
Cactus Blue (South
   Kensington)
Christopher's (Covent Garden)
Ed's Easy Diner (Chain)
Gaucho Grill (Piccadilly Circus)
Henry J Beans Bar & Grill
   (Chelsea)
Montana (Fulham Broadway)
La Perla (Covent Garden)
Texas Lone Star Saloon
   (Paddington/Bayswater)

ASIAN

Tiger Lil's (Fulham Broadway)

BELGIAN

Belgo Centraal (Covent Garden)
Belgo Noord (Chalk Farm)

BRASSERIE/BISTRO/BAR

Browns (Oxford Circus)
Cafe Delancey (Camden)
Gilberts (South Kensington)
Pitcher & Piano (Soho)
Tuttons (Covent Garden)

BRITISH/MODERN BRITISH

Andrew Edmunds Wine Bar &
   Restaurant (Soho)
Bow Wine Vaults (City)
The English House (Chelsea)
Monkeys (Sloane Square)
Plummers (Covent Garden)
Porters English Restaurant
   (Covent Garden & the Strand)
Rules (Covent Garden)
Simpson's in the Strand
   (Charing Cross)
The Star Café (Soho)
Steph's (Soho)
Stockpot (chain)
Veronica's (Bayswater)

CAFES/LIGHT FARE

Amato (Soho)
Bar Italia (Soho)

Bluebird Cafe (Sloane Square/
   South Kensington)
Books for Cooks (Notting Hill)
Cafe Boheme (Soho)
Cafe Bruno (Soho)
Café in the Crypt (Charing
   Cross/Strand)
Cafe San Martino (Covent
   Garden)
Caffe Uno (chain)
Capital Radio Cafe (Leicester
   Square)
Cyberia Cyber Cafe (Bloomsbury)
Farmer Brown's (Covent Garden)
Fifth Floor Cafe (Knightsbridge)
Fortnum & Mason (Piccadilly)
Intercafe (Oxford Circus)
Mad Dog Cafe (Bond St.)
Mille Feuille (Covent Garden &
   the Strand)
Neal's Yard Beach Café (Covent
   Garden & the Strand)
October Gallery Cafe (Holborn)
Vingt Quatre (Gloucester
   Road/Fulham Broadway)
The Well (Victoria)
Wooley's Catering (Holborn)
Zoe (Oxford Circus)

CHAINS

Aroma (Cafe)
Cranks (Vegetarian)
Ed's Easy (American)
Flo (Cafe)
My Old Dutch (Crepes)
Pierre Victoire (French/European)
Pizza Express (Pizza)
Pret à Manger (Cafe)
Seattle Coffee Company (Cafe)
Spaghetti House (Pasta/Italian)
Stockpot (British)

CHINESE

Chuen Cheng Ku (Soho)
Dragon Inn (Soho)
Fung Shing (Soho)
Harbour City (Soho)
Poons (Soho)
Wong Kei (Soho)
YMing (Soho)
Young Cheng (Soho)

CREPES
L'Ecluse (Camden)
Le Shop (Chelsea)

DESSERT
Maison Bertaux (Soho)
Patisserie Valerie (chain)

DINER/COFFEESHOP
Chelsea Kitchen (Chelsea)

EAST EUROPEAN
Gay Hussar (Soho)
Trojka (Chalk Farm)

ECLECTIC
Capital Radio Cafe (Leicester
Square)

EUROPEAN/MODERN EUROPEAN
Alastair Little (Soho)
Aubergine (Sloane Square)
Frederick's (Angel)
French House (Soho)
Granita (Angel)
Justin de Blanc (Bond Street)
Lola's (Angel)
Museum Street Cafe (Holborn)
Odette's (Chalk Farm)
Oxo Tower (Blackfriars)
Pont de la Tour (London Bridge)
St. John (Clerkenwell/Farringdon)
Stephen Bull (Bond Street)
Union Cafe (Bond Street)

FILIPINO
Josephines (Goodge St)

FISH & CHIPS
North Sea Fish Bar (Bloomsbury)
The Rock and Sole Plaice (Covent
Garden & the Strand)
Sea-Shell (Marylebone)
Upper Street Fish (Angel)

FOOD & FUN
Rainforest Cafe (Piccadilly Circus)

FRENCH
Au Jardin des Gourmets (Soho)
Brasserie St. Quentin (Knights-
bridge)
Criterion Brasserie (Piccadilly)

L'Escargot (Soho)
L'Estaminet (Leicester Square)
Le Mercury (Angel)
Le Metro (Knightsbridge)
Maison Novelli (Clerkenwell)
Mon Plaisir (Covent Garden)
Novelli (Notting Hill)
Pelican (Covent Garden)
Pret à Manger (chain)
Thierry's (Chelsea)

GREEK/GREEK CYPRIOT
Daphne (Camden)
Jimmy's (Soho)
Kalamaras (Bayswater)
Konaki (Bloomsbury/Euston)
Lemonia (Camden)
Nontas (Camden Town)

INDIAN
Abladin (Aldgate East)
Anwar's (Bloomsbury)
Cafe Lazeez (South Kensington)
Cafe Spice Namaste (Tower Hill)
Chutney Mary (Fulham Broadway)
Gopal's (Soho)
Grand Indian (Covent Garden)
Malabar Junction (Tottenham
Court Road)
Noor Jehan (South Kensington)
Red Fort (Soho)
Soho Spice (Soho)
Veeraswamy (Piccadilly Circus)
Woodlands (Bond Street)

INDONESIAN
Nusa Dua (Soho)

INTERNATIONAL
Camden Brasserie/Underground
Café (Camden)
Kartouche (South Kensington)

ITALIAN
Amalfi (Soho)
Assaggi (Notting Hill)
La Bersagliera (Chelsea)
Bertorellis (Covent Garden)
Casa Becci (Baker Street)
Casale Franco (Angel)
Cosmoba (Bloomsbury)
Pollo (Soho)
Riccardo's (South Kensington)

Trattoria Cappucetto (Soho)
Vasco & Piero's Pavilion (Soho)

JAPANESE/SUSHI

Inaho (Notting Hill)
Moshi Moshi Sushi (City)
Tokyo Diner (Piccadilly)
T'su (South Kensington)
Wagamama (Bloomsbury/Euston)
Yo Sushi (Soho)

LEBANESE

Byblos (Kensington)

MALAYSIAN/SINGAPOREAN

Rasa Sayang (Edgware Road)

MEDITERRANEAN

Dell Ugo (Soho)
The Eagle (Clerkenwell)
Market Place Café (Chelsea)
Mash (Oxford Circus)
Middle Eastern/North African
Momo (Piccadilly Circus)

NEPALESE

Great Nepalese
    (Bloomsbury/Euston)

PACIFIC RIM

Vong (Green Park)
Wok Wok (South Kensington)

PASTA

Palms Pasta (Covent Garden)
Pasta Prego (Knightsbridge)

PIZZA/LIGHT FARE

Kettners (Soho)
Oliveto (Victoria)
Pizza Express (chain)
Pizza on the Park (Hyde Park
    Corner)
Spighetta (Baker Street)

POLISH

Daquise (South Kensington)

PORTUGUESE

O Fado (Knightsbridge)

PUBS

All Bar One (chain)
The Australian (Chelsea)

The Black Friar (The City)
De Hems (Soho)
The Chapel (Edgware Rd.)
The Eagle (Clerkenwell)
The Engineer (Chalk Farm)
The Lamb and Flag (Covent
    Garden)
The Sun (Bloomsbury)

SANDWICH SHOP

Alberto's (Soho)

SEAFOOD

Cafe Fish (Soho/Piccadilly)
Livebait (Covent Garden)
Lou Pescadou (Earl's Court)

SPANISH

Cambio de Tercio (South Kens-
    ington)

SZECHUAN-VEGETARIAN

Veg (Knightsbridge)

THAI

Bahn Thai (Soho)
Busabong Tree (Chelsea)
Chiang Mai (Soho)
Sri Siam (Soho)

TURKISH

Efes Kebab (Oxford Circus)
Pasha (Angel)
Sofra (Covent Garden)

VEGETARIAN

Cranks (Chain)
Food for Thought (Covent Garden)
The Greenhouse Basement
    (Bloomsbury)
The Place Below at St. Mary
    Le Bow (The City)
Veg (Knightsbridge)

VIETNAMESE

Cam Phat (Soho)
Saigon (Soho)
Vietnamese (Soho)

WINE BARS

Corney & Barrow (chain)
Dover Street (Green Park)
Ebury Street (Sloane Square)
Shampers (Soho)

West End Restaurants

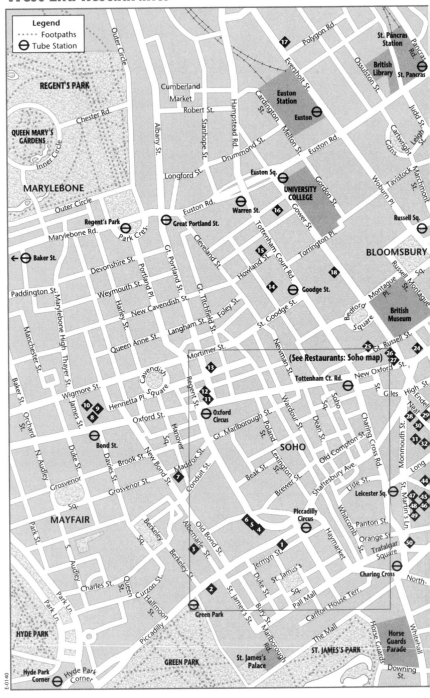

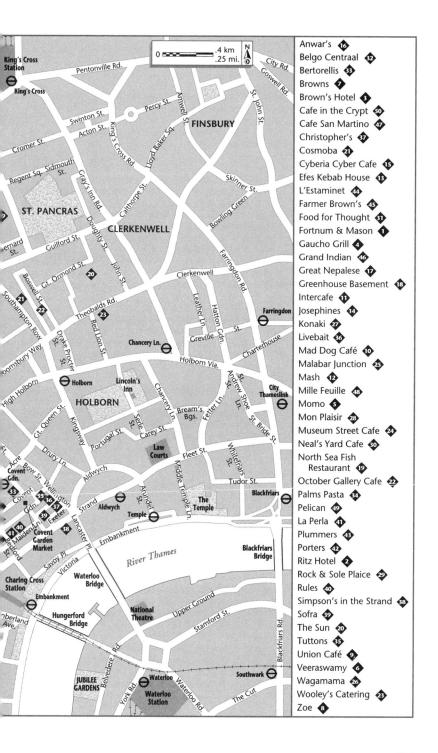

Anwar's **16**
Belgo Centraal **32**
Bertorellis **33**
Browns **7**
Brown's Hotel **3**
Cafe in the Crypt **50**
Cafe San Martino **47**
Christopher's **37**
Cosmoba **21**
Cyberia Cyber Cafe **15**
Efes Kebab House **13**
L'Estaminet **44**
Farmer Brown's **45**
Food for Thought **31**
Fortnum & Mason **1**
Gaucho Grill **4**
Grand Indian **46**
Great Nepalese **17**
Greenhouse Basement **18**
Intercafe **11**
Josephines **14**
Konaki **27**
Livebait **36**
Mad Dog Café **10**
Malabar Junction **25**
Mash **12**
Mille Feuille **48**
Momo **5**
Mon Plaisir **28**
Museum Street Cafe **24**
Neal's Yard Cafe **30**
North Sea Fish
   Restaurant **19**
October Gallery Cafe **22**
Palms Pasta **34**
Pelican **49**
La Perla **41**
Plummers **43**
Porters **42**
Ritz Hotel **2**
Rock & Sole Plaice **29**
Rules **40**
Simpson's in the Strand **38**
Sofra **39**
The Sun **20**
Tuttons **35**
Union Café **9**
Veeraswamy **6**
Wagamama **26**
Wooley's Catering **23**
Zoe **8**

3 Around Victoria

SUPER-CHEAP EATS

The Well. 2 Eccleston Place, SW1. ☎ **0171/730-7303.** £4.50 ($7.20) for a hot dish and salad. No credit cards. July–Sept Mon–Fri 9am–6pm, Sat 9:30am–5:30pm; Oct–June Mon–Sat 9:30am–5:30pm. Tube: Victoria. CAFE.

This is a handy spot near Victoria and one of the few better places to enjoy lunch or a slice of cake during the day. The place is light and airy and furnished with bentwood chairs and tables, where you're invited to linger as long as you wish. Pastries are available every day, but the hot dishes (which change daily) are offered only Monday to Friday. Then you'll find such items as quiches, jacket potatoes with a variety of toppings, lasagne, soups, salads, and sandwiches, all served cafeteria-style.

FOR A FEW POUNDS MORE

Oliveto Pizza. 49 Elizabeth St., SW1. ☎ **0171/730-0074.** Main courses £7–£10 ($11.20–$16). MC, V. Daily noon–3pm, 7–11:30pm. Tube: Victoria. PIZZA.

Another example of the sleek blond look that seems to be taking over so many London restaurants, this offshoot of Olivo's is good to know about. The pizzas are wonderfully crisp and this is one place where fashionable Belgravian families come to enjoy themselves. A few pasta dishes are offered too—a delicious linguine *al granchio* made with fresh crabmeat, garlic, and chili, for example. There are more than a dozen pizzas. Our favorites are the four *stagioni* made with mozzarella, tomato, sausages, prosciutto, mushroom, and squash; and one made with Gorgonzola, arugula, tomato, and mozzarella.

4 Bloomsbury & Fitzrovia

SUPER-CHEAP EATS

Anwar's. 64 Grafton Way, W1. ☎ **0171/387-6664.** Main courses £4–£6 ($6.40–$9.60). No credit cards. Daily noon–11pm. Tube: Warren St. INDIAN.

Anwar's not only maintains very high standards of quality but is one of the cheapest Indian restaurants in London. Few dishes top £5 ($8), and most cost just £4 ($6.40). Select from a wide choice of meat and vegetable curries and other Indian specialties, such as tandoori chicken. Service is cafeteria-style; help yourself and bring your meal to a basic Formica-covered table.

✪ **The Greenhouse Basement.** 16 Chenies St., WC1. ☎ **0171/637-8038.** Main courses £5–£8 ($8–$12.80). No credit cards. Mon–Fri 11am–8:30pm, Sat 11am–8pm. Tube: Goodge St. VEGETARIAN.

Candles on the harvest tables and fresh flowers make for a casual atmosphere reminiscent of the '60s. At the counter, choose from a variety of salads, quiches, pizzas, and vegetarian dishes. Chickpea or bean-sprout salad might be offered, and perhaps lasagne or a mixed-vegetable *masala* with black-eyed peas. Teas and vegetable and fruit juices are available.

North Sea Fish Restaurant. 7–8 Leigh St., WC1. ☎ **0171/387-5892.** Main courses £7–£8.50 ($11.20–$12.80). AE, DC, MC, V. Mon–Sat noon–2:30pm and 5:30–10:30pm. Tube: Russell Sq. or King's Cross. FISH & CHIPS.

Locals love North Sea's version of what is, of course, the national dish. Cod, scampi, skate, and many other selections are offered for take-out. One of the best chippies around.

✪ **October Gallery Café.** 24 Old Gloucester St., WC1. ☎ **0171/242-7367.** Main courses £4.40–£5.60 ($7.05–$8.95). AE, MC, V. Tues–Sat 12:30–2:30pm. Closed Easter week, August, and Christmas Week. Tube: Holborn. CAFE/LIGHT FARE.

Walk through the October Gallery to this cafe with its polished pinewood floors and tables. The garden courtyard setting is charming. The menu changes daily, but will most likely include a vegetarian and meat dish and a salad or two, plus dessert. The inspiration for the cuisine is global. Get here early, as the food usually runs out before 2pm. The gallery shows transvangarde (cross-cultural avant-garde) art.

Wooley's Catering Company. 33 Theobalds Rd., WC1. ☎ **0171/405-3028.** Sandwiches and specials £1.10–£3.30 ($1.75–$5.30). Mon–Fri 7am–3:30pm. Tube: Holborn. LIGHT FARE.

This is a first-rate food vendor selling primarily freshly made vegetarian dishes and homemade breads. Although the emphasis is vegetarian, among the weekly specials you might find poached salmon, house-roasted pork, and Stilton cheese with port chutney. Currently it's a take-out place, which unfortunately offers no seating (although renovations are under way to make maximum use of the glass-roofed space and to add some seating). The short and long roll sandwiches are filled with such great ingredients as roast chicken breast and crispy bacon, mozzarella with tomato and fresh basil, or scotch smoked salmon. Hot and cold fillings are provided for baked potatoes and there are also 10 or so salads offered made with rice, pasta, and vegetables.

FOR A FEW POUNDS MORE

Great Nepalese. 48 Eversholt St., NW1. ☎ **0171/388-6737.** Main courses £4.35–£10.95 ($6.95–$17.50); set meal £11.95 ($16.95). AE, DC, MC, V. Daily noon–2:30pm and 6–11:30pm. Tube: Euston. NEPALESE.

A unique spot to sample authentic Nepalese dishes and traditional Indian cuisine. Start with the *masco-bara*, Nepalese pancakes made with black lentils or, if you like mutton, the barbecued diced mutton with hot spices, garlic, and ginger. Follow with a traditional Indian dish or one of the Nepalese specialties like the Bhutuwa chicken, which is cooked in ginger, garlic, and spice and flavored with green herbs. *Aloo bodi tama* is a vegetarian dish similar to *aloo gobi* (potato and cauliflower stew) but made with potato, bamboo shoots, and beans. The best value is the set lunch or dinner, which includes a choice of curry, black dal, *aloo bodi tama, sag* (spinach), rice, and a dessert like mango *kulfi*. The service is attentive but there's virtually no ambience.

Josephine's. 4 Charlotte St., W1 ☎ **0171/580-6551.** Main courses £5–£11 ($8–$17.60). AE, DC, MC, V. Mon–Sat noon–3pm and 6–11pm. Tube: Goodge St. FILIPINO.

Scenes from the Philippines decorate the walls of this small restaurant that has a cozy charm with its blue-and-wood-slatted ceiling. It's one of the few Filipino restaurants in London and worth visiting to try the spicy cuisine. Start with the refreshing nourishing *sinigang* soup, made from rice soured with green tamarind fruit, plus slices of fresh radish and beans. You can have it with either king prawn, pork, or milkfish. The seafood dishes are first class, like the sweet-and-sour St. Peter fish. The pork adobo is made with a blend of garlic, salt, pepper, oregano, onion, paprika, and other spices that give it a wonderful flavor and tenderizes it at the same time. Rice, noodle, and sizzling dishes round out the menu. For dessert try the Halo-halo, which is made with shredded coconut, tropical fruit, and crushed ice.

Malabar Junction. 107 Great Russell St., WC1. ☎ **0171/580-5230.** Main courses £3.50–£8 ($5.60–$12.80). AE, MC, V. Daily noon–3pm and 6–11:30pm. Tube: Tottenham Court Rd. INDIAN.

This attractive restaurant offers excellent South Indian cuisine. The domed atrium dining room is furnished with elegant potted palms and shrubs, and a languid tropical air hangs over the place. Tables are large, well spaced, and covered with tablecloths and graced with fresh orchids. The house specialties include *masala dosa,* a traditional Kerala pancake made of rice and lentil flour, filled with potato *masala* and served with *sambar* and chutney; and *utthappam,* a cross between a pizza and an open pancake, which is also made of rice and lentil flour and topped with chopped onions, green chilies, and tomatoes, and flavored with curry and ginger. The cuisine definitely leans to the vegetarian, but there are also such delights as Malabar chicken chili, which is cooked with chilies, onion, curry leaves, tomatoes, pepper, ginger, and garlic; or the unusually rich lamb *kurma* prepared with cashew nuts, sultanas, and tomatoes in a creamy sauce. Fish lovers will want to sample the superbly flavored Malabar fish curry, which is marinated and cooked in coconut milk with tamarind, coriander, chilies, garlic, curry leaves, and onions. Among the more unusual vegetable dishes—and there are plenty of them—try the green bananas flavored with spices and onions, or *Kalan,* which is sweet mango and yam cooked with coconut, yogurt, cumin, and green chilies. It has a great sweet-and-sour flavor.

✪ **Wagamama.** 4a Streatham St. (off Coptic St.), WC1. ☎ **0171/323-9223.** Main courses £4.50–£7 ($7.20–$11.20). AE, MC, V. Mon–Sat noon–11pm, Sun 12:30–10pm. Tube: Tottenham Court Rd. JAPANESE NOODLES.

This is one of London's hot spots (in fact, on a recent trip a fellow traveler wearing a Wagamama t-shirt told me it was his all-time London favorite). Essentially, it's a noodle bar modeled on the traditional Japanese ramen shop. Stone stairs lead down to a dining room with long, family-style tables. Wait staff punch orders into handheld electronic keypads. These are sent via radio signal to the appropriate station in the kitchen. The Chinese-style thread noodles are served in soups, pan fried, or else served with various toppings. As it suggests on the menu, the way of the noodle is to make slurping noises as you eat, the extra oxygen adding to the taste. For a delicious, hearty dish, try the chili beef ramen—char-grilled sirloin, chilies, red onion, parsley, and spring onions served in a soup base that includes vinegar and chili sauce. It's served with parsley, pickled pepper, bean sprouts, and lime, which you add to the dish. A noodle dish accompanied by an order of *gyoza* (chicken, vegetable, or prawn dumplings served with a red chili and garlic sauce) should make a filling meal. Wine, sake, beer, and raw healthful juices are available. Each dish is cooked and served immediately, so if you're dining with a group, be prepared for individual meals to arrive at different times. And don't expect to linger too long either. The restaurant is strictly no smoking.

Another equally sleek but larger version is located at 10a Lexington Street in Soho. More branches are on the way.

MODERATELY PRICED CHOICES

Cosmoba. 9 Cosmo Place (off Southampton Row), WC1. ☎ **0171/837-0904.** Main courses £8–£14 ($8.50–$18.50). MC, V. Mon–Sat 11:30am–3pm and 5–11pm. Tube: Russell Sq. ITALIAN.

An old-fashioned London Italian place—small and cozy up front with a dining room in the back. Choose a pasta (tagliatelle, penne, spaghetti), and then select one of the many sauces (arrabbiata, vongole, bolognese). Cannelloni and risotto are also available. Main dishes include scampi *fritti, pollo arrosto, pollo* Kiev, steak pizzaiola, escalope of veal Valdostan, and saltimbocca à la romana.

Konaki. 5 Coptic St., WC1. ☎ **0171/580-9730.** Main courses £8–£14.50 ($12.80–$22.40). AE, DC, MC, V. Mon–Fri noon–3pm and 6–11pm, Sat 6pm–midnight. Tube: Holborn or Tottenham Court Rd. GREEK.

Behind the façade of white classical pillars lies a typical Greek dining room with a beamed ceiling. Here you can secure a fair-priced and good-sized meal of fish or meat kebabs, and similar traditional Greek favorites including a fine moussaka. Additional choices include such casseroles as lamb cooked in tomato sauce with green beans (lamb *fassolaki*), and *afelia*, which is pork marinated in red wine and cooked with coriander and spices. Start with hummus or *taramosalata* or any of the extensive list of mezes from which you could in fact select a decent meal. Finish with a filling baklava.

5 Soho & Chinatown

SUPER-CHEAP EATS

Alberto's. 2 Kingly St., W1. ☎ **0171/734-3525.** Everything is under £4 ($6.40). No credit cards. Mon–Sat 6am–5:30pm. Tube: Oxford Circus/Piccadilly Circus. SANDWICH SHOP.

A plain, down-home cafe to which people come at lunchtime particularly and line up for sandwiches as well as pasta and other dishes. This is one place, too, where you can enjoy breakfast all day.

Amalfi. 29–31 Old Compton St., W1. ☎ **0171/437-7284.** Pasta £5.50–£5.75 ($8.80–$9.20); pizza £5–£7 ($8–$11.20), main courses £6–£11.95 ($9.60–$19.10). AE, DC, MC, V. Mon–Sat noon–11:15pm, Sun 10am–10pm. Tube: Leicester Sq. or Tottenham Court Rd. ITALIAN.

One side of Amalfi is an espresso bar that sells delicious pastries and coffee. On the other side, the restaurant has tile-top tables and offers diners a comfortable, casual room lit by lanterns and accented with a few plants. The menu offers five different kinds of pasta with a choice of sauces, such as napoletana and amatriciana. More substantial main courses include the veal dishes—marsala, milanese, and limone—steak pizzaiola with garlic and anchovy sauce, or steak cacciatore.

Amato. 14 Old Compton St., W1. ☎ **0171/734-5733.** Main courses £3.20–£5.70 ($5.10–$9.10); pastries 85p–£2.70 ($1.35–$4.30). MC, V. Mon–Sat 8am–10pm; Sun 10am–8pm. Tube: Leicester Sq./Tottenham Court Rd. CAFE.

Comfortable seating and tables plus fewer crowds than in similar cafes make this one of the most appealing cafes in Soho. The pastries are as good as those at neighboring patisseries—terrific lemon tarts, superb chocolate croissants, and cakes made with chocolate and coffee mousses and flavored with liqueurs. A light menu featuring eggs, toasted and focaccia sandwiches, quiche, omelets, and salads is also served.

Bar Italia. 22 Frith St., W1. ☎ **0171/437-4520.** Light fare £1.50 –£3 ($2.40–$4.80). No credit cards. Mon–Thurs 7am–5am, 24 hours Fri–Sun. Tube: Tottenham Court Rd. CAFE/LIGHT FARE.

Soho's most authentic Italian cafe features great espresso served in a loud and busy atmosphere with the late Frankie in the background. Parma ham and cheese sandwiches can be had at the bar, eaten standing up, or served at one of the few sit-down tables, all of which are usually taken on weekends. Still a cool place to hang.

Cyber Cafe. 39 Whitfield St., W1. ☎ **0171/681-4200.** Pastries and snacks from 95p ($1.50). MC, V. Mon–Fri 10am–8pm, Sat 11am–7pm, Sun noon–6pm. Tube: Goodge St. CAFE/LIGHT FARE.

This cafe has 13 computers which you can reserve ahead of time at £3 ($4.80) per half hour to get onto the Internet. While you're waiting for your turn at the keyboard, you can sample coffee, tea, toasties, quiche, and such desserts as apple pie, although this isn't really why you're here. T-shirts, e-mail, and training are all part of the service. An easy way to check your e-mail.

Jimmy's. 23 Frith St., W1. ☎ **0171/437-9521.** Main courses £5–£8.95 ($8–$14.30). MC, V. Mon–Sat noon–3pm and 5:30–11:30pm. Tube: Leicester Sq. GREEK/CYPRIOT.

Across from Ronnie Scott's jazz club (see chapter 9), Jimmy's is a popular basement bistro with good Greek/Cypriot food. *Kleftico* (baked lamb), moussaka, and other Mediterranean dishes cost about £5.50 ($8.50). Don't expect too much from the decor, which runs to linoleum and fake paneling.

Maison Bertaux. 28 Greek St., W1. ☎ **0171/437-6007.** Pastry £1.50–£2.50 ($2.40–$4). No credit cards. Mon–Sat 9am–8pm, Sun 9am–1pm and 3–8pm. Tube: Leicester Sq. DESSERT.

One of London's top French bakeries. Maison Bertaux draws in passersby with rich aromas and a window displaying pastries, brioches, and buns. Everything is freshly prepared on the premises and tastes sublime, from chocolate cake to Danish, although service can be spotty. The treats are served at small tables, in two dining rooms (one upstairs and one down). Meat-and-cheese-stuffed croissants and other light snacks are offered, too.

Nusa Dua. 11 Dean St., W1. ☎ **0171/437-3559.** Main courses £4.50–£7.80 ($6.20–$10.85). AE, MC, V. Mon–Fri noon–2:30pm; Mon–Thurs 6:30–11:30pm, Fri–Sat 6:30–midnight, Sun 6:30–10:30pm. Tube: Leicester Sq. INDONESIAN.

The fare is hot and spicy and includes a variety of dishes from the Malay Peninsula—chicken with spicy coconut, chicken Sumatra-style, Malaysian beef curry, and lamb chop in chili sauce. The fish dishes are extra-special; these include fried fish with pineapple in hot green chili sauce or steamed fish with spring onion in ginger and oyster sauce. My favorite, though, is the pomfret with shallots in a sweet soy sauce. The ambience is casual, the service relaxed, and the furnishings basic bamboo.

Patisserie Valerie. 44 Old Compton St., W1. ☎ **0171/437-3466.** Pastry £1–£2.50 ($1.60–$4); main dishes £4.50–£6 ($7.20–$9.60). No credit cards. Mon–Sat 8am–8pm, Sun 10am–6pm. Tube: Tottenham Court Rd. DESSERT/LIGHT FARE.

This eternally crowded bakery is the Soho cafe to see and be seen in. Frequented by local film and theater types, Valerie is not the cheapest place for coffee and cake, but its chocolate truffle cake is almost world-famous. Delectable, too, are the florentines, lemon tarts, croissants, and brioches. Sandwiches, salads, omelets, and pasta dishes are also available.

✪ **Pollo.** 20 Old Compton St., W1. ☎ **0171/734-5917.** Main courses £3.40–£5.75 ($5.45–$12.70). No credit cards. Daily noon–midnight. Tube: Leicester Sq. ITALIAN.

Despite its name, locals flock here for the tasty pasta dishes, and you're likely to find a long line stretching out the door. The bustling atmosphere is appealing, and the prices are embarrassingly low. As for the pasta sauces, florentina, romana, slavia, Alfredo—you name it, they serve it—and the helpful staff is happy to explain it all. Chicken, though, is the specialty of the house, and it's served in a variety of ways—cacciatore, principessa (with asparagus), and milanese. Upstairs are small, round, marble-top tables, while downstairs there's a small, attractive restaurant. The list of Italian desserts includes a fair tiramisu.

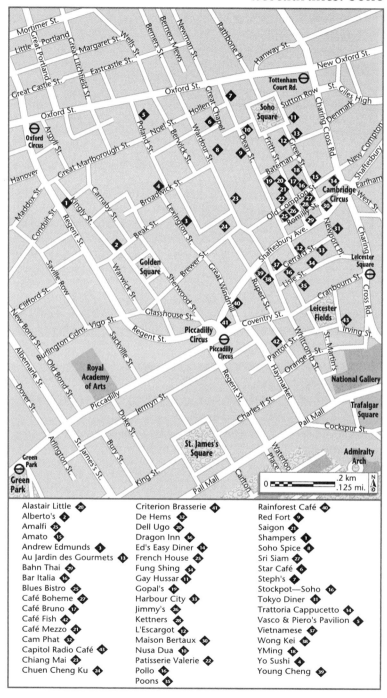

Alastair Little	**20**	Criterion Brasserie	**41**	Rainforest Café	**40**
Alberto's	**2**	De Hems	**12**	Red Fort	**9**
Amalfi	**25**	Dell Ugo	**20**	Saigon	**21**
Amato	**15**	Dragon Inn	**36**	Shampers	**1**
Andrew Edmunds	**3**	Ed's Easy Diner	**14**	Soho Spice	**8**
Au Jardin des Gourmets	**13**	French House	**25**	Sri Siam	**23**
Bahn Thai	**29**	Fung Shing	**34**	Star Café	**6**
Bar Italia	**16**	Gay Hussar	**11**	Steph's	**7**
Blues Bistro	**25**	Gopal's	**19**	Stockpot—Soho	**16**
Café Boheme	**27**	Harbour City	**33**	Tokyo Diner	**51**
Café Bruno	**17**	Jimmy's	**26**	Trattoria Cappucetto	**14**
Café Fish	**42**	Kettners	**28**	Vasco & Piero's Pavilion	**5**
Café Mezzo	**21**	L'Escargot	**12**	Vietnamese	**37**
Cam Phat	**32**	Maison Bertaux	**30**	Wong Kei	**38**
Capitol Radio Café	**43**	Nusa Dua	**10**	YMing	**18**
Chiang Mai	**23**	Patisserie Valerie	**22**	Yo Sushi	**4**
Chuen Cheng Ku	**24**	Pollo	**16**	Young Cheng	**39**
		Poons	**15**		

✪ **Poons.** 4 Leicester St., WC2 ☎ 0171/437-1528. Main courses £4–£7 ($6.40–$11.20). MC, V. Daily noon–11:30pm. Tube: Leicester Sq. CHINESE.

Poons is one of the London's most venerable Chinese restaurants. This branch is modern and comfortable and offers such grace notes as art on the walls. It features a full menu of Chinese dishes, but my vote goes for the crispy duck.

Another Poons around the corner, at 27 Lisle St., is very down-home and some people have a hard time with the cramped dining, spartan decor, and gleaming ducks hanging virtually under your nose. Still the prices are right—£3–£6 ($4.80–$9.60) for anything on the menu.

Saigon. 45 Frith St., W1. ☎ **0171/437-7109.** Main courses £4.80–£8 ($7.70–$12.80); set menu from £17 ($27.20). AE, DC, MC, V. Mon–Sat noon–11:30pm. Tube: Leicester Sq./ Tottenham Court Rd. VIETNAMESE.

This small, low-lit restaurant offers wonderful Vietnamese food. Try the spiced crab with garlic, lemongrass, and herbs; or the sliced duck with coriander in a special sauce. Also exciting is the spiced lamb with satay sauce, stir-fried prawns with spring onion and chili, and rice noodles with spring onion and mixed meat.

The Star Café. 22 Great Chapel St., W1. ☎ **0171/437-8778.** Main courses £4.25–£5.95 ($6.80–$9.50). MC, V. Mon–Fri 7am–6pm, Sat 10:30am–4:30pm. Tube: Tottenham Court Rd. BRITISH.

This greasy spoon is a favorite of film and media folk working in the area—it's just off Oxford Street near the Tottenham Court Road Underground. The cafe is good for breakfast and its daily luncheon specials such as roast chicken with crispy bacon stuffing, steak and onion pie, or salmon fillet with broccoli. Pasta, salads, and a vegetarian dish of the day are offered, too.

Tokyo Diner. 2 Newport Pl., WC2. ☎ **0171/434-1414.** Main courses £6–£13 ($9.60–$20.80); £5.95 ($9.50) set lunch. MC, V. Daily noon–midnight. Tube: Leicester Sq. JAPANESE.

This tiny hole-in-the-wall offers decent Japanese cuisine and in fact caters to many Japanese customers. The wooden tables are small and cramped, but nobody seems to mind. The bento boxes are great values, given that they include rice, noodle salad, salmon sashimi salad, and a main dish which might be pork or chicken *tonkatsu* or chicken, salmon, or mackerel teriyaki. If you're really on a strict budget you can make a meal from the *donburi,* which are boxes filled with rice that is topped either with such items as seasoned egg with chicken or chicken flambeed in teriyaki sauce. Sushi and sashimi are also served.

Vietnamese. 34 Wardour St., W1. ☎ **0171/494-2592.** Main courses £3.80–£6.50 ($6.10–$10.40); set menus from £6.50 ($10.40). AE, DC, JCB, MC, V. Mon–Sat 11:30am–11:30pm, Sun 11am–11pm. Tube: Leicester Sq. VIETNAMESE.

The decor is minimal but the food is good and cheap. Choose from the 16 soups and as many noodle and rice dishes. Enjoy such tasty dishes as sweet-and-sour chicken or prawns, beef with ginger and onions, sizzling beef with chili and black-bean sauce, or stuffed tofu with aubergine (eggplant) and peppers.

Wong Kei. 41–43 Wardour St., W1. ☎ **0171/437-8408.** Main courses £3.20–£7.50 ($4.65–$10.85); set menus from £6 ($9.60). No credit cards. Daily noon–11:30pm. Tube: Leicester Sq. or Piccadilly Circus. CHINESE.

Wong Kei is one of the most inexpensive restaurants in the area and it attracts mobs to its bustling dining rooms behind storefront windows where the cooks hack, chop, and stir fry. The menu is extensive, featuring lemon chicken, beef with ginger and green onion, braised duck with assorted vegetables, and baked crab in black bean sauce. Dine upstairs or downstairs at cloth-covered tables with glass overlays.

Sarah Bernhardt laid the foundation stone and fellow actor Henry Irving the coping stone of the building in 1905. The stylish associations have no influence on the service inside, which is notoriously brusque and considered part of the restaurant's charm.

FOR A FEW POUNDS MORE

Andrew Edmunds Wine Bar & Restaurant. 46 Lexington St., W1. ☎ **0171/437-5708.** Reservations recommended. Main courses **£**6.50–£9 ($10.40–$14.40). AE, MC, V. Mon–Fri 12:30–3pm, Sat–Sun 1–2:30pm; Mon–Sat 6–10:45pm, Sun 6–10:30pm. Tube: Oxford Circus or Piccadilly Circus. MODERN BRITISH.

Small and atmospheric with a low, wood-slatted ceiling, the dining room features butcher paper–covered tables lit by candles in wine bottles. Fresh is the keyword to describe the cuisine. The menu might offer a confit of duck with gratin dauphinoise, wild rabbit stew with mash and roast swede (rutabaga), baked cod fillet with sweet potatoes and peppers, and a stew made with lamb shank flavored with peppers and red onions. For dessert try the tiramisu, plum and almond tart, or a portion of Stilton. Among the appetizers, opt for the smoked salmon.

✪ **Cafe Boheme.** 13 Old Compton St., W1. ☎ **0171/734-0623.** Main courses £5–£11.50 ($8–$17.60). AE, DC, MC, V. Mon–Wed 7am–3am, Thurs–Sat 24 hours, Sun 8am–-10:30pm. Tube: Leicester Sq. CAFE/LIGHT FARE.

One of my favorite Soho hangouts. Full of atmosphere, it attracts a mixed crowd of hip young things as well as older couples. The food is classic French bistro—duck confit, lobster, smoked salmon, and brandy terrine, plus an assortment of char-grilled dishes. You can also secure an omelet for about £5 ($8). At night it gets very crowded; it seems you can watch the whole world drift in and out. More relaxing during the day but still very cool, funky, and relaxed. Worthy of its name.

✪ **Cafe Bruno.** 63 Frith St., W1. ☎ **0171/734-4545.** Main courses £5.50–£10 ($8.80–$16). AE, DC, V. Mon–Fri 12:15–2:30pm; Mon–Sat 6:15–11:30pm. Tube: Leicester Sq. or Tottenham Court Rd. FRENCH.

This primarily gay cafe which is an adjunct of the more expensive restaurant next door offers typical French bistro dishes. You'll find *moules marinières* to start and such dishes as steak and frites, roast *poussin au gratin dauphinois*, or fish cake with mushy peas and a salad. It has an attractive ambience. Rush-seated chairs are combined with brightly colored painted wood tables. At night the sconce lighting gives it a warm glow.

Cam Phat. 12 Macclefield St., W1. ☎ **0171/437-5598.** Main courses £5–£9 ($8–$14.40). MC, V. Sun–Thurs 11:30am–11:30pm, Fri–Sat 11:30–midnight. Tube: Leicester Sq. VIETNAMESE.

A good choice for a budget meal. There's always an £8 ($14.40) special that includes a starter like crispy aromatic Szechuan duck, a main course of sweet-and-sour pork or stir-fried chicken with cashew nuts, and fresh fruit for dessert. If you don't want to narrow your sights like this, there are plenty of delicious options on the menu. Among my favorites are the sizzling prawns with garlic sauce, the baked crab with lemongrass and chili, and the fried veal with honey sauce.

Capital Radio Cafe. Leicester Sq., WC2. ☎ **0171/484-8888.** Main courses £7.25–£11.50 ($11.60–$18.40). AE, CB, MC. Mon–Sat 11:45am–midnight, Sun 11:45am–10:30pm. Tube: Leicester Sq. ECLECTIC.

Young kids and teens love to visit this loud glitzy emporium created by Britain's popular Capital Radio station. DJs spin disks all day. If you can eat in this frenzied atmosphere, the food is decent. You could compile a list of teenage and youth favorites from the broad selection on the menu—satay, nachos, coconut shrimp to start, followed by burgers with a variety of toppings, fajitas, and barbecued chicken.

Chiang Mai. 48 Frith St., W1 ☎ **0171/437-7444.** Main courses £6.95–£8.95 ($11.10–$14.30). AE, MC, V. Mon–Sat noon–3pm and daily 6–11pm. Tube: Leicester Sq. THAI.

This small storefront restaurant attracts plenty of lunchers who are drawn by the quality and price of the food and the simple ambience. The menu offers a full range of Thai specialties, from a delicious *tom yam gai* soup, which zings with the flavor of lemongrass, to *pla lat prik,* which is fried fish with a wonderful combination of hot chili and tamarind flavors. There are also classic red and green curries and many rice and noodle dishes. A separate vegetarian menu is also offered featuring a full selection of dishes, including a piquant green papaya salad and spicy stir-fried long beans with bean curd. A short wine list is available.

Chuen Cheng Ku. 17 Wardour St., W1. ☎ **0171/437-1398.** Main courses £5.50–£9.95 ($8.80–$16). AE, DC, MC, V. Daily 11am–11:45pm; dumplings served until 5:45pm. Tube: Leicester Sq. CHINESE.

This is one of the few restaurants in London that offer the classic experience of dim sum served from rolling carts. This huge restaurant serves close to 30 kinds of steamed, fried, or boiled dim sum (dumplings). Favorites include steamed pork buns and shrimp dumplings, both £1.75 ($2.80). It takes a few servings here to satisfy the appetite, but it can be done for about £7.50 ($12). There's also a very extensive regular menu.

Dragon Inn. 12 Gerrard St., W1. ☎ **0171/494-0870.** Main courses £3.80–£11 ($6.10–$17.60); £5.50 ($8.80) dim sum set menu; £6 ($9.60) set lunch 11am–5pm; £7 ($11.20) happy-hour menu 5–7pm Mon–Thurs; set dinners from £8.50 ($13.60). AE, MC, V. Daily 11am–midnight. Tube: Leicester Sq. CHINESE.

Far from fancy, this small, low-ceilinged restaurant offers some great Chinese food. Baked chicken in soya sauce, prawn with cashew nuts, steamed fish with chili and black bean sauce, and duck flavored with ginger and pineapple are among the fine dishes on the broad menu. The noodles in soup (crabmeat noodle in soup) and the rice dishes on a plate (beef and vegetables with rice) make tasty, adequate meals for the truly budget-conscious.

Gopal's. 12 Bateman St., W1. ☎ **0171/434-1621.** Main courses £6.95–£13.50 ($11.10–21.15). AE, DC, V. Daily noon–3pm; 6–11:30pm. Tube: Piccadilly Circus or Tottenham Court Rd. INDIAN.

The atmosphere here is pleasant, with cane-backed upholstered chairs and tables covered with salmon-pink cloths. The food is not drenched in ghee or oil as at so many Indian restaurants, and the spice flavors are distinctive. A substantial number of traditional vegetarian, seafood, and meat dishes are featured. Two specialties of the house are *dum ka murg* (steamed chicken cooked on the bone in a sealed pot with Hyderabadi spices and herbs) and mutton *xacutti* (a Goan dish of hot lamb cooked with coconut, vinegar, and spices).

Harbour City. 46 Gerrard St., W1. ☎ **0171/439-7859.** Main courses £6.20–£12.50 ($9.90–$20). AE, DC, MC, V. Mon–Thurs noon–11:30pm, Fri–Sat noon–midnight, Sun 11am–11pm. Tube: Leicester Sq. CHINESE.

One of the most comfortable restaurants in Chinatown. Downstairs is a candlelit dining room; upstairs the tables are set with crisp white tablecloths and have black lacquered chairs. More than a dozen soups are offered, plus a variety of noodle, meat, and seafood dishes like duck in lemon sauce, moo shu pork, and Singapore-style vermicelli. Great dim sum is also offered until 5pm at an average price of £1.60 ($2.55) each.

Kettners. 29 Romilly St., W1. ☎ **0171/734-6112.** Main courses £6.50–£13.95 ($10.40–$22.30). AE, DC, MC, V. Daily 11am–midnight. Tube: Leicester Sq. or Tottenham Court Rd. PIZZA/LIGHT FARE.

Good, reasonably priced simple food in an haute cuisine atmosphere is what attracts people to Kettners. The dining rooms and bar retain their paneled walls, mirrors, and sconce lighting from the days when it was an elegant French restaurant. Although the menu offers a broad selection of dishes, from steaks, pizza, and pasta to chili, burgers, and sandwiches, we suggest concentrating on the pizzas, which are great. One pizza has such unusual toppings as sultanas, capers, onions, pine kernels, and olives, and there are several other rare combinations.

Pitcher & Piano. 40–42 William IV St., W2. ☎ **0171/240-6180.** Main courses £5–£8 ($7.75–$12.40). AE, V. Mon–Thurs noon–10:30pm, Fri–Sat noon–9pm, Sun noon–10pm. Tube: Charing Cross. BISTRO/BAR.

This light and airy bar occupies a very large space with polished wood floors and a grand piano. Steak frites, salads, sandwiches, and snacks plus other grills are offered at okay prices.

Rainforest Café. 20 Shaftesbury Ave., W1. ☎ **0171/434-3111.** Main courses £7.95–£14.95 ($12.70–$23.90). AE, DC, MC, V. Daily noon–midnight. Tube: Piccadilly Circus. FOOD & FUN.

The latest themed dining/shopping experience to arrive in London from the Minneapolis Mall of America, where it was launched in 1994. Kids love it. Walk into the downstairs dining room and you're enveloped by lush vegetation, rocks and waterfalls, tropical birds and animatronic animals that wail or scream, and thunderclaps and sudden storms. It's all set against a backdrop of salt-water aquariums filled with tropical fish. As if this isn't enough, kids are given a free coloring and puzzle pack to entertain them. A special menu offers them Jurassic chicken—breaded dinosaur-shaped chicken pieces served with fries and baked beans—and other items like pizza and dogs. For the adults there's a whole range of pizzas, pasta, wok dishes, and burgers, plus a 12-ounce New York strip served with poblano chile butter, as well as some alarming concoctions like the Chicken Bombay, a coconut milk curry served on a bed of mixed greens tossed with soy vinaigrette and rice with Thai peanut sauce. You might prefer to take one of the "animal" seats at the bar and bolt down one of the tropical drinks available to recover from this somewhat overwhelming experience.

The street level is devoted to a store selling casual clothes and accessories for that trip to Costa Rica or similar. Your shopping will be encouraged by the live parrots and the not-so-live crocodile in the swamp in the front window.

Shampers. 4 Kingly St., W1. ☎ **0171/439-9910.** Main courses £8–£12 ($12.80–$19.20). AE, DC, MC, V. Mon–Sat 11am–11pm. Tube: Oxford Cicus/Piccadilly Circus. WINE BAR.

Unlike most of London's wine bars, which are found in basements or cellars, Shampers has a light and airy upstairs dining room. Tables sport white tablecloths, and the atmosphere is casual yet stylish. It gets very crowded at lunchtime when businesspeople crowd in for the good selection of wines (more than 20 by the glass) and the reasonably priced cuisine, which consists of hearty salads made with guinea fowl, squid, and other more mundane ingredients, plus hot dishes like calves' liver, pastas, and mussels in a tarragon cream sauce. There's always a casserole of the day and a pasta and vegetarian dish of the day. The downstairs dining room has a slightly higher-priced menu and more ambience, even though it is only open for lunch.

Soho Spice. 124–6 Wardour St., W1. ☎ **0171/434-0808.** Main courses £8–£14 ($12.80–$22.40); 2-course lunch £8.50 ($13.60); 3-course seasonal menu £15.95 ($25.50). AE, DC, MC, V. Mon–Wed 11:30am–midnight; Thurs–Sat 11:30am–3am, Sun 12:30–10:30pm. Tube: Leicester Sq./Tottenham Court Rd. INDIAN.

This new-style Indian restaurant, which caters to a young crowd in search of casual spontaneous dining, is decked out in a strong palette of aqua, turquoise, deep blue, and terra-cotta red. Throughout the restaurant, spices accent the theme, from the antique spice jars and brilliantly colored spices in the window, to the pictures on the columns and the walls, to the spice cards (each elaborating on a particular spice) attached to the menu. Waiters wearing brightly colored kurtas serve diners seated at wood tables in this sleek, modern room. The food is more familiar —chicken *tikka*, tandoori lamb, and spicy prawn curry—supplemented by a seasonal three-course menu featuring a particular Indian regional cuisine. A Punjabi menu, for example, features such dishes as *rara gosht*, lamb cooked in the tandoor and then stir-fried with cardamon and dried ground ginger *masala*. The two-course lunch offers a choice of a couple of appetizers like *aloo palak Bhaji* (potatoes and spinach blended with spicy graham flour) or crisp fried chicken drumsticks. These are followed by a choice of three main dishes. One is always vegetarian.

The basement bar resonates with the colors of paprika, chili, and saffron. Snacks are available to accompany the spicy drinks, including one called the Bollywood Buzz, a combination of apricot brandy and sweet vermouth spiced with a ginger stuffed apricot and topped with ginger ale. Not for my taste but right on for the combination of Bombay and Hollywood. Happy hour runs Monday to Saturday from 5:30 to 7:30pm, when cocktails are all £2.50 ($4) instead of the usual £4.95($7.90). The reasonably priced and decent quality food plus the sleek decor make this a winner.

Sri Siam. 16 Old Compton St., W1. ☎ **0171/434-3544.** Main courses £7–£9 ($11.20–$14.40). AE, DC, V. Mon–Sat noon–3pm and 6–11:15pm, Sun 6–10:30pm. Tube: Leicester Sq. THAI.

This long, narrow dining room, which has been divided into several more intimate dining areas, is softly lit with sconces. Black lacquer chairs are set at tables decked with fine white tablecloths. Banana leaves painted on the walls convey a tropical ambience. The dishes here are well spiced and nicely presented. Try the delicious marinated fish grilled in banana leaf and served with two sauces (chili or tamarind plum); or the spicy dishes of stir-fried pork with basil, chili, and garlic; or diced chicken with lemongrass and red chili. Thai noodle dishes like *pad thai* are worth trying, too.

Steph's. 39 Dean St., W1. ☎ **0171/734-5976.** Main courses £6.95–£15 ($11.10–$24). AE, MC, V. Mon–Fri noon–3pm; Mon–Thurs 5:30–11:30pm, Fri–Sat 5:30pm–midnight. Tube: Leicester Sq. or Piccadilly Circus. MODERN BRITISH.

A fun spot, where the walls are painted with frolicking flamingos. The eclectic menu offers bangers and mash, pie of the day, burgers, fishcakes with parsley sauce, a lime-flavored chicken breast, and filet steak. Desserts include a fine key lime pie and the ubiquitous bread-and-butter pudding. Start with baked mushrooms with Stilton. There's a short, eclectic, and reasonably priced wine list.

Trattoria Cappuccetto. 17 Moor St., W1. ☎ **0171/437-2527.** Main courses £8.20–£13 ($13.10–$20.80); 3-course lunch £7.95 ($12.70). AE, MC, V. Daily noon–3pm and 5:30–11pm. Tube: Tottenham Court Rd. or Leicester Sq. ITALIAN.

Both the upstairs and downstairs dining rooms at this trattoria are small and intimate. The food is well prepared, particularly the veal dishes—*saltimbocca alla romana, carciofo, funghetto, limone,* or *marsala.* Other dishes like *pollo cacciatore* and *pollo sorpresa* stuffed with cheese, ham, garlic, and butter; steak in barolo sauce; and scampi and calamari round out the menu.

Yo Sushi. 52 Poland St., W1. ☎ **0171/287-0443.** Sushi selections from £1.95–£4. AE, DC, MC, V. Daily noon–midnight. Tube: Oxford Circus. JAPANESE.

This is one of the new, up-to-the-minute Japanese snack bars featuring a revolving sushi bar, robotic drinks bar, and music videos. It's sleek and modern, decorated in blond wood and tubular steel, and attracts a young, fashionable crowd who perch on the stools, selecting the dishes as they pass by. The price of your meal will be calculated in Japanese style by the number and colors of the dishes that you have in front of you at the end of the meal. They range from £1 ($1.60) for lime to £3.50 ($5.60) for pink, with blue, purple, and orange somewhere in between. Baby corn *maki* or similar is at the cheaper end of the scale, while scallops sashimi is at the more expensive. You'll be offered a full selection of *maki,* sushi and sashimi, the majority turned out by the robotic sushi maker.

Young Cheng. 76 Shaftesbury Ave., W1. ☎ **0171/437-0237.** Main courses £6–£12 ($9.60–$19.20); set menus from £8 ($12.80). AE, MC, V. Daily noon–11:20pm. Tube: Leicester Sq. CHINESE.

This small, plain restaurant with Formica-topped tables is always crowded with Chinese diners. The menu is more limited than most—Szechuan chicken, tofu with prawn and spicy sauce, chicken with black-bean sauce, and sweet-and-sour pork—but the quality is good.

MODERATELY PRICED CHOICES

Au Jardin des Gourmets. 5 Greek St., W1. ☎ **0171/437-1816.** Express 2-course lunch £10 ($16); 2-course lunch or dinner £25 ($40); 3-course lunch or dinner £30 ($48). AE, DC, MC, V. Open Mon–Fri noon–2:30pm and Mon–Sat 6–11:15pm. Tube: Tottenham Court Rd. FRENCH.

This is one of those lovely, old-style French restaurants featuring heavy drapes with tassels and Louis XVI chairs combined with exquisitely set extra-large tables. It attracts a lot of businesspeople from nearby Soho Square. It offers several good dining deals. The best is probably the two-course lunch for only £10 ($16), an excellent value which offers a choice of two appetizers and two main courses, like rib eye steak with Pommery mustard and grilled salmon with herb butter. The two-course and three-course lunch and dinner menus offer a balanced selection of fish and meat dishes, including steamed fish with ginger, spring onion, and vermouth; or filet of beef with Camembert and port wine sauce. To finish try the warm chocolate and praline fondant with pistachio sauce and chocolate ice cream.

✪ **Bahn Thai.** 21A Frith St., W1. ☎ **0171/437-8504.** Main courses £9.95–£18 ($15.90–$28.80). AE, DC, MC, V. Mon–Sat noon–2:45pm; Sun 12:30–2:30pm; Mon–Sat 6–11:15pm, Sun 6:30–10:30pm. Tube: Tottenham Court Rd. THAI.

Right in the middle of Soho is one of the best Southeast Asian restaurants in London. Decorative wall hangings give this exceptional place a totally authentic feel, but it's the food you come for, and you won't be disappointed. Excellent soups, seafood, and rice dishes are featured on the huge and creative menu. Try the crispy fried pomfret or a good green curry.

✪ **Blues Bistro and Bar.** 42–43 Dean St. W1. ☎ **0171/494-1966.** Main courses £10–£15.50 ($16–$24.80); 3-course lunch or dinner Mon/Tues £10 ($16). AE, DC, MC, V.

Mon–Thurs noon–11pm; Fri–Sat noon–1am; Sun noon–4pm. Tube: Leicester Sq./Tottenham Court Rd. AMERICAN.

An example of the new sleek Soho joint frequented by showbiz and media types. They gather upfront at the serpentine steel bar or in the rear dining room on the blue banquettes which contrast with the rich raspberry-colored walls. Huge modernist paintings and Venetian glass add striking decorative accents. The cuisine is up-to-the-minute American style. At lunch or dinner you'll find good tasting Maryland crabcakes with coriander and lime tartare sauce and Maryland chicken served with corn fritter and bacon. Fish dishes are well prepared, like the salmon in a polenta crust served with green olive tapenade. Simple grilled dishes are moist and well flavored. For example, try the spring chicken with morels, asparagus, fava beans, and tomato and basil sauce.

If you come for Sunday brunch, you can sample some of the above dishes at slightly lower prices, along with such items as grilled tuna steak with lemon and chive vinaigrette served with a warm potato salad, plus the usual eggs Benedict or a full English breakfast. Key lime pie and white chocolate and strawberry torte with a strawberry coulis are just two of the great desserts that will complete your meal. On Thursday to Saturday nights a small jazz combo entertains.

Cafe Fish. 39 Panton St., SW1. ☎ **0171/930-3999.** Main courses £7.85–£16.95 ($12.55–$27.10). AE, DC, MC, V. Mon–Fri noon–3pm and Mon–Sat 5:45–11:30pm; wine bar Mon–Sat 11:30am–11pm. Tube: Leicester Sq. SEAFOOD.

Cafe Fish is conveniently located between Leicester Square and Piccadilly Circus. People crowd in for the reasonably priced, decently prepared fish. The space upstairs is tiny and the tables are small and somewhat cramped, but it's still popular because the fish is fresh and you can have it prepared in a variety of ways, from deep fried (gasp!) to grilled and steamed for the more health conscious. There's even a whole Dover sole for £16.95 ($27.10), which is at least £10 ($16) less than you'd pay at a more fancy restaurant. Among the specialties, my favorite is the strongly flavored baked monkfish with smoked bacon, mushrooms, and spinach served on a potato galette. To start, there are plenty of local oysters and other shellfish, and to finish you can't beat the tart citron. The basement wine bar serves a shorter similar menu.

Dell Ugo. 56 Frith St., W1. ☎ **0171/734-8300.** Main courses £9–£14 ($14.40–$22.40). AE, DC, MC, V. Downstairs Mon–Sat 11:30am–11:30pm; upstairs Mon–Fri noon–3pm and Mon–Sat 7pm–12:30am. Tube: Leicester Sq. MEDITERRANEAN.

This fashionable place attracts a crowd of suits at lunchtime. On the walls are wildly colorful abstract murals, and seating is at black tables and chairs. The wide menu ranges from pasta (farfalle with Gorgonzola, spinach, and pine nuts; gnocchi with chorizo, olives, and tomatoes) to plain grills (rump steak and frites; lamb shank with flageolets, garlic, and rosemary). For dessert, there's an enticing double chocolate terrine with coffee and a lemon tart. A tapas menu is offered in the cafe downstairs.

L'Escargot. 48 Greek St., W1. ☎ **0171/437-2679.** 2-course set lunch £14.95 ($23.90), 3 courses £17.95 ($28.70); 2-course pre-theater £14.50 ($23.20), 3 courses £17.50 ($28); main courses £12.95 ($20.70). Picasso Room set lunch with 2 courses £25 ($40), 3 courses £30 ($48); 3-course set dinner £42 ($6.750). AE, DC, MC, V. Mon–Fri 12:15–2:15pm; Mon–Sat 6–11:15pm. Tube: Leicester Sq. or Tottenham Court Rd. FRENCH.

This restaurant recently received a one star Michelin rating; and it's worth splurging in the ground floor restaurant, where you can secure an excellent value lunch or dinner. Inside, cream-colored walls, fresh flower arrangements, handsome table settings, and leather upholstery set an elegant tone. The walls are decorated with works

---

Fish & Chips

Fast-food restaurants have replaced many a chippie, as the British call them, but they can still be found fairly easily. Nowadays, fish and chips may be served along with Chinese or Middle Eastern take-out, but the most authentic joints won't have a kebab in sight. Several kinds of fish are offered, but all taste similar—cod is the cheapest.

Sitting down will raise the price of the meal considerably, so do as the locals do, and take it away—wrapped in a paper cone, doused with malt vinegar, and sprinkled with salt. The bill should never top £6 ($9.60).

Two of the most popular chippies are **Upper Street Fish Shop,** 324 Upper St. (☎ **0171/359-1401**); and **North Sea Fish Restaurant** (see both listings above in this chapter under "Islington" and "Bloomsbury & Fitzrovia").

---

by Marc Chagall, Joan Miró, and David Hockney. Among the appetizers all £6.75 ($10.80), you're likely to find a smooth and flavorsome shellfish bisque enhanced by cognac and tarragon, or a parfait of foie gras and chicken livers served with brioche toast. Main course selections—all £12.95 ($20.70)—might include a pork chop, redolent with morels and Madeira jus, or rack of lamb with white bean jus. Fish dishes are also well prepared, like the roast wing of skate with a sauce diable and snails. A traditional peach melba or chocolate tart with orange sorbet is usually among the desserts. There's a fine, extensive wine list. Prices are higher in the upstairs Picasso, but the two-course £25 ($40) luncheon is worth going for and in the evening there's a pre-theater menu served from 6 to 7 which offers a short selection of fine dishes like gravlax with sweet dill dressing to start, and chicken chasseur with chanterelles or roasted red mullet served with great rosti potatoes and vermouth cream to follow.

✪ **French House.** 49 Dean St., W1. ☎ **0171/437-2477.** Main courses £8–£12 ($12.80–$19.20). AE, DC, MC, V. Mon–Sat noon–3pm; Mon–Sat 6–11:15pm. Tube: Leicester Sq. or Piccadilly Circus. MODERN EUROPEAN.

A legendary hangout for such British artists and Soho bohemians as Francis Bacon and Lucien Freud. In this plain dining room over a popular pub, an eclectic modern British menu is served. The menu changes daily but you might find carrot and dill soup and a rabbit terrine and pickled prunes to start. Main dishes will always include a vegetarian dish like roast tomato, goat cheese, and olives. The spring chicken and aioli is simple but very tasty. Other options might be boiled ham with swelled mash, rabbit with mustard and shallots, or roast pigeon and celeriac bake. Desserts run to lemon tart and a delicious chocolate terrine. Oak paneling, polished wood floors, and brass gas-style lamps make up the decor.

Fung Shing. 15 Lisle St., WC2. ☎ **0171/437-1539.** Main courses £8–£15 ($12.80–$24). Set meals from £16 ($25.60). AE, DC, MC, V. Daily noon–11:30pm. Tube: Leicester Sq. CHINESE.

This is one of the best Cantonese restaurants in the city—not the cheapest, but worth the splurge. On the very extensive menu there are some extra-special specialties, like the braised fresh carp with ginger and spring onion, a couple of shark's fin soups, and stir-fried crispy pigeon. These are the more expensive items on a menu that also offers delicious barbecued spare ribs, prawns with chili and black bean sauce, and beef with cashew nuts. The least expensive set-price menu provides soup and three dishes plus rice. It's much more comfortable here than at most Chinatown restaurants, and the skylit room at the back is particularly appealing.

Gay Hussar. 2 Greek St., W1. ☎ **0171/437-0973.** Main courses £12–£16 ($19.20–$25.60); 3-course lunch £17.50 ($28). AE, DC, MC, V. Mon–Sat 12:15–2:30pm and 5:30–10:45pm. Tube: Tottenham Court Rd. EAST EUROPEAN.

A venerable Soho locale with red tufted banquettes along each side of the dining room. Books line the shelves above the small bar in the back, many written by the left-wing trendies who have dined here for years. The food is hearty with such main dishes as pork schnitzel cooked with smoked sausage, paprika, and tomatoes; veal goulash; or medallions of pork cooked with diced bacon, onions, potatoes, and green paprika. Strudel and pancakes—*turos palacinta* made with sweet cheese—are among the traditional desserts. At lunch you can dine on many of the same dishes for less thanks to the three-course set menu for £17.50 ($28).

Red Fort. 77 Dean St., W1. ☎ **0171/437-2525.** Main courses £9–£19 ($14.40–$30.40); £12.50 ($20) 2-course pre-theater menu; £10 buffet lunch. AE, DC, MC, V. Daily noon–2:45pm and 5:30–11:30pm. Tube: Leicester Sq. or Piccadilly Circus. INDIAN.

The decor at this restaurant is refreshingly different from that of the traditional Indian restaurant. The chairs are well upholstered with rich red cushions setting off the pink tablecloths. Here you can experience a true Indian treat rarely found on menus outside of India—pomfret marinated in caraway seeds and spiced yogurt, then roasted or spiced with whole red chili, coconut, and lemon juice. Among the main courses try the chicken in a hot green peppercorn curry flavored with saffron and fennel, or the Punjabi chicken dish cooked with black cardamon. The *Gosht Kodar*—lamb in a curry made with spices, tomatoes, onions, and mint—is also super, and so too is Kerala prawn curry. Of course, there are tandoori specialties and plenty of vegetable dishes, too. The pre-theater menu consists of a chicken or vegetable starter followed by a chicken or vegetable main course accompanied by vegetables, rice, and bread.

Vasco & Piero's Pavilion. 15 Poland Street, W1. ☎ **0171/437-8774.** Reservations recommended. Main courses £8.50–£14.50 ($13.60–$23.20) at lunch; 2-course dinner £14.95 ($23.90); 3 courses £17.50 ($28). AE, DC, MC, V. Mon–Fri noon–3pm and 6pm–1am. Once a month it's open Saturday with special menu. Tube: Oxford Circus/Tottenham Court Rd. ITALIAN.

This small, comfortable Italian restaurant attracts a business and sophisticated older crowd, who consider it their secret favorite hideaway—folks like Ken Livingstone, Sir Clement Freud, and Stephen Fry. The room is warmly decorated in peach, the seats plush, and the tables attractively set. And it's all assembled under some trompe l'oeil that creates a "tent" effect. The welcome is sincere and the Umbrian cuisine finely prepared. Dishes are light and fresh and unpretentious. The flavors come through whether it's tomato and basil in a tomato sauce or asparagus that has been perfectly cooked al dente. The set menus are great values, offering as they do more selections than most. Some dishes to try? Pappardelle with peppers and red onions, calves' liver and sage, grilled sea bass with fennel, grilled beef with rosemary and green peppercorns; and to finish, if it's available, the pancake filled with grapes, apple, and cream and served with Amaretto liqueur and crumbled biscotti.

YMing. 35–36 Greek St., W1. ☎ **0171/734-2721.** Main courses £6–£12 ($9.60–$19.20); set meals from £15 ($24); pre-theater menu served noon–6pm £10 ($16). AE, DC, MC, V. Mon–Sat noon–11:45pm. Tube: Leicester Sq. CHINESE.

Light and airy and decorated elegantly and comfortably in pink and jade, YMing offers excellent Northern-style Chinese cuisine. The quality of the duck, prawn, and lamb are exceptional, and I recommend choosing a dish that contains one of these ingredients. Start with the delicious prawns in chili and spice salt and follow with one of the wraps like the shredded duck with ginger. The sizzling dishes are among the most popular—prawns with fresh mango or lamb with fresh leek or with ginger and spring onion. The pre-theater menu includes a choice of appetizer (crispy won ton, spring roll, tofu, or aubergine in spiced salt) followed by a main course like grilled fish with chili or chicken in hot sesame sauce, plus dessert and coffee. The large tables are prettily set with tablecloths, and the service is smooth and nonintrusive.

WORTH A SPLURGE

Alastair Little. 49 Frith St., W1. ☎ **0171/734-5183.** Reservations essential. 3-course lunch £25 ($40); 3-course dinner £33 ($52.80). AE, MC, V. Mon–Fri noon–3pm; Mon–Sat 6–11:30pm. Tube: Leicester Sq./Piccadilly Circus. MODERN EUROPEAN.

A plain storefront with little ambience. Still, Mr. Little is one of the city's gifted chefs, and the local media types come for the food. The menu changes daily, but will always feature about seven or so main dishes, many of them inspired by Italy. Among the starters you might find oysters with spicy sausages and shallot relish, or terrine of wild duck and foie gras served with toast and French beans. Fish and meat dishes are the choice selections—a loin of pork roasted in milk, for example, or sea bass with parsley salad. Desserts are classics, like crème brûlée and chocolate torte with espresso ice cream. If you're a cheese lover, this is the place to order a selection of British cheeses.

Criterion Brasserie. 224 Piccadilly, W1. ☎ **0171/930-0488.** Reservations essential. Main courses £12–£15 ($19.20–$24); 2-course lunch £14.95 ($23.90); 3-course dinner between 6 and 6:30pm £17.95 ($28.70). AE, MC, V. Mon–Sat noon–2:30pm, Sun noon–4pm; Mon–Sat 6pm–midnight, Sun 6–10:30pm. Tube: Piccadilly Circus. FRENCH.

If you want to try Michelin three-star chef Marco Pierre White's food, then this is probably the most economical place to do so. While everyone else is abandoning classic French cuisine, he sticks to it religiously at all of his restaurants, including Quo Vadis (now decorated with assistance from Damien Hirst) and the Cafe Royal (featured in the recent Stephen Fry movie *Wilde*). White operates an empire of top restaurants in London, but some are more affordable than others and, surprisingly, this stunning theatrical room is one of them. A dinner at his Oak Room in the Meridien Hotel runs $125 per person, but here at the Criterion you can sample some of the same dishes at a fraction (albeit still high for our budget) of the price— the caramelized wing of skate with winkles, capers, and parsley for £13.75 ($22), for example. You can enjoy them here in an exotic Moorish atmosphere of mosaic and plush fabrics and drapes.

6 Covent Garden & The Strand

SUPER-CHEAP EATS

✪ **Café in the Crypt.** St.Martin-in-the-Fields, WC2. ☎ **0171/839-4342.** £1.75–£2.20 ($2.80–$3.50) rolls and sandwiches; £5.50–£6.10 ($8.80–$9.75) main dishes. Mon–Sat 10am–8pm, Sun noon–8pm. Tube: Charing Cross. CAFE/LIGHT FARE.

Set in the church's brick-vaulted crypt, this self-service cafeteria offers freshly pre-pared meals in a unique atmosphere. Choices range from rolls filled with ham and cheese to more substantial hot dishes like poached salmon with a lemon-lime butter, chicken supreme in a white wine and asparagus sauce, or spinach and nut roulade. The soups and salads are excellent. Among the dessert selections there might be apple crumble, or bread-and-butter pudding (bread soaked in eggs and milk with currants or sultanas and then oven-baked). A good stop for coffee and breakfast. All profits are donated to the work of the church.

Late-Night Eating

Unlike many other cities, London's late-night dining is extremely limited, primarily because the Underground shuts down. Some of the restaurants that stay open until midnight or after include **Bar Italia** (p. 127), **Big Easy** (p. 154), **Ed's Easy Diner** (p. 176), **O Fado** (p. 161), and **Pelican** (p. 144). **Vingt Quatre** (p. 155) is one of the few to remain open 24 hours.

Café San Martino. 57 St. Martin's Lane, WC2. (No phone). Sandwiches/main dishes 90p–£2.50 ($1.45–$4). Mon–Sat 11am–8pm. Tube: Charing Cross. CAFE/LIGHT FARE.

Office workers and others line up at this tiny Italian take-out place for the big variety of sandwiches or any of the hot dishes like gnocchi, lasagne, or jacket potatoes. It's an additional 20p to eat in.

Farmer Brown's. 4 New Row, WC2. ☎ **0171/240-0230.** Salads £4–£7 ($6.40–$11.20); sandwiches £1.50–£4 ($2.40–$6.40). Mon–Wed 7:30am–7:30pm, Thurs–Sat 7:30am–8:30pm. Tube: Covent Garden. LIGHT FARE.

An atmospheric deli-restaurant with salami and hams and other Italian delicacies suspended from the ceiling. All sorts of salads and sandwiches—such as smoked salmon—are available. Make your selection from the blackboard menu behind the counter and enjoy it seated on the banquettes at one of the polished wood tables.

Food for Thought. 31 Neal St., WC2. ☎ **0171/836-9072.** Main courses £3–£5.50 ($4.80–$8.80). No credit cards. Mon–Sat 9:30am–8:30pm, Sun noon–4pm. Tube: Covent Garden. VEGETARIAN.

This smoke-free restaurant offers good vegetarian food at great prices. The space is somewhat cramped, but the daily selections of salads, quiche, pies, stews, and stir-frys are worth stopping for. The menu changes daily, but there might be flavorsome wild mushrooms baked in a brandy sauce and served with polenta; or zucchini, red pepper, and mushroom quiche; or a shepherd's pie made with leeks, mushrooms, swede (rutabaga), turnips, carrots, and lentils. There's a good selection of healthful desserts, too, like banana and strawberry scrunch and fresh fruit. Feel free to bring your own wine. The decor is simple, with pine tables and fresh flowers and original art on the fresh whitewashed walls. Neal Street is across from the Covent Garden Underground.

Mille Feuille. 39 St. Martin's Lane, WC2. ☎ **0171/836-3035.** Main courses £2–£3.95 ($3.20–$6.30). Mon–Sat 11am–8pm. Tube: Charing Cross. CAFE/LIGHT FARE.

A small place with tables covered by lace cloths and glass tops. The display case in the back showcases the fresh salads and sandwiches—avocado and prawn, chicken tandoori, or smoked salmon, for example. The quiches, chili, and lasagne are tasty and filling. About 15 or so pastries are offered too, including a decent rendering of California carrot cake, several cheesecakes, and, naturally, mille feuilles.

Museum Street Cafe. 47 Museum St., WC1. ☎ **0171/405-3211.** Main courses £4.50–£6.50 ($7.20–$10.40). AE, MC, V. Mon–Fri 8am–6pm, Sat 9am–6pm, Sun noon–6pm. Tube: Holborn/Tottenham Court Rd. MODERN EUROPEAN.

This is a small, quiet, and very unassuming place where you can enjoy a decent, primarily vegetarian lunch (spinach and olive tart; frittata with asparagus, potatoes, and sorrel) or secure an afternoon tea consisting of scones, jam, and cream, plus fruit cake and shortbread, for £8 ($12.80). Or you can structure your own tea and just have scones and jam for £3.50 ($5.60), or a slice of Linzertorte or Valrhona chocolate cake for the same price. Breakfast and Sunday brunch are also popular.

At the latter you'll find such dishes as red pepper soup, and asparagus with fennel, parmesan, and lemon basil vinaigrette, plus banana pancakes and smoked salmon with scrambled eggs.

Neal's Yard Beach Café. 13 Neal's Yard, WC2. ☎ **0171/240-1168.** Main courses £4–£5.25 ($6.40–$8.40). No credit cards. Mon–Sat 9:30am–8pm, Sun 11am–7pm. Tube: Covent Garden. LIGHT FARE.

Brilliantly colored murals and palm fronds transport you to tropical climes at this ground-floor courtyard cafe. And so does the food—an array of salads and focaccia sandwiches, such as the one with smoked guacamole and *pane farcito,* filled with mozzarella, spinach, tomato, and avocado. They are large, healthful, and well-priced. Carrot, apple, celery, and other juices are available. Better-than-average ice cream, too.

Palms Pasta on the Piazza. 39 King St., WC2. ☎ **0171/240-2939.** Main courses £4.40–£8.50 ($7.05–$13.60); 2-course lunch £6.95 ($11.10); pre- and post-theater dinner menu £7.95 ($12.70). MC, V. Daily noon–midnight. Tube: Covent Garden. PASTA.

As the name suggests, this place affects a Mediterranean air with its trompe l'oeil painted greenery and lush fruit. The pasta is quite good and the sauces flavorsome and fresh. Try the penne arrabbiata, which has a spicy edge thanks to the chili.

✪ The Rock & Sole Plaice. 47 Endell St., WC2. ☎ **0171/836-3785.** Main courses £3.50–£9 ($5.60–$14.40). No credit cards. Mon–Sat 11:30am–10:30pm; Sun noon–9pm. Tube: Covent Garden. FISH & CHIPS.

A tarted-up fish-and-chips spot outfitted with wood tables, white-tiled walls, and lots of theater posters. The downstairs dining room has an underwater theme. Select from halibut, mackerel, tuna, haddock, plaice, cod, and many more. If you've never tried skate, then why not do so now—it's a moist, flaky fish with a wonderful flavor. And the Dover sole has to be the cheapest in town at £11 ($17.60). For non–fish eaters there's steak-and-kidney pie and several other pies, plus sausage in batter.

FOR A FEW POUNDS MORE

Bertorellis. 44A Floral St., WC2. ☎ **0171/836-3969.** Cafe main courses £6.95–£9.70 ($11.10–$15.50); £9.95 ($15.90) set menu from 12–3pm and 5:30–6:30pm. Restaurant main courses £10.90–£14.50 ($17.45–$23.20). AE, DC, MC, V. Mon and Sat noon–3pm; Mon–Sat 5:30–11:30pm. Tube: Covent Garden. ITALIAN.

Head to the cafe downstairs because the dining room upstairs is more expensive. It has an attractive modern ambience. The ceiling is mirrored, giving a sense of space; the walls are painted bright colors and are decorated with modern collages. Best of all, it offers great value in a stylish atmosphere. The two-course meal might offer a delicious salad of warm roasted peppers, aubergines, and artichokes dressed in a fine warm vinaigrette, to be followed by chicken on rosemary potatoes with wild mushrooms, spinach, and anchovy butter. It's a steal for the price. Otherwise, you can select from the pizzas and pasta dishes like tagliatelle carbonara with pancetta and fresh parmesan, or gnocchi baked with mushroom and artichokes in a walnut pesto. Among the *secundi piatti* are such dishes as salmon and horseradish fish cakes on spinach leaves; or sun-dried tomato polenta with eggplant and roasted peppers topped with smoked mozzarella. There's another Bertorelli's at 19–23 Charlotte St., W1 (☎ **0171/636-4174**), which has a spectacular ambience and serves similar terrific cuisine at slightly higher prices.

Grand Indian. 6 New Row, WC2. ☎ **0171/240-0785.** Main courses £4.70–£10.95 ($7.50–$17.50). AE, DC, MC, V. Daily noon–3pm, 5pm–midnight. Tube: Covent Garden. INDIAN.

This pleasant restaurant offers a wide variety of vegetable and meat dishes, from a very hot beef vindaloo and *rogan josh*, to chicken *jalfrezi, masala* and Madras, and subtle prawn *biryani.* Some of the more unusual dishes are called *aacher* and they are cooked with green dried mangoes, tomatoes, and a touch of ginger and garlic, which gives them a subtle sweet-and-sour flavor. I also recommend the King Prawn delight, which is cooked in a mild sauce of fresh cream, almonds, sultanas, and red wine.

Mon Plaisir. 21 Monmouth St., WC2. ☎ **0171/836-7243.** Main courses £8.60–£13.95 ($13.75–$22.30); 3-course set lunch £14.95 ($23.90); pre-theater menu including glass of wine served 5:45–7:15pm: 2 courses £10.95 ($17.50), 3 courses £13.95 ($22.30); 3-course set dinner including glass of wine £19.95 ($31.90). AE, DC, MC, V. Mon–Fri noon–2:15pm, Mon–Sat 6–11:15pm. Tube: Covent Garden/Leicester Sq. FRENCH.

For good value classics it's hard to beat this long-standing favorite. It offers well-prepared, reasonably priced dishes like poached halibut with Hollandaise, breast of duck with sesame and honey sauce, or sliced filet of beef with a full-flavored wine sauce. The evening set menu (for two only) is a good value. It might start with snails in garlic butter, follow with prime rib with bearnaise sauce, and finish with choux pastry filled with Chantilly cream and hot chocolate sauce. A four-course vegetarian menu is also offered for £18 ($28.80). Sitting in the brick-walled dining room decorated with burnished copper pans is indeed a pleasure.

La Perla. 28 Maiden Lane, WC2. ☎ **0171/240-7400.** Main courses £6.95–£12.95 ($11.10–$20.70). AE, MC, V. Mon–Sat noon–11:45pm, Sun noon–8:30pm. Tube: Charing Cross/Covent Garden. AMERICAS.

Island colors (terra-cotta, peach, and purple), island music, and island drinks make the scene here while flying swordfish trophies contribute to the overall tropical decor. The food is lackluster—prawn, chicken, or vegetarian fajitas with all the traditional trimmings, plus enchiladas, burritos, and such dishes as char-grilled lamb with a chile sauce.

But they do know how to make a real margarita (without a mix), using a range of about 30 different tequilas. Tropical refreshers including daiquiris and caipirinas are also available. Happy hour is from 5 to 7pm, when margaritas sell for £2.85 ($4.55). It attracts a young mixed crowd plus a few suits.

Porters English Restaurant. 17 Henrietta St., WC2. ☎ **0171/836-6466.** Main courses £7.95–£10.95 ($12.70–$17.50); 2-course set meal £16.50 ($26.40) for a pie plus starter or pudding, tea/coffee, and a half-bottle of wine. AE, DC, MC, V. Mon–Sat noon–11:30pm, Sun noon–10:30pm. Tube: Covent Garden. BRITISH.

Unless you really like English food, don't come to Porters. The selections run from pies and heritage dishes to traditional winter warmers like steak-and-kidney pudding, pork and herb sausage with mash and onion gravy, and English fish pie made with salmon, prawns, and cod in a parsley and dill cream sauce with a cheese and potato topping. You can conclude the meal with equally British horrors like spotted dick and bread-and-butter pudding, or more happily with sherry trifle. The atmosphere is publike, and the dining rooms are encrusted with signboards and other fake historiana.

Tuttons. 11–12 Russell St., WC2. At the corner of the piazza. ☎ **0171/836-4141.** Main courses £8.60–£12.90 ($14.10–$20.65); fixed-price 2-course meal £10.90 ($17.55) available at lunch, pre-theater until 6:30pm, and post-theater (after 10:30pm); snacks £3.20–£6.50 ($5.10–$10.40). AE, DC, MC, V. Sun–Thurs 9:30am–11:30pm, Fri–Sat 9:30am–midnight. Tube: Covent Garden. BRASSERIE.

A great and convenient brasserie for breakfast, lunch, afternoon tea, or dinner. The decor is "elegant cafe," with a tile floor and high ceilings; there's also an attractive conservatory looking out onto the piazza. Main courses run from avocado and crispy bacon salad with a honey mustard vinaigrette, to such English staples as Cumberland sausage with red onion marmalade and bubble and squeak (mashed potatoes with greens). Such classics as steak and French fries as well as grilled tuna with sweet chile salsa are also offered all day. The cafe menu offers such light items as salads and egg dishes, plus a variety of desserts, pastries, and ice creams.

MODERATELY PRICED CHOICES

Belgo Centraal. 50 Earlham St., WC2. ☎ **0171/813-2233.** Main courses £7.95–£17.50 ($12.70–$28); lunch £5 ($8) daily noon–5:30pm, or Belgo *complet* set lunch and dinner £12.95 ($20.70). AE, DC, MC, V. Mon–Sat noon–11:30pm, Sun noon–10:30pm. Tube: Covent Garden. BELGIAN/MODERN EUROPEAN.

Belgium comes to London at this casual fun dining spot. It brings the nation's most famous fare—*moules, frites,* and *bières*—and serves it family style in a cellar basement at long wooden tables. The servers are monks in hooded habits. The youthful student crowd that jams in here loves the scene and the food, but for those who don't like to shovel their food down at a hectic crazy pace, it's not so appealing. The mussels are served in kilo pots with frites and mayo for only £12 ($19.20). They are prepared in a variety of ways—with coconut cream and lemongrass; with tomato, herbs, and garlic; or in classic marinière. Sometimes the stock seems more abundant than the fruits of the sea, however. The platters are served open-faced also in a variety of ways for only £9 ($14.40). Other dishes are also offered, like the traditional *carbonnades flamande,* which is beef braised in sweet Gueuze beer with apples and plums and served with frites. The set lunch is a good buy, consisting of a choice of wild boar sausages served with Belgian mash and a beer, or two lighter dishes served with mineral water. The Belgo *complet* similarly offers a *salade liègeoise* followed by a kilo pot of *moules marinières* or Provençale, plus either a beer or ice cream.

For fun there's also a Beat the Clock menu that is served Monday to Friday from 5 to 6:30pm. The price of your meal will be determined by the time shown on your food order, that is, anywhere from £5 to £6.30. Three dishes—half a roast chicken, a kilo pot of *moules marinières,* and wild boar sausages—are available. Several of the desserts of course, are slathered with delicious Belgian chocolate sauce.

Christopher's. 18 Wellington St., WC2. ☎ **0171/240-4222.** Reservations recommended. Main courses £10–£25 ($16–$40); 2-course pre-theater meal £12.50 ($20); brunch £5–£13. AE, DC, MC, V. Mon–Fri noon–3pm, Sun noon–4pm, daily 6–11:45pm. Tube: Covent Garden. AMERICAS.

A dramatic decor created largely by the structure of the building itself is what sets this restaurant apart from others in the area. At the top of the stone staircase of this former bank building complete with painted ceiling and niches, you'll enter a long room with ornate stucco carving and a soaring ceiling. The menu is extensive and supplemented by specials. The cuisine is largely regional American. The classic steaks and grills are supplemented by such specials as blackened salmon with arugula; and meat loaf with Monterey mash, Madeira, and wild mushrooms. There's even Maryland crab cakes and Maine lobster served with drawn butter. The brunch menu is spiced up with dishes like huevos rancheros and a lobster club sandwich. Finish with a key lime pie or the bourbon mint julep chocolate brownie with bourbon ice cream. The pre-theater menu is a good value, offering four main-course choices.

L'Estaminet/La Tartine. 14 Garrick St., WC2. ☎ **0171/379-1432.** Main courses £9–£15.50 ($14.40–$24.80); pre-theater 3-course menu £10.99 ($17.60) 5:45–7:30pm; wine bar £6–£8 ($9.60–$12.80). AE, MC, V. Mon–Fri noon–2:30pm, Sat noon–2pm; Mon–Sat 6–11pm. Wine bar Mon–Fri noon–11pm. Tube: Leicester Sq. FRENCH.

The elegant, comfortable, French upstairs restaurant is beyond our price range except for its pre-theater menu, but in the small downstairs wine bar you can secure such classics as an omelet paysan, croque monsieur, bangers and mash, salads, cheese plates, and sandwiches.

♻ **Livebait.** 21 Wellington St., WC2. ☎ **0171/836-7161.** Main courses £13–£18 ($20.80–$28.80); 2-course set lunch £15 ($24); pre/post-theater 2-course set menu £15 ($24). MC, V. Mon–Sat noon–3:30pm, 5:30–11:30pm. Tube: Covent Garden. SEAFOOD.

At Livebait you can experience fish cookery with a difference. You won't find grilled or fried here. Instead, you'll find such tempting dishes as turbot in turmeric, lime leaves, ginger, and lemon grass with sweet potato; or pan-seared tuna with caponata and black olive tapenade. Try the wonderful baked cutlet of hake or the roasted whole John Dory. There's also a full raft of crustacea, including cockles, whelks, and winkles, so dear to a Londoner's heart, plus crab from Dorset and oysters from Whitstable. The decor is far plainer than the food, and some people find it too reminiscent of a public convenience, with its ceramic tile, glass block, and mono-chromatic color scheme.

Pelican. 45 St. Martin's Lane, WC2. ☎ **0171/379-0309.** Main courses £10–£16 ($16–$25.60); 2-course fixed price £10.95 ($17.50). AE, MC. Mon–Sat 11am–midnight, Sun noon–10pm. Tube: Leicester Sq./Charing Cross. FRENCH/CONTINENTAL.

A very French brasserie with a long bar and cafe-style chairs. The menu features typical bistro dishes like *boeuf bordelaise,* steak au poivre, and confit of duck. Vegetarians will appreciate the *gratin de poireaux, celeriac, et pleurottes*—layers of oyster mushrooms, celeriac, and leeks, gratinéed and served with a tomato basil coulis. One of the better and more appealing spots (with its charming Gallic air) to secure a casual, good-tasting meal.

♻ **Plummers.** 33 King St., WC2. ☎ **0171/240-2534.** Set menus 1-course £8.90 ($14.25); 2-course £12.90 ($20.65); 3-course £16.90 ($27.05). Special lunch and pre-theater 2-course menu £9.90 ($15.85). AE, DC, MC, V. Mon–Fri noon–2:30pm; Mon–Sat 5:30–11:30pm; Sun noon–2:30pm and 6–10pm. Tube: Covent Garden or Leicester Sq. BRITISH.

A comfortable restaurant that is definitely worth a splurge. It's one of the few quiet retreats to be found in the Covent Garden area. Start with an apple-and-Stilton soup or the terrine of smoked salmon and turkey. The casserole dishes are excellent, such as lamb cooked with cider, honey, apricots, and rosemary; or the chicken breast cooked with butterbeans, tomatoes, chili, garlic, and white wine. Fish, too, is available, such as poached salmon and fish pie filled with smoked haddock, tuna, mussels, salmon, and onions with a white wine sauce and potato topping. Finish with a chocolate Grand Marnier mousse or the poached pears with orange and black currant sauce. The decor is calming—gray chairs, gray chintz wallpaper, and English prints hung on the walls.

Rules. 35 Maiden Lane, WC2. ☎ **0171/836-5314.** Reservations essential. Main courses £13.95–£15.95 ($22.30–$25.50); pre-theater Mon–Fri 3–6pm 2-course menu £15.95 ($25.50) and Sat–Sun 2-course lunch £17.95 ($28.70). AE, DC, MC, V. Tube: Charing Cross/Covent Garden. BRITISH.

It's been around for 200 years and likely to be around in another 200, or so it seems. This wonderful ultra-British restaurant, where certain wines are listed under Wines from the Former Colonies (and surprisingly they're not French; after all, they did own Bordeaux at one time), still offers a unique atmosphere and some terrific English dishes, particularly game. The pre-theater menu is a great deal because you can select anything from the menu. Start with such classics as Stilton-and-walnut tart with pear chutney or Morecambe Bay potted shrimps. Select one of the game dishes—the wild highland red deer with spiced red cabbage, blueberries, and bitter chocolate sauce is quite something; or you may prefer a fish or more familiar meat dish like the steak, kidney, and oyster pudding, which is loaded with the major ingredients, as it should be. Classic British desserts like sticky toffee pudding and treacle sponge are leavened by such dishes as caramelized vanilla and banana tart accompanied by banana ice cream. So comfortable are the banquettes and so historic the sense of place that you'll want to linger here awhile, much as did earlier literary and theatrical figures, including Lily Langtry and Edward VII, who trysted here.

Simpson's in the Strand. 100 The Strand, WC2. ☎ **0171/836-9112.** Main courses £12.50–£22.50 ($20–$36); set breakfast £12.95 ($20.70) or £14.95 ($23.90); 2-course set menu £13 ($20.80); 3-course menu £17.50 ($28), served at lunch and 5:30–7pm; Sunday 3-course menu £19.50 ($31.20) and £10.50 ($16.80) for children under 12. AE, DC, MC, V. Mon–Fri 7–11am; daily noon–2:30pm; Mon–Sat 5:30–11pm and Sun 6–9pm. Tube: Charing Cross. BRITISH.

If you want to experience classic, stylish, old-fashioned British dining, then you can't do better than ensconce yourself in this oak-paneled room and watch the joint trolleys being rolled by waiters turned out in coat and tails. It's expensive at dinner, but it's perfect for breakfast and worth considering at other times when set menus are offered. The Great British Breakfast starts with a bowl of porridge, cereal, or stewed fruit and follows with a plate filled with Simpson's sausage, scrambled eggs, streaky and back bacon (American and Canadian bacon), black pudding, grilled mushrooms, and tomato. Fresh juice, coffee, toast, and pastries are the accompaniments. Another £2 ($3.20) will bring such additions to the spread as lamb kidneys, deadly but delicious fried bread, bubble and squeak (mashed fried potatoes with greens), baked beans, and lamb's liver. The two- or three-course set lunch and early-bird dinner offer a selection of three or so main dishes like cod with parsley sauce or duck leg with duck livers and rosemary, plus starters that might include chicken wings with leeks and creamed Stilton sauce, and such puddings as plum and almond crumble. The Sunday meal features six or so main courses, including the traditional Simpson's favorites—roast beef with Yorkshire pudding and horseradish sauce, or roast saddle of lamb with redcurrant jelly. Start with the potted shrimps or the delicious smoked trout pâté wrapped in smoked salmon with a yogurt and dill sauce. Puddings are as traditional as ever too. You won't forget the sticky toffee and date pudding with butterscotch sauce or the bakewell tart with a vanilla sauce.

Sofra. 36 Tavistock St., WC2. ☎ **0171/240-3773.** Main courses £6.25–£16.60 ($10–$26.55) with most under £9 ($14.40); set lunch £9.95 ($15.90), set dinner £10.95 ($17.50). AE, DC, MC, V. Daily 12pm–12am. Tube: Covent Garden. TURKISH.

If you're searching for some reasonably priced cuisine served in a pleasant atmosphere, then head for Sofra. Although the cuisine isn't as spicy as you might expect or like, it's decent, moderately priced, and attractively presented. Essentially the cuisine is Greek with a twist. The menu is extraordinarily long. You could make a meal from the starters, which range from hummus and *taramasalata* to vegetarian moussaka and fried squid or mussels. The main courses are mainly meat or fish dishes that have been grilled over charcoal—chicken, lamb with oregano—or casseroles like the lamb fillets with onion, green pepper, tomatoes, mushroom, and oregano that have been wrapped in foil and then baked to retain the juices and the flavors. There are also vegetarian and steamed fish dishes. The set menu consists of 11 hot and cold mezes, or appetizers, and represents good value.

Other locations are: 1 St. Christopher's Place, W1 (☎ **0171/224-4080**); 18 Shepherd St., W1 (☎ **0171/493-3320**); and 17 Charing Cross Rd., WC2 (☎ **0171/930-6090**).

7 The City

SUPER-CHEAP EATS

Aladin. 132 Brick Lane, E1. ☎ **0171/247-8210.** Main courses £2.95–£6 ($4.70–$9.60). No credit cards. Sun–Thurs noon–11:30pm, Fri–Sat noon–midnight. Tube: Aldgate East. INDIAN.

This is one of the best choices along this street of Bangladeshi joints. The portions are large, the prices excellent, and the quality adequate for everything from curries to tandoori dishes. The current favorites are the Balti dishes, which are prepared in a cast iron pot or Balti. Bring your own wine, and don't focus on the plain decor and synthetic pine tables.

Corney & Barrow Wine Bar. 2b East Cheap, EC3. ☎ **0171/929-3220.** Sandwiches/snacks £2.70–£3.75 ($4.40–$6). Mon–Fri 11am–11pm. AE, DC, MC, V. Tube: Mansion House. WINE BAR.

One of the popular chains of city wine bars frequented by suits. Brick vaults and round tables combined with modern Milan-style chairs set the tone of this eclectic underground haven. Celebrate with a large glass of champagne or one of more than 40 wines available by the glass (£2.60–£10—$4.15–$16). The list is drawn from all over the world, from Australia and New Zealand to Chile, the United States, France, and Italy. The food is secondary, consisting of a selection of traditional sandwiches, plus finger-food dishes like breaded chicken breast with bacon and tomato dip, or prawn in ginger and garlic crumbs served with a sweet-and-sour sauce.

✪ **The Place Below at St. Mary Le Bow.** Cheapside, EC2. ☎ **0171/329-0789.** Main courses £5.95–£6.95 ($9.50–$11.10). No credit cards. Mon–Fri 7:30am–2:30pm. Tube: St. Paul's. VEGETARIAN.

This atmospheric, self-service cafe situated in the Norman crypt offers fine vegetarian cuisine. The menu changes daily, but you'll always find a hot dish of the day like the delicious aubergine and almond filo pie, and a quiche. When I was last there the quiche was especially full of flavor, combining the tartness of Stilton with the earthiness of field mushrooms. Salads are also always available, and you can finish off with the chocolate cake inspired by California's own Alice Waters. Takeout is available at slightly lower prices. No smoking.

FOR A FEW POUNDS MORE

Bow Wine Vaults. 10 Bow, EC4. ☎ **0171/248-1121.** Main courses £7–£9 ($11.20–$14.40). Mon–Fri noon–3pm. Tube: Mansion House/Bank. BRITISH/WINE BAR.

Located along a very attractive historic city pedestrian passageway, this is the place to enjoy some traditional but good English food. Pork and leek sausage and mash; liver and bacon; and steak with shallot, Worcester, and parsley sauce are just some of the delights on the menu. And the dessert menu continues the retro mood with treacle pudding and bread-and-butter pudding for died-in-the-English-wool folk. The atmosphere, though, is light and airy and distinctly upbeat.

Restaurants in & Around the City

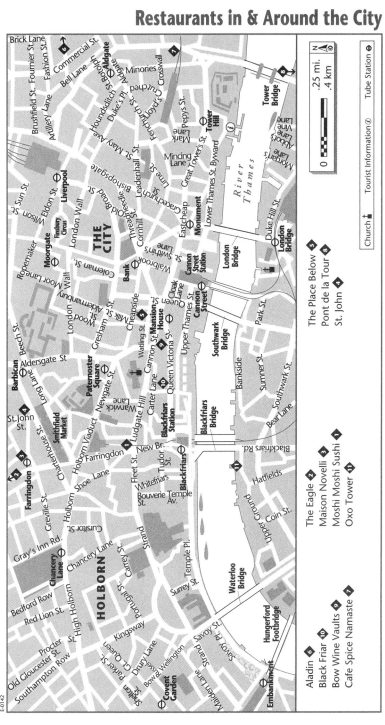

Tube Station ⊖

Tourist Information ⓘ

Church ✠

0   .4 km
    .25 mi.

N

The Place Below ⑤
Pont de la Tour ⑧
St. John ④

The Eagle ②
Maison Novelli ③
Moshi Moshi Sushi ①
Oxo Tower ⑪

Aladin ⑥
Black Friar ⑩
Bow Wine Vaults ⑨
Cafe Spice Namaste ⑦

E-0142

147

✪ **Cafe Spice Namaste.** 16 Prescot St., E1. ☎ **0171/488-9242.** Main courses £7.95–£10.50 ($12.70–$16.80). AE, DC, MC, V. Mon–Fri noon–3pm and 6:15–10:30pm, Sat 6:30–10pm. Tube: Aldgate/Tower Hill. INDIAN.

The Indian cuisine at this wonderful restaurant is some of the finest you will find in London, and that is saying something. Each dish has been subtly flavored with individually melded spices and herbs and is accompanied by superlative breads and chutneys. You'll find regional dishes from Goa, Hyderabad, Madras, and North India, plus some Parsee specialties. Begin with the tiger prawns tossed in hot sweet-and-sour *patia* and served on crisply fried poories. To follow, there are so many revelations—the *galinha xacutti*, a chicken curry which comprises more than 21 ingredients which are first roasted and then ground with browned onions and coconut; or the Goan prawn curry flavored with red chilies, garlic, cumin, and coriander in a coconut base. Finish with traditional *kulfis* or the house specialty, which is Parsee apricot toffee ice cream made with sun-dried Indian apricots, which have an intensely sweet flavor. The decor is equally extra-ordinary. Occupying a soaring space that once served as a court room, it has been decorated in brilliant colorful style. Walls are painted intense golds and blues and the arched doorways have been painted in a striped Alhambra style. The windows are draped also in purple and gold or magenta. A sumptuous revelation.

✪ **The Eagle.** 159 Farringdon Rd., EC1. ☎ **0171/837-1353.** Main courses £8–£11 ($12.80–$17.60). No credit cards. Mon–Sat 12:30–3:30pm and 6:30–10:30pm; Sun 12:30–4pm. Tube: Farringdon. PUB/MEDITERRANEAN.

Celebrated for its food, this pub, which is more like a cafe-restaurant than a traditional pub, is packed at lunch. The fresh ingredients are displayed in baskets at the bar. Always on hand is a hearty soup. A variety of Mediterranean-flavored delights come out of the kitchen, like the well-flavored *tagliata* (rare beef salad—rib eye steak combined with potatoes, capers, tarragon, rocket [arugula], and balsamic vinegar) or the grilled swordfish enhanced by the sweet-flavored salad of cauliflower, red onions, saffron, mint, pine nuts, raisins, and olive oil. A three-course meal can be had for £12 ($19.20) or less. About 14 wines are available by the glass from Chile, Spain, South Africa, and Italy.

✪ **Moshi Moshi Sushi.** 7–8 Limeburner Lane, EC4. ☎ **0171/248-1808.** Sushi 90p–£3.70 ($1.45–$5.90); lunch boxes £4.50–£8 ($7.20–$12.80). MC, V. Mon–Fri 11:30am–9pm. Tube: St.Paul's. SUSHI.

Super-fresh sushi with a London twist is found at this popular spot. At lunchtime, people converge around the large modern sushi bar to enjoy the fine lunch boxes filled with *nigiri* or *maki*. You can also order à la carte. All the traditional selections are offered, from California roll, tuna, salmon, octopus, and mackerel. Note though, that cockles add a distinct London flavor. Among the extraordinary range of vegetarian choices you'll find eggplant, asparagus, olive paste, and sun-dried tomato rolls. Some definitely work better than others.

A MODERATELY PRICED CHOICE

St. John. 26 St.John St., EC1. ☎ **0171/251-0848.** Reservations recommended. Main courses £9.60–£16 ($15.35–$25.60). AE, DC, MC, V. Mon–Fri noon–3pm; Mon–Sat 6–11:30pm. Tube: Farringdon. MODERN BRITISH.

This Smithfield venue concentrates on meat—and organ meats at that. Considered great delicacies by many gourmets, they are not for everyone. If you want to experiment, one of the best dishes to try is the oxtail with beans and the poached (would you believe) chicken. Other options might include duck leg and beetroot, kid fennel and aioli. To start there are winkles, langoustines, and grilled razor clams along with a skate and anchovy salad. Vegetables are additional.

WORTH A SPLURGE

Maison Novelli. 29 Clerkenwell Green, EC1. ☎ **0171/251-6606.** Reservations recommended. Main courses £15–£24.50 ($24–$39.20). AE, DC, MC, V. Mon–Fri noon–3:30; Mon–Thurs 6:30–11:15pm, Fri–Sat 6:30–midnight. Tube: Farringdon. FRENCH.

You can expect to enjoy a memorable meal at this, the most expensive and lavish of Jean-Christophe Novelli's restaurants. The cuisine is innovative, intensely flavored, and the fish dishes are miraculous. To start, try the brochette of salmon and scallop served on a warm citrus-infused couscous with oils of carrot, orange, cardamom, and coriander. Any one of the main fish dishes will be extraordinary, whether roast sea bass with chorizo oil, sun-dried tomato, eggplant, caviar, and picholine olives; or baked turbot with red pepper crust served with truffle-infused mash and red pepper oil. The meat is also extraordinarily good, like the filet with Parmesan crackling and cepe powder with soft wild mushroom polenta. Brilliant flavor combinations inform the desserts too. Try the plum tatin and Sambuca ice cream or the hot and cold, dark and white chocolate plate.

Nearby at Novelli EC1, 31 Clerkenwell Green EC 1, ☎ **0171/251-6606,** a more modest but still fresh and superbly prepared menu is priced from £9.50–£16 ($15.20–$25.60).

Oxo Tower. Oxo Tower Wharf, Barge House St, SE1. ☎ **0171/803-3888.** Reservations recommended. Restaurant, 3-course lunch £24.50 ($39.20); dinner main courses £12–£22 ($19.20–$35.20); brasserie main courses £10.50–£15 ($16.80–$24); brasserie pre-theater menu Mon–Sat 5:30–6:45pm, 2 courses £18.50 ($29.60) and 3 courses £21.50 ($34.40). Brasserie Mon–Sat 11am-11:30pm, Sun 11am–10:30pm; restaurant Mon–Fri noon–2:15, Sun noon–3:15pm; Mon–Sat 6–11pm and Sun 6:30–10:30pm. Tube: Blackfriars. MODERN EUROPEAN.

Grand panoramic views of the City and the River are offered from the huge terrace. Inside the dining room the revolving ceiling changes dramatically from white to blue at dusk. The most affordable menu offers a choice of four main dishes and a selection of five or so appetizers. For example, you might start with pappardelle with clams, mussel, lemon and garlic, cherry tomatoes, and arugula and follow with seared tuna with pancetta pesto and red wine jus, or roast rib of beef with sun-dried tomato and leek dauphinoise chive butter and Madeira jus. Close with a coconut and almond tart with vanilla sauce or some extremely fine ice cream. The other menus are really beyond our price range, but they will deliver a broader selection of similarly fine cuisine.

Le Pont de la Tour. Butler's Wharf, 36D Shad Thames, SE1. ☎ **0171/403-8403.** Reservations essential. 3-course lunch Mon–Fri £28.50 ($45.60); dinner main courses £16.50–£23.50 ($26.40–$37.60); pre/post-theater menu from 6–6:45pm and 10:30–11:30pm £19.50 ($31.20). Mon–Fri and Sun noon–3pm; Mon–Sat 6–11:30pm, Sun 6–11pm. Tube: Tower Hill/London Bridge. MODERN EUROPEAN.

This is the star in Conran's empire that Tony Blair chose to take Bill and Hillary too on one of their visits to London in 1998. It has a super romantic riverside location by Tower Bridge. The choice dining place is the hedge-lined terrace, which is more casual than the chic and lean dining room. The complex includes a restaurant, bar, and grill, plus a food and wine store and a bakery. The best deal is the pre- and post-theater menu which features a fish, meat, and poultry dish, like a pan-fried escalope of salmon with a shellfish bouillabaisse, or roast rump of lamb with ratatouille. You might start with an asparagus risotto and finish with chocolate marquise with roast pears and a hazelnut crust.

8 Mayfair

FOR A FEW POUNDS MORE

Browns. 47 Maddox St., W1. ☎ **0171/491-4565.** Sandwiches and main courses £6.95–£13.95 ($11.10–$22.30). AE, DC, MC, V. Mon–Sat noon–10pm. Tube: Oxford Circus. BRASSERIE.

One of a small chain of bar-restaurants occupying historic buildings that offer stylish surroundings, good value for money, and menus broad enough to satisfy everyone. This particular wood-paneled, skylit, and mirrored version affords comfort and decent food which ranges from pastas, salads, and sandwiches to such varied main courses as steak, mushroom, and Guinness pie; slow pot roasted gigot of lamb with flageolet beans; and baked cod with salsa verde. It offers a happy hour between 5 and 7pm when beer is £2 ($3.20) and spirits £3.95 ($6.30).

Also at 82 St. Martins Lane, Covent Garden, WC2 (☎ **0171/497-5050**), and 114 Draycott Ave., Chelsea SW3 (☎ **0171/584-5359**).

MODERATELY PRICED CHOICES

Dover Street Wine Bar. 8–9 Dover St., W1 ☎ **0171/629-9813.** Main courses £9.95–£15.95 ($15.90–$25.50). AE, MC, V. Mon–Fri noon–3pm; Mon–Thurs 5:30pm–2am, Fri–Sat 8pm–2am. Tube: Green Park/Piccadilly Circus. WINE BAR.

This is a serious party spot in Mayfair at which you can dine and dance and enjoy some decent food while partying with the business and celebrity set 'til the wee hours. The fare ranges from a simple ratatouille en croute (eggplant, mushrooms, squash, red peppers, cheese, and herbs in a pastry case) to saddle of venison on a bed of shallots and wild mushrooms in a port wine sauce. The music (live jazz, soul, and blues, plus DJs) starts at 10pm.

Fountain/Patio at Fortnum & Mason. 181 Piccadilly, W1. ☎ **0171/734-8040.** Main courses £7.50–£14.95 ($12–$23.90). AE, DC, MC, V. Daily 8:30–8pm. Tube: Green Park/Piccadilly Circus. CAFE/LIGHT FARE.

This famous cafe is mobbed at tea time but it's still a good place to come for breakfast when you can enjoy a full English breakfast served in style all day for £10.95 ($17.50). At lunch and early dinner it serves a limited menu featuring such dishes as steak-and-kidney pie along with Welsh Rarebit made tasty with the addition of Guinness stout and either back bacon or poached egg. There are salads and seafood too.

Gaucho Grill. 19 Swallow St., W1 ☎ **0171/734-4040.** Main courses £7.50–£17 ($12–$27.20). AE, DC, MC, V. Mon–Fri noon–3pm, Mon–Fri 5–11:30pm; Sat noon–midnight, Sun noon–10:30pm. Tube: Piccadilly Circus. AMERICAS.

Obviously meat is what this restaurant is all about and it satisfies any and all meat lovers who try the marbled Argentinean beef served here. The main features are the rump, sirloin, filet, and rib eye Argentinean steaks (223 gm/8 oz. or 300 gm/10oz.), which you can enjoy plain or with pepper, garlic, béarnaise, or mushroom sauce. Of course, there are some other dishes, like grilled lamb and calves' liver, plus vegetable couscous and a salmon steak, but meat is the real deal. Start with chorizos or empanadas. The decor, like the food, is old-fashioned with plenty of leather and brass. You'll find the restaurant downstairs in a barrel-vaulted basement.

Momo. 25 Heddon St., W1. ☎ **0171/434-4040.** Reservations essential. Main courses £8–£12 ($12.80–$19.20). 2-course lunch £12.50 ($20); 3 courses £15.50 ($24.80). AE, DC, MC, V. Mon–Fri 12:30–3pm; Mon–Sat 7–11pm. Tube: Piccadilly Circus. MIDDLE EASTERN/NORTH AFRICAN.

Momo is lavishly exotic and very fashionable ever since Madonna threw a bash here. Beaded curtains add a casbah mystique and so do the glowing lanterns that cast patterns on the stucco walls. The rich and romantic ambience is intensified by the use of elaborate sensual fabrics. The wait staff is also splendidly costumed. The North African dishes are delicate and inspired. Start with the paper-thin pastries filled with prawns and mushrooms or with chicken and saffron. *Tagines*—which are cooked in a clay pot and imbued with the flavor of a mix of sweet and spiced vegetables, are the main focus of the menu. They are cooked for a long time, resulting in tender meats and rich deep flavors. Try the tagine made with chicken, dates, and almonds, or the duck with apples, cinnamon, almonds, and orange blossom. Couscous and meat and fish dishes are also available. To finish, the salad of oranges with cinnamon and orange blossom water is wonderfully refreshing. The trendy bar downstairs is members only.

Veeraswamy. 99–101 Regent St., W1. ☎ **0171/734-1401.** Reservations recommended. Main courses £8.75–£13.50 ($14–$21.60); lunch and pre/post-theater menu 2 courses £12 ($19.20), 3 courses £14.75 ($23.60); Sunday special menu £15 ($24). AE, DC, MC, V. Mon–Fri noon–2:30pm, Sat 12:30–3pm, Sun noon–3pm; Mon–Sat 5:30–11pm and Sun 6–10pm. Tube: Piccadilly Circus. INDIAN.

This restaurant will surely prove the most extraordinary Indian restaurant you have ever encountered, at least as far as looks and style are concerned. It's vibrant, contemporary, and decorated in bright purples and saffrons—gold, orange, and yellow. Accents include frosted glass panels and some carved Indian wood pieces. Tables, chairs, and stools are ultra-modern. It is, in fact, one of the oldest Indian restaurants in London, having been established in 1926 by a general and an Indian princess. Over the years it has been frequented by princes and potentates, from the Prince of Wales to King Hussein and Indira Gandhi.

Today it still offers superb cuisine. Spices are prepared freshly for each dish. The menu offers about five each of southern Indian specialties and Northern dishes plus some grills, roasts, and vegetarian dishes. Try the *karwari* red fish curry made with kingfish, poppy seeds, and red chilies; or the delicious Malabar prawn curry with fresh turmeric and raw mango. For a Northern choice, the chicken curry flavored with almonds, cinnamon, cardamom, and green chilies is subtle and rich. To start, the stir-fried oysters with coconut and kerala spices are sublime.

9 Knightsbridge & Belgravia

SUPER-CHEAP EATS

Veg. 8. Egerton Gardens Mews, SW3. ☎ **0171/584-7007.** Main courses £4.50–£6.50 ($7.20–$10.40). No credit cards. Daily noon–2:30pm; Mon–Sat 6–11:15pm, Sun 6–11pm. Tube: Knightsbridge/South Kensington. SZECHUAN/VEGETARIAN.

Vegetarians will love this restaurant tucked away downstairs in a mews behind Knightsbridge only a few blocks from Harrods. The crispy duck is rendered here with beancurd and served in pancakes with hoisin sauce. A rendition of sesame prawns is made with mashed taro root. Other dishes, all made with vegetarian ingredients, include a lovely tofu flavored with ginger, onion, and soy sauce; broccoli in oyster sauce; and a meatlike *dow see* beef made with soy chuck, as it's called, flavored with ginger, onion, and soy sauce, and served with black bean sauce all topped with onions, chilies, and green and red pepper.

FOR A FEW POUNDS MORE

Le Metro. 28 Basil St., SW3. ☎ **0171/589-6286.** Main courses £7–£8.10 ($11.20–$12.95). MC, V. Mon–Sat 7:30am–10:30pm. Tube: Knightsbridge. FRENCH.

Where to Get That Good, Old-Fashioned Pub Grub

Pub fare can vary from snacks at the bar to a complete meal, but it's usually cheap, good, and filling. Most pubs offer food, and as there are so many pubs in the city, if you don't like what you see in one, you can always move on to the next. Don't hesitate to take a look at the food before purchasing—it's usually displayed under glass. When it's not, ask the bartender for a menu. Popular items include Scotch eggs (a hard-boiled egg surrounded by sausage meat and encased in bread crumbs), bangers and mash (sausages and mashed potatoes), meat pies (especially during colder months), and a ploughman's lunch (bread, cheese, salad, and pickles). Wash it all down with a beer.

The best pubs make their own dishes and keep the food hot on hotplates. Others offer only factory-made pasties (meat-filled pastry) and microwave them on demand. Note that food and drink are ordered and paid for separately. A good pub lunch will run from £4.50 to £7 ($6.40 to $11.20), and careful ordering can cut that amount almost in half.

Many popular pubs are listed in chapter 9. Pubs known especially for their food include **The Australian,** 29 Milner St., Chelsea, SW3 (☎ **0171/589-6027**), which has traditional but decent food; **The Black Friar,** 174 Queen Victoria St., EC4 (☎ **0171/236-5650**), near the Blackfriars Underground in The City, which has a terrace and also some fine art nouveau tilework; The Chapel, Chapel Street, NW1 (☎ **0171/402-9220**), just off the Edgware Rd., which serves some really good new pub food; ✪ **De Hems,** 11 Macclesfield St., W1 (☎ **0171/437-2494**), in Soho's Chinatown for its Dutch specialties; **The Eagle,** 159 Farringdon Rd., EC1 (☎ **0171/837-1353**), for new-wave pub food; **The Engineer,** 65 Gloucester Ave., NW1 (☎ **0171/722-0950**), in Chalk Farm; **The Lamb and Flag,** 33 Rose St., WC2 (☎ **0171/497-9504**), by Covent Garden Market; and **The Sun,** 63 Lamb's Conduit St., WC1 (☎ **0171/405-8278**), between Russell Square and Holborn Underground stations.

Around the corner from Harrods, this stylish subterranean wine bar consistently offers fresh food at reasonable prices. In fact it's one of the best wine bars in the city. The cuisine ranges from pasta dishes such as penne with king prawns, tomato, and chili, to a good beef onion and Madeira pie or baked halibut with lemon butter. Finish with a succulent treacle tart that only the English can love. This is also a good place to enjoy an afternoon tea of sandwiches, scone with jam and cream, and cakes for only £5.50 ($8.80). An added bonus are the more than 50 wines available by the glass.

Pasta Prego. 1A Beauchamp Place, SW3. ☎ **0171/225-1064.** Main courses £7–£8 ($11.20–$12.80); set lunch including soup or salad, pasta, and a glass of wine £8.50 ($13.60). AE, MC, V. Daily noon–3pm; Mon–Sat 6–11pm and Sun 6–10:30pm. Tube: Knightsbridge/South Kensington. PASTA.

This restaurant is so small that you can easily pass it by. It's a good place to retire after window shopping Harrods or Beauchamp Place; you can join the elegant suits and ladies who lunch. It's stylish and comfortable in an unassuming way. Breuer chairs are placed at tables set with white cloths. The pastas are well prepared and range from a rich lasagne to *paglie e fieno* and *amatriciana*.

Pizza on the Park. 11 Knightsbridge SW1. ☎ **0171/235-5273.** Main courses £6–£10 ($9.60–$16). AE, DC, MC, V. Mon–Sat 8:15am–midnight; Sun 9:15am–midnight. Tube: Hyde Park Corner. PIZZA.

This is an extra luxurious pizza restaurant that is also one of the hottest jazz spots in London. It occupies a large, high-ceilinged room featuring dramatic pillars and a mixture of smooth woods on floor and walls. The tables are elegantly set with tablecloths and fresh sprigs of flowers, and the waiters sport bow ties. The pizzas are as good as any in town. Just try the one with thinly sliced wild Scottish smoked salmon. The Music Room downstairs here is also one of London's top jazz spots featuring such singers as Annie Ross. A jazz brunch is served Sunday.

MODERATELY PRICED CHOICES

Brasserie St. Quentin. 243 Brompton Rd. SW3. ☎ **0171/589-8005.** Main courses £10.25–£17.50 ($16.40–$28). 2-course set lunch £13.50 ($21.60), 3 courses £16.50 ($26.40). AE, DC, MC, V. Daily noon–3pm and 6–11pm. Tube: Knightsbridge/S. Kensington. FRENCH.

Chandeliers, etched mirrors, and banquette seating provide all the hallmarks of a Paris brasserie, and indeed many French expats take refuge at this quintessentially French dining room. It offers a blend of classic and updated French fare featuring such dishes as grilled calves' liver with caramelized shallots and creamed potatoes, and roast rack of lamb with a rosemary sauce. The grilled tuna comes with tomato and pepper salsa, but there's also a wonderful skate with capers accompanied by Lyonnaise potatoes (fried with onions).

Ebury Wine Bar. 139 Ebury St., SW1. ☎ **0171/730-5447.** Main courses £9–£16 ($14.40–$25.60). AE, DC, MC, V. Mon–Sat 11am–11pm; Sun 11am–10pm. Tube: Sloane Sq. WINE BAR.

The Ebury, a stone's throw from Victoria Station, is an appealing wine bar which is very popular at lunch with executives from nearby investment banks. The food is well prepared, whether it's calves' liver with red currants and capers, seared salmon with mirin and soy, or lamb and pancetta meat loaf with Greek salad. Steaks are always available. Every Sunday at lunch a traditional roast is served.

Fifth Floor Cafe. Harvey Nichols, Knightsbridge, SW1. ☎ **017/235-5250.** Main courses £11–£18 ($17.60–$28.80); 2-course lunch £15.50 ($24.80), 3 courses £18.50 ($29.60). AE, DC, MC, V. Mon–Sat 10am–11pm, Sun 10am–6pm. Tube: Knightsbridge. CAFE/LIGHT FARE.

This is a buzzy place. It's glitzy and modern and offers a skylit cafe area, a revolving sushi bar, and a horseshoe bar where at lunchtime you can secure a sandwich like hot salt beef (£7 to £8.50; $11.20 to $13.60). The furnishings include sculptured "Swiss cheese" chairs in blue, red, and yellow arranged on a sleek teak floor. Among the favorite cafe dishes are native oysters served with grilled sausages; gambas fried with garlic, chili, and sherry; and grilled steak topped with Roquefort. For dessert try the bread-and-butter pudding or the raspberries and crème fraîche. Adjacent to the cafe, there's a gourmet food shopping area where the shelves are stocked with chutneys, preserves, pasta, and more. This is one place to put together a picnic. The cheese counter offers an array of British cheeses with wonderful names like Oxford blue, Lincolnshire poacher, and Lord of the Hundred that you've probably never encountered before. Deli meats are also offered. The pastry counter blossoms with brilliant-looking chocolate-glazed and other doughnuts, plus cheesecakes and much more.

WORTH A SPLURGE

✪ **Vong.** Berkeley Hotel, Wilton Place, SW1. ☎ **0171/235-1010.** Reservations essential. Main courses £12.75–£ 26.75 ($20.40–$42.80); black plate lunch £15 ($24), 2-course lunch £16.50 ($26.40), 3-course lunch £20 ($32); black plate menu pre/post-theater £17.50 ($28). Mon–Sat noon–2:30pm and 6–11:30pm; Sun 6–10pm. Tube: Green Park/ Knightsbridge. PACIFIC RIM.

This is the London outpost of Jean-Georges Vongerichten. Chic and streamlined, the multi-tiered room drops down from the reception area. It is super-modern with a flash of brilliant orange-mandarin used as a decorative element and such wonderful accents as gorgeous single-stem orchids. The cuisine is superb, a brilliant combination of Asian flavors and western produce. In every dish the flavors come through and the style of cooking enhances the basic ingredients perfectly—for example, the salmon, which is offered in a tomato galangal broth; or the tamarind-flavored duck breast served with sesame sauce. The desserts are similarly delicious Asian-Western inspired creations like the warm Valrhona chocolate cake accompanied by lemongrass ice cream or the raspberries in crisp rice crepes accompanied by coconut ice cream sorbet. The most affordable option is the Black Plate lunch, which will allow you to try the five heavenly (and most popular) appetizers—crab spring roll with tamarind dipping sauce, prawn satay with fresh oyster sauce, lobster daikon roll with rosemary ginger dip, tuna and vegetables wrapped in rice paper, and quail rubbed with Thai spices and served with a cress salad. Seafood lovers can skip the quail and enjoy instead salmon slices in a scallion pancake with green peppercorns, while vegetarians can also substitute a different selection.

10 Chelsea & South Kensington

SUPER-CHEAP EATS

Big Easy. 332–34 King's Rd., SW3. ☎ **0171/352-4071.** Main courses £6–£10 ($9.60–$16), £16–£20 ($25.60–$32) for steaks. AE, MC, V. Mon–Sat noon–11pm, Sun noon–10:30pm. Tube: Sloane Sq. AMERICAN.

Another retreat for homesick Americans. Business cards line the walls and paper lies over the wooden tables. The fare is typically American—burgers, barbecue ribs, crab claws, and serious steaks. Note the two-for-one happy hour.

Chelsea Kitchen. 98 Kings Rd., SW3. ☎ **0171/589-1330.** Main courses £2.25–£4 ($3.60–$6.40); set meals from £3 ($4.80). No credit cards. Mon–Sat 8am–11:45pm, Sun 10am–11:45pm. Tube: Sloane Sq. DINER/COFFEE SHOP.

The British version of a coffee shop. The wide menu offers everything from spaghetti bolognese, to braised lamb chops and goulash. The usual diner fare like omelets, burgers, and salads are served, too. Polished wood tables and booths make up the decor.

Henry J Beans Bar & Grill. 195–7 Kings Rd., SW3. ☎ **0171/352-9255.** Main courses £6.25–£7.25 ($10–$11.60). AE, DC, MC, V. Mon–Sat 11:45am–11pm; Sun noon–10:30pm. Tube: Sloane Sq. AMERICAN.

If you're a homesick American, then this is one place to visit. Festooned with commercial signs, it offers chili dogs, nachos, a variety of burgers, and all those other familiar fast-food favorites.

✪ **Le Shop.** 329 Kings Rd., SW3. ☎ **0171/352-3891.** Main courses £4–£8 ($6.40–$12.80). AE, MC, V. Daily noon–midnight. Tube: Sloane Sq. CREPERIE.

Galettes (Britanny pancakes made from wholemeal buckwheat flour) are the specialty here. These can be filled with ham, cheese, and spinach; chicken and asparagus; and prawn and ratatouille, which are some of the recommended combinations. Or you can create your own from a list of nearly 30 ingredients. Sweet fillings can be had, too, like the luscious flamed brandy, rum, kirsch, Grand Marnier, and calvados version. Round wooden tables, brick walls, and poster art make for a pleasant atmosphere.

Vingt Quatre. 325 Fulham Rd. SW10. ☎ **0171/376-7224.** Main courses £4–£9 ($6.40–$14.40). AE, MC, V. Open 24 hours. Tube: Gloucester Rd./Fulham Broadway. CAFE/LIGHT FARE.

This is one of the few places in London that stays open 24 hours, gathering a series of different crowds around the clock. Seated on the avant-garde chairs with their Swiss cheese holes, customers eat off the shining aluminum tables. You can secure breakfast, sandwiches, salads, and more substantial dishes.

FOR A FEW POUNDS MORE

La Bersagliera. 372 Kings Rd., SW3. ☎ **0171/352-5993.** Main courses £6.10–£13.50 (£9.75–£21.60); £4.90–£8.50 ($7.85–$13.60) for pasta; £5.10–£6.40 ($8.15–$10.24) for pizza. MC, V. Mon–Sat noon–3pm and 7pm–midnight. Tube: Sloane Sq. ITALIAN.

Murals of Italy, marble-topped tables, and rush-seat gateback chairs create an Italian atmosphere. The dishes range from steak pizzaiola made extra-piquant by the use of capers, to veal in marsala finished off with artichoke hearts. All the favorite pasta dishes are available (cannelloni, lasagne, spaghetti carbonara). Daily specials are offered, too.

Bluebird Cafe. 350 King's Rd., SW3. ☎ **0171/559-1000.** Tube: Sloane Sq./South Kensington. CAFE/LIGHT FARE.

Another Conran creation, incorporating a restaurant, cafe, food market, and wine shop, this is a good place to stop and put together a picnic or to relax outside at one of the cafe tables on this quiet oval courtyard. Inside there's a modern bar and round glass tables. The adjacent food store displays splendid salads, cheeses, deli items, pickles, breads, and pastries, all you need to put together a personal hamper and take it down to Cheyne Walk or the riverfront.

Busabong Tree. 112 Cheyne Walk, SW10. ☎ **0171/352-7534.** Main courses £4.95–£11.95 ($7.90–$19.10); set lunch £9.95 ($15.90); set menus from £22.25 ($35.60). AE, MC, V. Mon–Sat noon–3pm, 6–11:30pm. Tube: Sloane Sq. THAI.

This is a very appealing Thai restaurant. The room welcomes diners with its lush greenery and handful of graceful statues. The tables are nicely set with pale blue cloths, and the cane-seated chairs are equally elegant. The menu is very extensive, featuring a full range of Thai/Chinese meat, fish, poultry, vegetarian, rice, and noodle dishes. I suggest that you take the opportunity to try some of the more unusual specialties, like the braised monkfish in ginger sauce or the drunken lamb stir-fried with peppercorns, soy sauce, sake, garlic, and a little sesame oil. There's also a good roast duck red curry with pineapple, tomatoes, and holy basil, and delicious prawns in roasted chili paste. The set lunch menu is a good deal because it allows you to choose any dish up to £7.95 ($12.70), which includes 80% of the menu and adds two spring rolls or satay or chicken lemongrass soup.

Cafe Lazeez. 93–95 Old Brompton Rd., SW7. ☎ **0171/581-9993.** Main courses £6.95–£14.50 ($11.10–$23.20); 8-course buffet Sunday lunch. AE, DC, MC, V. Mon–Sat 11am–1am, Sun 11am–10:30pm. Tube: South Kensington. INDIAN.

In summer people like to hang out in the large outdoor dining area framed by flower boxes. Tiles and fabric-swathed chairs set the tone in the minimalist bar/brasserie on the ground floor, while the upstairs dining room has more

Restaurants from Knightsbridge to Earl's Court

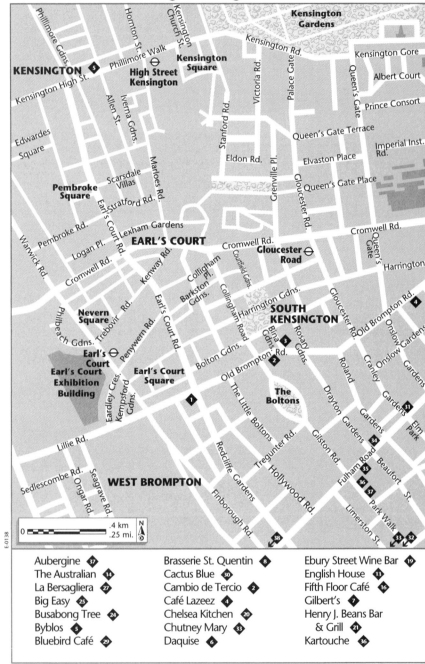

Aubergine	37	Brasserie St. Quentin	8	Ebury Street Wine Bar	19
The Australian	14	Cactus Blue	30	English House	13
La Bersagliera	27	Cambio de Tercio	2	Fifth Floor Café	16
Big Easy	25	Café Lazeez	4	Gilbert's	7
Busabong Tree	24	Chelsea Kitchen	20	Henry J. Beans Bar	
Byblos	5	Chutney Mary	33	& Grill	21
Bluebird Café	29	Daquise	6	Kartouche	36

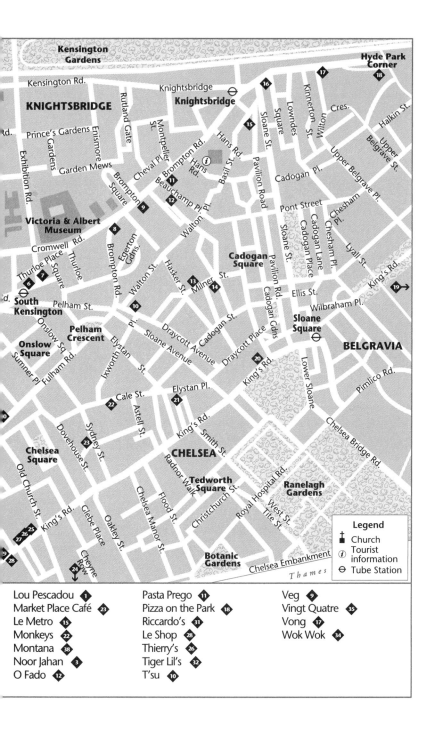

Restaurant		Restaurant		Restaurant	
Lou Pescadou	**1**	Pasta Prego	**11**	Veg	**9**
Market Place Café	**23**	Pizza on the Park	**18**	Vingt Quatre	**35**
Le Metro	**15**	Riccardo's	**31**	Vong	**17**
Monkeys	**22**	Le Shop	**28**	Wok Wok	**34**
Montana	**38**	Thierry's	**26**		
Noor Jahan	**3**	Tiger Lil's	**32**		
O Fado	**12**	T'su	**10**		

157

serene elegance. This is another of London's new wave Indian restaurants which offer fine Indian cuisine in a chic but casual atmosphere. The cuisine mixes such traditional dishes as lamb or chicken *korma* and red mullet *masala* with what Cafe Lazeez labels "evolved" dishes: such intensely flavored items as tuna in a sauce of onions, tomatoes, ginger, cinnamon, cloves, and black cardamom; and *pista* lamb, which has been marinated in a mixture of yogurt, lemon juice, saffron, and pistachio nuts. Puddings are a mixture of British favorites plus Indian rice pudding and mango-, almond-, or pistachio-flavored *kulfi*. There's jazz usually on Wednesday, Friday, and Saturday.

Another branch is located at 88 St. John St, Clerkenwell, EC1 (☎ **0171/ 253-2224**).

Daquise. 20 Thurloe St., SW7. ☎ **0171/589-6117.** Main courses £5.50–£12.50 ($8.80– $20); 2-course set lunch Mon–Fri £6.80 ($10.90). MC, V. Daily 11:30am–11pm. Tube: South Kensington. POLISH.

Daquise is a good budget standby that's been here keeping its clients happy for many years. It's very convenient for the major South Ken museums and is one of those old-fashioned places where you can linger for a while without being hustled out the door. The Polish food is hearty—stuffed cabbage, stuffed pepper, stews, pork knuckle with horseradish sauce, and kielbasa. A variety of Polish vodkas and beers is also served. Oilcloths cover the tables. On the wall, a picture of horses on the steppe evokes memories of Eastern Europe.

✪ The Market Place Restaurant. Chelsea Farmer's Market, 125 Sydney St., SW3. ☎ **0171/352-5600.** Main courses £7.50–£10.50 ($11.60–$16.30); 3-course barbecue £15 ($24). MC, V. Summer, daily 9:30am–5:30pm and 7pm–midnight; winter Tues– Sun 11am–3pm and 6pm–midnight. Tube: South Kensington or Sloane Sq. Bus: 11. MEDITER-RANEAN/ BARBECUE.

A great spot at the center of the Chelsea Farmer's Market. Here in summer you can sit outside at the wrought-iron tables in a patiolike setting and enjoy a unique (for London) three-course, all-you-can-eat barbecue hot off the coals. You'll start with a Mediterranean platter, follow with a trip or trips to the salad bar, and finish with a selection of super-tangy barbecue dishes—chops, ribs, steak, and Boer *ewors* (spicy South African sausage). This popular spot also offers a varied lunch menu of sandwiches and light fare like chicken on a baguette, and bacon, lettuce, and tomato sandwiches.

Noor Jahan. 2A Bina Gardens, SW5. ☎ **0171/373-6522.** Main courses £6.20–£12.90 ($9.90–$20.65); set menu £18.50 ($29.60). MC, V. Daily noon–2:30pm, Mon–Sat 6:30–11:30pm; Sun 6:30–11pm. Tube: South Kensington. INDIAN.

The tables are somewhat close together at this handsome restaurant, which features cloth-covered tables and banquettes. Chicken *dansak* and chicken *jalfrazi*, plus king prawns tandoori and heart warming *rogan josh*, are just some of the fine traditional dishes that are well rendered and served here in comfortable surroundings.

Riccardo's. 126 Fulham Rd., SW3. ☎ **0171/370-6656.** Main courses £3.95–£7.95 ($6.30–$12.70). AE, DC, MC, V. Daily 11:30am–3pm and 6pm–midnight. Tube: South Kensington. ITALIAN.

The most appealing aspect of this rather typical Italian restaurant is the glassed-in garden area. It caters to locals, offering a long menu consisting solely of Italian starters. Select two or three and you have a meal. You could start with the hearty Tuscan bean and cabbage soup and follow it with a chicken salad with roasted peppers, zucchini, and balsamic dressing; or Scottish salmon with pesto sauce; or prawns with garlic, lemon, rosemary, and chili.

T'su. 118 Draycott Ave., SW3. ☎ **0171/584-5522.** Sushi £2.75–£4.50 ($4.40–$7.20). AE, MC, V. Mon–Sat noon–11pm; Sun noon–10pm. South Kensington. JAPANESE/SUSHI.

This super-modern place with sleek wood-backed stools has a revolving sushi bar that brings everything from grilled fish *maki* and tuna sushi to a wonderful smoked salmon and avocado *maki.* More traditional dishes like teriyaki chicken are offered occasionally as specials. The price is determined by the color of the plates you select.

Wok Wok. 140 Fulham Rd., SW10. ☎ **0171/370-5355.** Main courses £6–£10 ($9.60–$16). AE, DC, MC, V. Mon–Fri noon–3pm; Mon–Thurs 6–11pm; Fri 6pm–midnight; Sat noon–midnight; Sun noon–10:30pm. Tube: South Kensington. PACIFIC RIM.

This popular place occupies a spare, modern, large space that has been painted in strong dramatic colors. Here at pedestal Formica tables you can enjoy some hot spicy food which draws on a variety of traditions, from Thai and Vietnamese, to Malaysian and Indonesian. You'll find the bowls of green vegetable curry or Malaysian king prawn curry very satisfying. So too are the *udon* noodles in broth with prawns, fish, chicken, squid, egg, and shiitake mushrooms.

MODERATELY PRICED CHOICES

Cactus Blue. 86 Fulham Rd., SW3. ☎ **0171/823-7858.** Main courses £10–£14 ($16–$22.40). AE, MC, V. Mon–Fri 5:30–11:45pm; Sat–Sun noon–4pm and 5:30–11:45pm. Tube: South Kensington. AMERICAN SOUTHWEST.

As you'd expect, this place has all the icons of the American Southwest—dhurrie-upholstered banquettes; copper tables, chairs, and bar; and large portraits of Native American leaders plus the usual complement of cactus. The food is far superior to that of most other similar American Southwest/Mexican ventures in London. Before you savor such dishes as char-grilled salmon with ancho chile and jalapeño creme, or chicken with barbecue glaze and ancho chile cornbread, try the avocado and lime vichyssoise or the tiger prawns tostaditas with chipotle honey mustard glaze. The tequila-cured wild salmon with potato flour tortilla, crème fraîche, and black caviar is also super-special. Happy hour goes from 5:30 to 7:30pm, when cocktails are £3.50 ($5.60) and bottled beer £2 ($3.20). Enjoy your pick from 40-plus tequilas.

Cambio de Tercio. 163 Old Brompton Rd. SW5. ☎ **0171/244-8970.** Main courses £8.50–£15 ($13.60–$24). AE, MC, V. Daily 12:30–2:30pm; Mon–Sat 7–11:30pm, Sun 7–11pm. Tube: South Kensington. SPANISH.

A small storefront restaurant that has been decorated in a rich yellow. Against this backdrop, tables spread with damask cloths are combined with chairs also swathed in burgundy fabric. Minimal decoration includes a matador's cloak and swords, plus one or two pieces of art. The Spanish cuisine is well prepared and full of flavor. The pig plays a major role, as suggested by the severed leg and trotter placed in the window. The most expensive appetizer is a plate of Jabugo ham derived from acorn-fed black pig. If you don't like ham, there are plenty of other seafood tapas and salads, like the griddled king prawns with sea salt and garlic lemon. Among the dozen main courses, the suckling pig Segovia style stands out, and so does the Basque-inspired poached eggs accompanied by grilled asparagus with Basque wine mousseline and sauteed foie gras. The filet of beef with Rioja jus and roasted piquillo peppers is soul satisfying.

Chutney Mary. 535 King's Rd., SW10. ☎ **0171/351-3113.** Reservations recommended. Main courses £9–£15.50 ($14.40–$24.80); £12.50 ($20) for 2-course lunch and also after 10pm. Sunday brunch 2 courses £13.95 ($22.30), 3 courses £16 ($25.60). Tube: Fulham Broadway. INDIAN.

An elegant Indian restaurant decorated in the Raj style with rattan chairs, lush floral tablecloths, and old prints of India. Potted tropical plants grace the large and comfortable upfront bar lounge. It draws a stylish crowd who enjoy the fine, carefully prepared Indian cuisine. Don't expect the vast menu of a standard curry house. The regional specialties prepared here are spectacular blends of spices and fresh authentic ingredients. This is one place to discover how sublime Indian food can really be. Try one of the regional specialties like the green chicken curry from Goa, which is flavored with a perfectly balanced combination of fresh coriander, green chili, mint, and tamarind. Each dish is a revelation, from the Syrian-Christian specialty roast duck curry made with coconut, pepper, tamarind, and chili, to the Hyderabad butterfly prawn curry with braised onion, tomato, and coconut milk. There are several vegetarian selections and some Anglo-Indian specialties like prawn kedgeree, a prawn stew topped with almonds, raisins, and crispy fried onions. The Sunday jazz brunch draws a stylish crowd who dine on many of the same dishes that are on the lunch/dinner menus.

Gilbert's. 2 Exhibition Road, SW7. ☎ **0171/589-8947.** Main courses £10.50–£16 ($16.80–$25.60). Set lunch and also 6:30–7:30pm 1-course meal £5 ($8); 2-course £7.75 ($12.40), 3-course £10.50 ($16.80). Tube: South Kensington. BISTRO.

A small bistro decked out in modern colors and style. Banquettes are combined with pine tables and set against mustard-yellow walls that are graced with large pictures. It's a decent place for a light meal. The set lunch, which changes weekly, is limited to a choice between soup of the day and deep fried mozzarella sticks to start, vegetable curry or poached salmon salad as a main course, and caramelized blackberries with vanilla ice cream or treacle tart for dessert. Five or so main courses are offered at dinner, always including a vegetarian choice. The food is typical bistro fare—breast of chicken with a lime and ginger sauce, or oregano and lemon marinated lamb cutlets in a coriander sauce. Finish with lemon tart set off well by a blackcurrant coulis, or the banana pancake with Muscat-marinated strawberries. There's a few tables outside too.

Kartouche. 329–331 Fulham Rd., SW10. ☎ **0171/823-3515.** Main courses £9–£13.20 ($14.40–$21.10); Mon–Fri 2-course lunch £11.50 ($18.40); 3-course lunch £14.50 ($23.20). AE, MC, V. Mon–Fri noon–3pm, Sat–Sun noon–3:30pm; Mon–Sat 6–11:45pm, Sun 6–10:45pm. Tube: South Kensington and Bus 14 toward Fulham. INTERNATIONAL.

The sexy fashion photographs add a frisson to this dining room's look, which already has a certain style with its antique red walls, tile floors, and rich blue decor. The cuisine is eclectic, drawing on many different traditions, modern and otherwise. For example, you could enjoy pea and ham soup as well as a herring and potato terrine with watercress dressing as appetizers. Among the main dishes, the poached cod is served with a red wine jus and artichoke mash, while the wood pigeon comes with celeriac, mushroom, and garlic, and the chump of pork with black pudding and apples. This around-the-world approach, though, does make the cuisine somewhat hit or miss with dishes often blander than you might like. The brunch menu ranges from pancakes with strawberries and cream and scrambled eggs with smoked salmon, to Thai fish cakes with sweet chili sauce and roast beef with Yorkshire pudding.

Lou Pescadou. 241 Old Brompton Rd., SW5. ☎ **0171/370-1057.** Main courses £10.80–£13.40 ($17.30–$21.45); 3-course lunch menu £9.90 ($15.85). AE, DC, MC, V. Daily noon–3pm and 7pm–midnight. Tube: Earl's Court. SEAFOOD.

You can't miss the porthole-style window in the facade of this fish restaurant. The marine theme is extended into the dining room. Scallop ashtrays and blue tablecloths grace the tables, and marine pictures hang on the walls. The floors are tile and there's an occasional decorative accent like a model boat. The main focus of the menu is obviously seafood—St. Peter's fish poached with tomato and basil, or turbot with capers, or salmon braised with vegetables and tomatoes. The meats are cooked in classical French style—steak with pepper or shallot sauce and chicken grilled with lemon. The set-lunch menu offers a starter like gazpacho followed by a choice of two main courses and two desserts. It's old-fashioned, but somehow comforting even if the prices are on the high side.

Montana. 125–129 Dawes Rd., SW6. ☎ **0171/385-9500.** Main courses £10–£14 ($16–$22.40); 2-course lunch on Friday £12.50 ($20). AE, MC, V. Mon–Thurs 6–11pm, Fri–Sat noon–midnight, Sun noon–10:30pm. Tube: Fulham Broadway. AMERICAS.

Rather off the beaten track but worth seeking out for the American Southwestern food, Montana occupies a large storefront that has been painted with antiqued, mustard-colored walls and a magenta ceiling. Tiny spotlights light the space filled with tables set with white tablecloths and coupled with modern-style chairs. A portrait of Crazy Horse surveys the scene. This is not your burrito and mush-style hash joint. Instead you will be served tamales with wild mushroom and chive and pasilla butter or with spinach and blue cheese. Fish dishes are equally inspired and innovative. For example, the Yucatán halibut will arrive fleshily moist in a green serrano broth with roasted poblano and peppers, while a grilled swordfish will be accompanied by chickpea stew and chipotle caramelized shallot and roasted corn salsa.

O Fado. 49–50 Beauchamp Place, SW3. ☎ **0171/589-3002.** Main courses £7.90–£12.80 ($12.65–$20.50). AE, MC, V. Daily noon–3pm; Mon–Sat 6:30pm–12:30am, Sun 6:30–11:30pm. Tube: Knightsbridge or South Kensington. PORTUGUESE.

If you choose a meat dish rather than fish, you can dine here on a modest budget. Tables covered with white cloths are paired with bentwood chairs for comfortable dining. Try the pork escalopes in a wine sauce; liver and onions; or breast of chicken in a mushroom sauce. For a real Portuguese treat, splurge on one of the sun-cured cod dishes like the one cooked with tomato, peppers, and clams, or the barbecued version. Fado, of course, is the traditional hauntingly soulful song of Portugal. These songs are performed at dinner accompanied by 12-string Portuguese guitars.

Thierry's. 342 King's Rd., SW3. ☎ **0171/352-3365.** Main courses £9–£19 ($14.40–$27.20). AE, DC, V. Mon–Sat 12:30–3:45pm and 7–10:45pm; Sun 12:30–3pm and 7–10:15pm. Tube: Sloane Sq. FRENCH.

Dark burgundy walls, gilt-framed pictures and posters, and wood tables make an elegant atmosphere at Thierry's. The cuisine is classic French bistro—*entrecôte bordelaise, coq au vin,* and beef bourguignon. At lunch there's a selection of hors d'oeuvres specially priced at £3 ($4.80) and main courses at £7 ($11.20). This menu changes weekly, but you might find such dishes as pan-fried cod with a garlic and herb crust prepared in a beurre blanc, or roasted chicken with polenta and fried sage. A special menu at dinner offers similar main courses for £8.50 ($13.60) and hors d'oeuvres for £3.50 ($5.60). These are excellent value. Has a good, reasonably priced French wine list.

Tiger Lil's. 500 King's Rd., SW10. ☎ **0171/376-5003.** Main courses £11 ($17.60). MC, V. Mon–Fri noon–3pm and 6pm–midnight; Sat noon–midnight, Sun noon–11pm. Happy hour Mon–Fri 5:30–7pm. Tube: Fulham Broadway/Sloane Sq. ASIAN.

A popular, fun restaurant that takes a modern approach to dining and delivers the kind of casual, good, and reasonably priced interactive food experience that many folks are looking for. The rice is delivered to your table, but you take the responsibility for selecting the ingredients for your meal and then the chefs cook it in their woks. There's a broad selection of ingredients: mussels, spare ribs, pork, chicken, beef, turkey, tofu, bok choy, and loads of other vegetables. You then select the seasonings—garlic, chili, or ginger—and the sauce. The sauces are all traditional Asian mixtures like teriyaki, satay, oyster, sweet and sour, plus a truly hot selection that blends galangal, lemongrass, and chili. Needless to say it helps to know what goes with what. You can eat as much as you like. It attracts a lively young crowd who also come for the happy hour on weekdays between 5:30 and 7pm when cocktails like Long Island spiced tea and mango margarita are two for one.

Other branches at 11–12 Russell St., WC2, ☎ **0171/240-3228;** 270 Upper St., N1, ☎ **0171/226-1118.**

WORTH A SPLURGE

✪ **Aubergine.** 11 Park Walk, SW10. ☎ **0171/352-3449.** Reservations essential. 3-course lunch £25 ($40); 3-course dinner £50 ($80); 6-course dinner £65 ($104). AE, DC, MC, V. Mon–Fri 12:15–2:30pm; Mon–Sat 7–10:30pm. Tube: Sloane Sq., then bus 11, 19, or 22. FRENCH/MODERN EUROPEAN.

Luxury makes its appearance here from the minute you enter the small bar-reception area with its plush couches. Beyond the grand floral bouquet the dining room is a study in creme deluxe. Tables boast fine settings and the chairs are beautifully and comfortably upholstered. And then there is the food, courtesy of Gordon Ramsay. The most affordable is the lunch menu, which offers two set menus, one with a fish main course and the other with a meat. For example, on this particular day you could have enjoyed a meal of *cappuccino de langoustines* and lentils followed by *jarret* of braised beef with a St. Emilion sauce, and finished off with either assorted cheese or passion fruit parfait with a chocolate sorbet. The other menu offered a terrine of foie gras and compote of figs as an appetizer, a main course of roast *lotte* in a *veloute* of *petits pois*, and a dessert of crème brûlée with the juice of Granny Smith apples, or assorted cheeses. Either one would have provided some great and very satisfying cuisine worth the price. Just think what inspired dishes you might be able to select from the seven or so starters at dinner—sauteed foie gras served on caramelized endives with a Sauternes sauce, or ravioli of lobster poached in lobster bisque and served with basil purée and confit tomatoes. Or from the eight main courses, which might feature a fillet of turbot poached in red wine and served with a St. Emilion sauce along with creamed leeks, baby spinach, and puréed potatoes, or an intensely flavored *ballottine* of Bresse chicken cooked in its own stock and served with a morel sauce. As for the desserts, what can you say about apricot souffle served with a bitter chocolate sorbet, or a pineapple tarte tatin with vanilla ice cream—just sublime.

The English House. 3 Milner St., SW3. ☎ **0171/584-3002.** Reservations recommended. Main courses £14.50–£17 ($22.40–$27.20); set lunch Mon–Fri 1 course £8.75 ($14), £12.25 ($19.60), £15.75 ($25.20); 3-course set lunch Sun £15.75 ($25.20). AE, DC, MC, V. Daily 12:30–2:30pm; Mon–Sat 7:30–11:30pm, Sun 7:30–10pm. Tube: South Kensington or Sloane Sq. BRITISH.

Set on a beautiful residential street in Chelsea, the English House upholds the fine traditions of English food and service. Many of the dishes have been adapted for 20th-century palates from 18th-century recipes. There are several intimate dining rooms, each furnished with antique pieces and fresh flowers. As a fire roars in the hearth on cold days, patrons are treated to beautifully prepared dishes, served by an expert staff. Even though the tables are close together, it's still a romantic dining spot. Menus change seasonally. Start with the full-flavored pea and ham soup, or crab cakes served with crab and whiskey sauce. Among the seven or so main courses you'll always find a vegetarian choice, like the braised endive with flageolet bean casserole. The other dishes will offer a good balance between fish (baked halibut with roasted spring vegetable and lemon pesto dressing), meat (say, roast rack of lamb with a sweet potato galette), and poultry (like roast Barbary duck breast with honeyed figs). The restaurant is also famous for such traditional English desserts as sticky toffee pudding with butterscotch sauce and steamed apple pudding with apple brandy custard. A traditional three-course English lunch is served Sundays.

Monkeys. 1 Cale St. at Markham, SW3. ☎ **0171/352-4711.** Reservations recommended. 5-course lunch £20 ($32) or £30 ($48); 5-course dinner £25 ($40) or £35 ($56). Tube: Sloane Sq. MODERN BRITISH.

A charmer. It's located in a tiny oasis of quiet in a venerable building that seems to list to one side. The dining rooms sport rich warm walnut paneling, which is decorated with pictures and mirrors. Tables are set with blue cloths and white overlays, and the whole place has an air of warmth, comfort, and hospitality. It offers two limited menus at different price levels. The more expensive offers one or two more appetizers and one more main course and features more expensive ingredients—filet steak compared to rump, sea bass compared to cod. On the £25 ($40) menu you might start with home potted shrimps and follow with baked fillet of cod with herbs and bread crumbs with a bearnaise sauce, or braised guinea fowl with muscat and grapes. On the £35 ($56) menu there might be hot foie gras salad, lobster ravioli, and dressed crab, which you can follow with sautéed sea scallops and ginger, or rack of lamb diable. The conclusion to either brings a sorbet and selection of puddings, or cheese plus coffee and petits fours. A great value and a chance to enjoy a romantic evening of quiet intimate conversation.

11 Kensington, Notting Hill & Bayswater

SUPER-CHEAP EATS

Byblos. 262 Kensington High St., W8. ☎ **0171/603-4422.** Set menus from £7.50–£10 ($11.60–$15.50); main courses £7.85–£10 ($12.55–$16). AE, DC, MC, V. Daily noon–11:30 pm. Tube: High St. or Kensington. LEBANESE.

You could select several cold and hot mezes—*sambouesek* (fried pastry with lamb and pine kernels), *labneh* (the soft Lebanese cream cheese), or the traditional hummus, falafel, or tabbouleh, and enjoy a satisfying meal for around £10 ($16). Or you can enjoy a heartier meal featuring any one of the kebab dishes or a great bowl of couscous.

Kalamaras Micro. 66 Inverness Mews, W2. ☎ **0171/727-5082.** Main courses £7–£11 ($11.20–$17.60). MC, V. Mon–Fri noon–2:30pm, 5:30pm–midnight. Tube: Bayswater. GREEK.

Authentic, competently prepared Greek cuisine is served in this traditional taverna, where the whitewashed walls are adorned with rugs and other Greek objets d'arts. The menu features close to 30 meze dishes, including salt cod and filo stuffed with lamb and spinach. The real specialties, though, are the fish dishes.

Mandola Cafe. 139–141 Westbourne Grove, W11. ☎ **0171/229-4734.** Main courses £4.95–£6.95 ($7.90–$11.10). No credit cards. Mon–Sat noon–11pm, Sun noon–10:30pm. Tube: Notting Hill Gate. AFRICAN/SUDANESE.

A Sudanese outpost. The food is simple and the menu short. You might select peanut and lentil to start and follow with a salad made with eggplant or with cabbage and peanuts. There are plenty of vegetarian dishes, including a lentil stew, a falafel dish, and fish with mixed vegetables in tomato. Many of the meat dishes are served in a spicy tomato sauce except for the lamb stew with *molokia*, which is a Sudanese vegetable similar to spinach.

FOR A FEW POUNDS MORE

Books for Cooks. 4 Blenheim Crescent, W11. ☎ **0171/221-1992.** Main courses are £6 ($9.60). AE, DC, MC, V. Mon–Fri 12:30–2:30pm; Sat sittings at noon and 1:45pm. Tube: Ladbroke Grove/Notting Hill Gate. CAFE/ECLECTIC.

This delightful store also has a little cafe in the back where, on a daily basis, different young professional chefs offer fresh light fare. You'll find great soups like herbed zucchini with mascarpone and salads like asparagus with couscous and a warm dressing. Main courses are typically chicken seasoned and flavored with spices and herbs and served with accompaniments like sweet potato. Desserts often have a distinct English flair, like the lemon and elderflower tart with cape gooseberries. Note it's BYOB.

☻ **Inaho.** 4 Hereford Rd., W2. ☎ **0171/221-8495.** Main courses £6.50–£13 ($10.40–$20.80). MC, V. Mon–Fri 12:30–2:30pm; Mon–Sat 7–11pm. Tube: Bayswater/Notting Hill Gate. JAPANESE.

A plain and simple small Japanese restaurant that produces fresh sushi and a short menu of classic Japanese dishes. Most people will want to plump for the assorted sushi and sashimi or individual rolls of sea eel, sweet prawn, and tuna. The tempura dishes are wonderfully light. The set lunches ranging in price from £8 ($12.80) for *tonkatsu* to £10 ($16) for beef teriyaki are excellent values.

MODERATELY PRICED CHOICES

Assaggi. 39 Chepstow Place, W2. ☎ **0171/792-5501.** Reservations recommended. Main courses £15.75–£18.50 ($25.20–$29.60). AE, MC, V. Tues–Fri noon–2:30pm; Sat 1–2:30pm; Sun 1–3pm; Tues–Sat 7:30–11pm. Tube: Notting Hill Gate. ITALIAN.

Located upstairs at a pub, this is a loud and buzzing dining room. Tables are large and well spaced and the crowd is chic and young. The Italian cuisine is equally robust, although many will consider the portions small. Still, it's the quality of the ingredients and the intensity of the flavors that count. The menu is short and concentrates on simple full-of-flavor dishes. For example, the veal cutlet with scent of *tartufo* (truffle), or the seasoned lamb, or *coda di rospo* with pancetta. A larger selection of starters is offered. If it's on the menu, opt for the fresh crab with celery lemon and olive oil dressing.

Texas Lone Star Saloon. 117A Queensway, W2. ☎ **0171/727-2980.** Main courses £8–£15 ($12.80–$24). MC, V. Mon–Wed 5–11:30pm, Thurs–Fri 5pm–12:30am, Sat–Sun 1pm–12:30am. Tube: Bayswater or Queensway. AMERICAN.

For those dying for American food and American-sized portions, this is the place to go for ribs, fried chicken, burritos, and burgers. Checkered tablecloths, ceiling fans, and country music set the tone.

☻ **Veronica's.** 3 Hereford Rd., W2. ☎ **0171/229-5079.** Reservations recommended. Main courses £10.50–£18.50 ($16.80–$29.60); two courses £12.50 ($20), three courses £16.50 ($26.40). AE, DC, MC, V. Mon–Fri noon–3pm; Mon–Sat 7pm–midnight. Tube: Bayswater/Queensway. BRITISH.

This is an authentic, inspiring dining experience. Veronica Shaw has won many awards for her celebration of traditional British cuisine. At this intimately and attractively appointed restaurant she replicates or adapts historic recipes and even adds historical notations to her menus. She is also health conscious and labels her dishes low fat, high fiber, vegan, and suitable for vegetarians. The set menus offer half a dozen main courses and such starters as an Oxford savory based on an 1870 recipe used at Balliol College. It consists of mushroom and anchovies blended on toast with chilled cream. It's delicious, at least for anchovy lovers like myself. Among the main dishes there might be Selsig Morgan, which is leek and Caerphilly sausages with minted apple and roasted potatoes. Choices on the à la carte menu run to China Cholla (lamb cutlets with mint and thyme on minted peas, lettuce, and spring onions with a hint of cream, a dish that dates back to the East India Company) and a char-grilled filet of beef (finished off between smoking planks of oak which impart a rich flavor to the meat). An appetizer of field mushrooms, blended with several herbs and spices, accompanied by fresh orange and drizzled with claret and horseradish sauce, will show you just what can be created with the humble fungus. The puddings naturally have wonderful names like Eton mess (a wonderful mess of strawberries, cream, and meringue) and Wet Nelly and Butterscotch, which surprisingly is a baked fruit pudding with whiskey and butterscotch sauce. They're great.

WORTH A SPLURGE

Novelli. 122 Palace Gardens Terrace, W8. ☎ **0171/229-4024.** Reservations recommended. Main courses £12.50–£14 ($20–$22.40); 2-course lunch £12.50 ($20), 3 courses £15.50 ($24.80). AE, DC, MC, V. Tues–Sat noon–3pm, Sun 12:30–3pm; Mon–Sat 6–11pm, Sun 7–10pm. Tube: Notting Hill Gate. FRENCH.

If you want to sample the cuisine of innovative chef Jean-Christophe Novelli, then this is the place to do so. It's an appealing restaurant with a long narrow dining room that is light and airy. On one side, banquettes line the wall, providing access to tables attractively set with crisp white tablecloths. Although all the cuisine is well prepared, the fish dishes stand out, whether it's roast mullet in a light anise broth accompanied by vanilla risotto, or the sea bream flavored with fennel, olives, tomato, and dried aubergine. The flavors are intense and the presentation superappetizing. Among the meat dishes the roast rump of lamb is combined with curry potatoes, baby leeks, and dried lamb, while the pork is enhanced by pancetta and a sage and Emmenthal glaze. The fixed-price menu offers a limited menu of one fish and one meat dish, plus such wonderful starters as the *mille feuille* of mackerel with aubergine caviar and roast plum tomato. Desserts are gorgeous and super-satisfying, whether it's a caramelized peach tatin with Grand Marnier ice cream or a hot and cold, light and dark chocolate plate.

12 Marylebone & Oxford Circus

SUPER-CHEAP EATS

Caffe Uno. 5 Argyll St., W1. ☎ **0171/437-2503.** Main courses £4–£9 ($6.40–$14.40). AE, DC, MC, V. Mon–Sat 10am–11:45pm, Sun 11am–10:45pm. Tube: Oxford Circus. PASTA/ LIGHT FARE.

This is an appealing casual eatery where young workers stop for a light lunch of pasta or pizza and such dishes as chicken marsala. The food is fresh and well prepared and the prices reasonable.

There are many other branches. Three of the most central are 64 Tottenham Court Rd., W1 (☎ **0171/636-3587**); 24 Charing Cross Rd., WC2 (☎ **0171/ 240-2524**); and 37 St. Martin's Lane, WC2 (☎ **0171/836-5837**).

Intercafe. 25 Great Portland St., W1. ☎ **0171/631-0063.** Snacks and sandwiches £2.50–£3.95 ($4–$6.30). MC, V. Mon–Fri 7:30am–7pm, Sat 9:30am–5pm. Tube: Oxford Circus. CAFE/LIGHT FARE.

A thriving cybercafe in which you'll find casual young sophisticates using the 10 computers available. They manage to connect against a rocking musical background. The cafe offers better food and more variety than most similar cyber spots—jacket potatoes, sandwiches, and salads plus croissants and pastries. There's plenty of space to dine, too, at deep purple tables combined with "Swiss cheese"–hole-style chrome chairs.

FOR A FEW POUNDS MORE

The Chapel. 48 Chapel St., NW1. ☎ **0171/402-9220.** Main courses £8–£12 ($12.80–$19.20). AE, MC, V. Daily noon–2:30pm and 7–10pm. Tube: Edgware Rd. PUB.

An example of London's new-style pub. It's light and airy with polished wood floors and scrubbed wood tables. Art photographs decorate the walls. The food is eclectic and the menu chalked on a board daily. The fare will range from baked Brie en croute to penne with pesto, and from a beef, mushroom, and wine stew, to pork with caramelized apples. In addition, this is one of the few pubs that offer a full range (12 to 15) of wines by the glass.

Efes Kebab House. 175–177 Great Portland St., W1. ☎ **0171/436-0600.** Main courses £5.80–£10.50 ($9.30–$16.80). AE, DC, MC, V. Mon–Sat noon–midnight, Sun noon–11:30pm. Tube: Great Portland St. TURKISH.

People come for the huge helpings of tasty Turkish-style dishes. The atmosphere is exotic. Diners sit on banquettes or on turquoise chairs under a deep blue ceiling that is strung with multicolored lights and lanterns that cast intricate patterns around the rooms. You can make a meal out of the more than 20 hors d'oeuvres, which include everything from prawn cocktail and hummus to avocado vinaigrette and diced lamb's liver. Main courses are mostly variations on a theme of kebabs, made with lamb, minced lamb, or chicken, and cooked on charcoal or roasted on an open spit. Steaks are also offered. The portions are large and the service prompt, but the food isn't exactly inspiring.

Mad Dog Cafe. 35 James St., W1. ☎ **0171/486-1511.** £4.95–£9.95 ($7.90–$15.90). AE, DC, MC, V. Mon–Sat noon–11pm, Sun noon–6pm. Tube: Bond St. CAFE/LIGHT FARE.

Church pew chairs at round wood tables or faux marble tables give this place an incongruous look. It serves a good hot dog and sausage dog, plus some other more exotic versions of the same. The latter are made with char-grilled lamb, chicken, steak, swordfish, or similar, which are then served in a baguette with onions, peppers, and barbecue sauce. You can choose to have the same ingredients served on a platter instead.

Rasa Sayang Restaurant. 22 Harcourt St., W1. ☎ **0171/723-8118.** Main courses £5.50–£8.80 ($8.80–$14.05). Buffet £3.95 ($6.30). AE, DC, MC, V. Daily noon–11:15pm (sometimes varies by location). Tube: Edgware Rd. MALAYSIAN/SINGAPOREAN.

A pleasant dining room furnished with marble tables and decorative images of Malaysia and Indonesia in which you can secure some very nicely cooked Southeast Asian cuisine. Main dishes will tweak the palate—Singapore beef curry, lemon chicken, *gado gado, nasi goreng*, and most of all the *sambals* (try the prawn version). A Malaysian buffet is served Sunday from 1 to 7pm for only £3.95 ($6.30).

Sea-Shell. 49–51 Lisson Grove, NW1. ☎ **0171/723-8703.** Main courses £7.95–£15 ($12.70–$24); 3-course set meal served until 7pm £9.50 ($15.20). AE, DC, MC, V. Mon–Fri noon–2pm, Sun noon–2:30pm; Mon–Fri 5:15–10:30pm. Tube: Marylebone. FISH & CHIPS.

Considered by many to be the best fish and chip emporium in town. Certainly it's fresh and in addition to the usual cod and chips you can also secure fish cakes and hot pots filled with marine life and crustaceans as well. The Dover sole tops the price list.

Spighetta. 43 Blandford St., W1. ☎ **0171/486-7340.** Main courses £5.50–£8 ($8.80–12.80). AE, MC, V. Daily noon–2:30pm and 6:30–10:30pm. Tube: Baker St. PIZZA/PASTA.

This small restaurant boasts little decor except for the wood-fired oven from which the terrific pizzas, about a dozen of them, emerge. They range from a simple margherita to one that is loaded down with tomato, arugula, cured beef, and goat cheese, and another with tomato, mozzarella, artichokes, ham, mushrooms, and olives. The rest of the menu features four or five main pasta dishes—linguine with clams and chili for example, and a selection of inspired appetizers. Try the warm goat cheese with potato and asparagus salad, or the wild mushroom and Asiago cheese wrapped in Savoy cabbage. Finish with ice cream or the tiramisu with espresso sauce. Good value indeed.

MODERATELY PRICED CHOICES

Casa Becci. 32 Paddington St., W1. No phone. Main courses £5–£13.50 ($8–$21.60) Tube: Baker St. ITALIAN.

A simple storefront restaurant frequented by many local Italians. Banquettes line both walls of the peach-toned room. Rush seat ladderbacks are set at tables sporting white tablecloths. The menu offers pastas with a choice of such sauces as arrabbiata and bolognese, plus such dishes as veal limone and veal pizzaiola. In addition, there are daily specials like saddle of lamb with garlic. Friendly service and cuisine with fresh, flavorful ingredients.

Justin de Blanc. 120–122 Marylebone Lane, W1. ☎ **0171/486-5250.** Main courses £8.25–£12.50 ($13.20–$20). AE, MC, V. Mon–Fri noon–3pm and 5:30–10pm. Tube: Baker St./Bond St. MODERN EUROPEAN.

A lofty storefront space furnished with zinc tables and bentwood chairs, this is a fun modern place that attracts both young and trendy as well as an older crowd. The food is well prepared and reasonably priced. The menu is limited, offering about seven dishes ranging from Wiener schnitzel served with mash, green beans, nut butter, and capers; to a classic tuna niçoise made with char-grilled tuna; to sausages in red wine, onions, and mushrooms served with a great mash. To start, try one of the fresh salads or a bowl of spicy carrot-and-coriander soup.

If you're a champagne fan you can order a magnum of champagne for only £29.70 ($47.50) between 5 and 7:30pm.

Mash. 19–21 Great Portland St., W1. ☎ **0171/637-5555.** Main courses £8–£13.50 ($12.80–$21.60). AE, DC, MC, V. Mon–Fri 8am–11pm, Sat 11am–11pm, Sun 11am–10:30pm. Tube: Oxford Circus. MEDITERRANEAN.

For shoppers Mash is an ideal stop just south of Oxford Street. This hip resto, deli, and microbrewery was opened by Oliver Peyton in 1998. Large and sleek with an abundance of glass and glass brick, it occupies a lofty and strikingly sculpted space. It's one of London's first microbreweries. You can see the huge tanks behind glass at the back of the first-floor cafe. Couches invite customers to linger awhile in another sunken sitting area. The same cutting-edge looks and orange and pistachio colors prevail in the upstairs restaurant. The cuisine is the requisite Mediterranean Italian fare requiring a wood-fired grill, from which appear paper-thin pizzas topped with such unusual ingredients as crispy duck, cucumber, Asian greens, and hoisin sauce. Main courses are either baked (like the sea bass accompanied by baby artichoke plum tomatoes and olive oil) or grilled (like the calves' liver served with a delicious

Marylebone, Paddington, Bayswater & Notting Hill Restaurants

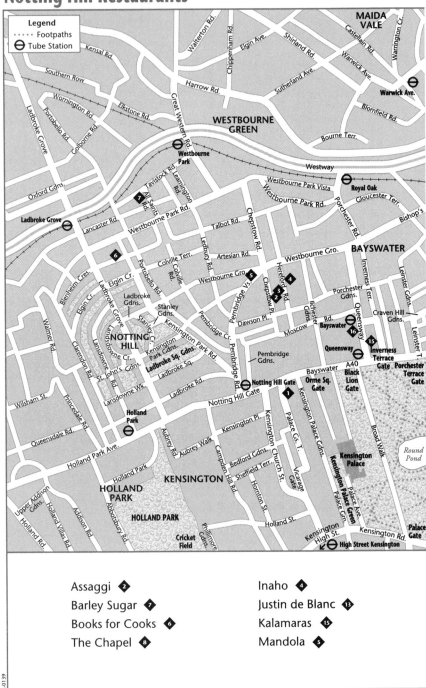

Assaggi **2**

Barley Sugar **7**

Books for Cooks **6**

The Chapel **8**

Inaho **4**

Justin de Blanc **13**

Kalamaras **15**

Mandola **5**

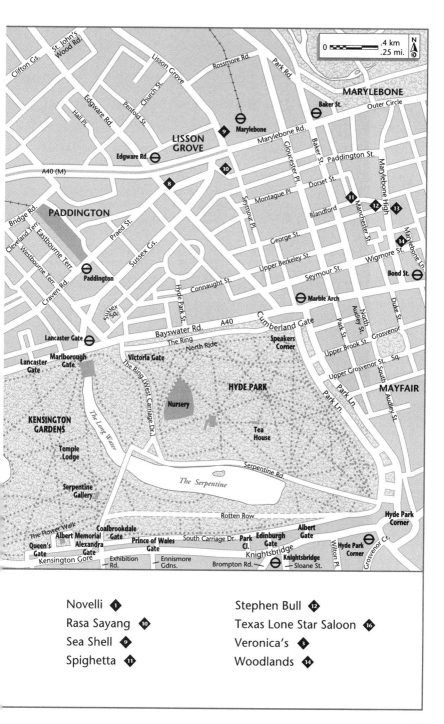

Novelli ◆1

Rasa Sayang ◆10

Sea Shell ◆9

Spighetta ◆11

Stephen Bull ◆12

Texas Lone Star Saloon ◆16

Veronica's ◆3

Woodlands ◆14

horseradish mash and crispy red onions). Wheat and fruit beers plus power quenchers like the Stamina Shake (ginseng, royal jelly and other Asian ingredients whipped up with apple juice and cream) are the order of the day. The other cool feature of this spot is the Love Machine at the entrance, which flashes romantic epigrams as people open the doors. One of the more flip is "The best way to a man's heart is to leave him."

Stephen Bull. 5–7 Blandford St., W1. ☎ **0171/379-7811.** Reservations recommended. Main courses £11.50–£15 ($18.40–$24). Pre/post-theater 2 courses £12.50 ($20). AE, MC, V. Mon–Fri 12:15–2:30pm; Mon–Sat 6:30–10:30pm. Tube: Bond St. MODERN EUROPEAN.

Decked out in avocado and turquoise, this sleek and modern establishment has all the right stylish accouterments—light wood floors, large impressive flower arrangements, a small pewter bar up front, and black banquettes in the mirrored dining room behind. Stephen Bull was one of the first chefs to prepare modern British cuisine and you can expect to enjoy richly flavored cuisine, like the rump of beef with morels, turnips, and foie gras butter. The menu changes at least twice a week, but you'll find eight or so main courses that might include a pot roast chicken full of flavor and enhanced by truffle mash and Vichy carrots. The fillet of salmon might be embellished with oyster cream. To start, try the goat cheese and ratatouille or, if it's the season, the warm langoustines with artichoke and tomato salad and shellfish jelly. As for the puddings, they are complete reinventions, like fig tart tatin and a delicious chocolate tart. For the best deal go between 5:45 and 7pm or 10:30 and 11:30pm for a limited menu featuring five or so main courses. The main courses are £10 ($16) and the starters and desserts £5.50 ($8.80), but you can enjoy starter and dessert for £9 ($14.40) and starter and main or main and dessert for £12.50 ($20).

Union Cafe. 96 Marylebone Lane, W1. ☎ **0171/486-4860.** Breakfast £2–£6.50 ($3.20–$10.40); main courses £9–£13.50 ($14.40–$21.60). MC, V. Breakfast Mon–Fri 9:30am–noon; lunch Mon–Fri noon–3:30pm and Sat 11am–5pm; dinner Mon–Sat 6:30–10:30pm. Tube: Bond St. MODERN EUROPEAN.

Innovative young chefs turn out some up-to-the-minute cuisine from the open kitchen at this lofty restaurant lit by Palladian windows. The room is simply furnished with wooden tables and chairs. The cuisine is simple and uses as many organic ingredients as possible. The menu changes daily but you'll find a pizza and pasta dish plus a meat and fish dish offered, along with half a dozen appetizers and a good selection of desserts. You might find a duck confit with dandelion, blood orange, fennel, and red onion salad; and roast turbot with steamed asparagus and sun-dried tomato pesto. Among the starters there might be coriander, leek, and potato soup and a selection of charcuterie. For dessert, if it's available, try the mascarpone and vanilla tart with mango and fresh berries.

It's a change to come here for breakfast when you can enjoy banana waffles and scrambled eggs with Heal Farm bacon or smoked salmon.

Woodlands. 77 Marylebone Lane, W1. ☎ **0171/486-3862.** Main courses £3.50–£10.95 ($5.60–$17.50). AE, DC, MC, V. Daily noon–2:30pm and 6–10:30pm. Tube: Bond St. SOUTH INDIAN/VEGETARIAN.

A London outpost of the famous Indian vegetarian restaurant empire. This is one place where you can enjoy such south Indian specialties as *dosas* and *uttapan*. The *dosas* may be filled with potatoes, onions, and snow peas, or with other vegetables and potatoes. Other dishes range from vegetable *korma* and *saag paneer* to a full-blown *thali*. There are several small dining rooms, each furnished with well-set tables and wooden chairs and some low-key wall decorations.

Zoe. St. Christopher's Place, W1. ☎ **0171/224-1122.** Main courses cafe £5.75–£10 ($9.20–$16); restaurant £9–£14.75 ($14.40–$23.60); 2-course cafe set lunch or dinner £10 ($16), 3 courses £12.50 ($20). AE, DC, MC, V. Restaurant Mon–Sat 12–3pm and 6–11:30pm; cafe daily 11:30am–11:30pm; bar noon–11pm. Tube: Bond St. LIGHT FARE.

Frenetic and noisy, this place is popular with businesspeople and shoppers because they can obtain an imaginative three-course meal here for £12.50 ($20). For example, you might select leek-and-potato tart with *tallegio* cream to start; follow it with *ciabatta* with mozzarella, hummus and arugula; and finish with a tangy lemon-and-lime tart with a citrus sabayon. Pretty good for the price. The ground-floor cafe offers soup, sandwiches, and such appetizing dishes as artichoke, wild mushroom, and pine nut risotto with crispy shallots; or chili chicken with *gado gado* vegetables and sesame crepe. The restaurant downstairs has good, occasionally inspired, food at fair prices. You might find on the menu a polenta-crusted salmon fillet with caramelized endive and sweet chili salsa; or grilled saddle of lamb, onion, and thyme confit served with fondant potatoes. Happy hour is from 5:30 to 6:30pm.

13 Islington

SUPER-CHEAP EATS

Le Mercury. 140A Upper St., N1. ☎ **0171/354-4088.** 3-course lunch £5.50 ($8.80); 3 courses until 7:15pm £5 ($8). MC, V. Mon–Sat 11am–1am, Sun noon–11:30pm. Tube: Islington/Highbury. FRENCH.

This attractive storefront restaurant offers some great food deals, which is why it gets so crowded. The room is upbeat with its yellow walls hung with mirrors and art. The white cloth-covered tables are somewhat close together and the gateback chairs are little hard on the back, but who cares when the food is good and so well priced. At lunch the set menu offers three courses selected from the à la carte menu. Thus you can begin with pork satay or grilled goat cheese and walnut salad, or another appetizer. Among main courses select such dishes as cod la Basquaisse, which is served with eggplant, parmesan cheese, and tomato coulis; rib eye steak with bearnaise sauce; or chicken forestière, which is chicken breast stuffed with spinach and cottage cheese and served with a cepe mushroom sauce. Desserts range from apple crumble to tiramisu and fresh fruit salad. The other set menu, which is available until early evening, offers a limited choice.

Upper Street Fish Shop. 324 Upper St., N1. ☎ **0171/359-1401.** Main courses £7.50–£10 ($12–$16). No credit cards. Tues–Fri noon–2:15pm, Sat noon–3pm; Mon–Thurs 6–10:15pm, Fri–Sat 5:30–10:15pm. Tube: Angel. FISH & CHIPS.

Marine paintings on the walls and blue-and-white check tablecloths provide a pretty but casual backdrop at this restaurant that serves, as its name states, fish and only fish. It's an upscale chippie, really, serving an A to Z of fish from cod to skate, all accompanied by good tasty chips. Good fish soup to start and suitable puddings to finish it all, too.

FOR A FEW POUNDS MORE

Pasha. 301 Upper St., N1. ☎ **0171/226-1454.** Main courses £6.95–£11.95 ($11.10–$19.10); quick lunch or dinner £9.95 ($15.90). 2-course set menu £5.50 ($8.80) served noon–3pm and 6–8pm Mon–Thurs and noon–3pm Fri–Sat. AE, MC, V. Mon–Sat noon–3pm; Mon–Thurs 6–11:30pm, Fri–Sat 6pm–midnight, Sun noon–11pm. Tube: Angel. TURKISH.

You can't beat the price-to-quality ratio at this simple Turkish restaurant. The room is decorated in a shade of purple and brightened with such accents as colorful plates and photographs. White cloths cover the tables; diners are invited to sit on bentwood chairs. The meze features good renderings of such traditional favorites as dolma, hummus, and tabbouleh, plus more unusual dishes like *barbunya pilahi,* which are Asian beans served with carrots, celery, and diced potatoes; and *sucuk,* which are spicy Turkish sausages cooked in foil and served with lemon, parsley, and tomatoes. Kebabs dominate the main courses and they are grilled carefully to retain succulence. There are also fish and vegetarian dishes. Try the char-grilled swordfish marinated in lime, bay leaf, and herbs; or the roasted green peppers stuffed with rice, pine kernels, and herbs. The quick lunch or dinner brings a dozen hot and cold mezes; the set meal is a soup followed by a simple roast chicken dish or similar with salad.

MODERATELY PRICED CHOICES

Casale Franco. 134–7 Upper St., N1. ☎ **0171/226-8994.** Main courses £11–£15.75 ($17.60–$25.20). Pizzas £6.70–£9.50 ($10.70–$15.20). MC, V. Fri–Sun noon–3pm; Tues–Sat 6:30–11pm and Sun 6:30–9:30pm. Tube: Angel. ITALIAN.

Tucked away off Upper Street, this restaurant has lots of atmosphere, and outside dining in summer is very pleasant. It's loaded with Italian atmosphere—flagstone floors, brick walls, and opera and Latin music playing in the background. Among the more creative decorative accents are the golf bags and tubas used as frond holders. The Italian cuisine is good, if not inspired, and ranges from grilled meat and fish dishes to cuttlefish in its own ink. Pizzas are available too.

Frederick's. 106 Camden Passage, N1. ☎ **0171/359-2888.** Main courses £9.50–£17 ($15.20–$27.20). 2-course British lunch £12 ($19.20); also offered 6–7:30pm. Mon–Sat 12–2:30pm and 6–11:30pm. Tube: Angel. MODERN EUROPEAN.

Right in the heart of Camden Passage Market, this is a large, stylish restaurant that offers dining in a light and airy conservatory and outside in a garden. Every week it offers a special Great British lunch featuring a variety of British classics, which is certainly the restaurant's best value. You might, for example, start with leek, potato, and bacon soup or black pudding with mustard sauce, and follow it with roast chicken with bread sauce or toad-in-the-hole with mash and onion gravy. If you like, you can accompany it with English wines by the glass. At dinner, the menu offers a mixture of traditional and more modern dishes. For example, there might be pan-fried veal chop with Parmesan, asparagus and gnocchi; or honey and roast monkfish with buttered cabbage, langoustine, and bacon. This is the place also to taste really fine British desserts like strawberry trifle, rhubarb crumble, or bread-and-butter pudding.

Granita. 127 Upper St., N1. ☎ **0171/226-3222.** Reservations recommended. Main courses £11–£13 ($17.60–$20.80). MC, V. Wed–Sun 12:30–2:30pm and Tues–Sun 6:30–10:30pm. Tube: Islington/Highbury. MODERN EUROPEAN.

This is the trendiest restaurant in Islington at the moment and was, it is said, one of Tony and Cherie's favorite dining places when they lived in the neighborhood. It's suitably modern, a study in blond on blond—blond floors, chairs, and tables all set against sky-blue walls. The menu is limited and only features about four main dishes. Inspiration for the cuisine is drawn from all over the world. For example, you might find an appetizer that combines carrot fritter, pine nuts, raisin, Lebanese yogurt sauce, red onion, and coriander salad alongside calves' liver, broad beans, mint, lemon, and arugula; or a leek-and-potato soup made more flavorsome by the addition of mushroom and dill. Among the main courses the Scotch rib eye might be flavored with coriander, nutmeg, and oregano marinade, and served with potato and tomato gratin and zucchini. Desserts also reflect this exciting approach to flavors. Here you can enjoy a trifle that is made with strawberry and cointreau, or a cherry and almond tart accompanied by cherry ice cream.

Lola's. The Mall Building, 359 Upper St., N1. ☎ **0171/359-1932.** Main courses £9.75–£14.50 ($15.60–$23.20); 2-course lunch £12 ($19.20), 3 courses £12.50 ($20). AE, DC, MC, V. Mon–Fri noon–2:30pm, Sat–Sun noon–3pm; Mon–Sat 6:30–11pm. Tube: Angel. MODERN EUROPEAN.

A lovely conservatory dining room set above the antiques mall below. It has a very elegant air. Club-style chairs are set at tables with cream tablecloths, and the room positively glows at night under the stars. The cuisine is light and fresh. The menu, which changes daily, will likely offer simple but really fine bistro dishes, like steak and frites, grilled tuna salad niçoise, and poached chicken breast with aioli and vegetable salads. On weekends it offers an excellent eclectic brunch to Camden Passage market visitors.

14 Camden/Primrose Hill & Hampstead

SUPER-CHEAP EATS

Street food is the cheapest option in this neighborhood. As you cruise the Camden Market there are loads of street vendors selling kebabs, hot dogs, falafel, and pizza usually for £1 ($1.60) a serving.

L'Ecluse. 3 Chalk Farm Rd., NW1. ☎ **0171/267-8116.** Main courses £5–£9.75 ($8–$11.35); 3-course lunch/dinner £10.95 ($17.50). AE, V. Mon–Fri noon–11pm, Sat 11am–11pm, Sun 10am–10:30pm. Tube: Camden Town or Chalk Farm. CREPES.

At L'Ecluse, the specialty is crepes, both savory and sweet, like *basquaise* or *forestière* (with mushrooms) or lemon chocolate. Other dishes are available, too, such as chicken in mushroom sauce, leg of lamb with rosemary, and pork in a spicy sauce. Brick walls and floral-printed tablecloths make for a rustic French atmosphere.

Nontas. 14–16 Camden High St., NW1. ☎ **0171/387-4579.** Main courses £6–£7.50 ($9.60–$12). AE, DC, MC, V. Mon–Sat noon–2:45pm, 6–11:30pm. Tube: Camden Town. GREEK.

There's a 1960s flavor to this spot, with its wooden tables lit by drop lamps. The food is mostly Greek—pork, lamb, chicken, and fish kebabs, moussaka, lamb cutlets, and rump steak. Good value.

FOR A FEW POUNDS MORE

✪ **Café Delancey.** 3 Delancey St., NW1. ☎ **0171/387-1985.** Main courses £6–£13 ($9.60–$20.80). MC, V. Daily 8am–11:30pm. Tube: Camden Town. BRASSERIE.

This very popular place is great for breakfast, which is served all day. At dinner, delicious main courses include rack of lamb with parsley and herb sauce; chicken in mushroom sauce; and sausage and onions with rôti potatoes. Salads and sandwiches like croque monsieur are available, too. The large tiled dining rooms are furnished with round marble-topped tables and bentwood chairs. At night the tables are covered and the rooms are transformed into charming candlelit spaces. In summer you can sit outside. Away from the main action of the market, it's a pleasant retreat.

Camden Brasserie/Underground Café. 214–216 Camden High St., NW1. ☎ **0171/482-2114.** Main courses £8–£13 ($12.80–$20.105). MC, V. Mon–Sat noon–3pm and 6–11:30pm; Sun noon–4:30pm and 5:15–10:30pm. Tube: Camden Town. INTERNATIONAL.

A large, popular bistro with a long, light oak bar. The antiqued walls are decorated with photographs and other art. On the wide-ranging menu, you'll find chicken rosemary, salmon hollandaise, lamb fillet with mint sauce, and rib eye steak with béarnaise. It's not exciting, but it's consistent and the locals swear by it.

Cottons Rhum Shop. 55 Chalk Farm Rd., NW1. ☎ **0171/482-1096.** Main courses £7.25–£12.25 ($11.60–$19.60). AE, DC, MC, V. Tues–Sun noon–4pm; daily 6:30–11:30pm. Tube: Chalk Farm. AFRICAN/CARIBBEAN.

Spicy Jamaican cuisine is what you'll find at this attractive restaurant with antiqued walls and wood tables. Try the okra and breadfruit curry, the jerk chicken, or the goat curry—a true specialty. Get high on the Caribbean atmosphere. Real reggae.

Daphne. 83 Bayham St., NW1. ☎ **0171/267-7322.** Main courses £6.50–£8.75 ($10.40–$14). MC, V. Mon–Sat noon–2:30pm and 6–11:30pm. Tube: Camden Town. GREEK.

This small restaurant has a tiny outdoor terrace embellished with vines and a more spacious roof terrace that is very popular in summer. Inside, the tables are covered with green gingham and the walls are decorated with scenes of Greece. The food is freshly and lovingly prepared by the Greek family-owners. Besides the traditional Greek specialties such as moussaka, *kleftiko* (joint of lamb baked with lemon and spices), and *afelia* (cubes of pork marinated in wine and cooked with coriander), the restaurant is known for its grilled seasonal fish—sea bass, mullet, and swordfish, for example. Specials are written on a blackboard. The wine list features Greek and Cypriot wines, plus a short selection of French bottles.

The Engineer. 65 Gloucester Ave., NW1. ☎ **0171/722-0950.** Main courses £8–£13 ($12.80–$20.80). MC, V. Mon–Sat noon–3pm, Sun noon–3:30pm; Mon–Sat 7–11pm; Sun 7–10:30pm. Tube: Camden Town/Chalk Farm. PUB.

A lovely spot to rest in summer, when you can relax in the backyard. The Engineer is another new pub with large glass windows, scrubbed tables, and the occasional couch. The food is more modern than most and there are lots of wines by the glass to accompany it. You might start with a hearty soup and follow it with some crispy prawns or an asparagus salad before tackling the main course, which might be glazed duck in noodle broth with shiitake and beansprouts, or breast of chicken with couscous. There's always a steak and a fish too.

Trojka. 101 Regent's Park Rd., NW1. ☎ **0171/483-3765.** Main courses £6–£10 ($9.60–$16); 2-course lunch £7.95 ($12.70). MC, V. Daily 9am–11pm. Tube: Chalk Farm. EAST EUROPEAN.

A local literary crowd gathers here for the superb blinis and borscht. The place has an Old World air about it, thanks to the mustard-colored walls hung with gilt framed pictures and the small, round wooden tables. Borscht, herring, goulash, blinis with smoked salmon, and latkes with mushrooms are a few of the well pre-pared and modestly priced dishes (given the location). Live Russian music draws the crowds.

MODERATELY PRICED CHOICES

Belgo Noord. 72 Chalk Farm Rd., NW1. ☎ **0171/267-0718.** Main courses £7.95–£17.50 ($12.70–$28). Lunch £5 ($8) daily from noon to 5:30 (4pm on weekends) or Belgo *complet* set lunch and dinner £12.95 ($20.70). AE, MC, V. Daily Mon–Fri noon–3pm, 6–11:30pm, Sat noon–11:30pm, Sun noon–10:30pm. Tube: Chalk Farm. BELGIAN/EUROPEAN.

This hip restaurant that has a cool industrial look can be easily missed because the facade is windowless. It attracts a youthful bohemian crowd to its cavernous sub-terranean dining room where diners sit at tables on benches in a monastic-communal style and are served by staff wearing voluminous black habits. The signature dish here is, naturally enough, the mussels, along with other crustaceans which appear on heaped steaming plates. There are other options too like *entrecôte* and *carbonnade flamande*, plus salmon and shrimp dishes.

Lemonia. 89 Regent's Park Rd., NW1. ☎ **0171/586-7454.** Reservations recommended. Main courses £7.25–£14.75 ($11.60–$23.60). DC, MC, V. Sun–Fri noon–3pm; Mon–Sat 6–11:30pm. Tube: Chalk Farm. GREEK.

This large restaurant with polished wood tables offers a classic Greek menu with many grilled meat and fish dishes. Start with a classic octopus salad or the charcoal grilled *hallonmi* (Cypriot cheese). Most of the fish dishes—salmon and Dover sole, for example—are grilled to maintain their flavor. And of course, there are several *shashliks* and kebabs. There's a delicious moussaka made with eggplant, zucchini, potatoes, tomatoes, and ground beef in a creamy sauce, and several other traditional dishes like the subtly flavored *afeila* (cubes of pork marinated in wine, coriander seeds, and spices), or the tender *kleftiko* lamb baked in lemon spices and herbs. It's very popular, so expect crowds of happy locals jamming the long wooden tables, especially on weekends. Still, it's a jovial dining experience.

Odette's. 130 Regent's Park Rd., NW1. ☎ **0171/586-5486.** Reservations recommended. Main courses £11–£16.50 ($17.60–$26.40). 3-course lunch £10 ($16). AE, DC, MC, V. Mon–Fri 12:30–2:30pm; Mon–Sat 7–11pm. Tube: Chalk Farm. MODERN EUROPEAN.

Gilded mirrors of all shapes and sizes cover the walls of this opulent Primrose Hill restaurant that draws a casually elegant clientele. The room is further enhanced by one or two pieces of classical statuary. What's affordable here is the three course, no choice set lunch, which might start with a butternut squash soup, followed by a roast loin of pork and finished with a plum and blueberry sorbet. The downstairs wine bar also offers well-prepared cuisine.

15 The Chains & Java Joints

The following chains are very popular with Londoners who appreciate their good value. They have numerous branches, most of which are conveniently located in the center of the city.

All Bar One. 1 Liverpool Rd., N1. ☎ **0171/843-0021.** Main courses £6–£9 ($9.60–$14.40). AE, MC, V. Daily 11:30–10pm. Tube: Angel. PUB/BAR.

This chain is the epitome of the new style bar-pub that has burst onto the scene. Each branch, and there are many, is furnished with plain wood tables and chairs and offers a moderately priced menu that is written on a blackboard. The young and the not-so-young flock into these bars at lunch and after work. The complimentary newspapers on sticks are a nice touch. There are too many bars to list. The most central are 48 Leicester Sq., WC2 (☎ 0171/839-0972); 36–38 Dean St., WC1 (☎ 0171/287-4641); and 3–4 Hanover St., W1 (☎ 0171/495-2216).

Aroma. 36A St. Martin's Lane, WC2. ☎ **0171/836-5110.** Sandwiches and salads £2.10–£3 ($3.35–$4.80). AE, DC, MC, V. Mon–Fri 8am–10pm, Sat 9am–10pm, Sun noon–8pm. Tube: Leicester Sq./Charing Cross. CAFE.

This chain of modern, bright, and airy cafes serves good, strong coffee in a dozen or so ways, some fine pastries, plus snacks and sandwiches. There are many branches, including one at the Bond Street Underground and the Royal Festival Hall. The most central are 120 Charing Cross Rd., WC2 (☎ 0171/240-4030); 273 Regent St., W1 (☎ 0171/495-4911); 1B Dean St., W1 (☎ 0171/287-1633).

Cafe Flo. 13–14 Thayer St., W1. ☎ **0171/935-5023.** Main courses £7–£15 ($11.20–$24). MC, V. Daily 9am–11:30pm. Tube: Bond St. CAFE.

This is my favorite low-cost brasserie. It has plenty of French style and ambience and decent casual cuisine. The fare consists of such stalwarts as *moules marinières*, steak frites, and *poule au pot*. The chain is not spread as thinly as many similar ones. Central locations include 51 St. Martin's Lane, WC2 (☎ **0171/836-8289**).

Cranks. 8 Marshall St., W1. ☎ **0171/437-9431.** Main courses £6–£9 ($9.60–$14.40); 2-course set meal £6.95 ($11.10). AE, DC, MC, V. Mon, Tues, Fri, Sat 8am–8pm; Wed, Thurs 8am–9pm. Tube: Oxford Circus. VEGETARIAN.

When Cranks opened its first health-oriented vegetarian restaurant in the early 1960s, the British public laughed. Today, more than half a dozen of these places serve no-longer-snickering Londoners innovative, high-quality cuisine at good prices. Cheesy lasagne, lentil-and-spinach quiche, satay vegetables, and other tasty dishes are well presented. The surroundings are modern, airy, and even decorous. A wide selection of herb teas, at about £1 ($1.60) per pot, is available. There's a good choice of reasonably priced organic wines.

This Cranks is three blocks east of Regent Street in Soho. Other downtown locations include the following: the Market, Covent Garden, WC2 (☎ **0171/379-6508**); 9–11 Tottenham St., W1 (☎ **0171/631-3912**), two blocks from Goodge Street Underground off Tottenham Court Road; and 23 Barret St., W1 (☎ **0171/495-1340**), across Oxford Street from the Bond Street Underground.

Ed's Easy Diner. 12 Moor St., W1. ☎ **0171/439-1955.** Main courses £6.50–£10 ($10.40–$16). AE, MC, V. Sun–Thurs 11:30am–midnight, Fri–Sat 11:30am–1am. Tube: Leicester Sq. AMERICAN.

Ed's Easy Diners are re-creations of 1950s-style American diners, complete with bobby-soxed waitresses, lots of turquoise and aluminum, and table jukeboxes. A good gimmick, but the burgers aren't for real unless you've been away for a real long time. With fries and a cola or a milk shake, a burger will cost about £8 ($12.80). Unless you're really homesick, there are tastier budget options.

Other central London locations include: 362 King's Rd., SW3 (☎ **0171/352-1956**), past the fire station in Chelsea; and 16 Hampstead High St., NW3 (☎ **0171/431-1958**).

My Old Dutch Pancakes. 221 King's Rd., SW3. ☎ **0171/352-6900.** Pancakes £2.95–£7 ($4.70–$11.20). AE, DC, MC, V. Daily noon–11pm. Tube: Sloane Sq. CREPES.

A Dutch ambience prevails at these establishments with wooden chairs and tables. The menu features a host of savory and sweet pancakes and waffles. I recommend the simple pancakes with lemon and sugar, or a stack accompanied with mandarin orange and curaçao, or those with chocolate sauce and cinnamon. The savory versions range from chili to vegetable. My favorite is the old Dutch savory filled with chicken, ham, bacon, sweet peppers, sweet corn, cheese, and mushrooms. Daily specials and a variety of special Dutch beers, too. Also at 131 High Holborn, WC1 (☎ **0171/242-5200**).

Pierre Victoire. 19–21 Notting Hill Gate, W11. ☎ **0171/460-4455.** Main courses £10–£16 ($16–$25.60); 3-course lunch £4.95 ($7.90); 3-course dinner £7.95 ($12.70). MC, V. Daily noon–3pm and 6–11pm. Tube: Notting Hill. FRENCH/EUROPEAN.

This chain now has scores of branches all over London. People are drawn by the low price set menus, which are fairly good values, although the cooking can be notoriously inconsistent and far from thrilling. Typical dishes include sole meunière, *moules marinières*, and lamb with blackcurrant sauce.

Other branches include 11 Charlotte St., W1 (☎ **0171/436-0248**); 42 New Oxford St., WC1 (☎ **0171/436-0707**); 5 Dean St., W1 (☎ **0171/287-4582**); and 6 Panton St., SW1 (☎ **0171/930-6463**).

✪ **Pizza Express.** 30 Coptic St., WC1. ☎ **0171/636-3232.** Pizzas £4.40–£6.75 ($7.05–$10.80). AE, V. Daily noon–midnight. Tube: Holborn. PIZZA.

Some of the best pizza in London can be enjoyed here. Black-tiled floors and black faux-marble tables create an elegant setting. The pies range from simple margarita to the veneziana with sultanas, capers, olives, onions, and pine nuts. Simple desserts are available. There are too many of these places to list—check the phone directory.

Pret à Manger. 77–78 Upper St. Martins Lane, WC2. ☎ **0171/379-5335.** Sandwiches and salads £1.75–£5.50 ($2.80–$8.80). No credit cards. Mon–Thurs 7:30am–9pm; Fri 7:30–11pm; Sat 9am–11pm, Sun 9am–9pm. Tube: Leicester Sq. or Charing Cross. FRENCH/LIGHT FARE.

A very successful chain of sandwich, salad, and dessert bars. They are all crisp and clean looking. Using super-fresh and good-quality ingredients, they make up a variety of sandwiches—salmon; watercress; pastrami with mustard mayonnaise; Brie and tomatoes; and tarragon chicken, to name only a few—on a variety of breads. Some branches have tables; others are strictly take-out. There are too many of these to list—check the telephone directory for the nearest one.

Seattle Coffee Company. 34 Great Marlborough St., W1. ☎ **0171/434-0778.** Coffees and snacks 90p–£2.50 ($1.45–$4). No credit cards. Mon–Thurs 7am–9pm, Fri 7am–10pm, Sat 8am–10pm, Sun 10am–8pm. Tube: Oxford Circus. CAFE.

This chain was begun by an American couple resident in London who picked up on the coffee craze in the United States. So successful have they been that they were recently purchased by none other than Starbucks itself. Besides the coffees—latte, mocha, and more—there are brownies and a full range of fresh sandwiches. Each branch sports a cool look with faux-marble tables, futuristic Italian-style chairs, leatherette couches in some places, and hot background colors.

Spaghetti House. 20 Sicilian Ave., WC1. ☎ **0171/405-5215.** Main courses £5.50–£12.50 ($8.80–$20). AE, DC, MC, V. Mon–Thurs noon–10:50pm, Fri–Sat noon–11:15pm. Tube: Holborn. PASTA.

This chain has been around for 50 years or more and yet it still manages to reinvent and mold itself to whatever is contemporary. So today it has a distinct antiqued Mediterranean ambience. The food is well prepared and you can secure a satisfying meal of cannelloni, eggplant parmigiana, or similar served by professional waiters in a pleasant atmosphere.

Stockpot—Soho. 18 Old Compton St., W1. ☎ **0171/287-1066.** Main courses £3–£5 ($4.80–$8). No credit cards. Daily 9am–11pm (sometimes varies by location). Tube: Leicester Sq. BRITISH.

The Stockpot restaurants feature contemporary decor and follow a generous, budget-minded philosophy. Menus change daily, but regularly feature two home-made soups; a dozen main-course selections such as chili, roast chicken, fish and chips, and liver and bacon; and an excellent selection of desserts. The food can be uneven but the prices make all the 'Pots popular.

Central London locations include 273 King's Rd., SW3 (☎ **0171/823-3175**), in Chelsea, a few blocks past the fire station; 6 Basil St., SW3 (☎ **0171/589-8627**), in ultra-fashionable Knightsbridge, between Harrods and Sloane Street; and 40 Panton St., SW1 (☎ **0171/839-5142**), just off Haymarket, one block south of Piccadilly Circus.

16 Afternoon Tea

Afternoon tea can consist of a pot of tea and a pastry taken at a cafe or it can be an elaborate affair taken in a grand room accompanied by a small orchestra. Either way, afternoon tea is still very much a British tradition and makes for a mini-meal in the mid-afternoon. A proper tea will include a pot of choice tea, accompanied by scones, wafer-thin sandwiches minus their crusts, and a selection of pastries and cakes. Don't confuse this with high tea, which is a working person's supper consisting of a hot dish, followed by dessert or cookies—high tea is mostly had in Northern England and Scotland. In my opinion, afternoon tea on a grand scale is not really worth it, but if it's part of your dream London vacation, then by all means go ahead and blow the £20 ($32) or so on the places listed here.

Brown's Hotel. Albemarle and Dover Streets, W1. ☎ **0171/493-6020.** Reservations required for 3pm seating. £16.95 ($27.10) per person. AE, DC, MC, V. Daily 3–6pm. Tube: Green Park.

This quintessentially understated hotel—so English—has a reputation for its afternoon tea. It's served in the sitting room/lounge. Tailcoated waiters will bring tomato, cucumber, and meat sandwiches, as well as scones and pastries. Choose from a variety of teas from India and Southeast Asia.

Cafe Valerie. 8 Russell St., WC2. ☎ **0171/240-0064.** Coffees/teas £1.40–£1.60 ($2.24–$2.55); pastries £1.50–£2.70 ($2.40–$4.30); main courses £4.95–£7.25 ($7.90–$11.60). AE, MC, V. Mon–Sat 7:30am–11pm, Sun 9am–6pm. Tube: Covent Garden. CAFE/LIGHT FARE.

A great place to come for breakfast, lunch, afternoon tea, and light dinner. The pastries and tarts are luscious—chocolate eclair, baba au rhum, strawberry and lemon tarts—whatever you love. They can be accompanied by a range of coffees and teas. The croque monsieur made with ham and Emmenthal is very satisfying for lunch. Other main dishes served throughout the day include quiches, omelets, salads, and such dishes as salmon steak with new potatoes and French beans.

Fortnum & Mason/The Fountain. 181 Piccadilly, W1. ☎ **0171/734-8040.** Set teas £6.95–£12.95 ($11.10–$20.70). AE, DC, MC, V. Mon–Sat 3–6pm. Tube: Green Park/Piccadilly. CAFE/LIGHT FARE.

Because of the name, it's mobbed with tourists all enjoying tea and cakes, or tea plus sandwiches, cake, and fruit tarts, in a somewhat crushed and frenzied atmosphere. The more expensive tea includes a Valrhona chocolate ice cream dessert as well as scones and clotted cream and a fruit tartlet accompanied by their Royal Blend tea. There are about a dozen different teas available, plus some wonderful sundaes.

✪ **Maison Bertaux.** 28 Greek St., W1. ☎ **0171/437-6007.** Pastry £1.50–£2.50 ($2.40–$4). No credit cards. Mon–Sat 9am–8pm, Sun 9am–1pm and 3–8pm. Tube: Leicester Sq. CAFE.

This has some of the most wonderful pastries and cakes anywhere. Try the hunk of chocolate cake or even a simple Danish. Fruit tarts are another specialty. Service can be erratic, but this isn't the Ritz and the price is right. Authentic theatrical Soho.

✪ **Patisserie Valerie.** 44 Old Compton St., W1. ☎ **0171/437-3466.** Coffees/teas, £1.60–£2 ($2.55–$3.20); pastries, £2.30–£3 ($3.70–$4.80); cream tea, £4.50 ($7.20); main courses, £6–£7 ($9.60–$11.20). AE, MC, V. Mon–Fri 8am–8pm, Sat 8am–7pm, Sun 9:30am–6pm. Tube: Leicester Sq./Tottenham Court Rd. CAFE/LIGHT FARE.

This chain also offers really fine pastries, croissants, and Danish. Here you can assemble a tea of your own, starting with a pot of your choice and a tart or pastry— mille feuille, chocolate eclair, lemon and chocolate tarts, or an alluring chocolate truffle cake. Or, if you prefer, you can opt for the cream tea, which is only £4.50 ($7.20). Enjoy it at a marble table while seated on a bentwood chair. At breakfast the almond croissants are a great start to the day. These are also good spots for light fare—quiches, pasta dishes, salads, and crepes. Most of the dining rooms have a sense of Edwardian style, with handsome murals. There are branches throughout London. Two central locations are: 215 Brompton Rd., Knightsbridge (☎ 0171/ 823-9971), conveniently located for Harrods; and 105 Marylebone High St. (☎ 0171/935-6240).

Ritz Hotel. Piccadilly, W1. ☎ **0171/493-8181.** Reservations are essential; make them at least two weeks in advance. £23.50 ($37.60) per person. AE, DC, MC, V. Daily sittings at 3:30–5pm. Tube: Green Park.

The elaborate afternoon tea at the legendary Ritz is probably the most famous tea in the world. It's served in the glass-domed Palm Court, which is opulently decorated in Louis XVI style with soaring marble columns. A pianist or harpist accompanies the affair. There are two sittings daily.

6

What to See & Do in London

So now you're set to explore what is currently Europe's hippest capital, a city strong in tradition and history. It's an exciting time to be visiting. Everywhere you look, mega building programs are in full swing, at such attractions as the Wallace Collection, British Museum, Tate Gallery, and National Portrait Museum. Much of the construction now underway is to prepare London for its huge Millennium Celebration, which will focus on two temporary structures: the British Airways Millennium Wheel (a gigantic ferris wheel) on the South Bank, and the Millennium Dome being constructed at Greenwich. What will be underneath the huge dome is still being decided but it will celebrate Britain's culture and its role in the world just as the great Crystal Palace Exhibition did.

There is just so much to see and do in London—and happily, much of the very best is free. In fact, a first-time visitor could spend a whole week visiting only the free attractions and have a fabulously entertaining visit. But there are also myriad ways to save money on the must-see sights that charge admission. Many tips have already been spelled out in chapter 2, but such valuable information certainly bears repeating.

HOW TO SAVE ON SIGHTSEEING

As I mentioned, the prime way to save money is take advantage of **all the major sights and attractions and experiences that are free.** It's a long list: the British Museum, the National Gallery, the Tate, and the Wallace Collection; the half dozen or so lovely parks; the hundreds of churches, many of which offer free concerts; Portobello Road and other markets; the pageants conducted at the Old Bailey, the Houses of Parliament, Buckingham Palace, and Whitehall; and, of course, the city streets themselves, which are lined with buildings that resonate with literary and historical associations.

Another way to save is to **purchase a three- or seven-day White Card** which provides discounts to 15 major museums and galleries—in all, a savings of £50. Equally useful is the **London for Less discount card and guidebook,** which grants savings on hotels, restaurants, shops, tours, and more. (The discounts offered by each card don't really overlap, so you may want to get both.) For information on purchasing these cards, see the Money-Saving Tips in chapter 2.

Finally, to get around as cheaply as possible, be sure to purchase a **London Transport Travelcard** (see "Getting Around" in chapter 3 for more details).

So whether you choose to focus on the old or the new, the timeless and indestructable or the hip and hot, it would take a lifetime to explore every alley and court, every attraction, every street and square in this sprawling city that Dr. Johnson said has "all that life can afford." For the first-time visitor, the question is never what to do, but what to do *first*. Consulting the "Suggested Itineraries" below and "London's Top Attractions" in this chapter will help.

Americans are notorious for whizzing around Europe's major sights trying to squeeze in as many of the "hits" as their brief vacations will allow. Europeans, who enjoy longer holidays, often poke fun at the hectic pace of vacationing Americans. Yet, when you have only a few days, moving at a fast clip is in order. If you prefer a slower pace, simply modify the itineraries below.

SUGGESTED ITINERARIES

If You Have 1 Day

Take the tube to Charing Cross or Embankment (they are within one block of each other) and cross into Trafalgar Square, London's most famous square and the city's unofficial hub. Here, the commercial West End meets Whitehall, the center of government, and The Mall, the regal avenue that leads to Buckingham Palace. In the center of the square is Nelson's Column. The National Gallery is on the northern side of the square, while the northeast side is dominated by the Church of St. Martin-in-the-Fields.

Turn down Whitehall and enter the Banqueting House, in the middle of the block, to view the nine magnificent, allegoric ceiling paintings by Rubens. Across the street from the Banqueting House, visit the home of the Queen's Life Guards, to see the Changing of the Guard, Monday through Saturday at 11am and on Sunday at 10am and 4pm (not to be confused with the larger affair at Buckingham Palace). Farther down Whitehall, in the middle of the street, you'll see the Cenotaph, dedicated to the citizens of the United Kingdom who died in the two world wars. Just opposite it is 10 Downing St., the official residence of the British prime minister. At the foot of Whitehall lies Parliament Square, site of Big Ben and the spectacular Houses of Parliament. The famous Westminster Abbey is just across Parliament Square.

After a late lunch and a short rest, take the tube into The City and visit St. Paul's Cathedral.

If You Have 2 Days

Follow the itinerary described above but at a more leisurely pace. During your Whitehall stroll, cross the beautiful St. James's Park to arrive at Buckingham Palace for the 11am Changing of the Guard. Save St. Paul's for the morning of your second day.

You could begin your walk of Whitehall from Parliament Square and end up at the National Gallery in Trafalgar Square. After visiting the gallery, continue north along Charing Cross Road, turn right on Long Acre, and visit Covent Garden. On the afternoon of your second day, visit one of the museums listed in "London's Top Attractions," below.

Central London Sights

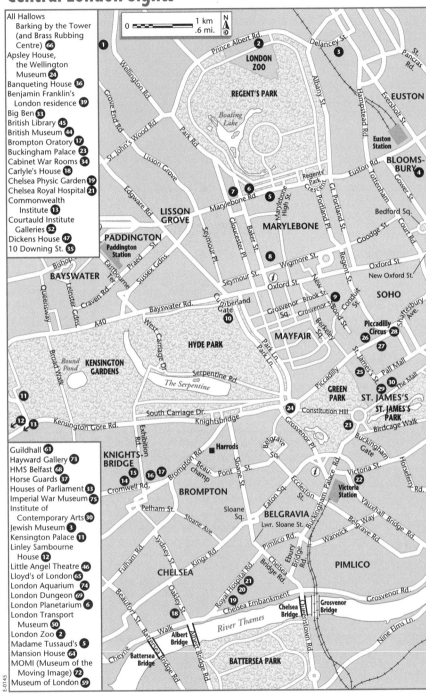

E-0145

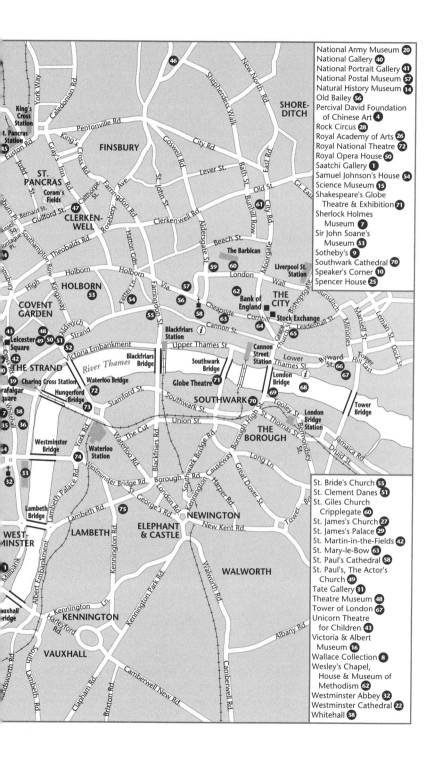

SHORE-
DITCH

King's
Cross
Station
t. Pancras
Station

FINSBURY

ST.
PANCRAS

Coram's
Fields

CLERKEN-
WELL

The Barbican

COVENT
GARDEN

Liverpool St.
Station

HOLBORN

Leicester
Square

Bank of
England

THE
CITY

Stock Exchange

Blackfriars
Station

Upper Thames St.

Cannon
Street
Station

River Thames

Blackfriars
Bridge

Southwark
Bridge

London
Bridge

Tower
Bridge

THE STRAND

Charing Cross Station

Waterloo Bridge

Hungerford
Bridge

Globe Theatre

SOUTHWARK

London
Bridge
Station

Westminster
Bridge

Waterloo
Station

THE
BOROUGH

Lambeth
Bridge

NEWINGTON

WEST-
MINSTER

LAMBETH

ELEPHANT
& CASTLE

WALWORTH

KENNINGTON

VAUXHALL

183

Cheap Thrills: What to See & Do in London for Free (or Almost)

- Visit **Sir John Soane's Museum,** the home of a remarkably ingenious architect and shrewd collector who does magic with mirrors.
- **Go to market.** Say it's antiques you're after—head to **Portobello Road.** If your taste runs more to funk and youth, spend early Saturday morning at Camden High Street. Both offer full days of fun.
- Wander through **Leighton House,** an Arabian Nights fantasy in Kensington that's filled with Victorian art.
- Sound off at **Speaker's Corner,** in the northeast corner of Hyde Park, where every Sunday anarchists, stand-up comics, religious fanatics, and would-be politicians spout their opinions and grievances on all subjects.
- Go to the **National Portrait Museum** and contemplate the visages of the great men and women who have contributed to Britain's history and culture.
- **Get outside.** London's sometime gloomy weather nonwithstanding, its parks definitely warrant a visit. Wander through **St. James Park,** across **Hampstead Heath,** or along the **Broad Walk** in Regent's Park.
- Visit the **Percival David Foundation of Chinese Art;** it's an opportunity to view one of the finest collections of Chinese ceramics anywhere in the world outside China.
- Go to the **Old Bailey** or the **Law Courts** to watch the black-gowned barristers weaving their arguments before even more grandly bewigged judges.
- Get a gardening fix at the **Museum of Garden History,** which offers historic gardens, gardeners, and botanists. A bonus: in the graveyard you'll find the tombstone of the infamous Captain Bligh.

If You Have 3 Days

Spend days one and two as described above. On your third day, visit the City of London and its host of interesting financial, legal, religious, and historical sights. Attractions include the Stock Exchange, the Royal Exchange, the Old Bailey, St. Paul's Cathedral, and St. Bride's Church, on Fleet Street. Try to time your sightseeing so that you are at St. Bride's for a free lunchtime recital (Tuesday, Wednesday, and Friday at 1:15pm, or Sunday at 11am and 6pm).

On the afternoon of your third day, visit the Museum of the Moving Image on the South Bank, then stroll over to the adjacent South Bank Arts Centre for a late-afternoon drink.

If You Have 5 Days

Spend your first three days as described above.

An extra couple of days will give you a chance to explore London's historic neighborhoods or to enjoy the city's cultural scene. If you like museums, be sure to make a pilgrimage to South Kensington. In addition to the Victoria and Albert Museum, no fewer than six other museums are found in this area, including the Natural History Museum, the Science Museum, the Geological Museum, and the Museum of Instruments. Diana fans will also want to stop at Kensington Palace, in Kensington Gardens.

- Explore the interior of **Westminster Cathedral,** ablaze with mosaics and columns in 100 different kinds and colors of marble.
- Pick up a snack or two at the city's **legendary food halls.** Harrods is a sensory experience as well as a remarkable study in lavish tile and decor. Fortnum & Mason, all red carpets and chandeliers, has a tradition that dates back almost three centuries. The Fifth Floor at Harvey Nichols, once Princess Di's favorite store, is the stylish latecomer.
- Hit the biggies: a morning at the celebrated **British Museum,** the standard bearer for major museums the world over; and the **Tate,** if only to see its Blakes and Turners.
- Sit in on **a session of Parliament** to see the PM answer questions (Wednesday at 2:30pm), or to see the antics of the MPs on both sides of the Speaker.
- Browse through the **Wallace Collection,** an amazing treasure trove amassed by the Marquesses of Hartford. Among the items on display are gorgeous Italian majolica and French Limoges, as well as some great paintings.
- Attend the **Notting Hill Carnival,** one of Europe's largest street festivals, featuring Caribbean music or food. Indeed, London hosts many other exciting **pageants and events,** from the Marathon to the Lord Mayor's Procession (see the Calendar of Events in chapter 2 for specifics).
- Take a trip to the **Geffreye Museum** to trace the arc of English domestic interior design from oak Tudor to art deco, all arranged in a beautiful historic complex of almhouse buildings.

1 London's Top Attractions

✪ **British Museum.** Great Russell St., WC1. ☎ **0171/636-1555;** 0171/580-1788 for recorded information. Main galleries free; £2 ($3.20) donation requested. Special exhibitions £4.50 ($7.20) adults, £3 ($4.80) students, seniors, and children under 16. Mon–Sat 10am–5pm, Sun 2:30–6pm. Tube: Holborn, Russell Sq., or Tottenham Court Rd.

Behind its classical facade, this museum is one of the richest storehouses of antiquities, prints, drawings, manuscripts, and objets d'art in the world. From a core collection purchased from Sir Hans Sloane in 1753, the museum has grown through acquisition and gifts. Celebrated objects and collections include: the **Rosetta Stone,** acquired from Napoleon after his defeat at Alexandria; **Lord Elgin's marbles** from the Parthenon and Erechtheum; **George III's library** (with almost 13,000 volumes); **Lady Raffle's Javanese collection; James Cook's South Sea Islands collection;** and the **Halicarnassus sculptures,** obtained by Sir Stratford Canning from Constantinople.

So much more is showcased today, too—the **Sutton Hoo** treasure hoard from the 7th century, a whole gallery of Egyptian mummies, Assyrian friezes, Babylonian astronomical instruments, the Diamond Sutra, and the world's oldest printed document, found in northern China.

Now that the British Library has decamped to its new premises, vacating 40 percent of the Bloomsbury complex, the British Museum has embarked on an ambitious program of expansion and renovation, which will be completed by 2003. Sir Norman Foster has been commissioned to create a Great Court, or covered square, at the center of the museum that will incorporate the Greek Revival courtyard designed by Sir Robert Smirke in 1823. A new elliptical building is also being constructed around the Reading Room that will house galleries, an educational center, bookshops, and a terrace restaurant.

The extraordinarily beautiful **British Library Reading Room** (constructed from 1852 to 1857), with its copper dome, which has been used by numerous scholars and writers, will be open to the general public for the first time in its history. Now you will be able to walk around the room that inspired so many, including Thomas Carlyle, Virginia Woolf, Mahatma Gandhi, Lenin, George Bernard Shaw, and Karl Marx (who wrote *Das Kapital* here).

The Department of Ethnography will return from the Museum of Mankind, and a series of permanent galleries for the display of the African, American, Pacific, European and Asian collections will be constructed.

Buckingham Palace. The Mall, SW1. ☎ **0171/930-4832;** 0171/799-2331 recorded info; 0171/321-2233 for credit card bookings 10am–4pm; 0171/839-1377 visitor office. Tours of the State Rooms £9.50 ($15.20) adults, £7 ($11.20) seniors, £5 ($8) children 5–17. Daily 9:30–4:15pm from second week in Aug to early Oct. Queen's Gallery £4 ($6.40) adults, £3 ($4.80) seniors, £2 ($3.20) children 5–17. Daily during exhibitions, 9:30am–4pm. Royal Mews £4 ($6.40) adults, £3 ($4.80) seniors, £2 ($3.40) children 5–17. Usually Tues–Thurs noon–4pm except Aug 3–Oct 1, 10:30am–4:30pm; times are very tentative so call ahead. Combined Gallery and Mews £6.50 ($10.40) adults, £4.50 ($7.20) seniors, and £3.50 ($5.60) children 5–17. Physically disabled visitors (only) can reserve tickets for palace tours directly from the palace (☎ **0171/839-1377**). Tube: Victoria, St. James's Park, or Green Park.

Buckingham Palace is the official London residence of Her Majesty the Queen; her personal standard flies when she is in residence. There are 600 rooms in the palace. The queen and the Duke of Edinburgh occupy a suite of just 12 rooms, and the remainder are used by the royal household or for affairs of state. Visitors can view the State Apartments—18 rooms in all—which are used for banquets, investitures, and other formal occasions. During the summer, the queen gives three famous parties in the 45-acre gardens. Attractively landscaped, the garden has one remaining mulberry tree planted by James I.

Buckingham House is reported to be the queen's least favorite residence. Originally the London home of the Duke of Buckingham, it was bought in 1762 by King George III and Queen Charlotte. King George IV converted it into a palace, commissioning John Nash to add some grandeur—which he did by adding wings at the front and extending those at the back, all for the astonishing sum of £700,000. Neither George IV nor his brother William IV lived here, though. By the time Queen Victoria came to the throne, the house was in a very poor state of repair: The drains were clogged, doors would not close, windows would not open, and bells would not ring. Nash was dismissed, and Edward Blore completed the repair work for Queen Victoria, who made it her official residence. It quickly became too small for the queen, and in 1847 the East Front, which faces The Mall, was constructed. At that time, the Marble Arch, which had stood in the palace's forecourt, was moved to its present position at the top of Park Lane. In 1913, a facade designed by Sir Aston Webb was placed here in the forecourt.

In 1962, the **Queen's Gallery** in the south wing was opened to the public. On view here are artworks from the royal collection—some of the finest pieces in the world. A recent show featured more than 400 pieces of Fabergé.

The **Royal Mews** is one of the finest working stables in the world today and well worth visiting. Housed here are the gilded and polished state carriages—such as the gold state coach used at every coronation since 1831—along with the horses that draw them.

In 1993, the queen opened the **State Rooms** at Buckingham Palace to the public to help raise money for the repair of Windsor Castle, which had been extensively damaged in a fire. Occupying the West Front, these include the **Throne Room** and other chambers in which ceremonial events take place. They are open during August and September when the royal family is on holiday. Overlooking the gardens, they are decorated with some of the finest pictures, tapestries, and furnishings from the royal collections. The queen's famous **picture gallery** is really worth seeing—it's a cache that includes Rembrandt's *The Shipbuilder and His Wife*, as well as works by Hals, Rubens, Van Dyke, and Claude Lorrain. Eager tourists start lining up at the palace gates at sunrise, and an hour-long wait is the rule. You must purchase a timed-entrance ticket on the same day you wish to take the palace tour (tickets go on sale at 9am).

The **Changing of the Guard** takes place daily from April through July at 11:30am, and on alternate days August through March. The ceremony is canceled during bad weather and for major state events. Always check ahead so you're not disappointed.

✪ **Hampton Court Palace.** East Molesey, Surrey. ☎ **0181/781-9500** for recorded information or 0181/781-9666. Admission £9.25 ($14.80) adults, £7 ($11.20) seniors, £6.10 ($9.75) children 5–15. Mid-Mar–mid-Oct Mon 10:15am–6pm, Tues–Sun 9:30am–6pm; mid-Oct–mid-Mar Mon 10:15–4:30pm, Tues–Sun 9:30am–4:30pm. Closed Dec 24–26. Train: From London Waterloo to Hampton Court (about 30 minutes). River launch: from Westminster Dock, Richmond, or Kingston. Call 0171/930-2062 or 930-4721 for information. The journey takes from 3 to 4 hours one-way, depending on the tide. Tickets cost £8 ($12.80) one-way, £12 ($19.20) round-trip for adults; £4 ($6.40) one-way, £7 ($11.20) round-trip for children under 15. Bus: 111, 131, 216, 411, 726, R68. Green Line Coach: 415, 416, 431, 451, 461.

On the banks of the Thames, about 15 miles southwest of London, sits this magnificent country palace, built originally in 1515 by Cardinal Wolsey as a retreat from the poisonous air and water and other inconveniences of London. He had it built to meticulous specifications. His plan called for 280 rooms and a staff of 500. When he fell into disfavor in 1525, he offered it to Henry VIII, who, despite the gesture, went ahead and confiscated all the cardinal's property anyway. Today, a visit to the Wolsey rooms and the Renaissance Picture Gallery will give you the aura of the period.

Henry VIII turned Hampton Court into an even grander pleasure palace. He constructed new courtyards and gardens, kitchens, galleries, a library, a covered tennis court, and a guard room. He also rebuilt the Great Hall with its splendid hammerbeam ceiling. Henry also loved to eat and entertain; the banquets that he presided over at Hampton Court were immense—a glimpse of the Tudor kitchens, where today costumed servants and wenches cook and entertain in traditional Tudor fashion, will give you some idea of their extravagance. The video offered in the state apartments will also provide some insight into what life was like at the Tudor court.

Queen Elizabeth I came to live at Hampton Court in 1559. She personally tended the gardens and planted them with new plants, such as tobacco and potatoes, brought back by Sir Francis Drake and Sir Walter Raleigh from their expeditions to South America.

During the Stuart period, especially under Charles I, the palace was further adorned with hundreds of paintings and other lavish objets d'art. Cromwell lived here, too, from 1651 to 1658. When Charles II moved in, the palace was once again buoyed up with a lively court. Pepys and Evelyn were regular visitors, as were the king's many mistresses.

William and Mary found the palace apartments old-fashioned and uncomfortable, so they commissioned Sir Christopher Wren to make improvements and asked such artists as Grinling Gibbons, Jean Tijou, and Antonio Verrio to decorate the rooms. Later, Anne redid the chapel and commissioned Thornhill and Verrio to paint murals in the drawing rooms. Under George I and II, restoration work continued, but with little personal attention from these monarchs. George II was the last monarch to live here. Supposedly, his successor, George III, hated the place ever since his grandfather boxed his ears as a boy in the State Apartments.

Among the highlights of the palace are the Tudor kitchens and the King's Apartments, as well as the Wolsey Rooms and Renaissance Picture Gallery. See, for example Andrea Mantegna's masterpiece, *Triumphs of Caesar*. Also, don't miss the phenomenal astronomical clock in Clock Court, which was created by Nicholas Oursian for Henry VIII in 1540.

The gardens are splendid too. Don't miss the famous maze and the Privy Garden. Capability Brown, who designed the gardens, planted the Great Vine in 1769. It still bears fruit today—fruit that is sold to visitors.

Three dining facilities are available for anything from a full meal to a snack.

✪ **Houses of Parliament.** Bridge St. & Parliament Sq., SW1. House of Commons ☎ **0171/219-4272;** House of Lords ☎ **0171/219-3107.** Free admission. House of Commons: public admitted Mon, Tues, Thurs starting at 2:30pm; Wed 9:30am–2pm and 2:30pm onwards; and Fri 9:30am–3pm. House of Lords: public admitted Mon–Wed from about 2:30pm, Thurs from about 3pm, and on some Fridays from 11am. Line up at St. Stephen's entrance, just past the statue of Oliver Cromwell. Debates usually run as late as 10pm and often into the night, and lines shrink after 6pm. If you want to attend the weekly Prime Minister's question time on Wednesday from 3pm, secure a ticket from your local MP (if you're a British resident), or from your embassy (if you are an overseas resident). Tube: Westminster.

Located in the Palace of Westminster, the Houses of Parliament, along with their trademark clock tower, are the ultimate symbol of London. Before the Norman Conquest of 1066, a palace built for Edward the Confessor stood on this site; it remained the home of the monarchy and the court until Henry VIII's time. Westminster Hall (1097) is the only part of that palace still standing today, but it's not open to the general public. The current Gothic Revival buildings of the Houses of Parliament date from 1840 and were designed by Charles Barry. (The earlier buildings were engulfed in flames in 1834—a fire to burn the tally sticks used to keep the Exchequer accounts got out of control.) Assisting Barry was Augustus Welby Pugin, who designed the paneled ceilings, tiled floors, stained glass, clocks, fireplaces, umbrella stands, and even inkwells. There are more than 1,000 rooms, 100 staircases, and two miles of corridors. The clock tower at the eastern end houses the world's most famous timepiece. **"Big Ben"** refers not to the clock tower, as many people assume, but to the largest bell in the chime, which weighs close to 14 tons and is named for the first commissioner of works. At night, a light shines in the tower whenever Parliament is in session.

Visitors may observe parliamentary debates from the **Strangers' Galleries** in both the Commons and the Lords—the Commons being of the greatest interest. Sessions usually begin in mid-October and run to the end of July, with recesses at Christmas and Easter.

Most visitors are struck by how small the **Commons chamber** is. When it was rebuilt in 1950 after being destroyed during the Blitz in 1941, the chamber was re-created in precise detail. Only 437 of its 651 members can sit at any one time, the rest must crowd around the door and the **Speaker's chair.** The ruling party and the opposition sit facing one another, two sword lengths apart, and on the table of the House sits the **mace,** a symbol of Parliament's authority.

Opulently decorated with frescoes and mosaics, the **House of Lords** seems almost sacrosanct. Debates here are not as interesting or lively as those in the Commons, but the line for admission is usually shorter. A visit here will give you an appreciation for the pageantry of Parliament. In front of the throne is the **Woolsack,** seat of the lord chancellor, who presides over the house; it's a reminder of the source of Britain's original great wealth, the wool trade.

National Gallery. Trafalgar Square, WC2. ☎ **0171/747-2885.** Main galleries free; Sainsbury wing, £3–£7 ($4.80–$11.20) during some special exhibitions. Mon–Sat 10am–6pm (Wed until 8pm), Sun noon–6pm. Closed Dec 24–26, Jan 1, and Good Friday. Tube: Charing Cross or Leicester Sq. Bus: Any bus going to Trafalgar Square; 3, 12, 24, 29, 53, 88, 159, 176, and many more.

This gallery houses Britain's collection of more than 2,200 paintings dating from 1260 to 1900. It's arranged by period in four wings. The **Sainsbury Wing** shows paintings from 1260 to 1510. Here you'll find works by Giotto, Masaccio, Piero della Francesca, Botticelli, Leonardo da Vinci, and Raphael. The **West Wing** displays paintings dating from 1510 to 1600 with examples of works by Cranach, El Greco, Holbein, Bruegel, Michelangelo, Titian, and Veronese. The **North Wing** offers masterpieces by 17th-century masters like Rubens, Van Dyck, Poussin, Velázquez, Rembrandt, and Vermeer. Works by such artists as Gainsborough, Constable, Turner, Hogarth, Canaletto, Goya, Ingres, Delacroix, Corot, Monet, Renoir, Cézanne, and Van Gogh are all found in the **East Wing.**

An audio guide to every painting on the main floor (about 1,000) is available for free, although a donation is suggested. Free guided tours are given, too. In the Sainsbury Wing, stop in the Micro Gallery and use one of the 12 workstations to view the visual encyclopedia containing background and other information on every painting in the collection. Look for special temporary shows from the museum's collection and visiting exhibits.

The Gallery has two excellent restaurants: the **Brasserie** in the Sainsbury Wing and the **Pret à Manger Cafe** in the Main Building.

✪ **Natural History Museum.** Cromwell Road, South Kensington, SW7. ☎ **0171/938-9123.** Admission £6 ($9.60) adult, £3.20 ($5.10) seniors, £3 ($4.80) children 5–17. Mon–Sat 10am–6pm, Sun 11am–6pm. Closed Dec 23–26, Jan 1, and Good Friday. Tube: South Kensington.

With towers, spires, and a huge navelike hall, this terra-cotta building is a wonder in itself. Designed by Alfred Waterhouse and opened in 1881, the museum is one of the finest of its kind. The core of the collection came from Sir Hans Sloane.Today, only a fraction of the museum's natural treasures—fossils, animal and plant life exhibits, and minerals—can be displayed. Among the highlights are the **dinosaurs** in the main hall, the **Human Biology exhibit** that features many interactive displays, an **ecology exhibit,** and "Discovering Mammals." In the Earth Galleries you can experience an **earthquake** and also walk under a volcano. Kids seem to love the creepy-crawly **insect display.**

✪ **St. Paul's Cathedral.** Ludgate Hill, St. Paul's Churchyard, EC4. ☎ **0171/248-2705.** Cathedral: £4 ($6.40) adults, £3.50 ($5.60) students and seniors, £2 ($3.20) children 6–16. Mon–Sat 8:30am–4pm. Galleries and crypt: £3.50 ($5.60) adults, £3 ($4.80) seniors, £1.50 ($2.40) children. Mon–Sat 10am–4pm, Sun for worship only. Tube: St. Paul's or Mansion House.

This is the place where Lady Diana Spencer and Prince Charles celebrated their marriage vows in 1981. The image of the carriage approaching the twin towers, and of Diana climbing the steps with her splendid train behind her, are indelibly imprinted on the minds of those who watched the most extravagant event in the recent history of this church.

St. Paul's stands on the site of 11th-century Old St. Paul's, which was destroyed in the Great Fire. After the fire, Christopher Wren cleared the site with a battering ram and set about rebuilding this magnificent building with its huge dome that at that time dominated the city skyline. More than 515 feet long and 365 feet high, the church took Wren 35 years to build, from 1675 to 1710. Anticipating that the commissioners overseeing the project might cut his budget, Wren, rather than starting at one end or the other, constructed the base first and worked from the ground up. Wren's anxiety was justified. He was constantly harassed by the commission, which cut his salary in half and obstructed his genius at every turn.

The **outer dome** of St. Paul's is so huge and heavy that Wren devised a smaller interior dome and a brick cone, sandwiched between the two, to support it. The cross on top is 365 feet above the sidewalk.

The **inner dome** is embellished with **frescoes depicting the life of St. Paul** by Sir James Thornhill—who narrowly escaped death while painting them. One day while standing on a high scaffolding, Thornhill stepped back to contemplate his work. Seeing Thornhill about to plunge to the church floor, an assistant smeared the wet paint of the fresco with a brush, and this caused Thornhill to jump forward angrily and safely back to the platform. These frescoes are best viewed from the **Whispering Gallery,** famous for its acoustics that enable a whisper to be heard 107 feet away on the opposite side of the gallery.

From the Whispering Gallery, a second steep climb leads to the **Stone Gallery.** Here visitors are presented with a fine view of the city. An additional 153-step climb brings you to the **Inner Golden Gallery** at the top of the inner dome and an even more dramatic view.

The two **west towers** were added as an afterthought. The southern one contains the famous **Great Tom,** which is rung when a member of the royal family, a Bishop of London, the Dean of St. Paul's, or the serving Lord Mayor dies.

The cathedral's ornamentation was completed by several artists. Grinling Gibbons carved the choir screens and stalls and the organ case. Francis Bird sculpted the statues of St. Paul, St. Peter, and St. James that grace the west front pediment. Tijou is responsible for the gates to the chancel aisles. Caius Gabriel Cibber executed the phoenix above the motto "Resurgam" on the pediment of the south door. The master mason William Kempster designed the geometrical staircase in the southwest tower.

It's amazing to think that Wren completed this masterpiece at the same time that he was working on 50 or more other churches. He's buried in **the crypt.** On his tombstone is inscribed *"Lector, si monumentum requiris, circumspice"* ("Reader, if you seek his monument, look around you"). Nelson is also buried in the crypt, marked by a sarcophagus that was originally created for Cardinal Wolsey. Wellington rests here, too. In the ambulatory, the American Memorial Chapel pays tribute to the American soldiers who lost their lives during World War II.

The cathedral has been the setting of some dramatic ceremonies, notably a thanksgiving in 1704 for the victory at Blenheim and another celebration a century later for Waterloo; and the funerals of Nelson (1806), Wellington (1852), and Winston Churchill (1965).

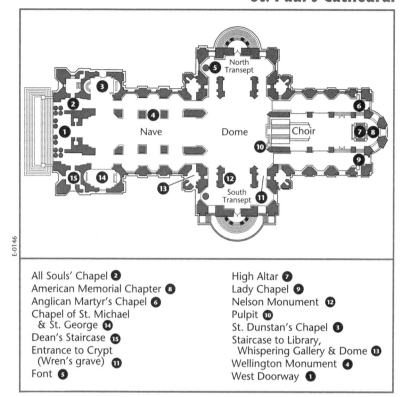

E-0146

All Souls' Chapel ❷
American Memorial Chapter ❽
Anglican Martyr's Chapel ❻
Chapel of St. Michael
  & St. George ⓮
Dean's Staircase ⓯
Entrance to Crypt
  (Wren's grave) ⓫
Font ❺

High Altar ❼
Lady Chapel ❾
Nelson Monument ⓬
Pulpit ❿
St. Dunstan's Chapel ❸
Staircase to Library,
  Whispering Gallery & Dome ⓭
Wellington Monument ❹
West Doorway ❶

✪ **Royal Botanic Gardens at Kew.** Richmond, Surrey. ☎ **0181/940-1171.** Information: Visitor Centre at Victoria Gate. Admission £5 ($8) adult, £3.50 ($5.60) senior, £2.50 ($4) children 5–16. Open daily 9:30am–4pm in winter, to 6:30pm in summer; Queen Charlotte's Cottage is open summer Sat–Sun and bank holidays only 11am–5:30pm. The Palace is currently closed for renovations until 2000. When it reopens, joint admission will be charged for Palace and Gardens. Tube: Kew Gardens. Train: From Waterloo to Kew Gardens or Kew Bridge. Bus: 65, 391. River Launch: from Westminster Pier (☎ **0171/930-2062**) to Kew Pier (☎ **0181/940-3891**).

Originally laid out by William Chambers and Capability Brown in the 17th and 18th centuries, these riverside gardens are world-renowned. More than 35,000 plants from all over the world grow at this 300-acre garden.

The most famous of the several glasshouses that incorporate four whole acres is the **Palm House** (1844–48) built by Decimus Burton and engineer Richard Turner. They also designed the **Temperate House.** John Nash designed the **Aroid House,** which now houses plants indigenous to a tropical rain forest. The newest and largest glasshouse is **the Princess of Wales Conservatory** (1987). The gardens are dotted with a variety of temples and sculptures, including the ten-story **Pagoda,** which was designed by Sir William Chambers and, more recently, a semi-reclining abstract figure by Sir Eduardo Paolozzi, which graces the Woodland garden. Most notable are the **Aquatic Gardens** and the **Orangery,** also designed by Chambers (1761). **Queen Charlotte's Cottage,** a timber-and-frame house with a thatched roof, dates from around 1771; it was first opened to the public in 1899. On the garden's eastern border, don't miss the **Marianne North Gallery,** which houses more than

800 oil paintings by this artist with an enthusiasm for botany. Also worth a visit is the refurbished museum overlooking the lake opposite the Palm House. Designed by Decimus Burton, the building houses displays of tools, ornaments, clothing, food, medicines, and other plant-related materials. Among the more unusual artifacts on display here are a Pacific Islands newspaper printed on beaten bark, rubber dentures, and a shirt made from pineapple fiber.

The gardens surround **Kew Palace** (☎ 0181/940-3321), the smallest of the royal palaces. Originally known as the Dutch House because of its sturdy gables, it was built in 1631. It was bought in 1781 by George III and became his and Queen Charlotte's favorite residence. Two floors are open to the public; in the **Queen's Drawing Room,** you can see the harpsichord played by J. C. Bach for the royals' entertainment.

✪ **Science Museum.** Exhibition Road, SW7. ☎ 0171/938-8000/8 or 0171/938-8123. Admission £6.50 ($10.40) adult, £3.50 ($5.60) seniors and children 5–17. Daily 10am–6pm. Closed Dec 24–26. Tube: South Kensington.

Britain was at the center of the first Industrial Revolution, and this museum won't let you forget it. Here are arrayed many of the early pioneering machines that ushered in the Industrial Age: the *Puffing Billy* (1813), one of the oldest locomotives still in existence; Stephenson's *Rocket* (1829); Arkwright's spinning machine; Wheatstone's electric telegraph; Fox Talbot's first camera; Edison's original phonograph; the Vickers "Vimy" aircraft, which made the first Atlantic crossing in 1919; and Sir Frank Whittle's turbo-jet engine. More modern examples of technology include the Apollo 10 command module and a fleece taken from "Dolly," the famous Scottish clone. Three new galleries are designed to appeal to children. The garden provides water, construction, sound and light shows, and games for 3- to 6-year-olds. The other two galleries appeal to 7- to 12-year-olds, allowing them to play on networked terminals and also to investigate the way things work through interactive exhibits.

✪ **Tate Gallery.** Millbank, SW1. ☎ 0171/887-8000. Permanent collection free; temporary exhibits £4–£7 ($6.40–$11.20). Daily 10am–5:50pm. Tube: Pimlico. Bus 77A, 88.

Founded in 1897 and endowed by sugar magnate Sir Henry Tate, this gallery displays two major collections. The first is a collection of **British art from the 16th to the late 19th centuries.** It consists of paintings, sculptures, and engravings by such major artists as Hogarth, Joshua Reynolds, John Constable, Thomas Gainsborough, William Blake, and the Pre-Raphaelites. This collection includes more than 300 brilliant oils and 30,000 watercolors by Turner—exhibited on a rotating schedule in the **Clore Gallery.** The second, the **Modern Collection,** includes works by British artists from 1880, as well as painting and sculpture done by international artists from the impressionist period and beyond. The Tate's permanent galleries are rehung every year to rotate the collection. The museum has an inspiring restaurant, decorated by Rex Whistler.

When the new Tate Gallery of Modern Art opens in spring 2000, across the river in the converted Bankside Power Station, the Millbank Tate will become the national repository of British art from 1500 to the present day.

The Power Station was originally designed by Sir Giles Gilbert Scott, who also designed Waterloo Bridge and the famous British red telephone box. The redesign is being completed by Swiss architects Herzog & de Meuron and will incorporate two additional floors with glass walls that will afford extraordinary views of the river and cityscape. The gallery will display 20th- and 21st-century art.

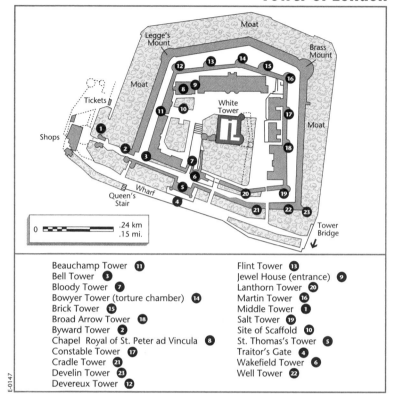

Tower of London

Beauchamp Tower **11**
Bell Tower **3**
Bloody Tower **7**
Bowyer Tower (torture chamber) **14**
Brick Tower **15**
Broad Arrow Tower **18**
Byward Tower **2**
Chapel Royal of St. Peter ad Vincula **8**
Constable Tower **17**
Cradle Tower **21**
Develin Tower **23**
Devereux Tower **12**

Flint Tower **13**
Jewel House (entrance) **9**
Lanthorn Tower **20**
Martin Tower **16**
Middle Tower **1**
Salt Tower **19**
Site of Scaffold **10**
St. Thomas's Tower **5**
Traitor's Gate **4**
Wakefield Tower **6**
Well Tower **22**

E-0147

Tower Bridge. SE1. ☎ **0171/378-1928.** Admission £5.95 ($9.50) adults, £3.95 ($6.30) seniors and children 5–15. Apr–Oct, daily 10am–6:30pm; Nov–Mar, daily 9:30am–6pm. Last entry is 1¼ hours before closing. Closed Dec 24–26, Jan 1, and the 4th Wed in January. Tube: Tower Hill.

Here's a lyrical London landmark you can't miss—possibly the most celebrated and most photographed bridge in the world. It's the one that a certain American thought he'd purchased instead of the one that spanned the Thames farther upriver. Despite its Gothic appearance, the bridge was built in 1894 and designed by Horace Jones, who died before its completion. The two towers are steel, clad in stone. Inside the towers, interactive exhibits trace the bridge's construction and its history.

Electrical power now raises and lowers the drawbridges, but the original hydraulic system (pre-1976) was preserved. In the south tower, you can see how that system worked—but unless you're a dedicated engineer, it might not thrill you that much.

Visitors can also climb onto the pedestrian walkways, where you'll find great views up- and downriver to St. Paul's, the Tower, and, in the distance, the Houses of Parliament.

The drawbridges are raised several hundred times a year to allow vessels to pass—in summer, about five times each day. Opening times change daily and are only announced one day in advance; call for information.

Tower of London. EC3. ☎ **0171/709-0765.** Admission £9.90 ($15.85) adults, £7.15 ($11.45) students and seniors, £6.25 ($10) children 5–15. March–Oct Mon–Sat 9am–6pm,

---

The Ceremony of the Keys

Plan in advance to attend the **Ceremony of the Keys** at the Tower of London. Every night for the past 700 years, the gates of this ancient fortress have been ceremoniously locked. At ten o'clock, the chief yeoman warder marches out across the causeway to the entrance gate, which he locks. From there the guard returns, locking the gates of the Byward Tower. As they approach the Bloody Tower, the sentry on duty confronts them and demands, "Halt, who goes there?" The chief yeoman warder replies "The Keys." "Whose keys?" demands the sentry. "Queen Elizabeth's keys," replies the chief warder. The sentry presents arms. The chief warder removes his Tudor bonnet and yells, "God preserve Queen Elizabeth." To which the whole guard replies, "Amen." You can watch this half-hour ritual if you request permission in writing at least one month in advance. Tickets are free. Write to: Ceremony of the Keys, 2nd floor, Waterloo Block, HM Tower of London, London EC 3N 4AB. Include an International Reply Coupon.

Sun 10am–6pm; Nov–Feb Mon–Sat 9am–5pm, Sun 10–5. Last tickets sold 1 hour before closing. Last entry to buildings 30 minutes before closing. Visitors should allow at least 2 hours to tour. Tours are given every half hour, starting at 9:30am. Closed Dec 24–26 and Jan 1. Tube: Tower Hill. Bus: 15, 25, 42, 78, 100, D1, D9, D11. Docklands Light Railway: Tower Gateway. River Launch: From Westminster Pier to Tower. For info call ☎ 0171/237-5134. A catamaran also operates from Charing Cross to the Tower. For info call ☎ 0171/987-1185.

The focal point of this perfect medieval fortress—the White Tower—was initially built by William I to protect London and to awe his new subjects. Each succeeding monarch added to it until the outer walls, built by Edward I, enclosed 18 acres. Long a royal palace and prison, during its history the Tower has also contained the royal mint, royal menagerie, royal armories, and royal observatory.

The massive impregnable tower at its center, dubbed the **White Tower** after a 1240 whitewashing, has walls 15 feet thick. Probably built about 1078 by order of William I, it remains one of the finest examples of Norman military architecture anywhere. Prison cells were on the first floor; soldiers' and servants' quarters on the second floor; and a banqueting hall, the Chapel of St. John and nobles' quarters on the third floor along with the royal bedrooms and the council chambers. Today, the White Tower houses the Royal Armouries Collection, an impressive array of armor—including a suit made to accommodate the massive girth of Henry VIII—artillery, weapons, and instruments of torture.

The **Bloody Tower** has a gruesome history worthy of its name. Here two princes, the 10- and 12-year-old sons of Edward IV, were imprisoned in 1483 by their Uncle Richard of Gloucester, who was off at Westminster having himself crowned King Richard III. Although the bodies of two children were later found near the White Tower in 1694, the mystery of the disappearance and possible murder of the princes has never been solved. Prisoners destined for the cells in the Bloody Tower passed through **Traitor's Gate** on the riverfront south of the tower. They were many and famous. Sir Walter Raleigh spent 13 years here living with his family and writing his *History of the World* before he was executed in 1618 at Westminster for treason.

Some prisoners were kept in **Beauchamp Tower.** Its interior walls are covered with their inscriptions, the most moving of which is "Jane," thought to have been carved by Lord Guilford Dudley of his beloved, Jane Grey, the "Nine Days' Queen." King Henry VI was imprisoned in **Wakefield Tower** in 1464. Rescued by Warwick the Kingmaker, he was later recaptured and returned to the Tower, where he was killed at prayer in 1471.

Executions were most frequent during the Reformation. The majority took place on **Tower Hill.** In 1535, John Fisher, Bishop of Rochester, and Sir Thomas More were both put to death here for refusing to sign the Oath of Supremacy making Henry VIII head of the Church. Fisher was so weak he had to be carried to the scaffold. Only a few were allowed the privacy and seclusion of being executed on Tower Green, including Henry VIII's second wife, Anne Boleyn, whose pretty head rolled in 1536. Losing favor with Henry for arranging his marriage to Anne of Cleves, Thomas Cromwell, who had brought the adultery charges against Anne, was beheaded in 1540. Sentenced to death that same year, the Countess of Salisbury, mother of Cardinal Pole, refused to place her head on the block. She ran screaming until she was dispatched standing up—or "fetched off slovenly," as it was described at the time. In 1542, Catherine Howard was beheaded for her adultery with Thomas Culpepper.

Before she became queen, Elizabeth I was briefly imprisoned in the **Bell Tower** after being implicated in a plot against Mary. Later, the Earl of Essex was executed for his aborted rebellion, as was the Duke of Monmouth, who chastised the executioner because the ax blade was so dull that it took three attempts to complete the deed. In the 18th century, numerous Jacobites were executed, except for lucky Lord Nithsdale, who escaped in 1716 dressed as his wife's maid.

After some valuables were stolen from Westminster Palace while King Edward I was away, the **Crown jewels** were moved to the Tower in 1303. Today, they're displayed in the ✪ **Jewel House** (1994). The collection includes several magnificent crowns, among them the Imperial State Crown encrusted with 3,200 jewels, including a ruby given to the Black Prince. In the late 17th century, an extraordinary attempt was made to steal the Crown jewels by an Irishman named Captain Blood and an accomplice. They posed as a parson and his wife, befriended the keeper, and then proposed to introduce their nephew to the keeper's daughter for a possible marriage. At this introduction, they requested to see the Crown jewels, attacked the keeper, and tied him up. The heist was foiled when the keeper's son returned unexpectedly, and the robbers were chased and captured. Charles II, though, was so charmed by Blood that he pardoned him, granted him estates in Ireland, and settled a £500 pension upon him. Some say that the king, who was short of money at the time, was in on the plot. Today visitors can also see a video of the 1953 coronation of Queen Elizabeth II. Note that despite the moving walkway (installed to handle the perpetual crowds who want to see the crown jewels), the wait can still be long and the experience wearing.

The **yeoman warders** who guard the Tower are not to be confused with the yeoman guard, established sometime before 1485. They are not and never should be referred to as "beefeaters." They are all highly decorated retired warrant officers or noncommissioned officers.

The **legendary ravens** are all that remain of the **royal menagerie,** which was kept at the Tower for hundreds of years. This zoo was begun in 1235 when the Holy Roman Emperor gave Henry III three leopards. Later, a polar bear was presented by the king of Norway and an elephant arrived from King Louis IX of France. In 1834, when it was removed to Regent's Park and became London Zoo, the menagerie had almost 60 animals.

The **Chapel of St. John** in the White Tower is a fine example of a Norman chapel; it's only 55 feet long and 36 feet wide. With their cubiform capitals, the massive columns supporting the nave are typically Romanesque. In the **subcrypt,** 600 Jews were imprisoned in 1278 for supposedly clipping the coinage. Of them, 267 were hanged, and the rest were banished. During the Peasants' Revolt in 1381, the king's ministers were dragged from the chapel's altar to Tower Hill and beheaded. In the hall off the chapel, Henry IV initiated the Ceremony of the Bath on the night before his coronation; an elite corps took baths and were invested into the knighthood Order of the Bath.

Among those buried at the Royal Chapel of St. Peter ad Vincula (St. Peter in Chains) are John Fisher, Thomas More, Anne Boleyn, Catherine Howard, and Lady Jane Grey.

Every three years on Ascension Day, a ceremony called the **Beating of the Bounds** is conducted. The Tower is not under the jurisdiction of the city, so its liberties have to be confirmed and its boundaries set by a painter who marks them on the ground.

During the Tower's long and bloody history, torture played a major part. Today, the instruments used are on display: bilboes that shackled ankles; thumbscrews; the Scavenger's Daughter that fastened the neck, wrists, and ankles; and the rack that reduced Guy Fawkes to confession in 30 minutes.

See the box, **"The Ceremony of the Keys,"** above for information on attending the Tower's nightly ceremony.

✪ **Victoria & Albert Museum.** Cromwell Rd., SW7. ☎ **0171/938-8500** (8441 for general information; 8349 for current exhibitions). Admission £5 ($8) adults, £3 ($4.80) seniors, free for children under 18. It's free 4:30–5:45pm. Mon noon–5:45pm, Tues–Sun 10am–5:45pm, with late admission on Wed 6:30–9:30pm to selected galleries for only £3 ($4.80). Closed Dec 25–27. Tube: South Kensington.

Named after Queen Victoria and her consort, the V&A is an enormous treasure house devoted to the decorative and fine arts. Huge, in both size and scope, the museum has 7 miles of galleries. They hold fabulous collections of sculpture, furniture, fashion, textiles, paintings, prints, photographs, silver, glass, ceramics, and jewelry—from Britain and all over the world. The **Dress Court** shows the history of fashion from 1500 to the present day. (Check out Vivienne Westwood's gigantic blue mock-crocodile platform shoes from which supermodel Naomi Campbell fell during a Paris fashion show.) The **Furniture Collection** has pieces by designers from Chippendale to Charles Rennie Mackintosh. The **National collection of British watercolors** has one of the finest collections of Constables. The **Devonshire Hunting Tapestries** date from the 15th century. The **Medieval Treasury** includes the Gloucester Candlestick (1105). Of the museum's collection of Renaissance and Victorian sculpture, the most valued piece to date is *The Three Graces* by Antonio Canova, for which £7.6 million was paid. The Canon Gallery is the latest to open, showcasing selections from the museum's world-class photography collection. Special collections feature the work of William Morris, the Arts and Crafts movement, and the Pre-Raphaelites. The **Great Bed of Ware** is here; it's referred to by Shakespeare in *Twelfth Night*. Raphael's famous *Cartoons* are beautiful—seven designs for tapestries commissioned by Pope Leo X in 1514 to hang in the Sistine Chapel. The Nehru Gallery of Indian Art displays Shah Jahan's jade cup. The Tsui Gallery is rich in Chinese art. The 20th-century Gallery is devoted to contemporary art and design. The Glass Gallery displays 7,000 objects, among them ancient Egyptian perfume bottles and the Luck of Eden Hall Vase, which had a curse laid on it when it was brought to England from the Holy Land by a 14th-century crusader. The Ironwork Gallery displays English and continental decorative ironwork spanning eight centuries—everything iron from balconies to cookie tins. Another gallery is devoted to Frank Lloyd Wright. In addition there are always fascinating temporary exhibits on display.

Westminster Abbey

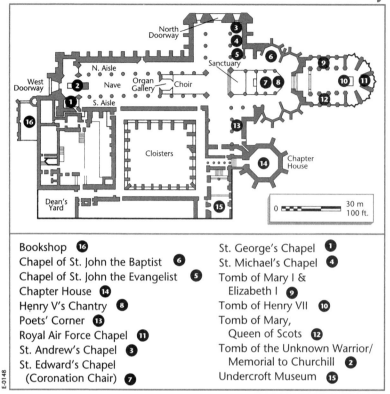

Bookshop **16**
Chapel of St. John the Baptist **6**
Chapel of St. John the Evangelist **5**
Chapter House **14**
Henry V's Chantry **8**
Poets' Corner **13**
Royal Air Force Chapel **11**
St. Andrew's Chapel **3**
St. Edward's Chapel
　(Coronation Chair) **7**

St. George's Chapel **1**
St. Michael's Chapel **4**
Tomb of Mary I &
　Elizabeth I **9**
Tomb of Henry VII **10**
Tomb of Mary,
　Queen of Scots **12**
Tomb of the Unknown Warrior/
　Memorial to Churchill **2**
Undercroft Museum **15**

E-0148

The collections are displayed in two ways. The Art and Design Galleries are arranged by place or date showing their visual relationships and cultural influences; the Materials and Techniques Galleries trace the developments in form, function, or technique of the particular material. The cafe here offers fine cuisine and an appealing ambience plus an extra-special jazz brunch on Sunday for £8.50 ($13.60).

✪ **Westminster Abbey.** Dean's Yard, SW1. ☎ **0171/222-5152.** Abbey, £5 ($8) adults, £3 ($4.80) seniors/students, £2.50 ($4) children 11–15. Abbey, Mon–Fri 9:20am–4pm, Sat 9:20am–1:45pm; Cloisters, Mon–Sat 8am–6pm. Brass rubbing center open Mon–Sat 9am–5pm. For times of daily services call **0171/222-5152.** Comprehensive guided tours are given by the abbey's vergers for £3 ($4.80) per person. Apr–Oct they leave weekdays at 10, 10:30, and 11am, and 2, 2:30, and 3pm (except Fri); Sat at 10 and 11am and 12:30pm. Nov–Mar, they leave weekdays 10 and 11am and 2 and 3pm (except Fri); Sat at 10am, 11am, and 12:30pm. Tube: Westminster/St. James's Park.

Neither a cathedral nor a parish church, Westminster Abbey is a "royal peculiar," under the jurisdiction of a dean and chapter and subject only to the sovereign. An architectural masterpiece, the Gothic abbey dates largely from the 13th to 16th centuries. The first church on the site was built in the 7th century by King Sebert of the East Saxons, on the instruction of St. Peter—who is said to have materialized at its consecration given by Mellitus, the first bishop of London. In 1050, Edward I built his palace and a church here in Westminster. Much of what visitors see today, however, dates from the reign of Henry III, who began rebuilding the existing edifices around 1245. Every coronation since 1066 has taken place at Westminister Abbey, and so have many seminal events in the life of the nation, including, most recently, the funeral of Princess Diana.

The **nave** soars 106 feet, the highest in Britain. It contains the **grave of the Unknown Warrior,** representative of all those who fell in World War I. The soldier was buried here in 1920 in soil that was brought from French battlefields, and the stone is from Belgium. Today, the nave is lit by six Waterford chandeliers, donated by the Guinness family to celebrate the abbey's 900th anniversary.

The **cloisters,** which were rebuilt after a fire in 1298, contain illuminated panels by David Gentleman on the East Walk. These show the various stages in the abbey's construction. Today, visitors can make a rubbing at the cloister's **Brass Rubbing Center** (☎ **0171/222-2085**). Also in the east cloister is the **Chapter House** (1245–55). The king's great council gathered here for the first time in 1257, during the reign of Henry III. From the middle of the 14th century to 1547, the Chapter House was used as a Parliament House for the Commons. Close by is the **Pyx Chamber,** where the standards for the coinage were kept. It displays the plate of the abbey and of St. Margaret's Church.

The **Norman Undercroft** houses a display of famous royal and nonroyal effigies, which were carried on the tops of coffins in funeral processions. Other exhibits include replicas of the coronation regalia.

In the south transept, **Poets' Corner** contains a veritable literary history of Britain. It originated in 1400, when Geoffrey Chaucer was buried here with a simple memorial. He was, in fact, interred here not because he was a famous poet, but because he worked for the abbey. Among other famous literary figures buried here are Ben Jonson (standing upright), Dryden, Samuel Johnson, Sheridan, Browning, and Tennyson. The practice of placing memorials to literary greats began in earnest in the 18th century. The first was the full-length figure of Shakespeare. The others that followed are to Eliot, Auden, Dylan Thomas, Lewis Carroll, William Blake and, more recently, Virginia Woolf (1991) and Oscar Wilde, whose memorial window was unveiled finally in 1995.

Many other famous people are buried or memorialized throughout the abbey. The politicians Castlereagh, Canning, Peel, Palmerston, and Gladstone are all buried here. The ashes of politicians Andrew Bonar Law, Neville Chamberlain, Clement Attlee, and Ernest Bevin are ensconced here, too. Scientists resting here include Sir Isaac Newton, Lord Rutherford, Robert Stephenson, and Thomas Telford. So, too, are the architects Robert Adam, Sir William Chambers, Charles Barry, and Sir George Gilbert Scott. The explorer David Livingston and theatrical greats David Garrick and Henry Irving lie here. Yet, there's only one painter, Godfrey Kneller.

Behind the high altar stands the **Shrine of Edward the Confessor,** who founded the abbey. He died only a few days after it was consecrated on December 28, 1065. The shrine was built by Henry III. Buried near the shrine are five kings and four queens, including Henry III, Edward III, and Richard II. The **Henry VII Chapel** (1519) has an extraordinary Tudor vaulted roof. Since 1725, it's been used as the **Chapel of the Order of the Bath;** their colorful banners, crests, and mantlings adorn the wooden stalls, which have beautifully carved misericords underneath their seats. In the north aisle of this chapel is the **grave of Elizabeth I,** who lies in the same vault as her half-sister Mary. The white marble effigy is reckoned a faithful likeness of the queen. Behind the altar is the final resting place of King Henry VII and his consort, Elizabeth of York, marked by a monument by Torrigiani. At the east end is the **Royal Air Force Chapel,** containing a memorial window that incorporates the crests of the 68 Fighter Squadrons which took part in the Battle of Britain in 1940.

The **Coronation Chair,** an oak chair made for King Edward I by Master Walter of Durham, was designed to hold the ancient **Stone of Scone,** seized from the Scots in 1296. The stone, on which Scottish kings were crowned, had been stolen back by Scottish nationalists several times—and recently it was, in fact, finally returned to Scotland. The chair has been used at every coronation since 1308.

2 Historic Buildings & Monuments

✪ **Cabinet War Rooms.** Clive Steps, King Charles St., SW1. ☎ **0171/930-6961.** Admission £4.80 ($7.70) adults, £3.60 ($5.75) students and seniors, £2.40 ($3.85) children 5–16. Daily Apr–Sept, daily 9:30am–6pm (last admission 5:15pm); Oct–Mar, daily 10–6pm (last admission 5:15pm). Closed Dec 24–26. Tube: St. James's Park or Westminster.

This warren of underground rooms served as the British government's headquarters during World War II. They were the nerve center of Churchill's government during the fight against the Nazis and are preserved exactly as they were back then. Crucial decisions were made here in the Cabinet Room; the progress of the war and the status of the military campaigns were plotted in the Map Room. You can see the Telephone Room, too, where so many calls were placed and received from FDR, plus Churchill's Emergency Bedroom. It's eerie and oddly exciting imagining Churchill and his staff installed here living a subterranean life for so long during their battle against Hitler.

Jewel Tower. Abingdon St., Westminster, SW1. ☎ **0171/222-2219.** Admission £1.50 ($2.40) adults, £1.10 ($1.75) seniors, 80p ($1.30) children. Apr–Oct, daily 10am–1pm and 2–6pm; Nov–March, daily 10am–1pm and 2–4pm. Closed Dec 24–26. Tube: Westminster.

Opposite the Houses of Parliament, this is the only surviving portion of the medieval Palace of Westminster dating from 1365 to 1366. The tower houses an exhibition about Parliament, which includes a virtual reality tour of both houses.

Kensington Palace State Apartments and Court Dress Collection. Kensington Gardens. ☎ **0171/937-9561.** Admission £7.50 ($12) adults, £5.90 ($9.45) seniors and students, £5.35 ($8.55) children 5–15. Summer daily 10am–6pm; winter Wed–Sun 10am–4pm. Tube: Queensway or Bayswater.

This palace surrounded by beautiful gardens has become a pilgrimage site ever since Princess Diana's death in August 1997. At the time, people flocked to the palace gates after the news was announced and carpeted the ground with hundreds of flower tributes. According to an announcement made in late 1997 by the Queen, the Palace will become a memorial to the late Princess as well as home to the Royal Collection of Art.

Originally a modest Jacobean home, it was purchased by William and Mary from the Earl of Nottingham in 1689. William suffered from asthma, and sought an escape from the putrid air that enveloped Whitehall. The royal couple then commissioned Sir Christopher Wren to make some alterations. Queen Anne, who succeeded William III in 1702, found the palace comfortable, too. Anne laid out the gardens in English style; she had the Orangery House built after designs of Nicholas Hawksmoor. The queen spent many happy times at Kensington Palace with her friend Sarah Churchill, the Duchess of Marlborough, until one of the most legendary tiffs between friends occurred. One day the duchess complained to the Queen that she had been "kept waiting like a Scotch lady with a petition," to which the queen replied by asking her to put it in writing; the duchess did and they never associated again. Queen Anne died here in 1714 from apoplexy brought on by overeating. The first two Georges lived at the palace, but George III abandoned it in favor of Buckingham House, and so the palace fell into disrepair. Edward, duke of Kent, the fourth son of George III, did have apartments here, though. His daughter, the future Queen Victoria, was born and baptised here on May 24, 1819. She also heard of her succession to the throne here on June 27, 1837, when the archbishop of Canterbury and the Lord Chamberlain roused her from her sleep to inform her that she had succeeded her uncle William IV to the throne. That night, she slept outside her mother's room for the first time in her life. Three weeks later, she moved into Buckingham Palace. Today, Princess Margaret, the Duke and Duchess of Gloucester, and Princess Michael of Kent all have apartments here.

Only the **State Apartments** and **Court Dress Collection** are open to the public. Among the highlights in the first are the Cupola Room, where Queen Victoria was baptized and where she was told that she was queen, and the King's Gallery, which features among others seven ceiling paintings depicting the journeys of Ulysses. These are stunning enough, but even more so are the Pompeiian-style ceilings painted by Kent in the Presence Chamber and the illusionist gallery (also painted by Kent) on the walls of the King's Staircase. The dress collection displays court fashions and uniforms from 1760 to 1950. The gardens and parkland surrounding the palace are beautiful, and you can have lunch or tea in the Orangery, which was designed by Hawksmoor and Vanbrugh for Queen Anne.

Mansion House. Bank, EC4. ☎ **0171/626-2500.** Free admission. Tours given on Tues, Wed, and Thurs at 11am and 2pm for groups only. They must be booked in advance by writing to the Principal Assistant-Diary, Mansion House, London EC4N 8BH. Tube: Mansion House.

This is the official residence of the lord mayor of London during his annual term of office. The original plans of this impressive Palladian building were executed by George Dance. The foundation stone was laid in 1739 but the building was not completed until 1753. The 103-foot-wide facade has a raised portico supported by six Corinthian columns. On the pediment, sculptures depict London trampling Envy and leading in Plenty, while Father Thames stands by. In 1768, when John Wilkes was elected to Parliament, a mob of his supporters broke the windows and chandeliers of Mansion House because the lights were not illumined to celebrate his victory. The house has several prison cells, one of which housed suffragette Emmeline Pankhurst in 1914 for demonstrating outside Buckingham Palace. Today the Mansion House houses the staff of the Lord Mayor's Office.

Spencer House. 27 St. James's Place, SW1. ☎ **0171/499-8620.** Admission £6 ($9.60) adults, £5 ($8) seniors and children under 16; children under 10 not allowed. Sun 10:45am–4:45pm. Closed Jan and Aug. Tube: Green Park.

This is one of the city's most beautiful buildings, with sumptuous, classically inspired interiors. It was built in 1756–1766 for John, the first Earl Spencer, an ancestor of Princess Diana. He was the great-grandson of Sarah Churchill, Duchess of Marlborough. He had secretly married his sweetheart Goergiana Poyntz at Althorp and soon after set about building a splendid new London house in St. James. They were a very wealthy couple; the diamond buckles on his honeymoon shoes alone were valued at £3,000. By 1927, it was no longer a private residence and has experienced a checkered history since then. At various times, it was rented to the Ladies' Army and Navy Club, Christie's, and British Oxygen Gases Ltd. In 1987, a painstaking restoration was begun which has returned it to the full splendor of its late-18th-century appearance. The eight state rooms were some of the first neoclassical interiors created in London by John Vardy and James Stuart. The series of gilded palm trees make the Palm Room spectacular; the Painted Room contains superb gilded furniture set against a backdrop of elegant mural decoration celebrating the Triumph of Love. The other rooms are all richly decorated and furnished, especially the Great Room, which has a lavish painted ceiling. Each also contains pictures from a fine collection of art that includes five portraits by Benjamin West.

3 Churches, Cathedrals & a Cemetery

Many of the churches listed below offer free **lunchtime concerts**—it's customary to leave a small donation. A full list of churches offering lunchtime concerts is available from the London Tourist Board.

All Hallows Barking by the Tower of London. Byward Street, EC3. ☎ **0171/481-2928.** Free admission. Museum Mon–Fri 11am–4:30pm; Church Mon–Fri 11am–6pm, Sat–Sun 10am–5pm. Tube: Tower Hill.

Through excavation work, archaeologists have determined that a church has stood here since Saxon times. In 1644, William Penn was baptized here. The following year, Archbishop Laud was buried here after he was executed; later his body was removed to St. John's College, Oxford. In 1797, John Quincy Adams got married at All Hallows. Bombs destroyed the church in 1940, leaving only the tower and walls standing. Rebuilt from 1949 to 1958, the church now has a brass rubbing center.

✪ **Brompton Oratory.** Brompton Road, SW7. ☎ **0171/589-4811.** Free admission. Daily 6:30am–8pm. Tube: South Kensington.

This Roman Catholic Church served by the priests of the Institute of the Oratory founded by St. Philip Neri was settled in 1849. The baroque-style building was designed by Herbert Gribble from 1880 to 1884, and modeled after the mother church of Rome's Chiesa Nova. Inside, it has the third widest nave in Britain after Westminster Cathedral and York Minster. The marble statues of the Apostles are by Mazzuoli and were brought from Siena Cathedral. The Oratory is famous for its **musical services** and for the solemn mass celebrated in Latin at 11pm on Sunday. Its organ has nearly 4,000 pipes.

Highgate Cemetery. Swain's Lane, N6. ☎ **0181/340-1834.** East cemetery £2 ($3.20); west cemetery £4 ($6.40). Apr–Sept, daily 10am–5pm; Oct–Mar, daily 10am–4pm. Tours at noon, 2pm, and 4pm weekdays, every hour on weekends, although call ahead and make an appointment before trekking out to Highgate. Avoid Sunday, when it's very crowded. Tube: Archway.

Serpentine pathways wind through this beautiful cemetery, laid out around a huge, 300-year-old cedar tree. Lined with tombs, **Egyptian Avenue** stretches beyond an archway—supported by two Egyptian columns and obelisks—to the **Circle of Lebanon.** This circular passageway is lined with catacombs. The cemetery was so popular and fashionable in the Victorian era that it was extended on the other side of Swain's Lane in 1857. Among the famous buried in the old western cemetery—which is only accessible if you take a guided tour, given hourly in summer—are scientist **Michael Faraday** and poet **Christina Rossetti.** In the eastern cemetery lie **Karl Marx,** marked by a gargantuan bust; novelist **George Eliot;** and philosopher **Herbert Spencer.** The grave of Marx is popular with government delegations visiting from China; in fact, the Chinese government helps pay for its upkeep. The cemetery is still very much in use and the proper respect is appropriate. *Note:* No children under 8 are allowed into the cemetery. Only small cameras are permitted, at the discretion of the wardens.

St. Bride's Church. Fleet St., EC4. ☎ 0171/353-1301. Free admission. Weekdays 8:30–4:30pm, Sat 9am–4:30pm, Sun 9:30am–12:30pm and 5:30–7:30pm. Concerts at 1:15pm on Tues, Wed, and sometimes Fri. Tube: Blackfriars. Bus 4, 11, 17, 15, 23, 26, 45, 63, 76, 172.

Known as the "the church of the press," St. Bride's is a remarkable landmark. The current church is the eighth one that has stood here. After it was bombed in 1940, an archaeologist excavated the crypts and was able to confirm much of the site's legendary history: A Roman house was found preserved in the crypt, and it was established that St. Brigit of Ireland had founded the first Christian church here. Among the famous parishioners have been writers John Dryden, John Milton, Richard Lovelace, and John Evelyn. The diarist Samuel Pepys and his eight siblings were all baptized here. The novelist Samuel Richardson and his family are buried here. After the Great Fire destroyed it, the church was rebuilt by Sir Christopher Wren for £11,430, excluding the spire. This was added later and has been described as a "madrigal in stone." The spire has four octagonal tiers capped by an obelisk that's topped off with a ball and vane. This soaring confection (234 feet tall) supposedly inspired the wedding cakes of a pastry cook who lived on Fleet Street in the late 17th century. The crypts had been used as burial chambers and a charnel house for centuries; today, they're a museum. **Concerts** are given on Tuesday and Friday, and an **organ recital** is given on Wednesday.

St. Clement Danes. Strand, WC2. ☎ 0171/242-8282. Free admission. Daily 9am–5pm. Tube: Temple.

It's not known for certain why Danes is part of the church's name, but we do know that there was a Saxon church on this site. In the late 10th century, that wooden church was rebuilt in stone. Although the church survived the Great Fire, it was declared unsafe, and Sir Christopher Wren was commissioned to rebuild it. The spire was designed by James Gibbs. The interior is decorated with ornate plasterwork. Samuel Johnson attended services here regularly. Robert Cecil, later Earl of Salisbury, was baptized here in 1563. Bishop George Berkeley and the wife of poet John Donne are buried here. The Blitz totally gutted the church, and it was rebuilt in the late 1950s. Today, this is the central church of the RAF. It contains memorials to the British, Commonwealth, and American airmen who flew in World War II. The church is often believed to be the source of the nursery rhyme, "Oranges and lemons say the bells of St. Clements," a ditty still memorialized by the gift of an orange and a lemon to each child of the attached primary school after a special annual service. (The rhyme, though, more likely refers to St. Clement Eastcheap, located on the riverfront, where citrus fruits were unloaded.)

St. Giles Church Cripplegate. Corner of Fore and Wood Sts., London Wall, EC2. ☎ 0171/606-3630. Free admission. Mon–Fri 9am–5pm, Sat 9am–noon, Sun for services. Tube: Moorgate or Barbican.

Named for the patron saint of cripples, St. Giles was founded in the 11th century. The church survived the Great Fire, but the Blitz left only the tower and walls standing.

Betrothed here in 1620 was Oliver Cromwell to Elizabeth Bourchier. John Milton, author of *Paradise Lost*, was buried here in 1674. More than a century later, someone opened the poet's grave, knocked out his teeth, stole a rib bone, and tore hair from his skull.

St. James's Church. 197 Piccadilly, W1. ☎ 0171/734-4511. Free admission. Recitals Wed–Fri at 1:10pm. Tube: Piccadilly Circus.

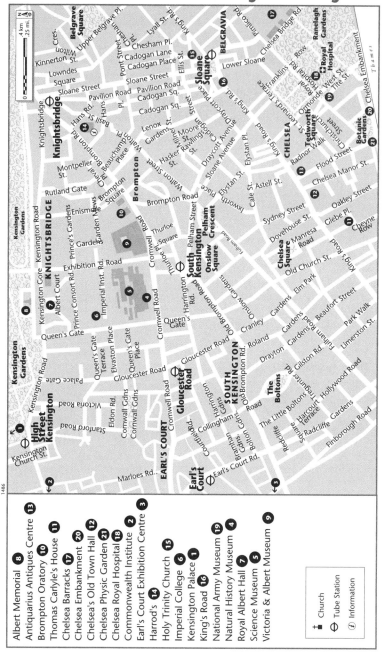

Albert Memorial **8**
Antiquarius Antiques Centre **13**
Brompton Oratory **10**
Thomas Carlyle's House **17**
Chelsea Barracks **20**
Chelsea Embankment **12**
Chelsea's Old Town Hall **21**
Chelsea Physic Garden **18**
Chelsea Royal Hospital **2**
Commonwealth Institute **3**
Earl's Court Exhibition Centre **14**
Harrod's **15**
Holy Trinity Church **6**
Imperial College **1**
Kensington Palace **16**
King's Road **19**
National Army Museum **4**
Natural History Museum **7**
Royal Albert Hall **5**
Science Museum **9**
Victoria & Albert Museum

＋ Church
Φ Tube Station
ⓘ Information

When the aristocratic area known as St. James was developed in the late 17th century, Sir Christopher Wren was commissioned to build its parish church. Diarist John Evelyn wrote of the interior, "There is no altar anywhere in England, nor has there been any abroad, more handsomely adorned." The reredos, the organ case, and the font were all carved by Grinling Gibbons. As might be expected, this church has rich historical associations. Baptized here were the poet William Blake and William Pitt (the first Earl of Chatham, who became England's youngest prime minister at age 24). Caricaturist James Gillray, auctioneer James Christie, and coffeehouse founder Francis White are all buried here. One of the more colorful marriages celebrated here was that of explorer Sir Samuel Baker and the woman he had bought at a slave auction in a Turkish bazaar.

Lunchtime recitals are given, as are inexpensive evening concerts as well.

St. Martin-in-the-Fields. Trafalgar Sq., WC2. ☎ **0171/930-1862.** Free admission. Daily 8am–7:30pm. Tube: Charing Cross, Leicester Sq., or Embankment.

Famous for its music, this is one of London's most beautiful and best-loved churches. Handel played on its first organ, and it's said Mozart performed here, too. Today, **free lunchtime concerts** are given Monday, Tuesday, and Friday beginning at 1:05pm. **Candlelit evening concerts** are performed, too. (Tickets cost around £12/$19.20; for information, call ☎ **0171/839-8362.**) The three Sunday services offer great **choral music,** often featuring choirs visiting from other countries. If I had to choose one quintessential Anglican service, it would be **Evensong,** usually at 5pm, but call ahead for specific times.

A place of worship has stood here since 1220; the current church, designed by James Gibbs, was completed in 1726. Its simple nave is enhanced by an intricate plasterwork ceiling. Curiously, the parish boundary passes through the middle of Buckingham Palace, and the names of many royal children appear on the baptismal registry. The Queen Mother, who resides at Clarence House, is also a parishioner.

In the crypt, there's an atmospheric cafe, shop, and the **London Brass Rubbing Centre** (open Mon–Sat 10am–8pm, Sun noon–6pm; see "Especially for Kids," below, for more information).

St. Mary Le Bow. Cheapside, EC2. ☎ **0171/248-5139.** Free admission. Mon–Thurs 6:30am–6pm, Fri 6:30am–4pm. Closed major holidays and week after Christmas and Easter. Lunchtime concerts are usually given Thurs at 1:05pm. Tube: St. Paul's/Bank. Bus 8, 25.

A true Cockney is said to be born within hearing distance of the famous Bow bells of this church. Destroyed in the Blitz, those bells have been replaced. The church's history has been marked by a series of somewhat disturbing and gruesome incidents. The first occurred in 1091, when its roof was ripped off in a storm, the second when the church tower collapsed in 1271, killing 20 people. In 1331, Queen Philippa and her ladies-in-waiting fell to the ground when a wooden balcony collapsed during a joust celebrating the birth of the Black Prince. The Great Fire destroyed the church, and it was rebuilt by Wren. The church was rededicated in 1964 after extensive restoration work.

St. Paul's, The Actors Church. Covent Garden, WC2. Free admission. Tube: Covent Garden.

As the Drury Lane Theatre, the Theatre Royal, and the Royal Opera House are all within its parish, St. Paul's has long been associated with the theatrical arts. Inside, you'll find scores of memorial plaques dedicated to such luminaries as Vivien Leigh,

Laurence Harvey, Boris Karloff, Margaret Rutherford, and Noël Coward, to name only a few. Designed by Inigo Jones in 1631, this church has been substantially altered over the years, but it retains a quiet garden-piazza in the rear. Among the famous who are buried here are wood-carver Grinling Gibbons, writer Samuel Butler, and actress Ellen Terry. Landscape painter J. M. W. Turner and librettist W. S. Gilbert were both baptized here.

Southwark Cathedral. Montague Close, London Bridge, SE1. ☎ **0171/407-2939.** Free admission. Suggested donation £2 ($3.20). Daily Mon–Sat 8:30am–6pm, Sun 9:30am–4pm. Tube: London Bridge.

There has been a church on this site for more than a thousand years. The present one dates from the 15th century; it was partially rebuilt in 1890. The previous one was the first Gothic church (1106) to be built in London. In the heart of London's first theatrical district, Shakespeare and Chaucer both worshipped here, and to this day a Shakespeare birthday service is held annually. Among the noteworthy attributes of the church are the carved memorial to Shakespeare and the wooden effigy of a knight dating to 1275. Illustrious events have been celebrated too. In 1424, James I of Scotland married Mary Beaufort here. During the reign of Mary Tudor, Stephen Gardiner, the Bishop of Winchester, held a consistory court in the retro choir. This court condemned seven of the Marian martyrs to deaths. Later, the same retro choir was rented to a baker and even used as a pigsty.

Organ recitals are given on Monday at 1:10pm and musical recitals on Tuesday at 1:10pm.

Wesley's Chapel, House & Museum. 49 City Rd., EC1. ☎ **0171/253-2262.** Chapel is free; house and museum £4 ($6.20) adult, £2 ($3.10) children 5–17. House and museum Mon–Sat 10am–4pm (closed Thurs 12:45–1:30pm). Tube: Old St. or Moorgate. Bus: 5, 43, 55, 76, 141, 214, 243, 271, 505.

John Wesley, the founder of Methodism, established this church in 1778 as his London base. The man who rode on horseback throughout the English countryside and preached in the open air is buried in a grave behind the chapel. (He lived at no. 47 City Road.) Surviving the Blitz, the church later fell into serious disrepair; major restoration was completed in the 1970s. In the crypt, a museum traces the history of Methodism to today. Across the road in Bunhill Fields is the Dissenters Graveyard where Daniel Defoe, William Blake, and John Bunyan are buried.

Westminster Cathedral. Ashley Place, SW1. ☎ **0171/798-9055.** Cathedral free; tower, £2 ($3.20). Cathedral, daily 7am–7pm; tower, Apr–Nov, daily 9am–5pm, otherwise Thurs–Sun only. Tube: Victoria.

This spectacular brick-and-stone church (1903) is the premier Roman Catholic Church in Britain. Designed in Byzantine style by John Francis Bentley, it's massive—360 feet long and 156 feet wide. One hundred different marbles compose the richly decorated interior. Eight dark-green marble columns support the nave. The 14 Stations of the Cross by the sculptor Eric Gill are renowned and controversial. The huge balacchino over the high altar is lifted by eight yellow marble columns. Mosaics emblazon the chapels and the vaulting of the sanctuary. Visitors can climb to the top of the 273-foot-tall campanile; they're rewarded with a sweeping view over Victoria and Westminster. Here in 1903, composer Sir Edward Elgar conducted the first performance of his celebrated choral work, the oratorio setting of Cardinal Newman's *The Dream of Gerontius* (a piece initially regarded as a failure but later acclaimed).

4 Institutions as English as Shepherd's Pie

BBC Visitor Centre. Broadcasting House, Portland Place, W1. ☎ **0171/580-4468.** Admission £5.75 ($9.20) adults, £4.35 ($6.95) seniors, £4 ($6.40) children. Daily 10am–5:30pm. Tube: Oxford Circus.

If you want to see how the BBC operates—whether it be producing radio broadcasts, soap operas, or its worldwide news service—then the BBC Experience will give you a glimpse into this quintessential British institution, which the locals, for some reason, call "Auntie." The exhibits include models, replica studios, archives, and interactive displays relating to radio and TV. You actually can join in a radio show and direct a scene from the *East Enders* as well as see historic footage. The building itself was designed by G. Val Myers in 1932. It was soon outgrown by the network, but remains the center of the operation. Note the sculptures of Ariel by Eric Gill on the exterior.

Law Courts. Strand, WC2. Free admission. Sessions Mon–Fri 10:30am–1pm and 2–4pm. Tube: Holborn or Temple.

At these 80 or more courts presently in use, all civil (and some criminal) cases are heard. Visitors can check themselves through the metal detectors and take a seat in the back of a courtroom to observe justice being served (or so we hope). Designed by G. E. Street, the neo-Gothic buildings (1874–82) contain more than 1,000 rooms and 3.5 miles of corridors. Sculptures of Christ, King Solomon, and King Alfred grace the front door; Moses is depicted at the back entrance. On the second Saturday in November, the annually elected Lord Mayor of the city of London is sworn in by the lord chief justice.

Lord's Cricket Ground. St. John's Wood, NW8. ☎ **0171/432-1033;** ☎ 0171/266-3825 for tours; ☎ 0171/432-1066 for tickets. Tickets £7–£45 ($11.20–$72); tours £5.80 ($9.30) adults, £4.20 ($6.70) seniors and children. Box office, Mon–Fri 9:30am–5:30pm. Tube: St. John's Wood or Marylebone.

The only way to see this hallowed cricket ground is to attend a match or to take the guided tour. Lord's is the elegant home of English cricket, where the first test against the Australians was played in 1884. Originally, Thomas Lord founded the Marylebone Cricket Club in 1787 on a site in Dorset Square. In 1811, the club was relocated to St. John's Wood, and it came to its current location in 1816. On the tour you'll see the pavilion, including the dressing room; the museum where the famous trophy the Ashes (for which the Australians and the English compete) is displayed, along with other exhibits on such legendary cricketers as W. G. Grace; a closed-in court used for playing "real tennis," a precursor to modern-day tennis; the indoor cricket school; and Lord's tavern. For additional information, see "Spectator Sports," below.

✪ **Old Bailey.** Newgate St., EC4. ☎ **0171/248-3277.** Free admission. Mon–Fri 10:30am–1pm and 2–4pm. Tube: St. Paul's.

This is the nation's Central Criminal Court, affectionately known as the Old Bailey after a street that runs nearby. Today, it's a fascinating experience to observe the bewigged barristers presenting their cases to the high court judges, who include the lord chancellor and the lord chief justice.

Built on the site of Newgate Prison, it opened in 1907. Added to in the 1970s, it now has 19 courtrooms and holding cells for 70 prisoners. Among the famous trials that have been heard here are those of Oscar Wilde, Lord Haw Haw, and the Yorkshire Ripper. Justice crowns the dome and a Recording Angel supported by Fortitude and Truth stands above the entrance.

Note: No cameras, electronic equipment, large bags, food, or drink are allowed in the building. No children under 14 are admitted. These rules are strictly adhered to.

5 More Museums & Galleries

Apsley House/Wellington Museum. 149 Piccadilly, Hyde Park Corner, W1. ☎ **0171/ 499-5676.** Admission £4.50 ($7.20) adults, £3 ($4.80) seniors, free for children under 12. Tues–Sun 11am–5pm. Closed Dec 24–26, Jan 1, Good Friday, and May 1. Tube: Hyde Park Corner.

Apsley House, nicknamed "No. 1 London," is a magnificent residence that has been the home of the Dukes of Wellington since 1817. The original was designed by Robert Adam between 1771 and 1778 and was later enlarged to house the first Duke's collections. Today it contains the Duke's great collection of silver, porcelain, sculpture, furniture, medals, and memorabilia along with his 200 or more paintings including works by Velázquez, Goya, Rubens, Brueghel, Steen, and de Hooch. The eighth Duke of Wellington and his son retain private apartments in the house, making it one of the great town houses in London where the collections remain intact and the family is still in residence. The house was built originally for the second Earl of Bathurst, Baron Apsley, which is when it acquired its nickname as Number One, because it was the first house beyond the tollgate at the entrance into London. Wellington lived here from 1817, returning here from a triumphant military career in India, Spain, and Portugal, which culminated in his victory over Napoleon at Waterloo. He was a hero whose military success had earned him the respect of kings and emperors who showered him with gifts. Here at Apsley House he entertained lavishly and the dinner services that he used can be seen, including the gorgeous Sèvres Egyptian Service that Napoleon had commissioned for Josephine and a vast silver Portuguese service with a 26-foot long centerpiece. The highlights of the first duke's memorabilia are his death mask as well as an illustration of the massive funeral carriage—it was drawn by twelve horses; the streets of London were lined with more than a million people for that grand procession. Note the nude statue of Napoléon by Canova on the main staircase.

Bank of England Museum. Threadneedle St., EC2. ☎ **0171/601-5545.** Free admission. Mon–Fri 10am–5pm. Closed major holidays. Tube: Bank.

This museum housed in the Bank of England provides insight into the institution that's long been the powerhouse of England's empire. It traces the history of the bank from its foundation by Royal Charter in 1694 to its role today as the nation's central bank. Displays include gold bars dating from ancient times to the modern market bar, bank notes, coins, and the pikes and muskets used to defend the bank. Documents relating to the business dealings and accounts of such famous clients as the Duchess of Marlborough, George Washington, and Horatio Nelson are also on display. An interactive presentation allows visitors to observe the intricacies of bank note design and production plus other workings of the central bank.

Fun Fact

The Duke of Wellington (he of Waterloo fame) was nicknamed the "Iron Duke" *not* because of his fortitude, but because he reinforced the house with iron shutters after mobs broke the windows during the Reform Bill riots.

Barbican Art Gallery. Level 3, Barbican Centre, EC2. ☎ **0171/382-7105,** 0171/588-9023 for recorded information. Admission £5 ($8) adults; £3 ($4.80) students, seniors, and children; reduced admission from 5pm weekdays, £3 ($4.65). Mon, Thurs–Sat 10am–6:45pm, Tues 10am–5:45pm, Wed 10am–7:45pm, Sun noon–6:45pm. Tube: Moorgate, Barbican, St. Paul's, Bank. The main entrance is on Silk St.

The main gallery of the Arts Center, this space regularly exhibits challenging and exciting shows of historic and contemporary works. Among recent highlights have been such shows as *Impressionism in Britain* and exhibitions built around works by Andy Warhol and Cindy Sherman.

Ben Uri Art Society. 126 Albert St., London, NW1. ☎ **0171/482-1234.** Free admission. Mon–Thurs 10am–4pm, Sun 2–5pm. Tube: Camden Town. Bus: 24, 27, 29, 31, 124, 168, 214, 253 to Camden High St.

This museum is temporarily housed here until the opening of a new Jewish Arts & Cultural Centre, which will include a performance space. The society is named after Beaelel Ben Uri, who crafted the tabernacle in the Old Testament. It has played a central role in the cultural life of Anglo Jewry and is one of the most prominent Jewish art collections in Europe. It has regular exhibitions of works by Jewish artists, many from the Ben Uri collection of more than 700 works, including works by David Bomberg, Mark Gertler, Jacob Epstein, Leon Kossoff, Jacob Kramer, Frank Auerbach, and R. B. Kitaj.

The British Library. 96 Euston Rd., NW1. ☎ **0171/412-7000.** Admission free. Galleries are open Mon, Wed–Fri 9:30am–6pm, Tues 9:30am–8pm; Sat 9:30am–5pm, Sun 11am–5pm. Tube: St. Pancras.

As it was being erected, this brand-new library, designed by Colin St. John Wilson, was condemned as an eyesore. Since it opened, it has gathered accolades, particularly for the galleries. The three galleries now display the rare books and manuscripts that were on view in the British Museum. Among the priceless collection are the Magna Carta, Tyndale's New Testament, and Shakespeare's first folio. Throughout, there are audio stations where visitors can listen to poets and writers reading from their works (James Joyce from *Finnegans Wake,* for example) or to other archival recordings. Truly amazing, though, are the interactive exhibits that allow you to flip through an illuminated manuscript which—until now—could only be viewed under glass open at a single page. Now you can flip through the *Lindisfarne Gospel* and Leonardo's *Notebooks* freely, an exciting prospect. Other galleries are devoted to the book as art and to exhibits about the craft of making books and paper.

Commonwealth Institute. Kensington High St., W8. ☎ **0171/603-4535.** The galleries are currently closed for refurbishment and are slated to reopen sometime in 1999. Tube: High St. Kensington.

This organization has exhibits on the culture and history of the 50 commonwealth countries.

Courtauld Gallery. Somerset House, the Strand, WC2. ☎ **0171/873-2526.** Admission £4 ($6.40) adults, £2 ($3.20) students and seniors, free for children 5–15. Mon–Sat 10am–6pm, Sun 2–6pm. Closed Dec 24–26, Jan 1. Tube: Temple or Covent Garden.

Named for its chief benefactor, textile mogul Samuel Courtauld, who collected impressionist and post-impressionist paintings, this museum is housed in the elegant Somerset House, a neoclassical masterpiece itself. Some fine Renaissance paintings are on view, including the intense *Master of Flemalle Triptych* and works by Tintoretto and Veronese. Among the remarkable works are Bruegel's *Christ and the Woman Taken in Adultery* and Cranach's *Adam and Eve.* Almost a whole gallery is

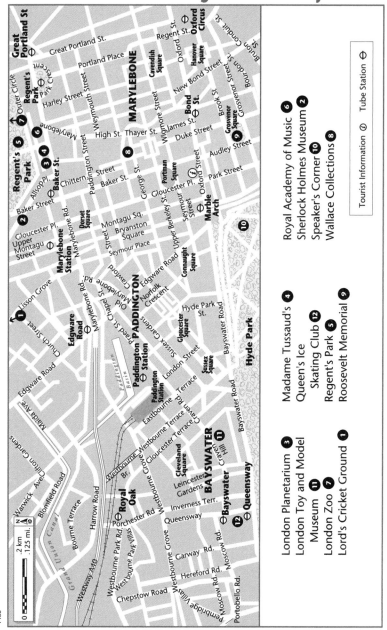

Tourist Information ⓘ   Tube Station ⊖

Royal Academy of Music ⑥
Sherlock Holmes Museum ②
Speaker's Corner ⑩
Wallace Collections ⑧

Madame Tussaud's ④
Queen's Ice
Skating Club ⑫
Regent's Park ⑤
Roosevelt Memorial ⑨

London Planetarium ③
London Toy and Model
Museum ⑪
London Zoo ⑦
Lord's Cricket Ground ①

devoted to Rubens. The collection also includes works by Gainsborough, Raeburn, Ramsay, Romney, and Turner (watercolors), as well as paintings by Ben Nicholson, Graham Sutherland, and Larry Rivers, but they are not currently on display.

The glory of this collection, though, is the impressionist works—Manet's *Bar at the Folies Bergères;* Monet's *Banks of the Seine at Argenteuil; Lady with Parasol* by Degas; *La Loge* by Renoir; Van Gogh's *Self-Portrait with Bandaged Ear;* and a number of Cézannes, including *The Card Players.* The gallery has been closed for renovations, but will reopen in late 1998.

Design Museum. 28 Shad Thames, at Butler's Wharf, London, SE1. ☎ **0171/378-6055.** Admission £5.25 ($8.40) adults, £4 ($6.40) students and children. Daily 11:30am–6pm. Tube: Tower Hill (then walk over the bridge) or London Bridge (then walk along the Silver Jubilee Walk Way). Docklands Light Railway: Tower Gateway (then walk over the bridge). Bus: 15, 78, 47, 42, or 188.

This is a place to view an aspect of the hip and happening London, including the current trends in design as well as innovative concepts and prototypes that provide a foretaste of the future. Part of the new Docklands development, this museum occupies a riverfront warehouse. It displays all kinds of manufactured products that have won love and acclaim for their design—cars, furniture, domestic appliances, audio-visual equipment, cameras, graphics, and ceramics (the Volkswagen Bug and the anglepoise lamp are just two examples). The museum really underlines the role that design plays in our daily lives. On the top floor, the series of thematic displays, which are historical in emphasis, further clarify this impact. Each showcase illustrates the many factors which influence design and affect the way products look and are used.

The museum shop is great browsing territory and has everything from designer socks to sleek alarm clocks. Want a cutting-edge souvenir? Look for the Millennium Kettle, touted as the fastest boiling kettle available (thus saving power and time) or perhaps the Baygen Freeplay radio, which operates without electric power or battery; just wind it up and the power is stored for use.

Dulwich Picture Gallery. College Rd., SE21. ☎ **0181/693-5254.** Admission £3 ($4.80) adults, £1.50 ($2.40) seniors and students, free for children under 16; free on Friday. Tues–Fri 10am–5pm, Sat 11am–5pm, Sun 2–5pm. Closed Dec 24–26, Good Fri, Easter Sun. Tube: Brixton, then P4 bus. Train: West Dulwich.

Dating to 1817, this is the oldest public picture gallery in England. It houses a fine collection of Old Masters, including works by Canaletto, Gainsborough, Poussin, Rembrandt, Rubens, and Van Dyck. It's one of London's few remaining buildings designed by Sir John Soane.

Fenton House. Hampstead Grove, NW3. ☎ **0171/435-3471.** Admission £4 ($6.40) adults, £2 ($3.20) children, £10 ($16) family. Mar, Sat–Sun 2–5pm; Apr–Oct, Sat–Sun 11am–5pm, Wed–Fri 2–5pm. Closed Nov–Feb. Tube: Hampstead.

Music lovers and fans of historic homes will want to visit this 1693 residence that once belonged to an 18th-century merchant named Fenton. In the 1950s, the house was left to the National Trust by then-owner Lady Binning to display her collection of furniture and porcelain. It's famous for the Benton Fletcher collection of musical instruments, all in working order, including a 1612 harpsichord that was probably used by Handel.

Florence Nightingale Museum. St. Thomas' Hospital, 2 Lambeth Palace Rd., SE1. ☎ **0171/620-0374.** Admission £3.50 ($5.60) adults, £2.50 ($4) seniors and children. Tues–Sun 10am–5pm. Closed Easter, Dec 25–26, and Jan 1. Tube: Waterloo.

Florence Nightingale founded her School of Nursing here in 1860. She dedicated her life to improving the standards of hospitals, the quality of nursing, and public health. How she did it is illustrated in the exhibits at this museum.

Freud Museum. 20 Maresfield Gardens, Hampstead, NW3. ☎ **0171/435-2002.** Admission £3 ($4.80) adults, £1.50 ($2.40) students, free for children under 12. Wed–Sun noon–5pm. Tube: Finchley Rd.

This was briefly the London home of Sigmund Freud after he and his family fled Vienna and the Nazis in 1938. He only lived here for one year, completing *Moses and Monotheism* and entertaining such friends as H.G. Wells. The rooms display memorabilia including furniture, paintings, photographs, and letters. Freudians will enjoy seeing the replica of his Viennese consulting room (complete with famous couch) and some of his collection of Egyptian, Roman, and Asian antiquities. Archive film programs are also given.

Geffrye Museum. Kingsland Rd., E2. ☎ **0171/739-9893.** Free admission. Tues–Sat 10am–5pm, Sun and holidays 2–5pm. Closed Good Friday, Dec 24–26, Jan 1. Herb garden open Apr–Oct. Tube: Liverpool St. Bus: 242, or 149 from Bishopsgate.

This museum is devoted to the history of English domestic interiors. It's a gem of a museum and worth a visit for its architecture alone, housed as it is in the former almshouses of the Ironmongers' Company, a harmonious grouping of buildings dating to 1715. The gardens in front, especially the herb garden, are used to enhance the period rooms. A series of period rooms traces the history of English domestic interior design from 1600 to the present—from Jacobean oak through fine Georgian and ornate Victorian to art deco and postwar utility. Special exhibitions explore a wide variety of themes. In December, the rooms sparkle with festive decorations, as 400 years of Christmas tradition come to life. New galleries displaying 20th-century furniture are scheduled to open in late 1998. The extension will also house a design center and restaurant.

Hayward Gallery. South Bank Centre, SE1. ☎ **0171/928-3144.** Admission varies but is usually around £6 ($9.60). Mon, Thurs–Sun 10am–6pm; Tues–Wed 10am–8pm. Tube: Waterloo or Embankment.

Part of the South Bank Centre, this gallery puts on a variety of fine contemporary, historical, and international shows. Expect to see single shows devoted to such British sculptors as Anish Kapoor and such avant-garde American artists as Bruce Nauman, plus other thematic shows. Call for schedule of exhibits.

Imperial War Museum. Lambeth Rd., SE1. ☎ **0171/416-5000.** Admission £5 ($8) adults, £4 ($6.40) seniors, £2.50 ($4) children 5–16, £13 family ($20.80). Daily 10am–6pm. Closed Dec 24–26. Tube: Lambeth North or Elephant & Castle. Bus: 1, 3, 12, 45, 53, 63, 68, 159, 168, 171, 172, and more.

This museum tells the story of 20th-century conflict from World War I to the present day through the use of artifacts, documents, paintings, sound recordings, photographs, and interactive exhibits. Visitors particularly appreciate the dramatic re-creations of an air raid on London—complete with sounds, scents, and other special effects—and of trench life during World War I.

The museum occupies an 1815 building that was part of Royal Bethlehem Hospital (Bedlam), where "distracted" patients were kept chained to the walls, dunked in water, or whipped when they became violent. In the 17th and 18th centuries, Bedlam was one of the major London "sights," and visitors paid a hefty entrance fee.

The museum is currently undergoing major redevelopment, so if there's a particular display you want to see, it's best to call ahead to make sure that it is open.

Institute of Contemporary Arts (ICA). The Mall, SW1. ☎ **0171/930-3647** or 0171/930-6393 for recorded information. Galleries, weekdays £1.50 ($2.40) adults, £1 ($1.60) seniors; weekends £2.50 ($4) and £2 ($3.20) respectively. Daily noon–7:30pm. Tube: Piccadilly Circus or Charing Cross.

Publicly assisted, ICA is a major forum for the arts. It maintains a theater, cinema, media center, cafe, bar, bookshop, lecture program, and two galleries showing contemporary art. Many artists have received their first solo shows at this gallery since it opened in 1948. Among the more recent are Damien Hirst, Helen Chadwick, Gary Hume, and Steve McQueen. See also "Fringe Theater" in chapter 9 for more information.

Jewish Museum. 129 Albert St., Camden Town, NW1. ☎ **0171/284-1997.** Admission £3 ($4.80) adults, £1.50 ($2.40) children, £7.50 ($12) family. Sun–Thurs 10am–4pm. Closed Jewish holidays and public holidays. Tube: Camden Town.

This museum opens a window onto the history and religious life of the Jewish community. The museum includes a History Gallery which features such highlights as medieval notched wooden tax receipts and loving cups presented to the Lord Mayors of London by the Spanish and Portuguese Synagogue. The exceptional Ceremonial Art Gallery features ritual objects of great beauty like a 16th-century Italian synagogue ark, Nathan Meyer Rothschild's *Book of Esther,* and some silver Torah bells crafted in London.

Another branch of the museum in Finchley contains an Oral History and Photographic Archive plus displays about Jewish social life in London that include reconstructions of East End tailoring and furniture workshops. It's located at 80 East End Rd. (☎ **0181/349-1143;** Tube: Finchley Central) and is open Sunday 10:30am to 4:30pm and Monday to Thursday 10:30am to 5pm. Admission is £2 ($3.20) for adults, £1 ($1.60) for seniors.

London Canal Museum. 12–13 New Wharf Rd., King's Cross, N1. ☎ **0171/713-0836.** Admission £2.50 ($4) adults, £1.25 ($2) seniors and students. Tues–Sun 10am–4:30pm. Closed Dec 25, 26, and Jan 1. Tube: King's Cross.

This museum is housed in a warehouse on the Regent Canal in which Carlo Gatti stored ice that he had shipped from Norway in the mid–19th century. The museum tells the story of Gatti and others like him who made their living along and on the canals.

London Transport Museum. Floral Market, Covent Garden, WC2. ☎ **0171/379-6344.** Admission £4.95 ($7.90) adults, £2.50 ($4.70) seniors and children 5–15, £12.85 ($20.55) family. Sun–Thurs 10am–6pm, Fri 11am–6pm, and Sat 10am–6pm (last admissions 45 minutes earlier). Closed Dec 24–26. Tube: Covent Garden or Charing Cross.

With the aid of a collection of omnibuses, paintings, and models, this museum traces 200 years of London transport history. Kids love it. The story is enlivened by actors who play such characters as a 1906 tunnel miner and a World War II clippie (bus conductor to you), and also by several interactive video exhibits—you can put yourself in the driver's seat of a bus or tube train, for example. Throughout the museum there are also 15 or so KidZones specially designed to aid learning with plenty of switches, buttons, and things to push and pull. Kids learn the secrets of horsepower and how to work out bus fares using giant tickets and much more. There's a good gift shop known for models, posters, and other original gifts, too.

Madame Tussaud's & the Planetarium. Marylebone Rd., NW1. ☎ **0171/935-6861.** Madame Tussaud's admission £9.25 ($14.80) adults, £6.95 ($11.10) seniors, £6.10 ($9.75) children 5–15. Planetarium admission £5.85 ($9.35) adults, £4.50 ($7.20) seniors, £3.85 ($6.10) children 5–15. Combined ticket for Madame Tussaud's and the planetarium is £11.50 ($28.25) adults, £8.75 ($14) seniors, £7.55 ($12.10) children 5–15. Madame Tussaud's open July–Aug, daily 9am–5:30pm; Sept–June, Mon–Fri 10am–5:30pm, Sat–Sun 9:30am –5:30pm. Closed Dec 25. Planetarium daily 10am–5:30pm. Shows run every 40 minutes, 12:20–5pm, weekends and holidays from 10:20am. Tube: Baker St. Bus: 2, 13, 18, 27, 30, 74, 82, 113, 159, 176.

Eerily lifelike figures have made Madame Tussaud's century-old waxworks world-famous. The figures from the original molds of Voltaire and members of the French court, to whom Madame Tussaud had direct access, are fascinating. Unfortunately, however, this "museum" gives the lion's share of its space to images of modern superstars like Michael Jackson, Liz Taylor, the late Princess Diana, and Brad Pitt, plus political figures like Bill Clinton, Margaret Thatcher, and Saddam Hussein. The dungeon-level **Chamber of Horrors,** which features famous criminals and killers from the French Revolution to today's serial killers, is the stuff tourist traps are made of. It features Charles Manson, Jack the Ripper, and Dracula, as well as audio-visual tableaux of Joan of Arc being burned at the stake and Guy Fawkes being hung, drawn, and quartered—pretty grisly stuff. The tour ends in a time travel ride in a black taxi that takes you though 400 years of London life past animatronic figures and sound effects. Despite the fact that Madame Tussaud's is expensive and overrated, it attracts more than 2.5 million visitors annually. If you go, get there early to get a jump on the crowds.

Next door, the **Planetarium** explores the mysteries of the cosmos in new galleries featuring interactive exhibits, models and displays (see "Especially for Kids," below).

Museum of Garden History. St. Mary-at-Lambeth, Lambeth Palace Rd., SE1. ☎ **0171/ 401-8865.** Free admission. Mon–Fri 10:30am–3:45pm, Sun 10:30am–4:45pm (closed Sat). Closed second Sun of Dec to the first Sun in March. Tube: Waterloo or Victoria, then bus 507. Bus: C10, 3, 77, and 344.

This museum is devoted to the British passion of gardening, and the gardeners and botanists or plant collectors who have nurtured it. The garden here is planted in a 17th-century Knot Garden design and contains many rare plants introduced into the country by the Tradescants, royal gardeners to Charles I and Charles II, who are in fact buried here. Another garden inspired by Persian gardens of old is open on Wednesdays and the first Sunday of the month from April to October. The museum houses displays relating stories about great plant gatherers like the Tradescants and Captain Bligh (the same who was abandoned by his mutinous crew), and such beloved English gardeners as Gertrude Jekyll. Also on display is a collection of historic garden tools and artifacts. The museum is located south of the Thames, in a historic church and churchyard. Morning coffee and lunchtime snacks are served daily.

✪ **Museum of London.** 150 London Wall, EC2. ☎ **0171/600-3699.** Admission £5 ($8) adults, £3 ($4.80) seniors, £2 ($3.20) children, £12 ($19.20) families (valid for 3 months). Free from 4:30pm. Tues–Sat 10am–5:50pm, Sun noon–5:50pm. Tube: Barbican, Moorgate, St. Paul's. Bus: 4, 56, 172.

For anyone interested in the city's history, this is the place to begin. It's one of the most engaging and creative museums in the city. Two floors of exhibits trace the city's development from Roman times to the 1990s using models, artifacts, reconstructions, and audio-visual presentations. Appropriate period background music makes for an even more evocative tour. Among the highlights are a reconstruction of a Roman interior and a Roman complex; a bedroom in a merchant's house from the Stuart period; the lord mayor's coach; a brilliant audio-visual dioramic presentation on the Great Fire, with voice-over reading diarist Samuel Pepys' account; a Victorian barber's shop; and the original elevators from Selfridges department store.

✪ **Museum of the Moving Image (MOMI).** National Film Theatre, South Bank, SE1. ☎ **0171/928-3535,** 0171/401-2636 for recorded information. Admission £6.25 ($10) adults, £5.25 ($8.40) students and seniors, £4.50 ($7.20) children 5–16. Daily 10am–6pm; last admission 5pm. Tube: Waterloo is closer, but the short walk over Hungerford Bridge from the Embankment Underground station is more scenic.

This lively, "hands-on" celebration of film and television is one of the city's best museums. Fifty chronologically organized exhibits are designed to captivate and encourage participation. They're staffed with outgoing, costumed actors, who never step out of character. Visitors can read the news from a TelePrompTer, create their own animated strip, fly with Superman, and play around with many interactive exhibits. Films are shown daily.

National Army Museum. Royal Hospital Rd., Chelsea, SW3. ☎ **0171/730-0717.** Free admission. Daily 10am–5:30pm. Closed Dec 24, 25, 26, Jan 1, Good Friday, early May public holiday. Tube: Sloane Sq. Bus: 11, 19, 22, and 211.

This museum tells the story of the British army from the raising of the Yeoman of the Guard in 1485 to the modern British army serving in Bosnia and elsewhere today. Many of the displays focus effectively on the everyday lives of the soldiers of different eras—Henry V's archers shivering at Agincourt, Wellington's troops standing shoulder to shoulder at Waterloo, and British Tommies scrambling over the top at the Somme. Visitors can actually experience what it was like to live and work in a World War I trench. Displays include life-size models, medals (including 30 original Victoria Crosses), paintings of battle scenes, weapons, and uniforms. Among the highlights are a 420-square-foot model of the Battle of Waterloo which contains more than 70,000 model soldiers; the skeleton of Napoleon's horse, Marengo; and the saw that was used to amputate the leg of Lieutenant-General The Earl of Uxbridge during the battle. Other offbeat exhibits include a stuffed cat that was rescued from Sebastopol by a sentimental officer during the Crimean War and brought back to England. Video presentations are given.

National Portrait Gallery. St. Martin's Place, WC2. ☎ **0171/306-0055.** Free admission. Mon–Sat 10am–6pm, Sun noon–6pm. Closed Dec 24–26, Jan 1, Good Friday, May 1. Tube: Charing Cross or Leicester Sq.

A great place to see the history of the nation writ large on the faces of its key personalities. This gallery has more than 9,000 paintings and 500,000 photographs in its collection. The permanent collection is displayed in chronological order from the Middle Ages down to Brian Organ's portrait of Princess Diana. Along the way you'll encounter Henry VII, Henry VIII, and Sir Thomas More all painted by Holbein, the only extant portrait of Shakespeare, and T.S. Eliot by Sir Jacob Epstein. Some of the portraits have been made by endearing amateurs, including one of Jane Austen by her sister. A major extension is planned to open in 2000, though the museum already has a spectacular 20th-century gallery in which the pictures are suspended on glass walls.

National Postal Museum. King Edward Building, King Edward St., EC1. ☎ **0171/776-3636.** Free admission. Mon–Fri 9:30am–4:30pm. Closed all bank holidays. Tube: St. Paul's, the Barbican. Bus: 4, 8, 11, 15, 17, 22B, 23, 25, 26, 76, 172, 501, 521.

In 1840, Britain introduced the world's first postage stamp, the Penny Black, but for 200 years before that a postal service of sorts was operating. In the main gallery, all the stamps of Britain are on display. One exhibit shows original art compared with the issued stamps. Also displayed are valentines and other greeting cards; scales and handstamps; and letter boxes, which were introduced by the Post Office surveyor and novelist Anthony Trollope in 1852.

Old Royal Observatory. Flamsteed House, Romney Rd., Greenwich Park, SE10. ☎ **0181/858-4422.** Admission £5 ($8) adults, £4 ($6.80) students, £2.50 ($4) children 5–16 (includes National Maritime Museum and Queens House). Daily 10am–5pm. Closed Dec 24–26. Rail: Charing Cross to Maze Hill. Docklands Light Railway: Island Gardens. Bus: 53, 177, 180, 188.

This is where the countdown for the millennium will take place on December 31, 1999, for all time is measured from the Prime Meridian Line here at Greenwich. Located high on a hill with magnificent views across the Thames, this is the original home of Greenwich Mean Time. It was founded in 1675 by Charles II as part of his quest to determine longitude at sea. The problem was eventually solved in 1763 by clockmaker John Harrison, who received £20,000 for his pains. The observatory has the largest refracting telescope in the United Kingdom and a collection of historic timekeepers and astronomical instruments. You can stand astride the meridian (with a foot in each hemisphere) and set your watch precisely by the falling time-ball. Wren designed the Octagon Room. Here the first royal astronomer, Flamsteed, made his 30,000 observations that formed the basis of his *Historia Coelestis Britannica*. Edmond Halley, who discovered Halley's Comet, succeeded him. In 1833, the ball on the tower was hung to enable shipmasters to set their chronometers accurately.

Percival David Foundation of Chinese Art. 53 Gordon Sq., WC1. ☎ **0171/387-3909.** Free admission. Mon–Fri 10:30am–5pm. Closed bank holidays. Tube: Russell Sq., Euston Sq., Euston, Goodge St. Bus: 7, 8, 10, 14, 18, 19, and many more.

Sir Percival David presented this fine collection of Chinese ceramics and a library of books relating to Chinese art and culture to the University of London in 1950. The more than 1,700 objects date mainly from the 10th to 18th centuries. They're not only exquisitely beautiful, but some bear important inscriptions by such emperors as Qianlong (1736–95). The stonewares from the Song (960–1279) and Yuan (1279–1368) dynasties are exceptional, and include examples of rare Ru and Guan wares. Most familiar are the blue-and-white porcelains. Polychrome wares are also represented, including examples of the doucai wares from the Chenghua period (1465–87) as well as a group of 18th-century porcelains known as Gu yue xuan.

Royal Academy of Arts. Burlington House, Piccadilly, W1. ☎ **0171/300-8000.** Admission varies, depending on the exhibition. Daily 10am–6pm. Closed Dec 25, Good Friday. Tube: Piccadilly Circus or Green Park.

The Royal Academy, which opened in 1768, was the nation's first art school and the first institution to hold an annual art exhibition. Among its founding members were Sir Joshua Reynolds, Thomas Gainsborough, and Benjamin West. The annual exhibition (held in June and July) continues to this day and is one of the world's largest open contemporary art exhibitions showing paintings, sculptures, and drawings, most of which are for sale. During the RA Schools Final Years Show (usually held in January), this is also the place to see (and purchase) the latest work by some of the nation's most promising young artists who have completed three years of postgraduate work at the RA schools. There are always interesting special exhibits on display.

✪ **Saatchi Gallery.** 98A Boundary Rd., NW8. ☎ **0171/624-8299.** Admission £4 ($6.40), £2 ($3.20) seniors. Thurs–Sun noon–6pm. Tube: St. John's Wood.

Charles Saatchi has amassed one of the largest collections of contemporary British and international art in the world. The museum is famous for introducing major new British artists and for its Young Americans shows, which do the same for American artists. The museum features rotating displays from Saatchi's vast holdings. Enter through the unmarked metal gateway of what was once, appropriately enough, a paint warehouse.

Sherlock Holmes Museum. 221B Baker St., NW1. ☎ **0171/935-8866.** Admission £5 ($8) adults, £3 ($4.80) children 7–16. Daily 9:30am–6pm. Tube: Baker St.

Dedicated Holmes fans will want to visit the literary address of their hero-detective who "resided" here from 1881 to 1904. It's not really a museum, but a re-creation of Victorian chambers occupied by Holmes and Watson. In the living room you can pick up Holmes's pipe, don a deerstalker, and take a photograph of yourself horsing around. Other "exhibits" include Dr. Mortimer's stick from *The Hound of the Baskervilles,* and numerous letters written to Holmes asking him to solve individual mysteries and the amusing "replies" he wrote. It's not worth the ticket unless you're a real Holmes freak.

✪ **Sir John Soane's Museum.** 13 Lincoln's Inn Fields, WC2. ☎ **0171/405-2107** or 0171/430-0175 for recorded information. Free admission (donation requested). Tues–Sat 10am–5pm; first Tues of each month also 6–9pm. Tube: Holborn.

An enchanting and edifying place to visit, the home of collector and architect John Soane. Soane (1753–1837) was the son of a bricklayer who apprenticed himself to George Dance the Younger and Henry Holland before opening an architectural practice of his own. He married into great wealth and began collecting the objects displayed in this wonderful house, which he designed and where he resided. It's stuffed full with all kinds of fascinating pieces—architectural fragments, casts, bronzes, sculpture, and cork models. Take special note of Soane's use of colored glass and mirrors to create reflections of architectural details and other dramatic effects. The collection of paintings includes works by Turner, three Canalettos, and two series of paintings by Hogarth, *An Election* and *The Rake's Progress.* Other works, including a wonderful group of Piranesi drawings, are ingeniously hung behind special movable panels in the Picture Room. Of special note is the sarcophagus of Seti I (Pharaoh 1303–1290 B.C.), which Soane bought for £2,000—a price so steep that it deterred the British Museum from its purchase. A gallery opened in April 1995 displays changing exhibitions of architectural drawings from Soane's collection of over 30,000, which includes works by Dance, Sir Christopher Wren, Sir William Chambers, and Robert and James Adam. It's particularly entrancing when it's candlelit during the evening opening time.

Theatre Museum. Russell St., WC2. ☎ **0171/836-7891.** Admission £3.50 ($5.60) adults, £2 ($3.20) seniors and children 5–17. Tues–Sun 11am–7pm. Closed Dec 25, 26, and Jan 1. Daily guided tours at 11:30am, 2pm, and 4pm; makeup demonstrations at 11:15am, noon, 1pm, 2:30pm, 3:30pm, and 4:15pm; and costume workshops at 12:30 and 3pm. Tube: Covent Garden or Charing Cross.

Lovers of the performing arts and British theater in particular will not want to miss this museum. A branch of the Victoria and Albert Museum, it contains the national collections of the performing arts encompassing theater, ballet, opera, music hall, pantomime, puppetry, circus, and rock and pop music. The costume collection is amazing and so are the other collections of paintings, photographs, and theatrical memorabilia. The museum also tells the story of the development of the British stage, from Shakespeare to the present day, using stage models, posters, props, audio-visual displays, and memorabilia of such legendary British thespians as Garrick, Kean, and Irving. In daily makeup demonstrations, you can become a model for the creation of special effects; costume workshops offer the opportunity to try on costumes from the Royal Shakespeare Company and the Royal National Theatre. The museum also has a major Diaghilev archive which is the basis of a display about the Ballets Russe and the revolutionary influence that it had (thanks to choreographer Michael Fokine and costume and set designer Leon Bakst) on dance in the West.

Wallace Collections. Hertford House, Manchester Sq., W1. ☎ **0171/935-0687.** Free admission (donation requested). Mon–Sat 10am–5pm, Sun 2–5pm. Tube: Bond St.

This is an often-overlooked cultural joy. Beginning in the 18th century, four generations of the Marquesses of Hertford amassed this varied and discriminating collection of exquisite furniture, armor, paintings and decorative arts. There's so much to pleasure the eye—Sèvres porcelain, Limoges enamels, 17th-century Dutch paintings, 18th-century British paintings, 18th-century French art (Watteau, Fragonard, and Boucher), and Italian majolica. It will be undergoing major expansion to coincide with the millennium.

Whitechapel Art Gallery. Whitechapel High St., E1. ☎ **0171/522-7888.** Free admission. Tues, Thurs–Sun 11am–5pm, Wed 11am–8pm. Closed holidays. Tube: Aldgate East.

This is one of London's leading art galleries and the place to see up-and-coming British contemporary artists. It hosts the biannual Whitechapel Open and Open Studios, which exhibits juried selected works plus works by more than 1,000 artists. This gallery exhibited Picasso's haunting *Guernica* in 1939 and has been on the cutting edge ever since. It introduced such British artists as Tony Bevan, Lucian Freud, and Cathy de Monchaux to the public. It also exhibits such international contemporary artists as Frida Kahlo.

6 Architectural Highlights

Banqueting House. Opposite Horse Guards Parade, Whitehall, SW1. ☎ **0171/930-4179.** Admission £3.25 ($5.20) adults, £2.50 ($4) seniors and students, £2 ($3.20) children. Mon–Sat 10am–5pm. Closed Sun, Dec 24–26, Jan 1, Good Friday. Note, too, that it is often closed at short notice for government functions, so always check the hours ahead of time. Tube: Charing Cross or Embankment.

This is all that remains of the great palace of Whitehall (the rest burned in 1698). A masterpiece of English Renaissance (1619–22) architecture, it was designed by Inigo Jones for James I. In the main hall, see the nine magnificent, allegorical paintings by Rubens depicting the Divine Right of Kings—they're fantastic. The bust of Charles I above the entrance reminds visitors that he was beheaded in front of this building. Designed for sumptuous royal banquets, balls, and concerts, it is still used for many functions today.

Chelsea Royal Hospital. Royal Hospital Rd., SW3. Free admission. Mon–Sat 10am–noon and 2–4pm, Sun 2–4pm except in winter when it's closed. Tube: Sloane Sq.

This dignified institution was founded by Charles II in 1682 as a home for veteran soldiers and designed and completed by Sir Christopher Wren in 1692. There's been little change to Wren's design, except for minor work done by Robert Adam in the 18th century and the addition of the stables, designed by Sir John Soane, in 1814. The main block containing the hall and chapel is flanked by east and west wings that are dormitories. A few hundred pensioners still live here today. They are easily identified by their everyday blue uniforms, replaced with red ones on ceremonial occasions. The Duke of Wellington lay in state in the hall here from November 10 to 17, 1852. So many people thronged to see him that two were crushed to death. Note the statue of Charles II by Grinling Gibbons in the courtyard.

Guildhall. Off Gresham St., EC2. ☎ **0171/606-3030.** Free admission. Daily 10am–5pm (Mon–Sat only in winter). Closed Dec 24–26, Jan 1, Good Friday, and Easter Mon, and for ceremonial occasions. Tube: Bank.

This has been the seat of local government for more than 800 years. The Guildhall itself dates from 1411 and has been restored on several occasions, notably after the Great Fire and again after the Blitz. Among the decorations in the building are the banners of the 100 Livery Companies and window inscriptions of all the Lord Mayors since 1189. Among the stranger inhabitants are the legendary giants Gog and Magog who guard the institution. The Court of Common Council meets here presided over by the lord mayor at 1pm on the third Thursday of each month. The meetings are open to the public.

Lloyd's of London Building. Lime St., EC3. ☎ **0171/623-7100.** Tube: Monument.

Designed by Richard Rogers (co-architect of the Pompidou Center in Paris), the Lloyd's of London Building opened in 1986 to much critical controversy. All the "guts" of the building (elevators, water pipes, electrical conduits) are on the exterior. Cranes are permanently stationed on the roof—ready to help with further expansion, should it become necessary. At night, special lighting lends it an extraterrestrial quality. Unfortunately, it's currently closed to visitors, over worries that it might be considered a terrorist's target.

Lloyd's, of course, is the famous British insurance company begun in 1688, whose members undertake to insure all kinds of items that most companies would shun. Even though it's housed in this ultra-modern building, traditions are still upheld, like the tolling of a ship's bell once for bad news and twice for good.

Queen's House. Romney Rd., Greenwich, SE10. ☎ **0181/858-4422.** Admission £5 ($8) adults, £4 ($6.40) seniors, £2.50 ($4) children. (*Note:* this admission currently includes the National Maritime Museum and Old Royal Observatory but this policy may change when the greatly expanded National Maritime Museum reopens in Easter 1999.) Daily 10am–5pm. Train: From Charing Cross to Maze Hill. Docklands Light Railway: Island Gardens.

Designed by Inigo Jones, Queen's House (1616) is a fine example of this architect's innovative style. It is most famous for the cantilevered tulip staircase, the first of its kind. Carefully restored, the house contains a collection of royal and marine paintings and other objets d'art.

Note: It will be closed for much of 1999 for renovations.

St. Pancras Station. Euston Rd., NW1. Tube: St. Pancras.

The London terminus for the Midland Railway, St. Pancras Station (1863–67) is a masterpiece of Victorian engineering. Designed by W. H. Barlow, the 689-foot-long glass-and-iron train shed spans 240 feet in width. It rises to a peak of 100 feet above the rails. The platforms were raised 20 feet above the ground because the tracks ran over the Regent's Canal before entering the station. The pièce de résistance, though, is Sir George Gilbert Scott's fanciful Midland Grand Hotel. Done in high Gothic style, it's graced with pinnacles, towers, and gables; it now functions as office space. The facade runs 565 feet and is flanked by a clock tower and a west tower.

7 Markets & Auction Houses

Auction houses are great fun to visit. Before the auction, you can inspect the merchandise; during it, you can share in the excitement of the bidding and buying. Items on sale at the three houses listed below may range from fine paintings, furniture, and jewelry to wines, stamps, cars, toys, valentines, and fans. Check out: **Christie's,** at 8 King St., St. James's, SW1 (☎ **0171/839-9060**) and at 85 Old Brompton Rd., SW7 (☎ **0171/581-7611**); **Phillips,** 101 New Bond St., W1 (☎ **0171/629-6602**); and **Sotheby's,** 34 New Bond St. (☎ **0171/493-8080**).

As for markets, here's a very short list of London's best.

Bermondsey. Bermondsey Sq., SE1. Fri only 5am–1pm. Tube: Elephant & Castle or Borough.

Get here early (it opens at 5am) to uncover the bargains at this antique market. It's been going strong for almost 50 years and still attracts dealers. It's also known as the New Caledonian market.

Billingsgate. North Quay, West India Docks Rd., Isle of Dogs, E14. Tues–Sat 5–8:30am. Docklands Light Railway: West India Quay.

This ancient fish market, which has operated since Saxon times, relocated to a warehouse here in 1982. Although the porters no longer wear their "bobbing" hats (so named after the amount—one shilling or a bob—they charged to carry the boxes of fish from the wholesaler to the retailer), it's still a fascinating place to come early in the morning. Forklifts now do the duties that were performed by porters wearing leather and wood hats that were supposedly modeled after the helmets bowmen wore at the Battle of Agincourt.

Camden Markets. Off Camden High St., NW1. Camden Market Thurs–Sun 9am–5:30pm; Camden Lock indoor stalls Tues–Sun 10am–6pm, outdoor Sat–Sun only; The Stables Sat–Sun 8am–6pm; Camden Canal Sat–Sun 10am–6pm; and Electric Market Sun 9am–5:30pm. Tube: Camden Town.

A London youth scene. On weekends—especially Sunday—this market is flooded with young people checking out the stalls that stock crafts, bric-a-brac, clothes (a lot of leather, jeans, tie-dyed items, Doc Martens, and vintage clothing at the Electric Market), and furniture. The market is held in several spaces and courtyards off Camden High Street. Tucked away on the side streets at the east end of Camden High are some decent restaurants. Get there early if you want to be able to move.

Greenwich Antiques Market. Greenwich High Rd. (opposite St. Alfeges Church), SE10. Sat–Sun 9am–5pm. Rail: Greenwich. Docklands Light Railway: From Tower Gateway to Island Gardens, then cross river via pedestrian tunnel.

This market has everything—books, furniture, crafts, and all kinds of bric-a-brac. A fun experience.

Leather Lane. EC1. Mon–Fri 10:30am–2pm. Tube: Chancery Lane.

This lively lunchtime market is close to Hatton Garden. It's London's diamond center.

New Covent Garden. Nine Elms, SW8. Mon–Fri 3:30–10:30am. Tube: Vauxhall.

The old Covent Garden market moved here in 1974 and became new. It's the biggest wholesale fruit, vegetable, and flower market in the nation and still worth visiting.

Petticoat Lane. Middlesex St., E1. Sun only 9am–2pm. Tube: Liverpool St. or Aldgate.

Not what it used to be, now that London has Sunday shopping and other events to draw the crowds. Still a London scene, though, and good for budget clothes and shoes. You'll find leather fashions at the Aldgate end of the market.

Portobello Antiques Market. Portobello Rd., W11. Sat 7am–6pm. Flea market at the northern end on Fri and Sat. Tube: Ladbroke Grove or Notting Hill Gate.

Atmospheric and fun. Antiques, clothes, and bric-a-brac along a road that never seems to end. There is also a daily market featuring fruits and vegetables. Saturday is the antiques day. Check out the many antique stores along Westbourne Grove too.

8 Neighborhoods & Villages of Note

Bankside. Tube: London Bridge.

Bankside, clustered along the south side of the river at the end of Southwark and London Bridges, is once again becoming the tourist attraction it was during Shakespeare's time. At its heart stands the dramatic Southwark Cathedral. Nearby lies the Golden Hinde, Shakespeare's Globe Theatre, and the new Tate Gallery of Modern Art, which will open in 2000. Beyond London Bridge stands the new Hay's Galleria and the HMS *Belfast*. Two historic inns, the George Inn and the Anchor Inn, offer welcome rest and victuals.

Bloomsbury. Tube: Russell Sq. or Holborn.

Bloomsbury is a great neighborhood to explore if you appreciate bookish and intellectual pursuits. Of course, it's most often associated with the Bloomsbury group of artists and intellectuals. (The area is bounded by Tottenham Court Road on the west, Euston Road on the north, Gray's Inn Road on the east, and Bloomsbury Way and Theobalds Road on the south.) The focal points of this neighborhood are the British Museum and the University of London. Elegant town houses edge the neighborhood's famous squares—Russell, Gordon, Tavistock, Bedford, and Bloomsbury. Antiquarian book and map shops, art galleries, and small affordable hotels fill the area.

According to the Domesday book, a survey of England written by officials of William the Conqueror in 1086, the area had vineyards and woods for 100 pigs. In the 13th century, the land became part of the manor Blemondsburi. Edward III gave the land to the Carthusian monks of Charterhouse in the 14th century. Later, it was acquired by the Earl of Southampton. The fourth earl laid out Southampton Square, which today is Bloomsbury Square, and constructed a magnificent home. Other aristocrats built similar homes in the neighborhood, including Montague House, now the British Museum. Until the 18th century, Bloomsbury was a rural retreat.

Among the great names associated with the area are Thomas Gray, the poet, who lived on Southhampton Row; Sir Hans Sloane, physician and British Museum benefactor; diarist and novelist Fanny Burney, who lived on Queen Square; Lord Chief Justice Mansfield, whose house was sacked during the Gordon Riots (the ringleaders were hanged in Bloomsbury Square); and that celebrated group of friends including art critic Clive Bell, married to Vanessa, Virginia Woolf's sister; novelist and R.A.F. pilot David Garnett; novelist E. M. Forster; artist and art critic Roger Fry, founder of the Omega Workshop that encouraged young modern designers; painter Duncan Grant, a pioneer of abstract art who lived with Vanessa Bell; Lytton Strachey, biographer of Queen Victoria; economist and author John

Bloomsbury, Covent Garden, & the South Bank

British Library ❷
British Museum ❽
Courtauld Institute
 Galleries ⓯
Dickens's House ❻
Globe Theatre ㉑
Gray's Inn ❾
Hayward Gallery ㉔
Inner Temple ⑳
Inns of Court
 & Chancery ⑱
King's College ⑯
Lincoln's Inn ❿
London Central
 YMCA ❼
London Transport
 Museum ⑭
Middle Temple ⑲
MOMI (National Film
 Theatre) ㉓
National Theatre ㉒
Percival David
 Foundation
 of Art ❸
Queen Elizabeth
 Hall ㉖
Royal Academy of
 Dramatic Arts ❹
Royal Courts
 of Justice ⑰
Royal Festival Hall ㉕
St. Paul's, The Actor's
 Church ⑬
Sir John Soane's
 Museum ⑪
Somerset House ⑮
Theatre Museum ⑫
University College ❶
University of
 London ❺

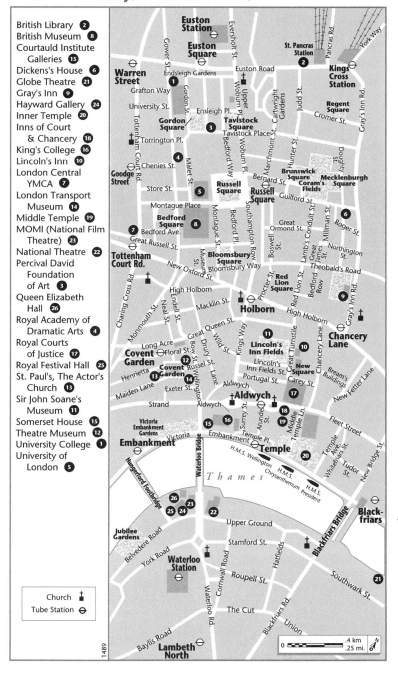

Church ✝
Tube Station ⊖

1489

221

Maynard Keynes; and novelist Virginia and her husband Leonard Woolf, author, editor, and art critic. The Bloomsbury group subscribed to G. E. Moore's dictum that "by far the most valuable things are the pleasures of human intercourse and the enjoyment of beautiful objects." Not a bad philosophy of life.

Chelsea. Tube: Sloane Sq.

Even though Chelsea no longer officially exists as an independent borough—it was formally amalgamated with Kensington in 1965—it retains a character all its own, thanks to its streets lined with pastel-colored residences that are often blessed with lovely gardens filled with wisteria and other flowering shrubs and plants. The origin of its name is uncertain, although early references to *Chelched* suggest that it may mean chalk wharf. Its reputation was firmly established when Thomas More built a retreat here. That was followed by homes for the Duke of Norfolk and King Henry VIII.

In the 17th and 18th centuries, Chelsea attracted a great number of writers and intellectuals, including Swift, Addison, Carlyle, and Leigh Hunt. Its association with art and artists began with the foundation of the Chelsea Porcelain works (1745–84) and the illustrations done for the publications of the Chelsea Physic Garden. In the late 19th century, such dramatic figures as Whistler and Rossetti gave the district a great reputation for style.

Although many of the 19th-century Chelsea homes have been replaced by ugly, blasted modern blocks, there are still plenty of residential streets with elegant town houses and well-tended front gardens to stroll along and enjoy.

Covent Garden. Tube: Covent Garden.

Long Acre, St. Martin's Lane, Drury Lane, and the Strand mark the boundaries of today's Covent Garden. Originally, it belonged to the Convent of St. Peter at Westminster, but after the dissolution of the monasteries, it was granted to John Russell, first Earl of Bedford, and it has remained in this family's hands. In 1627, the fourth earl hired Inigo Jones to lay out a new square consisting of St. Paul's Church and three sides of a square of tall terraced houses. Considered odd at the time, the houses had front doors that opened on vaulted arcades, but they were soon occupied by fashionable tenants. In the middle of the 17th century, a market developed here, encouraging some of the more fashionable folks to move to the new and more attractive district of St. James. The market continued to grow and new, more substantial shops were built. In the mid-18th century, coffeehouses opened up, too, and these were frequented by such literary figures as Fielding, Boswell, Goldsmith, Pope, Garrick, Sheridan, and Walpole. The Bedford was the most famous coffeehouse. The area has always been associated with the theater, and many of the early 18th-century theater actors and managers lived here.

By the mid-18th century, cheap lodging houses, gambling dens, and brothels dotted the area. Dubbing Covent Garden the Square of Venus, Magistrate John Fielding said, "One would imagine that all the prostitutes in the kingdom had picked upon the rendezvous." By the early 19th century, the market had become so disorderly that the Duke of Bedford applied to Parliament for authority to collect tolls and to build a new market building. Constructed in the early 1830s, the Bedford's new market thrived. Nearly 1,000 porters were employed when the market was at its height, earning between 30 and 45 shillings a week. It was still very disorderly, and the 11th Duke of Bedford eventually sold it in 1918 to a private group. Although it was condemned in 1920, the market continued to operate here until 1974. It was then refurbished and converted into the lively tourist-filled shopping mall that it is today. The Flower Market (1870) is now occupied by the National

Transport Museum. The Jubilee Market (1904) now features a covered street market.

Docklands, Isle of Dogs. Tube: Tower Hill or London Bridge. Docklands Light Railway: Tower Gateway For Isle of Dogs or DLR Crossharbour.

In the 1970s, the dockers fought stubbornly against containerization and in a few short years most London docks, except for Tilbury, had closed. When they died, the 55 miles of waterfront between the Tower of London and Greenwich were redeveloped by the government. Begin your visit of this large area at the **London Docklands Visitor Centre** (☎ **0171/512-1111**) in Limeharbour, Isle of Dogs (open Mon to Sat). A 16-minute video recaps the area's redevelopment. *Financial Times* walking-tour maps are available at the center; you can explore the area either by foot or bicycle. **Canary Wharf** is a shopping and office complex that incorporates **Cesar Pelli's** dramatic 800-foot-tall **tower** which is reputedly the tallest building in Europe. Old sugar warehouses stand at Port East.

To get there, take the Docklands Light Railway (DLR) from Tower Gateway station or catch it from Bank or Tower Hill tube stations to Crossharbour. Travelcards are valid on the DLR.

✪ **Greenwich.** Rail: Network Southeast train from Charing Cross to Maze Hill. Docklands Light Railway: Island Gardens. Bus: 53, 177, 180, 188.

Henry VIII, and later his daughter Elizabeth I, ruled England from a medieval palace in Greenwich. Today, Greenwich is a harmonious architectural treasure that is home to the **Royal Naval College** (1694); the elegant **Queen's House;** and the **Old Royal Observatory** (see individual listings in this chapter). The **Greenwich Tourist Information Centre** is at 46 Greenwich Church St., SE10 (☎ 0181/858-6376); it's open daily from 10am to 5pm. To get to Greenwich via the Thames, launches can be had from Westminster, Charing Cross, and Tower piers.

✪ **Hampstead.** Tube: Hampstead

Since earlier times, especially during the Great Plague, Hampstead has served as a rural escape for Londoners. In the late 17th century, London taverns sold water from Hampstead, and this helped to make the area fashionable. In 1700, John Duffield built a pump room in Well Walk, and stylish society began to flock to the tearooms, racetrack, and taverns of Hampstead.

Among its diverse residents have been navigator Martin Frobisher; Prime Minister William Pitt; poet and essayist Leigh Hunt; the romantic poets Byron and Keats; landscape painter John Constable; Kate Greenaway (at no. 39 Frognal); father of psychoanalysis Sigmund Freud (at no. 20 Maresfield Gardens); Nobel Prize–winning author Rabindranath Tagore (at no. 3 Villas on the Heath); ballet star Anna Pavlova (at Ivy House North End Road); biologist Julian Huxley; writers D. H. Lawrence, H. G. Wells, Katherine Mansfield, and John Galsworthy (at Grove Lodge); photographer and designer Cecil Beaton; and rock stars Boy George and George Michael. Today it's still home to the celebrity set.

The **800-acre heath** has been left to the public in perpetuity and is a wonderful place to walk or fly a kite. Great views are had from **Parliament Hill.** You could spend the day just strolling the village streets or visiting Heathside pubs, which include **Jack Straw's Castle,** the **Spaniards,** and the **Old Bull and Bush.** Specific sights to see include **Keats House** and **Freud Museum** (see individual listings for both of these in this chapter). The **Iveagh Bequest Kenwood,** at Hampstead Lane (☎ 0181/348-1286), is Lord Iveagh's collection of paintings; this includes works by Rembrandt, Vermeer, Turner, and Reynolds. It's open daily 10am to 6pm in summer, 10am to 4pm in winter; admission is free.

Impressions

In people's eyes, in the swing, tramp, and trudge; in the bellow and uproar; the car-
riages, motor cars, omnibuses, vans, sandwich men shuffling and swinging; brass
bands; barrel organs; in the triumph and the jingle and the strange high singing of
some aeroplane overhead was what she loved; life; London; this moment in June.

—Virginia Woolf, *Mrs. Dalloway*

Highgate. Tube: Archway.

Highgate was named after a tollgate high up on one of its hills. In the 14th century, a poor boy named Dick Whittington, resting at the bottom of that hill, heard the famous call to "Turn again, Whittington, Lord Mayor of London," or so the legend goes. The young man went to London with only his cat, believing the streets were paved with gold and silver. He became a cloth merchant and then thrice the lord mayor of London. Today, Highgate is discreet, low-key, WASPy, and right-wing. The streets are lined with elegant Georgian, terraced Victorian, and Edwardian homes. The district is known for its wealth of intellectual societies—debating, reading, and choral singing. The famous cemetery of the same name was laid out in the 19th century (see individual listing, above in this chapter). The poets A. E. Housman and John Betjeman and ethnologist Mary Kingsley are among the vil-lage's famous sometime residents.

✪ **Soho.** Tube: Oxford Circus, Tottenham Court Rd., or Piccadilly Circus.

A cosmopolitan neighborhood with a fascinating history, Soho was used for hunting in the Tudor era. This may explain its name, as *So ho!* was a common hunting cry. Residential development began in the early 17th century and acceler-ated in the 1670s. In the 18th century, many French Huguenots settled in the area, lending it a Gallic ambience—so much so that in 1749, William Maitland wrote that in Soho, you could easily imagine yourself in France. To this day, some fine charcuteries can be found in the district. While Soho's wealthier residents eventu-ally moved on, its foreign communities remained and were joined by artists. In the 19th century, Soho became one of the most densely populated areas of London. Cholera and other epidemics swept through the neighborhood and into other parts of London. Yet, at this time, Soho was London's entertainment center, filled with theaters, music halls, and some more disreputable pursuits.

In *The Forsyte Saga* (1922), John Galsworthy described Soho as: "Untidy, full of Greeks, Ishmaelites, cats, Italians, tomatoes, restaurants, organs, colored stuffs, queer names, people looking out of upper windows, it dwells remote from the Body Politic."

Soho's reputation as a fashionable but inexpensive dining area was well estab-lished by the 1920s. People flocked to restaurants and new theaters along Shaftes-bury Avenue and Charing Cross Road. In the 1960s, sex clubs proliferated and Soho gained an unsavory reputation. The few residents who did remain fought to save their neighborhood. A series of police corruption trials and a law requiring the licensing of sex clubs has reduced their number—dramatically. Today, Soho is one of the liveliest and most interesting areas of London. Wander along Dean and Frith Streets and into Soho Square (see also chapter 5 for Soho restaurants) to absorb the bohemian flavor of the area.

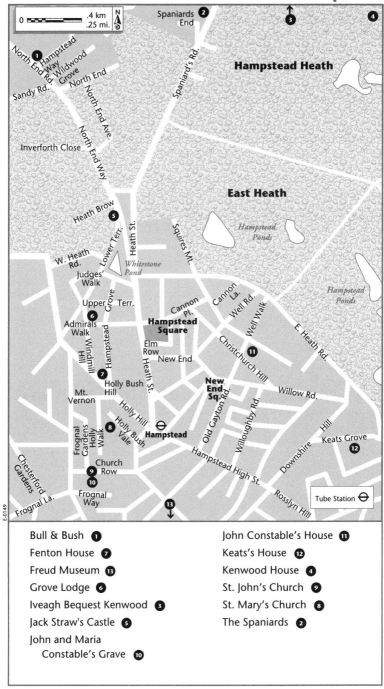

Bull & Bush ❶

Fenton House ❼

Freud Museum ⓭

Grove Lodge ❻

Iveagh Bequest Kenwood ❸

Jack Straw's Castle ❺

John and Maria
   Constable's Grave ❿

John Constable's House ⓫

Keats's House ⓬

Kenwood House ❹

St. John's Church ❾

St. Mary's Church ❽

The Spaniards ❷

9 Maritime & Waterfront Sights

Butlers Wharf. On the South Bank of the Thames, SE1. Tube: Tower Hill.

Near Tower Bridge, this complex of shops and restaurants has river views. The prime attraction here is the Design Museum and the warehouses themselves, which have been carefully and artfully restored. It's also home to one of Terence Conran's gourmet food complexes, including the Pont de la Tour restaurant.

Cutty Sark. King William Walk, Greenwich, SE10. ☎ **0181/858-3445.** Admission £3.50 ($5.60) adults, £2.50 ($4) children. Mon–Sat 10am–6pm (5pm in winter). Sun noon–6pm (to 5pm in winter). Closed Dec 24–26. Docklands Light Railway: Island Gardens. Bus: 177, 180, 188, 199. River launches: Greenwich Pier.

This 19th-century sailing clipper is one of the most famous to have survived its era. Built in Dumbarton and launched in 1869, it arrived too late to succeed in the tea trade, which by then had been taken over by steamers after the opening of the Suez Canal. Instead it entered the Australian wool trade, circling the globe round the Cape of Good Hope on the outward journey and Cape Horn on the homeward journey. She was designed for speed, able to cover almost 400 miles per day at sea. Restored in 1922, the ship has been in dry dock since 1954. On board you'll gain some insight into the life of Victorian sailors and how crew and officers lived during a voyage. Other highlights include the Long John Silver Collection of merchant ships' figureheads (the most extensive collection in the country), plus a fine collection of maritime paintings and prints.

HMS *Belfast*. Morgan's Lane, Tooley St., SE1. ☎ **0171/407-6434.** Admission £4.70 ($7.50) adults, £3.60 ($5.75) seniors, £2.40 ($3.85) children 5–17. Daily Mar–Oct 10am–5:15pm, Nov–Feb 10am–4:15pm. Closed Dec 24, 25, 26 and June 1999. Tube: Tower Hill or London Bridge. River launches: Tower Pier.

A World War II cruiser armed with 32 guns, the HMS *Belfast* played a leading role in the Normandy landings and the destruction of the *Scharnhorst* at the Battle of North Cape, and served on the terrible Arctic convoy route to North Russia. There are nine decks to explore, from the Bridge to the boiler and engine rooms. Along the way visitors can operate anti-aircraft guns and imagine what life was like for the crew in the cramped Mess decks. Among some of the more interesting statistics is one that states that from 1950 to 1952, when the ship served in the Far East, the crew consumed 56,000 pints of Navy rum along with 134 tons of meat and 625 tons of potatoes.

✪ **National Maritime Museum.** Romney Rd., Greenwich, SE10. ☎ **0181/858-4422.** Admission £5 ($8) adults, £4 ($6.80) seniors, £2.50 ($4) children 5–16. The admission includes the Queen's House and the Old Observatory. Daily 10am–5pm. Closed Dec 24–26. Rail: Charing Cross to Maze Hill. Docklands Light Railway: Island Gardens. Bus: 177, 180, 188. River service to Greenwich Pier.

This museum, adjoining the Queen's House, is currently being expanded; the new galleries will open in spring 1999. New themed exhibits will include "Liners, Art and the Sea," "Trade and Empire," "Maritime London," and an interactive area called "The Bridge." One of the largest maritime museums in the world, the collection contains 2,500 ship models, 4,000 paintings, 50,000 charts, and 750,000 ship plans plus hundreds of scientific and navigational instruments. The Nelson gallery displays many priceless items associated with Horatio Nelson, including the coat with the hole made by the bullet that killed him. The 20th-century gallery shows modern naval warfare illustrated with videos, paintings, and ship models both merchant and military.

Royal Naval College. King William Walk, off Romney Rd., Greenwich, SE10. ☎ **0181/ 858-2154.** Free admission. Daily 2:30–5pm. Closed Dec 24–26, Good Friday. Rail: Charing Cross to Maze Hill. Riverbus to Greenwich. Bus: 177, 180, 188.

This complex designed by Sir Christopher Wren in 1696 occupies four blocks named after King Charles, Queen Anne, King William, and Queen Mary. Formerly, Greenwich Palace stood here from 1422 to 1640. See the magnificent Painted Hall by Thornhill where the body of Nelson lay in state in 1805 and also the Georgian chapel of St. Peter and St. Paul.

Thames Barrier. Unity Way, Woolwich, SE18. ☎ **0181/305-4188.** Admission £3.40 ($5.45) adults, £2 ($3.20) seniors or children 5–17. Mon–Fri 10:30am–5pm; Sat–Sun 10:30am–5:30pm. River launches: From Westminster, Charing Cross, Tower, and Greenwich piers. Bus: 177, 180.

This giant feat of engineering opened in 1984 to protect London from flooding. It consists of four huge gates, each weighing 3,000 tons, and six smaller ones. When closed, these 10 gates seal the upper river off from the sea. The Visitor Centre on the south bank has exhibits that illustrate the operation of London's tidal flood defenses.

10 For Art and Literary Enthusiasts

England has a long and rich literary tradition, and walking the streets of London can bring you to homes of writers and artists and to the setting of scenes from novels that have become part of our personal myths. The curious may want to secure a guide to all the blue plaques in London, marking historically significant spots. Geoffrey Chaucer lived above Aldgate, in the easternmost part of the city, until 1386. Playwright Joe Orton lived on Noel Road in Islington until his death in 1967. Oscar Wilde, Dylan Thomas, Agatha Christie, George Orwell, D. H. Lawrence, George Bernard Shaw, Rudyard Kipling, William Blake—the list of writers who made London their home goes on and on. Usually, the blue plaque is, unfortunately, all that's left to mark the past, but there are some exceptions.

Dickens's House. 48 Doughty St., WC1. ☎ **0171/405-2127.** Admission £3.50 ($5.60) adults, £2.50 ($4) students and seniors, £1.50 ($2.40) children, £7 ($11.20) families. Mon–Sat 10am–5pm. Tube: Russell Sq.

Home to Victorian London's quintessential chronicler, this terraced house is on the outskirts of Bloomsbury. Dickens only lived here for two years (1837–39), but in that time, he produced some of his best-loved works, including a portion of *The Pickwick Papers, Nicholas Nickleby,* and *Oliver Twist.* The author's letters, furniture, and first editions are displayed in glass cases. The rooms have been restored to their original appearance.

Dr. Johnson's House. 17 Gough Sq., Fleet St., EC4. ☎ **0171/353-3745.** Admission £3 ($4.80) adults, £2 ($3.20) students and seniors, free for children under 10. May–Sept, Mon–Sat 11am–5:30pm; Oct–Apr, Mon–Sat 11am–5pm. Tube: Blackfriars, Temple, or Holborn.

The house is tucked away behind Fleet Street, on an intimate square at the end of a labyrinth of alleys and passages that are loaded with atmosphere. Samuel Johnson lived here from 1748 until 1759, compiling the first comprehensive English dictionary, published in 1755. Here, too, he greeted such friends as Joshua Reynolds, David Garrick, Edmund Burke, Oliver Goldsmith, and, of course, James Boswell. In the top garret, six copyists stood transcribing the entries for the dictionary while elsewhere Johnson sat reading and compiling lists of words from the best literature of the time. The original dictionary is on display along with letters, prints, portraits, and other memorabilia, but very few furnishings.

Keats House. Wentworth Place, Keats Grove, NW3. ☎ **0171/435-2062.** Free admission. Apr–Oct, Mon–Fri 10am–1pm and 2–6pm, Sat 10am–1pm and 2–5pm, Sun 2–5pm; Nov–Mar, Mon–Fri 1–5pm, Sat 10am–1pm and 2–5pm, Sun 2–5pm. Closed Dec 24–26, Jan 1, Good Friday, Easter Eve, and May 1. Tube: Hampstead/Belsize Park.

Romantic poet John Keats (1795–1821) lived and worked in this unassuming home in tranquil Hampstead. "Ode to a Nightingale" was penned here, and a first edition of this is displayed along with books, diaries, letters, memorabilia, and some original furnishings.

Note: The house is currently closed for major repairs and, at press time, no reopening dates had been determined.

Leighton House. 12 Holland Park Rd., W14, off Melbury Rd. ☎ **0171/602-3316.** Free admission. Guided tours £1.50 ($2.40) Wed and Thurs at noon, Mon–Sat 11am–5:30pm. Closed Sun and major holidays. Tube: High St. Kensington. Bus: 9, 9a 10, 27, 33, and 49.

This fine example of high Victoriana was the home of Frederic, Lord Leighton (1830–96), a classical painter and president of the Royal Academy. Built between 1867 and 1879 to designs by George Aitchison, it expresses Leighton's vision of a private palace devoted to art. The most stunning element of the house is the exotic Arab Hall with a fountain at the center and a remarkably beautiful gilt mosaic frieze depicting birds and animals. The authentic Iznik tiles add their own brilliance to the space. Similar fantasy infuses the artist's studio featuring a gilded dome and apse. The house also displays a fine collection of Victorian art, including works by Leighton, Edward Burne-Jones, Millais, and their contemporaries. Temporary exhibitions are mounted throughout the year.

Linley Sambourne House. 18 Stafford Terrace, W8. ☎ **0181/994-1019** or 0171/937-0663. Admission £3 ($4.80) adults, £2.50 ($4) seniors, £1.50 ($2.40) children under 16. Mar–Oct only, Wed 10am–4pm, Sun 2–5pm. Tube: High St. Kensington.

This was the home of Edward Linley Sambourne (1844–1910), a leading cartoonist for *Punch* magazine in the late Victorian and Edwardian era. The house is deliciously Victorian and cluttered. It retains most of the original decor including wall decorations, fixtures, furniture, and paintings made by Linley and his friends.

Thomas Carlyle's House. 24 Cheyne Row, SW3. ☎ **0171/352-7087.** Admission £3.20 ($5.10) adults, £1.50 ($2.55) children under 17. Apr–Oct, Wed–Sun 11am–5pm. Closed Nov–Mar. Tube: Sloane Sq.

Writer and historian Thomas Carlyle lived in this Queen Anne terrace house from 1834 until his death in 1881. Many a famous figure visited him here, including Chopin, Dickens, Tennyson, and George Eliot, who lived just around the corner on Cheyne Walk. The virtually unaltered house contains the original furniture and many books, portraits, and mementos from his day. The walled Victorian garden has also been restored and is a delight.

William Morris Gallery. Lloyd Park, Forest Rd., Walthamstow, E17. ☎ **0181/527-3782.** Free admission. Tues–Sat and first Sun of each month, 10am–1pm and 2–5pm. Closed Mon and all bank holidays. Tube: Walthamstow, then bus 34, 97, 215, or 257.

Designer, socialist, poet, publisher, and manufacturer of furniture and wallpaper, William Morris was an extraordinarily talented man. Fascinated by the medieval period and the richness of craftsmanship that prevailed back then, he became a prime leader in the Arts and Crafts movement. Fans of Morris will not want to miss the permanent collection here which traces his career through his work and writing.

Sights For Visiting Americans

Grosvenor Square, W1, has strong U.S. connections and is referred to by some as "Little America." John Adams lived on the square when he was the American ambassador to Britain, a statue of Franklin Roosevelt stands in the center of the square, General Eisenhower headquartered here during World War II, and the entire west side is occupied by the U.S. Embassy.

The former **home of Benjamin Franklin,** 36 Craven St., WC2 (steps from Trafalgar Square), is just one of many houses formerly occupied by famous Americans. For a complete list, pick up *Americans in London* (Queen Anne Press, 1988), by Brian Morton, an excellent anecdotal street guide to the homes and haunts of famous Americans.

Upstairs, temporary exhibits highlight the work of his circle, the Pre-Raphaelite artists, such as Edward Burne-Jones and Dante Gabriel Rossetti.

11 Zoos & Aquariums

London Aquarium. County Hall Riverside Building, Westminster Bridge Rd., SE1. ☎ **0171/ 967-8000.** Admission £7 ($11.20) adults, £6 ($9.60) seniors, £5 ($8) children. Daily 10am–6pm. Tube: Westminster/Waterloo.

When the Greater London Council was abolished by Maggie Thatcher, the office building at the end of Westminster Bridge on the south bank of the Thames was purchased and converted into this aquarium. It features two massive tanks that contain hundreds of varieties of fish and marine life hailing from the Pacific and the Atlantic. Kids enjoy the shallow Beach pier where they can touch stingrays and other fish.

London Zoo. Regent's Park, NW1. ☎ **0171/722-3333,** for recorded information. Admission £8.50 ($13.60) adults, £7.50 ($12) students and seniors, £6 ($9.60) children 4–14. Apr–Oct daily 10am–5:30pm; Nov–Mar 10am–4pm. Closed Dec 25. Tube: Camden Town, Regent's Park. Waterbus: Service operates along Regent's Canal between Camden Lock or Little Venice and the zoo. From Apr to the end of Sept the boat departs on the hour 10am–5pm. In winter there is less frequent daily service.

It's far from the world's best or most humane zoo, but it makes a reasonable stab at being educational. The most recent excitement was the opening of the children's zoo (in 1994). The zoo offers the usual assortment of animal life behind bars or in compounds—elephants, lions, tigers, penguins, and chimps, plus a small aquarium, and reptile and insect houses. When you enter, pick up a copy of the daily events guide and check it out for demonstrations at the amphitheatre or the feeding times of your favorite animals. The zoo has six places to eat—for you, not the animals.

12 Parks & Gardens

Founded in 1673, the **Chelsea Physic Garden,** at 66 Royal Hospital Rd., SW3 (☎ **0171/352-5646**), is the second-oldest botanical garden in England. Behind its high walls is a rare collection of exotic plants, shrubs, and trees, many more than 100 years old. Originally founded by the Society of Apothecaries to teach their apprentices how to identify medicinal plants, it continues to function primarily as a research and educational facility. Among the labeled plants, you'll find those that gave us aspirin, steroids, and many other common medicines. Its resident English

Gardening School holds lectures throughout the summer; call for details. Admission is £3.50 ($5.60) for adults and £1.80 ($2.90) for students and children. It's open April through October, on Wednesday noon to 5pm and Sunday from 2 to 6pm. Take the tube to Sloane Square.

Behind Kensington High Street, **Holland Park** is one of the city's most entrancing parks—an oasis of woods and gardens set around Holland House. Here peacocks can be found roaming. In summer, open-air theater and opera are performed in the park. There's an adventure playground for kids, plus plenty of sports facilities (squash, tennis, cricket and golf nets, and football). Call ☎ **0171/602-2226** for reservations. Also worth seeking out is the Japanese Kyoto Garden. A summer ballroom has been converted into an upscale restaurant; there's also a cafe available. Take the tube to High Street Kensington.

Of all the city's parks, ✪ **Hyde Park** (☎ **0171/298-2100**) is the largest, the most popular, and the most symbolic of London. The aptly named Serpentine Lake, created in the 1730s, is the 340-acre park's most notable feature. Enjoy boating on the lake, lounging by its side or riding along Rotten Row (a corruption of *route du roi,* the pathway laid out by King William III from the West End to Kensington Palace). The small Serpentine Gallery (☎ **0171/402-6075**) exhibits contemporary art. It's open daily from 10am to 6pm.

As in other Royal Parks, wood-and-cloth deck chairs are scattered throughout Hyde Park, and fee collectors seem to appear from nowhere to extract 60p (95¢) from seated visitors who are usually ignorant of this cost. It's free to sit on the benches and grass. On Sunday the park really comes alive, when artists hang their works along the Bayswater Road fence. The northeast corner, near Marble Arch, becomes ✪ **Speaker's Corner.** Anyone can stand on a soapbox here and speak on any subject. Although this tradition is often touted as an example of Britain's tolerance of free speech, few people realize that this ritual began several hundred years ago when condemned prisoners were allowed some final words before they were hung on Tyburn gallows, which stood on the very same spot. Take the tube to Hyde Park Corner.

Originally a private hunting ground of Henry VIII, today **Regent's Park** (☎ **0171/486-7905**) is London's playground. In summer, you'll see people walking their dogs; playing cricket, soccer, and baseball; doing gymnastics; and throwing Frisbees. Besides the zoo, it's famous for summer brass band concerts on Holme Green; Shakespeare in the open-air theater (☎ **0171/486-2431**); and a boating lake. Among the thousands of blooms found here are the 30,000 blossoms and 400 varieties of roses in Queen Mary's rose garden; the Italianate decorations in the Avenue Gardens; the Japanese Gardens; and the wildflowers that grow along the banks of Regent's Canal. In the northwestern corner of the park stands Winfield House, the home of the American Ambassador, while a short distance south of it is the London Mosque. The park was conceived in 1811 by the Prince Regent and John Nash as part of an elaborate remodeling of London, and originally incorporated grand villas (including a second home for the Prince Regent himself). Get there by tube to Regent's Park, Baker Street, or Camden Town (to Camden Town for the zoo).

With its trademark Round Pond, where model boat enthusiasts sail their barks, **Kensington Gardens** (☎ **0171/298-2100**) abuts the western perimeter of Hyde Park. The gardens which stretch beside and behind Kensington Palace were laid out in the early 18th century. You can wander around the edges of the sunken gardens, enjoy lunch or tea at the Orangery, and while away some time on one of the many

Where to Get Picnic Supplies

Most London supermarkets offer picnic fixings, but for the ultimate grocery shopping experience, go to **Harrods Food Hall,** 87–135 Brompton Rd., SW1 (☎ **0171/730-1234;** Tube: Knightsbridge), where you'll find fresh breads and other baked goods, prepared foods, and luxury comestibles of all types. Similarly sumptuous is **Fortnum & Mason,** 181 Piccadilly, W1 (☎ **0171/734-8040;** Tube: Piccadilly Circus or Green Park). In Soho, **Randall & Aubin,** on the north side of Brewer at no. 16 (☎ **0171/287-4447;** Tube: Picadilly Circus) is a characterful boucherie/charcuterie. Here you can assemble a feast of bread, cheese, and sausage.

If you're in Hampstead and want to take a picnic up to the Heath, then head to the **Rosslyn Hill Deli,** 56 Rosslyn Hill, NW3 (☎ **0171/794-9210;** Tube: Hampstead). It ain't cheap, but you can splurge a little on a picnic, no?

For a Chinese-inspired picnic, try the big and fascinating **Loon Fung Supermarket** at 42–44 Gerrard St., W1 (☎ **0171/437-7332;** Tube: Leicester Sq.), right in the heart of Soho's Chinatown. The most adventurous will try the black jelly fungus. The rest of us can settle for enjoying some dried cuttlefish, a traditional snack. Loon Fung is open daily from 10am to 7pm.

benches available. Near the Long Water, the famous statue of Peter Pan with attending bronze rabbits is the garden's most popular feature for children.

Opposite Buckingham Palace, **St. James's Park**, The Mall (☎ **0171/930-1793**), is perhaps the most beautiful of all of London's parks. It was landscaped by Le Notre and John Nash. The famous lake is a sanctuary for all kinds of waterfowl, including coots and white and Australian black swans, which give the park a romantic atmosphere. From the bridge that arches over the lake is the best view of Buckingham Palace. Numerous benches and plenty of grass and shade make this an ideal picnicking place. Take the tube to St. James's Park.

Named for its absence of flowers (except for a short time in spring), **Green Park** (☎ **0171/930-1793**) provides ample shade from tall trees that make it a picnic bower.

13 Organized Tours

Although the image of a tour group is repugnant to most independent travelers, guided tours do offer benefits, especially as an introductory orientation or for visitors with limited time.

WALKING TOURS

London's most interesting streets are best explored on foot, and several inexpensive walking-tour companies will lead you along some fascinating routes.

The Original London Walks, P.O. Box 1708, London NW6 4LQ (☎ **0171/ 624-3978**) offers an amazing array of themes, from the Beatles to pub walks to ghosts to literary heroes. Their Jack the Ripper walk (which leaves daily at 7:30 pm from Tower Hill Underground) is led twice a week (usually Sunday and Monday) by Donald Rumbelow, a retired member of the City Police force and an authority on the subject. Tours generally cost £4.50 ($7.20) adults, £3.50 ($5.60) seniors and students; they represent one of the best bargains in London. This company also offers **Explorer Day** tours to such places as York, Oxford, Bath, and Salisbury. Winnie the Pooh fans will want to take the special tour to East Grinstead, home to A. A. Milne's country house, Cotchford Farm. The charge for these is £9.50 ($15.20) adult and £8.50 ($13.60) seniors and students for the guide, plus the cost of rail fare.

For a few dollars more, you can enjoy **Discovery Walks,** led by author and historian **Richard Jones,** 67 Chancery Lane, London WC2A 1AF (☎ **0181/ 530-8443;** disctourlo@aol.com). Jones offers more than 30 different itineraries for £4.50 ($7.20) per person. Among the most popular is the London Theatrical Ghost Walk led by the spooky guide Thomas Bodie. Other companies worth contacting include **Historical Walks of London** (☎ **0181/668-4019**) and **Londoner Pub Walks** (☎ **0181/883-2656**).

One of London's most popular walks follows the route from Trafalgar Square to Parliament Square and is outlined in chapter 7. Other enjoyable walks are also described in that chapter, as well as in *Frommer's Memorable Walks in London* (Macmillan Travel).

For a slightly faster pace, join one of the weekend tours given by **London Bicycle Tour Company** (☎ **0171/928-6838**). The tours cost £11.95 ($19.12) plus bike rental of £9.95 ($15.90) per day or £2 ($3.20) per hour.

BUS TOURS

If your time is more limited than your budget, a comprehensive bus tour may be your best bet. The **Big Bus Company** (☎ **0181/944-7810**) leaves from Green Park and Victoria and from Marble Arch daily on several 30-mile routes that take anywhere from 1 to 2 hours. Tickets are £12 ($19.20) adults and £6 ($9.60) children. They are valid for 24 hours and allow you to hop on and off at 60 different locations. The **Original London Sightseeing Tour** (☎ **0181/877-1722**), operated by London Coaches, is a 90-minute tour that departs from Piccadilly Circus, Victoria, Baker Street, or Marble Arch. The cost is £12 ($19.20) for adults, £6 ($9.60) for children, and tickets can be purchased on board or at any London Transport or London Tourist Board office. The **London Plus Tour** (same price) allows you to get on and off at about 20 stops.

Do-it-yourselfers should purchase a **Travelcard** (see "Getting Around" in chapter 3) and climb aboard a red double-decker bus. One of the most scenic routes is taken by bus no. 11, which travels between Liverpool Station and Fulham Broadway. Along the way it travels via King's Road, Victoria Station, Westminster Abbey, Whitehall, Horse Guards, Trafalgar Square, the National Gallery, the Strand, Law Courts, Fleet Street, and St. Paul's Cathedral.

BOAT TOURS/CRUISES

The Thames has always served as the city's highway, and some of the most vivid experiences can be enjoyed on the river launches that still take visitors and commuters on the river from Westminster east to the Tower (all year, call ☎ **0171/ 237-5134**); Greenwich (all year, call ☎ **0171/930-4097**); and the Thames Barrier (March–Nov only, call ☎ **0171/930-3373**) and west to Hampton Court and Kew (Easter–Oct call ☎ **0171/930-2062** or 930-4721).

Other companies operate a variety of other cruises including lunch and dinner trips: **Catamaran Cruisers Ltd.** (☎ **0171/987-1185**), Campion Launches (☎ **0181/305-0300**); Woods River Cruises (☎ **0171/481-2711**), and **Bateaux London Ltd.** (☎ **0171/925-2215**).

Several companies offer boat tours on the Regent's Canal. **Jason's Trip** (☎ **0171/ 286-3428;** Tube: Warwick Ave.) operates a 90-minute tour in narrow boats from the wharf opposite no. 60 Blomfield Rd. in Little Venice. Trips go along the Regent's Canal, past Brownings Island (so called because Robert Browning lived there), through the Maida Hill Tunnel, into Regent's Park, and thence to Camden Lock. The round-trip price is £5.95 ($9.50) for adults and £4.50 ($7.20) for children; £4.95 ($7.90) and £3.75 ($6) respectively, one-way. Lunch and dinner cruises are offered, too. **London Waterbus Company** (☎ **0171/482-2660;** Tube: Warwick Ave. or Camden Town) operates similar trips between Little Venice and Camden Lock as well as cruises on the River Lea and to Limehouse. These canal trips operate from April to September only, daily on the hour from Camden Lock and Little Venice. The fares are as follows: one-way £3.80 ($6.10) adult, £2.40 ($3.85) seniors and children; round-trip £5 ($8) and £3 ($4.80). You can also include a stop at the zoo, which will cost £10.30 ($16.50) and £6.60 ($10.55) from Little Venice, and £8.50 ($13.60) and £6 ($9.60) from Camden Lock. The prices include admission to the zoo.

14 Especially for Kids

Kidsline (☎ **0171/222-8070**) offers advice on current happenings for youngsters. It operates during school holidays weekdays 9am to 4pm and during term from 4 to 6pm.

Obvious choices for children include touring the **Tower of London,** seeing Buckingham Palace's **Changing of the Guard,** climbing to the top of both **Tower Bridge** and **St. Paul's Cathedral,** and visiting the **Museum of the Moving Image.**

Other hits (see write-ups above in this chapter) are the *Cutty Sark,* HMS *Belfast,* Imperial War Museum, London Transport Museum, London Zoo, Madame Tussaud's, Natural History Museum, and Science Museum.

STILL MORE HITS FOR CHILDREN

Bethnal Green Museum of Childhood. Cambridge Heath Rd., E2. ☎ **0181/980-2415.** Free admission. Mon–Thurs, Sat 10am–5:50pm, Sun 2:30–5:50pm. Closed Fri, Dec 25–26, Jan 1, and May bank holiday. Tube: Bethnal Green.

A great collection of toys, dolls, dollhouses, games, puppets, children's costumes, and other kids' items.

✪ **Little Angel Theatre.** 14 Dagmar Passage, Islington, N1. ☎ **0171/226-1787.** Tickets £4.50–£6.50 ($7.20–$10.40). Tube: Angel, Highbury, or Islington.

A unique and wonderful puppet theater, featuring a variety of puppet and marionette groups performing such tales as *Blue Beard, Jack and the Beanstalk, Pinocchio, Rumpelstiltskin,* and *The Selkie Bride.* Performances are given on weekends at 11am and 3pm and during school holidays. No children under 3 are permitted, and some shows are recommended for certain age groups; children under the recommended age will not be accommodated.

London Brass Rubbing Centre. In the crypt of St. Martin-in-the-Fields Church, Trafalgar Sq., WC2. ☎ **0171/930-9306.** Free admission. Brass rubbings cost from £2.50 ($4). Mon–Sat 10am–6pm, Sun noon–6pm. Closed Dec 25 and Good Friday. Tube: Charing Cross.

Inside one of London's landmark churches, both adults and children can make rubbings of about 100 replicas of medieval church brasses—knights, ladies, kings, merchants, and heraldic animals—or any of several unusual Celtic designs and early woodcuts of the zodiac. It's fun, historical, and artistic. Materials and instruction are provided. The gift shop stocks Celtic jewelry as well as model knights and other mementos.

London Dungeon. 28–34 Tooley St., SE1. ☎ **0171/403-7221,** or 0171/403-0606 for recorded information. Admission £8.95 ($14.30) adults, £7.95 ($12.70) seniors, £6 ($9.60) children 5–14. Daily Apr–Sept, 10am–6:30pm; Oct–Mar, 10am–5:30pm. Closed Dec 24, 25, 26. Tube: London Bridge.

Some children may appreciate this state-of-the-art horror chamber in which the goriest events from British history are reenacted in the dark. The Theatre of the Guillotine and the Jack the Ripper Experience are particularly spine-chilling and may frighten and upset young children.

London Planetarium. Marylebone Rd., NW1. ☎ **0171/486-1121.** Admission £5.85 ($9.35) adults, £4.50 ($7.20) seniors, £3.85 ($6.10) children 5–15. Combined tickets for Madame Tussaud's and the planetarium are £11.50 ($28.25) adults, £7.55 ($12.10) children 5–15. Daily 10am–5:30pm. Shows run every 40 minutes 12:20–5pm, weekends and holidays from 10:20am. Tube: Baker St. Bus: 2, 13, 18, 27, 30, 74, 82, 113, 159, 176.

The planetarium explores the mysteries of the cosmos in new galleries featuring interactive exhibits, models, and displays. In these galleries visitors can hear Stephen Hawking talk about the mysterious black holes and also experience what shape or weight they would be on other planets. In the domed auditorium, catch a showing of *3D Planetary Quest*, which takes you on a journey through the solar system to distant galaxies. Along the way you cruise across the canyons of Mars and encounter exploding nebulae, comets, asteroids, and plenty of constellations, all thanks to the amazingly powerful Digistar II projector, which is able to project 9,000 stars.

Polka Theatre for Children. 240 The Broadway, SW19. ☎ **0181/543-4888.** Tickets £5–£7 ($8–$11.20). Performances are given during the day, with most around 11am and 12:30pm; last show at 5:30pm. Call for specific schedule. Closed Sept, Dec 25, Jan 1. Tube: South Wimbledon or Wimbledon. Bus: 57, 93, 155.

This company presents plays for young people and special shows for those from 3 to 13 years old in two theaters. Recent productions have included dramatizations of the *House at Pooh Corner, Beowulf the Dragon Slayer*, and *The Hare and the Tortoise*.

Rock Circus. London Pavilion, Piccadilly Circus, W1. ☎ **0171/734-7203.** Admission £7.95 ($12.70) adults, £6.90 ($11.05) seniors/students, £6 ($9.60) children 5–15. Sun–Mon, Wed–Thurs 11am–9pm, Tues noon–9pm, Fri–Sat 11am–10pm. Extended hours in summer 10am–10pm except Tues noon–9pm. Closed Dec 25. Tube: Piccadilly Circus.

An audio-animatronic show that tells the story of rock from the 1950s to today. Visitors don headphones catching song snippets along the way as they file past a series of wax dummies including Phil Collins, the Beatles, and Madonna. It's a high price to pay for poor camp.

SegaWorld. Trocadero Centre, Piccadilly Circus, W1. ☎ **0990/505040** or 171/734-2777. Admission is free but video games cost 20p–£1 (32¢–$1.60) and rides are £3 ($4.80) each. Sun–Thurs 10am–midnight, Fri–Sat 10am–1am. Occasionally it's closed for private parties so if you're making a special trip, call ahead. Tube: Piccadilly Circus.

SegaWorld is seven floors of electronic wizardry. In addition to vast banks of video games there are seven rides, including Emaginator (☎ 0171/437-5806), which offers two simulated rides—one aboard a runaway mine train, another on a craft racing through space. The Emaginator is open Sunday to Thursday 11am to 10:15pm, Friday to Saturday 11am to 10:30pm. Closed December 25. Note that at Segaworld there is a height restriction of 110cm (43 in.) on all rides and that kids under 16 must be accompanied by an adult.

Unicorn Arts Theatre. 6–7 Great Newport St., WC2. ☎ **0171/379-3280;** box office 0171/836-3334. £5–£9.50 ($8–$15.20). Tube: Leicester Sq./Covent Garden.

From September to June, this professional theater company presents plays for 4- to 12-year-olds. The plays may be adaptations of old favorites like *Cinderella* and *Hansel and Gretel,* or specially commissioned new plays. Performances are given Saturday and Sunday morning and afternoon.

15 Staying Active

Two organizations can help you find places to keep up an exercise routine: the **Sports Council,** 16 Upper Woburn Place, WC1 (☎ **0171/273-1500**) has information on sports centers; while **Sportsline** (☎ **0171/222-8000**) will answer any and all questions about sports in general, and direct you to the nearest swimming pool or any sport facility.

CHESS

Amateurs and grand masters lock horns at the Durham Castle, Alexander Street, in Paddington (no phone). Sets and clocks can be rented from the bar for £1 ($1.60) plus a £5 ($8) returnable deposit, and there's always someone looking for a game. The club is open during pub hours. Tube to Bayswater.

HORSEBACK RIDING

Hyde Park Riding Stables, 63 Bathurst Mews, W2, ☎ **0171/723-2813;** and **Ross Nye Stables,** 8 Bathurst Mews, W2, ☎ **0171/262-3791.** These are the places to go if you want to join a group horseback ride around Hyde Park. Hyde Park charges £25 ($40) per hour, Ross Nye charges the same. Both get booked up early for weekends. No galloping or jumping are allowed. Get there by tube to Lancaster Gate or Paddington.

ICE SKATING

Broadgate Ice Rink. Broadgate Circus, 3 Broadgate, EC2. ☎ **0171/505-4068.** Admission £5 ($8) adults, £3 ($4.80) seniors and students; skate rental £2 ($3.20) adults, £1 ($1.60) students and seniors. Nov–Apr, Mon–Thurs noon–2:30pm and 3:30–6pm; Fri noon–2:30 pm, 3:30–6pm, and 7–10pm; Sat–Sun 11am–1pm, 2–4pm, and 5–7pm. Tube: Liverpool St.

You can also to the hits at England's only open-air rink. This tiny but modern rink is surrounded by wine bars and features a state-of-the-art sound system that will knock your skates off.

Queen's Ice Skating Club. 17 Queensway, W2. ☎ **0171/229-0172.** Admission £4–£6.50 ($6.40–$10.40) adults and children 5–15, depending on the session. Mon 10am–noon is the cheapest at £4 ($6.40); Wed and Sun 8–10pm it's £5 ($8). Open daily 10am–11pm. There are several sessions daily; call for exact times. Tube: Bayswater or Queensway.

Weekend disco nights are especially crowded at this large indoor rink right in the heart of Bayswater. The basement-level rink can handle about 1,000 skaters, and often does.

SWIMMING/FITNESS

Brittania Leisure Centre. 40 Hyde Rd., N1. ☎ **0171/729-4485.** Admission 60p (95¢) adults, 40p (65¢) children. Mon–Fri 9am–10pm, Sat–Sun 9am–6pm. Tube: Old St.

A modern public sports facility with a swimming pool, badminton and squash courts, and soccer and volleyball fields.

Chelsea Sports Centre. Chelsea Manor St., SW3. ☎ **0171/352-6985.** Pool £2.30 ($3.70). Call for prices on classes; you have to be a member to use the weight room. Pool, Mon 7:30am–7pm, Tues–Wed and Fri 7:30am–10pm, Thurs 7:30am–2pm and 3–8pm, Sat 8am–5pm and 6–10pm, Sun 8am–6:30pm. Tube: Sloane Sq.

A community fitness center, this tri-level spa has a pool, sauna, and solarium as well as badminton, basketball, and volleyball courts. Aerobics classes are given.

London Central YMCA. 112 Great Russell St., WC1. ☎ **0171/637-8131.** Admission £15 ($24) per day, £35 ($56) per week. Mon–Fri 7am–10:30pm, Sat–Sun 10am–9pm. Tube: Tottenham Court Rd.

Snazzy for a Y, this top facility has a pool, weight room, squash/badminton, cardiovascular equipment, sauna, and solarium. Beauticians, massage therapists, and other specialized staff members are also on hand.

16 Spectator Sports

The English are passionate about sport and there is no better way to get to know and understand them than to watch them at play. The list that follows will help you in this endeavor. Questions about any spectator or participatory London sport will be answered free of charge by **Sportsline** (☎ **0171/222-8000**), Monday through Friday from 10am to 6pm. A good start is to drop by Regent's Park on a weekend and just ask to join one of the casual soccer or other games you'll find being played there.

CRICKET
Cricket is played at Lord's and the Oval. County games and international test series against a variety of countries—Australia, India, South Africa, the West Indies, and New Zealand, for example—are played during the summer. Check the newspapers or call Sportsline (see above) or the tourist board for information on current matches.

The Foster's Oval Cricket Ground. The Oval Kennington, SE11. ☎ **0171/582-6660.** Tickets £10–£47 ($16–$75.20). Box office, Mon–Fri 9:30am–4pm. Tube: Oval.

Less stodgy, pretty, and classy than Lord's, the Oval is still a great cricket ground. Home to Surrey CCC, this field traditionally hosts the final match in the international test series that are played during the summer. For international tests, you'll need to book tickets in advance.

Lord's Cricket Ground. St. John's Wood Rd., NW8. ☎ **0171/289-1611;** box office 0171/289-8979. Tickets £7–£45 ($11.20–$72). Box office, Mon–Fri 9:30am–5:30pm. Tube: St. John's Wood.

Cricket's national shrine. It's the home of the Marylebone Cricket Club (which governs the game) and also of the Middlesex County Cricket Club, which plays county matches on this hallowed ground. International tests are also played here and games take on the aura of society events. You'll need to reserve tickets for international tests, but for the county matches you can purchase tickets at the gate. Guided tours are given. Call for information.

FOOTBALL (SOCCER)
England's soccer (called "football") season runs from August to April and attracts fiercely loyal fans. The hooliganism, drunkenness, and fan violence long associated with British football has declined somewhat with the abolition of the stands in favor

of all-seat stadiums. The introduction of serious money (Mohammed Al Fayad, owner of Harrods, also owns Fulham, for example) and international players from the continent have added glamour to the game and created mega stars like David Beckham (suitor to Posh Spice). Games usually start at 3pm and are played on Saturday. London has more than a dozen clubs in several different leagues. Tickets range from £7 ($11.20) at lower league clubs to £50 ($80) for the most expensive seats at those in the premier league. Centrally located premier-division football clubs include current champions **Arsenal,** Arsenal Stadium, Avenell Road, N5 (☎ **0171/704-4000,** box office 704-4040; Tube: Arsenal); **Tottenham Hotspur,** White Hart Lane, 748 High Rd., N17 (☎ **0181/365-5000,** box office **396-4567;** Tube: Seven Sisters); and **Chelsea,** Stamford Bridge, Fulham Road, SW6 (☎ **0171/385-5545,** box office 0891/121011; Tube: Fulham Broadway).

GREYHOUND RACING

There is no horse racing in London proper, but **Ascot, Epsom,** and **Sandown** are within easy reach. Bettors may also want to try one of the greyhound dog tracks below for an exciting alternative night out. Races run throughout the year.

Catford Stadium. Ademore Rd., SE26. ☎ **0181/690-8000.** Tickets £4 ($6.40). BritRail: Catford.

A party atmosphere prevails at Catford, one of London's busiest tracks. There are usually races on Thursday and Saturday, the first one beginning at 6:30pm.

Wembley Stadium. Wembley. ☎ **0181/902-8833;** box office 0181/902-0902. Tickets £3–£5 ($4.80–$8) for the dogs; £4–£45 ($6.40–$72) for major events. Tours are usually given daily summer 10am–4pm and winter 10am–3pm. Call ahead to make sure there is no major event interrupting tours. The cost is £6.95 ($11.10) adults, £5.50 ($8.80) students, £4.75 ($7.60) seniors and children 6–15, £19 ($30.40) family. Tube: Wembley Park.

The soccer field is partitioned every Friday and Saturday evening to make way for the dogs. The first race usually begins at 7:30pm. At other times this is a venue for major national and international sports and performing events of all sorts, ranging from concerts by Michael Jackson, Tina Turner, and the Three Tenors to the F.A. Cup Final and World Cup. Guided tours are given of the stadium's facilities, including the England soccer team's changing room, the royal box, the players' tunnel, the executive and other suites, and the TV studios—call for information.

RUGBY

Twickenham. Rugby House, Rugby Rd., Twickenham, Middlesex. ☎ **0181/892-2000** or 0181/744-3111 for box office.

Twickenham is the headquarters of the Rugby Football Union where local and international games are played. The season lasts from September to April. Tickets to international and other big games sell out well in advance and are also expensive, but tickets for lesser matches start from £20 ($32). Take the tube to Richmond, then the Southern Railway.

Fun Fact ──────────────────────────────────────

Rugby is believed to have been invented by William Webb Ellis who, as a schoolboy playing soccer at Rugby, infringed upon the rules when he picked up the ball and ran with it, then decided that might be a good way to play the game. Ellis later became a rector at St. Clement Danes church in London.

TENNIS

Center-court seats for the **Wimbledon Championships** are sold by lottery. Write between September 1 and December of the preceding year for an application form for inclusion in the ticket ballot. A (very) few center-court seats are sold on the day of the match. To get these seats, camping out in line the night before is usually in order; prices range from £23 to £46 ($36.80–$73.60).

Tickets for the outside courts, where you can see all the stars in earlier rounds of play, are usually available at the gate. Expect long lines. Ground entrance for these outside courts costs £3 to £10 ($4.80–$16), depending on the day. The lower price is for the last Sunday, when few outside courts are in play. For further information, write or call the **All England Lawn Tennis and Croquet Club,** Church Road, Wimbledon, SW19 5AE (☎ **0181/946-2244**). To get there, take the tube to Wimbledon.

Strolling Around London

7

London is a walker's city. It's the only way to discover the many passageways, alleyways, squares, and parks that make up this wonderful capital. The walking tours outlined below are designed to acquaint you with the diverse neighborhoods of the city. And indeed, many of the sights, museums, churches, and such that are mentioned on these walks also appear in chapter 6, "What to See & Do in London." For additional itineraries, consult *Frommer's Memorable Walks in London* (Macmillan Travel), or take one of the excellent guided walks offered daily by a number of specialized companies (see "Organized Tours," in chapter 6).

WALKING TOUR 1
Knightsbridge & Kensington

Start: Hyde Park Corner.
Finish: Kensington High Street.
Time: 2½–3 hours (not including museum stops).
Best Times: When the museums are open, daily from around 10am to 6pm.
Worst Times: Before 10am Sunday, when the museums are closed; and on Monday morning, when the Victoria & Albert Museum is closed.

This long-ish tour offers up two slices of history—one recent, one a tad more aged. You'll stroll past the haunts and homes of Princess Diana; see the restaurants she loved to eat at and the boutiques she used to shop at. At the same time, the tour takes you past the grand museums, halls, and memorials that commemorate Prince Albert, husband to Queen Victoria, a legendary patron of the arts.

Begin your tour at:

1. **Hyde Park Corner.** To the north of this traffic circle stretches 340-acre Hyde Park, London's largest park. Originally a hunting ground for both Henry VIII and Elizabeth I, it was opened to the public in the early 17th century. Duck into the park just to see Rotten Row, where you'll likely see some riders and their horses kicking up the dust on their morning exercises. (If you want to ride yourself, contact either Richard Briggs Stables, ☎ 0171/723-2813; or Ross Nye Stables, at ☎ 0171/262-3791.) It's believed that "Rotten Row" is a corruption of the rue du roi, the route laid out by King William from Kensington Palace to

Hyde Park Trivia

Rotten Row was the first lighted route in London. Hundreds of lanterns were strung along its way in an effort to deter the highwaymen, one of whom was hanged in 1687 for killing a woman who had swallowed her wedding ring to prevent him from stealing it.

St. James's Palace. To enter the park you will have passed through the Decimus Burton screen erected in 1826 to 1829, notable for its friezes. Go far enough into the park to see the Statue of Achilles created by Sir Richard Westmacott in 1822 in honor of the Duke of Wellington. Farther west in the park, along Serpentine Road, lies Serpentine Lake, with its Lido (open June to mid-Sept 10am to 5pm) and its Boathouse (where you can also rent rowboats). Come back out of the park and turn to the left, and you'll find yourself standing in front of:

2. **Apsley House,** the grand mansion occupied by the victorious Duke of Wellington and the Ducal family ever since. It was referred to as No. 1 during his lifetime because it was the first house that travelers encountered when they entered London from the then villages of Knightsbridge and Kensington. The house is a classical beauty designed by Robert Adam between 1771 and 1778 for Henry Bathurst. Benjamin and Philip Wyatt enlarged it for the Duke of Wellington, who gave lavish parties here when he was being feted by the whole of Europe (with the exception of France) for his defeat of Napoléon. He amassed a huge collection of paintings and objets d'art, most of them gifts from grateful princes and potentates, the rest taken from Joseph Bonaparte at the Battle of Vitoria. Inside, you can view the collections and the magnificent, classically proportioned rooms.

Take the pedestrian subway (noting the many caricatures and other depictions of the Grand Duke along the way) to the center of Hyde Park circle, where you have a finer view of the grand facade of Apsley House and where you can also get a closer look at:

3. **The Duke of Wellington Monument,** the **Constitution Arch** on the south side, and the **Royal Artillery Monument** on the west side across from the Lanesborough Hotel. The statue of Wellington on his favorite horse, Copenhagen, is supported by carefully crafted figures in military regalia representing the 42nd Royal Highlanders, the 23rd Royal Welsh Fusiliers, the 6th Innikilling Dragoons, and the First Guards. The Constitution Arch, designed by Decimus Burton and erected in 1828, has incredible ornate wrought-iron gates and is surmounted by a bronze sculpture, *Quadriga,* showing a young boy at the reins of four horses with Peace descending from above. From here there's a good view down Constitution Hill toward Buckingham Palace. The Royal Artillery monument memorializes the 49,076 of the royal regiment of artillery who fell between 1914 and 1919 in such remote battle zones as Mesopotamia, Palestine, Macedonia, and the Dardanelles. Another panel recalls the 29,924 who died between 1939 and 1945, naming the places where they fell—from France and Belgium to Abyssinia, Java, and the High Seas. From here take the pedestrian subway marked Victoria and follow the signs to Belgravia and to Grosvenor Crescent. Walk southwest along this street past:

4. **The Royal College of Psychiatrists,** which has evolved from a group originally named the Association of Medical Officers of Asylums and Hospitals for the Insane when it was founded in 1841. Ahead lies a series of classic terraced residences with pillared porticoes and steep mansard roofs. Note Grosvenor

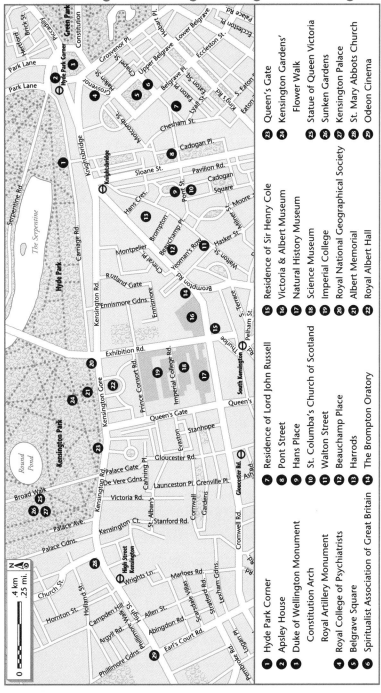

1. Hyde Park Corner
2. Apsley House
3. Duke of Wellington Monument
   Constitution Arch
4. Royal Artillery Monument
5. Royal College of Psychiatrists
6. Belgrave Square
7. Spiritualist Association of Great Britain
8. Residence of Lord John Russell
9. Pont Street
10. Hans Place
11. St. Columba's Church of Scotland
12. Walton Street
13. Beauchamp Place
14. Harrods
15. The Brompton Oratory
16. Residence of Sir Henry Cole
17. Victoria & Albert Museum
18. Natural History Museum
19. Science Museum
20. Imperial College
21. Royal National Geographical Society
22. Albert Memorial
23. Royal Albert Hall
24. Queen's Gate
25. Kensington Gardens'
    Flower Walk
26. Statue of Queen Victoria
27. Sunken Gardens
28. Kensington Palace
29. St. Mary Abbots Church
30. Odeon Cinema

Crescent Mews on the right, an attractive little private cul-de-sac. Continue along the street and you'll pass the British Red Cross Society, an organization to which Princess Diana devoted much of her time. Continue until you come to:

5. **Belgrave Square,** at the heart of this aristocratic enclave, whose residents at one time or another have included Lord Sefton, Lord Brownlow, the Duke of Bedford (who lived at no. 15), the Earl of Essex, and Earl Grey. Queen Victoria rented no. 36 for £2,000 per year for her mother the Duchess of Kent, while Kensington Palace was being readied for her. Earls and dukes continued to live on the square through the 19th century. Today, the primary tenants are foreign embassies, although in fact it was in an apartment on the square rented by Americans Pat and Mary Robertson that Diana Spencer worked as a nanny befor her engagement to Prince Charles. (Later, when they moved, she continued working at 11 Eaton Mews South, south of Belgrave Square on the other side of the King's Road.) As you enter the square, note the magnificent architectural sweep of Wilton Crescent on your right. Many embassies and consulates are located in this elegant square. At the center of the square the gardens contain several statues and sculptures recalling such figures as General Joséde San Martín (1778–1850), the father of Argentine independence who also granted freedom to Chile and Peru.

Walk around the square in a clockwise direction past the grand white buildings with their Palladian windows fronted by elegant balconies, rows of Corinthian pilasters, and roof balustrades surmounted with urns. Along the way you'll pass the High Commission of Malaysia, the Turkish Embassy, and the High Commission of Trinidad and Tobago. Opposite the last in the gardens is an intriguing sculpture called the *Homage to Leonardo, the Vitruvian Man,* from an original by Enzo Plazotta (1921–81). It represents the circle, the square, and Man with outstretched arms and legs trying to connect the two. Another statue recalls Simon Bolívar, the liberator of Venezuela, Colombia, Ecuador, Peru, and Panama. On the southeast side of the square past the Royal Agricultural Society you'll come to:

6. **The Spiritualist Association of Great Britain,** at no. 33. Drop in if you like and check out the books or see what lectures are being given. A portrait of Sir Arthur Conan Doyle, founder of the society, stares down from above the mantel in the foyer. You can also make an appointment to consult a psychic—it's a very reasonable £16 ($24.60). Continue on around the square past the Saudi Arabian embassy. At the southwestern corner of the square, note the reliefs that adorn the Norwegian Embassy. They depict cherubs representing painting and sculpture and were taken from the 1776 Danish-Norwegian consulate in Wellclose Square, in Stepney. Exit the square via Chesham Place. On the right you'll pass the German Embassy and on the left the Spanish Embassy. At no. 36 is:

7. **The residence of Lord John Russell** (1792–1878), who was twice prime minister and who worked long and hard for political reform. He lived here from 1841 to 1857 and from 1859 to 1870. A more recent resident of Chesham Place was Pete Townshend of The Who, who lived at no. 8 in 1965. Continue west and enter Pont Street. In this street are some legendary institutions and fine windows to browse.

🙂 **TAKE A BREAK**   The **Sheraton Hotel** on the corner of Belgrave Square and Chesham Place makes a welcome rest stop. **Drones** of Pont Street has a take-out next door to the restaurant of the same name if you want to pick up some delicious salads, sandwiches, and pastries.

Along Pont Street you'll find:

8. **Anya Hindmarch**, which sells brilliant satin and leather purses; Rachel Riley, the place for cool kid's clothes; Agent Provocateur, home of stunning lingerie; and Jeeves of Belgravia, London's finest dry cleaner (check the Wodehouse reference in the front window). Cross Cadogan Place (which leads south to Cadogan Square, where Lady Diana lived briefly in her mother's apartment when she first came up to London). On the other side of Pont Street you can also take a detour down into:

9. **Hans Place,** which has several associations. Jane Austen stayed at no. 23 with her brother Henry from 1814 to 1815. Shelley lived at no. 1 in 1817. Hill House School at no. 17 was attended by the Prince of Wales. Back across the street stands:

10. **St. Columba's Church of Scotland,** the headquarters of the kirk in London. The original building was totally destroyed in 1941 by a bomb; the current building dates from 1950 to 1955. Turn left down:

11. **Walton Street,** which is a legendary shopping street lined with fashion, jewelry, and accessory designer boutiques. Go down one side as far as you like and back up the other side before turning left into:

12. **Beauchamp Place.** Walk up this street filled with such fashion names as Bruce Oldfield, the couturier famous for Princess Diana's glamorous "Dynasty" gowns; Catherine Walker, another designer favored by Diana; John Boyd, milliner to the late Princess; and many others, from Caroline Charles and Isabel Kristensen (a Duchess of York favorite) to Nejoud Boodai. On the right is San Lorenzo, the restaurant once frequented by Princess Diana and still the haunt of numerous celebrities. (Don't overlook the Designer Sale Shop, which is also on Beauchamp Place.) Also in Beauchamp Place is The Occasional and Permanent Nannies Agency, employers of one Diana Spencer, who signed on in 1980 under the condition that she work only in SW1, SW3 or SW7.

   TAKE A BREAK **Pizza Express** has a very elegant branch furnished with marble-topped tables right here in Beauchamp Place, or you can enjoy a lunch at **Pasta Prego.** The **Bottega at San Lorenzo** also has great stuff to go.

At the end of Beauchamp Place, turn right onto Brompton Road to:

13. **Harrods,** the shopper's paradise, staffed by 4,000 or more working in close to 250 departments. It was originally a grocery store that was taken over by a wholesale tea merchant from East Cheap named Henry Charles Harrod. In 1861, his son Charles Digby Harrod bought the store from his father; he was the one who built up the business and vastly extended it to the point that by 1880 he had 100 assistants. In December 1883, fire destroyed the building, but Harrod still managed to deliver his Christmas orders, and for this accomplishment he was rewarded with even more customers. Here the first escalator was installed in 1898, complete with an official stationed at the top who administered brandy to the most anxious customers. The great terra-cotta food halls were built between 1901 and 1905 and they are not to be missed.

   Today, of course, the store is owned by the al-Fayed brothers, who bought it in 1985 for £615 million, much to the horror of the British Establishment. Mohamed Al Fayed's son Dodi was, of course, killed with Princess Diana in the Paris car crash. In their memory, Mohamed al-Fayed has erected a tribute to Diana and Dodi in one of the shop windows that faces Brompton Road.

Exit Harrods and turn left down Brompton Road to:

14. The Brompton Oratory, which has the third largest nave in the nation after Westminster Cathedral and York Minster, and which is famous for its High Latin Mass celebrated on Sunday at 11am. Turn right and continue along Thurloe Place until you come to a little garden and a house on the left marked with a plaque:

15. The residence of Sir Henry Cole (1808–82), the first Director of the Victoria and Albert Museum. The garden is dedicated to all those who suffered or were killed under Communism after repatriation at the end of World War II. Note the horse trough on the street that now serves as a planter. Across the street is:

16. The Victoria & Albert Museum, the fabulous 12-acre repository of all manner of decorative arts that have been assembled in a haphazard way since its founding in 1852 as the Museum of Manufactures. The current building, designed by Aston Webb, opened in 1909. The collections include such diverse objects as the Great Bed of Ware mentioned in *Twelfth Night*, Raphael's tapestry cartoons, paintings, fashions, Chinese art, and the collections of the East India Company. Turn right and continue down Cromwell Gardens onto Cromwell Road and walk to Exhibition Road. At this corner stands the:

17. Natural History Museum, easily identified by its variegated terra-cotta building designed in 1881 by Alfred Waterhouse. The cathedral-like central hall holds a mammoth life-size skeleton of a dinosaur. The other Life Galleries contain amazing collections of birds, insects, and mammals. The Earth Galleries focus on earthquakes, volcanoes, and other aspects of geology using plenty of hands-on exhibits.

Turn right onto Exhibition Road. As you walk, look more closely at the facade of the Henry Cole wing of the V.&A. It has a lovely classical roof line and a series of Roman arches and mosaic decoration. Continue to:

18. The Science Museum, which celebrates science and the development of technology. It was started with a collection of naval models and artifacts from the Great Exhibition of 1851 held at the Crystal Palace. In the galleries today you can see Stephenson's *Rocket*, Arkwrights' spinning jenny, Wheatstone's telegraph, plus Fox Talbot's first camera, and the Vickers *Vimy*, the plane in which Alcock and Brown made the first transatlantic flight. The Apollo 10 module is another highlight and there are plenty more spread over the six floors. Many of the galleries contain interactive displays that help visitors understand basic scientific principles. Don't miss the new gallery dedicated to the Science of Sport.

From the museum continue up Exhibition Road past:

19. Imperial College, established in 1907, one of the earliest institutions anywhere devoted to advanced technological education. Two members of the rock group Queen attended—guitarist Brian May studied physics and astronomy while drummer Roger Taylor studied biology.

Cross Prince Consort Road past the Jamaican High Commission and the National Sound Archive at no. 29 (open Mon–Fri 10–5pm) and continue until you reach Kensington Gore. At no. 1 stands:

20. The Royal National Geographical Society, marked by busts of two great explorers—David Livingstone, who sought the source of the Nile, and Sir Ernest Shackleton, who explored the Arctic. This society, founded in 1830 as the Geographical Society of London, received a royal charter from Queen Victoria in 1859 and moved to this building designed by Norman Shaw in 1912. Many expeditions led by such great figures as Burton, Speke, Stanley, Livingstone, and Scott have been undertaken under the auspices of the society, which continues to sponsor expeditions and advise explorers. Livingstone lay in state here in the Map Room. This room, which is open to the public, houses the largest private collection of maps (more than 900,000) in the world.

Cross into Hyde Park/Kensington Gardens. Turn left and walk down to:

21. **The Albert Memorial,** recently restored to its Victorian splendor. It honors Prince Albert, beloved husband of Queen Victoria and the epitome of Sober Britannia. He was the driving force behind the Great Exhibition of 1851, held in Kensington Gardens under the canopy of the Crystal Palace, and it was Albert who saw to it that the profits were used to develop the museum complex in South Kensington. At his death, in 1861, people wallowed in grief, and memorabilia flooded the market—jugs, lamps, a tape measure, even lithographs of the death bed. Statues were erected throughout the land to the extent that Dickens wrote to a friend: "If you should meet with an inaccessible cave anywhere to which a hermit could retire from the memory of Prince Albert and testimonials to the same, pray let me know of it. We have nothing solitary and deep enough in this part of England." This Albert Memorial, encrusted with statuary, was designed by George Gilbert Scott and completed in 1872; John Foley's statue of the prince was not added until 1876. The Gothic canopy is inlaid with mosaics, enamels, and polished stone and topped by an inlaid cross. Seven tiers of statuary rise from the base, including allegories depicting Asia, Europe, and America and everything from Agriculture to Commerce and Engineering. Around the base are 169 life-size figures of the prominent painters, architects, musicians, poets, and sculptors of the period. Prince Albert is holding the catalog of the Great Exhibition.

This luscious monument faces the:

22. **Royal Albert Hall,** which was, as it says on the frieze, "erected for the advancement of the arts and sciences and work of industry of all nations." After the great Crystal Palace Exhibition, Prince Albert proposed using the profits to build a complex of museums in South Kensington, including a central hall. It took many years before Albert's dream was to be realized. Eventually Henry Cole, chairman of the Society of Arts, managed to raise enough money by selling seats entitling holders to free seats for 999 years. Queen Victoria laid the first stone in 1867 and surprised everyone by prefacing the name of what was supposed to be the Hall of Arts & Sciences with Royal Albert. When it opened in 1871 she was too overcome to attend the ceremony; instead her son did the honors. This inspiring hall can hold up to 7,000 under its vast glass and iron dome. The frieze around the dome illustrates the Triumph of Arts and Sciences. The stage has been the scene of many great cultural moments and events. Wagner conducted here. Adelina Patti sang here. Paul McCartney met his first girlfriend, Jane Asher, after a concert in 1963 when she came to interview him for the *Radio Times*. John and Yoko sat in a black bag doing "Bagism" in 1968 as part of the Alchemical Wedding Christmas Party. Prince Charles brought Diana here to a performance of Verdi's *Requiem* on one of their early dates. Since 1941, the famous Henry Wood Promenade concerts have been held here annually. The hall always had a pronounced echo which made it a very poor venue for music. It was only corrected in the mid-'sixties, when the acoustics were improved by suspending triangular objects from the ceiling.

Stay in the park and walk down to:

23. **Queen's Gate,** which is decorated with a charming doe and kid and the royal coat of arms. Take the bike path that leads deeper into the park and turn left into:

24. **Kensington Gardens' Flower Walk,** which is fenced off. The sweet air is filled with the scent of flowers and the beds are filled with well-tended pansies, blue-bells, rhododendron, horse chestnut, and laburnum, depending on the season.

Exit Flower Walk and turn right, following the signs to Round Pound. As you walk up the Broad Walk on your left you will see:

25. **Queen Victoria's statue,** which was sculpted by HRH Princess Louise, Queen Victoria's daughter, and erected here in 1893. Kensington Palace is behind the statue.

Continue along the Broad Walk and turn left and enter:

26. **The Sunken Gardens.** Walk around the perimeter and rest on one of the benches as you go. The hedges are neatly trimmed and mark off an area that has a sunken pond, with fountains and a colorful display of flowers and shrubs. Diarist John Evelyn described the gardens as "very delicious" and indeed they are. Exit the gardens and turn left up to the entrance to:

27. **Kensington Palace,** associated most closely today with Princess Diana. It was from here that her funeral cortege departed, taking her on her last journey to Westminster Abbey and ultimately to her final resting place at Althorp. People lined the route 30 or 40 deep, and 30,000 had camped out overnight to assure a place on the sidewalk. It was to the gates of this palace that the people flocked to leave their floral tributes and messages like, "Born a lady, became a princess, died a saint" when they heard the news of her death. More than a million bouquets were left behind, by official count.

From the outside, the palace looks rather dreary built as it is of graying brick, only relieved by the glowing golden weathervane on the roof. When William and Mary bought it to escape from Whitehall, it was a plain Jacobean house. Wren and Hawksmoor renovated and extended it and Queen Anne continued the process until she died here from apoplexy brought on by overeating. George I restored the house with the help of William Kent, William Benson, and Colen Campbell. The Broad Walk and the Round Pond were laid out under George II and his wife, Queen Caroline. After George II's death, George III disliked the house so much that he abandoned it for Buckingham Palace.

Still, it was here that Queen Victoria was born on May 24, 1819 to George III's son, the Duke of Kent, who had abandoned his mistress, married Princess Victoria of Saxe Coburg Saalfeld, and returned from abroad to Kensington Palace. Only 18 years later, on June 20, 1837, Victoria was roused from her sleep by the Lord Chamberlain and the Archbishop of Canterbury and told of her accession to the throne. Queen Mary was born here in 1867 and Princess Louise lived here from 1880 to 1939. The house was opened to the public and a portion of the house served as the Museum of London. Today, the Princess Margaret, the Duke and Duchess of Gloucester, and Prince and Princess Michael of Kent have apartments here. The interiors are lavish, especially the King's Gallery, the King's Drawing Room, the Cupola Room, and the Pompeiian-style ceiling in the Presence Chamber, painted by William Kent.

From the palace, exit back out into the Broad Walk and take it around to the palace gates and then out into Kensington High Street.

London's Best Buys

The smart shopper will seek out those quintessential items that you can find only in Britain, or that are made better here than anywhere else. Here are just a few ideas for the best of Britain.

- **Jams, pickles, sauces,** or **preserves** that you either won't find at home or won't find made with the particular fruits or other ingredients—look for preserves made with damson, blackcurrant, greengage, and quince. Crosse & Blackwell's Branston pickles and anchovy paste are two other good bets. I also love the creamy horseradish that you can purchase here.

- You can be sure the British know their **teapots.** Go to any tea store, like Whittards or Twinings, or look in other homeware stores for reasonably priced teapots.

- **Tea** is another good buy—not so much the teas that you can buy at home from Twinings and Jacksons, although they are slightly cheaper here—but the tea the average Brit drinks. It's superior in flavor and punch to anything on your own supermarket shelves. Look for PG Tips and Typhoo.

- **Biscuits** are another good purchase. Pick up packets of chocolate covered digestives or Cadbury's orange creams, or just browse the shelves for anything you can't get at home. **Shortbread** is also reasonably priced.

- Good quality **woolens** can still be secured in Britain. Look for sale markdowns or visit stores like Scotch House. The other place to look is Westaway, on Russell Street. Their fashions aren't exactly hip, but Westaway does sell fine quality Scottish wools at much lower prices than elsewhere.

- **Stationery** is another item that the British seem to do well. Look in Rymans for good quality leather-bound address books or similar items.

- And then there are the splurge items so well made they will last a lifetime—like an **umbrella** from James Smith & Sons or a Burberry trenchcoat at Westaway & Westaway.

- Although the French are the great perfumiers, you'll find wonderful **aromatherapy oils** in London, made by Neal's Yard Remedies, which are packaged in attractive keepsake bottles. And for a special treat stop in at Penhaligon's and pick up something unique, like the Blenheim Bouquet aftershave or any of their handmade scents that appeal to you.

- Finally, even though you can't take it with you, **theater, concert,** and **dance** tickets are still some of Britain's best buys. Make sure you see a lot of performances (see chapter 9 for information on securing tickets).

purchase amounts. To reclaim your VAT, you need to show identification at the store and fill out a VAT form. Make sure you keep your receipt and form. On your departure, show your form and receipt to British customs and they will stamp it. Then mail the stamped form back to the store and eventually you'll receive a refund. For more information contact the BTA.

TRADITIONAL SALES

January sales are as British as Christmas pudding—and this dessert is usually reduced by 30% after the holiday, too. All the big department stores start their annual sales just after Christmas; the smaller shops usually follow suit. For Londoners, the January sales are a rite. Visitors are certainly not immune to this shopping fever. Offering one or two remarkable specials, Harrods and Selfridges may have people lined up all night long to get in the doors the morning of the sale. But buyer beware: Some goods are shipped into the stores especially for sales, and these goods may not be of a quality as high as what's carried year-round.

1 The Shopping Scene

The **West End** is the heart of London shopping; its main artery is mile-long **Oxford Street,** lined with stores including John Lewis, Selfridges, and Marks & Spencer, where the latest in fashions is on display. At the eastern end of Oxford Street, St. Giles Circus is the gateway into the area around **Covent Garden,** a warren of narrow streets lined with eye-catching stores, many of which showcase the current fashion trends. Covent Garden's **Piazza** has become a focal point for visitors drawn by the concentrated energy of the place; clowns, mimes, singers, and other artists regularly perform in or around the square.

At its midpoint, Oxford Street is crossed by **Regent Street,** a more elegant shopping street, which is noted for such clothiers as Aquascutum, Austin Reed, and Burberry. Farther west on Oxford Street, New Bond Street leads south, changing its name to Old Bond Street before it reaches Piccadilly. It's a wonderful street to amble down, window-shopping for fine antiques, art, and jewelry. Sotheby's auction house is about halfway down.

Both Regent Street and Old Bond Street run into Piccadilly. South of Piccadilly, **St. James's Street, Jermyn Street,** and Savile Row offer some of the finest shopping anywhere in the world. Here you'll find Hatchard's for books; Swaine, Adeney Brigg & Sons for fine leather goods, riding equipment, and umbrellas; and Fortnum & Mason, a department store with a renowned food hall. Jermyn Street is famous for shirtmakers; its other fine shops include Paxton & Whitfield, a specialist cheesemonger, and Floris, which has been blending perfume since 1730.

Continue west from Piccadilly and Hyde Park Corner and you'll enter **Knightsbridge,** home to Harrods department store, on **Brompton Road.** The store has become even more a destination for many people, because its owner is the father of Dodi Fayed, who died along with Princess Diana in Paris in 1997. **Sloane Street,** which comes off Knightsbridge and Brompton Road, is a designer row lined with names like Joseph, Armani, Valentino, and Kenzo. It runs down to Sloane Square and **King's Road,** which was once the center of Swinging London and now straddles the fashion fence between trendy and traditional. In the 1970s, this was the center of punk fashion. Things have quieted down somewhat, but mainstream boutiques are still mixed with a healthy dose of the avant-garde.

Young fashion flourishes, too, on **Kensington High Street** in general, and in Hyper DF (see "Fashion, Contemporary," below) and the Kensington Market in

What's in a Name? The Royal Warrant

Henry II is thought to have granted the first royal warrant in recognition of personal service to himself or to members of his family or household. A warrant entitles certain tradesmen to the court to display the royal coat of arms on their merchandise or a particular product. The warrant technically lapses after the death of the royal family member in whose name it was granted; however, the grantee may continue to use the phrase "by appointment to His or Her Late Majesty" on the relevant products. Approximately one thousand firms have the privilege of displaying the royal coat of arms; others use a royal badge.

Fashion Hits the Street: London Designers of the Moment

In London, the transfer of fashion from the couturier runways to the street is incredibly fast. Reproduction of the latest styles in less expensive materials can appear in a few months or even weeks. For the newest in British fashions, check out the folks who stayed home and haven't headed off for Paris along with Alexander McQueen and Stella McCartney. Look for Ally Capellino, Amanda Wakeley, Pearce Fonda, Antonio Berardi, David Emanuel, Ben de Lisi, Jasper Conran, and Ghost. If you're trolling the stores, head for Kensington Market and Hyper DF, such department stores as Debenhams, and chains like Dorothy Perkins, all of which are working with contemporary British designers. In the Covent Garden area, look for such names as Big Apple, Red or Dead, Nick Coleman, or the Duffer of St. George. On Oxford Street drop into Top Shop and Mash.

And it's not just clothes; British accessory designers are hot. Hats are still big business in London, and Britain has some very trendy milliners. Philip Treacy has sculpted headgear for the royals as well as for Boy George and Diana Ross, and Stephen Jones works with the top French couturiers. Georgina von Etzdorf has revolutionized scarf design with her jewel-like colors and printed velvet designs, while Jimmy Choo (who designed many a pair of evening shoes for Princess Diana) now has a Knightsbridge boutique. Jewelry trendsetters include Solange Azagury-Partridge, whose bold gems are worn by Madonna, and Dinny Hall, who crafts exquisite, more organic pieces. Lulu Guinness's satin and embroidered or velvet brocade bags are sought after and have already been purchased by the V&A for its collection.

Most of these upscale designers have boutiques of their own in Mayfair, Brompton-Chelsea-Belgravia, or Notting Hill. Among them are **Georgina von Etzdorf,** Burlington Arcade, W1 (☎ 0171 245-1066); **Jimmy Choo,** 20 Motcomb St., SW1 (☎ 0171/235-6008); **Amanda Wakeley,** 80 Fulham Rd., SW3 (☎ 0171/584-4009); **Ally Capellino,** 66 Sloane Ave, SW3 (☎ 0171/488-9777); **Patrick Cox,** 129 Sloane St., SW1 (☎ 0171/730-8886); **Philip Treacy,** 69 Elizabeth St., SW1 (☎ 0171/259-9605); **Solange Azagury-Partridge,** 171 Westbourne Grove, W11 (☎ 0171/792-0197); **Dinny Hall,** 200 Westbourne Grove, W11 (☎ 0171/792-3913) and 54 Fulham Road, SW3 (☎ 0171/589-9192); **Lulu Guinness,** 66 Ledbury Rd., W11 (☎ 0171/221-9686); and **Ghost,** 36 Ledbury Rd., W11 (☎ 0171/229-1057).

particular. Adjacent Notting Hill has also become a stylish shopping area, especially along Ledbury Road and Westbourne Grove. See listings below for information on specific shops.

MARKETS

Outdoor markets are where knowledgeable Londoners and bargain-hunting visitors shop for food, clothing, furniture, books, antiques, crafts, and, of course, junk. Dozens of markets cater to different communities. For shopping or just browsing, markets offer a unique and exciting day out. Only a few stalls officially open before sunrise, but that doesn't stop the flashlight-wielding professionals who'll snap up gems even before they reach the display table. During wet weather, stalls may close early. See below for detailed information on specific London markets.

2 Shopping A to Z

ANTIQUES

Although there are legions of antiques stores everywhere in London, many congregate in particular neighborhoods. **Portobello Road** is obviously one place to go (see "Markets," below), but you should extend your explorations also along Westbourne Grove, where there are numerous stores (take the Tube to Bayswater or Notting Hill Gate). In Islington, Camden Passage is another great hunting ground (see also "Markets," below). It offers several dealer-packed arcades, and this is one place to look for some incredible art nouveau jewelry and other decorative arts. Chelsea has several large antiques "malls" on the King's Road. **Antiquarius,** 131–41 King's Rd. (☎ **0171/351-5353**), features more than 120 sellers hawking everything from books and prints to scientific instruments, glass, and jewelry. **Chelsea Antique Market,** 245A–253 King's Rd. (☎ **0171/352-5689**), has been around since 1964 and is known for fair prices on decorative objects, jewelry, books, and film and theater memorabilia. These venues are open Monday through Saturday from 10am to 6pm; take the Tube to Sloane Square or South Kensington.

And of course check out all the flea markets as well, from Camden to Bermondsey.

ART

Galleria Charlick. 138 Gray's Inn Rd., WC1. ☎ **0171/713-6206.** Tube: Chancery Lane.

This gallery is an extension of the takeaway foodstore next door. Here food is served among the work of young photographers, painters, and sculptors.

October Gallery. 24 Old Gloucester St., WC1. ☎ **0171/242-7367.** Tube: Russell Sq. or Holborn.

This gallery is dedicated to exhibiting art from all cultures and to advancing its appreciation. It shows artists of the transvangarde or the cross-cultural avant-garde. In the past the gallery has exhibited everyone from William Burroughs to Kenji Yoshida, Aubrey Williams, and Sokari Douglas Camp and has also hosted group exhibitions from Tibet, South Africa, Haiti, and Oceania. You'll always find something interesting to see. There are often performances, as well.

BATH & BODY

The Body Shop. 32–34 Great Marlborough St., W1. ☎ **0171/437-5137.** Tube: Oxford Circus.

Now famous internationally, this British chain sells organically based lotions, shampoos, and beauty aids. Prices on some popular products are lower here than in the U.S. This is but one of numerous branches that dot the city.

Crabtree & Evelyn. 6 Kensington Church St., W8. ☎ 0171/937-9335. Tube: High St. Kensington.

Fans of Beatrix Potter and Laura Ashley are also undoubtedly loyal to this purveyor of fanciful English-design toiletries. Pastel-colored soaps, powders, and potpourri are beautifully packaged.

Lush. Units 7 and 11, The Piazza, Covent Garden, WC2. ☎ **0171/240-4570.** Tube: Covent Garden.

You've probably never seen anything quite like Lush—it's a beauty shop that takes "organic" to a whole new level. Huge slabs of soap burst with items like pineapple slices (good for the skin) and poppy seeds (a great exfoliator). Facial masks are whipped up fresh, then placed in bowls over ice for preservation (just scoop some into a take-home container and keep refrigerated). It's an excellent source for sweet-smelling gifts, especially the "bath bombs," fragrant, orange-sized balls that fizz and smell up the bath when placed under running water. There's a branch in Chelsea, at 123 Kings Rd., SW3 (☎ **0171/376-8348**), and one in Soho, at 40 Carnaby St., W1 (☎ **0171/287-5874**).

✪ **Neal's Yard Remedies.** 15 Neal's Yard, WC2. ☎ **0171/379-7222.** Tube: Covent Garden.

Founded in 1981, this is still London's best shop for packaged herbal medications, aromatherapy oils, homeopathic hair remedies, and other alternative medicines. Most of the products come in fetching, intensely blue glass bottles that make for attractive and reasonably priced gifts. The latest products include organic floral waters and some wonderful essential oils including grapefruit, geranium, and sweet marjoram. The store is located at the end of a short cul-de-sac off Short's Gardens, two blocks north of Covent Garden Market.

✪ **Penhaligon's.** 41 Wellington St. (Covent Garden), WC2. ☎ **0171/836-2150.** Tube: Covent Garden.

Barber William Penhaligon opened this business in 1841, and the scents sold here today are still made by hand according to his formula. Penhaligon's is a lavish store selling soaps, eau de cologne, and scents, as well as a fine selection of antique scent bottles and such silver accessories as boxes, mirrors, and manicure sets. The most famous women's scents are Violetta and Bluebell.

BOOKS/MAGAZINES

London is one of the best places in the world for books—new, used, and anti-quarian—but the prices are comparable to prices Stateside these days. A great many of the city's 1,000 or so booksellers are clustered in and around **Charing Cross Road.** Look for entire shops devoted to art, science fiction, religion, medicine, cookery, crime, government, sport, and travel. Browsers should start from the Leicester Square Tube station and work their way north along Charing Cross Road. Don't ignore side streets like St. Martin's Court and Cecil Court. Bloomsbury, too, has many booksellers, especially scholarly antiquarian dealers.

To find specialist shops, check the phone book or ask a local bookseller.

Ballantyne Way. 38 Museum St., WC1. ☎ **0171/242-4249.** Tube: Holborn.

This store specializes in antiquarian and new books on art design, architecture, pho-tography, and the decorative and applied arts. It also sells prints, some of which can be purchased for as little as £17 ($27.20).

Beaumont. 31 Museum St., WC1. ☎ **0171/637-5862.** Tube: Holborn.

A great store selling rare and out-of-print travel books. Wonderful stock in good condition.

There's another branch at 40 Museum St. (☎ **0171/831-1600**), which carries a large stock of modern first editions and illustrated books. Rare and fine books are a specialty, but there are also less expensive books in the basement.

Books for Cooks. 4 Blenheim Crescent, W11. ☎ **0171/221-1992.** Tube: Ladbroke Grove.

A cook's paradise. This store stocks books on practically every ethnic cuisine in the world, as well as classic books on entertaining and more. Cooking demonstra-tions are given a couple of times a week. Call for information. Small cafe in the back, too, where the menu changes daily and includes a set three-course meal for £12 ($19.20).

✪ **Compendium Bookshop.** 234 Camden High St., NW1. ☎ **0171/485-8944.** Tube: Camden Town.

A terrific shop with exhaustive sections on politics, psychology, women's issues, and New Age. All the alternative and anarchist magazines can be found here. This is the place to come for what was once termed "underground" lit.

✪ **Dillons the Bookstore.** 82 Gower St., WC1. ☎ **0171/636-1577.** Tube: Goodge St.

An extremely helpful staff, terrific indexing, and almost a quarter of a million books makes Dillons one of the best bookshops anywhere. This branch is right across from the University of London Union and services thousands of students. Good stock of magazines and a secondhand section on the second floor.

✪ **Edward Stanford.** 12–14 Long Acre, WC2. ☎ **0171/836-1915.** Tube: Covent Garden.

One of the best travel bookshops in the world, Stanford's is known for its exhaustive collection of maps, atlases, travel guides, and travel literature. They appear to have large-scale maps of every region of the world as well as specialty hiking, biking, maritime, historical, and other maps. A good selection of globes, too. Oddly enough, though, there are few guidebooks on London—not exotic enough, obviously.

Foyles. 119 Charing Cross Rd., WC2. ☎ **0171/437-5660.** Tube: Leicester Sq. or Tottenham Court Rd.

The largest bookseller on the strip, famous Foyles has the best-sellers along with a good collection of hard-to-find titles. Once the best in town, and still very well stocked, it has today been surpassed—at least in efficiency—by such chains as Waterstones and Dillons. Still, it's the place to find fiction and literary titles you can't find elsewhere.

✪ **Hatchards.** 187 Piccadilly, W1. ☎ **0171/439-9921.** Tube: Piccadilly Circus or Green Park.

A holder of all four Royal Warrants, Hatchards has been trading for nearly 200 years. It carries all the latest releases and popular fiction and nonfiction titles. It's a pleasure to climb the creaking stairs and browse here among the venerable wooden stacks.

Jarndyce. 46 Great Russell St., WC1. ☎ **0171/631-4220.** Tube: Tottenham Court Rd.

An antiquarian bookseller with a specialty collection of 19th-century English literature. Also in the same building upstairs, **Fine Books Oriental** has just that, a superb collection of Orientalia.

Offstage Theatre and Film Bookshop. 37 Chalk Farm Rd., NW1. ☎ **0171/485-4996.** Tube: Camden Town or Chalk Farm.

A great selection of books on drama and film, including screenplays and plays. Special sections on stagecraft, cinematography, circus, and commedia dell'arte. A large secondhand department, too.

The Travel Bookshop. 13–15 Blenheim Crescent, W11. ☎ **0171/229-5260.** Tube: Ladbroke Grove.

This little gem carries a variety of travel literature and guidebooks, both old and new.

Vintage Magazine Shop. 39–43 Brewer St., at Great Windmill St., W1. ☎ **0171/439-8525.** Tube: Piccadilly Circus.

A great place to pick up a gift mag at a bargain price. You'll find classical music, newspapers, and film and music magazines. Prices start at £3 ($4.80). Film buffs love the movie posters. There's another branch at 247 Camden High St.

✪ **Waterstones.** In Harrods, 87–135 Brompton Rd., SW1. ☎ **0171/730-1234.** Tube: Knightsbridge.

This is my favorite chain bookstore in London. They have a tremendous stock and the service is swift, expert, and friendly. The store makes special recommendations and holds frequent author signings. Other branches can be found at 9–13 Garrick St., WC2 (☎ **0171/836-6757**); 121 Charing Cross Rd., WC2 (☎ **0171/ 434-4291**); 193 Kensington High St., W8 (☎ **0171/937-8432**); 99 Old Brompton Rd., SW7 (☎ **0171/581-8522**); and 128 Camden High St., NW1 (☎ **0171/284-4948**).

CHARITY SHOPS

Don't overlook charity shops (i.e., thrift shops), especially those in well-heeled neighborhoods like Knightsbridge, Kensington, and Chelsea. The stock can be exceptional in quality. It's a transient business, however, so check the yellow pages to find the locations for shops operated throughout London by the following: Bernardo's, Imperial Cancer Research Fund, Scope (cerebral palsy), Notting Hill Housing Trust, Oxfam, and Unicef. Some, like Sue Ryder, a charity for the disabled, take short leases and move frequently.

CRAFTS

Galerie Singleton. 40 Theobalds Rd., WC1. ☎ **0171/831-6928.** Tube: Holborn.

A good selection of modern arts and crafts items—night-lights for under £10 ($16), pewter, soft toys, glass, metal, and ceramic objects, and picture frames.

The Kasbah. 8 Southampton St., WC2. ☎ **0171/240-3538.** Tube: Covent Garden or Charing Cross.

Good-quality Moroccan leather, glass, textiles, rugs, clothing, and furniture. A set of six decorated tea glasses is about £18.75 ($30). There's also a wide selection of affordable boxes—metal, juniper wood, and camel bone.

Tibet Shop. 10 Bloomsbury Way. ☎ **0171/405-5284.** Tube: Holborn.

Filled with jewelry, rugs, crafts, musical instruments, Thangka paintings, books, and cards. Proceeds go to help the Tibetan cause.

DEPARTMENT STORES

Department stores are the city's most famous shopping institutions, and a handful stand out as top visitor attractions as well.

Barkers of Kensington. 63 Kensington High St., W8. ☎ **0171/937-5432.** Tube: High St. Kensington.

This store was the last survivor of the dowdy, frumpy '50s Britain. In 1998, it has undergone a makeover and has been transformed and reenergized. Though Barkers reopened to some acclaim, it's too soon to know if the makeover will give it a permanent lease on life.

Debenhams. 333–348 Oxford St., W1. ☎ **0171/580-3000.** Tube: Bond St. or Oxford Circus.

Debenhams was one of the first department stores to hustle new fashions into its stores and to team up with designers who produce a line for it each season. The store now features such British fashion names as Ben de Lisi, Jasper Conran, and Jeff Banks, plus milliner Philip Treacy, jewelry designer Dinny Hall, and bag designers Lulu Guinness and Bill Amberg. Its prime focus is clothing.

✪ **Harrods.** 87–135 Brompton Rd., SW1. ☎ **0171/730-1234.** Tube: Knightsbridge.

By many estimates, Harrods is the largest department store in the world, selling everything from pins to pianos. The store claims that anything in the world can be bought here. Even if you're not in a shopping mood, the incredible ground-floor food halls are a must. Other departments worth visiting for the Harrods experience are the formal wear departments and the children's department complete with theater, cartoon cafe, and specialty hairdresser.

✪ **Liberty.** 210–214 Regent St., W1. ☎ **0171/734-1234.** Tube: Oxford Circus.

London's prettiest department store and great to browse through for its classic and original merchandise. Everything that you find here is beautiful and stylish. In addition to colorful clothing separates with the famous Liberty imprint, this old-world store features an incomparable Asian department and women's fashions by well-known and up-and-coming designers. It's world famous for its fabrics, so don't miss the fabric or the furniture department. Though it's far from budget in pricing, if you're after small souvenirs or bric-a-brac, you can usually pick up a thing or two here.

Marks & Spencer. 458 Oxford St., W1. ☎ **0171/935-7954.** Tube: Marble Arch.

England's largest and best-known department store chain is headed by this flagship store in the heart of Oxford Street. Mid-priced British designs run the gamut from traditional to trendy. The store is most famous for its excellent underwear and intimate apparel departments. This is where the average Brit seeks low prices and high quality on standard clothing items—shirts, pants, skirts, and jumpers. M&S, though, is no slouch when it comes to style. It consults regularly with the leading lights of British fashion—Paul Smith, Ghost's Tanya Sarne, and Caroline Charles among them. A slinky jersey dress usually goes for £70 ($112), and suits go for about £100 to £120 ($160–$192).

Selfridges. 400 Oxford St., W1. ☎ **0171/629-1234.** Tube: Marble Arch or Bond St.

Selfridges seems almost as big as, and more crowded than, its chief rival, Harrods. Opened in 1909 by Harry Selfridge, a salesman from Chicago, this department store revolutionized retailing with its variety of goods and dynamic displays. The ground-floor perfumery is one of London's best. The upper floors are well stocked with top designer fashions. Younger people from their teens to mid-twenties will want to check out Miss Selfridge—a store-within-the-store that's also opened up some satellite branches around town.

FASHION
CONTEMPORARY

The following listings are "warehouse" shops, each encompassing dozens of small, individually owned and managed stalls.

Hyper DF. 48–52 Kensington High St., W8. ☎ **0171/938-3801.** Tube: High St. Kensington.

Spread over three floors, Hype DF features stands that display cutting-edge British designer fashions and accessories from the likes of Ally Capellino, Biba, and Red or Dead. It's not cheap, but it's filled with some of Britain's most interesting and esoteric fashions—definitely worth a visit.

Kensington Market. 49–53 Kensington High St., W8. ☎ **0171/938-4343.** Tube: High St. Kensington.

A labyrinthine multilevel emporium selling a lot of trashy looks, plus some cutting-edge street fashion. Look for the latest in nightclub fashions, gothic garb, period clothing, and leather and fetish stuff. It's often packed. Some stalls accept credit cards.

Oasis. 13 James St., WC2. ☎ **0171/240-7445.** Tube: Covent Garden.

The young and trendy pile into this chain store, putting together the very latest retro combinations before a night on the town; it's all very au courant. Check the telephone directory for the many other branches.

Warehouse. 25 Long Acre WC2. ☎ **0171/240-8242.** Tube: Covent Garden.

One of the more reasonably priced emporiums for the latest trendsetting fashions. Warehouse has everything from safari garb to the retro look.

DISCOUNT

Amazon. 1–3, 7a, 7b, 19–22 Kensington Church St. ☎ **0171/376-0630.** Tube: High St. Kensington

Seconds and closeouts by top name designers. Worth browsing.

Browns Labels for Less. 50 South Molton St., W1. ☎ **0171/491-7833.** Tube: Bond St.

Here you'll find an assortment of designer names at 50% off—among them Missoni and Issey Miyake.

Designer Sale & Exchange Shop. 61d Lancaster Rd., W11. ☎ **0171/243-2396.** Tube: Notting Hill.

Great off-price samples and secondhand items from the likes of Vivienne Westwood.

Designer Sale Studio. 201 King's Rd., SW3. ☎ **0171/351-4171.** Tube: Sloane Sq.

Armani, Versace, Bagutta, Aspesi, and other high-fashion designer women's wear are sold here for anywhere from 30% to 60% off their original ticket price. Younger looks from Byblos, Complice, and Moschino are here too. Much of the stock is made up of hits from last season, though current samples and timeless accessories from Prada are also usually on hand. There's also a menswear department. It's worth cruising regularly because new stock is always arriving.

Designer Secondhand Store. 132 Long Acre, WC2. ☎ **0171/240-8765.** Tube: Covent Garden.

Loads of great clothes to pick over. Worth doing given the prices. It stocks everything from Yves Saint Laurent to biker garb and street cred clothes.

French Connection/Nicole Farhi Factory Outlet. 75–83 Fairfield Rd., E3. ☎ **0181/981-3931.** Tube: Bow Rd.

Here you can pick up some old stock, seconds, and samples of these two designers. If you wear either label, it's worth coming all the way out here.

Paul Smith Shop. 23 Avery Row, W1. ☎ **0171/493-1287.** Tube: Bond St.

Three floors stocking this hot British menswear designer at a discount. Most of the suits and other clothes are from last season. You'll also find such discounted accessories as hats, belts, and socks.

Shop 70. 70 Lamb's Conduit St., WC1. ☎ **0171/430-1533.** Tube: Holborn/Russell Square.

Primarily an outlet for men's clothes, it sells overstock from the top designers' less conservative lines. Giorgio Armani and Paul Smith are labels that you'll frequently come across here, along with Moschino and Stone Island. Knowledgeable salespeople and contemporary ambience.

VINTAGE/SECONDHAND CLOTHES

Blackout II. 51 Endell St., WC2. ☎ **0171/240-5006.** Tube: Covent Garden.

Pick up your club costume at this fun emporium, where you'll find everything from feather boas to PVC coats. Whether you're looking for glam or kitsch, you'll find it here. Bell bottoms and other retro stuff, all at decent prices.

Cobwebs. 60 Islington Park St., N1. ☎ **0171/359-8090.** Tube: Highbury/Islington.

This store has a broad range of stock starting at reasonable prices; day dresses, for example, can be had for under £18 ($28.80). Looking for cavalry twills and Harris tweed from the '50s? This is the place. The stuff dates from the turn of the century to the '60s and includes lacy and frilly gear, too—anything from slips to evening gowns.

Cornucopia. 12 Upper Tachbrook St., SW1. ☎ **0171/828-5752.** Tube: Victoria.

You'll have to look for the bargains here, but they do exist. It's a wonderful agglomeration of costumes from the 1920s on, all arranged by era. Plenty of evening wear and other unusual items and accessories, including loads of costume jewelry.

Merchant of Europe. 232 Portobello Rd., W11. ☎ **0171/221-4203.** Tube: Notting Hill.

Search the racks for secondhand clothes dating from the turn of the century to that disco decade, the '70s.

66 Fulham High Street. 62–66 Fulham High St., SW6. ☎ **0171/736-5446.** Tube: Putney Bridge.

A full range of retro upscale tailoring. Good suits in good condition for men. The prices are very fair.

✪ **Steinberg & Tolkien.** 193 King's Rd., SW3. ☎ **0171/376-3660.** Tube: Sloane Sq.

This is perhaps the best place to head if you have limited time and want to peruse the vintage clothing racks. A vast array of well-organized clothing is found here on two floors. The clothes, which are organized by era and designer, date from the mid–19th century to contemporary times and are in prime condition. You may well secure a designer outfit here from such legendary names as Chanel, Balenciaga, or Vivienne Westwood.

FOOD

✪ **Fortnum & Mason.** 181 Piccadilly, W1. ☎ **0171/734-8040.** Tube: Green Park.

It may be small compared to Harrods, but it's still a first-rate place to browse and shop, selecting from the magnificent displays of foods. Fortnum & Mason knows everything there is to know about tea; their house brand is a bit pricey, but the quality is outstanding. In fact, it's said that if you were to take a sample of your water to them they would know which tea to pair it with. Don't miss the truffles—they are the best anywhere in town.

Harrods. See "Department Stores," above.

This is the king of food halls par excellence. The food that is on display, the way it's displayed, and the decor of the halls themselves make a visit totally spectacular. It's huge and has close to 20 departments. The meat, fish, and poultry room is the most amazing; mosaics depict peacocks and wheat sheafs, along with grand assemblages of ceramic fish, scallop shells, boars, and more. The best buys are such items as jams made with fruits rarely found at home, like gooseberries, greengage, and blackcurrant. Also within the hall are plenty of food service counters, selling everything from a humble BLT on a baguette for £1.99 ($3.15) to £13 ($20.80) for steamed, grilled, or teppan-style fish. In all, a positively Bacchanalian experience.

Harvey Nichols. 109–125 Knightsbridge, SW1. ☎ **0171/235-5000.** Tube: Knightsbridge.

The store has received a lot of kudos for its supermodern fifth floor foodie addition. It's certainly stylish. The metal racks are stocked with a selection of unusual and often exotic prepared foods. In addition, you'll find meat and fish counters and a first-rate cheese counter where you can sample some of the unique British cheeses never seen across the pond.

Marks & Spencer. 458 Oxford St., W1. ☎ **0171/935-7954.** Tube: Marble Arch.

Less celebrated than the aforementioned halls, M&S holds a place in the hearts of most Brits for supplying a whole range of quality goods, including tasty, conveniently packaged sandwiches and salads.

Neal's Yard Dairy. 17 Shorts Gardens, WC2. ☎ **0171/379-7646.** Tube: Covent Garden.

This is the place to come for any and all British and Irish cheeses—since that is all they sell. There are the very best familiar traditional cheeses plus an array of goat cheeses and some more unusual special cheeses—about 40 or 50 varieties in all.

Paxton & Whitefield. 93 Jermyn St., W1. ☎ **0171/930-0259.** Tube: Green Park.

London's most venerable cheese shop, established in 1797, it concentrates on English and French farmhouse cheeses—about 200 in all—and offers a selection of wines and ports to go with them.

Selfridges. 400 Oxford St., W1. ☎ **0171/629-1234.** Tube: Bond St./Marble Arch.

If you can't visit the other food halls but happen to be near Selfridges, pop in to see the full range of products offered here. It will give you some insight into how the British attitude to food has changed in the last few years. Selfridges has great fish, meat, and cheese counters, plus gourmet meals to go and caviar of all qualities.

GIFTS/SPECIALTIES

Anything Left Handed. 57 Brewer St., W1. ☎ **0171/437-3910.** Tube: Oxford Circus.

"Righties" will be amazed at how much they take for granted when they visit this unusual shop. Scissors, rulers, kitchenware, corkscrews, mugs, and books—all made for the southpaw. It's off Regent Street, four blocks south of Oxford Circus.

Architectural Components Ltd. 4–8 Exhibition Rd., SW7. ☎ **0171/581-2401.** Tube: South Kensington.

Ever yearned for those very English hearth implements, period door knockers, snuffers, fireplace implements, and shaving stands? Here's where to find them. Some are quite reasonably priced.

The Back Shop. 14 New Cavendish St., W1. ☎ **0171/935-9120.** Tube: Bond St.

The Back Shop claims to stock the largest range of ergonomic products for backache sufferers in Europe—chairs, pillows, massage equipment, writing desks, and other comfort-inducing devices.

The Chelsea Gardener. 125 Sydney St., SW3. ☎ **0171/352-5656.** Tube: Sloane Sq.

In addition to mature garden plants, this store offers a wide variety of functional and decorative items for the garden, including urns, pots, trellises, sculpture, benches, and furniture. A visit will inspire any gardener and stimulate innovative ideas. Among possible small gift items are pretty herb labels and huge candles that look like birch logs.

Coincraft/Lobel. 44–45 Great Russell St., WC1. ☎ **0171/636-1188.** Tube: Tottenham Court Rd.

For an unusual gift, check out some of the coins and archaeological objects here. You can pick up a Victorian silver sixpence dated 1887 for as little as £10 ($16), a genuine 1,600-year-old terra-cotta Roman oil lamp for only £30 ($48), or a small Roman vase for £45 ($72).

The Filofax Centre. 21 Conduit St., W1. ☎ **0171/499-0457.** Tube: Oxford Circus.

Nothing was more emblematic of the booming 1980s than the Filofax loose-leaf organizers found under almost every Yuppie arm. They're not cheap, but they're handy. Here at the British headquarters, you can pick up every insert ever made for the filers. There's another branch at 69 Neal St., Covent Garden, WC2 (☎ **0171/ 836-1977**).

London Tourist Board Shop. In the Tourist Information Centre, Victoria Station Forecourt, SW1. No phone. Tube: Victoria.

A variety of books, gifts, and souvenirs, such as T-shirts, key rings, teapots, and coasters.

MARKETS

Please note that additional markets are listed in chapter 6.

Brixton Market. Electric Avenue, SW9. Tube: Brixton.

Brixton is the heart of African-Caribbean London, and the Brixton Market is its soul. Electric Avenue (immortalized by Jamaican singer Eddie Grant) is lined mostly with fruit and vegetable stalls selling Afro-Caribbean ingredients. If you continue to its end and turn right, you'll see a terrific selection of the cheapest second-hand clothes in London. Take a detour off the avenue through the enclosed **Granville Arcade** for African fabrics, traditional West African teeth-cleaning sticks, reggae records, and newspapers oriented to the African-British community. Open Monday to Tuesday and Thursday to Saturday 8am to 5:30pm, Wednesday 8am to 1pm.

Camden Markets. Along Camden High St., NW1. Tube: Camden Town.

Don't confuse Camden Markets with the Camden Passage Market (below). This trendy collection of stalls—in parking lots and empty spaces along Camden High Street all the way to Chalk Farm Road—incorporates several markets. The stalls at the Stables concentrate on clothing, 20th-century collectibles, and other bric-a-brac that appeals to people of all ages. Head to Canal Market for essentially more of the same plus old LPs. Vintage clothing can best be found at the Camden Market at Buck Street and Camden High. Cafes and pubs (some offering live music) line the route, making for an enjoyable if very crowded day out. When you've had enough of shopping here, turn north and walk along the peaceful and pretty Regent's Canal. Open Saturday and Sunday 8am to 6pm only. Get there as early as you can if you want to avoid the biggest crowds.

✪ **Camden Passage Market.** Off Upper St., N1. ☎ **0171/359-9969.** Tube: Angel.

The Market at Camden Passage is a wonderful place to browse. There are several arcades/malls to explore plus the passageway itself, which is lined with specialty stores. Wednesday and Saturday are the best days to look for bargain jewelry, silverware, and trinkets, when the outdoor market stalls are open. Open Tuesday to Saturday 10am to 5pm.

Petticoat Lane. Middlesex St., E1. Tube: Liverpool St. or Aldgate.

Located in the East End, this is London's best market for inexpensive fashions. A terrific variety of new, contemporary styles hangs on racks all along the street. Visitors also flock here to experience the Cockney scene and try some whelks and jellied eel, the local East End delicacy. Open Sunday 9am to 2pm only.

✪ **Portobello Market.** Along Portobello Rd., W11. Tube: Notting Hill Gate (ask anyone for directions from there).

The big day at this famous market is Saturday, when the antiques market holds sway and more than 2,000 dealers put out their wares for sale. You'll find every conceivable collectible somewhere along the route that never seems to end. During the week it's mostly a fruit and vegetable market.

MUSEUM SHOPS
✪ **British Museum Shop.** Great Russell St., WC1. ☎ **0171/323-8587** or 0171/323-8422. Tube: Tottenham Court Rd.

Like most museum shops, this is an inspired place to find a gift. Books, reproductions, and replicas are all beautifully crafted. A pair of earrings or a brooch or pendant copied from ancient Egyptian or Greek designs make lovely gifts. Browse the jewelry cases anyway because they feature some stunning (and pricey) pieces.

London Transport Museum Shop. The Piazza, Covent Garden. ☎ **0171/379-6344.** Tube: Covent Garden.

A wide selection of offbeat souvenir items: T-shirts, models, toys, posters, and reproductions of Underground maps the size you see in the station.

Science Museum. Exhibition Rd., SW7. ☎ **0171/938-8187.** Tube: South Kensington.

This shop is filled with books, high-tech games, puzzles, and other gimmickry (moon mud that glows in the dark, for example) that helps explain scientific phenomena. It also sells serious scientific instruments, including oddball clocks and telescopes.

✪ **Victoria & Albert Museum.** Cromwell Rd., SW7. ☎ **0171/938-8434.** Tube: South Kensington.

Plenty of beautiful replicas of museum treasures, even if they are pricey. It stocks a full range of pewter, glass, ceramics, china, jewelry, and inspired silk designs including ties and scarves. There are books, games, and edibles too.

RECORDS, CDS, TAPES
A good place to head if you're in a music frame of mind is the area around Notting Hill. Here you'll find a small coterie of places that specialize in secondhand albums, CDs, musical instruments, and equipment, both for purchase and exchange. Such exchange marts are great places to look for bargains.

NEW
HMV. 150 Oxford St., W1. ☎ **0171/631-3423.** Tube: Tottenham Court Rd. or Oxford Circus.

HMV is known for its particularly vast collection of international music and spoken-word recordings, downstairs. Look for contemporary sounds from Europe, Africa, India, and the Caribbean. The ground floor features new releases, rock, soul, reggae, and pop music.

London by Design

London shops have a different look and feel today than they did a few years ago, when they often lacked style and could rightly be described as fuddy-duddy. Now, everywhere you go, you encounter the pared-down, sleek, minimal look—stripped wood, stone, whitewashed walls, and frosted glass. Interior design has become big business and it shows.

To see what's happening in British design, check out the Design Museum (see "More Museums & Galleries" in chapter 6) and also stop in at such stores as Habitat, Bhs, Next and Allders. For the latest trend in fabrics, furniture shapes, and crafts, don't miss the Designers Guild, at 267–271 and 275–277 King's Road. This is the domain of Tricia Guild, the cutting-edge designer who has pioneered so many "looks," including the distressed look in the '80s. Numerous other design stores can be found along the Fulham Road and in Pimlico—among them, at 60 Pimlico Rd., SW1, the furniture design store of David Linley, son of Anthony Armstrong Jones and HRH Princess Margaret (☎ **0171/730-7300**).

Tower Records. 1 Piccadilly Circus, W1. ☎ **0171/439-2500.** Tube: Piccadilly Circus.

A veritable warehouse of sound, Tower has four floors of records, tapes, and compact discs. Pop, rock, classical, jazz, bluegrass, folk, country, soundtracks, and more—all in separate departments. Downstairs you'll find a broad selection of international music magazines.

Virgin Megastore. 14–16 Oxford St., W1. ☎ **0171/631-1234.** Tube: Oxford Circus or Tottenham Court Rd.

Virgin is particularly strong on new releases. Customers can listen to their selections on headphones before paying. The store now carries videos and has a Virgin Atlantic airline ticket office.

USED

Harold Moore's Records. 2 Great Marlborough St., W1. ☎ **0171/437-1576.** Tube: Oxford Circus.

Classical heaven. It's full of stock ranging from 78s to LPs and CDs, some rare and precious to the tune of thousands of pounds.

Mole Jazz. 311 Gray's Inn Rd., WC1. ☎ **0171/278-8623.** Tube: Chancery Lane.

Jazz fans come here for historic recordings that are out of print, whether it be New Orleans traditional, swing, or modern.

Music and Video Exchange. 38 and 56 Notting Hill Gate, W11. ☎ **0171/243-8573** and 0171/229-4805. Tube: Notting Hill Gate.

This series of stores is amazing for the broad selection of all kinds of music from classical to rap. The stock is regularly marked down to encourage purchase. You need to know what you're looking for and to take the time to really browse. There's soul, dance, funk, LPs, and CDs, with CDs from £2 ($3.20) to £10 ($16). The classical store has wonderful historic LPs for £3 ($4.80) plus boxed opera CDs for £35 ($56).

Out on the Floor. 10 Inverness St., NW1. ☎ **0171/267-5989.** Tube: Camden Town.

Mainly rock and roll, pop, soul, and jazz. Good prices.

Reckless Records. 30 Berwick St., W1. ☎ **0171/437-4271.** Tube: Oxford Circus.

Great selection of dance, punk, rock, soul, and pop.

SHOES

Shoe stores almost outnumber pubs and churches in London. In general, check Brompton Road and Sloane Street for high fashion, King's Road for trendy styles, and Oxford Street for mid-priced popular footwear. In Covent Garden, there's also **Dr. Marten's Department Store,** 1–4 King St. (☎ **0171/497-1460**), where you can pick up a pair of their basic shoes for £40 ($64). They're also sold in Camden Market at a discount.

Natural Shoe Store. 21 Neal St., WC2. ☎ **0171/836-5254.** Tube: Covent Garden.

Not the most beautiful shoes in the world, but the most comfortable. Full lines of Dexter, Ecco, Birkenstock, Arche, and Timberland. Shoes with specialized contours, arches, and soles are carried.

Red or Dead. 33 Neal St., WC2. ☎ **0171/379-7571.** Tube: Covent Garden.

Out-of-sight shoes for the future, from clogs to sandals to whatever fashion trend is on the horizon.

Wannabe. 129 Sloane St. SW1. ☎ **0171/730-8886.** Tube: Sloane Sq.

Everyone, it seems, lusts for a pair of mock crock or fake snake or any kind of loafer designed by Patrick Cox.

TOYS

✪ **Hamley's.** 188–196 Regent St., W1. ☎ **0171/734-3161.** Tube: Oxford Circus or Piccadilly Circus.

Its antecedent was named Noah's Ark and was founded in 1760 by William Hamley. On seven floors, Hamley's has more than 35,000 toys, games, models, dolls, stuffed animals, and electronic cars—one of the largest, if not the largest, toy stores in the world.

TRADITIONAL BRITISH GOODS

Frank Johnson Sports. 187–189 Ferndale Rd., SW9. ☎ **0171/733-1722.** Tube: Brixton.

Darts fans and other sports enthusiasts will want to visit this most British of sports shops. All types of darts and accessories are sold. Boards can be shipped home from the store. Open Monday to Saturday 9:30am to 6pm.

James Smith & Sons. 53 New Oxford St., WC1. ☎ **0171/836-4731.** Tube: Tottenham Court Rd.

Few things are more British than the umbrella, and James Smith & Sons, one of London's premier purveyors, has been making them since 1830. Traditional "brollies" come in nylon or silk, and they're stretched over wood or metal frames. Prices start from about £30 ($48). A fancy umbrella or cane can set you back £300 ($480) or more.

Royal Doulton. 154 Regent St., W1. ☎ **0171/734-3184.** Tube: Piccadilly Circus.

A venerable English store that stocks such famous British chinas as Royal Doulton, Minton, Royal Albert, and Royal Crown Derby.

Fun Feet Fact

Doc Martens—those funky, clunky boots with the air-cushioned soles that have become requisite street wear for cool kids the world over—were invented by Dr. Klaus Maertens in postwar Germany as a comfort shoe for old ladies.

Reject China Shop. 33 Beauchamp Pl., SW3. ☎ **0171/581-0737.** Tube: Knightsbridge.

These stores carry a wide range of English china. As the name suggests, most of the stock is seconds. Shoppers who know the going prices in the United States may pick up some bargains here. Other branches are at 183 Brompton Rd. and 134 Regent St.

The Scotch House. 2 Brompton Rd., SW1. ☎ **0171/581-2151.** Tube: Knightsbridge.

Good-quality sweaters and vests begin at about £50 ($80). Prices go up with the quality and complexity of design. The emphasis here is on hand-knit Shetlands and cashmeres, as well as machine-made woolens. Kilts, hats, socks, and scarves can be bought off-the-rack or made-to-order with your desired pattern.

The Tea House. 15 Neal St., WC2. ☎ **0171/240-7539.** Tube: Covent Garden.

Besides teapots and tea balls, this wonderful-smelling shop sells more than 70 varieties of tea from India, China, Japan, and the rest of the world. Available loose or in bags, traditional English blends make excellent, light, and inexpensive gifts, all under £2 ($3.20).

Waterford Wedgwood. 173 Piccadilly, W1. ☎ **0171/629-2614.** Tube: Piccadilly Circus or Green Park.

Waterford crystal and Wedgwood china share the same table at this upscale shop. Fine cut-glass vases, platters, and objets d'art in a wide range of prices. Complete sets of the famous powder-blue-and-white Jasper china are available, along with many other styles and patterns.

The flagship store, which is at 158 Regent St. (☎ **0171/734-7262**) stocks an even wider selection and is open seven days a week.

Whittard of Chelsea. 184 King's Rd., SW1. ☎ **0171/351-3381.** Tube: Sloane Sq.

Everything you need to make tea or to accompany it. It also sells a full range of coffees, as well as colorful ceramics like large coffee bowls that make appealing inexpensive gifts. Other branches can be found at 33 Bedford St., WC2; 43 Carnaby St., W1; and 209 Kensington High St., W8.

WINE

Oddbins.

With more than 50 branches, this chain of wine stores carries a broad range of reasonably priced wines from all over the world. It really keeps up to date with the latest sources for new inexpensive wines, and you'll find selections from Languedoc, Chile, Uruguay, and South Africa, along with the more common wine regions. Centrally located stores include Brewer Street, W1; Brompton Road, SW3; Ebury Street, SW1; and Southampton Row, WC1.

WOOLENS

Westaway & Westaway. 62–65 Great Russell St., WC1. ☎ **0171/405-4479.** Tube: Tottenham Court Rd.

An old-fashioned country store that stocks good Shetland wool sweaters and cardigans, plus Burberry and tartans. The prices are old-fashioned too, and the store is worth a visit if that's your style.

London After Dark

9

London's cultural life is on an upswing—particularly in the theater, where a new wave of young playwrights is making its mark—notably Brian Friel, Mark Ravenhill, and Sara Kane. You can see an intelligent, exciting play every night in London, and every one is well attended by a young audience.

Opera and ballet are suffering a little, in the wake of the closure of the Royal Opera House for refurbishment and of the financial scandals recently reported. But contemporary dance continues to grow and thrive. London's classical music scene, of course, has always been extraordinary, given the number of orchestras and small ensembles that call the city home.

On the popular music front, jazz continues to enjoy a loyal following, and now that the mid-'90s wave of Britpop has put London again on the rock map, dance music is sure to follow suit. London club life is quite diverse and trendsetting; new sounds like drum 'n' bass boast more than a distinct trace of Indian and Caribbean influence.

1 London's Theater Scene

TICKETS Attending a play in London is an experience that should not be missed. More theatrical entertainment is offered here than in any other city, and at prices that are well below those in New York. About 40 West End stages operate, with tickets ranging from £7 to £35 ($11.20–$56). Tickets for musicals are the most expensive, since demand for them is highest; but why see them here when you can see them on tour in your hometown? Instead, check out some great British actors in dramas, for a fraction of what you'd pay for a Broadway ticket. Moreover, even deeper discounts are available at the half-price booth in Leicester Square, and also at the individual theaters which often offer day-of-performance tickets and discounted tickets to students and seniors. When available, these tickets are sold either early in the day or as late as 30 minutes prior to curtain time; line up early for popular shows.

At the **Society of London Theatre half-price ticket booth** in Leicester Square (☎ **0171/836-0971**), tickets for many shows are available at half price, plus a £2 ($3.20) service charge. Tickets are sold only on the day of performance, and there is a limit of four per person. You cannot return tickets, and no credit cards are accepted.

Entertainment on a Shoestring: London's Nightlife Bargains

The good news is that nightlife here is a lot more affordable than in other big cities around the world. Even better, with all the additional ways to cut costs, you'll see more than you might otherwise. So let us count the savings.

First, the theater. Check out what's available at the Society of London Theatre's **half-price ticket booth** in Leicester Square. (But please beware of ticket scalpers in offices around Leicester Square and those that work the crowds outside theaters; they will sell you tickets at horrendously inflated prices.)

If nothing on offer there strikes your fancy, consider another tactic. Opting for a **matinee** instead of an evening performance will save you at least £5 ($8). If you're interested in great performances of cutting-edge theater, go to the **Royal Court Theatre** on Monday night, when all tickets are £5 ($8). Or check out what's happening at one of the fringe venues; **Almeida** is the most exciting, and tickets start at just £6.50 ($10.40).

Music lovers should check the listings magazines to see where **free or low-cost church lunchtime concerts and recitals** are being performed. There are also free concerts at the Barbican, the National Theatre on the South Bank, and the Royal Festival Hall. If you're here in summer during **the Proms,** at the Royal Albert Hall, purchase a £3 ($4.80) standing room ticket—hey, who wants to sit in a box, anyway?

Free street theater and **musical entertainment,** from classical to South American, abound in the streets around the piazza at Covent Garden. At dance clubs take advantage of the discounts to those who go early or super-late. Also look for **coupons for discounted admission** at such stores as the Tower Records at Piccadilly Circus. Similarly, if the **movies** are on your mind, **go early;** you'll pay £5 ($8) instead of £8 ($12.80) or £9 ($14.40). And if your evening fun consists of having a few drinks, then look for the many bars that have **happy hours.** We've noted them in the entries in chapter 5 as well as in this chapter. In London, entertainment is the biggest deal of all.

The booth is open Monday through Saturday from noon on matinee days (which vary with individual theaters), and from 2:30 to 6:30pm for evening performances. All West End theaters are closed Sunday.

MAJOR COMPANIES

Three major world-class theater companies can be enjoyed in London—the Royal Shakespeare Company, the Royal National Theatre, and the Royal Court Theatre. Try to fit at least one of them into your schedule plus a performance at Shakespeare's Globe.

Royal Shakespeare Company. Barbican Centre, Silk St., EC2. ☎ **0171/638-8891.** Barbican Theatre £8–£25 ($12.80–$40); The Pit £12–£19 ($19.20–$30.40). Tube: Barbican or Moorgate.

Where to Get Your Culture Info

The best source of information about what's on is *Time Out* magazine, a weekly that comes out on Wednesday. Also, the *Evening Standard* publishes a supplement every Thursday that lists the week's happenings. The arts section of the weekend *Independent* is also a good reference.

Central London Theatres

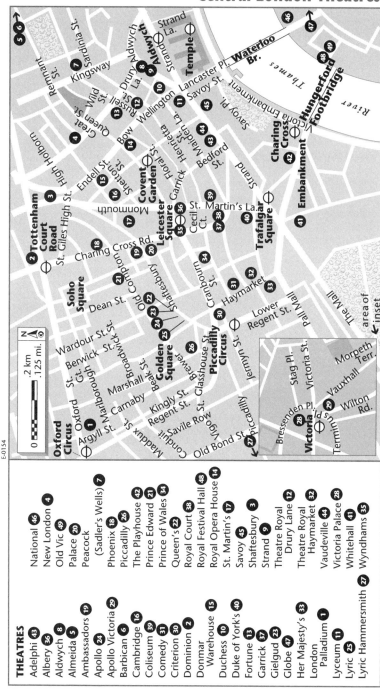

271

E-0154

Ticket Buyers Beware

The kiosk in Leicester Square run by the Society of London Theatres is the *only* legitimate discount ticket service. Avoid other booths in the vicinity with signs that boast "half-price tickets;" these are run by ticket brokers who charge exorbitant scalper prices. Should you fall victim to this practice, be sure to report it to the Society of London Theatres.

This is the London home of the world-renowned Royal Shakespeare Company from October to May. The company stages the classics in the Barbican's 1,200-seat main auditorium. It also performs the works of other historic and contemporary playwrights in a smaller studio space called The Pit. Box office open daily 9am to 8pm. The company's headquarters is in Stratford-upon-Avon, the bard's birthplace, where many of its productions originate. (See chapter 10, "Easy Excursions from London," for details on Stratford-upon-Avon.) Backstage tours are offered for £4 ($6.40) adults, £3 ($4.80) seniors and students.

✪ **Royal Court Theatre Downstairs.** St. Martin's Lane, WC2. Royal Court Theatre Upstairs; West St., WC2. ☎ **0171/565-5000.** Fax 0171/565-5001. Downstairs tickets £5–£19.50 ($8–$31.20); matinees £5–£15 ($8–$24); Mon evenings, all seats are £5 ($8). Students under 21 and seniors and disabled can secure discount tickets for £9 ($14.40) in advance and £5 ($8) standby from 10am on the day of performance. The best culture buy are the bench seats, available from 6:30pm for only 10p (16¢). Upstairs tickets £5–£10 ($8–$16), with all seats £5 ($8) Monday nights and matinees. SRO available for 10p (16¢). Tube: Leicester Sq.

While the old original Sloane Square site is being rebuilt and readied for an early 1999 reopening, this legendary controversial theater company operates at the two addresses above. It has always been a leader in the production of provocative, cutting-edge new drama ever since it staged the plays of the angry young men of the 1950s (John Osborne, Arnold Wesker, et al.) and later works by Caryl Churchill and Mark Ravenhill. Today the tradition is being continued with such controversial and acclaimed modern works as *The Beauty Queen of Leenane*, *The Chairs*, *Cleansed*, and *The Old Neighborhood*.

Note: The incredibly cheap bench seats can be purchased in person only from 6:30 pm. Whatever the current production, it will certainly be controversial and excitingly staged.

✪ **Royal National Theatre.** South Bank, SE1. ☎ **0171/452-3000** box office; fax 0171/452-3030; 0171/452-3400 information and backstage tours. Tickets £8–£27 ($12.80–$43.20); weekday matinees £8–£16 ($12.80–$25.60). Tickets in Cottlesloe are £12 ($19.20) with restricted view and £17 ($27.20). All unsold tickets in the Olivier and Lyttleton theaters are sold two hours before curtain at discounted prices. Student standby may also be available for £8 ($12.80) 45 minutes before curtain at all three theaters. Box office open Monday to Saturday 10am to 8pm. Tube: Waterloo.

An evening spent here at Britain's national drama house is a wonderful experience (you can even dine at the Mezzanine Restaurant). The lobby is filled with musical performers and people browsing the bookstore or enjoying coffee or dinner in the restaurants. Others are outside strolling the riverfront terrace. The center contains three performance spaces: the two large **Olivier** and **Lyttelton** theaters and the smaller, studio-style **Cottesloe.** At any one time, as many as six different plays are being performed, from new stagings of classics to premieres of contemporary plays, from musicals to shows for young people.

FRINGE THEATER

Some of the best and most original theater in London is performed on the "fringe"—at the dozens of so-called fringe theaters devoted to "alternative" plays, revivals, contemporary dramas, and musicals that exist throughout the city. Tickets for these productions are lower in price than those in the West End, so you can expect to pay from £4 to £20 ($6.40 to $32). Most theaters offer discounted seats to students and seniors.

Check the weekly listings in *Time Out* for schedules and show times. Some of the more popular and centrally located fringe theaters are listed below. Call for details on current productions.

✪ **Almeida Theatre.** Almeida Street, N1. ☎ **0171/359-4404.** Tickets £6.50–£19.50 ($10.40–$31.20).The cheapest seats have restricted view. Tube: Angel/Highbury.

Over the last decade this theater has developed a notable reputation for producing top shows with talented actors, among them *Hamlet* with Ralph Fiennes and *Medea* with Dame Diana Rigg, both of which transferred to Broadway. More recently Kevin Spacey's *The Iceman Cometh* has generated much excitement and so, too, has David Hare's *Judas Kiss,* starring Liam Neeson. The theater is also home to the annual Festival of Contemporary Music, a.k.a. Almeida Opera, from mid-June to mid-July. Performances are usually given Monday through Saturday. Box office open Monday to Saturday 10am to 6pm.

The Gate. The Prince Albert Pub, 11 Pembridge Rd., W11. ☎ **0171/229-0706.** Tickets £6–£10 ($9.60–$16). No credit cards. Tube: Notting Hill Gate.

This tiny room above a pub in Notting Hill is one of the best alternative stages in London. Popular with local cognoscenti, the theater performs historic and contemporary international drama. Performances are usually held nightly at 7:30pm. Box office open Monday to Friday 10am to 6pm.

ICA Theatre. The Mall, W1. ☎ **0171/930-3647.** Tickets average £6–£8 ($9.60–$12.80). Tube: Charing Cross or Piccadilly Circus.

In addition to a cinema, cafe, bar, bookshop, and two galleries, the Institute of Contemporary Arts (ICA) has one of London's leading theaters for experimental drama. The box office is open daily noon to 9:30pm.

The King's Head. 115 Upper St., N1. ☎ **0171/226-1916.** Tickets £10–£11 ($16–$17.60). MC, V. Tube: Angel/Highbury and Islington.

Arguably London's most famous fringe venue, the King's Head is also the city's oldest pub-theater. Despite its tiny stage, the popular theater produces lively musicals and revues; some that originated here have gone on to become successful West End productions.

Both matinee and evening performances are usually held Tuesday through Friday. Evening performances Tuesday to Saturday, plus matinees Saturday and Sunday. Box office open Monday to Friday 10am to 6pm, Saturday 10am to 8pm, Sunday 10am to 4pm.

Know Your Lingo

When queuing up to buy your tickets for a London show, be sure you know what types of seats you're purchasing. **Stalls** are the equivalent of orchestra seats in an American theater; the **Dress Circle** is comparable to seats in the front balcony.

Young Vic. 66 The Cut, SE1. ☎ **0171/928-6363.** Fax 0171/928-1585. Tickets £5–£15 ($8–$24). MC, V. Tube: Waterloo.

Adjacent to the Old Vic, a major venue that once was home to the Royal National Theatre, the Young Vic endeavors to introduce and hone new stage talent in its resident company. A theater in the round, it stages an eclectic variety of productions from *King Lear* to *The Comedy of Errors, More Grimm Tales*, and *As I Lay Dying*. Touring companies also appear here. Box office open Monday to Saturday 10am to 7pm.

A RE-CREATED CLASSIC

✪ **Shakespeare's Globe Theatre.** New Globe Walk, Bankside, SE1. ☎ **0171/902-1500.** Fax 0171/902-1515. Box office 0171/401-9919. Tickets £5– £20 ($8–$32), standing room in the yard £5 ($8). Discounted seats £9–£17 ($14.40–$27.20) available to seniors, students, disabled, and anyone under 16. Tours £5 ($8) adults, £4 ($6.40) seniors and students, £3 ($4.80) children, £14 ($22.40) family ticket. The tour includes admission to the museum. Call for the schedule, which is affected by matinees. Tube: Mansion House/Cannon St./London Bridge.

Just across the river by Southwark Bridge, this reconstructed replica of Shakespeare's original ampitheater (standing on the site where the original burned down, in 1613) is the place to see the plays of Shakespeare performed as they would have been in his era. They are staged in Elizabethan style, without lighting or scenery, or such luxuries as cushioned seats and protection from the elements. Ticket prices vary depending on the performance. In the undercroft, the **Globe Exhibition** will clue you into such subjects as bear baiting and stews, inter-theater rivalries on Bankside, penny stinkards, bodgers, and other such esoteric topics. It's open daily, May to September 9am to 12:15pm and 2 to 4pm, and October to April 10am to 5pm. Entry to the exhibit includes a guided tour of the theater.

2 The Performing Arts

OPERA & BALLET

London has a long and venerable opera history. The first theater at Covent Garden was built in 1734, and Handel wrote several operas and oratorios that were performed there. Under the musical direction of Covent Garden's Henry Bishop, Mozart was performed in English for the first time in 1817, but it wasn't until 1849 that the theater became devoted exclusively to opera. Adelina Patti made her English debut at Covent Garden in *La Somnambula* in 1861. Since then, most, if not all, of the great opera singers have performed here. The London premieres of works by several British composers, notably Sir Arthur Bliss, Sir Ralph Vaughan Williams, Sir Benjamin Britten, Sir Michael Tippett, and Sir William Walton, have been performed here. The two major British companies performing in London are the Royal Opera, which was granted a charter in 1968, and the English National Opera.

Ballet has had a venerable history in London, too, although in the last decade the scene has changed, leaving the city with only one major ballet company, the Royal Ballet. The old Sadler's Wells Ballet moved out to Birmingham; it's now called the Birmingham Royal Ballet. The only other ballet company performing occasionally in London is the Rambert Dance Company (formerly the Ballet Rambert); it doesn't have a city home base but tours the United Kingdom and internationally. Of course, many international dance companies perform regularly in London, also, and the modern dance scene has become extremely hot.

The English National Opera. London Coliseum, St. Martin's Lane, WC2. ☎ 0171/ 632-8300. Fax 0171/379-1264. Tickets £5–£55 ($8–$88). Discounted day-of-performance tickets for weekday performances and Saturday matinees only in the Dress Circle (£25/$40) and for all performances in the Balcony (£2.50/$4) go on sale at the box office at 10am or by telephone 12 noon for matinees and 2:30pm for evening performances. Three hours before the performance, any unsold tickets are offered for £18 ($28.80) to seniors and students; similarly, on Saturday, any unsold tickets in the Dress Circle or Stalls are offered at £28 ($44.80). Note: children under 18 are half price with an adult in the Stalls or Dress Circle. AE, DC, MC, V. Tube: Charing Cross, Leicester Sq.

The English National Opera (ENO) is an innovative company that continually thrills enthusiasts and rocks traditionalists with its lively, theatrical, and often updated reinterpretations of the classics like Jonathan Miller's recent production of *Carmen,* which was set in 1930s Spain. The company also performs such new works as the recent world premier of *Doctor Ox's Experiment,* by British composer Gavin Bryars and directed by Canadian filmmaker Atom Egoyan. Operas are always sung in English, and many productions have been transported to Germany, France, and the United States. The ENO performs in the 2,350-seat London Coliseum. Their season lasts from August to May.

✪ **The Royal Ballet.** In the Royal Opera House, Bow St., Covent Garden, WC2. ☎ 0171/304-4000 or fax 0171/497-1256 for box office, which is open for telephone bookings. Tickets £9–£70 ($14.40–$112) depending on the venue (the Barbican is cheaper than the Coliseum). Tube: Covent Garden.

While the Royal Opera house is closed for refurbishment until December 1999, Britain's leading ballet company performs at a variety of venues around town, including the Barbican (☎ 0171/638-8891), the London Coliseum (☎ 0171/ 632-8300), and Royal Festival Hall. For additional information call ☎ 0171/ 240-1066. Currently under the direction of Anthony Dowell, the company performs a varied ballet repertory with a tilt toward the classics and works by its earlier choreographer-directors Sir Frederick Ashton and Kenneth Macmillan. The season lasts from September to early August.

✪ **The Royal Opera.** In the Royal Opera House, Bow St., Covent Garden, WC2. ☎ 0171/304-4000. Fax 0171/497-1256 for telephone bookings. Tickets £2–£150 ($3.20–$240). Tube: Covent Garden.

The Royal Opera is currently without a permanent home, until the refurbishment of the opera house in Covent Garden is completed. The controversy that this extension caused made England's most elite opera the subject of scandal and ridicule. If the vision of a company tearing itself apart weren't so devastating, then it might have been described as soap-opera hilarious. The company is currently performing at different venues around town—Royal Albert Hall, Barbican, and the Shaftesbury Theatre among them— and will continue to do so until the Opera House (hopefully) reopens in 1999. Performances are usually sung in the original language, but supertitles are projected, translating the libretto for the audience.

CLASSICAL MUSIC

Currently, London supports five major orchestras—the **London Symphony** at the Barbican Centre, the **London Philharmonic** at the South Bank Centre, the **Royal Philharmonic,** the **Philharmonia Orchestra,** the **BBC Symphony,** and the **BBC Philharmonic**—several choirs, and many smaller chamber groups and historic instrument ensembles. Among them look out for the **London Sinfonietta,** the **English Chamber Orchestra,** and the **Academy of St. Martin-in-the-Fields.**

Major orchestras perform in the South Bank Centre, the Barbican, and the Royal Albert Hall. For smaller recitals, there's Wigmore Hall and St. John's Smith Square.

Tickets usually range in price from £6–£30 ($9.60–$48). The **British Music Information Centre,** 10 Stratford Place, W1 (☎ **0171/499-8567**), is the city's clearinghouse and resource center for "serious" music. The center provides free telephone and walk-in information on current and upcoming events. Low-cost (£5/$8, £3/$4.80 seniors and students) contemporary music recitals are offered here weekly, usually on Tuesday and Thursday at 7:30pm; call for exact times. Take the tube to Bond Street.

London Symphony Orchestra. Barbican Centre, Silk St., EC2. ☎ **0171/638-8891.** Tickets £6–£30 ($9.60–$48). Tube: Barbican or Moorgate.

London's top orchestra is currently under the musical direction of Sir Colin Davis. Reduced-price student standby tickets are sometimes available 90 minutes prior to the concert. The most taxing part of the evening will be finding your way around the labyrinthine arts complex, so allow plenty of time.

DANCE

Dance in London is thriving; new venues, companies, and events are bursting onto the city scene. Tickets are reasonably priced and at most major venues, inexpensive standby seats are sold on the day of performance only), while prices at fringe theaters rarely top £10 ($16) for adults and £6 ($9.60) for seniors and students at any time. Major international dance companies like Merce Cunningham, Twyla Tharp, and Trisha Brown appear at the **Barbican Centre,** Silk Street, EC2 (☎ **0171/ 638-8891**); **South Bank Centre,** South Bank, SE1 (☎ **0171/928-8800**); and **Sadler's Wells Theatre,** Rosebery Ave., EC1 (☎ **0171/713-6000**). The last is temporarily housed at the Peacock Theatre, on Portugal Street, until the Rosebery Avenue theater opens. Smaller dance venues include **The Place,** 17 Duke's Rd., WC1 (☎ **0171/387-0031**); **ICA,** The Mall, SW1 (☎ **0171/930-3647**); and **Riverside Studios,** Crisp Road, Hammersmith, W6 (☎ **0181/237-1000** or 0181/237-1111 for the box office). For ballet information, see above.

The Place. 17 Duke's Rd., WC1. ☎ **0171/387-0031.** Tickets £10–£14 ($16–$22.40). Tube: Euston.

This is London's showplace for contemporary dance, and has been since it was founded in the late '60s by Robert Cohan of the Martha Graham Company. Today, it's the home base of the Richard Alston Dance Company, and also home to a professional school, a theater, and a community center for dance. It schedules 32 weeks a year of British and international dance. Each season focuses on a particular aspect of dance. "Resolution," in January and February features up-and-coming British and European companies; "Spring Loaded" (Feb–May) presents the very best in contemporary British dance; "The Turning World" (May–June) offers cutting-edge international companies; and "Re:Orient" (Oct) showcases rarely seen companies from the Asian-Pacific region. Box office open Monday to Friday (and Saturday performance days) 10am to 6pm.

Dance Umbrella. 20 Chancellor's St., W6. ☎ **0181/741-4040,** 0181/741-5881. Tickets £8–£35 ($12.80–$56).

This company's fall season showcase becomes the contemporary dance event in London. During its six-week season, new works by up-and-coming choreographers are featured along with such companies as Merce Cunningham and Ballet Frankfurt. Seats, except for the blockbuster companies, are usually available on the day of performance and can be secured for as little as £8 ($12.80). Performances are given at a variety of theaters.

MAJOR CONCERT HALLS & ALL-PURPOSE AUDITORIUMS

✪ **Barbican Centre.** Silk St., EC2. ☎ 0171/638-8891. Reduced-price student standby tickets sometimes available. Tube: Barbican or Moorgate.

Reputedly the largest arts complex in Europe, the Barbican is so mazelike that yellow lines have been painted on the sidewalk to help visitors negotiate their way from the Underground to the box office. The architecture of the sprawling center has long been the object of critical attention, most of it negative.

Even its detractors, however, agree that the Barbican has an acoustically excellent concert hall that is home to the London Symphony Orchestra. It hosts festivals and other large-scale events when the orchestras are not performing. It's also the London home of the Royal Shakespeare Company. The complex contains two theaters, two art galleries, three cinemas, and several dining facilities.

Free concerts are performed in the foyer weekdays from 5:30 to 7:30pm. The program, which alternates between classical and jazz, is repeated on Sunday from 12:30 to 2:30pm. Box office open daily 9am to 11pm.

London Coliseum. St. Martin's Lane, WC2. Box office ☎ **0171/632-8300.** Tube: Leicester Sq. or Charing Cross.

Home to the English National Opera, the Coliseum is one of London's most architecturally spectacular houses. During summer and other times when the opera is off or out of town, visiting companies (often dance) perform. Box office open Monday to Saturday 10am to 8pm.

Royal Albert Hall. Kensington Gore, SW7. ☎ **0171/589-3203;** box office 0171/589-8212. MC, V. Tube: South Kensington or Kensington High St.

In summer, during the the Henry Wood Promenade Concerts (nicknamed "the Proms"), a £3 ($4.80) standing room spot on the floor in front of the orchestra has to be one of the best buys of the cultural season. For 124 years, the 5,000-seat Royal Albert Hall has been host to some of the finest international talent in the world, from Frank Sinatra and Liza Minnelli to Eric Clapton. It's most famous, though as the home of the most famous classical music festival in the world, the Proms, held every year from mid-July to mid-September. The Proms cover all musical bases, so there's something to appeal to everyone. The Last Night is usually televised, and includes some wild, jingoistic flag-waving, with standees swaying to the sounds of Elgar's most famous *Pomp and Circumstance*. Box office open daily 9am to 9pm.

Sadler's Wells Theatre. Rosebery Ave., EC1. ☎ **0171/713-6000.** Fax 0181/741-7902. Tube: Angel.

This is one of the busiest stages in London, and also one of the best. Host to top-visiting opera and dance companies from around the world, the theater offers great sight lines and terrific prices from £9 ($14.40). Box office open Monday to Saturday 10:30am to 8pm. It has been recently refurbished and will reopen in late 1998. The temporary site at the Peacock Theatre, on Portugal Street off Kingsway, will be retained.

St. John's Smith Square. Smith Square, SW1. ☎ **0171/222-1061.** Tube: Westminster/St. James' Park.

A slightly larger space than Wigmore Hall, it features many chamber groups, choirs, and voice soloists. The Thursday lunchtime concerts at 1pm are a steal at £4 ($6.40) and so, too, are the occasional BBC Monday lunchtime concerts costing £6 ($9.60). Otherwise, tickets range from £4 ($6.40) to £18 ($28.80). The performances are given in one of London's baroque masterpieces designed by Thomas Archer.

South Bank Centre. South Bank, SE1. Box office ☎ **0171/960-4242.** Discounted student and senior standby seats are sometimes available 2 hours before performance. Tube: Waterloo is closest, but the short walk over Hungerford rail bridge from Embankment Underground station is more scenic.

The South Bank Centre, London's flagship performing arts complex, includes three well-designed, modern concert halls. The **Royal Festival Hall** is the usual site for major orchestral performances. Smaller **Queen Elizabeth Hall** is known for its chamber-music concerts, and the intimate **Purcell Room** usually hosts advanced students and young performers making their professional debut. All three stages are lit almost every night of the year, and it's not all classical music; ballet (including the Royal Ballet), jazz, pop, and folk concerts are also staged here.

The foyer of the Royal Festival Hall is one of the city's hardest-working concert halls in and of itself. Regular, free, informal lunchtime music recitals are scheduled here, in front of the Festival Buffet cafe, daily from noon to 2pm. A Friday evening Commuter Jazz series is also held during summer months only from 5:15 to 6:45pm. Box office open daily 10am to 10pm.

Wigmore Hall. 36 Wigmore St., W1. ☎ **0171/935-2141.** Discounted student standby tickets sometimes available. Tube: Bond St. or Oxford Circus.

Considered by many to be the best auditorium in London for both intimacy and acoustics. Buy the cheapest seats, as it really doesn't matter where you sit. The Sunday Morning Coffee Concerts (all seats £7) are a great buy. Box office open Monday to Saturday 10am to 8:30pm; Sunday 45 minutes before performance.

3 The Club & Music Scene

CABARET & COMEDY

In addition to the clubs listed below, keep an eye out for performances at the **Comedy Café,** 66 Rivington St., EC2 (☎ **0171/739-5706,** Tube: Old St.), where there's no admission charge on Wednesday and it's only £2 ($3.20) on Thursday nights; and at the **Comedy Spot,** Maiden Lane, WC2 (☎ **0171/379-5900;** Tube: Covent Garden), which offers good value.

The Comedy Store. 1A Oxendon St., SW1. ☎ **0142/691-4433.** Cover £10–£12 ($16–$19.20). Tube: Piccadilly.

Thursday, Friday, and Saturday nights this is the place to see current as well as up-and-coming comedy stars. Launched in 1979, The Comedy Store is still London's premier comedy club, having nurtured such talents as Rik Mayall, Keith Allen, Dawn French, Ben Elton, Paul Merton, Jack Dee, and Eddie Izzard. On Tuesday nights the Cutting Edge performs a topical satirical revue. An improv group, The Comedy Store Players, perform on Wednesday and Sunday. Performances are given Tuesday to Sunday at 8pm with additional midnight shows on Friday and Saturday.

Oranje Boom Boom. At De Hems Dutch Bar, Macclesfield St., W1. ☎ **0171/437-2494.** Cover £5 ($8). Tube: Leicester Sq.

This West End pub/theater shop is typical of the smaller venues where you can find good, offbeat comedy. Performances happen usually Wednesday, except during June and July. Call the club for details.

ROCK & POP

Rock-and-roll may not have been invented in Britain, but in the 1960s the English fine-tuned a style that engulfed the world in waves of sound provided by the Beatles, the Rolling Stones, the Who, Led Zeppelin, and the Yardbirds. Glam rock led by Elton John, David Bowie, and Queen dominated the '70s, until the Sex Pistols ushered punk into the UK in the '80s, followed closely by New Wave (think early Wham!, Duran Duran, Culture Club, et al). Britpop emerged in the late '80s and early '90s as an anti-American, anti-grunge movement; it blossomed in the pubs of Camden, where the members of Oasis, Blur, and Pulp hung out. The scene has faded somewhat; there are still some good music venues, although how good they are really depends on who's performing.

Although Britpop has come and gone, London and the UK are still producing new sounds and crazes, like drum 'n' bass, that have emerged from the stew of Anglo and Asian and Caribbean cultures. Archaic drinking laws (which, rumor has it, are about to be abolished) require most late-opening clubs to charge admission; unfortunately, that often gets pricey. Most clubs stay open until 2 or 3am weekdays and to the wee hours on Friday and Saturday.

The club and music scene in London is lively and truly megacultural. The roster of currently trendy clubs changes so rapidly that, as one London newspaper recently reported, by the time you get there the blasé and bored will have moved on. In a way, that's a blessing—they'll have left the place as good as it ever was, so you can enjoy a good night out without having to suffer that jaded, been-there-done-that attitude.

The Bull & Gate. 389 Kentish Town Rd., NW5. ☎ **0171/485-5358.** Admission £5 ($8). No credit cards. Tube: Kentish Town.

Smaller, cheaper, and often better than its competitors, the Bull & Gate is the unofficial headquarters of London's pub rock scene. Independent and unknown rock bands are often served up back-to-back by the half dozen. It's open pub hours, with music Monday to Saturday 8:45pm to 11:30pm.

Rock Garden. 6–7 The Piazza, Covent Garden, WC2. ☎ **0171/240-3961.** Cover £2–£10 ($3.20–$16). Tube: Covent Garden.

The quality of music varies at this small basement club in Covent Garden. In the good old days new talents like Dire Straits, the Police, and others played here before they became famous. Today groups are run of the mill but the triple and quadruple bills ensure variety. The place is usually filled with foreigners. Open Monday to Thursday 5pm to 3am, Friday to Saturday 5pm to 5am, Sunday 7:30pm to midnight.

The Wag Club. 35 Wardour St., W1. ☎ **0171/437-5534.** Cover £5–£10 ($8–$16). No credit cards. Tube: Leicester Sq. or Piccadilly Circus.

The split-level Wag club is still good for live music. The downstairs stage usually attracts newly signed, cutting-edge rock bands, while dance disks spin upstairs. Open Wednesday and Thursday 10pm to 3am, Friday 10pm to 4am, and Saturday 10pm to 5am.

FOLK

Cecil Sharp House. 2 Regent's Park Rd., NW1. ☎ 0171/485-2206. Admission £3–£5 ($4.80–$8). Tube: Camden Town.

CSH was the focal point of the folk revival in the 1960s. The English Folk Dance and Song Society is based here, and the place continues to treasure this music and to document and nurture it. Here, you'll find a whole range of traditional English music and dancing performed. Call to see what's happening.

JAZZ

You can get information on jazz concerts and events from **Jazz Services** (☎ **0171/405-0737**) and the listings magazines. Another jazz organization worth contacting is the Jazz Umbrella, an organization of jazz musicians. For information, call **0171/729-0631.** Free jazz is usually offered every Sunday from 12:30 to 2:30pm on level 0 of the Barbican Centre, Silk Street, EC2 (☎ **0171/638-4141**); tube to Barbican or Moorgate. For fun, why not attend the Sunday morning jazz brunch at the Victoria and Albert Museum, which runs from 11am to 5pm and has featured such greats as Django Reinhart? Cost is £8.50 ($13.60). For info, call **0171/581-2159.**

Jazz Cafe. 5 Parkway, NW1. ☎ **0171/916-6060.** Cover £7–£15 ($11.20–$24). Tube: Camden Town.

The jazz/soul sounds are so great here that it's worth booking a table if you really want to hear anything and everything from rap to Latin jazz.

The 100 Club. 100 Oxford St., W1. ☎ **0171/636-0933.** Admission £5–£10 ($8–$16); student discount available. Tube: Tottenham Court Rd.

An austere underground club, the 100 usually hosts traditional jazz nights on Monday, Wednesday, Friday, and Saturday. The stage is in the center of a smoky basement—looking just the way a jazz club is *supposed* to look. On Tuesday and Thursday nights it's a rock venue for Britpop and retro bands. Open Monday to Thursday 7:30pm to midnight, Friday 8:30pm to 3am, Sat 7:30pm to 1am, Sunday 7:30 to 11pm.

Pizza Express. 10 Dean St., W1. ☎ **0171/437-9595.** Cover £8–£20 ($12.80–$32), plus food. Tube: Tottenham Court Rd.

One of the city's most popular jazz rooms finds an unlikely location in the basement of this chain restaurant. The house band shares the stage with leading traditional and contemporary jazz names. Open Sunday to Thursday 9 to 11:30pm, Friday to Saturday 9pm to 12:30am.

✪ **Ronnie Scott's.** 47 Frith St., W1. ☎ **0171/439-0747.** Cover £15 ($24) Mon–Sat. Students under 26 £8 ($12.80). Mon–Thurs. Tube: Leicester Sq.

Ronnie Scott's is the capital's best-known jazz room. It opened in 1959 and has featured all the greats of jazz, from Ella Fitzgerald and Dizzy Gillespie to Hugh Masekela, Roy Ayers, Charlie Watts, and Elvin Jones. For a Saturday show you'll need to reserve 2 weeks in advance. Be aware that the bill can add up as the evening goes on. Shots are £2.50 ($4) and a glass of house wine runs £2 ($3.20). There's dancing upstairs Wednesday and Thursday to jazz, soul, and funk, and on Friday and Saturday to salsa (cover is only £6/$9.60). On Sunday it's not a jazz club; a variety of acts do appear. Open Monday to Saturday 8:30pm to 3am, Sunday 8 to 11pm.

Vortex. 139–141 Stoke Newington Church St., N16. ☎ **0171/254-6516.** Cover £3–£10 ($4.80–$16). British Rail Stoke Newington.

Some of the most original and talented jazz musicians in Britain and Europe perform in the laid-back jazz bar here. The music starts at 9pm and continues till 11pm weekdays and midnight on Saturdays.

Attention Club Hoppers: How to Save a Few Quid

Even though most clubs charge hefty door charges, the most reliable way to save money is to go early (or late) when charges drop. Discount passes to clubs are also sometimes available just inside the front door of Tower Records on Piccadilly Circus. *But keep in mind:* Cocktails can run as high as £5 ($8).

DANCE CLUBS & DISCOS

The hippest Londoners attend club nights or "one-nighters," which are dance events held at established clubs on a rotational basis. The pickings are slender early in the week but swell considerably Thursday to Saturday. As the "hot" celebrations change from one week to the next, it's impossible to make reliable recommendations (best to consult the weekly listings in *Time Out* for the latest roster). But some of the groovier events on Saturday are **Blow Up** at The Wag Club, 35 Wardour St. (☎ 0171/437-5534); **Carwash** at The LA2, 157 Charing Cross Rd., WC2 (☎ 0171/434-0403); **Happiness Stan's** at Smithfields, 334–338 Farringdon St., EC1 (☎ 0171/236-8112); **Freedom** at Bagleys Studios, Kings Cross Freight Depot, N1 (☎ 0171/278-2777); **It's On Up West** and **Reggae with Rodigan** at Gossips, 69 Dean St., W1 (☎ 0171/434-4480); **Revolution** at Cuba, 11–13 Kensington High St., W8 (☎ 0171/938-4137); **Rulin** at the Ministry of Sound, 103 Gaunt St., SE1 (☎ 0171/378-6528); and **Spacey** at **The Hanover Grand,** 6 Hanover St., W1 (☎ 0171/499-7977). Meanwhile, the listings below have stood the test of time and survived the transformation from glitterati flash-in-the-pans to long-term popular venues.

The Aquarium. 256 Old St., EC1. ☎ **0171/251-6136.** Admission £7–£12 ($11.20–$19.20). Sat 10pm–4am, Sun 7pm–midnight. Tube: Old St.

Shades of the Continental baths at this venue with swimming pool. No jeans and no sneakers allowed, though, at this basically-scruffy-but-still-hot spot, which attracts everyone from flamboyantly dressed transvestites to the merely glamorous.

Bagley's Studios. King's Cross Freight Depot, off York Way, N1. ☎ **0171/278-2777.** Admission £7–£15 ($11.20–$24). Open Sat 10pm–6am. Tube: Kings Cross.

A large warehouse that throws gay/straight parties on weekends and also attracts young ravers.

✪ **Bar Rumba.** 36 Shaftesbury Ave., W1. ☎ **0171/287-2715.** Admission £3–£10 ($4.80–$16). Open Mon–Thurs 10pm–3am, Fri 10pm–4am, Sat 9pm–6am, Sun 8pm–1am.

This place is popular for its Monday night "That's How It Is" party, its steamy jazzy sounds, and its drum 'n' bass night on Thursday. Friday night is another winner, when The Next Level plays everything from funk to disco to hip hop to drum 'n' bass. Definitely worth visiting.

✪ **Bluenote Night Club.** 1 Hoxton Sq., N1. ☎ **0171/729-8440.** Admission £3–£10 ($4.80–$16). Open Mon–Wed 10pm–3am; Fri–Sat 10pm–5am; Sun 7pm–midnight. Tube: Old St.

This hip club has hosted some of Britain's hottest bands, including Pulp, Ronni Size, Monkey Mafia, and Allsorts. It attracts an 18-to-35 crowd to its three-story space with the main dance floor in the basement. Different DJ productions and live bands take over on different nights playing and spinning everything—breakbeat, house, disco, funk, new soul, drum 'n' bass, hip hop, reggae, and garage. It's a definite trend setter on the club scene, and a lot of fun on any night. You may have to wait but you *will* get in—no exclusive velvet-rope treatment here. Definitely the one scene to visit.

Cafe de Paris. 3 Coventry St., W1. ☎ **0171/734-7700.** Admission £5–£15 ($8–$24). Open Mon–Fri 5pm–4am, Sat 8pm–4am, Sun 3–6pm. Tube: Piccadilly Circus.

This is where glamorous and moneyed London gathers. Plenty of celebrities pull up to this fantastic showplace that dates back to the 1920s. It has been lavishly updated and blessed with a superb sound system and spacious dance floor. Go-go girls perform, the crowd shows off its bronzed flesh, and everyone has a fun evening. The only way to skirt the members-only policy is to book a dinner table and pick up a tab of about $130 for two.

Camden Palace. 1A Camden High St., NW1. ☎ **0171/387-0428.** Admission £5–£20 ($8–$32). Open Tues–Thurs 9pm–2am, Fri 10pm–6am, Sat 10pm–8am. Tube: Mornington Crescent or Camden Town.

A Britpop legend but far from a pleasure palace. Depending on the night, you'll hear indie rock, house, and garage. Whatever the rhythms, the feet of the 18-to-30-year-old crowd keep moving to the beat, especially during Tuesday night's Feet First and Friday night's Peach.

The Clinic. 13 Gerrard St., W1. ☎ **0171/734-9836.** Admission £4–£9 ($6.40–$14.40). Open Thurs 10pm–3am, Fri–Sat 10pm–4am.

This small, comfortable club gets an exclusive crowd because not many people know about it. The music is good. It's worth exploring.

The Complex. 1–5 Parkfield St., N1. ☎ **0171/288-1986.** Admission £10–£12 ($16–$19.20). Open Fri–Sat 10pm–7am. Tube: Angel.

A four-story party venue offering a whole menu of cultural rhythms, from African drumming to Latino beat. Its Saturday night Camouflage Party is particularly popular, when the top floor Love Lounge is filled with a motley youthful crowd. Another good bet.

The End. 16A West Central St., WC1. ☎ **0171/419-9199.** Admission £8–£12 ($12.80–$19.20). Open Fri 10pm–6am, Sat 9pm–7am. Tube: Tottenham Court Rd.

At this large, cutting-edge club the main sounds are house and drum 'n' bass; it gets all the young things going. Excellent.

Hanover Grand. 6 Hanover St., W1. ☎ **0171/499-7977.** Admission £3– £10 ($4.80–$16). Open Wed–Thurs 10pm–3:30am, Sat 11pm–4:30am. Tube: Oxford Circus.

Here's the scene: A dress-conscious crowd cavorts around a renovated theater. It's the home of youth, glitter, and glam—the kind of place to go when you've put on your best high heels and sequined outfit. Saturday night is the big one.

The Hippodrome. Charing Cross Rd., WC2. ☎ **0171/437-4311.** Admission £4–£12 ($6.40–$19.20). Open Mon–Thurs 9pm–3am, Fri–Sat 9pm–3:30am. Tube: Leicester Sq.

Located near Leicester Square, the popular Hippodrome is London's big daddy of discos, with a great sound system and lights to match. Very touristy, fun, and packed on weekends.

Iceni. 11 White Horse St., W1. ☎ **0171/495-5333.** Admission £10–£12 ($16–$19.20). Open Fri–Sat 9pm–3am. Tube: Green Park.

A Mayfair club for the chic. Good fun, though. From Monday to Thursday they play Arabic music. Friday is VIP night, which attracts a cosmopolitan crowd of all ages; on Saturdays the crowd is slightly younger and more downmarket. On both Friday and Saturday nights the music ranges from swing, hip hop, and R&B on the ground floor, to house and garage on the second floor, to '70s and '80s disco on the top floor.

Legends. 29 Old Burlington St., W1. ☎ **0171/437-9933.** Admission £6–£15 ($9.60–$24). Open Thurs–Fri 10:30pm–3:30am, Sat 10pm–5am. Tube: Green Park/Oxford Circus.

One of the city's more lavish but intimate spots. A place to show off your assets and your world weariness at the same time. If there are any Sloane Rangers left, they're here.

Limelight. 136 Shaftesbury Ave., WC2. ☎ **0171/434-0572.** Admission free to £12 ($19.20). Free admission before 11pm on Monday and Thursday. Early door specials available—£5 ($8) before 10:30 on Friday and £6 ($9.60) before 10pm on Sat. Discounts are also offered if you have a flyer on other nights. Open Sun–Fri 10pm–3am, Sat 9pm–3am. Tube: Leicester Sq.

This large dance club, located inside a Welsh Presbyterian Chapel, offers at least two floors featuring different kinds of music every night of the week. The Dome and Gallery bar are where the main action occurs; a smaller dance area is available downstairs in the basement Club VIP. The music varies: house and garage on Monday; rap, ragga, swing, and bhangra on Tuesday; retro-disco on Wednesday; and house garage and soul on Thursday, Friday, and Saturday. Sunday's Gay Tea Dance from 6 to 11pm is a blast. Its well-known name has made it a big tourist scene.

Ministry of Sound. 103 Gaunt St., SE1, WC2. ☎ **0171/378-6528.** Admission £10–£20 ($16–$32), reduced after 5am (it stays open 'til 9am). Open Fri 10:30pm–6:30am, Sat 10pm–9am. Tube: Elephant & Castle.

Even though it's been around for a number of years and the trendy have moved on, this is still one of the clubs to visit in London. It has a large bar and an even larger sound system that blasts garage and house music to enthusiastic, energetic crowds who fill the two dance floors or who relax in the cinema room. It's not cheap and it can afford to be selective. Not a place you'd come for friendly conversation.

Stringfellows. 16–19 Upper St. Martin's Lane, WC2. ☎ **0171/240-5534.** Admission £10–£15 ($16–$24). Open Mon 9pm–3:30am; Tues–Thurs 6pm–3:30am; Fri–Sat 8pm–3:30am. Tube: Leicester Sq.

Live music plays until 11:30pm, when couples take to the club's famous glass dance floor. This is a members-only club for the nouveaux riches, a scattering of celebs, but you can usually join temporarily if you want.

Subterania. 12 Acklam Rd., W10. ☎ **0181/960-4590.** Admission £8 ($12.80). Open Mon–Thurs 8pm–2am, Fri–Sat 10pm–3:30am. Tube: Ladbroke Grove.

A mixed crowd dances to regular live shows and to London's best party vibes created by DJs. The stylish, minimalist decor attracts a lively twenty-something crowd.

333 Club. 333 Old St., EC1. ☎ **0171/739-5949.** Admission £4–£8 ($6.40–$12.80). Open Mon–Wed 9pm–3am, Thurs 9pm–4am, Fri–Sat 10pm–5am, Sun 7pm–1am. Tube: Angel.

Another Hoxton Square club that takes the overflow from the Blue Note. A bit on the scruffy side.

4 The Gay & Lesbian Scene

Old Compton Street in Soho is the equivalent of Christopher Street in New York City, although there are plenty of gay bars and clubs in other areas. In the clubs, gay nights are often one-nighters like the youth party **Popstarz** at the Leisure Lounge, 121 Holborn, EC1 (☎ 0171/738-2336), which romps to the top tunes from the '80s and '90s; or the serious beautiful body crowd that flocks to **Trade** at Turnmills, 63B Clerkenwell Rd., EC2 (☎ 0171/250-3409) from 3am Saturday to noon Sunday; or the lighter and fun gathering **G.A.Y.** held Monday, Thursday, Friday, and Saturday at LA1 and LA2, 157 Charing Cross Rd., WC2 (☎ 0171/734-6963). A similar lesbian event, **Kitty Lips,** is held at Gray's, 4 Gray's Inn Rd., WC1 [no phone], the first and third Saturday of each month. To find out what's going on, pick up one of the gay newspapers that can be found in many if not all of the bars and venues listed below. Look for *The Pink Paper* and *Boyz* in particular.

The Box. Monmouth St., WC2. ☎ **0171/240-5828.** Tube: Leicester Sq.

A small, comfortable and modern cafe-bar where people hang out during the day and gather for drinks in the evenings. Women's night is Sunday night. Food is available.

Brief Encounter. 41 St. Martin's Lane, WC2. ☎ **0171/240-2221.** Tube: Leicester Sq.

Everyone in the gay community seems to gather here. It becomes so crowded that it's hard to find elbow room in the bi-level bars. The crowd is varied—from leather and jeans to suits.

Coleherne. 261 Old Brompton Rd., SW5. ☎ **0171/373-9859,** 244-5951. Tube: Earl's Court.

The leather bar. Serious cruising. Crowded.

Compton's. 53 Old Compton St. ☎ **0171/437-4445.** Tube: Piccadilly.

A lively, cruisey bar frequented by a more mature crowd.

The Edge. 11 Soho Sq., W1. ☎ **0171/439-1313.** Tube: Tottenham Court Rd.

A mixed gay/straight cafe/bar where you can lunch and hang out all day. A four-level venue for the trendy and fashionable that stays open until 1am (until 10:30pm on Sunday).

Freedom Cafe. 60–66 Wardour St., W1. ☎ **0171/734-0071.** Tube: Piccadilly.

A large, comfortable cafe and bar where people meet during the day over late breakfast or lunch and coffee (salads, sandwiches, and pastries available, priced from £3 [$4.80] to £6.30 [$10.40]). At night, the music gets hyped up and the place is jammed (with dancing downstairs). You can even down a Long Island iced tea here.

The Fridge. Town Hall Parade, Brixton Hill, SW2. ☎ **0171/326-5100.** Admission £8–£12 ($12.80–$19.20). Open Fri–Sat 10pm–7am. Tube: Brixton.

One of the oldest gay dance clubs in town. It features two bars and a restaurant, which attract a mixed lesbian/gay and straight crowd. Video, live performance, and go-go dancers add an extra dimension to the multiracial scene. It's a 30-minute trek out to this spot; take a cab.

G.A.Y. at LA 1 and LA 2. 157–165 Charing Cross Rd., WC2. ☎ **0171/734-6963.** Cover free–£10 (free–$16). Tube: Tottenham Court Rd.

Loud music, colossal dance floor, and a trendy crowd makes GAY one of the best dance spots in the city. About 75% men, 25% women. Open Monday to Thursday 10:30pm to 4am, Friday to Saturday 10:30pm to 5am.

Heaven. Under the Arches, Craven St., WC2. ☎ **0171/930-2020.** Admission £6–£8 ($9.60–$12.80). Discounts before 11pm. Open Tues–Thurs and Sat 10:30pm–3am, Fri 10:30pm–5am, Sun 9pm–1am. Tube: Embankment or Charing Cross.

Hands-down, this is the most famous gay club in the city. A stage, where live bands sometime perform, overlooks a huge dance floor. The crowd varies from drag to Asian (Wednesdays and Fridays are well attended by straights), but the sound system is always great. Three floors offer different sounds—oldies and disco top floor, house and R&B mid floor, and techno on the first floor. The club entrance is on a small street between Charing Cross and the Embankment Underground stations.

The King's Arms. 23 Poland St., W1. ☎ **0171/734-5907.** Tube: Oxford Circus.

A busy gay men's pub on two levels, with good food and cheap double-measures in both bars.

Madame Jo Jo's. 8–10 Brewer St., W1. ☎ **0171/734-2473.** Admission £3–£22.50 ($4.80–$36). Open daily from 9 or 10pm until 2 or 3 am. Tube: Piccadilly Circus.

This is London's most popular transvestite showplace, famous for its flamboyant drag cabaret shows. They're usually featured on Thursday to Saturday nights (cover £17.50 to £22.50 ($28–$36) or £10 to £15 ($16–$24) for standing room; student discounts on Thursday only for £8). The latest extravaganza, "Return to Planet JoJo" was largely inspired by *Star Wars* and *Barbarella,* with a dash of *101 Dalmatians.* Other forms of entertainment, from funk to disco and soul to easy listening and comedy, are provided during the week. Tuesday nights Indigo reprising Burt Bacharach and other easy listening is popular. Call to see what's on the calendar.

Turnmills. 63 Clerkenwell Rd., EC1. ☎ **0171/250-3409.** Admission £3–£12 ($4.80–$19.20). Open Mon 7pm–2am, Thurs 10pm–4am, Fri 10pm–7am, Sat 9pm–3:30am, Sun 3:30am–1:30pm and 6pm–6:30am.

The labyrinthine venue for Heavenly Juke Box on Saturday; it's a rip-roaring party to all kinds of sounds—techno, indie, and house.

The Yard. 57 Rupert St., W1. ☎ **0171/437-2652.** Tube: Piccadilly Circus.

A stylish spot that attracts an after-work professional crowd to its patio courtyard and upstairs bar.

5 The Pub Scene

There is nothing more British than a pub. The public house is exactly that, the British public's place to meet, exchange stories, tell jokes, and drink. Many people outside Britain have tried to build something that looks like a pub, but all fail to capture the unique flavor and atmosphere of the indigenous version. Today even the pubs are changing and many have been refurbished and lightened up in look and decor. Even though they're listed here under evening entertainment, the Brits frequent pubs at lunch and in the evenings. At noon, they often repair to the pub for a glass of beer, or something similar, and a pub lunch. Later after work, they may stop in for an early evening drink before going home. (*Note:* Children under 14 are not allowed in pubs at all, and no one under 18 may legally drink alcohol.)

Beer is the main drink sold in pubs. Since January 1995, alcohol has been sold in metric measures: quarter-, half-, and liter-measures. The old imperial half-pints and pints have technically disappeared. The choice is usually between lager and bitter, and the locals more often than not opt for the latter. Expect to pay between £2 ($3.20) and £3.50 ($5.60) for a pint. Many pubs serve particularly good "real" ales, distinguishable at the bar by handpumps that must be "pulled" by the barkeep. Real ales are natural "live" beers, allowed to ferment in the cask. Unlike lagers, English ales are served at room temperature and may take some getting used to. For an unusual and tasty alternative to beer, try cider, a flavorful fermented apple juice that's so good you'll hardly notice the alcohol—until later.

As a rule, there is no table service in pubs; drinks and food are ordered at the bar. Tipping at a pub is unusual and should be reserved for exemplary service. A meal will cost anywhere from £3–£6 ($4.80–$9.60).

Pubs are allowed to stay open from 11am to 11pm Monday through Saturday, and from noon to 10:30pm on Sunday. Not all pubs take advantage of this freedom, however; some still close daily between 3pm and 7pm.

Carpeted floors, etched glass, and carved-wood bars are the hallmarks of most London pubs, but many have been made over recently. Each pub, though, looks different, and has a particular flavor and clientele. Greater London's 5,000-plus pubs ensure that you never have to walk more than a couple of blocks to find one, and part of the enjoyment of "pubbing" is discovering a special one on your own. A few tried and true favorites are listed below to help you on your way.

The Alma Tavern. 41 Spelman St., E1. ☎ **0171/247-5604.**

A traditional East End "boozer," the Alma was opened in 1854 by Edward Tilney, a soldier who had just returned from the Crimean War. On the site of an old brewery, its back garden still sports a wellhead from which water for brewing was drawn. Steve Kane, the ultra-friendly owner, is a former actor who loves to talk about his establishment's, as well as his own, eventful past. Tell him I sent you, and he'll invite you to take a photo of yourself pulling an English pint behind his bar.

Cittie of Yorke. 22–23 High Holborn, WC1. ☎ **0171/242-7670.** Tube: Holborn.

Walk through the narrow stone passageway into this pub, and you'll be standing in a soaring high-gabled room, which must contain the longest bar in England. Above can be seen huge vats that the original company used to dispense wine and liquors. Along one wall are private wood-carved cubicles, supposedly designed for lawyers who maintain chambers in the neighborhood to meet with their clients. Each features a *Vanity Fair* caricature. The pub dates from 1430 but has been rebuilt since.

De Hems. 11 Macclesfield St., W1. ☎ **0171/437-2494.** Tube: Piccadilly or Leicester Sq.

A Dutch outpost in the city. It's decorated in Dutch style and serves Dutch food and beers and even draught Dutch gin. Of course, English food and beer are available, too. First Thursday of the month draws a crowd of Dutch folks who are living and working in London.

✪ **The Dove.** 19 Upper Mall, W6. ☎ **0181/748-5405.** Tube: Ravenscourt.

A perfect riverside pub with a terrace for watching the Boat Race or just the river life. Along with what must be one of the smallest bars in the world, it has a series of comfortable oak-paneled rooms with copper tables and settle seating.

Ferret and Firkin. 114 Lots Rd., SW10. ☎ **0171/352-6645.** Tube: Sloane Sq., then bus no. 11 or 22 down King's Rd.

One of a popular chain of pubs that attracts young people for the fun offered usually on weekends when pianists or guitarists or some other musicians provide sing-along entertainment. There are now going on 30 Firkin pubs like the Finnock & Firkin in Islington.

The Flask. 77 Highgate West Hill, N6. ☎ **0181/340-7260.** Tube: Archway.

Creaky floors, winding corridors, and plenty of tradition give this a definite village pub flavor. Frequented by Hogarth, who used the locals as subjects for his sketches of drunken revelry, and John Betjeman, who lived just up the road. Take the no. 271 or 143 bus from the tube station.

The French House. 49 Dean St., W1. ☎ **0171/437-2799.** Tube: Tottenham Court Rd.

Opened by a Belgian, it became the center of French life, especially during World War II when de Gaulle and his circle gathered here. Today, it still attracts a substantial number of French-speaking visitors.

✪ **The George.** 77 Borough High St., SE1. ☎ **0171/407-2056.** Tube: London Bridge.

A real coaching inn. Although the George dates back to 1542—possibly earlier than that—the current building was constructed in 1676. Here in the galleried courtyard, it's believed Shakespeare's plays were performed, and today they still are during the summer. Dickens is also associated with the place.

The Grenadier. 18 Wilton Row, SW1. ☎ **0171/235-3074.** Tube: Hyde Park Corner.

This mews pub is always crowded. It was an officers' mess in the Duke of Wellington's time, and the downstairs lounge originally housed the bar and skittles alley they used when they were on leave. It's filled with Wellington memorabilia.

The Jamaica Wine House. St. Michael's Alley, off Cornhill, EC3. ☎ **0171/626-9496.** Tube: Bank (Exit 5).

This is one of the oldest bars in the city, where Caribbean merchants met to make deals over coffee and rum. Today, investment bankers gather at the ground-floor bar or in the more cozy downstairs area to sip good wines, port, or beer.

The Lamb. 94 Lamb's Conduit St., WC1. ☎ **0171/405-0713.** Tube: Oxford Circus.

A Victorian pub with decent food and an unmarred atmosphere. The etched and hinged glass screens that extend around the bar are called snob screens; they were installed so that customers didn't see the bartender. Apparently, they were the cat's pajamas at the turn of the century when such niceties really mattered.

Lamb & Flag. 33 Rose St., WC2. ☎ **0171/497-9504.** Tube: Leicester Sq.

The Lamb & Flag is an old timber-framed pub in a short cul-de-sac off Garrick Street in Covent Garden. The pub was dubbed the "Bucket of Blood" by the poet Dryden after he was almost beaten to death here (no doubt for being too witty at someone else's expense). The pub can be hard to find, but its great atmosphere makes the search well worth the effort. The food is traditional (sausage, chips, and beans, toasted and doorstep sandwiches, and ploughman's). There's live jazz on Sunday evening.

Museum Tavern. 49 Great Russell St., WC1. ☎ **0171/242-8987.** Tube: Holborn.

As you'd expect from its location opposite the British Museum, it's frequented by writers, publishers, and scholars using the library. Etched glass and oak provide Victorian atmosphere, but the pub dates further back to the early 18th century.

Prospect of Whitby. 57 Wapping Wall, E1. ☎ **0171/481-1095.** Tube: Whitechapel, and then East London line to Wapping. Turn right and walk along river.

Named after a coal barge that operated between Yorkshire and London, this is an atmospheric riverside pub that offers a fine prospect of the river. Once frequented by smugglers and thieves and most of London, it dates back to 1520. Take a cab from the tube station.

The Punch Tavern. 99 Fleet St., EC4. ☎ **0171/353-6658.** Tube: Blackfriars.

England's satirical magazine *Punch* was founded here by a group that included Charles Dickens. The tavern, one of the oldest in London, is also known for its Victorian gin palace interior—extraordinarily impressive. Today, the Punch is popular with local office workers. It serves simple pub grub and a variety of ales, bitters, and lagers. Next door to St. Bride's Church and within walking distance of St. Paul's Cathedral.

Salisbury. 90 St. Martin's Lane, WC2. ☎ **0171/836-5863.** Tube: Leicester Sq.

This popular Victorian pub has elaborately etched glass and a lincrusta ceiling. Radiant, it's lit by bronze art nouveau lamps with figures as bases.

Shepherd's Tavern. 50 Hertford St., W1. ☎ **0171/499-3017.** Tube: Green Park.

Tucked away in a warren of streets off Park Lane, this early 18th-century pub has a warm and snug air. Among its more interesting features is the telephone booth, which is actually a sedan chair that once belonged to the Duke of Cumberland, son of George III. During World War II, it was a popular haunt for RAF pilots.

The Spaniard's Inn. Spaniard's Rd., NW3, Hampstead. ☎ **0181/731-6571** Tube: Hampstead.

A romantic heathside pub that has a lovely garden in summer and hearthside drinking in winter. Part of it dates back to 1585, and many a famous Brit has dallied here—from Keats and Shelley to Dickens and the highwayman Dick Turpin.

Star Tavern. 6 Belgrave Mews West, SW1. ☎ **0171/235-3019.** Tube: Knightsbridge.

If your idea of a pub in winter is one that is warmed by a glowing fire, then this is the place to come, for it has two fires going. A Victorian atmosphere prevails.

Ye Olde Cheshire Cheese. Wine Office Court, 15 Fleet St., EC4. ☎ **0171/353-6170.** Tube: Blackfriars.

Open since 1667, this historical wooden pub is where Dr. Johnson took his tipple, and it's a sightseeing attraction in its own right. Ducking through the low doors will transport you back in time, as the wood benches and narrow courtyard entrance give it authentic period charm. Meals here are traditional and filling, but expensive.

Ye Olde Mitre. 1 Ely Court, Ely Place off Hatton Garden, EC1. ☎ **0171/405-4751.** Tube: Chancery Lane.

This place is so well tucked away in a dingy little alley that first-time visitors often turn back halfway along the passageway, fearing they've gone the wrong way. It's understandable why Ye Old Mitre is often referred to as London's "best-kept secret." It has a delightful, snug Elizabethan interior.

6 Wine Bars

Wine lovers will appreciate these welcome alternatives to pubs. Although not as common as pubs, there are plenty to choose from throughout London. Most have a good selection of wines by the glass and the bottle, and food is almost always served. Menus tend to have a continental flavor, with standards and prices that are higher than at most pubs. You don't have to eat, however, and a bottle of the house wine, usually costing £7 to £9 ($11.20–$14.40), shared between two or three people, may come out cheaper than a visit to a pub. Most wine bars keep pub hours.

✪ **The Cork and Bottle Wine Bar.** 44–46 Cranbourn St., WC2. ☎ **0171/734-7807** or 0171/734-6592. Tube: Leicester Sq.

Located between Leicester Square and Charing Cross Road, this small basement bar is in the heart of the theater district and gets very crowded in the early evenings. It's cozy, the food is decent and reasonably priced, and there are about 25 wine selections available by the glass. Go after 8pm if you want a seat.

The Ebury Wine Bar. 139 Ebury St., SW1. ☎ **0171/730-5447.** Tube: Victoria or Sloane Sq.

The Ebury, a stone's throw from Victoria Station, is an appealing wine bar which is very popular at lunch with executives from nearby investment banks. The food is well prepared (priced from £9–£12 or $14.40–$19.20). Every Sunday at lunch a traditional roast is served.

Olde Wine Shades. 6 Martin Lane, Cannon St., EC4. ☎ **0171/626-6876.** Tube: Monument.

One of the oldest wine bars that's survived the many disasters that have struck the city. Dickens is rumored to have frequented the place. It still has a 19th-century air, with its oil paintings and political cartoons.

Vats. 51 Conduit St., WC1. ☎ **0171/242-8963.** Tube: Oxford Circus.

It looks very plain from the outside—just a few benches and tables and minimal decoration—but it's the wine selection and the prices that draw folks here. There are about 15 wines offered by the glass and a similar number of half-bottles available. The food ranges from £8 to £14 ($12.80–$22.40).

10 Easy Excursions from London

Even if you're only staying a short time in London, try to make some time to get out of the city into the English countryside—"the green and pleasant land." Before you go, visit the **British Travel Centre, 12 Lower Regent St., W1** (no phone), just south of Piccadilly Circus, for information and advice. They will also book trains, buses, and tours for you.

For train journeys under 50 miles, the cheapest tickets are called "cheap day returns." Try to avoid day-trips on Friday, when fares increase to profit on the mass exodus of city-dwellers. If you're planning to do a lot of traveling by train in the southeast, then purchase BritRail's regional pass. The Southeast Pass will allow you to travel as far west as Exeter, as far south as Brighton and Eastbourne, as far north as Kings Lynn and Northampton, and as far east as Canterbury. These flexipasses cost $69 adult, $18 child for three days out of eight, $94 adult and $18 child for four days out of eight, and $126 adult and $18 child for seven days out of fifteen. For information on these (and other passes that can be purchased only outside Britain), call ☎ **800/677-8585.** For specific trains to the destinations below, contact the British Travel Centre or call ☎ **0345/484950.**

Since the denationalization of the railways, there are no longer uniform fares and routes. Depending on the destination the following kinds of fares will be offered: a **standard return** allows you to go and return whenever you like; an **off-peak return** can be used only outside of morning and evening rush hours; an **APEX** must be purchased a week in advance with firm departure and return dates and times; a **super APEX** must be bought by 2pm before the day of departure; and the **Network Away Break** requires you to return within five days. I have quoted those that currently apply, but always ask for the least expensive ticket and then decide if it suits your travel plans. Note too, that thanks to diversification you can now travel to the same destination via different routes. Paradoxically, though, instead of the shortest and fastest route being the most expensive, it's the slowest and longest that costs the most. For example, you can be routed to Stratford via Banbury or via Birmingham. The Banbury route, which is the fastest, is also the cheapest.

National Express (☎ **0990/808080**), the country's primary long-haul bus line, operates coaches to almost every corner of

Britain. If you're planning to do a lot of touring, you may want to take advantage of their Tourist Trail Pass, which allows for unlimited travel within either 2, 7, or 14 days, costing £49 ($78.40), £120 ($192), and £187 ($299.20) respectively. The first segment must be used within three consecutive days, the second in 21 days, and the third in 30 days. National Express also offers discounts to seniors, families, and youths. Victoria Coach Station, located one block west of Victoria Rail Station, is the line's London hub.

All of the destinations listed below are close enough to visit in one day, but each warrants a more thorough exploration; make an overnight visit if you have the time.

1   Windsor & Eton

21 miles W of London

Surrounded by gentle hills and lush valleys, this pretty riverside town—which was known to ancient Britons as Windlesore—is famous today for two things: a castle and a prep school.

ESSENTIALS
GETTING THERE

By Train   Trains depart from Paddington Station and make the journey in about 50 minutes with a change at Slough. Trains leave 13 times each day, and tickets cost £5.60 ($8.95) round-trip.

By Bus   Green Line buses (☎ **0181/668-7261**) leave once an hour from London's Eccleston Bridge, behind Victoria Station. Day-return tickets cost £6.50 ($10.40) round-trip.

ORIENTATION

From the station (which has been attractively modernized and features cafes and such upscale stores as Jaeger and Liberty), you walk out into the High Street and turn right for the **Windsor Information Centre,** at 24 High St. (☎ **01753/743900**).

WHAT TO SEE & DO

✪ **Windsor Castle** (☎ **01753/868286**) claims to be the largest inhabited castle in the world. For more than 900 years, English monarchs have made a home on this site. On a bend in the Thames, the castle is surrounded by 4,800 acres of lawn, woodlands, and lakes. The damage caused by the fire late in 1992 has been repaired, and the castle is now fully operational.

When the Royal Standard is not flying, the **State Apartments** are open to the public. They are worth seeing. On your way through the many rooms you'll see fabulous furnishings, tapestries, and paintings that include Rembrandts, Canalettos, Van Dycks, Rubenses, and such portraits as those of Henry VIII and Thomas Howard by Holbein. In the **Queen's Ballroom** hang some marvelous portraits by Van Dyck of Charles I and his family, and the Duke of Buckingham. **St. George's Hall** displays the heraldic arms of 800 plus Knights of the Garter going back to the founder, the Black Prince. Each of the arms is numbered and it's fun to try and

Windsor Fun Fact

The painter of the extraordinary pagan feast depicted on the ceiling in the **King's Dining Room** has actually placed himself in the picture. See if you can find his visage or ask one of the guards to point it out.

figure what some of them represent. The **Lantern Room** holds displays of some fabulous silver by Paul de Lamerie and George Wickes, as well as other decorative objects including a gorgeous 16th-century shell piece by Nicolaus Schmidt.

The **Changing of the Guard** ceremony takes place outside the Guardroom in the Lower Ward at 11am Monday to Saturday April to June and then alternate days for the remainder of the year. To find out if the ceremony is taking place on the day of your visit, call the castle number and ask for extension 2235.

A favorite highlight at the castle is the spectacular **Queen Mary's Doll House.** Designed by Sir Edwin Lutyens, it took more than a thousand artisans more than three years to create. It's built on a scale of 1:12, and everything in it actually works, from the miniature plumbing to a tiny electric iron. Even the bottles in the wine cellar contain vintage wine of its era.

✪ **St. George's Chapel** (☎ 01753/865538), within the precincts of the castle, was founded by King Edward IV in 1475 and completed in 1528 by Henry VIII. It is one of the finest examples of late Gothic architecture in the nation and the resting place of 10 sovereigns, including Henry VIII and his third wife, Jane Seymour. The chapel is named after the patron saint of the Most Noble Order of the Garter, Britain's highest Order of Chivalry. Here in the choir you can see the banners, swords, helm, and crests of each current member above the stalls below, plus the metal stall plates of more than 700 members of the Garter, the oldest dating back to about 1390. Sadly, many of these have been lost, including those of the original founders in 1348. Some of the heraldic symbols are extraordinary—ranging from sea monsters to boars and all manner of wild beast and bird. Visitors are welcome to Sunday services and also at daily Evensong.

Unless the queen is in residence, the castle is open March to October daily from 10am to 5:30pm, and 10am to 4pm the rest of the year. The State Apartments are open March to October 10am to 4:30pm and November to February 10am to 3:30pm. St.George's Chapel is open Monday to Saturday March to October from 10:45am to 4pm and the rest of the year till 3:45 pm.

After visiting the castle, take some time to wander the cobblestone streets—which are referred to as Guildhall Island—opposite the gatewayand then turn down the High Street. At the bottom of the street cross the bridge over the Thames into Eton High Street, which will lead eventually to **Eton College** (☎ 01753/671-0000). You can walk there easily from the city center or you can hop on one of the courtesy-free shuttles that operate around Windsor/Eton. Eton is one of (if not the most) prestigious British public schools. During term you'll see the boys going through the streets in their white collars and tails. Many members of the British Establishment have been educated at Eton, including nineteen former prime ministers. Other illustrious alumni include George Orwell and Aldous Huxley. The **Lower School** houses one of the oldest classrooms in the world, dating from 1443.

The school is open for visitors from Easter to the end of September daily from 2pm to 4:30pm. During summer holidays, hours are extended from 10:30am to 4:30pm.

En route to the college you can browse in the many antiques stores and galleries like **J Manley** at no. 27 (☎ 01753/865647), where you might find a traditional print.

Families come to Windsor also to visit **Legoland** (☎ 0990/040404), an innovative, creative, even educational, theme park sponsored by the Lego company. On hand are 21 rides (including roller coaster and water rides), shows, and entertainment, plus an imagination center and freestyle workshops where the kids can build whatever fires their imagination. Miniland was created using an astonishing

20 million blocks—you'll never look at Lego in quite the same way again. Admission is £16 ($25.60) adults, £13 ($20.80) children 3–15, and £10 ($16) seniors. If you book in advance (a free service) you'll be guaranteed admission. Open from mid-March to November 1 from 10am to 6pm, and from 10am until 8pm from mid-July to the end of August.

WHERE TO EAT

In addition to the restaurants listed here, there are a couple of decent chain restaurants, as well as a pub called **The Two Brewers** at the top of Park Street, which is worth a visit. **Pierre Victoire** is at 6 High St. (☎ **01753/833009**), where you can secure a one-course lunch for £3.90 ($6.25), two courses for £4.90 ($7.85), and three courses for £5.90 ($9.45). From 6 to 7:30pm there's also a special £6.90 ($11.05) menu. Open daily for lunch and dinner. **Cafe Rouge** is located in the station and offers main courses priced from £6 to £10 ($9.60–$16).

Eton Wine Bar. 82–83 High St., Eton. ☎ **01753/854921.** Main courses £7–£13 ($11.20–$20.80). AE, DC, MC, V. Mon–Sat noon–2:30pm and 6–11pm; Sun noon–2:45pm and 7–10:30pm. WINE BAR.

This attractive restaurant with tile floors and wooden tables serves typical bistro fare—steak and frites, calves' liver and bacon, and salmon fillet on spicy Asian vegetables—to go with the several wines they offer by the glass. In summer dine in the rear garden.

Jake's. Upstairs at 10 High St., Eton. ☎ **01753/832222.** Main courses £7.50–£13.75 ($12–$22). AE, MC, V. Mon–Sat noon–2:30pm and 6:30–11pm; Sun noon–4pm.

This comfortable dining room offers something to please everyone, from a vegetarian dish of the day to stir-fry to pan-fried filet of beef with an oyster, mushroom, and Madeira sauce. You can start with some smoked salmon or the chicken, bacon, and roasted pepper terrine, and finish with one of the traditional treacle puddings or the vanilla crème brûlée.

The Punter Wine Bar & Restaurant. 50 Thames St., Eton. ☎ **01753/865565.** Main courses £5.95–£13.25 ($9.50–$21.20). AE, DC, MC, V. Mon–Sat noon–2:30 and 6–11pm; Sun noon–9pm.

This is an atmospheric dining room that offers, as its name suggests, a full complement of wines by the glass plus some good quality casual dining. You can choose to have a perfectly tasty Stilton and mixed-vegetable omelet at one end of the price range, or an eight-ounce filet plain or au poivre at the other. In between, there are such innovative dishes as calves' liver and bacon with a port and pickled cranberry gravy, and grilled fillet of haddock with a red pepper sauce.

2 Bath

110 miles W of London

Bath is an extraordinarily beautiful town and one of the most popular excursions from London. The well-preserved remains of the original Roman baths are the town's primary tourist draw and are one of the finest Roman sites in England.

ESSENTIALS
GETTING THERE

By Train   Trains depart from Paddington, making the trip in about 1¼ hours. Round-trip off-peak day return fares are £20.60 ($32.95); APEX fare is £17.50 ($28), and an open return is £59 ($94.40). For national rail inquiries call ☎ **0345/ 484950.**

By Bus   National Express (☎ **0990/80 8080**) buses leave daily from London's Victoria Coach Station and make the trip in about 3 hours. Special day return is £10.75 ($17.20), while a standard return is £18.50 ($29.60).

By Car   From London, take the M4 motorway to Exit 18.

ORIENTATION

Bath (pop. 83,000) is situated in a steep valley along the River Avon. Most of the city's main sights, including the abbey and baths, are clustered near the two bridges that span the river. Both the bus and train stations are located at the end of Manvers Street, within easy walking distance of the city center.

VISITOR INFORMATION

Bath's **Tourist Information Centre,** Abbey Church Yard (☎ **01225/477101**), outside the Roman baths, will provide information and help you find accommodations at any one of a number of local bed-and-breakfasts. The center is open May through October, Monday to Saturday from 9:30am to 6pm, Sunday from 10am to 4pm; November through April, Monday to Saturday from 9:30am to 5pm, Sunday from 10am to 4pm.

WHAT TO SEE & DO

According to legend, Bath was founded by King Lear's father, Bladud, who was miraculously cured of leprosy after immersing himself in the town's legendary hot springs. In actuality, however, the warm waters of Bath have been a resort site since Roman times. Although it was founded in A.D. 75, Bath didn't become a popular resort until the beginning of the 18th century, when Queen Anne came to take the waters and made it the country's most fashionable spa. Society flocked to the Assembly and Pump Rooms to take the foul tasting but supposedly curative waters, which you can still taste today for 45p (72 cents) per glass. The grottoes and pavilions of Sydney Gardens played host to balls, concerts, firework displays, and other entertainments. Bath's reputation as a resort meant that it soon became a magnet for artists, musicians, and social climbers. Gout sufferers like Queen Anne would arrive early in the morning to bathe and to drink her prescribed amount of water, anywhere from a pint to a gallon. Fashions and trends were set from Bath buns to Bath chairs and over it all presided the dashing figure of dandy Beau Nash, who served as society's Master of Ceremonies. Jane Austen came here regularly, and Gainsborough made his name here as a portrait painter.

Not everyone subscribed to the delights of Bath. Daniel Defoe was of the opinion that "people go to Bath to commit the worst of all murders—to kill time." The fun lasted until the end of the 18th century, when the benefits of sea bathing surpassed the importance of Bath in the public consciousness.

The splendid town planning and architecture of this 18th-century gem was conceived and executed by John Wood and his son, who laid out a series of elegant interconnected squares and crescents stretching from Queen Square to the Circus and the Royal Crescent. Bath was heavily bombed by the Germans in 1942 and the Assembly Rooms were destroyed, but they have since been rebuilt.

The best way to see Bath is to take one of the free walking tours that leave daily, except Saturday, from the Abbey Church Yard.

Otherwise, begin your tour at the ✪ **Roman Baths and Museum** (☎ **01225/47785**). The baths were originally dedicated to Sulis, a local Celtic goddess who is closely identified with the Roman goddess Minerva. Hot mineral water still rises and gurgles into a series of pools and fills the main bath, which is quite remarkable.

Impressions of Bath

What a delicate beverage is every day quaffed by drinkers medicated with sweat and dirt and dandruff, and abominable discharges of various kinds from twenty different diseased bodies parboiling in the kettle below.

—Matthew Bramble, a character in Tobias Smollet's *The Expedition of Humphry Clinker* (1771), assessing the curative powers of the waters of the Roman Baths

---

The baths were built between A.D. 65 and 75. You can just picture the Romans used to a Mediterranean climate relishing the hot water in this alien, cold climate. The spring pumps out 240,000 gallons a day. On the tour you can still see the sauna and steam rooms plus the dry heat rooms where massages were given. In the museum, computer-animated reconstructions and wooden models show the site as it probably looked in Roman times.

The museum also contains some striking finds from the excavation, including a gilt-bronze head of Minerva, 13,000 coins, soles of sandals, a magnificent Gorgon's Head, and several mosaics and stone carvings. Among the most fascinating oddities unearthed are the many curses inscribed on pewter or lead items recovered from the spring. "Whoever stole my gloves, may he lose his mind and his eyes in the temple," is just one example. It's open April to September daily 9am to 6pm; August daily 8am to 10 pm; October to March daily 9:30am to 5pm. Admission is £6.30 ($10.10) adults, £3.80 ($6.10) children.

The 18th-century **Pump Room,** which overlooks the baths, is a beautiful example of a Georgian interior designed between 1786 and 1795 by Thomas Baldwin and John Palmer. People still come to see it and to have lunch or tea accompanied by the strains of the Pump Room Trio. You can also sample the foul-smelling waters (which contain 43 minerals) for yourself for a small sum. It's open daily from 9:30am to 4:30pm. Admission is free.

Bath Abbey, located across from the Pump Room, dates from the late 16th century, although there were earlier Abbeys on the site from the 8th century. In fact, the first Christian community here dates to 676; it was a convent headed by the Abbess Bertana. The most striking aspect of the exterior is the west front; its series of angels climbing a ladder to heaven is said to depict a dream of Bishop Oliver King, a dream that exhorted him to restore the church, which he did in 1499. Inside, the stained-glass windows (note the East window containing 56 scenes from the life of Christ) and fan vaulting are stunning. The abbey also includes some interesting memorials, including one to Isaac Pitman, inventor of Pitman Shorthand; and also to Richard Beau Nash and U.S. Senator William Bingham (1754–1804). Other memorials recall the deaths of soldiers in Guadeloupe, India, and elsewhere throughout the Empire. It's open Monday to Saturday 9am to 6pm (November to Easter 9am to 4:30pm); Sunday 1:30 to 2:30pm and 4:30 to 5:30pm, although you can also attend any one of six services.

More of Bath's architectural heritage can be seen by visiting the **Pulteney Bridge,** which is near the Abbey. It was designed by Robert Adam and finished in 1774. It's unusual for being lined with a series of small shops. Also visit the **Circus,** which is a circle of 30 three-story town houses divided by 114 Ionic columns and built around a central green. Each column supports different carvings. The Circus was begun by John Wood the Elder in 1754 and completed by his son. The most famous architectural feature of the city is the **Royal Crescent,** a crescent of 30 houses built between 1767 and 1775 by John Wood the Younger. If you want to see an example of the interiors of this splendid row of homes, then visit **Royal**

Crescent House (☎ 01225/428126), which is furnished in late-18th-century style. Period furnishings, kitchen implements, and paintings give the house an air of lived-in authenticity. It's open mid-February through October, Tuesday to Sunday 10:30am to 5pm; November, Tuesday to Sunday from 10:30am to 4pm; last admission is a half hour before closing. Admission is £3.80 ($6.10) adults, £3.50 ($5.60) seniors and children.

Bath has several other sites and attractions, but two in particular stand out. The **Holburne Museum & Crafts Study Centre,** Great Pulteney Street (☎ 01225/466669), is located in a lovely 18th-century building at the end of the splendid and once very fashionable 100-foot-wide Great Pulteney Street. It contains a wonderful collection of decorative and fine arts, including stunning jewelry, silver, Italian majolica, porcelain (Meissen, Bow, and Chelsea), and furniture, plus paintings by Gainsborough, Turner, Stubbs, and Ramsay, and a collection of stunning miniatures. Among the portraits is one of Dr. Rice Charlton, a medical practitioner who helped build the reputation of Bath and its waters as a health-giving resort. What makes the displays particularly interesting is the method of arrangement. New and old pieces are juxtaposed so that you can compare the two and clearly see how the particular craft developed. The display also exhibits the ceramics, textiles, and furniture of contemporary arts-and-crafts people like Bernard Leach and Katherine Pleydell Bouverie. Open mid-February to mid-December Monday to Saturday 11am to 5pm and Sunday 2:30 to 5:30pm. Admission is £3.50 ($5.60) adults, £3 ($4.80) seniors and students, £1.50 ($2.40) children. Across from the museum, Jane Austen resided from 1801 to 1805 at no. 4 Sydney Place.

The **Museum of Costume & The Assembly Rooms,** Bennett St. (☎ 01225/477752), traces the history of fashion and accessories from the 1600s to today. Visitors can enjoy a personal audio tour that takes them through the collection decade by decade, from the silver tissue dresses of the 1660s through the beaded chiffon dresses of the '20s to the 1991 dress of the year designed by Karl Lagerfeld for Chanel. Open Monday to Saturday 10am to 5pm, and Sunday 11am to 5pm. Admission £3.80 ($6) adults and £2.70 ($4.30) children. Unless you're staying in town, you won't be able to enjoy this final recommendation. It's called **Bizarre Bath** (☎ 01225/335124) and indeed it is just that. This walking tour takes an irreverent look at Bath and takes you on a hilarious trip filled with comic antics and tomfoolery. Lighthearted and fun, it's an entertaining piece of street theater that uses passersby as well as you, the audience, for some classic British lunacy and sharpedged wit. Cost is £3.50 ($5.60). Assemble at the Huntsman Inn at 8pm. And don't forget your sense of humor.

WHERE TO STAY

The **Tourist Information Centre** (☎ 01225/477101) offers an exceptionally efficient accommodations booking service. Reservations for local hotels and B&Bs—in all price ranges—are made with a 10% deposit and a £3 ($4.80) booking fee. The largest cluster of budget-priced B&Bs is located along Newbridge Road, but the best quality operations are south of the city along streets like Wells Road. Except during festival time, when hotels of all description are booked solid, you can usually get a room without prior reservations.

Leighton House. 139 Wells Rd., Bath, Avon, BA2 3AL. ☎ **01225/314769.** Fax 01225/443079. 8 units (all with tub and shower). TV TEL. £47 ($75.20) single; £60–£75 ($96–$120) double. All rates include English breakfast. MC, V.

Proprietors Marilyn and Colin Humphrey offer terrific value in their spacious 1870s Victorian, set on a knoll from which there are views over the city of Bath. The gardens are well maintained and the front door entrance is made more welcoming with all the potted plants and hanging baskets. All rooms are nicely decorated, some with period pieces like marble-top tables, and are well equipped with hair dryer and tea/coffeemaking facilities. They are super-clean and comfortable. There's a large, comfortable lounge furnished with sofas and armchairs around the fireplace. The breakfast is à la carte. Choose from traditional eggs cooked any style, kippers, or smoked haddock for your main course, and help yourself to cereals, fruits, and yogurt. The house is only a 10-minute walk from the town center, located on a bus route.

Oldfields. 102 Wells Rd., Bath, Avon, BA2 3AL. ☎ **01225/317984.** Fax 01225/444471. www.oldfields.co.uk. E-mail: info@oldfields.co.uk. 14 units (all with private bathroom). TV TEL. £50 ($80) single; £60–£70 ($96–$112) double or twin; four-poster room from £80 ($128). AE, JCB, MC, V.

This friendly and well-run hotel occupies a large, elegant, Victorian honey-colored stone residence that has views over the city. The rooms have lofty ceilings, and both the public spaces and the rooms have been attractively decorated and thoroughly modernized. Additional amenities include hair dryers and tea/coffeemaking facilities. An excellent breakfast is included, which is cooked to order and offers a full selection from a menu. Fruit, breads, cereals, and yogurt are put out on a large sideboard. There's a large sitting room for guests and off-street parking. It's only 10 minutes' walk from the city center.

✪ **The Old Red House.** 37 Newbridge Rd., Bath, Avon, BA1 3HE. ☎ **01225/330464.** Fax 01225/331661. 5 units, all with private bathrooms. TV. £45 ($72) single, £40–£60 ($64–$96) double. Discounts on three nights or more. MC, V.

This is my favorite B&B in Bath, mainly because the owner has such charm and the rooms have been decorated in such a fetching personal style, often with treasures brought from places far afield like India. The house itself is unique. It is a gingerbread house that is indeed red and has some compelling features, including stained glass. My favorite room is privately situated in the back, in a separate little lodge. Each room has been attractively decorated, perhaps with a tented fabric treatment above the bed or similar. Furnishings are antique and eye catching. The largest room boasts stained-glass windows and a marble fireplace. Additional amenities include hair dryers and tea/coffeemaking facilities.

WHERE TO EAT

In addition to the listings below, the **Puppet Theatre Cafe** (☎ 01225/480532) is a charming little hole-in-the-wall tucked down off Pulteney Bridge facing out to the river. It's good for a spot of tea or light meals like toasted sandwiches, quiche, and jacket potatoes priced around £3 ($4.80).

Coeur de Lion. Northumberland Place, ☎ **01225/463568.** MC, V. Mon–Sat 11am–11pm and Sun noon–6:30pm. Lunch only. PUB.

This has to be the smallest pub in Bath and one of the most charming. The ground floor bar is behind a storefront window and boasts a fireplace. The food consists of sandwiches and cheese and pâté plates, plus dishes like beef and stout pie and *moules marinières*.

Crystal Palace. 11 Abbey Green. ☎ **0225/423944.** Main courses £3–£4.95 ($4.80–$7.90). V. Mon–Sat 11am–11pm, Sun noon–3pm and 7–10:30pm. ENGLISH.

This large 18th-century pub features traditional English fare such as steak-and-mushroom pie, breaded plaice, chili, quiches, and a variety of sandwiches. It's a large, modernized pub that also features several fruit machines. During winter, try to get a table beside the paneled fireplace, which has a coal fire burning. In summer, the best dining is alfresco, on the outdoor garden patio. The Crystal Palace is one of the few places in England where you can order Thomas Hardy Ale, a strong brew claiming the highest alcohol content of any beer in the world.

Fodders. Cheap St. ☎ **01225/462165.** £2.10–£2.85 ($3.40–$4.60). No credit cards. Mon–Fri 10am–4pm, Sat 10am–4pm. SANDWICHES.

This is a casual place that offers 24 fillings ranging from a pâté de campagne to a BLT and from cheddar and guacamole to club, made with your choice of bread—malted wheat, white, brown, pita, and more.

George I. Mill Lane at Bathampton off the A 36. ☎ **01225/425-079.** £5–£9($8–$14.40) MC, V. PUB.

This canalside pub is a short distance from Bath. It sits right on the Kennett and Avon canal. Inside there are a series of stone-walled rooms, some with fireplaces. The eye-catching decor is an eclectic mix of paintings, mirrors, and other decorative objects. The food is traditional but well prepared. Try the steak and kidney pie, cod and chips, or roast beef and Yorkshire pudding, all served with an excellent selection of fresh vegetables. No muzak or fruit machines either. You can, if you like a healthy walk, hike along the towpath; otherwise, you really need a car.

Old Green Tree. 12 Green St., Bath. ☎ no phone. £3.30–£6 ($5.30–$9.60) MC, V. PUB.

This small, friendly pub consists of two paneled rooms and a bar. Low-ceilinged and cozy with wood tables and stools and no fruit machines, it also offers some good food. You can have a half pot of prawns (shells on) with a garlic mayonnaise, or a delicious oak-smoked trout sandwich and salad. The bangers and mash are served with a Somerset sauce made of apple cider, whole grain mustard, and cream; and the ploughman's consists of a huge doorstep of whole grain bread and a very generous portion of cheese, pickled onions, and chutney.

Pierre Victoire. 16 Argyle St. ☎ **01225/334334.** Main courses £6– £9 ($9.60–$14.40); 2-course set lunch £4.90 ($7.85), 3-course £5.90 ($9.45); set dinner before 7:30pm £8.90 ($14.25). MC, V. Daily noon–3pm and Mon–Sat 6–11pm.

This branch of the chain overlooks the river, with some tables by the window looking out over the weir below the Grand Parade. Here you can secure a decent meal that might begin with a salad of scallops with lemon zest and dill mayonnaise or duck terrine with port and honey sauce. Follow it with roast poussin with blueberry and cassis sauce. Cheese or a dessert like profiterole would conclude the meal. If you don't opt for the prix fixe, other typical bistro dishes are offered.

Sally Lunn. North Parade Passage. ☎ **0225/461634.** Main courses at dinner £7–£9 ($11.20–$14.40). Mon–Sat 10am–11pm, Sun noon–11pm. BAKERY.

Sally Lunn buns are famous outside Bath. They are named after the woman who established herself as a baker in the 1680s in this house, which is said to be the oldest in Bath. The buns are similar to brioche but extra large, almost loaf size. And they can be filled with a variety of meats, cheeses, and salads and served either cold or toasted. They can also be topped with such sweets as lemon or orange curd and hazelnut and coffee. This is the place to come for morning coffee, light meals, and afternoon cream tea during the day, or a candlelit dinner at night. A downstairs museum features the original kitchen (admission 30p/48¢).

The Walrus and the Carpenter. 28 Barton St. ☎ **0225/314864.** Reservations recommended. £8–£12.50 ($12.40–$20). MC, V. Mon–Sat noon–2:30pm and 6–11pm, Sun noon–11pm. CONTINENTAL.

A casual, reasonably priced restaurant where the tables are covered in gingham-check tablecloths and the walls with posters. The food is adequate. An extensive menu offers everything from steaks, burgers, and kebabs to salads and vegetarian dishes.

3 Cambridge

55 miles N of London

Cambridge competes with Oxford in everything. It loses in age—and usually in boat races—but it wins in beauty and charm. Unlike Oxford, which was a thriving center of car manufacture and other industry, and was a thriving town before the first college was founded, Cambridge has a somnolent air, immediate captivating beauty, and a romance that can easily be felt on the banks of the Cam or standing on the Bridge of Sighs at St. John's College.

Settled by the Romans, who bridged the River Cam, the city did not begin to flourish until the 13th century, when the first college was founded here. Cambridge University now has 31 colleges. Year-round, the college grounds are open to the public. Some are worth visiting; others are less so and the admission fees can quickly add up. We recommend that you visit the Fitzwilliam, Kettle's Yard, and then one or two of the colleges before taking a stroll along the backs or a punt on the river. During the summer months when the schools are closed for vacation, the colleges are crowded with visitors.

ESSENTIALS
GETTING THERE

By Train   Trains depart from London's Paddington, Liverpool Street, and King's Cross stations every 20 minutes and make the trek in about an hour. The day-return fare is £15.50 ($24.80); off-peak £13.20 ($21.10) and Network Away Break £17.80 ($28.50). From Cambridge station, ☎ **0345/484950,** take the Cityrail link bus to Market Square, in the center of the city. For national rail inquiries call ☎ **0345/484950.**

By Bus   National Express (☎ **0990/808080**) buses leave from London's Victoria Coach Station 13 times each day, take an hour and 50 minutes, and cost £11 ($17.60) return, £8 ($12.80) same-day return.

By Car   From London, take the M11 motorway to Exit 11.

ORIENTATION

Cambridge (pop. 103,000) has two main streets. Trumpington Road—which becomes Trumpington Street, King's Parade, Trinity Street, and finally St. John's Street—runs parallel to the River Cam. It's close to several of the city's colleges. Bridge Street, the city's main shopping street, starts at Magdalene Bridge; it becomes Sidney Street, St. Andrew's Street, and finally Regent Street.

VISITOR INFORMATION

The **Tourist Information Centre,** Wheeler Street (☎ **01223/322640;** fax 01223/457588), located behind Guildhall, offers transportation and sightseeing information, as well as maps and accommodations lists. The office is open November through March, Monday through Friday 9am to 5:30pm, Saturday 9am to 5pm; April through June and September through October, Monday through Friday 9am to 6pm, Saturday 9am to 5pm, Sunday 10:30am to 3:30pm. It also sponsors walking tours which leave from here daily. At least two tours a day are scheduled from April to October—more at the height of the summer and fewer in the fall/winter. Tickets are £6.25 ($10) and include entrance to King's College. The other way to get around is on a bike, which can be rented from **Cambridge Recycles** (☎ **01223/506035**) or **Geoff's Bike Hire** (☎ **01223/365629**). Average cost is £6 ($9.60) per day.

WHAT TO SEE & DO

You won't have time to see all the colleges. Note that admission ranges from £1.50 ($2.40) to £3 ($4.80) and it can mount up. Some, quite frankly, in our opinion, are not worth the money, so here are a few brief recommendations. Do stroll the backs and take a walk across Jesus Meadow to a pub that we'll list below.

✪ **King's College** (☎ **01223/31100,** or **01223/331447** for the chapel), founded by Henry VI in 1441, is worth seeing. The chapel is internationally famous for its choir and the traditional Festival of Nine Lessons and Carols broadcast annually on Christmas Eve. Some notable features are the incredible fan vaulting, beautiful stained-glass windows, and a screen given by Henry VIII bearing his initials and those of his queen at the time, Anne Boleyn. Behind the altar you can see Rubens's *Adoration of the Magi,* painted in 1634. During term go for a choral service (Tuesday to Saturday at 5:30pm and Sunday at 10:30am and 3:30pm) to experience the true beauty of this chapel and its choir. A small exhibition hall features pictures and commentary on how and why the chapel was built. It's open during school term Monday through Saturday 9:30am to 3:30pm, Sunday 1:15 to 2:15pm. During vacation, it's open Monday through Saturday 9:30am to 4:30pm, Sunday 10am to 4:30pm. The chapel is closed December 26 through January 1, and occasionally without notice for recording sessions and rehearsals.

From the chapel, you can walk around the front court, pass the neo-Gothic gatehouse and screen, go through the passageway between the Gibbs's and Wilkins's, buildings, and find the back lawn and the bridge that crosses the River Cam before you leave via the North Gate.

Trinity College (☎ **01223/338400**) was founded by Henry VIII in 1546 and is the largest and wealthiest of Cambridge's colleges. It has produced 29 Nobel Laureates; among its famous alumni are scientists Sir Isaac Newton and Lord Rutherford; poets and writers Francis Bacon, Lord Tennyson, Lord Byron, Andrew Marvell, and John Dryden; and philosopher Bertrand Russell. The courtyard is particularly impressive, covering as it does two acres. Traditionally, students try to run around this court before the clock finishes striking 12 (it strikes the hours twice)—a scene recalled in the movie *Chariots of Fire.* More rakishly, it's said that the poet Byron used to bathe naked in the large fountain at its center. Note the statue of Henry VIII on the Great Gate clutching a chair leg instead of a sword—the result of a student prank.

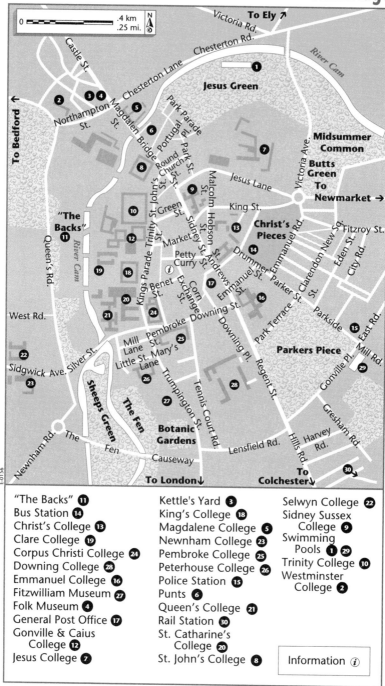

Cambridge

Jesus Green

Midsummer Common

Butts Green

To Newmarket →

Christ's Pieces

"The Backs"

Parkers Piece

West Rd.

Botanic Gardens

To London ↓

To Colchester ↓

To Ely ↗

To Bedford ←

To Newmarket →

The college's impressive **Wren Library** was designed by Sir Christopher himself and possesses many original works by famous former students.

Queens' College (☎ 01223/335511) is arguably the prettiest of all of Cambridge's colleges. Founded in 1448, it is named for two queens, Margaret of Anjou, wife of Henry VI; and Elizabeth, wife of Edward IV. The most spectacular college building is the half-timbered **President's Lodge,** which dates from the beginning of the 16th century. The Tower is where the great scholar resided from 1510 to 1514.

Other colleges worth visiting include **Magdalene,** to view the Pepys Library, the diarist collection of 3,000 volumes; and **Jesus College,** for the chapel's stained-glass windows by Edward Burne-Jones and its ceiling by William Morris, plus the college's association with Samuel Taylor Coleridge.

Stroll along the backs by the river Cam for magnificent views of the colleges, particularly **St. John's,** famous for the Bridge of Sighs replica of the Venetian original.

"Punting," or pole-boating, on the River Cam is a Cambridge tradition. So is **Scudamore's Boatyards,** Granta Place (☎ 01223/359750) by the Anchor Pub, which has been renting punts and rowboats since 1910. All boats rent for £8 ($12.80) per hour, and require a £30 ($48) refundable deposit. It's open during summer only, daily from 10am to 7pm.

If you enjoy museums and galleries, there are two exceptional collections to visit here in Cambridge. The **Fitzwilliam Museum,** Trumpington Street (☎ 01223/332900), is a remarkable collection that can be divided into antiquities, decorative applied arts, coins, manuscripts, and paintings. Among the antiquities highlights are the Roman marble Pashley Sarcophagus depicting the triumphal return of Bacchus from India; a plastered and painted wood figure of an Egyptian official dating to the 23rd century B.C., and many other treasures. Chinese jades and bronzes, pages from beautiful Books of Hours and the first draft of Keats's "Ode to a Nightingale," china, glass, majolica, silver, clocks, and many other beautiful objects are displayed in the museum. The Egyptian collection is superb. The paintings are also extraordinary. They range from medieval and Renaissance works to contemporary canvases. For example, you can feast your eyes on Simon Martini's *St. Geminianus;* Titian's *Tarquin and Lucretia;* stunning Tudor, Stuart, and other miniatures; Rubens's *The Death of Hippolytus;* brilliant etchings by van Dyck; Dutch landscapes and still lifes; rare Hogarths; 25 Turners; many extraordinary painted works by William Blake; examples of the impressionists; and more recent paintings by Paul Nash and Sir Stanley Spencer. See in particular *John Donne Arriving in Heaven* and *Making Columns for the Tower of Babel* by Spencer. It's an amazing collection and offers many masterpieces that you won't see elsewhere. Open Tuesday to Saturday 10am to 5pm, and Sunday 2:15 to 5pm. Admission is free.

Any art lover will not want to miss **Kettle's Yard,** Castle Street (☎ 01223/352124), a complex that embraces an extraordinary home that houses an even more amazing collection of art, furniture, and decorative objects, as well as a gallery that shows changing exhibitions of 20th-century art. There will certainly be a stimulating show in the gallery, but the house is an absolute treasure, the vision and creation of Jim Ede and his wife Helen. He was the curator at the Tate during the 1920s and 1930s and acquired the collection that is displayed as he arranged it in his home. The way everything is displayed is an art form in itself; sometimes pictures are hung low on walls so that they can be viewed from a strategically placed wing chair; likewise, furniture and objects are carefully arranged throughout. You'll find numerous paintings by Ben Nicholson, Christopher Wood, and Alfred Wallis, and many sculptures by Henry Moore, Henri Gaudier-Brzeska, Brancusi, and Barbara Hepworth, plus other striking pieces. Admission is free. Open April to September 1, Tuesday to Sunday 1:30 to 4:30pm and 2 to 4pm in winter.

WHERE TO STAY

Some of the city's best B&Bs are clustered along Chesterton Road, not far from the train station.

Ashley Hotel. 74 Chesterton Rd., Cambridge, Cambridgeshire, CB4 1ER. ☎ **01223/ 350059.** 10 units (8 with shower or tub). TV. £28.50 ($45.60) single; £49.50–£59.50 ($79.20–$95.20) double. All rates include English breakfast. MC, V.

This good bed-and-breakfast is located close to the city center, between the River Cam and Jesus Green. Extra amenities in the rooms include hair dryers as well as tea/coffeemakers. If you want a single room, make reservations well in advance, as there are only two available.

Cambridge Youth Hostel. 97 Tenison Rd., Cambridge, Cambridgeshire, CB1 2DN. ☎ **01223/354601.** Fax 01223/312780. 102 units (none with bathroom). £11 ($17.60) per night with an IYHF card. MC, V. Walk straight from the train station, and turn right onto Tenison Rd.

This is a comfortable hostel conveniently located close to the train station. It offers a full range of amenities, including kitchen and laundry facilities, TV lounge, and games room. There's also a licensed cafeteria where you can enjoy a three-course evening meal for only £4.35 ($6.95), and there's a small shop. If space permits, couples may share a room.

Fairways Guest House. 143 Cherryhinton Rd., Cambridge, Cambridgeshire, CB1 4BX. ☎ **01223/246063.** 15 units (8 with bathroom). TV TEL. £24 ($38.40) single without bathroom, £32 ($51.20) with bathroom; £37 ($59.20) double without bathroom, £50 ($80) with bathroom. MC, V.

The rooms in this handsomely restored Victorian are cozy and feature tea/coffeemakers. Hair dryers, ironing board, and iron will be provided on request. A lobby bar serves drinks. Located about 1.5 miles from the heart of the city.

WHERE TO EAT

The Anchor. Silver St. ☎ **0223/353554.** £3.95–£4.50 ($6.30–$7.20). MC, V. Mon–Sat noon–11pm, Sun noon–3pm and 7–10:30pm; food served daily Sun–Thurs noon–2pm, Fri–Sat noon–5pm. ENGLISH.

One of the city's most popular riverside pubs, the Anchor has several split-level bars including the river view, which looks out on a raft of punts and the willow-fringed river. It's loaded with atmosphere—beams, sloping ceilings—and filled with odds and ends like cider pots, jugs, and prints. It serves such traditional English specialties as battered cod, plaice, lamb and vegetable pie; leek and potato pie; and sausage, egg, and chips. Traditional hand-pulled "real" ales are also available, along with the usual selection of lagers and bitters.

The Baron of Beef. Bridge St. ☎ **0223/505022.** Main courses £3–£5 ($4.80–$8). Food served daily from 11:30am. PUB.

Despite its name, this pub is rigged out with fishing baskets and fishing traps suspended from a ceiling that has been painted red and gives the pub a warm glow. It's frequented by folks from St. John's across the street. The food includes a good beef casserole and roast beef as well as the usual dishes.

The Champion of the Thames. King St. ☎ **0223/352043.** Main courses £3–£5 ($4.80–$8). Food served daily noon–2pm. PUB.

This 13th-century pub is decked out with plenty of sculling memorabilia. It's cozy and has low-ceilinged rooms with large beams furnished with leather banquettes and wood stools and settles.

The Eagle. Benet St. ☎ **0223/505020.** Main courses £3.25–£4.95 ($5.20–$7.90). Food served daily noon–2:30pm and Mon–Thurs 5:30–8:45pm.

An ivy-covered pub with a lovely galleried courtyard that serves as a beer garden. Inside are two bars and three sitting areas with scrubbed wood tables. The Air Force bar has the names and numbers of wartime officers burned into the ceiling. The pub offers good and traditional pub fare.

✪ **Fort St. George.** Midsummer Common. ☎ **0223/354327.** Main courses £2.80– £6.95 ($4.50–$11.10). Food served daily noon–2:30 and 5:30–9pm (7–9pm in winter). PUB.

This is my favorite pub in Cambridge. It's across Jesus Common alongside the river. It has several bars, including a snug with high back settles and a dining room that looks out over the river and several of the boathouses. From here you can watch the crews practicing or kayakers honing their skills. The food is really good. It ranges from abbot's pie (filled with steak, mushrooms, and onions in an Abbot ale gravy), pork loin Dijonnaise, Cumberland sausage, scampi, and open sandwiches. Breakfast is served all day. The public bar has a pool table.

The Granta. Newnham Rd. ☎ **0223/50516.** £2–£5.95 ($3.20–$9.50). Daily noon–2pm and Mon–Sat 6–8pm. PUB.

This appealing pub has a patio overlooking the mill pond and meadows. It offers a mixed menu featuring burgers, hot dogs, BLTs, and open sandwiches (with shaved ham, turkey, or pastrami), plus the usual cod, haddock, chili, and steaks.

Hobbs Pavilion. Park Terrace. ☎ **01223/367480.** Reservations recommended. £4.95–£11.50 ($7.90–$18.40). 2-course lunch £6.75 ($10.80); 3-course meal anytime £8.75 ($14). No credit cards. Tues–Sat noon–2:15pm and 7–9:45pm. Closed mid-Aug to mid-Sept. CREPES.

Located in a historic building, Hobbs is known for its imaginative crepes, more than 40 of them. They're stuffed with everything from vegetarian and hot chilied lamb to Dijon chicken and black pudding; from banana, ginger, and cream to lemon, sugar, and butter. Soups, salads, and char-grilled meats and fish are also available. Try the chicken breast marinated with lemon and herbs or the duck marinated in red wine. The ice cream is made here in flavors such as lavender and honey. No smoking is allowed.

The Mitre. Bridge Street. ☎ **0223/358403.** Food served Mon–Fri 11:30am–2:30pm and 6–8:30pm, Sat noon–4pm, Sun noon–6pm. PUB.

This venerable Cambridge pub dating from 1754 has a storefront window looking out onto the street. Inside, tables are scrubbed and a coke fire burns. Classical music, yes, classical music, plays in the background. The food consists of the usual favorites—sausage, chips, and peas; steak and mushroom pie; and cauliflower cheese.

4 Oxford

57 miles NW of London

Oxford contrasts dramatically with Cambridge. It is a modern, crowded, and busy place where town seriously competes with gown. The town existed two centuries before the founding of the first college and it does not forget this fact. Oxford does not reveal its beauty easily; you have to look a little more deeply and if you do it will yield enchantment. If you really want to uncover the nooks and crannies of the city's history and personalities, then read *Oxford* by the wonderful writer Jan Morris. Wedged between the Thames and Cherwell Rivers, the city has more than 600 buildings listed for their historical or architectural interest.

ESSENTIALS
GETTING THERE

By Train   Trains depart from London's Paddington Station and make the trip to Oxford in about an hour. Day-return tickets are £28.10 ($44.95); off-peak day return £13.50 ($21.60); APEX (purchased by 2pm day before departure) £11.70 ($18.70); and Network Away Break £17.50 ($28).

By Bus   National Express (☎ **0990/808080**) round-trip fares from Victoria Coach Station are £9 ($14.40) with day returns for under £7 ($11.20).

By Car   From London, take the M40 to the A40, to the A420 (or the A423, the scenic route via Windsor and Henley). Don't drive into the city center, however, as parking and traffic are horrific. Free **Park and Ride** car parks are located on the main approaches to the north, south, and west sides of the city. These are regularly served by buses that run into the heart of the city (there's a small charge).

ORIENTATION

Carfax, the city center, is surrounded by the colleges of Oxford, and intersected at right angles by Cornmarket Street, St. Aldate's Street, Queen Street, and High Street. Magdalen Bridge lies past the east end of High Street; the train and bus stations are located to the west of High Street.

VISITOR INFORMATION

The **Oxford Information Centre,** The Old School, Gloucester Green (☎ **01865/ 726871;** fax 01865/240045), can provide you with maps, brochures, and accommodations information. They also have a lot of information on local sights and attractions. Tours costing £4 ($6.40) leave from the center daily at 11am and 2pm. The office is open May through September, Monday through Saturday 9:30am to 5pm, Sunday 10:30am to 3:30pm; October through April, Monday through Saturday 9:30am to 5pm (closed Sunday).

Most colleges open their quads and chapels in the afternoon except for Christ Church, Hertford, New College, St. Hugh's, and Trinity College, all of which are also open in the mornings.

WHAT TO SEE & DO

Before setting out, you may want to see the multimedia presentation at **The Oxford Story,** 6 Broad St. (☎ **01865/728822**), which relates the history of Oxford and student life. It's open April through October, daily 9:30am to 5pm; November through March, daily 10am to 4pm. Admission is £4.95 ($7.90) adults, £4.25 ($6.80) seniors, and £3.95 ($6.30) students.

For a bird's-eye view of the lay of the land, climb the 97 steps to the top of Carfax Tower for a panorama across the college buildings and quads. The attendant at the entrance will provide a map identifying the individual rooftops. It's open March through October only, daily 10am to 5:30pm. Admission is £1.20 ($1.90) adults, 60p (95¢) children.

Although scholars and students were congregating here as early as the 12th century, Oxford University wasn't formally established until 1214, when it received its first charter from the Papal Legate. From then on, a series of colleges was founded beginning in 1249 with University, then Balliol in 1263 and Merton in 1264. Originally the colleges were for men only, and separate colleges for women were opened much later. The first, Lady Margaret Hall, was established in 1878 and followed by Somerville in 1879. In 1975 some of the men's colleges began admitting women, and the rest followed their lead. Today there are 35 colleges scattered throughout the city. Obviously you can't visit all of them, so what follows are merely suggestions for a short visit.

Founded in 1458, **Magdalen** (pronounced "*Maud*-len") is one of the largest and most beautiful of the colleges. Its belltower (dated 1492–1509) is a city landmark from which on May mornings the sounds of a hymn sung by the choir are heard followed by the pealing of bells. The hall has some lovely carved wood paneling. The adjacent Botanic Gardens, meadows, and Grove (where deer have roamed since the 1700s) make it a peaceful retreat. Among its more famous alumni are Thomas Wolsey, Edward Gibbon, Oscar Wilde, and Edward, Prince of Wales. The tower is open daily from 2 to 6:15pm.

Christ Church (1546) is both college and cathedral. The cathedral was built on the site of St. Frideswide's Monastery. It contains some beautiful medieval stained glass, including one depicting the martyrdom of Thomas à Becket, plus the St. Frideswide and St. Catherine windows by Edward Burne-Jones. Charles I established his residence in the Deanery during the civil war, when Oxford was his military headquarters. At the entrance to the college, **Tom Tower,** containing the beloved 7-ton bell "Great Tom," was built by Sir Christopher Wren in 1682. The bell tolls 101 times at 9:05 pm every day—a tradition that derives from the time when one chime represented one scholar and the tolling marked the closing of college. Christ Church possesses a fine collection of portraits, displayed in the hall. They include such notable graduates as William Penn, W. E. Gladstone, John Wesley, Anthony Eden, and Lewis Carroll. The cathedral is open in summer, Monday through Saturday 9:30am to 4:30pm, Sunday 1 to 4:30pm. Visitors are welcome to attend the four services held on Sunday, and evensong at 6pm weekdays.

All Souls (1438) is notable for a variety of attributes. No undergraduates are admitted. The chapel has a striking hammerbeam ceiling and finely carved reredos and misericords. The Great Quad was designed by Nicholas Hawksmoor, a pupil of one of the college's most famous graduates, Sir Christopher Wren.

New College (1379) is a harmonious collection of English Perpendicular buildings. The chapel contains some notable sculpture and art, including Epstein's *Lazarus* and El Greco's *St. James,* plus some fine stained-glass windows and woodwork, particularly the carving of the choir stalls. The Hall is the oldest in Oxford and has fine paneling, while the gardens are some of the most beautiful.

Oxford

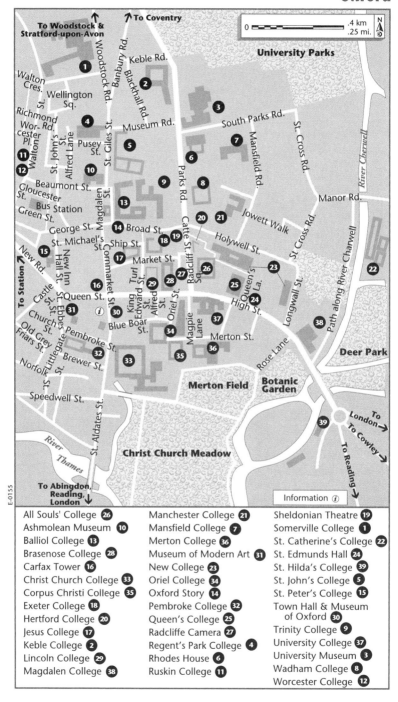

To Woodstock &
Stratford-upon-Avon

To Coventry

Keble Rd.

University Parks

0   .4 km
     .25 mi.

N

Walton
Cres.

Wellington
Sq.

Woodstock Rd.

Banbury Rd.

Blackhall Rd.

Keble Rd.

South Parks Rd.

St. Cross Rd.

River Cherwell

Richmond
Rd.
Wor-
cester
Pl.

Museum Rd.

Mansfield Rd.

Walton St.

St. John's St.

Alfred Lane

Pusey St.

St. Giles St.

Beaumont St.

Magdalen St.

Gloucester
St.

Bus Station

Green St.

George St.

St. Michael's St.

Ship St.

Broad St.

New Rd.

New Inn
Hall St.

Cornmarket St.

Market St.

Turl St.

Parks Rd.

Catte St.

Holywell St.

Jowett Walk

Manor Rd.

St. Cross Rd.

Path along River Charwell

To Station

Castle St.

St. Ebbes
St.

Queen St.

Church
St.

Old Grey
Friars St.

Pembroke St.

Brewer St.

Norfolk
St.

Littlegate

Speedwell St.

St. Aldates St.

King
Edward
St.

Alfred
St.

Blue Boar
St.

Oriel St.

Magpie
Lane

Merton St.

Radcliffe
Sq.

Queen's
La.

High St.

Longwall St.

Rose Lane

Merton Field

Botanic
Garden

Deer Park

Christ Church Meadow

River
Thames

To Abingdon,
Reading,
London

To
London →

To Cowley →

To Reading →

Information ⓘ

E-0155

All Souls' College **26**	Manchester College **21**	Sheldonian Theatre **19**
Ashmolean Museum **10**	Mansfield College **7**	Somerville College **1**
Balliol College **13**	Merton College **36**	St. Catherine's College **22**
Brasenose College **28**	Museum of Modern Art **31**	St. Edmunds Hall **24**
Carfax Tower **16**	New College **23**	St. Hilda's College **39**
Christ Church College **33**	Oriel College **34**	St. John's College **5**
Corpus Christi College **35**	Oxford Story **14**	St. Peter's College **15**
Exeter College **18**	Pembroke College **32**	Town Hall & Museum
Hertford College **20**	Queen's College **25**	of Oxford **30**
Jesus College **17**	Radcliffe Camera **27**	Trinity College **9**
Keble College **2**	Regent's Park College **4**	University College **37**
Lincoln College **29**	Rhodes House **6**	University Museum **3**
Magdalen College **38**	Ruskin College **11**	Wadham College **8**
		Worcester College **12**

Impressions

The world, surely, has not another place like Oxford: it is a despair to see such a place and ever to leave it.

—Nathaniel Hawthorne, *Notebooks*, 1856

The **Hall at Jesus** (1571) has some fine portraits, including one of Charles I by Van Dyck and another of Sir Harold Wilson by Ruskin Spear. It also displays a couple of fine busts—one of Elizabeth I and the other of poet Edward Thomas.

Corpus Christi (1517) is a small college. Somehow it managed to retain most of its silver and other plate; it has a charming sundial surmounted by a pelican at the center of the Front quad and an altarpiece in the chapel, *The Adoration of the Shepherds,* attributed to Rubens.

At **Exeter** (1314), the neo-Gothic chapel redesigned by Sir Giles Gilbert Scott contains a tapestry by William Morris and Edward Burne-Jones, who developed a friendship while they were undergraduates here.

Hertford (1874) has its own Bridge of Sighs and an unusual octagonal chapel now used as a common room. St. John's (1555) gardens, laid out by Capability Brown, are beautiful. Bill Clinton was a Rhodes Scholar at University College in 1968. Balliol (1263) may well be the most influential college, having what seems to be the longest list of famous scholars and politicians, including Herbert Asquith, Lord Curzon, Harold Macmillan, Edward Heath, Denis Healey, and Roy Jenkins.

In addition to the colleges, Oxford has some other architectural highlights. The **Sheldonian Theatre** (1669) was Sir Christopher Wren's first building. Today it's used as a concert hall and for such university ceremonies as the Encaenia, when honorary degrees are bestowed. The interior is entirely of wood except for the ceiling, which consists of 36 panels painted by Robert Streeter, court painter to Charles II. It's open Monday to Saturday 10am to 12:30pm and 2 to 4:30pm. Admission is £1.50 ($2.40) adults, £1 ($1.60) children.

Next door, the old Ashmolean building houses the **Museum of the History of Science** (☎ **01865/277280**) displaying scientific and medical instruments, plus clocks, cameras, and other equipment (open Tues to Sat noon to 4pm). Behind is the famous **Bodleian Library** (1602) containing over five million books (☎ **01865/277165**). It's open for tours; admission is £3.50 ($5.60). The **Radcliffe Camera** (1748), designed by James Gibbs, is used as a reading room.

Founded in 1683, the **Ashmolean Museum,** Beaumont Street (☎ **01865/ 278000**), is England's oldest public museum. In addition to housing a terrific archaeology collection—with Egyptian mummies and casts of Greek sculptures— the galleries contain fine collections of silver, ceramics, and bronzes, as well as paintings including works by da Vinci, Raphael, and Rembrandt. It's open Tuesday through Saturday 10am to 4pm, Sunday 2 to 4pm.

The **Museum of Modern Art** on Pembroke Street (☎ **01865/722733**) contrasts with Oxford's antiquity. It's a leading center for contemporary visual arts. Exhibitions change regularly, and include sculpture, architecture, photography, video, and other media. Call for an exhibition schedule. It's open Tuesday through Sunday 10am to 6pm (until 9pm Thursday). Admission is £2.50 ($4) adults, £1.50 ($2.40) seniors, children under 16 free. It's free on Wednesday 11am to 1pm and Thursday 6 to 9pm.

WHERE TO STAY

Accommodations in Oxford are limited, especially during the school term. The main roads out of town are lined with affordable bed-and-breakfasts; these are fine if you don't mind a healthy walk.

In addition to the listings below, the **Oxford Information Centre,** The Old School, Gloucester Green (☎ **01865/726871;** fax 01865/240045), will book accommodations for a £3 ($4.80) fee.

Adams Guest House. 302 Banbury Rd., Summertown, Oxford, Oxfordshire, OX2 7ED. ☎ **01865/556118.** 6 units (all with showers). £25–£30 ($40–$48) single; £40–£42 ($64–$67.20) twin. All rates include breakfast. No credit cards.

Located in Summertown, 1.25 miles from Oxford, this is one of the best B&Bs around. Rooms are comfortable and cozy. From this quiet neighborhood with a number of restaurants, shops, and a laundry, a bus runs every few minutes to the city center. It's opposite the Midland Bank.

Lonsdale Guest House. 312 Banbury Rd., Summertown, Oxford, Oxfordshire, OX2 7ED. ☎ **01865/554872.** 8 units (5 with shower). TV. £28 ($44.80) single without bathroom; £45 ($72) double with bathroom (shower only). All rates include English breakfast. No credit cards. Bus: 7, 7A, 2A, or 2B.

About 10 minutes by bus from the city center, the Lonsdale has comfortably furnished rooms. With down comforters and central heating, it's one of the nicest B&Bs in town. Most rooms have a private shower and all have tea/coffeemaking facilities. Tennis courts, a heated indoor swimming pool, and a Laundromat are all a 2-minute walk away.

WHERE TO EAT

In addition to the restaurants and pubs listed below, there is also a branch of the chain **Pierre Victoire,** 9 Little Clarendon St. (☎ **01865/316616**), and of **Pizza Express,** at The Golden Cross in Cornmarket St. (☎ **01865/790440**).

The Bear. Alfred St., off High St. ☎ **01865/721783.** Main courses £2–£5 ($3.20–$8). No credit cards. Food served daily noon–3pm. PUB.

This tiny old pub has four low-ceilinged and partly paneled rooms covered with the ends of neckties that have been clipped off in the course of an afternoon or evening here at this famous Oxford institution; the ties are permanently displayed with the owners' names. The menu is restricted to sandwiches and such dishes as salmon cakes, scampi, and sausage and chips. The bear, by the way, was the heraldic emblem of the Earls of Warwick.

Browns Restaurant & Bar. 5–11 Woodstock Rd. ☎ **01865/511995.** Main courses £6.50–£12 ($10.40–$19.20). Mon–Sat 11am–11:30pm, Sun noon–11:30. ENGLISH.

This large, casual, upbeat brasserie is one of the best places to eat in Oxford. It serves good quality food, including a good traditional cream tea. It has a large convivial bar and a very pleasant outdoor terrace.

Munchy Munchy. 6 Park End St. ☎ **01865/245710.** Lunch £5–£12 ($8–$19.20). Tues–Sat noon–2pm and 5:30–10pm. Closed 2 weeks in September and 3 weeks in December. INDONESIAN/MALAYSIAN.

People line up here for some of the best budget dining in the city. Dishes change daily depending on the chef's inspiration. But whether it's a *sambal* or a curry or some other spicy concoction, it will stimulate the palate and offer some unusual combinations of sour and sweet.

St. Aldates Coffee House. 94 St. Aldates. ☎ **0865/245952.** Main courses £1.80–£2.50 ($2.90–$4); buffet £4.75 ($7.60). Summer Mon–Sat 9:30am–5:30pm, and winter Mon–Sat 10am–5pm. COMFORT FOOD.

Right opposite Christ Church, this pleasant restaurant has good-value hot dishes at lunchtime—chicken and almond bake, country hot pot, and honey pork. Cream teas are served from 2pm and coffee and cakes all day.

The Turf Tavern. 4 Bath Place. ☎ **01865/243235.** Main courses £2–£5 ($3.20–$8). Food served daily noon–3pm and 6–8pm. PUB.

This delightful pub, tucked away down a cobblestone alley, gets very crowded, no doubt because of its excellent food. The building has three or so bars and a series of long, low-ceilinged rooms which are decorated with plenty of rowing crew portraits and other Oxford memorabilia. The food ranges from steak-in-ale pie and fish and chips to sandwiches. It also offers a good selection of cask ales and has pleasant beer gardens.

5 Stratford-upon-Avon

92 miles NW of London

The Bard was born here. But even if Stratford-upon-Avon were not Shakespeare country, this appealing town would still draw visitors. Picture-perfect, half-timbered houses are shaded by statuesque chestnut and poplar trees, while lazy willows skim the surface of the River Avon. In spring and summer, roses and honeysuckle seem to bloom everywhere, filling the air with a sweet fragrance.

ESSENTIALS
GETTING THERE

By Train   Depending on the route taken, trains make the trip in anywhere from 1½ to 2½ hours from London's Paddington Station. Round-trip tickets cost from £35 to £59 ($56 to $94.40); day return from £18 to £26 ($28.80 to $41.60).

By Bus   National Express (☎ **0990/808080**) buses run every two hours or so. Departing from London's Victoria Coach Station, they make the trip in about 3.5 hours. Tickets cost £11 ($17.60) for a same-day return and £14.50 ($23.20) for an open return.

By Car   From London, take the M40 motorway, then head north on A34.

ORIENTATION

Little changed since the Middle Ages, Stratford's simple layout is an important component of its charm. Just three streets run parallel to the river, and three streets at right angles to it. Buses stop at the corner of Guild Street and Warwick Road.

A Money-Saving Ticket

Collectively referred to as the "Shakespeare Properties," Stratford's five most important restored sites are administered by the Shakespeare Birthplace Trust. A money-saving ticket, good for admission to all five, can be purchased at any site for £10 ($16) adults, £5 ($8) for children under 15. The ticket saves £8 ($12.80).

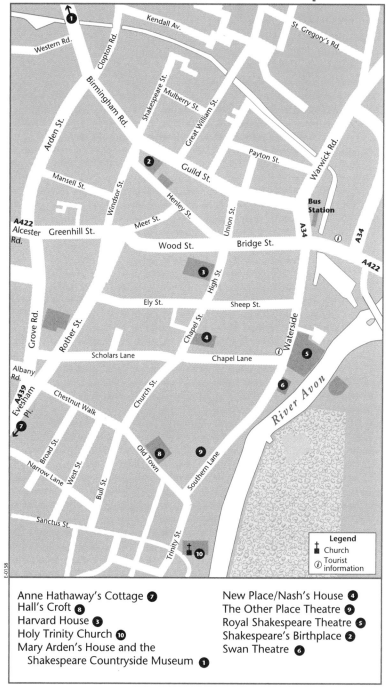

Legend
† Church
ⓘ Tourist information

Anne Hathaway's Cottage ➐
Hall's Croft ➑
Harvard House ➌
Holy Trinity Church ➓
Mary Arden's House and the
    Shakespeare Countryside Museum ➊

New Place/Nash's House ➍
The Other Place Theatre ➒
Royal Shakespeare Theatre ➎
Shakespeare's Birthplace ➋
Swan Theatre ➏

Visitor Information

The Information Centre, Bridgefoot (☎ **01789/293127;** fax 01789/259262), offers tourist information, maps, and a helpful accommodations booking service. It's open April through October, Monday to Saturday 9am to 6pm, Sunday 11am to 5pm; November through March, Monday to Saturday from 11am to 4pm and Christmas Sundays (closed other Sundays).

WHAT TO SEE & DO

Begin at the beginning, at **Shakespeare's Birthplace,** on Henley Street. The famed playwright was born in this three-gabled, half-timbered house on St. George's Day (April 23) in 1564. Today the house features some period furniture and an exhibition about Shakespeare's "life-and-times." Get there before 11am, when the masses of day-trippers arrive. It's open late March to mid-October, Monday to Saturday 9am to 5pm, Sunday 9:30am to 5pm; mid-October to mid-March, Monday to Saturday 9:30am to 4pm, Sunday 10am to 4pm. Admission is £4.50 ($7.20) adults and £2 ($3.20) children.

Two miles west of Stratford, in Shottery, **Anne Hathaway's Cottage** (☎ **01789/204016**) is certainly a pretty thatched cottage surrounded by lovely gardens and an orchard. Inside, a large open fireplace and ceilings with massive beams have been preserved along with many original furnishings. If the weather is good, walk to the cottage from Stratford, across the meadow, along the marked pathway from Evesham Place. Or take the bus from Bridge Street. The cottage is open late March to mid-October, Monday to Saturday 9am to 5pm, Sunday 9:30am to 5pm; mid-October to mid-March, Monday to Saturday 9:30am to 4pm, Sunday 10am to 4pm. Admission £3.50 ($5.60) adults, £1.50 ($2.40) children.

Shakespeare's daughter Susanna lived in **Hall's Croft, Old Town,** ☎ **01789/204016,** with her well-to-do husband, Dr. John Hall. The Tudor home is traditionally furnished with oak and also features an exhibit about Elizabethan medical practices. In back, the walled garden is worth visiting. The adjoining Hall's Croft Club serves morning coffee, lunch, and afternoon tea. It's open late March to mid-October, Monday to Saturday 9:30am to 5pm, Sunday 10am to 5pm; mid-October to mid-March, Monday to Saturday 10am to 4pm, Sunday 10:30am to 4pm. Admission is £3 ($4.80) adults, £1.50 ($2.40) children.

New Place, on Chapel Street, was the Bard's retirement home and when he purchased it in 1597 it was one of Stratford's most impressive homes. Unfortunately, only the foundation and gardens remain. **Nash House** is the 16th-century home next to New Place. It was owned by Thomas Nash, first husband of Shakespeare's granddaughter Elizabeth. Between the two houses lies the Elizabethan **Knott Garden,** and the Great Garden which has a mulberry tree said to have grown from a cutting planted by Shakespeare himself. It's open late March to mid-October, Monday to Saturday 9:30am to 5pm, Sunday 10am to 5pm; mid-October to mid-March, Monday to Saturday 10am to 4pm, Sunday 10:30am to 4pm. Admission £3 ($4.80) adults, £1.50 ($2.40) children.

Located in Wilmcote, five miles north of Stratford, **Mary Arden's House** was probably the home of Shakespeare's mother, Mary Arden, before she married John Shakespeare and moved to Stratford. It's a fine Tudor farmhouse with many outbuildings and an adjacent working farm. Visitors can see displays that bring rural work and traditions to life from Tudor times to now. On the property visitors can watch falconry demonstrations, blacksmithing, and livestock farming. It's open late March to mid-October, Monday to Saturday 9:30am to 5pm, Sunday 10 to 5pm; mid-October to mid-March, Monday to Saturday 10am to 4pm, Sunday 10:30am to 4pm. Admission is £4 ($6.40) adults, £2 ($3.20) children.

Shakespeare is buried in **Holy Trinity Church** (☎ **01789/266316**). The grave is marked with a small plaque bearing the words, ". . . and cursed be he who moves my bones." Anne Hathaway is also buried here. It's open April through October, Monday to Saturday 8:30am to 6pm, Sunday noon to 5pm; November through March, Monday through Saturday 8:30am to 4pm, Sunday 2 to 5pm.

You may also want to go by **Harvard House,** on the High Street, which was the home of Katherine Rogers, mother of John Harvard. Today it houses a collection of pewter. Admission is free. It's open May 1 to late October, Monday to Saturday 10am to 4pm and Sunday 10:30am to 4pm.

ATTENDING THE THEATRE

Founded in 1961 by Sir Peter Hall, the **Royal Shakespeare Company** is Stratford's repertory theater company. In addition to Shakespeare, it performs other classical plays as well as contemporary works. The main stage is at the **Royal Shakespeare Theatre,** which is located on the banks of the Avon and seats 1,500. The season usually features five different plays and extends from early April to late January. The smaller **Swan Theatre** is designed in a neo-Elizabethan style, complete with gallery, and seats 430. The plays of post-Shakespearean playwrights are staged here during a similar season. Again, about five plays rotate. A third small and modern theater, The Other Place, where the seating arrangements can be rearranged easily, is used for experimental productions. Tickets range from £13 to £20 ($20.80 to $32).

Backstage tours of the Royal Shakespeare Theatre are available but must be booked two weeks in advance. They're usually scheduled Monday through Saturday at 1:30 and 5:30pm, and Sunday at 12:30, 2:15, 3:15, and 4:15pm. They're also offered after some evening performances. Tours cost £4 ($6.40) adults, £3 ($4.80) for students and seniors. For information call ☎ **01789/412602.**

Making Advance Reservations   To obtain good seats, tickets should be purchased in advance from the theater box office, which starts taking reservations in early March. You can either call ☎ **01789/295623** (Mon to Sat 9am to 8pm), fax to 01789/261974, or write with credit card details and an SAE with international postal coupon to Box Office, Royal Shakespeare Theatre, Stratford-upon-Avon, CV37 6BB. In the United States, tickets are available from Keith Prowse (☎ **800/ 669-8687** or 212/398-1430). A small fee will be charged.

Getting Tickets on the Day of the Performance   Occasionally you can secure good matinee seats on the morning of a performance. Standing room and returned tickets may also be available on the day of an evening performance. At the Royal Shakespeare Theatre, ticket prices range from £7 to £48 ($11.20 to $76.80). At the Swan Theatre, tickets range from £10 to £32 ($16 to $51.20). Discounted tickets for seniors are available for some performances at both the Royal Shakespeare Theatre and the Swan. Also at both theaters, standby tickets for students are sometimes available on the day of performance.

WHERE TO STAY

Although there are many bed-and-breakfasts in town , during the summer it's wise to book ahead. **The Information Centre,** Bridgefoot, Stratford-upon-Avon, Warwickshire, CV37 6GW (☎ **01789/293127;** fax 01789/295262) can help you find accommodations on short notice.

The Hollies. 16 Evesham Place, Stratford-upon-Avon, Warwickshire, CV37 6HT. ☎ **01789/ 266857.** 6 units (3 with shower). TV. £36 ($56) double without bathroom, £45 ($72) with bathroom. All rates include English breakfast. No credit cards.

Located in an old 3-story schoolhouse, this spacious guesthouse offers comfortable rooms kept spotlessly clean by the resident mother-and-daughter proprietors. Each room has been attractively decorated with duvets and curtains that match. All of the rooms have tea/coffeemakers; hair dryers are available on request. The sunny breakfast room is decorated with hand-cut crystal.

Royalyn House. 17 Evesham Place, Stratford-upon-Avon, Warwickshire, CV37 6HT. ☎**01789/262295**. 5 units (all with private bath). TV. £45 ($72) double, £60 ($96) triple. All rates include English breakfast. MC, V.

The friendly Dempsters operate this sparkling B&B in which all the rooms have been furnished with good-quality beds and duvets and decorated in a color-coordinated, stylish way. The rooms have tea/coffeemaking facilities.

Salamander Guest House. 40 Grove Rd., Stratford-upon-Avon, Warwickshire, CV37 6PB. ☎ **01789/205728** (also fax). 7 units (all with shower). TV. £22 ($35.20) single; £44–£48 ($70.40–$76.80) double. All rates include English breakfast. No credit cards.

Fronting a wooded park, this homey guest house is efficiently run by Maurice and Ninon Croft. Home-cooked dinners are available from £8 ($12.80). A five-minute walk from the town center.

IYHF Youth Hostel. Hemmingford House, Wellesbourne Rd., Alveston. Stratford-upon-Avon, CV37 7RG. ☎ **01789/297093**. 130 beds. £13.45 ($21.50) per night with an IYHF card. Also 6 units with private bathroom £32 ($51.20) double, £56 ($89.60) family (quad). DC, MC, V. Closed early Dec to early Jan. Bus 18 from Stratford Station.

This busy hostel is 2 miles from the city center. The large 18th-century building has 20 rooms set up in dorm fashion with 4 to 12 beds in each room. Six private rooms are available. Guests have full use of kitchen facilities. There's also a cafeteria serving decent inexpensive meals. The large game room offers pool table, video games, and reading/game tables; there's also a separate TV lounge. It's open 24 hours. Nonsmoking.

WHERE TO EAT

Black Swan. Southern Lane, Waterside. ☎ **01789/297312**. £8–£16 ($12.80–$25.60)). MC, V. Pub food 11am–9pm; restaurant Tues–Sun noon–2pm and Mon–Sat 5–10pm. ENGLISH.

Affectionately known as the Dirty Duck, this popular pub has been a regular hangout for local actors since the 18th century. Autographed photos of patrons, including Lord Olivier, adorn the walls. English specialties like braised kidneys are served, as well as steaks and the true specialty of the house, a honey roast duck. During cold weather, an open fire blazes. When it's nice out, you can take your drinks onto the terrace overlooking the river.

The Old Thatch. At the corner of Rother and Greenhill Sts. ☎ **01789/295216**. Main courses £4.45–£8.95 ($7.10–$14.30). MC, V. Meals served daily 11am–2:30pm and 6– 8:30pm. PUB.

From the outside, it's clear that this thatched-roof building lists decidedly to one side. Inside, it's warm and comfortable. The bars have flagstone floors, low-beamed ceilings, and a gas fire glowing in the brick hearth. The food is decent, ranging from cottage and steak and kidney pies to steak and the most expensive item on the menu, a mega-mixed grill consisting of a 6-ounce rump, 6-ounce gammon steaks, Cumberland sausage, lamb chop, kidney, chips, and peas. That should fill your protein quota for the next few weeks.

Queen's Head. Ely St. ☎ **01789/204914.** Main courses £2.25–£5 ($3.60–$8). MC, V. Meals served daily 11am–2:30pm and from 6pm. PUB.

This snug, two-bar pub attracts a local older crowd. The bar menu offers an extensive choice of baguette sandwiches and jacket potatoes, plus such dishes as scampi and chips.

Slug & Lettuce. 38 Guild St. ☎ **01789/299700.** Main courses £6–£10 ($9.60–$16). MC, V. Mon–Wed noon–2pm, Thurs–Sat noon–9pm, Sun noon–3 and 7–9pm. PUB.

This new-wave pub has a traditional front section complete with small fireplaces and warm paneling, which contrasts with a back area's incongruous zebra-skin couches. You can watch the chefs cooking the better-than-usual fare—such dishes as breast of chicken stuffed with avocado and garlic, or roulade of whiting with basil and bacon in a creamy spinach sauce, as well as more traditional items like bangers and mash. The menu is supplemented by specials, which might include pork with apple and calvados. Sometimes the combinations aren't always successful, like the shoulder of lamb stuffed with spinach and mint and served with a curry sauce.

The Windmill Inn. Church St. ☎ **01789/297687.** Main courses £2.45–£6.75 ($3.90–$10.80). MC, V. Mon–Wed noon–3pm, Thurs–Sun noon–2:30pm.

This lovely old pub was built in 1599 and became an inn a year later. It offers three spacious bars. One has old, highback settles, another has a large inglenook fireplace complete with cooking spit, and the third has a copper-hooded fireplace. The menu offers a broad selection, from sandwiches and jacket potatoes to lasagne and chili, plus steaks and barbecued ribs. There's also a decent selection of wines by the glass. Check out the list of licensees dating back to James Biddle, who was behind the bar in 1720.

Index

See also separate Accommodations, Restaurant, and Afternoon Tea indexes, below.
Page numbers in italics refer to maps.

AFTERNOON TEA

The English House

Please mention this coupon when you are making your dinner reservations. If you have any trouble with the validity of the coupon, please ask to speak to the manager.

The English House Restaurant Limited
3 Milner Street, London SW3
Tel: 0171/584-3002
Fax: 0171/584-2848

Aster House

Phone: 44(0) 171/581-5888
Fax: 44(0) 171/584-4925
asterhouse@btinternet.com
www.Welcome2London.com

Rates include breakfast.
MasterCard, and VISA are accepted.

Take Tube to South Kensington.
Walk 3 blocks down Old Brampton Road
to Sumner Place (on your left).

The English House

The English House is pleased to offer Frommer's readers one free bottle of House Wine for every couple dining with us.

The English House Restaurant Limited
3 Milner Street, London SW3
Tel: 0171/584-3002
Fax: 0171/584-2848

Aster House

Come ride The Big Bus Company's Hop-On/Hop-Off London Tour Bus. Pay half price for a tour ticket with a minimum stay of two nights.

3 Sumner Place
London SW7
For reservations, call 44(0) 171/581-5888

FOR RESERVATIONS CALL:
1-800-4-CHOICE

CHOICE HOTELS
INTERNATIONAL

Advance reservations are required. Discounts are based on availability at participating hotels and cannot be used in conjunction with other discounts or promotions.

20% Off SuperValue Rates The United Kingdom.

Terms and Conditions:
The 20% discount off the time and mileage portion of a SuperValue rate is available on rentals starting on or before December 31, 1999, at participating Avis locations in the United Kingdom when using Avis Worldwide Discount (AWD) number **B688900**. Cars and rates subject to availability. **An advance reservation is required**. Local taxes, VAT, theft protection, local government surcharges and optional items, such as CDW, additional driver fee and fuel service are extra. Renter must meet Avis age, driver and credit requirements. Minimum age is 23 in United Kingdom.

Avis features GM cars from Opel and Vauxhall.

Travel Certificate

5% Off
Any European
Car Rental

Or

$20 Off
Any Air Fare
To Europe

Or

$5 Off
Per Night, Any
European Hotel

auto ⓐⓔ europe®

Contact Your Travel Agent
Reservations: 1-800-223-5555
www.autoeurope.com

FROMMER'S® COMPLETE TRAVEL GUIDES

Alaska
Amsterdam
Arizona
Atlanta
Australia
Austria
Bahamas
Barcelona, Madrid & Seville
Belgium, Holland &
    Luxembourg
Bermuda
Boston
Budapest & the Best of
    Hungary
California
Canada
Cancún, Cozumel &
    the Yucatán
Cape Cod, Nantucket &
    Martha's Vineyard
Caribbean
Caribbean Cruises & Ports
    of Call
Caribbean Ports of Call
Carolinas & Georgia
Chicago
China
Colorado
Costa Rica
Denver, Boulder &
    Colorado Springs
England
Europe
Florida
France

Germany
Greece
Greek Islands
Hawaii
Hong Kong
Honolulu, Waikiki & Oahu
Ireland
Israel
Italy
Jamaica & Barbados
Japan
Las Vegas
London
Los Angeles
Maryland & Delaware
Maui
Mexico
Miami & the Keys
Montana & Wyoming
Montréal & Québec City
Munich & the Bavarian Alps
Nashville & Memphis
Nepal
New England
New Mexico
New Orleans
New York City
New Zealand
Nova Scotia, New Brunswick
    & Prince Edward Island
Oregon
Paris
Philadelphia & the
    Amish Country
Portugal

Prague & the Best of the
    Czech Republic
Provence & the Riviera
Puerto Rico
Rome
San Antonio & Austin
San Diego
San Francisco
Santa Fe, Taos &
    Albuquerque
Scandinavia
Scotland
Seattle & Portland
Singapore & Malaysia
South Pacific
Spain
Switzerland
Thailand
Tokyo
Toronto
Tuscany & Umbria
USA
Utah
Vancouver & Victoria
Vermont, New Hampshire
    & Maine
Vienna & the Danube Valley
Virgin Islands
Virginia
Walt Disney World &
    Orlando
Washington, D.C.
Washington State

FROMMER'S® DOLLAR-A-DAY GUIDES

Australia from $50 a Day
California from $60 a Day
Caribbean from $60 a Day
England from $60 a Day
Europe from $50 a Day
Florida from $60 a Day

Greece from $50 a Day
Hawaii from $60 a Day
Ireland from $50 a Day
Israel from $45 a Day
Italy from $50 a Day
London from $75 a Day

New York from $75 a Day
New Zealand from $50 a Day
Paris from $70 a Day
San Francisco from $60 a Day
Washington, D.C.,
    from $60 a Day

FROMMER'S® PORTABLE GUIDES

Acapulco, Ixtapa &
    Zihuatanejo
Alaska Cruises & Ports of Call
Bahamas
California Wine Country
Charleston & Savannah
Chicago

Dublin
Las Vegas
London
Maine Coast
New Orleans
New York City
Paris

Puerto Vallarta, Manzanillo
    & Guadalajara
San Francisco
Sydney
Tampa & St. Petersburg
Venice
Washington, D.C.

FROMMER'S® NATIONAL PARK GUIDES

Family Vacations in the
National Parks
Grand Canyon

National Parks of the
American West
Yellowstone & Grand Teton

Yosemite & Sequoia/
Kings Canyon
Zion & Bryce Canyon

FROMMER'S® MEMORABLE WALKS

Chicago
London

New York
Paris

San Francisco
Washington D.C.

FROMMER'S® IRREVERENT GUIDES

Amsterdam
Boston
Chicago

London
Manhattan

New Orleans
Paris

San Francisco
Walt Disney World
Washington, D.C.

FROMMER'S® DRIVING TOURS

America
Britain
California

Florida
France
Germany

Ireland
Italy
New England

Scotland
Spain
Western Europe

THE COMPLETE IDIOT'S TRAVEL GUIDES

Boston
Cruise Vacations
Planning Your Trip to Europe
Hawaii

Las Vegas
London
Mexico's Beach Resorts
New Orleans

New York City
San Francisco
Walt Disney World
Washington D.C.

THE UNOFFICIAL GUIDES®

Branson, Missouri
California with Kids
Chicago
Cruises
Disney Companion

Florida with Kids
The Great Smoky &
Blue Ridge
Mountains

Las Vegas
Miami & the Keys
Mini-Mickey
New Orleans

New York City
San Francisco
Skiing in the West
Walt Disney World
Washington, D.C.

SPECIAL-INTEREST TITLES

Frommer's Britain's Best Bike Rides
The Civil War Trust's Official Guide
to the Civil War Discovery Trail
Frommer's Caribbean Hideaways
Frommer's Gay & Lesbian Europe
Israel Past & Present
Monks' Guide to California
Monks' Guide to New York City
New York City with Kids
New York Times Weekends
Outside Magazine's Adventure Guide
to New England
Outside Magazine's Adventure Guide
to Northern California

Outside Magazine's Adventure Guide
to Southern California & Baja
Outside Magazine's Adventure Guide
to the Pacific Northwest
Outside Magazine's Guide
to Family Vacations
Places Rated Almanac
Retirement Places Rated
Washington, D.C., with Kids
Wonderful Weekends from Boston
Wonderful Weekends from New York City
Wonderful Weekends from San Francisco
Wonderful Weekends from Los Angeles

ODDLY ENOUGH, GETTING YOUR SCHEDULE STRAIGHT HELPS YOU KEEP YOUR PRIORITIES STRAIGHT.

Palm III
Connected Organizer

It fits in your pocket. It's elegantly simple. The Palm III™ connected organizer keeps names, phone numbers, schedules, memos, and e-mail right at your fingertips. And HotSync® technology lets you exchange all that information back and forth with your PC. You can even personalize your organizer with thousands of available applications. Wherever your life takes you, your Palm III organizer can come along. Palm Computing® connected organizers start as low as $249.* To learn more visit www.palm.com or call 1-800-861-2529.

Finally,
Vacations for Real People.

Save 37% off the newsstand price! **Subscribe Today!** **Only $14.95.**

You've read the guides, now check out the magazine...

Arthur Frommer's **BUDGET TRAVEL** magazine is your top source for hardhitting, practical info you can really use to plan your next affordable getaway. Each issue is crammed with hot tips, cool prices, and useful facts. After reading your very first issue, you'll undoubtedly save many times the cost of the subscription on your next vacation.
